For my family, who makes life so sweet

Contents

Acknowledgments

First of all, I wish to thank publisher Bruce Shaw and editor Pam Hoenig of The Harvard Common Press, who had the vision and then gave me the opportunity to do a book with such a wide scope. Copy editor Deborah Kops did a painstaking and thorough job, whipping recipes from multiple sources into shape and holding my hand a time or two. My gratitude also goes to Jodi Marchowsky, Valerie Cimino, Skye Stewart, Beatrice Wikander, Chris Alaimo, Betsy Young, and everyone else at The Harvard Common Press who makes it all happen.

Next I want to thank my family—Jean and Jack Merkle, and Julie and John Fox—who have made my kitchen a very special place to be. I apologize to my daughter Sarah for ruining her taste for cheesecake and marzipan with too much of a good thing, and to my son Nick for even attempting tomato ice cream (you'll notice it's not in the book). I'm grateful to Altha Fertig and Bev Fertig for their recipe contributions and our ongoing relationship.

My deepest thanks to all the contributors, past and present, who have given this book its depth and richness, and to the librarians overseeing the extensive culinary collection at the Kansas State University Library. I'm grateful for professional advice and information from Shirley Corriher and John T. Edge, and for the work of Jane Grigson, James Deetz, David Hackett Fischer, and Henry Glassie, which opened my eyes to the importance of American foodways as cultural touchstones.

Thanks to all the testers and tasters who, with good humor and great sense, have helped me make each dessert recipe the best it can be: Mary Bandereck, Jean and Jack Merkle, Julie Fox, Karen Adler, Reene Jones, Mary Pfeifer, Mary Ann Duckers, Dee Barwick, everyone in the test kitchens at *Mary Engelbreit* and *Better Homes & Gardens* magazines, the Heart of America Chapter of Les Dames D'Escoffier, and the Kansas City Cookbook Club.

American desserts are truly a national treasure.

What makes a dish American?

For Julia Child, it's simple. "As far as I'm concerned, it is American food, cooked in America by Americans with American ingredients," she says.

Boston chef Lydia Shire agrees: "American cooking is really the creative cooking of good, simple food, using American products and infusing some kinds of classical preparations."

I would add that an American dessert is one that was either adapted from other culinary traditions to suit American ingredients or tastes, or one that was created by an American cook using American ingredients.

Since Europeans first landed on Northern American shores, we've amassed a staggering number of desserts that we can proudly call American. You'll find around 400 of them in this book, which could easily have grown into a multivolume set with thousands of recipes.

The trick for me has been to carefully select or develop the recipes that best showcase what American desserts are all about. In choosing these recipes, I have to confess a bias. I can easily decline any old cookie, brownie, piece of cake or pie, mousse, or ice cream. For me, dessert has to be really, really good to pique my interest. And if I fall into one of the classic trio of dessert divisions—those people who prefer chocolate, cream, or fruit-based desserts—it is probably fruit for me.

That said, I think my bias has made me develop, choose, and adapt recipes with better, fresher, or richer flavor in mind. For example, instead of a classic carrot cake with cream cheese frosting (for which everyone has a recipe), I was inspired by an American quilt design to create my three-layer Praise and Plenty Cake (page 174), which includes grated yellow squash and green zucchini, as well as carrots. Fruit crisps and crumbles get a squeeze of lemon to accent the flavor. Homemade ice creams such as Summer Melon Ice Cream (page 429) and Lemony Blackberry Crumble Ice Cream (page 450) capture the essential flavor of the main ingredient. Brownies are richer, more chocolaty. Rootin' Tootin'

Texas Chocolate Sheet Cake (page 217) is exactly that. American desserts should be the best they can be.

Even historic recipes have had to prove themselves for inclusion in *All-American Desserts*. They have to have a reason for appearing on the American table beyond their historic value because not all of them appeal to contemporary tastes. Journalist Peter Nulty sums up our take on most seventeenth-century fare: "I guess people who wore armor weren't fussy eaters. They just added tons of cinnamon and cloves. Everything tasted like Christmas." The handful of hardy Pilgrim housewives who had to cater the first Thanksgiving dinner probably served a dessert that did taste like Christmas, at least to us today. Their dessert was most likely full of rosewater, dried fruit, and spices, and definitely not pumpkin pie, which came later.

But it's hard to beat Monticello Vanilla-Flecked Ice Cream (page 425), based on a recipe that Thomas Jefferson had his cooks prepare at his Virginia plantation. Amelia Simmons's Coriander Spice Cookies (page 132) are still appealing over 200 years after she included them in the first truly American cookbook. Transparent Tartlets (page 327) are still as delicious and as well loved as when their early makers crossed the Atlantic from Britain centuries ago.

Transparent Tartlets, which my family has enjoyed on weekends spent in Kentucky, provided the breakthrough I was looking for in this book. I wanted to know where most of our classic American dessert templates—the patterns for pies, puddings, cakes, cookies, etc.—originated. During my years of living in England, I noted that British desserts were similar but still different from ours. In researching this book, I reread Jane Grigson's *The Observer Guide to British Cookery* and found her mention of transparent tarts. They turned out to be originally English, but are now found only in Kentucky and the Carolinas. People don't make transparent tarts, or tartlets, in Kansas City or Boston or San Francisco unless they were born and raised in the above-mentioned states. Why only there?

That question sent me back to *Albion's Seed* by David Hackett Fischer, a scholarly but readable tome on how and why the cultures of various British regions were transplanted to American shores.

The Roots of American Desserts

Puritans who settled Massachusetts from 1629 to 1641 were originally from the region of East Anglia (the counties of Suffolk, Essex, and Norfolk). Not only did they rename the New World with their old place names (Boston, Boxford, Andover, Cambridge, Ipswich), but they also brought their preferred style of cooking—English tastes mixed with Puritan austerity—for example, cold baked beans and brown bread and the classic New England boiled dinner. The New England climate is not kind to growing wheat, so the precious wheat flour was used only on a top crust for a pie—hence the term "upper crust." Cornmeal replaced it in many desserts like Indian pudding and hasty pudding. Indeed, baking was the most popular form of cooking. Writes Fischer, "The austerity of New England's foodways was softened by its abundance of baked goods." The classic American fruit-filled and pumpkin pies, small cakes (or what the Dutch called cookies), baked Indian pudding, and later Toll House cookies, betties, cobblers, crumbles, crisps, and Boston Cream Pie have all evolved from these English roots.

Distressed cavaliers, or younger sons of the Royalist gentry who fought for King Charles I and lost to the Puritans in the English Civil War (1642 to 1649), tried to recoup their fortunes and start anew in Virginia from 1642 to 1675. Mainly from southern England (Northampton-shire, Gloucestershire, Somerset, Hampshire, Wiltshire, Oxfordshire, Surrey), these gentlemen brought servants from the lower ranks of British society. Instead of developing small farmsteads and larger cities as the colonists did in New England, these cavaliers established plantations—English manors in the New World. Shunning Puritan austerity, these planters wanted the good life in everything, including food. They tucked into roast beef, fried chicken, fresh oysters from the shore, and fresh asparagus and strawberries from their gardens. Baking took a back seat to boiling, grilling, roasting, and frying. From this region, we get classic American recipes for ice cream, sweet desserts enriched with sherry or rum, trifle, fruit compotes, and liqueurs.

Quakers, persecuted for their religious beliefs, relocated to the Delaware Valley from 1675 to 1725. These were mainly poor farmers and craftsmen from the north of England (Cumber-land, Yorkshire, Lancashire, Cheshire), as well as tradesmen and artisans from London. Quakers from Wales and others persecuted for their religious beliefs also found a haven in what is now western New Jersey, Delaware, and Pennsylvania. Northern England places names, such as Chester, Carlisle, York, and Lancaster, echo throughout Pennsylvania. From this region, we get the classic American cheesecake, lemon curd, lemon meringue pie, apple dumplings, and apple butter. Later on, the German separatist group that became known as the Pennsylvania Dutch added shoofly pie and fried pastries.

The last British group migrated to the colonies from 1717 to 1775. They came from the hill country of northern England, western Scotland, and Northern Ireland—the rough and ready borderlands, where blood feuds, mournful ballads, and serious whisky drinking were the norm. High rents, heavy taxes, low wages, and the infamous Highland Clearances—during which clans were broken up when tenants were removed from their ancestral lands by their lairds or lords—prompted thousands to leave the old country for a new start. Pride and poverty went hand in hand with this group of settlers, who found that the wild mountain country of the Appalachians suited them just fine. Because of their geographic isolation and strong traditions, many very old British dessert recipes still remain in the repertoire of their descendants, such as stack cake, miniature fried pies, and desserts flavored with bourbon.

As each new immigrant group arrived, the American dessert pantheon became further enriched. There were northern European tortes and rice puddings, Italian cookies and panna cotta, Spanish flan, and Greek pastries. Over the years, American cooks invented new recipes that have become classics: the hot fudge sundae, layer cakes, angel food cake, brownies, and chocolate chip cookies.

Distinctly American ingredients transformed early British recipes and fueled resourcefulness in American cooks to create new ones. From the earliest days to the present, these ingredients included molasses, pure cane syrup, and maple syrup; cornmeal; pecans and black walnuts; Concord grapes; American varieties of apples, pears, and peaches; California wines and Kentucky bourbons; New Mexican chiles and pine nuts; wild fruits, such as the persimmon, Juneberry, chokecherry, and beach plum; orchard fruits from around the Great Lakes; citrus fruits from California, Florida, and Arizona; tropical fruits and coconuts from Florida, Puerto Rico, and Hawaii; unsweetened cocoa powder; and even Marshmallow Fluff, Cool Whip, and Jell-O.

Throughout *All-American Desserts*, there are always plenty of stories to tell. As in my previous books, *Prairie Home Cooking* and *Prairie Home Breads*, I weave stories throughout the recipes to tell the sweet and sometimes bittersweet tale of American life.

All-American Desserts is edible history, a sweet bite of the past, a showcase of the best loved American ingredients and our collective culinary skill at its finest.

All-American Desserts

Paradise was the furthest thing from William Bradford's mind when the *Mayflower* finally reached the shores of Cape Cod on November 11, 1620. Speaking for all the sea-weary Pilgrims who were expecting a latter-day Promised Land, Bradford sadly recalled, "What could they see but a hideous and desolate wilderness, full of wild beasts and wild men." Before the *Mayflower* finally reached Plymouth Bay in a snowstorm on December 11, Bradford's wife had been lost overboard. Arriving at the wrong place in the wrong season, struck by tragedy, disillusioned, Bradford's steadily shrinking group clung to their religion for hope and strength. Plymouth may have been their "promised land," but it was no Eden.

The next wave of immigrants, led by John Winthrop in 1630, had read everything they could about their future home and were the first to understand the terms of entry

Almost Paradise Fruit Preserves and Desserts

into this new Eden. They could expect no gold, no help from the Indians, and no easy life. They would have to build their own homes, clear their own land, and grow their own food. The Puritans brought what they needed to sustain them for a year and got right to work transforming the wilderness into a garden.

For guidance, these seventeenth-century practical idealists brought their Bibles and their herbals: gardening was serious business and taming the land was a God-given prerogative. The wilderness had to be improved, cultivated, civilized. This was an early manifest destiny, and what better place to begin than the New World?

In *Early American Gardens: "For Meate or for Medicine,"* gardener and writer Ann Leighton painstakingly chronicles the plants that were native to America when these early colonists arrived, and those they brought or had sent from England. Wild strawberries, native persimmons, wild grapes, and beach plums helped sustain the colonists while they waited for their gardens and orchards to mature. From grafting and happy accident, the Bartlett pear, Concord grape, and Newtown Pippin apple grew in these new gardens and began to grace American tables.

In 1803, right from the start of the Lewis and Clark exploration of the Louisiana Purchase, George Rogers Clark also noted, day by day, the wild berries and fruits along the Missouri River from Missouri to the Pacific Northwest. Soon waves of pioneers would tame this broad expanse of land as well.

"There seemed to be nothing to see; no fences, no creeks or trees, no hills or fields," wrote Willa Cather about homesteading in Nebraska in her novel *My Antonia*. "If there was a road, I could not make it out in the faint starlight. There was nothing but land: not a country at all, but the material out of which countries are made. No, there was nothing but land."

But soon this vast area west of the Mississippi also became a fruited plain. German immigrants who planted vineyards in the rolling prairie west of St. Louis soon transformed this area into the country's major wine-producing region, until California took precedence after Prohibition ended. There were orchard fruits in the cool climate of the Pacific Northwest, citrus fruits in the newly irrigated groves of southern California, and berries of all kinds everywhere.

Before the advent of refrigeration and air transport, fresh fruits were enjoyed only during their brief seasons or as preserved foods. Methods of preserving fruit changed over time. The earliest including drying and sugaring or cooking in a sugar syrup. Early colonial households had stores of dried apple rings, raisins, dried berries, and crocks full of fruits preserved in sugar syrup and sometimes rum. Early receipt books are replete with recipes for preserving all kinds of fruits in the form of marmalades, conserves, and jellies. Before the advent of paraffin or the canning jar, pots of jellies would have been topped with a round of cloth dipped in candle wax and tied onto the jar.

It's still worth seeking out locally grown fruit for the best-tasting desserts, no matter what fruits are available year-round at the grocery store. We're still looking for that culinary Garden of Eden that Governor Bradford sought in 1620.

Strawberry Spoon Fruit

When Mary Todd Lincoln was married and living in a two-story Federal-style house in Springfield, Illinois, her June social calendar revolved around strawberries. In a letter to her friend Hannah Shearer on June 26, 1859, she describes the height of strawberry season: "For the last two weeks, we have had a continual round of strawberry parties, this last week I have spent five evenings out." *So many strawberries, so little time* must have been the thinking back then. That's why vintage cookbooks are full of recipes like spoon fruit, which captures the delicious yet fleeting treasure of strawberries to enjoy throughout the year. Spoon fruit, or softly set preserves, used to be eaten by the spoonful with after-dinner coffee as a kind of dessert. Today, it's still made by American Spoon Foods in Michigan and by home cooks like Charlotte Flichler of Strawberry Point, Iowa.

Here I've added a touch of rosewater, which is available at Asian markets or gourmet shops. This old-fashioned flavoring gives Strawberry Spoon Fruit a flavor like the tiniest, most aromatic *fraises des bois* (wild strawberries). Serve with Wildflower Honey Cream (page 348), dolloped on homemade bread, or simply by the spoonful.

MAKES 4 CUPS

1 quart fresh strawberries, hulled and cut in half

2 tablespoons fresh lemon juice

4 cups sugar

1 teaspoon rosewater

1 Place the strawberries in a large heavy saucepan over medium-low heat. Pour the lemon juice over the berries and cover with the sugar. Stir to blend with a wooden spoon. Bring the mixture to a full boil and continue boiling for exactly 8 minutes. Watch the saucepan carefully to make sure the mixture does not boil over. If you boil the mixture longer than 8 minutes, you may end up with traditional preserves and not spoon fruit.

2 Remove the mixture from the heat and stir in the rosewater. Transfer to a glass or crockery bowl. Let cool for 15 minutes, then cover with plastic wrap and set aside at room temperature until the berries have plumped and the mixture has thickened to a syrup-like consistency. Transfer to a clean glass jar. Will keep, tightly covered in the refrigerator, for up to 3 months.

Fresh Orange Marmalade

In the hill country of Tennessee and the Carolinas, where appliquéd and patchwork quilts hang on wash lines to air, cooks salute their British and Scots-Irish descent by making orange marmalade. Made with fresh, carefully peeled Valencia or navel oranges, this marmalade is not bitter like that made with Seville oranges can be. Besides being delicious on toast, Fresh Orange Marmalade is also wonderful as the basis for a pie filling or as a golden surprise in the middle of a layer cake, like the orange marmalade cake that made Esther Bortnick famous in author Jan Karon's fictional town of Mitford, North Carolina. This also makes a wonderful topping for rice pudding or creamy custard.

MAKES ABOUT 2 CUPS

4 medium-size Valencia or navel oranges, washed and patted dry

1 cup water

$\frac{1}{2}$ cup sugar

2 tablespoons fresh lemon juice

2 tablespoons orange liqueur (optional)

1 Carefully peel the oranges with a paring knife so that you get the orange zest, but not the white pith beneath. Finely chop the zest, then section the oranges and cut away any white membrane. Finely chop the orange sections, removing any seeds.

2 In a medium-size heavy saucepan, combine the zest, orange sections, water, sugar, and lemon juice. Bring to a boil over medium-high heat and cook at a boil for 15 minutes. Remove from the heat, and stir in the liqueur, if using. Pour into a clean pint-size jar, and let cool at room temperature. Cover tightly and store in the refrigerator until ready to use. Keeps indefinitely.

Cranberry-Chokecherry Conserve

This is a tart and rosy sauce made with cranberries and wild chokecherry or red currant jelly. It is wonderful as a side dish for Thanksgiving dinner, as a cake filling, or as a sauce for Wildflower Honey Cream (page 348), ice cream, or pound cake.

MAKES ABOUT 4 CUPS

One 12-ounce bag cranberries, picked over for stems and rinsed
¼ cup water

¾ cup sugar
½ cup chokecherry or red currant jelly

In a medium-size heavy saucepan bring the cranberries, water, and sugar to a boil. Reduce the heat to medium-low and simmer until the cranberries are tender and burst, about 10 minutes. Stir in the chokecherry jelly and heat through until completely melted. Serve warm or at room temperature. Will keep in the refrigerator, tightly covered, for up to 2 weeks.

Green Tomato and Apple Mincemeat

The American palate has moved away from the rich taste of mincemeat. The British, however, still love it—especially at Christmas and on Boxing Day, when they gobble up mincemeat tarts. But the true indicator of popularity is the package of mincemeat tarts available at every corner shop in Britain, like packaged Hostess cupcakes here. Still, there are plenty of Americans who love mincemeat. In the 1945 film *State Fair*, the fortunes of the Frake family at the Iowa State Fair revolve around "Blue Boy," the prize Hampshire boar, and Mrs. Frake's pickles and mincemeat. She wins a special award of distinction when one of the judges just can't get enough of her mincemeat, liberally flavored with brandy (thanks to Mr. Frake sneaking in more when the missus wasn't looking).

Made with either small green tomatoes or tomatillos and apples, this mincemeat has a fresher flavor than traditional kinds made with chopped beef and shredded beef suet, and it's delicious in Amish Mincemeat Cookies (page 106). You decide on how liberal you want to be with the rum or brandy. This recipe makes enough to fill four mincemeat pies. **MAKES 3 TO 4 PINTS**

Cranberries

New kinds of pilgrims—340,000 every year—now land in Plymouth, Massachusetts to visit Cranberry World, a museum devoted to everything cranberry. A fruit native to the swampy bogs of Cape Cod, the cranberry still packs 'em in, so to speak. Cranberries were also known as bear berries to early colonists because the bears liked them, too. The Pilgrims learned all about cranberries from the Native Americans, who recognized the natural preservative power (benzoic acid) in the berries and often mixed them with dried venison to make a kind of pemmican—high-energy food with a long shelf life. When sugar became readily available, colonists boiled cranberries with water and sugar to make a drink that could be preserved. That's probably the way that the first cranberry conserve began as well. A 1663 receipt book descended from a Pilgrim family lists a recipe that sounds a lot like our cranberry sauce.

By the late 1600s, oranges from the West Indies arrived in port cities in time for Christmas. Fresh orange juice and grated orange rind gradually became part of many cranberry conserve and relish recipes. General Ulysses S. Grant ordered cranberry sauce served to his troops during the siege of Petersburg in 1864.

In 1816, the first commercial cranberry operation began on Cape Cod near what is now Harwich. Captain Henry Hall noticed that covering wild cranberry vines with sand encouraged their growth. A few years later, he was in business. Cranberry cultivation is still big business there. In 1912, cranberry sauce was first commercially canned by the Cape Cod Cranberry Company, which marketed the product as Ocean Spray Cape Cod Cranberry Sauce.

The cranberry (Vaccinium macrocarpon) grows on creeping evergreen vines that just love the acidic peat soil of swampy bogs, freshwater, and sand. It takes five years for plants to mature enough to bear fruit. A late frost in spring can freeze the pink blossoms. We've all experienced the deprivation of a bad cranberry year, when there's not a bag to be had after Thanksgiving.

Cultivated cranberry bogs have ditches down the middle and around the sides to act as canals so that the water level can be changed. The water level is raised during harvest, from late September through early December, so the berries float and can be scooped up. The water level can also be raised to flood the bog to avoid frost damage.

Today, fresh cranberries add a festive touch to side dishes, baked goods, and desserts from Thanksgiving through Valentine's Day. Enjoy them in Winter Ruby Molded Gelatin (page 21), Cranberry-Chokecherry Conserve (page 7), Wintertime Cranberry and Orange Cake (page 185), Spiced Cranberry Tea (page 493), and Festive Cranberry Tart (page 324).

15 small green tomatoes or 20 tomatillos (husks removed), cored and chopped

2 pounds tart apples (6 to 8), such as Granny Smith or Jonathan, peeled, cored, and chopped

1½ pounds raisins

1 cup packed dark brown sugar

2 cups apple cider

1 teaspoon freshly grated nutmeg

1 tablespoon ground cinnamon

½ teaspoon ground cloves

½ teaspoon ground ginger

Grated zest and juice of 2 lemons

Rum or brandy to taste

1 In a large heavy pot, combine the tomatoes, apples, raisins, brown sugar, cider, and spices. Bring to a boil, then reduce the heat to medium-low and simmer, covered, until the tomatoes and apples are soft and the mixture has thickened, about 1 hour.

2 Stir in the lemon zest and juice. Add rum or brandy and keep hot.

3 Bring a large pot of water to a boil and sterilize 3 or 4 pint-size jars for 5 minutes.

4 Remove the jars from the hot water with tongs. Quickly ladle the mincemeat into the hot jars, leaving ½ inch of headspace. Seal by twisting on the lids tightly, then loosening a quarter turn. Place the filled jars back into the boiling water for 10 minutes. Remove the jars and let cool. Store the mincemeat in a dark, cool place, where it will keep indefinitely.

Dried Fruit Compote with Brown Sugar Syrup

Compotes are fruits cooked in a syrup just until softened, so they still retain their form. So popular have they been that the name also refers to the footed dish—usually glass—that is used to serve them. A European tradition transplanted to America, compotes were possible when sugar became available to wealthy households in the 1500s.

Dried fruits have always been an essential part of the American larder. Before electricity reached rural communities in the 1940s, fruits were canned, preserved in sugar, or dried in the sun to keep during cold weather. Today, we appreciate dried fruits in dishes like this compote—a winter dessert served with a scoop of homemade ice cream or Wildflower Honey Cream (page 348), or as an accompaniment to a rich baked custard. The recipe may also be adapted to any variety of dried fruits you have on hand.

MAKES 8 SERVINGS

1 cup packed dark brown sugar

3 cups water

1 cup dried apricots

1 cup dried pear slices

1 cup dried apple slices

1 cup pitted prunes

1 cup dried cherries

Juice of 1 orange

Juice of 1 lime

1 Simmer the brown sugar and water together in a large saucepan over medium-low heat until the sugar has dissolved, about 5 minutes. With kitchen shears, snip the apricots, pears, apples, and prunes into quarters.

2 Place all the fruit in the sugar syrup and gently poach until the fruits have softened, 15 to 20 minutes. Remove from the heat and stir in the orange and lime juices to blend. Serve warm or cold.

Quince Compote

Quinces, argued by some scholars to be the real "apple" in the Garden of Eden, had long been established in Europe before English colonists brought them to New England. Old varieties like Smyrna, Champion, and Orange traveled westward to central Ohio. Prized for their high pectin and setting properties, quinces began to fall out of favor when Charles Knox developed granulated gelatin in 1890. The fruit is making a comeback now and is grown around the Great Lakes and in California.

In the fall, a bowl of knobby yellow quinces can perfume a room with a sweet, apple-like scent. In north central Ohio, near Wooster, quince trees with golden fruit clinging to bare branches bring a kind of poetry to abandoned farmsteads. Quinces also work some magic in this recipe. When their juices and peels cook with sugar, the syrup turns a deep ruby red. Serve this compote with the vanilla bean still in it for a dramatic contrast. With its pineapple-like flavor, Quince Compote is a delicious accompaniment to a homemade ice cream, Luscious Cream Cheese Pound Cake (page 203), or whipped cream. **MAKES 8 SERVINGS**

4 large quinces, peeled, quartered, and cored (reserve the peels and cores)

Juice of 1 lemon

4 cups sugar

1 vanilla bean

1   Place the quince peels, quarters, and cores in a large saucepan with enough water to cover. Bring to a boil, then reduce the heat to medium-low, and simmer until the water turns red, 10 to 15 minutes. Transfer the quince quarters to a separate plate and set aside. With a slotted spoon, remove the peels and cores and discard.

2   Add the lemon juice, sugar, and vanilla bean to the cooking water and bring to a boil, stirring until the sugar dissolves. Reduce the heat to a simmer. Cut the quince quarters into thinner slices and return to the cooking water. Simmer, uncovered, until the quinces are softened and the syrup is a deep red, about 20 minutes. Remove the vanilla bean and serve warm or cold.

Oranges in Cardamom Syrup

The fresh taste of oranges is a welcome foil to all the rich foods served during the winter holidays. This recipe was inspired by desserts served in Swedish-American communities and adapted from one by Raphael Kadushin. It looks wonderful served in a glass compote. Carefully peel one of the oranges in one long, curling strip. Brush fresh sage leaves with slightly beaten egg white and dust with sugar. Then use the curled strip of orange peel and the sugar-frosted sage leaves to garnish the compote dish or individual servings. **SERVES 8**

6 oranges

1 cup sugar

$^1\!/_2$ teaspoon cardamom seeds

1   Grate the zest of 1 orange and set the zest aside. Using a sharp paring knife, peel all the oranges over a large bowl to catch the juice (including the one you grated), then remove the pith. Cut between the membranes to separate the orange segments, discarding the membranes, and place the segments in a serving bowl.

2   Place the orange zest, sugar, and cardamom in a small heavy saucepan. Pour the juice collected in the bowl holding the orange segments into a measuring cup and add enough water to make 1 cup. Pour the liquid over the sugar mixture in the saucepan. Bring to a boil and continue to boil for 5 minutes. Remove from the heat and strain the syrup through a fine-mesh strainer over the oranges. Serve warm or chilled.

Caramelized Orange Compote

This is so easy and so good—and so fat-free—that I could just eat it alone and feel virtuous. But it also makes a wonderful accompaniment to pound cake, ice cream, or a homemade butter cookie. Prepare this during the winter months when fresh citrus fruits are in season from Florida and California. Serve it in a footed glass compote dish and just enjoy. Grate the orange zest before you peel the oranges, then place the zest in sealable plastic freezer bags to save for other desserts. **MAKES 4 SERVINGS**

4 oranges, preferably seedless, peeled, white pith removed, and cut horizontally into $1/2$-inch-thick rounds

1 cup sugar
$1/2$ cup water

1   Arrange the orange slices in layers in a glass dessert compote or serving dish. Set aside.

2   In a small heavy saucepan over medium-high heat, stir the sugar and water together and bring to a boil. Continue to boil, without stirring, until the mixture turns golden brown and reaches a temperature of 329 degrees F on a candy thermometer, about 10 minutes. Watch carefully; once the mixture starts to turn color, it does so quickly. Remove from the heat.

3   Pour the hot caramel over the oranges. Serve warm or at room temperature.

Fresh Oranges in Bourbon Vanilla Syrup

In 1910, the majority of Americans still lived and worked on farms. By the 1950s, most people worked in factories or at other blue-collar jobs. In 2000, most of us worked in air-conditioned offices, reading and sending e-mail to do business. Our working lives have gotten more sedentary, so our desserts have gotten leaner and meaner to make up for it. A dessert like this one—under 150 calories and no fat—could be a nightly indulgence, with no ill effects. California chefs have paved the way for desserts like this one—high in flavor, pleasing to the eye, and guaranteed to keep budding starlets or middle-aged studio execs lean and mean. **MAKES 4 SERVINGS**

4 navel oranges

1 cup water

¼ cup sugar

16 coriander seeds

1 vanilla bean

1 tablespoon Kentucky bourbon

1   With a zester or a small, sharp knife, cut small strips of orange rind from half of 1 orange. Set the zest aside. With a sharp knife, peel the oranges, including the white pith. Slice each orange into ⅛-inch-thick rounds. Arrange the orange slices on four dessert plates. Cover the plates with plastic wrap and chill until ready to serve.

2   To make the syrup, combine the strips of rind with the water, sugar, and coriander seeds in a small heavy saucepan. Slice the vanilla bean in half lengthwise and scrape the seeds into the saucepan. Bring to a boil, then reduce the heat to medium-low and simmer until the syrup registers 220 degrees F on a candy thermometer. Stir in the bourbon and cook for 2 more minutes.

3   To serve, spoon the syrup over the oranges on each plate.

Kumquat Compote

When kumquats—small oval orange citrus fruits from Florida or California—are in season during the winter months, make this easy compote to have on hand the rest of the year. It is delicious over pound cake or ice cream, as the filling in a jelly roll or the topping on a tart, or as a grace note spooned around the base of a wobbling molded gelatin or a Bundt cake displayed on a cake stand. Use this as a flavorful building block to make your own layered trifle or individual parfaits with cubes of pound cake, Classic Crème Anglaise (page 369), and whipped cream. Star anise, available at Asian markets, not only adds visual appeal, but also a very slight licorice note.

MAKES ABOUT 2 CUPS

1 pound kumquats

2 tablespoons whole star anise

2 tablespoons coriander seeds

1 cup sugar

1 cup water

1   Cut each kumquat horizontally into 4 or 5 slices and remove any seeds. Trim off the ends, if desired. Place the kumquat slices, spices, sugar, and water in a medium-size heavy saucepan over

medium-high heat and bring to a boil, stirring to dissolve the sugar. Continue to boil until the kumquat slices are glistening and translucent, 15 to 20 minutes.

2   Let cool in the pan, then transfer to a pint-size jar with a lid. Seal the jar and refrigerate. Will keep indefinitely.

Peaches in Almond Syrup with Peach and Raspberry Granita

For a cool, toothsome dessert, nothing even comes close to this one—a whole, smooth, fragrant poached peach accompanied by a rosy, shaved-ice granita. A contemporary version of Escoffier's Peach Melba. **MAKES 4 SERVINGS**

1 recipe Almond Syrup (page 486)
4 large ripe peaches, still a little firm

1 cup fresh or frozen (thawed) raspberries
Fresh lemon balm or peach leaves for garnish

1   Place the almond syrup and whole peaches in a large saucepan and bring to a boil. Reduce the heat to medium-low and simmer until the peaches are tender when tested with a knife, 10 to 15 minutes. Remove from the heat and let the peaches cool in the syrup. When the peaches have cooled, peel away their skins (it will be easy). Transfer the poached peaches to a bowl, reserving the syrup.

2   Mash the raspberries in a small bowl and push through a fine-mesh strainer. Transfer to a blender or food processor, add ½ cup of the peach syrup, and puree. Pour into a container and freeze for about 1 hour, until frozen but slightly slushy.

3   Serve on chilled dessert plates: Place a whole poached peach on each plate accompanied by a scoop of granita and a sprig of lemon balm or fresh peach leaves. Alternatively, cut the peaches in half, remove the pits, and place a small scoop of granita in each peach half.

Sour Cherry and Almond Compote

At my local farmers' market, I can buy locally grown tart cherries that are pitted and frozen, so I stock up in order to serve this deliciously rosy compote year-round. Chilled, it makes a good filling for a meringue basket or a pastry tartlet, topped with a dollop of whipped cream, or a layer cake. Warm, it goes over pound cake or ice cream or graces a brunch table during the cold, gray days of February. MAKES ABOUT 4 CUPS

4 cups pitted sour cherries, fresh, canned
   (drained), or frozen (thawed)

2 cups sugar

$\frac{1}{2}$ cup water

2 tablespoons fresh lemon juice

2 tablespoons cornstarch

$\frac{1}{2}$ teaspoon almond extract

1   In a large saucepan, bring the cherries, sugar, and water to boil over medium-high heat. Stir to dissolve the sugar and continue to boil until the cherries start to release their juice, about 5 minutes.

2   Meanwhile, put the lemon juice and cornstarch in a jar, screw on the lid, and shake to blend until smooth. Whisk the lemon juice mixture into the boiling cherry compote and stir until thickened, about 2 minutes. Remove from the heat and stir in the almond extract. Serve warm or chilled.

Northwest Sweet Cherry Compote

I love it when sweet cherries from the Pacific Northwest come into the markets in July and August. I buy bags of cherries and we eat them like candy. I never really considered using them in desserts until pastry chef Emily Lucchetti demonstrated this dish in Kansas City for the Northwest Cherry Growers association. She serves this compote with her Almond Panna Cotta (page 363), but it is also delicious on ice cream, pound cake, or just by itself. I love to use several different kinds of sweet cherries: the dark Bing, the sweet Rainier dappled with gold and blush, the early Lambert, the large Lapin, and the bright red Sweetheart. Use a paper clip to pit the cherries.

MAKES ABOUT 4 CUPS

2 pounds sweet cherries, stemmed and pitted

2 teaspoons Grand Marnier

2 teaspoons vanilla extract

1/4 cup sugar

2 teaspoons fresh lemon juice

1/2 cup fresh orange juice, plus extra as needed

1/2 teaspoon cornstarch

1 Place the cherries, Grand Marnier, vanilla, sugar, and lemon and orange juices in a large nonstick skillet over medium heat. Cook until the cherries begin to release their juice and have softened, about 5 minutes.

2 Drain the cherries, reserving the liquid, and place them in a serving bowl or compote dish. Measure the cherry liquid, which should be about 1/2 cup. (If necessary, add enough extra orange juice to reach 1/2 cup.)

3 Return the cherry liquid to the pan and place over medium heat until hot. Transfer 1/4 cup of the hot liquid to a jar. Add the cornstarch to the liquid, screw on the lid, and shake to blend. Add the cornstarch mixture to the pan and whisk to blend. Cook, stirring, for several more minutes, until the liquid has thickened slightly. Pour the sauce over the cherries. Serve warm or at room temperature.

Strawberry and Lemon Compote

Italian immigrants to the East Coast, Midwest, and California wine country brought their love of lemon-kissed strawberries, or *fragole al limone*, with them. Deliciously simple, this compote tastes best with the first fresh strawberries of the season. Serve with cakes, cookies, puddings, or custards. **MAKES ABOUT 5 CUPS**

2 pints fresh strawberries, hulled

1 cup water

1 cup sugar

Four 2-inch lengths lemon zest

1 Place the strawberries in a glass bowl.

2 In a small saucepan, bring the water and sugar to a boil over high heat. Add the strips of lemon zest and cook in the syrup for 3 minutes. Set aside to cool.

3 Pour the cooled syrup over the berries and macerate at room temperature for at least 1 hour before serving. Will keep, covered, in the refrigerator for up to 2 days.

Fresh Mangoes in Lime Syrup

Mangoes, which are picked green in Florida and then shipped, are more widely available than ever before in grocery stores across the country. Allow an extra day or two for your mangoes to ripen on the kitchen counter in a paper bag—they're ripe when they turn a rosy orange color and feel a little soft when squeezed. Then use them to make this low-fat dessert with a wonderfully aromatic flavor. **MAKES 4 SERVINGS**

2 limes

2 tablespoons water

$\frac{1}{2}$ cup sugar

2 large or 4 small fresh mangoes

Fresh mint leaves for garnish

1 Using a paring knife, peel the limes, then cut the zest lengthwise into thin strips about 2 inches long. Squeeze the juice and combine in a small saucepan with the water and sugar. Bring to a boil over medium-high heat and continue to boil until syrupy, about 5 minutes. Stir in the strips of lime zest and set aside to cool slightly.

2 Peel the mangoes with a paring knife. Using a chef's knife, halve the mangoes lengthwise by cutting all around, as close as possible to the pit. Carefully twist off the two halves of each mango. Place the halves on a cutting board. Using the chef's knife, cut the mango halves into slices about $\frac{1}{2}$ inch thick. Taking care to keep the mango slices together, place each sliced half on a deep platter. Pour the syrup over the mangoes. Garnish with mint leaves and serve.

M. F. K. Fisher's Wartime Fruit Compote

Food writer M. F. K. Fisher spent years in France between the World Wars, which sharpened both her appetite and her pen. After World War II broke out, she wrote *How to Cook a Wolf* in 1942 as wartime shortages and dire headlines made it seem, indeed, as if the proverbial wolf were at the door. In *How to Cook a Wolf*, Fisher gives a recipe for a compote of nine different fruits doused with a wine glass each of seven different liqueurs, followed by a half-bottle of demi-sec champagne. Then she writes, "Yes, it is crazy to sit savoring such impossibilities, while headlines yell at you and the wolf whuffs through the keyhole." But if the reader could find these ingredients, "you are doubly blessed, to possess in this troubled life both the capacity and the where-withal to forget it for a time." In an article she wrote for *House Beautiful* magazine in November 1944, when the shortages were still on, Fisher offered this similar, but more practical compote, which I have updated. **MAKES ABOUT 3 CUPS; 6 SERVINGS**

¾ cup canned apricots with their juice

½ cup canned pears with their juice

½ cup canned plums with their juice

½ cup canned peaches with their juice

½ cup canned sour cherries with their juice

½ cup dark rum or 1 cup dessert wine, such as late harvest Riesling or Sauternes

Combine the fruits and their juices in a large saucepan over medium heat and bring to a simmer. Remove from the heat and stir in the rum or dessert wine. Chill before serving. Keeps, covered, in the refrigerator indefinitely.

Golden Apple Compote

This is a luscious, golden-hued compote perfect to serve as a cake or tart filling or as a warm sauce over ice cream or pound cake. Golden Delicious are the preferred apples because they're naturally sweet. **MAKES ABOUT 2 CUPS**

6 Golden Delicious or other sweet dessert apples (about 2 pounds), peeled, cored, and cut into ½-inch-thick slices

½ cup water

⅔ cup sugar

Juice of 1 large lemon

½ teaspoon ground cinnamon

1 tablespoon unsalted butter

Put all the ingredients in a large skillet and bring to a boil over medium-high heat. Reduce the heat to medium, cover, and simmer until the apple slices are tender but still intact, about 5 minutes. Uncover and continue to cook, stirring, until most of the liquid evaporates. Remove from the heat. Serve warm with ice cream or pound cake. Let cool to room temperature before using as a cake or tart filling. May be covered and refrigerated for up to 1 week.

Antique Apples

Horticultural anthropologists now think that the first apples grew wild in what is now Kazakhstan in central Asia. Over thousands of years, thousands of apple varieties were developed by accidents of nature or by careful propagation throughout the temperate regions of Europe and Asia.

Gerard's Herball, an influential gardening manual edited by Thomas Johnson in 1633, listed 60 different apple varieties that were known to grow in England, including "Queening or Queen of Apples," "Sommer Pearmaine," "Winter Permaine," "Pome Water," and the "Bakers ditch Apple tree."

Nearly every written seed list of the early English colonists mentions apple seeds, scions, or trees brought to New England. From John Winthrop, Jr., to Cotton Mather, Samuel Sewell to William Bradford, apples were essential. By 1970, Ann Leighton noted in her book *Early American Gardens*, you could still find descendants of those original apples—Queens, Pearmaines, Pommewaters, and even Baker's Sweet—in parts of New England. Colonists also grafted scions onto older native crab apple plants and created many new varieties based on older European ones.

Today, there is a newfound appreciation for the antique apples that bloomed and thrived where they were planted in America. Here is a selection of those still available:

★ *Baldwin:* A biennial apple (the tree bears fruit every other year), from Wilmington, Massachusetts, circa 1740. It is large, sweet, juicy, and good for cooking or eating as a dessert apple.

★ *Calville Blanc:* A late autumn French apple dating back to the late 1500s. It was brought to America by French and French-Canadian settlers. Very tart and aromatic, it is a good keeper and wonderful in apple tarts.

★ *Maiden Blush:* A summer apple and a favorite in Jefferson's Monticello orchards. It is pale yellow with a pink cheek, very aromatic, and good for drying in the sun.

★ *Newtown Pippin:* A late autumn apple first grown in the mid-1700s in the Huguenot settlement of Flushing, New York. It was a favorite of Thomas Jefferson at Monticello, and Benjamin Franklin had some shipped to him during a sojourn in London, England, in 1758. America's first fruit export to Europe, the Newtown Pippin is now grown in Oregon.

★ *Roxbury Russet:* Possibly the oldest apple in America. It was first grown in about 1630 in Roxbury, Massachusetts. This autumn apple has yellow skin and brownish markings, is good for frying and roasting, and is an excellent keeper.

★ *Stayman Winesap:* An autumn apple that is sharply tangy with a rosy fragrance. It is good for eating raw, cooking, and drying.

Winter Fruit Compote with Vanilla Rum Syrup

When Martha Dandridge married Daniel Custis in 1749, she brought along an heirloom receipt book that the women in her family had kept. It is full of recipes like this one for preserving fruits of all kinds for winter use. After Daniel Custis died, Martha took the book to her new household when she became the bride of George Washington. The receipt book finally went to her granddaughter, Nelly Custis, in 1799. What Martha Washington did of necessity centuries ago, we do now for convenience. This lusciously flavored compote keeps, refrigerated, for up to a year. It makes a great hostess gift. And it can be pulled out to reach room temperature, or warmed in a saucepan over low heat, to spoon over ice cream, pound cake, or Bundt cake, or to serve by itself with a crisp sugar cookie. **MAKES ABOUT 4 CUPS**

VANILLA RUM SYRUP
1 cup sugar
3/4 cup water
1 vanilla bean, split in half lengthwise

COMPOTE
1/2 cup dried figs
1/2 cup dried pineapple

1/2 cup dried peaches
1/2 cup dried apricots
1/2 cup dried sour cherries
One 5- to 6-inch strip lemon zest
1/4 cup dark rum

1   To make the syrup, dissolve the sugar in the water in a medium-size saucepan over medium-high heat, stirring. Scrape the seeds of the vanilla bean into the saucepan and add the vanilla bean. Bring the mixture to a boil and continue boiling for 1 minute, until the syrup reaches 220 degrees F on a candy thermometer, or until a drop placed on a chilled saucer and refrigerated for 1 minute is thick and syrupy. Remove from the heat and set aside until ready to use.

2   To make the compote, reheat the syrup, bringing it to a simmer over low heat. Add the figs and pineapple and poach for 15 minutes. Add the peaches and poach for 7 minutes more. Add the apricots and cherries and poach for 4 minutes more. Remove from the heat. The fruits should be softened, but still retain their shapes.

3   Transfer the fruit from the syrup to a glass jar or earthenware crock and add the strip of lemon zest. Stir the rum into the syrup and pour over the fruit in the jar. Cover and refrigerate until ready to use.

Southern Ambrosia

Sometimes the simplest dishes are the best. This ambrosia relies on only three ingredients, so find the best you can: juicy oranges with great flavor, toasted fresh (not rancid) pecans, and fresh coconut shredded with a vegetable peeler. A quintessential Southern fruit dish—especially for holiday buffet tables—ambrosia began appearing in American cookbooks at the beginning of the twentieth century. Some versions also include chopped bananas or miniature marshmallows. James Beard preferred sweetened, flaked coconut in his 1946 rendition. Add sugar to taste if your oranges aren't very sweet. **MAKES 8 SERVINGS**

4 large Valencia or navel oranges

1 cup toasted (see page 181) and chopped pecans

1 cup shredded fresh coconut or frozen (thawed) unsweetened shredded coconut (available in health food stores)

1   With a paring knife, peel the oranges over a large bowl to catch the juice. Remove and discard the white pith. Cut between the membranes to separate the orange sections, discard the membranes, and put the sections in the bowl with the juice.

2   In a large glass serving bowl, combine the orange segments and juice with the pecans and coconut. Cover with plastic wrap and refrigerate until chilled, or up to 4 hours before serving.

Winter Ruby Molded Gelatin

Shimmering on a glass cake stand surrounded by sugar-frosted branches of fresh rosemary and cranberries, this jewel-colored gelatin dessert catches the candlelight at the table. The grenadine and rosewater are available in Asian markets. (Grenadine is also available at liquor stores.) **MAKES 12 SERVINGS**

Two 12-ounce bags fresh cranberries, picked over for stems and rinsed

4 cups water

1½ cups sugar

⅓ cup grenadine (pomegranate) syrup

Two ¼-ounce packages unflavored gelatin

1 teaspoon rosewater

1   In a large saucepan, bring the cranberries and water to the boil. Reduce the heat to medium-low, cover, and simmer until the cranberries have softened, about 10 minutes. Remove the lid and mash the fruit against the sides of the pan. Place a large sieve lined with cheesecloth over a large mixing bowl. Pour the cranberries and their cooking liquid into the sieve. Leave to drip for 30 minutes. Discard the solids.

2   Rinse out the saucepan and pour the cranberry juice back in. Over low heat, stir in the sugar, grenadine syrup, gelatin, and rosewater. Heat until the sugar and gelatin have dissolved and the mixture is very warm (120 degrees F). *Do not let it boil or even begin to simmer.* Remove from the heat.

3   Pour the cranberry juice mixture into a decorative 2-quart mold or 12 individual dessert glasses. Cover with plastic wrap and chill until the gelatin has set, at least 4 hours.

4   To unmold the dessert, set the mold in a large bowl or pan with enough warm water to come halfway up its sides for 1 minute. Invert the mold onto a serving platter or cake stand and remove the mold from the gelatin. If the gelatin will not unmold the first time, place it back in the warm water for 30 more seconds and try again. Serve chilled.

Working with Gelatin

Creating your own refreshing molded desserts is easy once you learn the basics of working with unflavored gelatin. To avoid the two most common disasters—a lumpy concoction of stringy gelatin or a mixture that won't set and remains a liquid—it's good to know the three main rules:

1   Avoid using raw fruits containing enzymes that keep the gelatin from setting: figs, pineapple, kiwi, papaya, and mango. These fruits must be cooked (or canned) first before including in a gelatin recipe.

2   Sprinkle the gelatin over room-temperature water first and let it soak through. Then gently heat the gelatin-and-water mixture just enough to dissolve the gelatin, but not enough to simmer the mixture. It will be a clear beige color, a signal it is ready to be incorporated into the dish.

3   If you are adding gelatin to a juice-and-sugar mixture, boil the juice and sugar first in order to completely dissolve the sugar. Then add the gelatin.

You can't go wrong with a base of 2 cups of water, the juice and grated zest of 2 lemons, and 1/2 cup sugar, to which you can add raspberries, blueberries, strawberries, pomegranate seeds, or whatever you wish. You'll have a naturally flavored and colored homemade gelatin dessert that children and adults will love.

Fresh Peach and Blueberry Gelatin

Vintage cookbooks are replete with homemade gelatin desserts. The earliest, from about 1860 to 1880, call for Russian isinglass (which was made from the air bladders of freshwater sturgeon) as the setting agent. Around the turn of the century, Coxe's gelatin did the trick. And from about 1905 onward, just "gelatine" or Knox gelatin, owing to the popularity of the Knox booklet *Dainty Desserts for Dainty People*. The advent of iceboxes and refrigerators made gelatin desserts all the more popular. Today, we simply use a package of unflavored gelatin granules to set about 2 cups of liquid. The only tricky part it to make sure the gelatin is first dissolved in liquid to make an opaque mixture, then heated until the mixture becomes a clear beige. Then you can make a refreshing gelatin dessert like this one. **MAKES 8 SERVINGS**

One ¼-ounce envelope unflavored gelatin

1 cup water

½ cup sugar

Grated zest and juice of 1 large lemon

1 recipe Homemade Vanilla Bean Syrup (page 486)

1 cup peeled, pitted, and chopped ripe peaches, plus extra for garnish

1 cup fresh blueberries, picked over for stems, plus extra for garnish

Lemon balm or mint leaves for garnish

1. Sprinkle the gelatin over ¼ cup of the water in a small bowl. Set aside for several minutes, until the gelatin is soaked through.

2. Fill a small baking pan with enough hot water to come three quarters of the way up the side of the bowl of gelatin mixture. Set the bowl in the pan of hot water for several minutes, until the gelatin mixture is clear. Set aside.

3. In a medium-size saucepan, combine the remaining ¾ cup of water, the sugar, and lemon zest and juice and bring to a boil. Remove from the heat and whisk in the vanilla syrup and gelatin mixture. Chill in the refrigerator in the saucepan until the mixture just begins to set, about 2 hours.

4. Rinse out eight 4-ounce molds or a 9 x 5-inch loaf pan with cold water. Add the 2 cups of fruit to the molds or pan and pour the gelatin over it. Cover with plastic wrap and chill 2 more hours or overnight until set.

5. To serve, dip the molds or loaf pan into a pan of warm water to loosen the bottom and sides and turn out onto a serving plate. Garnish with fresh fruits and lemon balm or mint.

Strawberry Sour Cream Gelatin Mold

This is a refreshing, chiffon-like dessert that is great for the novice (as well as for the experienced) gelatin maker to prepare and enjoy. The lemon, sour cream, and strawberry are a great flavor combination. **MAKES 12 SERVINGS**

One 3-ounce package strawberry gelatin mix (Jell-O)

½ teaspoon salt

1 cup boiling water

¼ cup cold water

2 tablespoons fresh lemon juice

1 cup sour cream

One 10-ounce package frozen strawberries in syrup, thawed

1   In a medium bowl, dissolve the gelatin mix and salt in the boiling water. Whisk in the cold water, lemon juice, and sour cream and continue whisking until well blended. Pour into a 9 x 13-inch baking pan and place in the freezer until firm 1 inch around the edge and yet soft in the center, 20 to 25 minutes.

2   Transfer to a large mixing bowl and whip until fluffy with an electric mixer. Drain the strawberries, then chop fine and fold into the gelatin mixture. Pour into a 1-quart mold and chill until firm, about 3 hours.

3   To serve, dip the mold into a pan of warm water to loosen the bottom and sides, and turn out onto a serving plate.

There's Always Room for Jell-O

The story of Jell-O is a rags-to-riches, pull-yourself-up-by-your-bootlaces American success story involving inventors, doubters, flimflam patent medicine men, advertising whiz kids, and even artist Norman Rockwell.

In 1845, industrialist, inventor, and philanthropist Peter Cooper obtained the first patent for a gelatin dessert mix. He never promoted the product. Over 50 years passed before Pearle Wait, a carpenter by day and a maker of patent medicines and laxative teas by night, bought Cooper's patent and packaged his own gelatin dessert mix in LeRoy, New York, in 1897. His wife, May Davis Wait, named the product Jell-O. Although Wait tried to market his invention, he lacked the capital and the expertise. In 1899, Wait sold his formula to Orator Francis Woodward, also of LeRoy, for $450.

Orator Francis Woodward, a dropout, found success manufacturing and selling several patent medicines, Raccoon Corn Plasters, and a roasted coffee substitute made from cereal called Grain-O. He was also involved in the manufacture and sale of a composition nest egg with "miraculous power to kill lice on hens when hatching." In 1897, he combined all his businesses under one name: the Genesee Pure Food Company. But two years later, Jell-O almost did him in.

The first four Jell-O flavors were orange, lemon, strawberry, and raspberry. (Lime was introduced in 1930.) At first, Jell-O sales were dishearteningly slow. The public just didn't "get it." Woodward, in a fit of pique, offered to sell the Jell-O business to his plant manager for only $35, but then changed his mind. In the early 1900s, Woodward launched a vigorous "America's Most Favorite Dessert" advertising campaign for Jell-O, and used the words "Delicate. Delightful. Dainty." to describe the product. ("Dainty" must have been a buzzword in the early 1900s, because Knox Gelatin used the same term in their *Dainty Desserts for Dainty People* recipe booklet.) The first of the millions of Jell-O recipe booklets—illustrated by major artists such as Rose O'Neill of kewpie doll fame, Maxfield Parrish, and Norman Rockwell—found their way into American households. Jell-O sales took off.

Many of those recipe booklet desserts have become American favorites, such as layered gelatin dessert, strawberry chiffon pie, Easter "eggs," jigglers, and Jell-O shots (edible alcoholic "drinks"). In 1981, Jell-O introduced Moist and Fruity Rainbow Cake in *Bon Appétit* magazine—a two-layer white cake with holes poked in the surface with a fork or cake tester, liquid Jell-O poured into the holes, the whole thing chilled until the Jell-O set, and then frosted with Cool Whip. It became known as Poke Cake.

Blackberry and Lemon Molded Dessert

The deep, shimmery, reddish-purple color and vibrant, fresh flavor of this gelatin prove that you *can* have great no-fat desserts. **MAKES 12 SERVINGS**

6 cups fresh or frozen (thawed) blackberries, plus extra for garnish if desired

Juice of 2 lemons

2 cups sugar, plus extra for dusting lemon peel

2 cups water

Two 1/4-ounce packages unflavored gelatin

3 or 4 large lemons

Lemon balm or mint leaves for garnish (optional)

1   Put the blackberries, lemon juice, sugar, and 1½ cups of the water in a large saucepan over medium heat. Bring to a boil and continue to boil until the blackberries soften and release their juice, about 10 minutes. Remove from the heat.

2   Sprinkle the gelatin over the remaining ½ cup of water in a small bowl and let set until the gelatin is soaked through.

3   Rinse out a 2-quart mold or 12 individual ¾-cup molds with cold water. Strain the blackberry mixture through a fine-mesh sieve into a bowl; discard the solids. Stir the gelatin mixture into the hot blackberry juice. Spoon the blackberry mixture into the large mold or use a ½-cup measure to fill the individual molds two thirds full. Cover with plastic wrap and chill until firm, 2 to 3 hours.

4   To serve, dip the mold(s) into a pan of warm water to loosen the bottom and sides and turn out onto a serving plate or cake stand. With a paring knife, peel each lemon in one long, curling strip. Dust the strips with sugar and garnish the gelatin with them, along with additional fresh blackberries and lemon balm or mint leaves, if you like.

Red Summer Fruit Molded Gelatin

Dark, ruby red with a vibrant berry flavor, this light and refreshing dessert is a perfect ending to a summertime meal. I have a collection of vintage individual metal gelatin molds, and I like to make this gelatin using three different kinds of patterns. I unmold each one onto a silver serving tray garnished with fresh leaves and more berries, and a bowl of softly whipped cream next to it for guests to dollop on themselves. **MAKES 12 SERVINGS**

2 cups fresh or frozen (thawed) unpitted tart cherries

2 cups fresh or frozen (thawed) raspberries

2 cups fresh or frozen (thawed) red currants

Juice of 2 lemons

2 cups sugar

2 cups water

Two $\frac{1}{4}$-ounce packages unflavored gelatin

1   Combine the fruit, lemon juice, sugar, and $1\frac{1}{2}$ cups of the water in a large saucepan over medium heat. Bring to a boil and continue to boil until the cherries begin to lose their color and the skins crack, about 10 minutes. Remove from the heat.

2   Sprinkle the gelatin over the remaining $\frac{1}{2}$ cup of water in a small bowl and let sit until the gelatin is soaked through. Strain the fruit and cooking liquid into a metal bowl, pressing lightly on the fruit to release more juice; discard the solids. Stir the gelatin mixture into the hot juice to dissolve the gelatin.

3   Rinse out a 2-quart mold or 12 individual $\frac{3}{4}$-cup molds with cold water. Spoon the hot juice into the 2-quart mold or use a $\frac{1}{2}$-cup measure to fill each individual mold two thirds of the way full. Cover with plastic wrap and chill until firm, 2 to 3 hours.

4   To serve, dip the mold(s) into a pan of warm water to loosen the bottom and sides and turn out onto a serving plate.

Europeans find it curious that Americans consider sweetened fruit solidified by gelatin to be a salad. They don't think sweet and salad mix, and at one time we agreed with them.

In colonial days, "sallet" meant greens or cooked vegetables dressed with vinegar and oil. Southern households of the eighteenth century made gelatin from calves' feet and used it in molded wine or spiced fruit gelatins to accompany roast venison, beef, or ham.

The 1875 *Presbyterian Cook Book* from Dayton, Ohio, lists only one fruit gelatin recipe—"Orange or Lemon Gelatine" made with Coxe's packaged gelatin, sugar, and the juice and grated rind of oranges or lemons. The later *Capital City Cook Book* from Madison, Wisconsin, published in 1905, offers a fruit salad similar to ambrosia as well as wine, pineapple, and lemon gelatin desserts made in a mold.

Then all gel broke lose, as Laura Shapiro chronicles in *Perfection Salad: Women and Cooking at the Turn of the Century* (Modern Library, 2001). In those times, women wore girdles to mold their bodies and curling papers and later pin curls to tame their hair, worried about respectability, and had little power other than in the kitchen (not even in the bedroom, because they weren't supposed to know much about or like sex). So it's no wonder that perfect, tame, respectable, white sauce–dressed, carefully molded food became popular. A perfect example, according to Shapiro, is the lunch served to President Woodrow Wilson during his first day in office in 1913: "Cream of celery soup, fish with white sauce, roast capon with two white vegetables, a fruit salad, and a dessert made with gelatin, custard, and whipped cream."

"Dainty" was the operative word, and both Knox gelatin and Jell-O produced recipe booklets with that word in the title. "Dainty" got the stamp of approval from the Boston Cooking School and other institutions, which promoted Americanization of immigrants through cooking based on scientific principles, like the accurate measuring championed by Fannie Farmer. "Dainty" meant no aroma of garlic or spices in the house, although immigrants proved reluctant to give up their "coarse and unsavory" meals for prim and proper food served chilled or blanketed in white sauce—the dainty American way.

Cafeterias and tearooms evolved at the turn of the century from big-city lunchrooms serving office workers, railroad men, and shop girls. Decent working folk wanted a clean, socially appropriate place where they could eat nourishing, well-made food—not in a saloon, barroom, or tavern. When the "free lunch" saloons closed during Prohibition, cafeterias and tearooms thrived. The congealed or frozen fruit salad, made ahead and served attractively, was a natural. Southern cooks—with an already pronounced sweet tooth—were especially fond of these chilled or frozen molded salads. And in a hotter climate in which appetites could become jaded, these dishes were refreshing.

From 1920 to 1940, jelled or "congealed" salads became very popular; almost one third of the salad recipes in the average cookbook were gelatin based. This led to the introduction of lime Jell-O in 1930, a flavor well suited to salads, appetizers, relishes, and entrées.

Frozen or congealed fruit salads are still "tray chic" at places like Gray Brothers Cafeteria, right outside Indianapolis, or well-heeled establishments like the Swan Coach House in Atlanta.

Summertime Mango Gelatin Molds

Serve these light and refreshing molds as an accompaniment to chicken salad for a light lunch or as a dessert accompanied by fresh fruit on a hot summer night. Adapted from a dish served at Cappy's Restaurant in San Antonio, this easy-to-assemble, no-fuss dessert celebrates the American love for convenience foods, though here convenience takes a backseat to the delicious taste. **MAKES 8 SERVINGS**

2 cups water

Two 3-ounce packages lemon-flavored gelatin (Jell-O)

One 15-ounce can mangoes, with their liquid

4 ounces cream cheese ($\frac{1}{2}$ an 8-ounce package) at room temperature

Fresh mint sprigs for garnish

1   In a medium-size saucepan, bring the water to a boil, remove from the heat, stir in the gelatin, and continue stirring until dissolved. Set aside for 5 minutes to let the mixture cool slightly.

2   In a blender or food processor, process the mangoes and cream cheese together until smooth. Whisk the puree into the gelatin mixture until well blended. Pour the mixture into a 4-cup mold or into eight $\frac{3}{4}$-cup molds. Cover with plastic wrap and chill until set, about 4 hours.

3   To serve, dip the mold(s) into a pan of warm water to loosen the bottom and sides, then unmold onto a serving platter or dessert plate. Garnish with mint sprigs and serve.

Wine Country Lemon Muscat Molded Gelatin

Adapted from a recipe by Britain's Sophie Grigson, this wobbly gelatin dessert takes a leap across the great pond when made with a California dessert wine. My favorite dessert wines to pour (and use for this dessert) are the Sauternes-style Nightingale from Beringer Vineyards; Chateau St. Jean Select Late Harvest Johannisberg Riesling; and Bonny Doon's sweet orange Muscat, called Essensia. This is grown-up Jell-O, full of boozy charm. I like to make it a day ahead to let it firm up, then turn out this honey-colored molded gelatin onto a cake stand and surround it with an autumn-colored fruit compote, such as Dried Fruit Compote with Brown Sugar Syrup (page 9), Winter Fruit

Compote with Vanilla Rum Syrup (page 20), Kumquat Compote (page 13), or Oranges in Cardamom Syrup (page 11). To serve, just scoop the gelatin into a bowl, drizzle with cream, and spoon the fruit compote over it. Heaven. **MAKES 8 SERVINGS**

2 lemons

One 750-ml bottle dessert wine, such as
    Sauternes, Late Harvest Riesling, or Muscat

¾ cup water

1 cup sugar

Two ¼-ounce envelopes unflavored gelatin

1   Brush a 6-cup mold with sweet almond oil or an unflavored vegetable oil and set aside. With a paring knife, peel the rind from each lemon in a long strip. Juice the lemons into a bowl and set aside the juice.

2   Place the lemon peel and dessert wine in a large saucepan over medium heat. Cook until small bubbles form around the edge of the pan. Remove from the heat, cover, and let the mixture steep for 20 minutes.

3   Remove the lemon peel and discard. Stir the lemon juice, water, and sugar into the wine mixture and set over medium heat again. Cook, stirring, until the sugar has dissolved and small bubbles again form around the edge. Remove from the heat and sprinkle the gelatin over the liquid. When the gelatin has softened, whisk it into the hot liquid to dissolve. Pour the mixture into the prepared mold, cover with plastic wrap, and refrigerate until set, about 4 hours.

4   To serve, dip the mold into a pan of warm water to loosen the bottom and sides and then invert onto a serving platter or a cake stand. Surround the mold with a fruit compote, if you wish.

Frozen Fruit Salad

At the Swan Coach House in Atlanta's upscale Buckhead area, you can sit in floral splendor in a tearoom-style restaurant—open for lunch only—where the walls are upholstered in a botanical tulip fabric. Order a fried green tomato sandwich, chilled shrimp and chicken salad, or their famous frozen fruit salad from among the menu offerings and sit among very pale-complexioned Southern women who probably totally disregarded the prevailing social pressure to have a good tan in the '60s and '70s.

This fruit salad is an adaptation of the one served at the Swan Coach House. I think the cooks there freeze the fruit salad in hamburger patty molds—or else they cut taller frozen salads horizontally with a knife dipped in hot water. However you mold it, I would serve this frozen fruit confection as an ice cream–like dessert, perhaps topped with Classic Hot Fudge Sauce (page 427), Caramel Sauce (page 454), or a fresh raspberry sauce (see page 61, step 2). **MAKES 8 SERVINGS**

1 cup heavy cream

Two 3-ounce packages cream cheese at room temperature

1/4 cup cream sherry, white rum, or amaretto

1 cup crushed pineapple, with its juice

1/2 cup drained and snipped canned apricots

1/2 cup maraschino cherries, cut in half

1/2 cup chopped pecans

1 Rinse out the inside of a 6-cup mold or 3 empty 15-ounce cans that have been opened at one end only and cleaned. Set aside.

2 With an electric mixer, beat the cream in a medium-size mixing bowl until it holds stiff peaks. Set aside. In a large mixing bowl, beat the cream cheese and sherry together until smooth. Mix in the pineapple, apricots, maraschino cherries, and pecans and stir until well blended. Fold in the whipped cream with a rubber spatula until the mixture is smooth. Spoon into the prepared mold or cans and freeze until firm, 2 to 3 hours.

3 To serve, dip the mold into a pan of warm water to loosen the bottom and sides and then invert the dessert onto a serving platter or a cutting board. Use a serving spoon or a knife dipped in hot water to portion out the dessert. Serve cold.

Warm Brioche with Red Summer Fruits and Ice Cream

This is a delicious dessert with various components that can be made ahead, then assembled in minutes. Individual brioches are scooped out and filled with luscious poached raspberries, red currants, and strawberries, and are accompanied by a scattering of fresh berries and a scoop of homemade ice cream. Iced Berries 'n' Cream (page 428) is wonderful to serve with this, or simply use the best vanilla ice cream you can find. **MAKES 4 SERVINGS**

4 individual brioches made from Buttery Brioche
dough (recipe follows)

1 quart mixed summer fruits, such as raspberries,
sliced strawberries, and/or red currants

Juice of 1 lemon

$^1\!/_2$ cup sugar

1   With a serrated knife, cut off the top of each cooled brioche, then hollow out the brioche. Set aside the brioches and reserve the brioche tops for another use.

2   In a medium-size heavy saucepan, combine 3 cups of the berries, the lemon juice, and sugar over medium heat and cook until the sugar dissolves and the berries release their juice, about 5 minutes.

3   To serve, place each brioche on a dessert plate, spoon some warm berry compote into each one, and scatter the remaining 1 cup of berries on the plates.

Buttery Brioche

Teacher and college counselor Lorraine Gordon spends her days immersed in the English language—teaching, reading, writing, and grading it. Amazingly, though, English is not her first language. Lorraine's father met and married a young French woman during World War II and brought his bride and her mother back to live on a tiny farm in Wyandotte County, Kansas. "Both my mother and grandmother had come from Lorraine in northeastern France," says Gordon. "Until I was six, I spoke practically nothing but French." Gordon's grandmother Celestine, still clung to her peasant roots, easy enough to do on a farm. "My dad kept chickens and cows. We made our own butter, had our own fresh eggs and fresh chicken," says Gordon. "I vividly remember going to my grandmother's part of the house in the dead of winter, and there she would be—nursing a sick chicken. She never had any qualms about letting chickens in the house." Likewise, Celestine's cooking was more home style, less high style, with homemade breads like this brioche. Enjoy it with a cup of richly brewed coffee or as the basis for many different desserts. The baked brioche can also be frozen, then rewarmed, wrapped in foil, in a 350-degree-F oven. MAKES TWELVE 4-INCH BRIOCHES OR 1 LARGE LOAF

Two ¼-ounce packages or 1½ tablespoons instant or bread machine yeast

¼ cup lukewarm water

1 cup (2 sticks) unsalted butter at room temperature

2 large eggs

1¼ cups buttermilk

2 teaspoons baking powder

1½ teaspoons salt

2 tablespoons sugar

5 cups all-purpose flour, plus more as needed

3 large egg yolks

1   Preheat the oven to its lowest setting, around 150 degrees to 170 degrees F. Grease the inside of 12 fluted brioche molds, 4 inches in diameter; regular muffin cups; or a 9 x 5-inch loaf pan, place them on a large baking sheet, and set aside.

2   In the bowl of an electric stand mixer, beat together the yeast, water, butter, whole eggs, buttermilk, baking powder, salt, and sugar. Beat in 2½ cups of the flour and continue beating until smooth. Gradually beat in the remaining 2½ cups of flour, ½ cup at a time, plus additional flour, as needed, until you have a smooth dough that has lost its stickiness. Turn the dough out onto a floured work surface.

3   To make individual brioches: With a serrated knife, cut the dough into 13 equal pieces. Roll 12 of the pieces into balls and place each one in a prepared brioche mold or muffin cup. Cut the remaining piece of dough into 12 equal pieces and roll each piece into a small ball. Dust your thumb with flour and make a ½-inch indentation in the top of each large ball of dough in the pans. Place a small ball of dough in each depression. This creates the "crown" of the brioche.

   To make a loaf, form the dough into a loaf shape and place in the prepared pan.

4   Turn off the oven. Place the brioches in the oven to rise for 30 minutes.

5   Whisk the egg yolks until smooth. Remove the brioches from the oven, and raise the temperature to 350 degrees F. Use a pastry brush to brush the brioches with the egg yolk glaze, being careful not to dislodge the "crowns" of the small brioches.

6   When the oven temperature has reached 350 degrees F, bake the brioches until an instant-read thermometer inserted in the center registers at least 190 degrees F, about 30 minutes for the smaller brioches and 45 to 50 minutes for the loaf. Invert onto a wire rack and immediately turn right side up to cool. Serve warm or at room temperature.

Martha's Vineyard Summer Pudding

English settlers brought this simple cottage dessert to America—perfect for a mid-summer day. Home cooks can use their leftover homemade bread or Buttery Brioche (page 32) along with raspberries, red currants, blueberries, and strawberries from the garden or blackberries, elderberries, and mulberries from the wild. Jacqueline Kennedy's cook, Marta Sgubin, revealed the secret of the family's version of this dessert, served at their summer home on Martha's Vineyard—at least 1 cup of red currants among the berries. Any way you make this pudding, it's delicious served with a dollop of Wildflower Honey Cream or sweetened whipped cream. **MAKES 6 TO 8 SERVINGS**

6 to 8 slices good quality stale bread or Buttery Brioche loaf (page 32), crusts removed

6 cups fresh or frozen (thawed) mixed berries, such as raspberries, strawberries, and/or blackberries

¼ cup sugar, or to taste

Fresh lemon juice to taste

1 recipe Wildflower Honey Cream (page 348), sweetened whipped cream, crème fraîche, or yogurt for garnish

1   The night before serving, cut the bread to line the bottom and sides of a medium-size or small mixing bowl or pudding bowl, and cut a lid out of the brioche to fit. Cook the berries and sugar in a large heavy saucepan over medium heat, stirring constantly, until the mixture begins to boil. Reduce the heat to low and simmer the fruit, stirring frequently, for 5 to 10 minutes. Remove from the heat, add lemon juice to taste, and more sugar if the fruit is too tart.

2   Pour the fruit into the bread-lined bowl and top with the bread lid. Sit a plate on top of the bread lid and weight it down with a heavy can. Refrigerate overnight.

3   The pudding is ready when the juice has permeated the bread, turning it a reddish purple color. Invert the pudding onto a serving plate, cut into wedges, and serve with the garnish of your choice.

Creole Pain Perdu with Poached Sweet Cherries

In New Orleans, Creole *pain perdu* (literally, "lost bread" in French) is what we would call glorified French toast. Made with egg or brioche bread, butter, sugar, and spices, it is elevated to dessert status here. Use a paper clip to pit the cherries. If you don't want to serve this with cherries, top it with a squeeze of lemon juice and a dusting of confectioners' sugar. **MAKES 4 SERVINGS**

POACHED CHERRIES

2 cups sweet cherries, pitted

1½ cups water

1 cup sugar

Juice of ½ lemon

PAIN PERDU

Four ½-inch-thick slices Buttery Brioche (page 32) or store-bought egg bread, such as challah

1 large egg

5 tablespoons unsalted butter

3 tablespoons sugar

¼ teaspoon salt

½ teaspoon ground cinnamon

¼ teaspoon freshly grated nutmeg

⅓ cup all-purpose flour

¾ cup milk

¾ teaspoon vanilla extract

1   To make the poached cherries, place the cherries, water, and sugar in a medium-size heavy saucepan and bring to a boil over medium-high heat. Reduce to a simmer and cook until the mixture becomes syrupy and the cherries are soft but still hold their shape, 10 to 15 minutes. Keep warm.

2   To make the *pain perdu*, lay the bread out on a flat surface to dry a little while you make the batter. In a medium-size mixing bowl, whisk the egg. Melt 3 tablespoons of the butter in a small saucepan and allow to cool slightly. Whisk the sugar, salt, and spices into the egg. Slowly drizzle the butter into the egg, whisking constantly. Whisk the flour, 1 tablespoon a time, into the butter-and-egg mixture to make a smooth batter. Whisk in the milk and vanilla and set aside.

3   Heat the remaining 2 tablespoons of butter in a large skillet over medium heat. Dip each slice of the bread in the batter and allow to soak for 30 seconds. Remove from the batter and allow the excess to drip back into the bowl. Place the battered slices into the skillet and fry until golden on one side, then turn and cook on the other side, about 5 minutes total. (You may need to do this in two batches.)

4   Stir the lemon juice into the cherries and serve the *pain perdu* immediately with a generous spoonful of cherries on each plate.

A Dessert-Lover's Garden

Gardeners who love growing plants as well as making and eating great desserts make a point to grow fruits, herbs, and flowers that they use often or can't find commercially. You can create truly signature desserts simply by using just-picked sweet herbs, berries, flowers, fruits, and vegetables right from your garden.

In my garden, I have lemon-scented roses, lavender, honeysuckle, lemon balm, lemon verbena, scented geraniums, and other edible flowers that I use to infuse in syrups or as garnishes. Because I have sprayed no chemicals on them, they're safe to use in cooking. (It's a good idea to learn which plant leaves and petals are poisonous, such as lily-of-the-valley, oleander, foxgloves, and daffodils.)

The scented petals or leaves of these plants can also be infused to make scented creams of all kinds, such as Rose-Scented Crème Anglaise (see page 57) or Lemon Verbena Whipped Cream (see page 37). Scented petals can be candied (see page 177) or simply strewn fresh over a frosted or sugared cake. Scented leaves can line a buttered cake tin, creating an edible pattern around the cake's perimeter, as in Lemon Rose Geranium Layer Cake (page 178).

I also grow raspberries, red currants, mulberries, and small Kieffer pears. Every year I experiment with different vegetable varieties, but I usually grow green zucchini and yellow summer squash and sometimes small sugar or pie pumpkins. All of these homegrown products have worked their way into my own American dessert repertoire—the fruits in all manner of confections, such as Martha's Vineyard Summer Pudding (page 34) and Baked Lemon Spice Pears (page 67); the vegetables in Praise and Plenty Cake (page 174), Fresh Pumpkin Cake (page 241), and Garden Candy (page 482).

Summer Berry Cobbler with Lemon Verbena Whipped Cream

Deep blue sky, morning sun the color of lemons, warm air, fresh breeze. If a sunny summer day could be translated into a dessert, this would be it. Pastry chef Stephanie Settle of Kansas City, whose dessert I have adapted, loves to use seasonal ingredients. And she's especially fond of flavoring sugars and creams with old-fashioned herbs like lemon verbena, scented geranium, and other aromatic plants.

MAKES 8 SERVINGS

LEMON VERBENA WHIPPED CREAM

1 cup heavy cream

1/4 cup packed fresh lemon verbena leaves

3 tablespoons sugar

COBBLER

1/2 cup (1 stick) unsalted butter

2 1/2 cups sugar

1 1/2 cups all-purpose flour

2 teaspoons baking powder

1 cup milk

4 cups mixed berries, such as blackberries, raspberries, blueberries, and hulled and sliced strawberries

Whipped cream for serving

1   To make the whipped cream, combine the cream and lemon verbena leaves in a small saucepan and warm over medium heat. Do not boil. Strain the cream, discarding the leaves, and chill for several hours or overnight. After you have made the cobbler and are ready to serve, pour the cold infused cream into a chilled medium-size mixing bowl and beat until thickened. Gradually beat in the sugar until the cream holds stiff peaks.

2   To begin the cobbler, preheat the oven to 350 degrees F. Melt the butter in a 9 x 13-inch baking pan. In a large mixing bowl, whisk together 1 1/2 cups of the sugar, the flour, baking powder, and milk until you have a smooth batter. Pour the batter over the melted butter in the baking pan, but do not mix the two together. Sprinkle the berries in an even layer over the batter. Sprinkle the berries with the remaining 1 cup of sugar. Bake until a cake tester inserted in the center comes out clean, about 35 minutes.

3   Serve the cobbler, warm or at room temperature, with a dollop of the whipped cream on top.

Rich Berry Cobbler

This is my very favorite cobbler, adapted from a recipe by the late Lee Bailey. Unlike most cobblers, which have a drop biscuit–dough topping, this one has a rich top pastry that is rolled like a pie crust. The pastry doesn't have to be perfect because it practically melts into the berries as the cobbler bakes. This recipe also makes an incredible peach cobbler. Just replace the blackberries with an equal amount of peeled and sliced fresh peaches. A scoop of vanilla ice cream is wonderful with this served warm.

MAKES 8 SERVINGS

PASTRY TOPPING

⅓ cup all-purpose flour

⅛ teaspoon salt

2 tablespoons (¼ stick) unsalted butter, frozen and cut into small pieces

2 tablespoons vegetable shortening, frozen and cut into small pieces

2 to 2½ tablespoons ice water, as needed

FILLING

6 cups fresh or frozen (thawed) blackberries, red or black raspberries, whortleberries, or huckleberries

1 tablespoon fresh lemon juice

1 teaspoon grated lemon zest

⅔ cup sugar

1   To make the pastry topping, place the flour and salt in a food processor or blender. Add the butter and shortening and process with quick pulses until the mixture resembles small peas. Add the water, 1 tablespoon at a time, and continue to pulse until the dough forms a ball. Wrap the dough in plastic wrap and chill for 30 minutes.

2   Preheat the oven to 450 degrees F. Butter the inside of a 2-quart soufflé dish.

3   To make the filling, pour the berries into the dish, sprinkle with the lemon juice, zest, and sugar, and toss to blend.

4   Roll out the pastry to make a ragged circle large enough to cover the berries, then place on top of the berries.

5   Place the cobbler in the oven and immediately reduce the oven temperature to 425 degrees F. Bake until bubbling and the crust has browned, 40 to 45 minutes. Serve warm.

Pear and Maple Cobblers

Pears, skillfully grown and nurtured by the French on their own soil, were among the first fruits cultivated by New England colonists. In 1634, John Winthrop, Jr., learned that Joseph Downing was sending 100 apple and pear trees to Winthrop's father. On the voyage from England to New England, Downing sent instructions that the young trees should be aired on deck two or three days per week to survive the voyage. Survive they did, even in the cold New England winters. In this dessert, Old World pears are sweetened with New World maple syrup, bringing out the best in both. Serve each small cobbler with a dollop of whipped cream. **MAKES 6 INDIVIDUAL COBBLERS**

FILLING

3 pounds ripe Bartlett or Anjou pears, peeled, cored, and sliced

²⁄₃ cup pure maple syrup

1¹⁄₂ tablespoons all-purpose flour

¹⁄₂ teaspoon vanilla extract

¹⁄₄ teaspoon freshly grated nutmeg

¹⁄₂ teaspoon ground cinnamon

1¹⁄₂ tablespoons cold unsalted butter, cut into small pieces

TOPPING

1¹⁄₂ cups all-purpose flour

¹⁄₂ teaspoon baking powder

¹⁄₄ teaspoon freshly grated nutmeg

6 tablespoons (¾ stick) cold unsalted butter, cut into ¹⁄₂-inch pieces

1 cup half-and-half

¹⁄₂ cup pure maple syrup

1 teaspoon vanilla extract

Melted butter for brushing topping

Sugar for dusting topping

Whipped cream for serving

1   Preheat the oven to 425 degrees F.

2   To make the filling, combine the pears, maple syrup, flour, vanilla, nutmeg, and cinnamon in a large mixing bowl. Divide the mixture among 6 ovenproof bowls or soufflé dishes. Dot the tops with the butter and bake until the pears are tender and the filling is hot and bubbling, about 18 minutes. Set aside.

3   To make the topping, combine the flour, baking powder, and nutmeg in a food processor. Add the butter pieces and pulse the machine until the mixture resembles coarse crumbs. Transfer the mixture to a large mixing bowl. In a small mixing bowl, whisk together the half-and-half, maple syrup, and vanilla. Add this mixture, 1 cup at a time, to the pastry crumbs, mixing well with a fork until you have a soft batter. Spoon the batter over the fillings, brush the tops with melted butter, and dust with sugar.

4   Bake for 8 minutes, then reduce the oven temperature to 375 degrees F and continue baking until the topping is golden brown and firm to the touch, 10 to 15 minutes more. Serve warm with a dollop of whipped cream.

Sweet Cherry Cobbler with Snickerdoodle Topping

This is adapted from a recipe by pastry chef Jennifer Welshhons at Cory Schreiber's Wildwood restaurant in Portland, Oregon. Wildwood celebrates Northwestern regional foods, and Welshhons uses Hood River Valley orchard fruits in this homey dessert with the inspired topping of classic snickerdoodle cookie dough, a vintage American cookie dusted with cinnamon sugar. **MAKES 8 SERVINGS**

FILLING

6 cups pitted fresh sweet cherries, preferably Bing

3 tablespoons instant tapioca or cornstarch

1/2 cup packed light brown sugar

Juice of 2 lemons

TOPPING

1/2 cup plus 2 teaspoons granulated sugar

1/4 cup (1/2 stick) unsalted butter at room temperature

1 large egg

1 large egg yolk

1/2 teaspoon vanilla extract

3/4 cup all-purpose flour

1/4 teaspoon freshly grated nutmeg

1/2 teaspoon ground cinnamon

1/4 teaspoon baking soda

1/4 teaspoon salt

Vanilla ice cream for serving

1 Preheat the oven to 350 degrees F. Butter a 2-quart baking dish and set aside.

2 To make the filling, combine the ingredients in a large mixing bowl and stir gently to blend. Spoon the cherry mixture into the prepared baking dish.

3 To make the topping, cream together 1/2 cup of the granulated sugar and the butter in a food processor until fluffy. Add the whole egg, egg yolk, and vanilla and pulse to blend. Add the flour, spices, baking soda, and salt and pulse again to blend to a batter. Drop the batter by the rounded tablespoon onto the fruit filling. Sprinkle the batter with the remaining 2 teaspoons of granulated sugar.

4 Bake until the fruit is bubbling and the topping has browned, 40 to 45 minutes. Serve warm with a scoop of vanilla ice cream.

Springtime Strawberry and Rhubarb Pandowdy

When I create new recipes, I try not to take away from the natural flavors of the ingredients. "Sometimes, the less you do, the better," says Missouri-born Bradley Ogden, now chef-owner of One Market, Lark Creek Inn, and Lark Creek Cafe, all in the San Francisco Bay area. I've adapted his version of an old-fashioned pandowdy—a baked dessert with pie crust that is broken into the fruit filling so that it soaks up the juices, making it similar to a cobbler. Fresh and crystallized ginger take it to a new level.

MAKES 10 TO 12 SERVINGS

4 cups diced ($\frac{1}{4}$-inch) rhubarb stalks

4 cups hulled and sliced fresh strawberries

1 cup plus 2 tablespoons sugar

$\frac{1}{4}$ cup fresh lemon juice

1 tablespoon finely grated lemon zest

1 teaspoon peeled and finely grated fresh ginger

$\frac{1}{2}$ cup (1 stick) unsalted butter

4 ounces ($\frac{1}{2}$ an 8-ounce package) cream cheese at room temperature

1$\frac{1}{2}$ cups all-purpose flour

$\frac{1}{2}$ cup heavy cream

1 teaspoon vanilla extract

3 tablespoons chopped crystallized ginger

1   Butter a 9 x 13-inch baking pan. In a large mixing bowl, combine the rhubarb, strawberries, 1 cup of the sugar, the lemon juice and zest, and fresh ginger and spoon into the prepared baking pan. Set aside.

2   In another large mixing bowl, work the butter and cream cheese into the flour with your fingertips or a pastry cutter until there are pea-size bits of butter and cream cheese. Stir in the cream and vanilla and continue stirring until the dough forms a ball. Do not overmix. Cover with plastic wrap and refrigerate for 30 minutes.

3   Preheat the oven to 350 degrees F. On a lightly floured work surface, roll out the dough into a 9 x 13-inch rectangle about $\frac{1}{8}$ inch thick. Gently place the dough over the fruit mixture. Trim the edges so the dough fits within the baking dish. Lightly brush the top of the dough with water. Sprinkle with the remaining 2 tablespoons of sugar and the crystallized ginger.

4   Place the baking pan on a baking sheet and bake for 30 minutes. Remove from the oven. With a knife or a pizza wheel, score the crust, cutting it into large blocks, and gently press the crust pieces into the fruit until just moistened. Return to the oven and bake until the crust is golden brown and the fruit is bubbling, about 30 minutes more. Let cool slightly before serving.

Ginger Pear Crumble

This is another in the pantheon of homey American desserts that are currently being revived at upscale casual restaurants, where they are usually served warm in individual portions. Crumbles, betties, cobblers, and crisps have held on as comfort food for 300 years, and when you taste this one, you'll understand why. Process about 12 whole gingersnaps in the food processor to make the crumbs. A drizzle of cream or a scoop of ice cream takes this crumble into another dimension. **MAKES 6 SERVINGS**

1½ cups gingersnap crumbs

½ cup packed brown sugar

¼ teaspoon salt

¼ cup (½ stick) unsalted butter at room temperature

4 ripe dessert pears, such as Anjou or Bosc, peeled, cored, and sliced

1 tablespoon fresh lemon juice

Heavy cream or ice cream for serving

1   Preheat the oven to 350 degrees F. In a medium-size mixing bowl, combine the gingersnap crumbs, brown sugar, and salt with your fingers. Work in the softened butter until the mixture is dotted with large pea-size bits of butter. Arrange the pear slices in a 9-inch square baking pan and drizzle with the lemon juice. Spoon or drop the crumb mixture over the pears.

2   Bake until the pears are soft and the crumble is bubbling, 25 to 30 minutes. Serve warm with cream or ice cream.

I'm a Fool for Slumps, Grunts, Buckles, Betties, Crumbles, Cobblers, and Pandowdies

These centuries-old homey baked desserts with English country roots are very much at home in American kitchens today. Temporarily banished during the "dainty" years of congealed desserts and perfectly white frosted cakes, these have a rustic appearance that is once more appealing. What's even better, they taste great and are done when they look done—browned and bubbling. No inserting thermometers, tapping the sides of the pan, or testing with a toothpick. No one is really sure about the origin of these names, but they're in the English tradition of quirky dessert titles for homemade fare, such as Spotted Dick and Dead Man's Leg (both pale, steamed suet puddings with dried fruit).

★ *Betty:* A baked fruit dessert made with layers of buttered bread crumbs and sweetened and spiced fruit. Most betties are made with apples or pears.

★ *Buckle:* A baked, coffeecake-like dessert made with an egg and baking powder batter, with fruit—usually blueberries—scattered on the batter and a streusel mixture on top.

★ *Cobbler:* A baked dessert made with sweetened fruit topped with drop biscuits or pieces of rolled pastry dough to form "cobbles" on top.

★ *Crisp:* A baked dessert made with spiced and sweetened fruit, usually apples or berries, and a crunchy topping of cookie crumbs, flour, or oats blended with butter, sugar, and spices.

★ *Crumble:* A baked fruit dessert similar to a crisp made with sweetened fruit such as apple, pear, or berries, and topped with chopped nuts or bread crumbs mixed with sugar, spices, and butter. The name is more commonly used in England than in the United States.

★ *Grunt:* A fruit dessert cooked on the stove top or steamed, topped with dropped baking powder dumplings, or "grunts."

★ *Pandowdy:* A baked deep-dish fruit dessert topped with pieces of pastry that are pressed into the filling during baking. This softens the crust, but doesn't help the appearance of this dish. The original Middle English word *dowdy* went from meaning "slatternly" in the Middle Ages to "unfashionable" or "matronly" today.

★ *Slump:* A baked cobbler-like fruit dessert whose top crust appears to be slumping into the filling. *Little Women* author Louisa May Alcott loved this dessert, and she nicknamed Orchard House, her home in Concord, Massachusetts, "Apple Slump."

Lemon-Zested Blackberry Crisp with Lemon-Rose Geranium Whipped Cream

The trio of flavors in this dessert—blackberry, rose, and lemon—is a fabulous combination. This is yet another American dessert that brings the garden or farmers' market to the table. I loved the Lemon-Zested Mulberry and Rhubarb Crisp I created in *Prairie Home Cooking* so much that I adapted the recipe for blackberries here. The flavored whipped cream, inspired by pastry chef Stephanie Settle, is the crowning glory. Scented geraniums, available in the herb section of garden nursery shops, come in all kinds of flavors, from apple to peppermint, nutmeg to rose. The scent is in the leaves, not the flowers. Tender plants, they need to be brought indoors for the cold weather. My Rober's lemon rose geranium stays on my patio in warm weather, and basks indoors in a sunny window during the winter. **MAKES 8 SERVINGS**

LEMON-ROSE GERANIUM WHIPPED CREAM

1 cup heavy cream

$1/4$ cup packed fresh lemon-rose geranium leaves, or substitute $1/2$ teaspoon grated lemon zest mixed with $1/2$ teaspoon rosewater

3 tablespoons sugar

CRISP

6 cups fresh or frozen (thawed) blackberries

2 cups sugar

1 tablespoon quick-cooking tapioca

Grated zest and juice of 1 lemon

1 cup all-purpose flour

$1/2$ cup (1 stick) unsalted butter at room temperature

1   To make the whipped cream, combine the cream and lemon-rose geranium leaves in a small heavy saucepan and warm over medium heat. Do not boil. Strain the cream, discarding the leaves, and chill for several hours or overnight. (If using lemon zest and rosewater, simply combine all the ingredients when you're ready to whip the cream.) After you've made the crisp and are ready to serve, with an electric mixer, whip the flavored cream in a medium-size bowl until it holds stiff peaks.

2   To make the crisp, preheat the oven to 375 degrees F. Butter a 9 x 13-inch baking dish and set aside. In a large mixing bowl, combine the blackberries, 1 cup of the sugar, the tapioca, and lemon juice. Stir to blend, then turn into the prepared pan. In a medium-size mixing bowl, combine the remaining 1 cup of sugar, the lemon zest, and flour. Using your fingers, rub the butter into the

flour mixture to form large crumbs. Sprinkle these large crumbs evenly over the blackberries. Bake until lightly browned and bubbly, about 35 minutes.

3   Spoon the warm crisp onto dessert plates and serve with a dollop of flavored whipped cream.

Maple and Hickory Nut Apple Crisp

Odessa Piper, the celebrated chef-owner of L'Etoile in Madison, Wisconsin, started her food career as a hippie farmer. In 1976, Piper opened her restaurant and also had a market stall at the Madison Farmers' Market across the street. "I learned what I could about freezing, drying, and preserving. I thought about what Native Americans did in this cold climate, and began to see what I could do, very elegantly, in my own restaurant," she says. She installed an extensive root cellar in L'Etoile to store locally grown and harvested apples like Gravensteins or Winesaps, root vegetables, potatoes, onions, hams, and hickory nuts for her winter menus. She was then able to bake and serve homey desserts like this one, which I have adapted. Accompany it with Monticello Vanilla-Flecked Ice Cream.

Hickory trees are native to the United States and grow in many parts of the country, including Maine, Nebraska, Tennessee, and Minnesota. The nuts ripen and are shaken off the trees in fall. **MAKES 10 TO 12 SERVINGS**

1 cup shelled hickory nuts or pecans (see Sources)

1½ tablespoons plus 1 teaspoon vegetable oil

¼ teaspoon salt

1½ cups old-fashioned rolled oats

½ teaspoon pure maple extract

3 tablespoons pure maple syrup, plus more, warmed, for garnish

¼ cup (½ stick) unsalted butter at room temperature

3 tablespoons packed brown sugar

½ cup all-purpose flour

8 cups sliced apples, such as Gravenstein, Winesap, or Pippin

1 teaspoon cornstarch

⅓ cup granulated sugar

1 recipe Monticello Vanilla-Flecked Ice Cream (page 425)

1   Preheat the oven to 325 degrees F. Butter a 9 x 13-inch baking pan and set aside.

2   Toss the hickory nuts with 1 teaspoon of the vegetable oil and ⅛ teaspoon of the salt and spread out on a baking sheet. Toast in the oven for 10 minutes, then set aside.

3 In a large mixing bowl, combine the oats with the remaining 1½ tablespoons of vegetable oil, the remaining ⅛ teaspoon salt, the maple extract, and 2 tablespoons of the maple syrup. Spread out the oat mixture out on a baking sheet and toast in the oven until the oats turn golden, about 10 minutes. Set aside until cool enough to handle. Increase the oven temperature to 375 degrees F.

4 In a medium-size mixing bowl, combine the softened butter, brown sugar, and flour with an electric mixer until smooth. With your fingers, blend in the oat mixture until crumbly.

5 In a large mixing bowl, combine the apples, cornstarch, and granulated sugar and toss to coat. Spread the apples evenly in the bottom of the prepared pan, drizzle with the remaining 1 tablespoon of maple syrup, and top with the oat mixture. Bake for 20 minutes, then cover the pan with aluminum foil and bake until the apples are tender and juicy, about 10 more minutes. Remove the foil and let crisp, uncovered, for another 10 minutes. Serve warm, drizzled with warm maple syrup, and accompanied by the vanilla ice cream.

Shelburne Apple Crisp

During the mid 1970s, I worked at the Shelburne Museum in Vermont, first as a tour guide and then as a member of the office staff. This apple crisp comes from a recipe card the museum gave out during that time, and it's one I have adapted over the years. This is another example of a truly American dessert, close to but not the same as a softer British apple crumble. The British version usually features Bramley apples, which cook down to the consistency of applesauce. In this recipe, the topping melts into the fruit. Peaches, pears, nectarines, or berries can be used instead of apples. This is a great recipe to make with kids and a crowd pleaser for all ages. **MAKES 6 TO 8 SERVINGS**

TOPPING

¾ cup packed brown, turbinado ("raw" sugar), or maple sugar

¼ cup granulated sugar

½ cup all-purpose flour

½ cup old-fashioned rolled oats

1 teaspoon ground cinnamon

¼ teaspoon salt

½ cup (1 stick) unsalted butter at room temperature

FILLING

4 large tart apples, such as Jonathan, Empire, Cortland, or Granny Smith, peeled, cored, and sliced (about 4 cups)

1   Preheat the oven to 425 degrees F. Butter a 9-inch square baking pan and set aside.

2   In a large mixing bowl, whisk together the sugars, flour, oats, cinnamon, and salt and work in the butter with your fingers until the mixture resembles coarse crumbs.

3   Arrange the apples in the prepared baking pan and sprinkle evenly with the topping. Bake for 15 minutes, then reduce the oven temperature to 350 degrees F and bake until bubbling and the top has browned, about 35 more minutes. Serve warm.

New England Blueberry Grunt

From their English forebears, New Englanders inherited a love of unusual words, and the region has more than its share of funny-sounding desserts: snickerdoodle cookies, pandowdy, slump, and grunt—an old New England word for dumpling. This dessert is similar to a cobbler or crisp, but with cloud-like dumplings instead of a batter or crisp topping. Blueberry grunt is steamed on top of the stove, not baked, harking back to the nineteenth century, when large cast-iron stoves dominated the kitchen.

MAKES 10 TO 12 SERVINGS

DUMPLINGS
1 large egg
1/3 cup heavy cream
1 teaspoon vanilla extract
2/3 cup all-purpose flour
2 tablespoons sugar
1 teaspoon baking powder
1/4 teaspoon salt

FILLING
1/2 cup sugar
1/2 cup water
Grated zest and juice of 1 lemon
4 cups fresh or frozen (thawed) blueberries

1   To make the dumpling batter, beat the egg, cream, and vanilla together in a medium-size mixing bowl with a fork. Mix in the flour, sugar, baking powder, and salt until you have a thick batter. Set aside.

2   To make the filling, in an 11- or 12-inch skillet with a lid, bring the sugar, water, lemon zest and juice, and blueberries to a boil, stirring, over medium-high heat. Reduce the heat to low so that

the berries barely simmer. Drop in the batter by spoonfuls to make 12 to 14 dumplings, spacing them about ½ inch apart. Cover and cook, without lifting the lid, for 15 minutes. The grunts will have risen and the blueberries cooked down to a sauce. The grunts are done when a cake tester inserted in the center comes out clean. If it does not come out clean, cover, and cook for 5 minutes more. Serve in dessert bowls.

Buttery Pear Brown Betty

Betties, crisps, cobblers, crumbles, and slumps are relatively quick, cottage-style desserts, which were well suited to the New England settler's penchant for baking. They're so delicious and adaptable that they're still with us 300 years later. They're also easy—when they look done, they are. A betty is a baked dessert formed from layers of leftover homemade bread crumbs and stewed fruit mashed to a pulp. Traditionally, it was made with apples—and the apple betty even traveled as far west as Alaska—but I think that pears are particularly good this way. Like any other dessert, the quality of the ingredients is what makes for the best flavor. Use really good bread, not packaged crumbs. **MAKES 8 SERVINGS**

4 cups cubed Buttery Brioche (page 32), challah, or bakery butter-topped white bread, crusts removed

½ cup (1 stick) unsalted butter, melted

8 Bartlett pears, peeled, cored, and quartered

1¼ cups packed light brown sugar

1 cup water

½ teaspoon freshly grated nutmeg

½ teaspoon ground cinnamon

¼ teaspoon salt

Juice of 1 lemon

1 teaspoon vanilla extract

Vanilla ice cream or heavy cream for serving

1   Preheat the oven to 350 degrees F. Arrange the bread cubes on a baking sheet and toast in the oven until lightly browned, about 15 minutes. Remove from the oven to cool slightly, but leave the oven on. Butter a 2-quart baking dish and set aside.

2   Place the toasted bread cubes in a food processor and pulse to create coarse crumbs. Transfer the crumbs to a large mixing bowl and drizzle with the melted butter. Gently toss to blend.

3   In a large saucepan, combine the pears, brown sugar, water, spices, and salt and bring to a boil over medium-high heat. Lower the heat, and simmer the pears, covered, stirring occasionally, until they have softened, about 20 minutes. Remove from the heat and stir in the lemon juice and vanilla. Lightly mash the pears with a potato masher and set aside.

4   Spoon a third of the crumb mixture over the bottom of the prepared baking dish and top with half of the pear mixture. Repeat the layers and top with the remaining crumb mixture.

5   Bake until the top has browned and the fruit is bubbling, about 30 minutes. Serve warm with vanilla ice cream or heavy cream.

Farmhouse Peach and Blackberry Shortcakes with Warm Nutmeg Cream Sauce

This is what homemade dessert is all about. Forget the towering flights of fancy that dazzle the eye but have little flavor. American desserts are rooted in practical goodness: bringing out the maximum flavor from seasonal ingredients. In this case, shortcakes are drizzled with the simplest of sauces—rich, warm, sweetened cream scented with nutmeg—then scattered with freshly picked peaches and blackberries. **SERVES 8**

NUTMEG CREAM SAUCE
¼ cup (½ stick) unsalted butter
¼ cup sugar
2 cups heavy cream
⅛ teaspoon freshly grated nutmeg

SHORTCAKES
¾ cup all-purpose flour
¼ cup cake flour
1½ teaspoons baking powder
¼ teaspoon salt

¼ cup sugar
¼ cup (½ stick) unsalted butter at room temperature
1 large egg
3 tablespoons milk

TO ASSEMBLE THE DISH
4 large ripe peaches, peeled, pitted, and sliced
1 pint fresh blackberries, blueberries, or raspberries

1   To make the cream sauce, combine the butter, sugar, and cream in a heavy-bottomed, 2-quart saucepan. Over low heat, slowly bring the cream mixture to a boil and let it boil up to the top of the saucepan, about 15 minutes. Whisk the cream down, then let it come to a simmer and continue simmering until it coats the back of a spoon, 2 to 3 more minutes. Stir in the nutmeg. (You may make the sauce several hours ahead of time. Cover and chill it, then gently warm over very low heat to serve.)

2   Preheat the oven to 400 degrees F. Butter a baking sheet or line it with parchment paper and set aside. To make the shortcakes, sift both flours, baking powder, salt, and sugar into a small mixing bowl. Cut in the butter with a pastry blender, two knives, or your fingertips until the mixture resembles coarse crumbs. With a fork, beat the egg with the milk in a small bowl. Make a well in the dry ingredients and pour the egg mixture in. Using a circular motion, blend the dry ingredients into the egg mixture with a fork, just enough to make a moist dough.

3   Drop about 2 tablespoons of the dough at a time onto the prepared baking sheet to make 8 shortcakes. Bake until risen and browned, 12 to 15 minutes.

4   To assemble the dish, cut the warm shortcakes in half horizontally. Place each bottom shortcake half on a dessert plate or in a shallow bowl. Arrange several sliced peaches on the shortcake and top with the upper shortcake half. Pour about ¼ cup of warm sauce over each shortcake, then scatter more peach slices and the blackberries in the pool of sauce around the shortcake. Serve warm.

Classic Strawberry Shortcake

Buttery, biscuit-like shortcake. Tangy, fruity, lightly sweetened strawberries. Mounds of whipped cream. These three flavor notes combine to create an ode to summer celebrated in strawberry festivals from Vermont to California. Forget berries that still look good after traveling thousands of miles to your grocery store, but taste like cotton. Instead, find the best locally grown strawberries you can: Earliglow, Sparkle, and Jewel varieties in the Northeast and Midwest; Cardinal, Sweet Charlie, or Virginia native strawberry *(Fragonaria virginiana)* in the South; Chandler in the West; Totem and Redcrest in the Pacific Northwest. Roger Williams, who founded Rhode Island in 1636, loved strawberries. He noted, "This berry is the wonder of all the fruits growing naturally in those parts. . . . In some parts where the Indians have planted them, I have many times seen as many as would fill a good ship, within a few miles compass. The Indians bruise them in a Morter, and mix them with meale and make strawberry bread." Colonial cooks were already familiar with shortbread and "short" cakes—*short* meaning pastries made with almost equal parts butter and flour—and it didn't take long for strawberries and short-cake to combine in the classic American early summer dessert. Baking powder had to be invented in the mid-nineteenth century before we got the kind of shortcake we know today, the baking powder biscuit variety. **MAKES 4 SERVINGS**

BERRIES

3 cups strawberries, hulled and cut in half lengthwise

¼ cup plus 1 tablespoon sugar

SHORTCAKES

1½ cups all-purpose flour

2 teaspoons baking powder

1 teaspoon salt

1 tablespoon sugar

¼ cup (½ stick) cold unsalted butter, cut into cubes

¾ cup milk

Whipped cream for garnish

1   Toss the strawberries and sugar together in a medium-size mixing bowl. Set aside to macerate for 30 minutes.

2   Preheat the oven to 400 degrees F. Line a baking sheet with parchment paper and set aside. To make the shortcake, sift the dry ingredients into a medium-size mixing bowl. With a pastry blender, two knives, or your fingertips, work the butter into the mixture until it resembles coarse crumbs. Mix in the milk with a fork and continue stirring until you have a thick dough. Transfer the dough to a floured work surface and roll or pat to a thickness of 2 inches. Using a 3-inch biscuit cutter, cut out 4 rounds. Place each round on the prepared baking sheet. Bake just until golden, about 10 minutes. Remove from the oven and let cool slightly on the baking sheet.

3   Remove half the strawberries from the bowl. Using a potato masher, lightly mash the remaining strawberries. To serve, cut the warm biscuits in half horizontally and spoon a fourth of the mashed berries and their juice onto each biscuit half. Top with the other half of the biscuit and spoon a fourth of the halved strawberries and their juice over the top. Garnish with a dollop of whipped cream and serve immediately.

Fresh Berries with Lemon Whirligigs

I came across this intriguing dessert in the 1981 *Elsah Landing Restaurant Cookbook*. A Mississippi River port founded in 1853, Elsah Landing is on the Illinois side of Mark Twain country, still rife with limestone caves and berry patches, and windmills or whiligigs are still common features on the rolling prairie farms. Elsah Landing Restaurant founders Helen Crafton and Dorothy Lindgren developed quite a following for their delicious homemade breads and homey desserts like this one. Any kind of fresh berry will taste wonderful in this fanciful, lemony version of a shortcake, which I have adapted. A biscuit-like dough is spread with sweet lemon butter, then rolled up, jelly-roll style, and sliced. These whirligigs are then placed over the berry filling and baked.

MAKES 8 TO 10 SERVINGS

BERRY FILLING

⅔ cup sugar

2 tablespoons quick-cooking tapioca

½ teaspoon ground cinnamon

¼ teaspoon salt

¼ teaspoon freshly grated nutmeg

1 cup hot water

3 cups fresh or frozen (thawed) mixed berries, such as raspberries, blueberries, black raspberries, and blackberries

WHIRLIGIGS

1 cup all-purpose flour

2 teaspoons baking powder

½ teaspoon salt

3 tablespoons vegetable shortening

1 large egg, beaten

2 tablespoons heavy cream or half-and-half

¼ cup sugar

2 tablespoons (¼ stick) unsalted butter, melted

1 teaspoon grated lemon zest

Heavy cream for serving

1   Preheat the oven to 400 degrees F. Butter a 10-inch round baking pan and set aside.

2   To make the filling, in a medium-size saucepan, combine the sugar, tapioca, cinnamon, salt, and nutmeg. Whisk in the hot water and bring to a boil over medium-high heat. Whisk until the mixture thickens and the tapioca has softened, about 5 minutes.

3   Sprinkle the berries evenly over the bottom of the prepared baking pan and pour the hot sugar mixture over them. Set aside.

4   To make the whirligigs, in a large mixing bowl, sift together the flour, baking powder, and salt. Work in the shortening with a pastry blender, two knives, or your fingertips until the mixture is dotted with pea-size bits of shortening. Add the egg and cream and mix with a fork to make a stiff dough. Turn the dough out onto a floured work surface and roll out to a 6 x 12-inch rectangle.

5   In a small bowl, combine the sugar, melted butter, and lemon zest. Spread this mixture over the surface of the dough. Roll the dough up jelly-roll fashion, starting with a 12-inch side. Cut the roll into 20 slices and place on top of the berries. Bake until the whirligigs are golden brown, about 12 to 15 minutes. Serve with cream.

Bourbon-Laced Sautéed Apples

Weston, Missouri, a sleepy river town on the rolling prairie northwest of Kansas City, was settled by Kentucky and Virginia farmers in the 1840s. They were responsible for the elegant brick Federal-style houses as well as the black tobacco barns that dot the landscape. Burley tobacco is still grown there, with tobacco auctions from November through February. The early Westonians' taste for bourbon was encouraged by stagecoach king and business magnate Ben Holladay, who founded the McCormick Distilling Company in 1856. Despite a recent scandal improbably involving the Russian mafia, the distillery is still going strong, and produces a bourbon that goes well with Jonathan or McIntosh apples from Weston's apple orchards—and with those near you.

MAKES 4 SERVINGS

½ cup (1 stick) unsalted butter

¼ cup packed brown sugar

4 Jonathan or McIntosh apples, peeled, cored, and sliced

¼ cup bourbon

1 recipe Black Walnut and Honey Ice Cream (page 434) or vanilla ice cream for serving

In a large skillet, heat the butter and brown sugar together over medium heat until bubbling. Add the apples and sauté for 5 minutes. Pour the bourbon over the apples and stir to blend. Sauté until the apples are soft, but still somewhat firm, about 10 more minutes. Serve warm with ice cream.

Classic Bananas Foster

First created in 1950 for Rob Foster, a business friend of the famous Brennan restaurant family in New Orleans, this classic flaming dish adds a little dessert-time drama when you entertain. Before you flambé the bananas, however, take the precautions recommended on page 56, so you don't have more drama than you bargained for!

MAKES 4 SERVINGS

¼ cup (½ stick) unsalted butter

¼ cup firmly packed brown sugar

¼ teaspoon ground cinnamon

2 ripe but firm bananas, peeled and cut into
  ½-inch-thick slices

4 scoops best quality store-bought vanilla ice
  cream

½ cup dark rum

⅓ cup banana liqueur

1   In a large, heavy sauté pan, melt the butter, brown sugar, and cinnamon together over medium-high heat, stirring until the mixture bubbles. Add the bananas and sauté until softened and lightly browned, about 5 minutes.

2   Scoop the ice cream into four bowls or deep serving plates and set aside.

3   Pour the rum and liqueur over the bananas, tilt the pan slightly, and ignite the alcohol by placing a lit, long-handled butane lighter or fireplace match just above the liquor fumes. When the rum has ignited, carefully shake the pan to prolong the flames for about 10 seconds.

4   When the flame goes out, spoon the bananas and sauce over the ice cream and serve immediately.

Warm Persimmon and Apple "Pot Pie"

Native persimmons ripen throughout the Midwest and South in early fall, their orange flesh becoming mellow and sweet. Asian persimmons grown in California are more readily available, or you can get native persimmon pulp by mail order (see Sources). This light version of pot pie with a meringue top crust, from James Beard Award–winning chefs Debbie Gold and Michael Smith, is the perfect end to a typical Thanksgiving meal in which we're all tempted to overindulge. This dessert was served to a gathering of the American Federation of Food Journalists to rave reviews. The vanilla syrup and pastry cream can be made up to 3 days in advance. **MAKES 8 SERVINGS**

VANILLA BEAN SYRUP
1 vanilla bean

$1/3$ cup water

3 tablespoons granulated sugar

PASTRY CREAM
3 large egg yolks

$1/4$ cup granulated sugar

$1/8$ teaspoon salt

1 cup heavy cream

1 vanilla bean

TO ASSEMBLE THE POT PIE
$1^1/2$ cups pureed native persimmon pulp or pulp from 3 or 4 ripe Asian persimmons

4 Golden Delicious apples, peeled, cored, and cut into $1/4$-inch dice

4 large egg whites

$1/4$ cup granulated sugar

Confectioners' sugar for dusting

1   To make the vanilla syrup, combine the ingredients in a small saucepan, bring to a boil, and continue boiling until the sugar is dissolved, about 10 minutes. Let cool, remove the vanilla bean, and store in a covered jar in the refrigerator until ready to serve.

2   To make the pastry cream, whisk the egg yolks, granulated sugar, and salt together in a medium-size mixing bowl. In a medium-size heavy saucepan, combine the cream and vanilla bean and bring to a boil, then remove from the heat and set aside to steep for 5 minutes. Pour the warm cream into the egg yolk mixture, whisking constantly. Return the egg yolk–and-cream mixture to the saucepan and cook over low heat until it has thickened and coats the back of a spoon, 10 to 15 minutes. Remove the vanilla bean and pass the pastry cream through a fine-mesh strainer to remove any lumps. Cover with plastic wrap and chill until almost ready to serve. Let it come to room temperature before using in the recipe.

3 To assemble the pot pie, combine the persimmon pulp in a small saucepan with the vanilla syrup, bring to a boil over medium heat, and cook at a boil for 5 minutes. Stir in the diced apples, remove from the heat, and set aside. Preheat the oven to 400 degrees F. Butter and sugar the insides of 8 small ovenproof bowls or individual soufflé dishes and set aside. In a large mixing bowl with an electric mixer, whip the egg whites with the granulated sugar until they hold stiff peaks. With a rubber spatula, gently fold in the pastry cream until well blended. Divide the apple-and-persimmon mixture evenly among the prepared bowls. Spoon the meringue-and–pastry cream mixture over the fruit in each bowl. Bake until the meringue is firm and golden, about 6 minutes. Sprinkle with confectioners' sugar and serve immediately.

How to Flambé—Safely!

Flambéing, a technique brought to America by French chefs, can add a wonderful flavor note to desserts. It involves warming a liquor, for example cognac or rum, then setting it alight in the pan and finishing the rest of the sauce or pouring the flaming liquid over the dessert.

   If you don't want to flambé yourself along with your dish, take these precautions:

* Use a long-handled, deep metal saucepan or skillet.

* Turn off the fan over the stove, as it could draw up the flames.

* Use a match with a long stick or a long-handled butane lighter.

* Protect your hands with ovenproof mitts. Be watchful of long hair and long dangling sleeves.

* Point the match or lighter down into the pan, but not into the liqueur. The flame will ignite the fumes, which will then ignite the liquor.

* As you light the warm liquor, stand away from the saucepan. Do not bend over it.

* Let the flames die down naturally, which takes only seconds. If for some reason the flames do not die down in a minute or two, use the bottom of a baking sheet to smother the flames.

Blackberries with Rose-Scented Crème Anglaise

Near patches of wild blackberries, you will often find wild prairie roses like Queen of the Prairie, there for the taking, but some only bloom briefly in early summer. In Kansas, where I live, homesteading women planted Belle of Baltimore, Old Velvet, and Stamwell Perpetual roses for longer bloom, as well as some that have lost their original names, but have kept the names of the women who loved them. Rescued from oblivion by heirloom gardener Nancy Smith, Florence Henry's Rose from Esbon and May Zimm's Red Rose from Dennison now thrive in Smith's Kansas garden. From the same horticultural family, blackberries and roses go well together in this dessert, inspired by one from pastry chef Lindsey Shere, of Chez Panisse fame. **MAKES 6 TO 8 SERVINGS**

ROSE-SCENTED CRÈME ANGLAISE

2 highly fragrant organic, unsprayed roses or
  ½ teaspoon rosewater

1 cup heavy cream

3 large egg yolks

¼ cup sugar

⅛ teaspoon salt

1 quart fresh blackberries

1   To begin the crème anglais, with your fingers or scissors, remove the bitter-tasting white "'heel" from each of 16 rose petals. Reserve extra rose petals for a garnish.

2   In a medium-size heavy saucepan, combine the rose petals and cream and bring to a boil. Remove from the heat and set aside to steep until the mixture has the desired rose flavor (the longer you infuse it, the stronger it will taste), about 10 minutes. Whisk together the egg yolks, sugar, and salt in a medium-size mixing bowl. Pour the warm cream through a fine-mesh strainer into the egg yolk mixture, whisking constantly. Return the egg yolk–and-cream mixture to the saucepan and cook over low heat until the mixture has thickened and coats the back of a spoon, 10 to 15 minutes. Pass the pastry cream again through a fine-mesh sieve to remove any lumps. Cover with plastic wrap and chill until ready to serve. Let it come to room temperature before using in the recipe.

3   To serve, pour the chilled crème anglaise onto dessert plates or into bowls. Strew fresh berries on the cream and garnish with rose petals.

Natural Flavorings

Early cooks used fruits and blossoms from the orchard or the wild to replicate natural flavorings such as vanilla, almond, and honey when vanilla beans, almonds, or honey were unavailable. Covered with water or milk in a saucepan, brought to a boil, then removed from the heat and covered with a lid, the blossoms or leaves steep in the liquid, which can then be made into a flavored syrup or pouring custard. Make sure you use unsprayed, organic leaves and flowers—preferably from your own garden.

* *Elderflower blossoms.* With a flavor reminiscent of vanilla, the Queen Anne's lace–like elderflowers grow on bushes along fence lines and riverbanks and bloom in June. Use them fresh. They are also good cooked with gooseberries for a pudding or pie filling. Remove the elderflowers before serving.

* *Honeysuckle blossoms.* Wild or domestic honeysuckle blossoms make a delicate honey-flavored syrup when blended with sugar and lemon juice after the initial steeping. Honeysuckle syrup is delicious as a flavoring for lemonade or drizzled over fresh blueberries.

* *Fresh peach leaves.* These have a surprising almond flavor when steeped in water, then sweetened with sugar and spiked with lemon juice. Use peach leaves to create a peach leaf custard sauce and pour it over fresh peaches, or make a syrup from the leaves to drizzle over French toast or fresh raspberries or to flavor coffee.

* *Scented geranium leaves.* My favorite scented geranium is Rober's Lemon Rose, which has a haunting fragrance and flavor. Too much can be overpowering, so a little goes a long way.

* *Lemon verbena leaves.* A tender annual that is in my Midwestern climate zone, lemon verbena has to be brought indoors in winter. The leaves, which have a high concentration of oils, produce a wonderful citrus flavor in teas, syrups, and pouring custards.

* *Lemon balm leaves.* The leaves of this invasive perennial have a pleasant citrus scent and flavor. Fresh or dried, they are good in teas, syrups, and cookie batter.

* *Rose petals.* Just smell a rose and you'll be able to tell if the fragrance will transform into flavor. A weak scent won't do. I have David Austin English roses that work well, but the old-fashioned, deep red *Rosa rugosa* has been used by cooks and dessert makers for centuries.

Fresh Prickly Pear with Lemon and Piloncillo

Available in Hispanic markets from September through March, prickly or cactus pears are the wallflowers of the fruit world. In real estate terms, they don't have curb appeal. In fact, they're downright homely. Grown in desert areas of the Southwest, as well as in Mexico and Central and South America, prickly pears are very popular with Hispanic cooks. Once you get past their unappealing tough and prickly outer skin, you get sweet flavor—a taste that combines the best attributes of watermelon, banana, honeydew melon, and strawberry. The inner flesh ranges in color from magenta to pumpkin, so this dessert can dazzle on a glass platter. Fruits that gently give to the touch are ripe enough to eat. Piloncillo, a cone-shaped Mexican sweetener, is available in Hispanic markets. **MAKES 8 SERVINGS**

8 ripe prickly pears
Juice of 2 lemons

½ cup crumbled piloncillo or packed dark brown sugar
Fresh mint leaves for garnish

Halve the prickly pears lengthwise, then cut each half lengthwise into three sections. Carefully peel off the tough outer skin of each prickly pear section with a paring knife. Arrange the fruit on a dessert platter and drizzle with the lemon juice. Sprinkle with the piloncillo, garnish with the mint leaves, and serve.

Strawberries Bourbonnais

The rich Bourbonnais sauce that coats these fresh berries so deliciously is also wonderful on pound cake, ice cream, or stolen from the jar by the spoonful. Bourbonnais sauce became popular in the 1970s, showing up on restaurant dessert menus and even in fundraiser types of cookbooks. Fresh peaches with Bourbonnais would also be luscious. Use a good Kentucky bourbon because the flavor really comes through. **MAKES 12 SERVINGS (ABOUT 3 CUPS OF SAUCE)**

BOURBONNAIS SAUCE

2 cups sugar

2 tablespoons water

¼ cup (½ stick) unsalted butter

½ cup heavy cream

¾ cup bourbon

1 quart fresh strawberries, hulled

Toasted flaked almonds for garnish

1 To make the sauce, in a medium-size heavy saucepan, dissolve the sugar in the water over medium-high heat, then bring the mixture to a boil. Reduce the heat to medium and cook until the mixture turns golden brown and caramelizes, about 10 minutes. Remove from the heat immediately. Wearing oven mitts on both hands, stir the butter into the caramel with a wooden spoon. Add the cream, 2 tablespoons at a time, then the bourbon and stir to blend until smooth. (If the sauce is still not smooth, place over low heat and keep stirring until it is.) Keep the sauce warm or at room temperature.

2 Portion the strawberries into parfait glasses or dessert bowls. Pour the sauce over the berries. Garnish each dessert with toasted almonds and serve. (Any remaining sauce can be stored, covered in a jar, and refrigerated indefinitely.)

Fresh Nectarines with Warm Mint Syrup

When the temperature soars and your appetite is flagging, prepare this simple, no-fuss dessert, which just needs a mint sprig or two for garnish. It looks like an Impressionist painting when you serve it on a pastel plate, with the gentle colors favored by American painter Mary Cassatt. The flavor is also gentle but surprising. **MAKES 4 SERVINGS**

1 recipe Fresh Mint Syrup (page 487)

4 nectarines, left unpeeled, pitted and thinly sliced

4 to 8 fresh mint sprigs

Heat the syrup in a small saucepan over medium-high heat until it is almost hot, about 5 minutes. Arrange the nectarine slices on four plates or in four bowls. Pour 1/4 cup of the warm syrup over each serving, garnish with mint sprigs, and serve.

Summer Fruit Salad with Raspberry Sauce

When summer fruits are at their peak, I like to layer them in a glass trifle bowl and serve them with a raspberry sauce. Vary the fruits according to what you like and what is in season and layer them with the sturdier fruits at the bottom and the more perishable ones at the top. Pass the sauce at the table. **MAKES 8 SERVINGS**

Juice of 2 oranges

1/2 fresh pineapple, peeled, cored, and cubed

1 large ripe banana, peeled and sliced

1 pint fresh blueberries, picked over for stems

1 pint fresh strawberries, hulled and thickly sliced

2 large ripe peaches, peeled, pitted, and thickly sliced

1 medium-size bunch green grapes (about 8 ounces), cut in half

3 purple plums, left unpeeled, pitted and thinly sliced

RASPBERRY SAUCE

1 pint fresh raspberries or one 10-ounce bag frozen raspberries, thawed

Sugar to taste

1   Pour the orange juice into a shallow bowl. Arrange the pineapple in the bottom of a trifle bowl or a large, wide glass bowl. Dip the banana slices in the orange juice (to prevent browning) and arrange on top of the pineapple. Scatter the blueberries over the bananas. Layer the strawberries over the blueberries. Dip the peach slices in the orange juice and arrange on top of the strawberries. Add a layer of grapes, then arrange the plum slices attractively over the top of the fruit salad. Pour the remaining orange juice over the fruit. Cover with plastic wrap and chill until ready to serve.

2   When ready to serve, make the raspberry sauce: Puree the raspberries in a blender or food processor and sweeten to taste with sugar. Pass the sauce through a fine-mesh sieve into a bowl and discard the seeds. Pour the raspberry sauce in a sauceboat and pass at the table.

Fruit and Cream Trifle

During the 1970s, layered salads began to catch on, especially the kind with layers of spinach leaves, crisp bacon bits, red onion rings, frozen peas, and mayonnaise slathered over the top. If it works for salad, why not for dessert, some anonymous cook asked herself. And this recipe was born, a riff on the English trifle. This is a great dish to make for an informal gathering—say, at the lake cottage or the beach house—when you don't want to fuss. **MAKES 12 SERVINGS**

Two 3-ounce packages cream cheese at room temperature

2 tablespoons sugar

Two 8-ounce cartons strawberry yogurt

2 teaspoons fresh lemon juice

1 teaspoon almond extract

1 cup heavy cream, whipped until it holds stiff peaks

6 cups assorted fruit, such as sliced strawberries, blueberries, raspberries, peeled and sliced kiwi, sliced peaches, sliced nectarines, and red or green grapes (keep each fruit separate)

1   With an electric mixer, blend together the cream cheese, sugar, yogurt, lemon juice, and almond extract in a medium-size mixing bowl until smooth. Fold in the whipped cream and blend until smooth.

2   In the bottom of a large glass serving bowl, layer 2 or 3 different kinds of fruit separately, then cover with half of the cream cheese mixture. Add 2 to 3 more layers of fruit, then top with the remaining cream cheese mixture, smoothing it to the edge of the bowl. Cover with plastic wrap and refrigerate until ready to serve.

Poached Plums with Late Harvest Sabayon

A celebration of orchard and vineyard harvests, this dessert is best served warm. California late harvest Rieslings are made by allowing the grapes to remain on the vine for an extended period of time. Then, the fermentation process is stopped early on in the wine making process, encouraging more natural sweetness. Since the flavor of the wine really comes through in this dessert, why not use the best, then enjoy a sip as a wonderful accompaniment? I prefer to use either Chateau St. Jean Special Select Late Harvest Johannisberg Riesling from the Alexander Valley, or a Sauternes like Beringer Vineyards' Nightingale. Any sweet dessert wine will work. **MAKES 4 SERVINGS**

POACHED PLUMS

6 to 8 ripe red or purple plums

1 cup water

1/4 cup granulated sugar

1/2 teaspoon grated lemon zest

1 cinnamon stick

2 cloves

LATE HARVEST SABAYON

6 large egg yolks

1 cup superfine sugar

1 1/2 cups late harvest Riesling or other dessert wine

Grated zest of 1 lemon

1   Cut the plums into 1/2-inch-wide wedges, leaving the peel on and discarding the pits. In a medium-size heavy saucepan, combine the water, granulated sugar, lemon zest, and spices and bring to a boil. Reduce the heat to medium-low and add the plums. Simmer until the plums are tender, about 5 minutes. Remove from the poaching liquid and set aside. Return the saucepan with the poaching liquid to the heat, raise it to high, and boil the liquid until it has reduced to about 1/2 cup. Remove from the heat, strain out the spices, and pour the reduced liquid over the plums. Cover and set aside to keep warm.

2   To make the sabayon, whisk the egg yolks with the superfine sugar in a medium-size heavy saucepan. Cook over medium-low heat, whisking constantly, until thick and creamy, 5 to 8 minutes. Add the wine in a steady stream, whisking constantly. Add the lemon zest and continue whisking until the mixture froths to almost triple its volume. Remove from the heat and let stand, whisking occasionally, for about 10 minutes, until just slightly warm.

3   To serve, spoon the plums into four glass dessert or sherbet bowls, top with the sabayon, and serve warm.

Baked Amaretti-Stuffed Peaches

This is an Italian *casalinga*, or "home cooking" dessert, which tastes wonderful with fresh peaches or nectarines. Many Italian-American restaurants offer this treat during the summer months. **MAKES 4 SERVINGS**

2 tablespoons granulated sugar

2 large egg yolks, beaten

1 cup crushed homemade (page 96) or store-bought amaretti

1 tablespoon late harvest Riesling, golden sherry, or amaretto

6 large ripe peaches or nectarines, halved and pitted

2 tablespoons unsalted butter

Confectioners' sugar for dusting

1 Preheat the oven to 350 degrees F. Line a baking sheet with parchment paper and set aside.

2 In a medium-size mixing bowl, whisk together the granulated sugar and egg yolks until smooth and creamy. Fold in the amaretti and Riesling and set aside.

3 Peel 2 of the peach halves and finely chop. Fold into the amaretti mixture.

4 Place the remaining 10 peach halves on the baking sheet. Spoon some of the amaretti filling into each peach cavity and dot with a little butter. Bake until the peaches have softened and the filling is crusty, 25 to 30 minutes. Dust with confectioners' sugar and serve warm.

Apple Dumplings with Spiced Syrup

All the fragrant comforts of Grandma's kitchen in one recipe! Making these dumplings is a bit of a project, but it's a labor of love. This vintage recipe was popular from the last half of the nineteenth century through the 1960s. Today, it's still made in home kitchens and restaurants serving traditional American food. **MAKES 6 DUMPLINGS**

SPICED SYRUP

2 cups water

2 cups sugar

1 teaspoon ground cinnamon

$1/4$ teaspoon freshly grated nutmeg

$1/4$ cup ($1/2$ stick) unsalted butter

DOUGH

2 cups all-purpose flour

1 teaspoon salt

2 teaspoons baking powder

$3/4$ cup cold vegetable shortening

$1/2$ cup milk

FILLING

2 teaspoons sugar

1 teaspoon ground cinnamon

3 tart apples, such as Granny Smith, Braeburn, or Jonathan, peeled, cored, and quartered

1 tablespoon unsalted butter

Heavy cream or ice cream for serving

1 To make the syrup, place the water, sugar, cinnamon, and nutmeg in a large saucepan and bring to a boil, stirring constantly. Continue boiling and stirring for 1 minute, then add the butter, stir to melt, and set aside.

2 To make the dough, place the flour, salt, and baking powder in a medium-size mixing bowl. Using a pastry cutter or two knives, cut in the shortening until the mixture resembles coarse crumbs. Stir in the milk to form a rich, biscuit-like dough. Divide the dough into 6 portions.

3 Preheat the oven to 375 degrees F. Coat a 9 x 13-inch baking pan with nonstick cooking spray and set aside. Roll out each portion of dough into a 5- to 6-inch circle on a floured work surface.

4 To fill the dumplings, in a small dish, combine the sugar and cinnamon. Place 2 apple quarters, $1/2$ teaspoon of the butter, and $1/2$ teaspoon of the cinnamon sugar in the center of each dough circle. Wrap the dough around to enclose the filling and pinch the edges closed. (The dumpling will be sort of tulip shaped, like a beggar's purse.) Place each dumpling in the prepared pan. When all the dumplings are in the pan, pour the syrup over the dumplings.

5 Bake the dumplings until golden brown, about 35 minutes. Serve warm with cream or ice cream.

Spice and Honey Baked Apples

A tradition of baking apples came with the Pilgrims and Puritans to the shores of New England. In the seventeenth century, people ate them for breakfast or dinner, or immersed them in a flagon of warm spiced ale to make a winter drink called "lamb's wool," which got its name from the wooly appearance of the cooked apple pulp. Today, baked apples are still popular, especially with chefs or home cooks who want to serve their guests a deliciously comforting dessert with an impeccable American pedigree.

MAKES 6 SERVINGS

6 tart apples, such as Jonagold, Braeburn, or Gala, cored

$1/2$ cup clover or another light amber honey

$1/2$ cup apple cider

1 teaspoon ground cinnamon

$1/8$ teaspoon salt

$1/2$ cup dried apricots, snipped into small pieces, or raisins

Heavy cream for garnish

Chopped toasted pecans (see page 181) for garnish

1   Preheat the oven to 350 degrees F. Butter a 9-inch square baking pan. Trim the bottoms of the apples so they sit without wobbling and place them, top side up, in the pan. Set aside.

2   In a small heavy saucepan, bring the honey and cider to a boil. Stir in the cinnamon and salt and remove from the heat.

3   Spoon some apricots into the cavity of each apple, then spoon the cider and honey mixture into the cavity and over each apple. Cover the pan with aluminum foil.

4   Bake until the apples are almost tender when pierced with a fork, about 30 minutes. Remove from the oven, keep covered, and let stand for 30 minutes. Serve in individual bowls, drizzled with cream and topped with chopped nuts.

Baked Lemon Spice Pears

Sarah Gibbons Telfair came to Savannah, Georgia, as a new bride in 1774. Her husband, Edward Telfair, represented Georgia at the Continental Congress in Philadelphia in 1778, and so the Telfairs lived in that city for a while. After the Revolutionary War ended, they moved back to Savannah, where Sarah raised nine children and entertained her successful merchant husband's guests in the gracious tradition of the South. Her receipt book, containing her cache of recipes, has been preserved by the Georgia Historical Society. That is how we learned that Sarah and her kitchen staff made American classics such as brandied cheesecake, transparent tarts, and these luscious pears, baked with half a thinly sliced lemon, a stick of cinnamon, and a whole vanilla bean. Use a paring knife to cut a long, curling strip of lemon peel for this dish.

MAKES 4 SERVINGS

4 firm pears, peeled, cored, and cut in half lengthwise

$\frac{1}{4}$ cup sugar

1 vanilla bean

Five 2- to 3-inch-long strips fresh lemon zest

One 4-inch-long cinnamon stick

1 cup water

4 thin spice cookies

1   Preheat the oven to 325 degrees F. Coat the inside of a 9-inch square baking pan with nonstick cooking spray and set aside.

2   Place the pears cut side down in the prepared baking pan. Sprinkle with the sugar. Place the vanilla bean, 1 strip of the lemon zest, and the cinnamon stick around the pears. Pour the water over all, and cover the pan tightly with aluminum foil.

3   Bake until the pears are soft and fragrant, about $1\frac{1}{2}$ hours. Serve, garnishing each serving with a strip of lemon zest and a thin spice cookie.

Key West Baked Plantains

In the few pages of the 1948 *Key West Recipes*, compiled by Luise Putcamp and Virginia Z. Goulet, you get a glimpse of America before we really became homogenized, our landscape dotted with the familiar presence of a McDonald's, Wal-Mart, Holiday Inn, or Texaco almost everywhere. The compilers describe the backyard orchards dotting the two- by four-mile island at the southernmost tip of Florida, lush with sapodillas, soursops, papayas, guavas, and Key limes. Curiously, the dessert recipes include saltine crackers, for example queen of puddings (see page 416 for my version), possibly because well-wrapped crackers could withstand the humidity. One unique dessert is guava shells, or peeled and pitted guava, served with fingers of cream cheese and saltine crackers.

With West Indian plantains, a kind of starchy banana, now available even in the Midwest, this wintertime Key West fruit dessert doesn't have to remain on the island. Choose ripe, yellow-gold fruit. **SERVES 4**

1 teaspoon ground cinnamon

1 tablespoon sugar

4 ripe plantains, peeled and cut in half lengthwise

1 cup fresh orange juice

1 tablespoon cold unsalted butter, cut into small pieces

1 Preheat the oven to 350 degrees F. Butter a 9-inch square baking pan and set aside.

2 In a small bowl, combine the cinnamon and sugar until well blended. Arrange the plantains in the prepared baking dish, drizzle with the orange juice, and sprinkle with the cinnamon sugar. Dot them with the butter. Cover the baking dish with aluminum foil.

3 Bake until the plantains are soft and the juices are syrupy, about 45 minutes. Serve warm.

Mountain Berry Gratin with Sourwood Honey Sabayon

When I was a child, my family took several vacations to the Smoky Mountains in Tennessee. We learned to love grits, braised greens, dry-spiced Memphis-style smoked ribs, and sourwood honey on biscuits. Sourwood trees grow in the lower reaches of the southern Appalachian and Smoky Mountains and blossom in early summer, when bees make this light amber varietal honey. This contemporary dessert is best made with freshly picked berries. A drizzle of Sourwood Honey Sabayon pulls all the flavors together. **MAKES 4 SERVINGS**

4 cups mixed fresh berries, such as raspberries, blackberries, sliced strawberries, and blueberries

3 large egg yolks

$1/2$ cup sourwood or other amber honey

Juice of $1/2$ lemon

1 Preheat the broiler. Divide the berries among 4 heat-proof individual casserole dishes, gratin dishes, or bowls. Set aside.

2 Heat some water in the bottom of a double boiler until it begins to simmer. Raise the heat to medium-high and in the top of the double boiler, whisk together the egg yolks, honey, and lemon juice, using an up-and-down motion to beat air into the mixture. Keep whisking until the egg mixture has increased in volume to become a fluffy cream, about 5 minutes.

3 Remove the top of the double boiler and spoon the sabayon over the four bowls of berries. Set the bowls on a baking sheet and broil until the sabayon bubbles and turns a golden brown. Serve at once.

Cranberries in the Skillet

Arrived at Dr. Tuft's, where I found a fine Wild Goose on the Spit, and Cranberries in the Skillet for Dinner," noted John Adams on April 8, 1767. Those cranberries must have been stored in a cold room over the winter months, much as we freeze bags of cranberries when they're available in late fall. Cranberries, caramelized in a slow oven, are delicious served warm with whipped cream or over pound cake or ice cream. I use a cast-iron skillet with a cover (or foil) to make this dish, but you could also put the berries in a covered casserole dish. **MAKES 6 SERVINGS**

One 12-ounce bag fresh cranberries, picked over for stems and rinsed

¾ cup sugar

¼ cup kirsch, amaretto, or brandy (optional)

1   Preheat the oven to 250 degrees F. Spread the cranberries over the bottom of a large cast-iron skillet or shallow baking dish. Sprinkle the sugar evenly over the cranberries. Cover with a lid or with aluminum foil.

2   Bake until the cranberries have softened and caramelized, about 1 hour. Remove the lid and pour the kirsch into the skillet, if desired. Cover and return to the oven for 15 more minutes. Serve warm.

Grilled Fruit Kabobs with Honey Butter Glaze

When plums, peaches, and nectarines are at their juicy best, bring out their goodness with this simple treatment. **MAKES 4 SERVINGS**

¼ cup (½ stick) unsalted butter

¼ cup wildflower honey or another medium-colored honey

Juice of 1 lemon

8 medium-size ripe peaches, plums, or nectarines, cut in half and pitted

1   Prepare a medium-hot fire in a grill. Soak 4 wooden skewers in water for 30 minutes before grilling.

2   Combine the butter, honey, and lemon juice in a small saucepan and bring to a boil. Stir to blend, then set aside.

3   When ready to grill, skewer 4 fruit halves lengthwise on each skewer. Brush the fruit with the glaze and grill until golden brown and softened, 3 to 4 minutes per side. Serve each skewer with a small bowl of ice cream drizzled with a little of the remaining glaze.

Grilled Glazed Peaches and Blueberries with Fresh Ginger Sabayon

Use a medium-hot fire to grill fruits, after basting them with melted butter and brown sugar. Fresh ginger gives traditional sabayon a terrific flavor, which marries well with peaches and blueberries. Grilled fruit is also delicious served with Kentucky Bourbon Pouring Custard (see page 389) instead of the sabayon. **MAKES 8 SERVINGS**

FRUIT

1/4 cup (1/2 stick) unsalted butter, melted

1/2 cup packed brown sugar

4 ripe peaches, peeled, halved, and pitted

2 cups fresh blueberries, picked over for stems

GINGER SABAYON

3 large egg yolks

1/2 cup orange blossom, clover, or any light-colored varietal honey

1 tablespoon peeled and grated fresh ginger

1/2 teaspoon ground cinnamon

Juice of 1/2 lemon

1   Prepare a medium-hot fire in a grill.

2   To prepare the fruit, mix the melted butter and brown sugar together to make a glaze. Brush the cut sides of the peaches with half the glaze. Place each peach, cut side down, on the grill and cook until browned, 3 to 4 minutes. Use grill tongs to turn each peach over, place 1 tablespoon of blueberries in each peach cavity, and drizzle with the remaining glaze. Cover the grill and cook for 3 more minutes.

3   Make the sabayon right before serving. Heat some water in the bottom of a double boiler until it begins to simmer. Raise the heat to medium-high and in the top of the double boiler, whisk together the egg yolks, honey, ginger, cinnamon, and lemon juice, using an up-and-down motion to beat air into the mixture. Keep whisking until the egg mixture has increased in volume to become a fluffy cream, about 5 minutes. Set aside to cool slightly.

4   To serve, arrange a grilled peach on each dessert plate. Sprinkle the remaining blueberries on and around each peach, and spoon the warm sabayon over the peaches and berries.

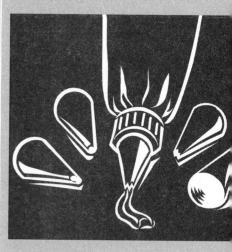

Cookie recipes—for what were then called "small cakes," "bisket bread," and "jumbles"—came over with the Puritans and Pilgrims in the early 1600s. *Elinor Fettiplace's Receipt Book*, handwritten around that time period, has several recipes for different types of bisket bread. One, much like our sponge ladyfingers, was flavored with anise and ground coriander; another, called French bisket bread, was similar to an almond macaroon; and a third, called white bisket bread, was similar to a meringue. She also has a recipe for small almond cakes, raised with "barme," or yeast left over from making ale. Eggs or yeast were the leavening agents of choice because baking powder had not been invented yet.

For the American colonists, almonds would have been hard to come by, as the trees could not survive the cold New England winters. Spices—which could be kept for a long time—were used instead. Likewise, for people not

The American Cookie Jar

living close to a port city, sugar was replaced by maple sugar or molasses. In contrast to the fine, light English bisket bread preferred by Lady Fettiplace, American cobblestones and hermits were dark with molasses and spice, and somewhat heavy and chewy.

Dutch colonists in what is now Manhattan and eastern New York State brought their tradition of cookie making, especially the ornately decorated letter cookies sometimes depicted in still-life paintings of the mid-seventeenth century. Amelia Simmons, who probably lived in the Hudson River Valley, was the first American cookbook author to use the word "cookie" (from the Dutch *koekje*, meaning "little cake") in 1796. Her Coriander Spice Cookies (page 132) are surprisingly good.

Waves of immigration since then have brought cookies from all over the world: dry, light, and not-too-sweet Italian cookies, such as St. Joseph's Day Vanilla Biscotti (page 92) and Calabrian Love Knots (page 117); German cookies like Vanilla Sticks (page 85), Grossmutter's Date-Filled Cookies (page 133), and Germantown Lebkuchen (page 123); and English and Scottish shortbreads of all kinds.

By the early twentieth century, Americans had invented brownies, chocolate chip cookies, filled cookies, peanut butter cookies, and lemon bars. And we're not finished yet!

The Cookie Exchange

With such a diversity of cookies from every conceivable ethnic background and family origin, it's no wonder that holiday cookie exchanges are still popular. Friends, families, and even communities get together and bake many different varieties, or each cook might make several dozen of her specialties. Then the cookies are ceremoniously displayed, and everyone who participated boxes up a half or full dozen of each kind to take home. It takes a village . . . .

Blue Ribbon Brownies

At the turn of the century and into the early 1900s, "brownie" referred to the deep brown chocolate squares that people had started making. ("Brownies" also referred to elves in popular art and to young girls getting ready to be Girl Scouts.) The first known published recipe for brownies appeared in the *Sears, Roebuck Catalogue* in 1897. Popular legend has it that brownies were created by accident, when a flustered cook failed to add baking powder to a chocolate cake batter, but who really knows?

Today, brownie lovers fall into two different camps—those who like cake-like brownies and those who like them moist. Brownie mix manufacturers even allow you to adapt the mix to yield either kind. For me, the epitome of a classic brownie is this recipe, which yields moist, dense, fudgy squares of America's favorite after-school treat. For those who prefer theirs cake-like, you'll get the same flavor and texture in Chocolate Drop Cookies (page 108). **MAKES 2 DOZEN BROWNIES**

1¼ cups unsweetened cocoa powder	1½ cups (3 sticks) unsalted butter, melted
1¼ cups all-purpose flour	3 cups sugar
½ teaspoon salt	7 large eggs
1 cup chopped nuts (optional)	2 teaspoons vanilla extract

1   Preheat the oven to 350 degrees F. Line the bottom and sides of a 9 x 13-inch baking pan with aluminum foil and grease the foil with butter.

2   Whisk together the cocoa, flour, salt, and chopped nuts, if using, in a large mixing bowl.

3   With an electric mixer, beat the melted butter and sugar together in another large mixing bowl. Beat in the eggs and continue beating until well blended. Beat in the vanilla. Add the egg mixture to the dry ingredients and beat on low speed until well blended. Pour into the prepared pan.

4   Bake until a toothpick inserted into the center comes out almost clean, 40 to 45 minutes. If brownies tend to burn on the edges in your oven, cover the perimeter of the brownies with strips of foil toward the end of the baking time.

5   Let the brownies cool in the pan, then cut into squares.

Blonde Brownies with Chocolate and Walnuts

Whimsical, elfin brownies got into all kinds of trouble in *The Brownie Year*, a children's book of poetry and prints by American author and artist Palmer Cox, published in the early 1900s. I remember seeing *The Brownie Year* in *The Illustrated History of Children's Literature* (1955), a wonderful book my sister and I grew up with, which I bought for my daughter when she was little. Around the time that Cox's brownies were delighting their first round of children, Hershey's cocoa powder became readily available to American households. And soon the chocolate brownie we know and love was created. Serve these rich, butterscotch-like brownies warm from the oven with a scoop of Toffee-Banana Ice Cream (page 439) or Monticello Vanilla-Flecked Ice Cream (page 425). Arrange them on a platter like a checkerboard with darker Blue Ribbon Brownies (page 75), or cut into rounds to form the foundation of individual Baked Alaskas (page 165). **MAKES 3 DOZEN BROWNIES**

2 cups all-purpose flour

1 teaspoon baking powder

$1/4$ teaspoon baking soda

1 teaspoon salt

1 cup chopped walnuts

$2/3$ cup ($10^1/2$ tablespoons) unsalted butter, melted

2 cups packed dark brown sugar

2 large eggs, lightly beaten

2 teaspoons vanilla extract

One 12-ounce bag semisweet chocolate chips

1 Preheat the oven to 350 degrees F. Grease a 9 x 13-inch baking pan and set aside.

2 Sift together the flour, baking powder, baking soda, and salt into a medium-size mixing bowl. Stir in the walnuts and set aside. With an electric mixer, beat the melted butter and brown sugar together in a large mixing bowl. Beat in the eggs and vanilla. Then beat in the flour mixture, $1/2$ cup at a time, mixing well after each addition. Fold in the chocolate chips to make a very thick batter. Spoon the batter into the prepared pan and then press it down.

3 Bake the brownies until a cake tester inserted in the center comes out clean, 20 to 25 minutes. Let cool in the pan and cut into bars.

Quilt Country Pumpkin Brownies

Quilters love to gather at a friend's house and work on their latest projects. But usually they don't just bring needlework with them—they also bring a dessert. Like a good quilt pattern, these cake-like brownies can be modified and adapted to suit your mood or the season. Whether you frost them or leave them plain, these moist and delicious morsels are good any time of year, but especially in the fall. I like to vary these from time to time by adding a cup of chopped nuts, dried cherries, or raisins to the batter. **MAKES 16 BROWNIES**

BROWNIES

2 cups granulated sugar

1½ cups all-purpose flour

1½ teaspoons baking powder

1½ teaspoons baking soda

1½ teaspoons ground cinnamon

½ teaspoon salt

¾ cup corn or canola oil

One 15-ounce can pumpkin puree

2 large eggs, lightly beaten

½ cup chopped pecans, dried cherries, or raisins (optional)

CREAM CHEESE FROSTING (OPTIONAL)

One 3-ounce package cream cheese at room temperature

½ cup (1 stick) unsalted butter at room temperature

1 teaspoon vanilla extract

2 cups confectioners' sugar

1   Preheat the oven to 325 degrees F. Coat a 9 x 13-inch sheet pan with nonstick cooking spray or line with parchment paper and set aside.

2   To make the brownies, sift together the sugar, flour, baking powder, baking soda, cinnamon, and salt into a large mixing bowl. Add the oil and beat with an electric mixer until the dry ingredients are moistened. Add the pumpkin puree and beat until smooth, then add the eggs and beat for 1 minute. Fold in the nuts if desired. Pour the batter into the prepared pan and smooth with a rubber spatula so that the brownies will be level when baked.

3   Bake until a cake tester inserted in the center comes out clean, about 30 minutes. Let cool in the pan.

4 To make the frosting, if using, put the cream cheese, butter, and vanilla in a large mixing bowl, and with the mixer, beat until light and fluffy. Sift in the confectioners' sugar, about 1 cup at a time, beating well after each addition, and continue beating until the frosting is smooth and thick.

5 When the brownies have cooled, use a rubber spatula to ice them, if desired.

Glazed Mexican Chocolate Brownies

When you need to bring a dessert for a potluck or a bake sale, make these oh-so-good brownies, a Southwestern version of the classic chocolate brownie. Dense, moist, and richly flavored with Mexican chocolate ingredients—ground almonds, cinnamon, and dark chocolate—these brownies also have a hint of coffee and a bite of black pepper. Serve as a miniature dessert cake, accompanied by a dollop of Cinnamon Whipped Cream (see page 317) or a scoop of Monticello Vanilla-Flecked Ice Cream (page 425). Cut these large, into 12 squares, or smaller, into 24.

MAKES 1 DOZEN LARGE OR 2 DOZEN SMALL BROWNIES

BROWNIES

1 cup flaked almonds

4 ounces bittersweet chocolate, broken into pieces

1 cup (2 sticks) unsalted butter

2 cups packed light brown sugar

4 large eggs

1 teaspoon instant espresso powder

1 teaspoon ground cinnamon

$1/2$ teaspoon freshly ground black pepper

1 teaspoon vanilla extract

$1/2$ teaspoon salt

1 cup unbleached all-purpose flour

GLAZE

1 cup heavy cream

6 ounces bittersweet chocolate, broken into pieces

2 tablespoons light corn syrup

1 teaspoon ground cinnamon

1 teaspoon instant espresso powder

Blanched almonds for garnish

1 Preheat the oven to 325 degrees F. To make the brownies, spread out the almonds on a baking sheet and toast for 10 minutes, or until lightly browned. Let cool slightly, then transfer to the bowl of a food processor and grind to a fine consistency; set aside. Coat a 9 x 13-inch baking pan with cooking spray and set aside.

2   Melt the chocolate and butter in a heavy-bottomed saucepan over low heat, stirring constantly until smooth.

3   In the bowl of an electric stand mixer or food processor, beat or process together the brown sugar and eggs until smooth. Beat in the melted chocolate mixture, then the espresso, cinnamon, pepper, vanilla, salt, and flour, or pulse after each addition. Continue beating or processing until well blended. Fold in the ground almonds, and spoon the batter into the prepared pan.

4   Bake the brownies for 35 minutes, or until a cake tester inserted in the center comes out clean. Let the brownies cool for 15 minutes in the pan.

5   Meanwhile, make the glaze: Heat the cream in a heavy-bottomed saucepan over medium heat until small bubbles form around the perimeter. Stir in the chocolate pieces. Let sit for 1 minute, then stir until the chocolate has melted. Stir in the corn syrup, cinnamon, and espresso powder and continue stirring until you have a smooth glaze.

6   To glaze the brownies, place two wire racks over sheets of parchment or waxed paper. Cut the brownies and place on the wire racks. Spoon or brush the hot glaze over each brownie, allowing the glaze to drip down the sides. When the glaze has cooled slightly, press a flaked almond in the center of each brownie and leave to cool. Wrapped in plastic wrap and stored in resealable plastic freezer bags, these will keep in the freezer for up to 3 months.

Chocolate-Raspberry Brownies

According to a 1997 *Bon Appétit* magazine poll, brownies were one of the top three chocolate desserts, right behind hot fudge sundaes and chocolate mousse. This take on the basic brownie blends chocolate with raspberry. These cut and freeze well.

MAKES 2 DOZEN LARGE OR 3 DOZEN SMALL BROWNIES

1¼ cups all-purpose flour

1 teaspoon baking powder

½ teaspoon salt

1 cup (2 sticks) unsalted butter

5 ounces unsweetened (not semisweet) chocolate, broken into pieces

2 cups sugar

4 large eggs

2 teaspoons vanilla extract

1 cup chopped toasted walnuts (see page 181, optional)

¾ cup raspberry preserves

1   Coat a 9 x 13-inch baking pan with nonstick cooking spray and set aside.

2   In a small mixing bowl, sift together the flour, baking powder, and salt. In a medium-size saucepan over medium-low heat, melt the butter and chocolate together, stirring constantly until smooth. Remove from the heat and whisk in the sugar, then the eggs and vanilla. Add the flour mixture to the chocolate mixture and blend. Stir in the nuts, if desired. Pour 2 cups of this batter into the baking pan, spreading it evenly over the bottom. Freeze just until firm, but not frozen through, about 10 minutes.

3   Spread the raspberry preserves over the frozen brownie batter in the pan. Spoon the remaining batter evenly over the preserves. Let stand 20 minutes at room temperature to thaw the bottom layer.

4   Preheat the oven to 350 degrees F. Bake the brownies until a cake tester inserted in the center comes out clean, about 35 minutes. Cool in the pan on a wire rack and cut into squares.

Emergency Substitutions

When you want to make a dessert but don't have all the ingredients you need, try some of these suggested substitutions:

INGREDIENT	SUBSTITUTION
1 cup unsalted butter	1 cup unsalted margarine or vegetable shortening
1 cup buttermilk	1 tablespoon lemon juice or cider vinegar plus enough milk to equal 1 cup (let stand 5 minutes before using)
1 cup cake flour	1 cup minus 2 tablespoons all-purpose flour
1 cup corn syrup	1 cup granulated sugar mixed with $\frac{1}{4}$ cup water
1 large egg	2 large egg whites, 2 large egg yolks, or $\frac{1}{4}$ cup frozen egg substitute, thawed
1 cup self-rising flour	1 cup all-purpose flour plus 1 teaspoon baking powder, $\frac{1}{2}$ teaspoon salt, and $\frac{1}{4}$ teaspoon baking soda
1 cup molasses	1 cup medium- to dark-colored honey or sorghum

Shortbread Lemon Bars

It's hard to beat a buttery yet sweet-and-sour lemon bar. This recipe, developed by my neighbor B. J. Shondell, is one of my favorites. **MAKES 3 DOZEN BARS**

SHORTBREAD CRUST

3 cups all-purpose flour

1½ cups (3 sticks) unsalted butter at room temperature

¾ cup confectioners' sugar

LEMON FILLING

3 large eggs

1½ cups granulated sugar

¾ teaspoon baking powder

¼ teaspoon salt

1½ tablespoons grated lemon zest

3 tablespoons fresh lemon juice

Confectioners' sugar for dusting

1   Preheat the oven to 350 degrees F.

2   To make the shortbread, mix the flour, butter, and confectioners' sugar together in a large mixing bowl just until the dough holds together. Press the dough into the bottom and halfway up the sides of an ungreased 16½ x 11½ x 1-inch jelly-roll pan. Bake until set, but not brown, about 15 minutes. Remove from the oven and set aside.

3   While the crust is baking, make the filling: With an electric mixer, beat the ingredients together in a medium-size mixing bowl and continue beating for 3 minutes. Pour the filling over the hot crust. Bake until firm in the middle, another 20 to 25 minutes. Let cool completely, then dust with confectioners' sugar and cut into bars.

Butter Pecan Turtle Bars

Who can resist a turtle, that decadent candy made from caramel, pecans, and a coating of chocolate? These bar cookies are just as addictive. You can't eat just one, so cut them small! **MAKES 2 DOZEN BARS**

2 cups all-purpose flour

1 cup packed light brown sugar

1¼ cups (2½ sticks) unsalted butter at room temperature

1 cup pecan halves

1 cup semisweet chocolate chips

1   Preheat the oven to 350 degrees F.

2   In a medium-size mixing bowl, whisk together the flour and ½ cup of the brown sugar. Cut 1 stick of the butter into chunks and, using a pastry blender or your fingertips, work the butter into the flour-and-sugar mixture to make a crust. Pat the crust mixture into the bottom of a 9 x 13-inch baking pan. Sprinkle the pecans evenly on top of the crust.

3   Melt the remaining 1½ sticks of butter with the remaining ½ cup of brown sugar in a medium-size saucepan over medium heat. Bring to a boil and continue boiling for 1 minute, then pour evenly over the crust.

4   Bake until the crust has browned, 18 to 20 minutes. Remove from the oven and sprinkle the chocolate chips over the hot bars. When the chocolate has melted, swirl the chocolate into the filling with a knife. Let cool in the pan, then cut into 24 bars.

Orange-Iced Banana Bars

Ooey and gooey, these tropical fruit bars are great to make on a winter day when the sun is trying to shine but not making much headway. With a great repertoire of bar cookies like these in your dessert file, you can face any bake sale, potluck gathering, or church supper with aplomb. Like the parable of the loaves and fishes, bar cookies can be cut so that everyone gets a piece. **MAKES 2 DOZEN BARS**

BARS

1 cup granulated sugar

$1/2$ cup (1 stick) unsalted butter at room temperature

1 large egg

$1^1/2$ cups mashed ripe bananas (about 3 medium-size bananas)

1 teaspoon vanilla extract

1 teaspoon baking soda

1 tablespoon hot water

$1^1/2$ cups all-purpose flour

1 teaspoon baking powder

2 cups miniature marshmallows

ICING

1 cup confectioners' sugar

$2^1/2$ tablespoons unsalted butter, melted

1 teaspoon grated orange zest

Juice of 1 orange

Sweetened flaked coconut (optional) for garnish

1 Preheat the oven to 350 degrees F. Coat a 9 x 13-inch baking pan with nonstick cooking spray and set aside.

2 To make the bars with an electric mixer, cream the granulated sugar and butter together in a large mixing bowl until light and fluffy. Beat in the egg, then the mashed bananas and vanilla. Dissolve the baking soda in the hot water, then add this to the batter. Beat in the flour and baking powder and continue beating until smooth. Spoon the batter evenly into the prepared pan.

3 Bake until a knife inserted in the center comes out clean, 25 to 30 minutes. Turn off the oven and sprinkle the marshmallows over the hot bars. Return the pan to the oven and leave it there until the marshmallows have melted, about 10 minutes. Set aside to cool in the pan.

4 To make the icing, with an electric mixer, beat together the confectioners' sugar, melted butter, and orange zest and juice in a medium-size bowl until smooth. Drizzle this over the cooled bars. Top with coconut, if desired. Cut into 24 bars.

Glazed Apple Bars

On crisp autumn Saturdays, I've picked up bags of local apples at orchards in Milford, Ohio; Nashville, Indiana; and Weston, Missouri. There's always the fragrant smell of an apple wood fire from the indoor farm stand and a cup of tart fresh cider to help you make your decision: Jonathan, Winesap, McIntosh, Red Delicious, or maybe crab apples? If I need to bring a casual dessert to a potluck gathering, I might make this apple bar recipe, from the apple country of central Illinois, which can be cut into small bars to feed a crowd. **MAKES 3 DOZEN BARS**

BARS

4 cups all-purpose flour

2 $\frac{1}{3}$ cups granulated sugar

$\frac{1}{2}$ teaspoon salt

1 $\frac{1}{2}$ cups (3 sticks) unsalted butter, cut into pieces

2 large eggs, beaten

6 to 8 tart apples (about 3 pounds), such as Jonathan or Granny Smith, peeled, cored, and thinly sliced

1 teaspoon ground cinnamon

ALMOND GLAZE

1 cup sifted confectioners' sugar

1 tablespoon heavy cream

1 teaspoon almond extract

1   Preheat the oven to 350 degrees F.

2   To make the bars, in a large mixing bowl, sift together the flour, 2 cups of the granulated sugar, and the salt. Work the butter into the mixture with a pastry blender, two knives, or your fingertips until it resembles coarse crumbs. With a fork, blend in the eggs until you have a moist, crumbly mixture. Spoon all but about 1 $\frac{1}{2}$ cups of this mixture into the bottom of an ungreased 12 x 17x 1-inch baking sheet with a 1-inch side. Pat the crust down gently with your hands.

3   Arrange the apple slices in rows over the bottom crust. Mix the remaining $\frac{1}{3}$ cup of granulated sugar with the cinnamon and sprinkle evenly over the apples. Crumble or spoon the remaining crust mixture over the tops of the apples. Bake until the apples are soft and the crust has browned, 40 to 50 minutes. Let cool in the pan on a wire rack.

4   To make the glaze, whisk the ingredients together in a medium-size bowl until smooth. With a whisk or your hands, drizzle the glaze over the cooled apple bars. Cut into pieces to serve.

Vanilla Sticks

Vanilla sticks, a German cookie originally called *Vanillefinger*, is one of many home-made varieties that lure folks to German Village from October to Christmas Eve. There, in the southern part of Columbus, Ohio, the Bierberg family bakes thousands of Christmas cookies made from German recipes passed down from Helen Bierberg's immigrant grandmother and offers them for sale to the throngs of people who line the street outside the bakery door. The holiday-only bakery sells more than 2,000 pounds of *pfeffernuesse*, *springerle*, and these vanilla sticks each fall. This cookie is now part of our family's holiday tradition, and we always have several tins on hand. They're light and crunchy—and addictive! **MAKES 12 DOZEN COOKIES**

1 pound whole natural almonds (skins on)

4 large egg whites

One 1-pound box confectioners' sugar, plus extra for dusting

1 teaspoon vanilla extract

1 Preheat the oven to 275 degrees F.

2 Grind the almonds to a fine paste in a food processor; set aside.

3 With an electric mixer, beat the egg whites in a large mixing bowl until they hold stiff, but not dry, peaks. Add the confectioners' sugar, 1 cup at a time, beating after each addition, then beat for 15 minutes more. Place half of the egg white mixture in a separate bowl to use for icing; set aside.

4 Dust a flat work surface with confectioners' sugar. With the electric mixer, beat the almond paste and vanilla with the other half of the egg-white mixture. Spread or roll out half of this dough out on the sugar-dusted surface to form a 6 x 18-inch rectangle. Spread half the reserved egg white icing over the almond mixture. With a paring knife, cut the dough into strips ½ inch wide and 3 inches long. Place on a baking sheet. Repeat the process with the remaining half of the almond mixture and egg-white icing.

5 Bake until the cookies are lightly browned, about 20 minutes. Let cool on wire racks. Store in airtight containers.

Holiday Baking

"Baking begins in earnest weeks ahead. Waves of cookies, enough to feed an army, enough to render any army defenseless, including powerful rumballs and fruit cakes soaked with spirits (if the alcohol burns off in the baking, as they say, then why does Arlene hide them from her mother?)."

GARRISON KEILLOR
LAKE WOBEGON

Walnut Grove Tea Squares

Small towns named Walnut Grove dot the country, from New England to the Pacific Northwest. "Grove" denotes a natural growth of wild trees, and there are many different types of walnut trees that are native to the United States. The unusual addition of brown sugar is responsible for this slightly sweet, somewhat crumbly pie crust, the foundation for these delicious glazed bar cookies. **MAKES 25 COOKIES**

CRUST

$1/2$ cup (1 stick) unsalted butter at room temperature

1 cup all-purpose flour

2 tablespoons packed dark brown sugar

FILLING

$1^1/2$ cups packed dark brown sugar

2 tablespoons all-purpose flour

$1/4$ teaspoon baking powder

$1/2$ teaspoon salt

2 large eggs, beaten

1 teaspoon vanilla extract

$1/2$ cup sweetened flaked coconut

1 cup chopped walnuts

ORANGE GLAZE

1 cup confectioners' sugar

2 tablespoons orange juice

2 tablespoons unsalted butter at room temperature

1 teaspoon fresh lemon juice

1 Preheat the oven to 350 degrees F.

2 To make the crust, in a medium-size mixing bowl, work the butter into the flour and brown sugar with your fingertips until well blended. Press into a 10 x 15-inch baking pan and bake until lightly browned, about 12 minutes.

3 While the crust is baking, make the filling: With an electric mixer, beat together the brown sugar, flour, baking powder, salt, eggs, and vanilla in a large mixing bowl until smooth. Fold in the coconut and walnuts. Pour evenly over the hot crust and bake until a cake tester inserted in the center comes out clean, 25 to 30 minutes. Let cool slightly in the pan before glazing.

4 To make the glaze, with an electric mixer, beat the ingredients together in a medium-size mixing bowl until smooth. Drizzle over the filling while it's still warm. Let cool completely in the pan, and cut into 2 x 3-inch squares.

Apricot-Almond Bars

Fresh apricots, grown in California and the South, always seem to have a disappointing flavor. Although luscious to look at, their taste is bland and cottony. Drying or cooking brings out their flavor. These almond-scented bar cookies have a lovely apricot filling. **MAKES ABOUT 2 DOZEN BARS**

⅔ cup dried apricots (half of an 8-ounce package)

½ cup (1 stick) unsalted butter at room temperature

¼ cup granulated sugar

1 cup all-purpose flour

2 large eggs

1 cup packed light brown sugar

1 teaspoon almond extract

½ teaspoon baking powder

¼ teaspoon salt

½ cup sliced almonds

1   Snip the dried apricots into small pieces with kitchen shears and put in a small saucepan with enough water to cover. Bring to a boil, reduce the heat to medium-low, and simmer the apricots, covered, until soft, about 10 minutes. Drain and set aside to cool.

2   Preheat the oven to 375 degrees F. In a large mixing bowl, work the butter into the granulated sugar and ⅓ cup of the flour with your fingertips until the mixture has a uniform consistency. Press into the bottom of an ungreased 12 x 17-inch baking pan and bake until lightly browned, about 20 minutes.

3   While the crust is baking, beat the eggs in a medium-size mixing bowl and add the brown sugar and almond extract. Sift the remaining ⅔ cup of flour, the baking powder, and salt into the egg mixture and beat well. Fold in ¼ cup of almonds and all the apricots. Pour the filling evenly over the hot crust, sprinkle the top with the remaining ¼ cup almonds, and bake until a cake tester inserted in the center comes out clean, 20 to 23 minutes. Let cool in the pan, then cut into squares.

Chewy Southern Chess Squares

English in origin and a relative of Transparent Tartlets (page 327) and Bakewell Tart (page 319), chess pie has become a beloved Southern dessert. All of these simple pastries feature butter, sugar, and eggs, which are cooked into a translucent custard filling. Chess pie usually contains an additional ingredient, such as cornmeal—or in this case, pecans—that gives the filling a little more texture. The original English ingredient would have been ground almonds, bread, or cake crumbs. But why the name "chess"? The story goes that a cook was once preparing chess pie when she was asked what she was making. "Jus' pie, honey," was her reply, and the name stuck. These squares have a chess filling, and you'll feel more virtuous just eating a square than a whole slab of rich, sweet chess pie. **MAKES 32 SQUARES**

1 cup (2 sticks) unsalted butter

One 1-pound box light brown sugar

4 large eggs

1 teaspoon vanilla extract

2 cups all-purpose flour

1 teaspoon baking powder

$\frac{1}{8}$ teaspoon salt

1 cup finely chopped pecans

Confectioners' sugar for dusting

1   Preheat the oven to 300 degrees F. Butter and flour a 16½ x 11½ x 1-inch jelly-roll pan, tapping out the excess, and set aside.

2   In a large saucepan over medium-high heat, melt the butter and stir in the brown sugar. Stir in the eggs and vanilla and continue stirring until well blended, then stir in the flour, baking powder, salt, and pecans. Spoon the mixture into the prepared pan and smooth the top.

3   Baker until a knife inserted in the center comes out clean, 35 to 40 minutes. Let cool for 20 minutes in the pan, then dust with confectioners' sugar and cut into squares.

Sunflower Cookie Brittle

Sunflowers, native to the American prairie, have become big business in the Dakotas. Grown for their rich oil, sunflowers look wonderful in their neat rows, heads turned toward the sun in late summer. Roasted sunflower seeds contribute a nut-like flavor and texture to this delicious unleavened cookie, which you just press into the pan and bake. A shorter baking time produces a chewier cookie; a longer baking time produces a crisper cookie. After the cookie has baked, you break it into irregular pieces like a nut brittle or like the irregular pattern of a crazy quilt. Substitute sliced almonds, chopped walnuts, or pecans for the sunflower seeds, if you prefer; this recipe is very adaptable.

MAKES ABOUT 3 DOZEN PIECES

1 cup (2 sticks) unsalted butter at room temperature

1 cup sugar

1 teaspoon salt

1½ teaspoons vanilla extract

2 cups all-purpose flour

1 cup salted and roasted sunflower kernels

1 cup semisweet chocolate chips

1 Preheat the oven to 350 degrees F.

2 Combine the butter, sugar, salt, and vanilla in a large mixing bowl and beat with an electric mixer until creamy. Stir in the flour gradually, beating until well blended. Fold in the sunflower kernels and chocolate chips, then press the dough into an ungreased 16½ x 11½ x 1-inch jelly-roll pan.

3 Bake 20 to 25 minutes, or until golden brown. Remove the pan from the oven and let cool. Break the baked cookie apart like peanut brittle. Store in an airtight container.

Coffee-Glazed Spice Bars

For many years, my Cincinnati-based parents had a weekend home across the Ohio River in the sleepy tobacco town of Augusta, Kentucky. Along the riverfront, late eighteenth-century brick townhouses lined the street to the ferry dock. My parents' riverfront stuccoed house, a former Methodist church built in the early nineteenth century, had a great view of the Ohio River. Once they crossed the river on the ferry to the Kentucky side, they really were in another world of Southern accents, sweet iced tea, small town scandals, cornbread, and soupy beans.

For your getaway weekend, take these portable cookies. They travel well, stay moist, and taste delicious. Rich with spices, nuts, and raisins, these cake-like bar cookies are finished off with a coffee glaze. Bake them in a pan that has a cover, so you can transport them easily. Cut them into bars when you get to your destination.

MAKES 2 DOZEN BARS

BARS
1 cup raisins
1 cup water
$1/2$ cup canola or other vegetable oil
1 cup packed light brown sugar
1 large egg, beaten
$1^{3}/4$ cups all-purpose flour
$1/4$ teaspoon salt
1 teaspoon baking soda
1 teaspoon baking powder
1 teaspoon ground cinnamon

$1^{1}/2$ teaspoons freshly grated nutmeg
1 teaspoon ground allspice
$1/2$ teaspoon ground cloves
$1/2$ cup chopped walnuts or pecans

COFFEE GLAZE
$1/4$ cup strong brewed coffee
1 teaspoon instant espresso powder
2 cups confectioners' sugar, sifted
1 teaspoon vanilla extract

1 Preheat the oven to 375 degrees F. Coat a 9 x 13-inch baking pan with nonstick cooking spray and set aside.

2 To make the bars, combine the raisins and water in a large saucepan and bring to a boil. Remove from the heat and stir in the canola oil with a wooden spoon. Let cool to lukewarm.

3 Stir the brown sugar into the saucepan, then the egg. Sift the dry ingredients, including the spices, into the saucepan and stir well to blend. Stir in the nuts, then pour or spoon the batter into the prepared pan.

4   Bake until a cake tester inserted in the middle comes out clean, about 20 minutes. Remove from the oven.

5   While the cookies are still hot, beat the glaze ingredients together in a medium-size mixing bowl to make a thin, smooth glaze. With a cake tester or a toothpick, poke holes halfway through the surface of the hot crust. Drizzle with the glaze and set aside to cool. Slice and serve.

Almond-Glazed Coffee Toffee Bars

These cookies may look innocent, but they're full of intrigue. They've been involved in an attempt to rig the outcome of a baseball game. When my friend Reene Jones and I were in high school in a suburb of Cincinnati, our boyfriends played on the school baseball team. Reene brought these cookies to a home game, thinking she'd give them to her boyfriend (and now husband), Tom, when the game was over. The hungry guys from the other team kept eyeing the cookies. "Can't we have one of those?" they asked. We didn't have to think too long. "You can if you strike out," we told them. I don't remember who won that game, but I do remember the taste of these cookies—definite bribery material. My thanks to Reene for sharing her recipe and a bit of our shameful past. **MAKES ABOUT 2 DOZEN BARS**

BARS
1 cup (2 sticks) unsalted butter at room temperature
1 cup packed light brown sugar
1 teaspoon almond extract
2 tablespoons instant coffee granules or espresso powder
$1/2$ teaspoon baking powder
$1/4$ teaspoon salt

$2 1/4$ cups all-purpose flour
One 6-ounce bag semisweet chocolate chips
$1/2$ cup chopped almonds

GLAZE
1 tablespoon unsalted butter at room temperature
$3/4$ cup confectioners' sugar
$1/4$ teaspoon almond extract
1 to 2 tablespoons milk

1   Preheat the oven to 350 degrees F. Coat a rimmed baking sheet with nonstick cooking spray or line with parchment paper and set aside.

2   To make the bars, with an electric mixer, cream the butter and brown sugar together in a large

mixing bowl until light and fluffy. Beat in the almond extract, coffee granules, baking powder, and salt. Add the flour, ¾ cup at a time, until you have a smooth, stiff batter. Fold in the chocolate chips and almonds. Press the dough evenly into the bottom of the baking sheet.

3   Bake until lightly browned, about 20 minutes.

4   To make the glaze, beat the ingredients together in a small mixing bowl until the glaze has a spreadable consistency. Spread evenly over the bars. Cut on the diagonal while still warm.

St. Joseph's Day Vanilla Biscotti

The Italian word for cookies is *biscotti*. Although we associate the word with those twice-baked pastries we love to dunk into coffee, the term *biscotti* includes so much more. The Feast of St. Joseph is observed in Sicilian Catholic congregations with a St. Joseph's table, a lavish display of foods to honor the hard-working carpenter, celebrate bounty and good fortune, and raise money for the needy. In many churches, pastel net bags of vanilla biscotti in shades of pale green, pink, and white are handed out to everyone who attends. They make a beautiful display.

MAKES 4 DOZEN BISCOTTI

BISCOTTI
2½ cups all-purpose flour
2½ teaspoons baking powder
2 tablespoons plus 1 teaspoon granulated sugar
½ cup vegetable shortening
¼ cup milk
3 large egg yolks, beaten
1 large egg, beaten

1 teaspoon vanilla extract
2 to 3 drops of red food coloring
2 to 3 drops of green food coloring

GLAZE
2 cups confectioners' sugar
⅓ to ½ cup heavy cream, as needed
1 teaspoon vanilla extract

1   Preheat the oven to 350 degrees F.

2   To make the biscotti, sift together the flour, baking powder, and granulated sugar into a medium-size mixing bowl. With your fingertips, rub in the shortening until the mixture has a uniformly crumbly consistency. In a small mixing bowl, beat the milk, egg yolks, whole egg, and vanilla together and add to the flour mixture. Mix until the dough holds together, then knead until smooth on a floured surface. Divide the dough into three equal parts. Mix in enough red food coloring to turn one third of the dough a pale pink. Mix in enough green food coloring to turn the second third of the dough a pale green. Leave the remaining third a pale white.

3   Pinch off about 1 teaspoon of dough at a time and roll into a ball. Place the cookies on an ungreased baking sheet and bake until the biscotti are very light brown, 8 to 10 minutes. Do not let them brown.

4   To make the glaze, mix the glaze ingredients together in a small bowl. Dredge the warm cookies in the glaze, then set them on wire racks to cool and dry.

Cinnamon-Oatmeal Cookies

Oats grown in Iowa ripen in late summer, when they're harvested with combines, which separate the oat kernel from the oat stalk and chaff. At lightning speed, the stalk and chaff are chopped up and blown back on the ground, while the brownish gray oat kernels fill up the storage area of the combine. When it's full, a grain truck pulls up alongside and the oat kernels are blown through a chute to fill up the truck bed. The grain truck then transports the oats to a grain co-op to be evaluated for moisture and protein content, weighed, and stored. Later on, the oat kernels are taken to processing plants, like those in Cedar Rapids, Iowa, where heavy metal rollers flatten the oat kernels into rolled oats. Just think of all the work that goes into a box of old-fashioned oatmeal! Celebrate your end of the food chain when you make these crisp, spicy oatmeal cookies, which will seem to disappear as quickly as you make them. **MAKES 6 DOZEN COOKIES**

$\frac{1}{2}$ teaspoon salt

$\frac{1}{2}$ teaspoon baking soda

$1\frac{1}{2}$ teaspoons ground cinnamon

2 teaspoons baking powder

$1\frac{1}{4}$ cups ($2\frac{1}{2}$ sticks) unsalted butter at room temperature

$2\frac{1}{2}$ cups sugar

2 tablespoons molasses

2 large eggs

$1\frac{1}{2}$ teaspoons vanilla extract

2 cups all-purpose flour

$2\frac{1}{2}$ cups old-fashioned rolled oats

1 cup finely chopped pecans

1   Preheat the oven to 375 degrees F. Coat several baking sheets with nonstick cooking spray or line them with parchment paper and set aside.

2   Whisk together the salt, baking soda, cinnamon, and baking powder in a small bowl. In a medium-size bowl, with an electric mixer, cream the butter and sugar together. Add the molasses and beat until light and fluffy. Beat in the eggs, one at a time, then beat in the cinnamon mixture and the vanilla. Gradually beat in the flour and then the oats. Stir in the pecans with a wooden spoon. You will have a thick dough.

3   Drop the dough by rounded teaspoonfuls, about 1 inch apart, onto the prepared baking sheets. Bake until lightly browned, 7 to 10 minutes. Let cookies cool on the baking sheets about 3 minutes, then transfer to wire racks to cool completely. Store in airtight containers.

> **VARIATION** You can also roll the dough into logs however thick you prefer, cover, and refrigerate for up to 1 week before baking. Just cut ¼-inch-thick slices from the dough, place them on a baking sheet, and bake as directed above.

Greek Almond Butter Cookies

Perhaps the greatest testament to ethnic and culinary diversity in this country is in the wide range of cookies welcomed into each household as part of Christmas baking. In the 1965 *McCall's Cookie Collection*, cookies from over different 20 different ethnic groups were featured, having become part of mainstream American culture. These delicate and flavorful cookies, called *kourabiedes* in Greek, come from an old Greek family recipe brought to this country in the early 1900s.

MAKES 3 DOZEN COOKIES

1 cup slivered almonds
2 tablespoons granulated sugar
1 cup (2 sticks) unsalted butter
1 tablespoon vegetable shortening
2 large egg yolks

½ teaspoon vanilla extract
1½ teaspoons baking powder
1⅔ to 2 cups all-purpose flour, as needed
Confectioners' sugar for dusting

1   Grind the almonds finely in a food processor or nut grinder, then set aside.

2   Put the granulated sugar in a small heavy saucepan and melt and then caramelize over medium heat until the sugar is golden brown, about 10 minutes. Quickly stir the ground almonds into the caramelized sugar with a wooden spoon. Set aside to cool, then crumble with your hands into tiny pieces.

3   While the caramelized sugar is cooling, in another small saucepan, melt the butter and shortening over low heat. Remove from the heat and clarify by skimming off the solids and foam. Let the clarified butter and shortening cool slightly.

4   Preheat the oven to 275 degrees F. With an electric mixer, beat the egg yolks and vanilla in a large mixing bowl until thick. Add the clarified butter and beat until thick and creamy. Beat in the baking powder, then stir in the crumbled caramelized sugar and almond mixture and enough of the flour so the dough will form a soft ball. Pinch off 1 tablespoon of dough at a time, shape into a ball, then flatten slightly with the palm of your hand to form an oval. Place 1 inch apart on an ungreased baking sheet.

5   Bake until lightly browned, about 20 minutes. Let cool slightly, then dust with confectioners' sugar. Store in layers between sheets of waxed paper in an airtight container.

Pecan Balls

Called by various names—Mexican or Portuguese wedding cookies or wedding bells—these small, delicious white orbs will not last long on your cookie plate. My family has been making these for the holidays since the late 1960s, but their origin is unclear. A version of this recipe called Mexican Wedding Cake was in *Favorite Recipes*, a cookbook compiled by the Smithfield Woman's Club in Smithfield, North Carolina, in the early 1940s (when local telephone numbers must have been very easy to remember—286 or 304-J, for instance—and ladies made their own household cleaning solution with a product called Chipso). Have some napkins ready when you serve these cookies because the confectioners' sugar has a tendency to cling to lips and fingers.

MAKES 2 DOZEN COOKIES

1 cup chopped pecans

1 cup sifted all-purpose flour

⅛ teaspoon salt

1 tablespoon granulated sugar

1 teaspoon vanilla extract

½ cup (1 stick) unsalted butter at room temperature

1 cup sifted confectioners' sugar

1 Preheat the oven to 375 degrees F. In a food processor, grind the pecans finely. Add the flour, salt, and granulated sugar and process for a few seconds. Add the vanilla, then the butter, and process until the dough holds together. Pinch off about 1 teaspoon of the dough at a time, roll into a ball, and place the balls on an ungreased baking sheet about 1 inch apart.

2 Bake until lightly browned, about 15 minutes. Remove from the oven and let cool 1 minute on the baking sheet. Put the confectioners' sugar in a shallow bowl. While the cookies are still warm, dredge them, one by one, in the sugar and place on wire racks to cool. Store in layers between sheets of waxed paper in an airtight container.

Amaretti

Originating in Turin, Italy, and brought to America by Italian bakers, these amaretti *morbidi* (meaning "sluggish") are softer and chewier than the more common Saronno amaretti from Milan. In Italian bakeries on "the Hill," an Italian enclave in St. Louis, you'll find cookies like these among many other delicious kinds. For special occasions, wrap each cookie in a twist of colored tissue and pile in a bowl, or tie with thin ribbons to hang on a small Christmas tree or a festive wreath.

MAKES ABOUT 4 DOZEN COOKIES

One 1-pound box confectioners' sugar, plus extra for dusting your hands

1 recipe Marzipan (page 481) made with almond extract at room temperature, or two 8-ounce cans almond paste

1 large egg white, beaten

1 Sift the confectioners' sugar onto a flat work surface. Place the marzipan on the confectioners' sugar and flatten slightly with your hands. Pour a little of the beaten egg white onto the marzipan and dust with confectioners' sugar. Knead the egg white and sugar into the marzipan by folding

the marzipan over the egg white and sugar, turning it a quarter turn, flattening the marzipan with the heel of your hand, and repeating the process. Keep dusting with confectioners' sugar. Repeat the process until all the egg white and sugar have been incorporated into the marzipan. The amaretti dough should be smooth and pliable.

2   Coat two baking sheets with nonstick cooking spray or line with parchment paper and set aside. Dust the palms of your hands with confectioners' sugar. Pinch off about 1 teaspoon of dough at a time and roll into a ball with your palms. Place the balls on the prepared baking sheets about 1 inch apart. Leave to dry at room temperature, uncovered, overnight. This drying is necessary to develop the chewy texture.

3   Preheat the oven to 325 degrees F. Bake the amaretti until lightly browned, 20 to 25 minutes. Amaretti can be wrapped in plastic and frozen for several months or stored in an airtight container.

Midnight Stars

In 1720, a pastry cook named Gasparini invented a confection of egg whites and sugar beaten to stiff peaks. He named his invention after the Swiss town Meiringen, where he first made this creation. Later, both French and Italian cooks adopted Gasparini's recipe. Over time, the French pronunciation and spelling won out, and "meringue" it was. American cooks from the late eighteenth century on have developed recipes with fanciful names for meringue cookies like these. Sometimes they're called Kisses for a Slack Oven (because you basically dry these out in a low oven rather than bake them), Sugar Kisses, or Dimples, for the dimpled appearance they can take on when baked. Piled high in a dark blue glass compote dish or arranged over an ice cream sundae or poached fruit, these crisp white meringue cookies piped in star shapes have many virtues: They can take on any number of flavorings, such as citrus, coffee, cinnamon, or black walnut; they are easy to make, low in fat, and keep well in an airtight container. And after a heavy meal, they're just the thing to serve with coffee. **MAKES 5 DOZEN COOKIES**

5 large egg whites

$1/4$ teaspoon cream of tartar

$1/2$ cup superfine sugar

$1/2$ cup confectioners' sugar

1 teaspoon finely grated lemon or orange zest

1   Preheat the oven to 200 degrees F. Line two baking sheets with parchment paper and set aside. Fit a pastry bag with a star tip, such as no. 8, and set aside.

2   With an electric mixer, whip the egg whites and cream of tartar in a large mixing bowl until they hold soft peaks. Beat in the sugars, ¼ cup at a time, and continue beating until the meringue turns glossy white and holds stiff peaks. With a rubber spatula, fold the grated zest into the meringue.

3   Quickly spoon the meringue into the pastry bag. Pipe stars about 1 inch apart onto the prepared baking sheets. Bake until the stars are dry and crisp to the touch, about 1 hour. Let cool on the baking sheets. Store in an airtight container.

> **VARIATIONS** For other flavorings instead of citrus, try
>
> *   1 tablespoon instant coffee
>
> *   1 teaspoon ground cinnamon
>
> *   1 cup very finely ground black walnuts

Tornadoes

In this whimsical dessert, funnel clouds of pecan meringue cookies touch down on dots of whipped cream and pools of brilliantly colored fruit sauce. It's not Oz, but it's close. These are much more friendly than real tornadoes, distinctly North American weather phenomena that can strike from Texas and Oklahoma eastward to New England and the Gulf States. If you've ever seen one, you never forget the experience.

MAKES 2 DOZEN COOKIES

PECAN MERINGUES
¾ cup pecans
5 large egg whites
¼ teaspoon cream of tartar
1 cup superfine sugar
1 teaspoon vanilla extract

BERRY SAUCE
2 cups fresh or frozen (thawed) raspberries, blackberries, or strawberries
⅓ cup granulated sugar
Juice of ½ lemon

Whipped cream for garnish

1   Preheat the oven to 300 degrees F. Line two large baking sheets with parchment paper and set aside.

2   To make the meringues, in a food processor, grind the pecans to a fine paste. With an electric mixer, whip the egg whites and cream of tartar in a large mixing bowl until the egg whites hold soft peaks. Beat in the superfine sugar, ¼ cup at a time, add the vanilla, and continue beating until the egg whites hold stiff peaks. Beat for 1 more minute. Fold in the pecan paste with a rubber spatula.

3   Fit a pastry bag with a no. 4 star tip and spoon the meringue mixture into the bag. Pipe twenty-four 2-inch mounds of meringue on the baking sheets to resemble inverted funnel shapes (the pointed end of each meringue will be the spout of the tornado).

4   Bake for 10 minutes, then turn off the oven and leave the meringues to crisp and dry out for 2 to 4 more hours with the oven door closed. If not using immediately, store in airtight containers.

5   To make the sauce, puree the ingredients in a food processor until smooth. If using fruit with seeds, pass the sauce through a sieve into a bowl.

6   To serve, place 3 teaspoonfuls of whipped cream in a random pattern on a dessert plate. Spoon about 3 tablespoons of the sauce in the center of the plate. Place the pointed end of each meringue into the whipped cream and serve.

Teatime Almond Macaroons

It was a cold, damp March weekend when I attended a food writer's conference at the Greenbrier Resort in West Virginia. The ghost of interior designer Dorothy Draper still lingers there in the cool green and abundant floral decor, as does the charm of Southern hospitality. These delicate cookies were on the teatime menu, and they also turned up as a topping for the Greenbrier's spectacular Grand Marnier soufflé. Whenever I make a batch of Marzipan (page 481), I save some to make these cookies. **MAKES ABOUT 75 SMALL COOKIES**

10 ounces Marzipan made with almond extract (page 481) or store-bought almond paste at room temperature

¾ cup granulated sugar

½ cup confectioners' sugar

Cookbook Collections

Many Americans not only use cookbooks for recipes, but they also read them like novels. Slowly, year by year, the odd book or two accumulates into a treasured collection. This domestic habit is not new, however. Since the founding of our country, cookbooks have passed the culinary culture of a certain time, place, and family down to others.

In early eighteenth-century Pennsylvania, the William Penn family kept a handwritten copy of Gulielma Penn's recipes. The first wife of William Penn and the mother of William Penn, Jr., Gulielma wrote down the recipes that had been used by her family and those she prepared at Worminghurst, the Penn family home in Sussex, England. Gulielma died in 1694 at the age of 50, before she was able to travel to her husband's New World settlement. When William Penn, Jr., was getting ready to depart Worminghurst for Philadelphia in 1702, he had someone copy his mother's recipes into a book to take with him to the New World.

In 1749, when Martha Dandridge married Daniel Custis, she brought a handwritten manuscript of family recipes written by an English ancestor, which she considered "quaint" even then, but also valuable as a family heirloom. *A Booke of Cookery* and *A Booke of Sweetmeats* might have come over to Virginia when Martha's Oxford-educated great-grandfather, the Reverend Rowland Jones, immigrated in 1633 to become the minister of Bruton Parish, in Williamsburg, Virginia. There are recipes for pickling broom buds, cooking roach (a carp-like fish), and making a cheesecake redolent with rosewater and nutmeg. When Martha married George Washington in 1759, she took the book with her to a new and improved Mt. Vernon, along with her children, Jacky (four) and Patsy (two). In 1799, she gave the cookbook to her granddaughter Nelly Custis.

During the 1780s, when she accompanied her husband on a diplomatic mission to England, Abigail Adams, the wife of one president and mother of another, bought a copy of Sarah Harrison's *The House-keeper's Pocket-book and Compleat Family Cook*, an English cookbook dating back to 1755. Imagine that an almost thirty-year-old cookbook was the best you could find! Gone are the days . . .

¼ cup plus 2 tablespoons sifted all-purpose flour

1 teaspoon grated lemon zest

½ cup egg whites (about 4 large)

Granulated sugar and/or chopped almonds for dusting

1   Preheat the oven to 350 degrees F. Line two baking sheets with parchment paper and set aside.

2   With an electric mixer, beat together the marzipan, both sugars, the flour, and the lemon zest in a large mixing bowl until smooth. Beat in the egg whites, 1 tablespoon at a time, until well blended.

3   Drop the batter by teaspoonfuls onto the prepared baking sheets or pipe them with a pastry bag. With a moistened spatula, flatten the peaks of the cookies, then dust with granulated sugar and/or chopped almonds.

4   Bake until lightly browned, 10 to 12 minutes. Let cool completely on the baking sheets. Place in a tightly covered container and store in the refrigerator for up to 1 month.

In 1843, author Nathaniel Hawthorne and his wife, Sophia, were setting up their newlywed household at the Old Manse in Concord, Massachusetts. During their idyllic honeymoon year, Hawthorne eked out a meager existence writing short stories such as the classic "The Celestial Railroad" and "Rapaccini's Daughter" for American magazines that didn't pay particularly well. Still, at Thanksgiving that year, the Hawthornes roasted a turkey by following the instructions "sentence by sentence" in *Miss Leslie's House Book*, written by the remarkable Eliza Leslie and published in 1840. Hawthorne was very complimentary about Sophia's first attempt at pumpkin pie.

When Willa Cather's family moved from Virginia to a homestead in Nebraska in the late nineteenth century, they brought with them *The Home Queen Cookbook*, published in 1893; *The White House Cookbook*, published in 1887; and *Domestic Cookery* by Elizabeth Ellicott Lea, published in Baltimore in 1853.

In my own family on my mother's side, my great-grandmother immigrated to the United States from Germany in the late nineteenth century. A farm girl, she knew how to cook German foods, but had to learn how to make American dishes with American ingredients. She didn't have a cookbook, nor did my grandmother, who wrote down her own recipes—gathered from her mother or other family members, friends, or the newspaper—in a brown composition school notebook.

When my mother married in 1949, however, she started housekeeping with *The American Woman's Cook Book*, published in Chicago in 1948. Some of our favorite family desserts, such as Blitz Torte (page 224) and Chocolate Drop Cookies (page 108), come from that book, chapters of which were also published in pamphlet form and given away as grocery store premiums in the 1950s.

When I married in 1972, I started with a file of family recipes, then cooked my way through Julia Child's *The French Chef Cookbook* (Knopf, 1968). In 1990, I started writing my own cookbooks.

Classic Butter Cookies

This is our family's favorite cookie, buttery and tender. (There is also the infamous family story of how our dog Jiggs scarfed a batch of these cookies, leaving nothing but incriminating dog drool on the plate.) The dough can be tinted, then pressed into any shape the occasion demands—flowers, holiday trees, hearts, swirls—or rolled into a log and cut into rounds. They're better than most bakery cookies because they have real butter and real flavor. **MAKES ABOUT 3 DOZEN COOKIES**

2½ cups all-purpose flour

½ teaspoon salt

1 cup (2 sticks) unsalted butter at room temperature

½ cup sugar

1 teaspoon vanilla or almond extract

Food coloring (optional) for tinting cookies

Flavored sugar (optional, see page 103) or colored sprinkles for garnish

1   Preheat the oven to 300 degrees F. Coat two baking sheets with nonstick cooking spray or line with parchment paper and set aside.

2   Sift the flour and salt together into a medium-size mixing bowl. With an electric mixer, cream the butter, sugar, and vanilla together in a medium-size mixing bowl until light and fluffy. If you wish, with the mixer going, add food coloring, a little bit at time, to tint the dough your preferred shade. Beat the flour into the butter mixture, ½ cup at a time, and continue beating until you have a smooth, thick dough.

3   Divide the dough in half. Wrap one half and refrigerate until ready to use. Place the other half in a cookie press. Press the cookies out onto the prepared baking sheets, about 1 inch apart. Decorate with flavored sugar or colored sprinkles, if desired.

4   Bake until slightly golden but not brown, 25 to 30 minutes. Let cool on wire racks.

Flavored sugars add a subtle nuance of taste and aroma to desserts. Sprinkle flavored sugar on top of cookies or pie crusts before baking, or use them to make flavored syrups or sorbets. For the Citrus Sugar, I prefer to use a microplane grater to zest the citrus fruit, so that I avoid the white pith underneath the rind. Citrus Sugar is wonderful on blackberries or blueberries. I especially like to use my rose petals to make Rose Sugar, then add it to strawberry or raspberry desserts or just sprinkle it over roasted pineapple. Lavender Sugar is delicious sprinkled over sliced white peaches.

Remember to keep homemade flavored sugars closed tightly in jars because they can quickly clump from humid air or lose their scent. Good quality commercial flavored sugars are available from Golden Fig Epicurean Delights and Pumpkin Hill Farm (see Sources, page 505).

Citrus Sugar MAKES 1 CUP

Grated zest of 2 oranges

Grated zest of 2 lemons

1 cup sugar

Put all the ingredients in a food processor and process until finely ground. Cover tightly and refrigerate; keeps indefinitely.

Rose Sugar MAKES 1 1/2 CUPS

1 cup packed fragrant organic, unsprayed rose petals

1 1/2 cups sugar

1   In a medium-size mixing bowl, stir the rose petals and sugar together. Tie a width of cheesecloth over the bowl and let sit at room temperature for 2 days, stirring once every day.

2   Stir the petals and sugar again, then cover tightly with plastic wrap and let sit at room temperature until the petals have dried, 4 to 5 days, stirring once every day.

3   Transfer the sugar to a food processor and process until finely ground. Store in a tightly covered jar; keeps indefinitely.

Lavender Sugar MAKES 1 1/2 CUPS

1/2 cup fragrant organic, unsprayed dried lavender buds

1 1/2 cups sugar

In a food processor, combine the lavender and sugar and process until finely ground. Store in a tightly covered jar; keeps indefinitely.

Ole Mole Cookies

With their intriguing flavor mix of chocolate and chiles, reminiscent of a traditional Mexican mole, these Southwest-inspired cookies can be habit-forming. The bitter and warm ancho chile (the dried form of a fresh poblano) accentuates these qualities in the chocolate, and the pine nuts add a rich, soft crunch. **MAKES 5 DOZEN COOKIES**

2 large ancho chiles

1¾ cups all-purpose flour

½ teaspoon baking powder

½ teaspoon baking soda

¼ cup unsweetened cocoa powder

8 ounces semisweet chocolate

1 cup (2 sticks) unsalted butter at room temperature

1 cup packed light brown sugar

1 cup granulated sugar

2 large eggs, beaten

1 tablespoon vanilla extract

1 cup pine nuts, toasted (see page 181)

1   Preheat the oven to 375 degrees F. Coat two baking sheets with nonstick cooking spray or line with parchment paper and set aside.

2   With kitchen scissors, snip the ancho chiles, except for their stems, into a clean spice or coffee grinder and grind to a coarse powder. Set aside.

3   Sift together the flour, baking powder, baking soda, and cocoa into a small bowl. Melt the chocolate in the top of a double boiler set over simmering water. With an electric mixer, cream together the butter and both sugars in a large mixing bowl. Beat in the eggs and vanilla. Beat in the melted chocolate, then the ground chile, and then beat in the flour mixture, ½ cup at a time. Fold in the pine nuts.

4   Using a 2-inch cookie scoop or a large serving spoon, drop about 2 tablespoons of batter at a time onto the prepared baking sheets, spacing the cookies about 2 inches apart. Bake until the cookies have a crinkled appearance, about 10 minutes. Let cool for 1 minute on the baking sheet. Then transfer the cookies to wire racks to cool. Store in an airtight container.

Orange-Glazed Marmalade Cookies

Whether you use homemade Fresh Orange Marmalade (page 6) or the commercial variety, you'll get cookies with the fresh taste of citrus in this recipe. These drop cookies are a welcome treat in winter and are especially good with a cup of spiced tea.

MAKES ABOUT 4 DOZEN COOKIES

COOKIES

2 cups all-purpose flour

½ teaspoon baking powder

½ teaspoon salt

2 cups quick-cooking rolled oats

1 cup granulated sugar

1⅓ cups (about 2⅔ sticks) unsalted butter at room temperature

2 large eggs

1 teaspoon vanilla extract

¼ cup Fresh Orange Marmalade (page 6) or store-bought marmalade

1 teaspoon grated orange zest

ORANGE GLAZE

2 cups confectioners' sugar

3 tablespoons fresh orange juice

1   Preheat the oven to 350 degrees F. Coat two baking sheets with nonstick cooking spray or line with parchment paper and set aside. Place wire cooling racks on top of sheets of parchment or waxed paper (not the ones lining the baking sheets).

2   Sift the flour, baking powder, and salt together into a medium-size mixing bowl. Stir in the oats and set aside. With an electric mixer, cream the granulated sugar and butter together in a large mixing bowl until light and fluffy. Beat in the eggs and vanilla, then add the dry ingredients, ½ cup at a time. Beat in the marmalade and orange zest and continue beating until you have a thick batter. Drop the batter by teaspoonfuls onto the prepared baking sheets, about 1 inch apart. Bake until lightly browned around the edges, 12 to 15 minutes. Transfer to the wire racks to cool.

3   While the cookies are still warm, make the glaze: Whisk the confectioners' sugar and orange juice together in a medium-size mixing bowl until smooth. Drizzle each cookie with the glaze and let the glaze dry and the cookies cool before storing. Cookies can be stored in an airtight container for up to 1 week.

Of Cookies and Baking Sheets

Cookies bake best on heavy, light-colored aluminum; a nonstick sheet; or an insulated, air-cushioned baking sheet. Air-cushioned baking sheets produce a more moist product. To keep buttery cookies from spreading, bake on a prechilled baking sheet. The night before baking, stack several sheets together and chill in the refrigerator.

Amish Mincemeat Cookies

Amish communities still "put up" canned goods like homemade mincemeat in the summer to have on hand for use in pies and cookies like these. Flavored with Green Tomato and Apple Mincemeat, these cookies won't last long. **MAKES 4 TO 5 DOZEN**

3¼ cups all-purpose flour

½ teaspoon salt

1 teaspoon baking soda

1½ cups sugar

1 cup (2 sticks) unsalted butter at room temperature

3 large eggs, beaten

1⅓ cups Green Tomato and Apple Mincemeat (page 7) or store-bought mincemeat

1 Preheat the oven to 400 degrees F. Coat several baking sheets with nonstick cooking spray or line with parchment paper and set aside.

2 Sift together the flour, salt, and baking soda into a medium-size mixing bowl. With an electric mixer, beat the sugar and butter together in a large mixing bowl until light and fluffy. Add the eggs and blend well. Beat in the flour mixture, ½ cup at a time. Fold in the mincemeat and blend well. Drop the batter by heaping tablespoonfuls onto the prepared baking sheets.

3 Bake until puffed and browned, 8 to 10 minutes. Transfer to wire racks to cool and store in an airtight container.

Southern Lemon Coolers

The Byrd Cookie Company in Savannah, Georgia, has been making benne seed wafers and lemon coolers like these since 1924. These snow-white cookies with a tart lemon flavor do seem very cooling, especially when served with iced tea or an *agua fresca* in the summer. The cornstarch gives these a powdery, light texture.
MAKES ABOUT 2 DOZEN COOKIES

½ cup slivered almonds

1 cup (2 sticks) unsalted butter, at room temperature

2 teaspoons finely grated lemon zest

¾ cup confectioners' sugar, plus extra for rolling cookies

2 tablespoons milk

1½ cups sifted all-purpose flour

¾ cup cornstarch

1   Preheat the oven to 350 degrees F. In a food processor, grind the almonds to a fine paste. Add the butter, lemon zest, and confectioners' sugar and process until smooth. Add the milk, flour, and cornstarch and pulse until you have a stiff dough. Pinch off teaspoon-size pieces of cookie dough, roll into a ball, then press the ball of dough down gently onto an ungreased baking sheet until slightly flattened, but still round.

2   Bake until very lightly browned, about 15 minutes. Carefully roll the warm cookies in a bowl of confectioners' sugar, then place on wire racks to cool.

KEY LIME COOLERS Substitute grated Key lime zest for the lemon zest.

Chocolate Crackle Cookies

In the early 1990s, I belonged to an online group whose members posted recipes once a week. At first, it was wonderful receiving (and giving) all types of recipes, including this one. But then the postings got bigger and bigger and I couldn't keep up. At least I have this recipe. These cookies look just as their name suggests—crackled. Make sure you remove them from the baking sheet while they're still warm, or they will stick to the pan. **MAKES 2 DOZEN COOKIES**

2 cups all-purpose flour

1½ teaspoons baking powder

½ teaspoon salt

2 cups semisweet chocolate chips

2 cups packed brown sugar

⅔ cup vegetable oil

3 large eggs

2 teaspoons vanilla extract

1 cup chopped nuts (optional)

1 cup confectioners' sugar

1 Coat a baking sheet with nonstick cooking spray or line it with parchment paper and set aside.

2 Sift together the flour, baking powder, and salt into a medium-size mixing bowl; set aside. Melt the chocolate chips over low heat in a large saucepan. Remove from the heat. Whisk in the brown sugar and oil, blending until well combined. Then add the eggs and vanilla, blending well. Gradually stir in the sifted dry ingredients, mixing well. Add the nuts, if desired, and blend well. Cover the dough with plastic wrap and refrigerate until firm, about 2 hours.

3 Preheat the oven to 325 degrees F. Put the confectioners' sugar in a bowl. Roll a tablespoon of the dough at a time into a ball, roll each ball in the confectioners' sugar, and place the balls on the prepared baking sheet about 2 inches apart. Bake until crackled in appearance, 8 to 10 minutes. Transfer the cookies while still warm to wire racks and let cool.

Chocolate Drop Cookies

Both my grandmother and mother made these quietly addictive cookies, soft pillows of cake-like chocolate. The rounded tops just beg for—and receive—a little pastel icing and some colored sprinkles, appealing to the child in all of us. A similar recipe appeared in the 1948 edition of *The American Woman's Cook Book*, edited by Ruth Berolzheimer. You can actually make these in a saucepan for easier cleanup.

MAKES 3 DOZEN COOKIES

COOKIES
2 ounces unsweetened chocolate

$1/2$ cup vegetable shortening

1 cup packed light brown sugar

$1/2$ teaspoon baking soda

1 large egg

3 to 4 tablespoons milk, as needed

1 teaspoon vanilla extract

2 cups all-purpose flour

PASTEL ICING
$1^1/2$ cups confectioners' sugar

1 to 2 tablespoons milk or heavy cream, as needed

1 teaspoon vanilla extract or $1/2$ teaspoon almond extract

Several drops of food coloring (optional) for tinting icing

Colored sprinkles for decorating

1 Preheat the oven to 375 degrees F. Coat two baking sheets with nonstick cooking spray or line with parchment paper and set aside.

2   To make the cookies, melt the chocolate and shortening together in a large saucepan over low heat. Set aside to cool slightly. Whisk in the brown sugar and baking soda, blending until smooth, then whisk in the egg, 3 tablespoons of the milk, and the vanilla. Beat in the flour, $\frac{1}{2}$ cup at a time, until you have a stiff batter that will drop from a spoon. Add a little more milk if the batter is too stiff. Let the batter rest for 10 minutes.

3   Drop the batter by rounded teaspoonfuls onto the prepared baking sheets, about 1 inch apart. Bake until the cookies are puffed and lightly browned at the edges, 12 to 15 minutes. Transfer to wire racks and let cool completely before icing.

4   To make the icing, whisk together the confectioners' sugar, 1 tablespoon of the milk, and vanilla in a medium-size mixing bowl until you have a smooth, spreadable icing. Add more milk if necessary. Add food coloring to tint it the shade you want, if desired. Ice the top of each cookie with a knife or small spatula, then decorate with colored sprinkles. Store in layers between sheets of waxed paper in an airtight container.

Simply Delicious Peanut Butter Cookies

How easy can it get? These flourless peanut butter cookies couldn't be simpler to make or more delicious to eat. **MAKES ABOUT 5 DOZEN COOKIES**

1 cup creamy or chunky peanut butter

1 cup sugar, plus extra for decorating cookies

$\frac{1}{2}$ teaspoon salt

1 large egg

1 teaspoon baking soda

1   Preheat the oven to 350 degrees F. Coat two baking sheets with nonstick cooking spray or line with parchment paper and set aside.

2   With an electric mixer, cream the peanut butter, sugar, and salt together in a large mixing bowl. Beat in the egg and baking soda, mixing until well combined.

3   Roll level teaspoonfuls of dough into balls and place about 1 inch apart on the prepared baking sheets. Moisten the tines of a fork, dip them in sugar, and make a crosshatch pattern on top of each ball of dough, pressing the cookies to a $1\frac{1}{2}$-inch diameter.

4   Bake until pale golden, about 10 minutes. Let cool for 2 minutes on the baking sheet, then transfer the cookies to wire racks to finish cooling. Store in an airtight container for up to 5 days (if they last that long!).

Peanut Butter–Oatmeal Cookies

For an after-school snack, a treat for a long car trip, or simply a sweet indulgence, these homey cookies taste just right with a glass of cold milk.

MAKES 6 DOZEN SMALL COOKIES

2 cups quick-cooking rolled oats

1¼ cups all-purpose flour

1 teaspoon baking powder

1 teaspoon baking soda

¼ teaspoon salt

1 cup (2 sticks) unsalted butter at room temperature

1 cup creamy or chunky peanut butter

Who Made the First Peanut Butter Cookie?

Peanut butter cookies are so common in America today that you can buy them fresh from a bakery, packaged at the grocery store, or even in boxes from your favorite Girl Scout. When I searched for the first mention of a peanut butter cookie recipe, however, I was surprised to find that they are a relatively recent addition to the American cookie jar. But upon further reading, it all began to make sense.

Peanuts traveled from Africa to the American South and improbably became a household commodity. Peanut butter as we know it was invented in 1890 by an unknown St. Louis physician, who wanted a nutritious soft food that his toothless, elderly patients could easily eat. A local food manufacturer ground the peanuts in a mill, kept the mixture in barrels, and sold it for 6 cents a pound. Around the same time, in Battle Creek, Michigan, Dr. John Harvey Kellogg of cereal fame also came up with a peanut butter. Kellogg, however, didn't roast the peanuts first and the resulting colorless, virtually tasteless paste did not catch on.

In 1903, Dr. George Washington Carver began his peanut research at Tuskegee Institute in Alabama, eventually developing more than 300 other uses for peanuts. In 1904, entrepreneur C. H. Sumner introduced peanut butter at the Universal World's Fair in St. Louis, the same fair that gave us ice cream cones and hot dogs. Peanut butter was new and cooks didn't know quite what to do with it yet. In the *P.E.O Cookbook* published in Iowa in 1910 by a parents and educators organization, several recipes are included for making your own peanut butter, which was considered a kind of condiment, like ketchup or mustard. Entrepreneurs and food manufacturers around the country began grinding their own brands of peanut butter. (I remember my mother talking about how, as a child growing up in Ohio during the Depression, she had to stir the peanut butter, bought in tins at the grocery store, to keep it from separating. But that was soon to change.)

In 1922, Joseph L. Rosefield began selling a number of brands of peanut butter in California. These were churned like butter so they were smoother and more homogenized than other, gritty peanut butters. He soon received the first patent for a shelf-stable peanut butter, which would stay fresh for up to a year

1 cup granulated sugar

1 cup firmly packed brown sugar

2 large eggs, beaten

1 teaspoon vanilla extract

1   Preheat the oven to 350 degrees F. In a medium-size mixing bowl, whisk together the oats, flour, baking powder, baking soda, and salt. Beat together the butter and peanut butter in a large mixing bowl until smooth. Gradually add both sugars, beating until smooth, then beat in the eggs and vanilla. Add the oat and flour mixture, a little at a time, beating until well combined. Drop the dough by rounded teaspoonfuls onto ungreased baking sheets about 1 inch apart.

2   Bake until lightly browned, about 12 minutes. Transfer to wire racks while still warm and cool completely. Store in airtight containers.

because the oil didn't separate from the peanut butter. One of the first companies to adopt this new process was Swift & Company, which made E. K. Pond peanut butter—renamed Peter Pan in 1928. In 1932, Rosefield had a dispute with Peter Pan and began producing peanut butter under the Skippy label in 1933. By 1935, Rosefield had also created the first crunchy-style peanut butter by mixing in chopped peanuts at the end of the manufacturing process.

Peanut butter was mostly a local or regional product, but it was catching on. During the Depression, two peanut butter mills in Brundidge, Alabama, did so well that they kept the town financially afloat.

Spread on bread, inexpensive peanut butter was becoming a household word, but was still not used much in cooking. I could find no peanut butter cookie recipes in the Depression-era cookbooks I consulted, but food historian Jean Anderson found one similar to the cookies we make now in a cookbook by Ruth Wakefield from that time period. Wakefield, as you may remember, found fame and glory as the inventor or the Toll House cookie—the Classic Chocolate Chip Cookie (page 112). But despite her creativity, the peanut butter cookie had not spread to the rest of the country.

After the Depression came World War I. Some GIs posted overseas had peanut butter, which was very portable, in their provisions, but back home, sugar rationing kept any new possibilities for baking with peanut butter in check. In the 1948 The American Woman's Cook Book—a large hardcover tome of over 824 pages— there are no recipes that include peanut butter. But in the American Family Cook Book, published in 1954, I finally found a rolled and cut-out peanut butter cookie made with only $\frac{1}{2}$ cup of peanut butter and 2 cups of flour—much milder in flavor than the sweetly peanutty cookies we know today.

Ruth Wakefield's recipe finally began to catch on by the '60s and '70s. Now we all enjoy those distinctive peanut butter cookies that are rolled into balls and flattened with a sugared fork or the bottom of a glass before baking.

Classic Chocolate Chip Cookies

In a 1997 survey of their readers, the editors at *Bon Appétit* discovered that the most popular American cookie was chocolate chip, hands down, followed by oatmeal or oatmeal raisin and shortbread. Who invented this delight? Food historians credit Ruth Wakefield, who owned the Toll House, an inn near Whitman, Massachusetts. In 1930, Wakefield was going to bake a brown sugar cookie with nuts, called a "Boston cookie," but she ran out of nuts. Looking around her kitchen, she found a Nestlé chocolate bar and got an idea. She chopped up the bar into "pieces the size of a pea," she related, and folded it into the batter. The rest is history. By 1939, Toll House cookies were so popular that Nestlé began to package chocolate morsels for baking them. And Americans continue to consume chocolate chips in variations of the original recipe as fast as Nestlé can make them—240 million morsels a day! I have updated the Toll House cookie to include more vanilla and a combination of unsalted butter and shortening (packaged in sticks for baking) so the cookies don't spread too much. I've also use less brown sugar.

MAKES ABOUT 4 DOZEN COOKIES

2¼ cups all-purpose flour

1 teaspoon baking soda

1 teaspoon salt

½ cup (1 stick) unsalted butter at room temperature

½ cup vegetable shortening

¾ cup granulated sugar

⅔ cup packed dark brown sugar

2 large eggs

2 teaspoons vanilla extract

One 12-ounce bag semisweet chocolate chips

1 cup chopped walnuts or pecans (optional)

1 Preheat the oven to 350 degrees F. Coat two baking sheets with nonstick cooking spray or line with parchment paper and set aside.

2 Sift together the flour, baking soda, and salt into a medium-size mixing bowl. Set aside.

3 With an electric mixer, cream together the butter, shortening, and both sugars in a large mixing bowl until light and fluffy. Add the eggs and vanilla and beat until smooth. With the mixer on low speed, add the flour mixture a little at a time and continue beating until well blended. With a rubber spatula, fold in the chocolate chips and the nuts, if using. Drop the dough by heaping tablespoonfuls onto the prepared baking sheets, about 2 inches apart.

4 Bake until golden brown around the edges and still soft in the center, 14 to 17 minutes. For chewier cookies, let cool on the baking sheets. For crispier cookies, cook on wire racks. Store in an airtight container.

Urban Legend Cookies

I have received this recipe from three different friends by e-mail in the past year, always in the same format. The story that precedes the recipe tells of a woman who was allegedly charged $250 for this cookie recipe by Nieman-Marcus. She vows to send the recipe on to everyone she knows and asks the recipients to send it on to friends as well—her revenge for having to pay for it. I have rearranged the recipe because the ingredients list in the original doesn't match up with the directions, and I have also cut the recipe in half. The urban legend goes on, but these cookies, loaded with chocolate chips as well as grated chocolate, are worth it. **MAKES ABOUT 4 1/2 DOZEN COOKIES**

3 cups old-fashioned rolled oats

1 cup (2 sticks) unsalted butter at room temperature

1 cup granulated sugar

1 cup packed brown sugar

2 large eggs

1 teaspoon vanilla extract

2 cups all-purpose flour

1/2 teaspoon salt

1 teaspoon baking powder

1 teaspoon baking soda

One 12-ounce bag semisweet chocolate chips

One 4-ounce milk chocolate candy bar, coarsely grated

1 1/2 cups chopped walnuts or pecans

1 Preheat the oven to 375 degrees F. Put the rolled oats in a blender or food processor and process to a fine powder. Measure 2 1/2 cups and set aside, and discard the rest.

2 With an electric mixer, cream the butter and sugars together in a large mixing bowl until light and fluffy. Beat in the eggs and vanilla. Beat in the flour, processed oats, salt, baking powder, and baking soda and continue beating until you have a thick, well-blended dough. Stir in the chocolate chips, grated chocolate, and chopped nuts. Pinch off about 1 tablespoon of dough at a time and roll into a ball. Place the balls on an ungreased baking sheet, about 2 inches part.

3 Bake until lightly browned, about 10 minutes. Transfer to wire racks to cool. Store in an airtight container.

Whoopie Pies

I lived for a short time in Vermont during the mid '70s, when whoopie pies were still popular in New England. Flat rounds of devil's food sponge cake with a Marshmallow Fluff and buttercream filling, these are messy but fun to eat, and they taste great. Marshmallow Fluff was concocted in 1917 by Allen Durkee and Fred Mower, who first sold it door to door in Lynn, Massachusetts. In 1930 the company produced its first cookbook extolling the virtues of their product, especially as the not-so-secret ingredient in Never-Fail Fudge and Whoopie Pies. I got this recipe from a neighbor in Burlington, Vermont, the year before we moved out and Ben and Jerry (of ice cream fame) moved in. **MAKES 12 LARGE SANDWICH COOKIES**

COOKIES
2¼ cups all-purpose flour
1¼ cups granulated sugar
½ cup unsweetened cocoa powder
1 teaspoon baking soda
2 teaspoons cream of tartar
1 teaspoon salt
⅔ cup vegetable shortening
2 large eggs

2 teaspoons vanilla extract
1 cup milk

MARSHMALLOW CREAM FILLING
½ cup (1 stick) unsalted butter at room temperature
1 cup confectioners' sugar
1½ cups Marshmallow Fluff
1 teaspoon vanilla extract

1   Preheat the oven to 350 degrees F. Coat two baking sheets with nonstick cooking spray or line with parchment paper and set aside.

2   To make the cookies, sift together the flour, granulated sugar, cocoa, baking soda, cream of tartar, and salt into a medium-size mixing bowl. Set aside.

3   With an electric mixer, cream the shortening, eggs, and vanilla together in a large mixing bowl until light and lemon colored. Add the dry ingredients, a little at a time, alternating with the milk until you have a smooth batter. Drop 2 tablespoons of the batter at a time onto the prepared baking sheets, about 2 inches apart. You should have 6 cookies on each sheet.

4   Bake until browned around the edges and the centers spring back when touched, 8 to 10 minutes. Transfer the cookies to a wire rack to cool. Bake another batch with the remaining batter.

5   To make the filling, with an electric mixer, cream the butter and confectioners' sugar together in a medium-size mixing bowl, then add the Marshmallow Fluff and vanilla and beat until you have a smooth filling. Spread 2 to 3 tablespoons of the filling on a cooled cookie and place another cookie on top to make each pie. The cookies may be individually wrapped and stored in an airtight container or in the refrigerator for 2 days.

I'm Just Dying for. . .

An RC and a moon pie. In the South during the Depression, two nickels could buy you a bottle of Royal Crown Cola and a moon pie—a chocolate-covered graham cracker sandwich cookie with a marshmallow filling. People in and around Chattanooga, Tennessee, where moon pies have been made by the Chattanooga Bakery since 1919, still consider this simple dessert a winner.

A Sonker. This deep-dish pie from the mountains around Mount Airy, North Carolina, is made with whatever is on hand: biscuit or pie dough or bread crumbs, fruit or sweet potatoes from the garden, and a "dip" or sauce, made with milk, sugar, and vanilla, to be poured over the sonker.

A King Cake. Louisiana bakers make over 250,000 king cakes between January 6, which is Three Kings Day, and Fat Tuesday, the day before the beginning of Lent. A king cake is brioche or puff pastry dough baked in a ring and filled with fruit or nut pastes—similar to the French *gâteau de Pithiviers*. But king cake goes all out in gaudy Mardi Gras fashion, and is decorated with purple (for justice), green (for faith), and gold (for power) frosting. A tiny plastic baby, symbolizing the Christ child, is baked inside the pastry. Whoever gets the baby in his or her slice of cake will have good fortune the rest of the year.

A Twinkie. During the Depression, James Dewar came up with a new sponge cake, pumped full of sweet fluff and selling two for a nickel, which could be baked in custom pans normally used for the very short strawberry shortcake season. The Chicago head of Continental Bakeries didn't know what to name this new product, though. He got inspired on a business trip when he saw the sign on a shoe factory for Twinkle Toe Shoes. Dewar changed the name to "Twinkie" and the rest is history.

A Chocolate Dip Cone. For me, memories of Creamy Whip chocolate dip cones are connected with my first brush with romance in eighth grade, a sort of *Wonder Years* experience I still fondly remember—and chuckle over. I still want one chocolate dip cone every summer, for old times' sake and because I still like them.

A Marshmallow Crispy Treat. Made with Rice Crispies cereal, melted butter, and marshmallows, these treats were created in 1939 by Mary Barber, a home economist for the W. K. Kellogg Company. The recipe started appearing on cereal boxes in 1941. Today, they can be bought already prepared and packaged.

A Black-and-White Cookie. A favorite of kids growing up in New York, these round, lemon-scented cookies are iced with white on one half, dark chocolate on the other half. They're still a popular bakery item today.

Benne Seed Wafers

Benne seeds, or sesame seeds, which Africans associated with good luck, were first brought to the Southern colonies by black slaves taken from the western coast of Africa during the seventeenth and early eighteenth centuries. Soon benne seeds were planted in gardens in Low Country (the coastal plains of the Carolinas and Georgia), and these traditional wafer cookies from Charleston, South Carolina, were created. They are crispy, with a flavor somewhat like peanut butter cookies. Toasting the sesame seeds to a medium brown brings out their best flavor. But I should warn you—these can be habit-forming! **MAKES 7 DOZEN WAFERS**

1 cup sesame seeds

1/4 teaspoon baking powder

1 1/4 cups all-purpose flour

1/4 teaspoon salt

3/4 cup (1 1/2 sticks) unsalted butter at room temperature

1 1/2 cups packed light brown sugar

2 large eggs

1 teaspoon vanilla extract

1 Preheat the oven to 350 degrees F. Sprinkle the sesame seeds on a baking sheet and toast in the oven until golden brown, 7 to 8 minutes. Set aside to cool. Reduce the oven temperature to 325 degrees F. Line two baking sheets with parchment paper and set aside.

2 Sift together the baking powder, flour, and salt into a small mixing bowl. With an electric mixer, cream the butter and brown sugar together in a large mixing bowl until light and fluffy. Add the eggs and beat until well blended, then beat the dry ingredients into the batter, 1/4 cup at a time. Beat in the vanilla, then the sesame seeds. Drop the batter, 1 teaspoonful at a time, onto the prepared baking sheets, about 2 inches apart because the batter spreads during baking.

3 Bake 8 minutes for softer cookies, 9 minutes for crispier cookies. They are done with they turn golden brown around the edges. Transfer the cookies to wire racks to cool. Store in an airtight container for up to 1 week.

Calabrian Love Knots

During the early 1900s, the height of Italian immigration to this country, many people came from Calabria in the "toe" part of boot-shaped Italy, right across the Mediterranean from the island of Sicily. When women of Calabrian descent become brides, beautifully arranged platters of these almond-flavored cookies are often served at the reception. Most Italian cookies seem a little dry to Americans, but these are meant to be dunked in sweet or sparkling wine or even dark, rich coffee. They freeze well and are also lovely to serve during the holidays. **MAKES 4 DOZEN COOKIES**

COOKIES

3 large eggs

$\frac{1}{2}$ cup vegetable oil

$\frac{1}{4}$ cup plus 2 tablespoons granulated sugar

$\frac{1}{4}$ teaspoon salt

$\frac{1}{4}$ cup milk

1 tablespoon almond extract

2 teaspoons baking powder

4 cups all-purpose flour

ALMOND SUGAR FROSTING

$\frac{1}{2}$ cup heavy cream

1 teaspoon almond extract

1 cup confectioners' sugar

1 Preheat the oven to 350 degrees F. Coat baking sheets with nonstick cooking spray or line with parchment paper and set aside.

2 To make the cookies, with an electric mixer, beat together the eggs, oil, granulated sugar, and salt in a large mixing bowl until smooth. Stir in the milk, almond extract, baking powder, and enough flour so that you have a stiff dough. Fit the mixer with the dough hook and knead the dough until smooth, or knead it by hand on a flat work surface. Pinch off about 1 tablespoon of dough and roll it into a rope that is $\frac{1}{4}$ inch wide and 4 inches long. Tie the rope into a knot like a pretzel and place on a prepared baking sheet. Repeat the process with the remaining dough. Bake until lightly browned, about 10 minutes. Meanwhile, place wire racks over sheets of parchment paper or waxed paper. Transfer the cookies to the wire racks to cool.

3 To make the frosting, whisk the cream and almond extract together in a small mixing bowl. Beat in the confectioners' sugar and continue beating until you have a smooth icing. Drizzle the icing over the cooled cookies. Store in airtight containers.

Swedish Wishing Cookies

On St. Lucia Day, in the homes of families of Swedish descent, the eldest daughter wears a white gown with a red sash and crown of tiny white lights. In the darkness of a December 13 morning, she brings a tray of saffron-flavored Lucia buns or cookies like these into her parents' bedroom. In public celebrations, a teenage girl playing the role of St. Lucia offers these cookies, called *pepparkakor*, to both adults and children who attend the festivities, which might include Swedish folk dancing and a pageant. When these spice cookies are rolled very thinly and cut out in heart shapes, they become "wishing cookies," a charming holiday tradition. St. Lucia gives a child a cookie to hold in the palm of one hand and tells the child to make a wish. With the index finger of the other hand bent, the child strikes the cookie with the knuckle. If the cookie breaks into three pieces, the wish will be granted. If not, there are still those delicious cookie pieces to gobble up. These can also be cut out with cookie cutters, baked, and then decorated or outlined with Decorating Icing (page 128).

MAKES 5 DOZEN COOKIES

3 1/2 cups all-purpose flour

1 teaspoon baking soda

1 1/2 teaspoons ground ginger

1 1/2 teaspoons ground cinnamon

1 teaspoon ground cloves

1/2 teaspoon ground cardamom

1/2 cup (1 stick) unsalted butter at room temperature

3/4 cup sugar

1 large egg

3/4 cup light molasses

2 1/2 teaspoons grated orange rind

1 Sift together the flour, baking soda, ginger, cinnamon, cloves, and cardamom into a medium-size mixing bowl. With an electric mixer, cream the butter and sugar together in a large mixing bowl. Beat in the egg, molasses, and orange rind. Add the dry ingredients, 1 cup at a time, beating well after each addition. Cover the dough with plastic wrap and refrigerate for several hours or overnight.

2 Preheat the oven to 375 degrees F. Coat several baking sheets with nonstick cooking spray or line with parchment paper and set aside. Divide the dough into 4 pieces. Roll out a piece on a floured work surface to a thickness of 1/8 inch. Cut out with a heart-shaped cookie cutter or the shape of

your choice and place on the prepared baking sheets, about 1 inch apart. Repeat the process with the remaining dough.

3   Bake the cookies until browned, 7 to 9 minutes. Transfer the cookies to wire racks to cool. Store in airtight containers.

Spices in the Baking Cupboard

Spices used in desserts need to be fresh to be flavorful. Throw out old spices from your baking cupboard, use whole spices as much as possible, and grind or grate spices right before using in a recipe. Below are some of the most common baking spices in the American kitchen.

★ *Whole white cardamom*, grown in India, can be used for Swedish-inspired ice creams, custards, syrups, cookies, and cakes. For the best flavor, remove the cardamom seeds from the pods and grind to a fine powder in a spice grinder or coffee grinder before using in baking recipes. Cardamom pods are available at gourmet shops or from spice emporiums.

★ *Ground cassia cinnamon*, the kind most commonly available, contributes a sweet-spicy flavor to recipes.

★ *Coriander* is the seed of the cilantro plant, which forms after the plant has flowered. With a hot citrus flavor, it pairs well with mellow persimmon, sweet potato, pumpkin, and other cooked squash fillings. Coriander seeds can be difficult to grind at home, so buy powdered coriander from a reputable spice company.

★ *Ground ginger*, made from drying and grinding fresh gingerroot, has a hot, lemony flavor to lend to cookie, cake, and bread recipes. It should be a pale yellow.

★ *Nutmeg*, native to the Moluccas and now grown on the Caribbean island of Grenada, tastes best when it is freshly grated right into a sauce or batter. The nutmeg, the small inner part of the seed from a tree, has a hard outer covering called mace, which is also used in cooking.

★ *Saffron*, the dried red stigma from the culinary crocus, imparts a honeyed and fragrant flavor and golden color to baked goods. Use whole saffron threads and infuse them in a liquid or batter to get the maximum flavor and color.

Buttery Tea Cakes

The Southern tradition of tea cakes—buttery, cake-like cookies that can be dunked into a hot beverage without crumbling—traveled north to places like Kent, Ohio, with freed black slaves who had worked in plantation kitchens. Kent resident Angela Johnson, a Coretta Scott King Award–winning children's book author, treasures her grandmother Mattie's tea cake recipe, from which this one is adapted.

MAKES ABOUT 3 DOZEN TEA CAKES

2 cups all-purpose flour

1$^1/_2$ teaspoons baking powder

$^1/_2$ cup (1 stick) unsalted butter at room temperature

$^3/_4$ cup sugar

2 large eggs

1 tablespoon heavy cream

1 teaspoon vanilla extract

1 Sift the flour and baking powder together in a small mixing bowl. With an electric mixer, cream the butter and sugar together in a large mixing bowl until light and fluffy. Add the eggs, heavy cream, and vanilla and beat well. Add the flour mixture, $^1/_2$ cup at a time, and beat until well blended. Shape the dough into a ball, cover with plastic wrap, and chill for several hours or overnight.

2 When ready to bake, preheat the oven to 350 degrees F. Coat a large baking sheet with nonstick cooking spray or line with parchment paper.

3 Divide the dough into 4 portions. On a lightly floured work surface, roll out each piece to a thickness of $^1/_4$ inch. Cut into rounds with a 3-inch cutter and place, 2 inches apart, on the prepared baking sheet. Repeat the process with the remaining dough.

4 Bake the cookies until the edges are lightly browned, 10 to 12 minutes. Transfer to wire racks to cool. Store in an airtight container.

Graham Cracker Toffee Pecan Cookies

Sylvester Graham, a nineteenth-century health food champion and physician, touted the benefits of whole grains so much that his name has been associated with whole wheat or "graham" flour and crackers ever since. He would be horrified at the richness of these cookies, but an occasional indulgence feeds the soul as well as the body. Try an ice-cream sandwich made with two of these cookies and a scoop of softened Toffee-Banana Ice Cream (page 439). **MAKES 2 DOZEN COOKIES**

24 double graham crackers
1 cup (2 sticks) unsalted butter

$1\frac{1}{2}$ cups packed dark brown sugar
$\frac{1}{2}$ cup finely chopped pecans

1 Preheat the oven to 350 degrees F. Coat a large rimmed baking sheet with nonstick cooking spray or line with parchment paper. Lay the graham crackers flat on the baking sheet.

2 Melt the butter in a large saucepan. Stir the brown sugar into the butter until dissolved and bubbling. Pour this mixture over the graham crackers and sprinkle evenly with the pecans. Bake until browned and bubbling, about 15 minutes.

3 Remove from the oven and let cool on the baking sheet for 5 minutes. Transfer the cookies to a wire rack, let cool completely, then store in layers between sheets of waxed paper in an airtight container.

Bohemian Lemon and Poppy Seed Hearts

The Eastern European affection for lemon and poppy seeds in baked goods lives on in this recipe from the Bonbonerie bakery in Cincinnati, Ohio. The hearts can be made as single cookies or sandwich cookies dressed up with icing flowers, if you wish. To make the flowers, double the recipe for the Lemon Frosting.
MAKES ABOUT 70 SINGLE, OR 35 SANDWICH, COOKIES

COOKIES

5 cups all-purpose flour

1 teaspoon salt

2 tablespoons poppy seeds, ground in a coffee or spice grinder

1 pound (4 sticks) unsalted butter at room temperature

1⅓ cups granulated sugar

2 large eggs

2 teaspoons vanilla extract

LEMON FROSTING

6 tablespoons (¾ stick) unsalted butter at room temperature

2 cups sifted confectioners' sugar

Juice of 3 lemons

1 To make the cookies, whisk together the flour, salt, and ground poppy seeds in a medium-size mixing bowl. With an electric mixer, cream the butter and granulated sugar together in a large mixing bowl until light and fluffy. Beat in the eggs and vanilla. Add the dry ingredients, ½ cup at a time, beating well after each addition. Form the dough into a ball, cover with plastic wrap, and refrigerate for 2 hours or overnight.

2 Preheat the oven to 350 degrees F. Coat a baking sheet with nonstick cooking spray or line with parchment paper and set aside.

3 Remove the dough from the refrigerator and cut in half. Wrap one half and return it to the refrigerator. Roll out the other half on a lightly floured work surface to a thickness of ¼ inch. Cut out the cookies with a 2-inch heart-shaped cookie cutter. With a lightly floured metal spatula, place the cookies on the prepared baking sheet and bake until light brown, about 11 minutes. Transfer to wire racks to cool. Continue to gather the scraps of dough, roll out, and cut out as many cookies as possible. Repeat the process with the remaining half of dough in the refrigerator.

4 To make the frosting, with an electric mixer, cream the butter and confectioners' sugar together in a medium-size mixing bowl. Add the lemon juice and beat until smooth and creamy. Spread about 1 teaspoon of the frosting on each cooled cookie. Or, if making sandwich cookies, frost half the cookies. Place an unfrosted cookie on top of a frosted one, gently pressing down until the frosting in the middle comes to the cookie's edge. Make sandwiches with the remaining cookies. Make a second batch of Lemon Frosting and pipe a frosting flower on the top of each cookie, if desired.

Germantown Lebkuchen

In German-style bakeries throughout America, the gingerbread-like lebkuchen cookies begin to appear in early November. Every baker has his or her own unique recipe, a closely guarded secret. In this one, from German Village, Ohio, the glaze is a later American addition, making the venerable cookie just a bit sweeter. For a very traditional cookie, roll out the dough on a floured surface and cut out the cookies with Santa Claus or angel cutters. Bake and glaze the cookies, and then affix a Victorian-style paper decoration to each one (the decorations easily peel off before eating). See Sources (page 505) for cookie cutters and paper decorations. **MAKES 4 DOZEN COOKIES**

2¾ cups all-purpose flour

1 teaspoon ground allspice

1 teaspoon ground cinnamon

1 teaspoon ground ginger

½ teaspoon baking soda

½ teaspoon salt

¾ cup packed brown sugar

1 large egg

1 cup wildflower or other medium-colored honey

1 tablespoon grated orange zest

1 cup slivered almonds

1 cup dried apricot halves, snipped into ¼-inch pieces

1 cup dried cranberries

ORANGE GLAZE
1 cup confectioners' sugar

3 tablespoons orange juice

1   Preheat the oven to 350 degrees F. Line a large baking sheet with parchment paper and set aside.

2   In a medium-size mixing bowl, sift together the flour, spices, baking soda, and salt. With an electric mixer, beat the brown sugar and egg together in a large mixing bowl until smooth; beat in the honey and orange zest. Add the flour mixture, 1 cup at a time, to the honey mixture, beating well after each addition. Stir in the nuts and dried fruit. Transfer the dough to a floured work surface and roll out to a thickness of ¼ inch. Cut out the dough with cookie cutters and place on the prepared baking sheet ½ inch apart.

3   Bake the cookies until lightly browned on the edges, 15 to 20 minutes. Cool the cookies in the pan on a wire wrack.

4   To make the glaze, whisk together the confectioners' sugar and orange juice in a small mixing bowl. Drizzle the glaze over the tops of the cookies. Let the glaze harden for 30 minutes. Store in an airtight container.

All the Pretty Houses

Crisp gingerbread or spice cookies have been American favorites from the earliest colonial days. But these first homemade cookies were not fancy creations. According to food historian William Woys Weaver, early American cooks cut out their cookies using only the simplest of tools—the drinking end of a glass or a tea cup, the sharp lid of a tin, or perhaps a pie crimper. In the mid-nineteenth century, children cut out paper shapes, then placed them on rolled-out cookie dough and cut out the dough with a knife. Gingerbread houses are still made that way.

Special cookie cutters and molds were the province of the confectioner or professional baker, especially those in the Philadelphia area. Not until the late nineteenth century were tin cookie cutters mass produced, and thus more affordable. Today, we can choose from these inexpensive metal cutters or from well-crafted cookie cutters in unusual shapes, which carry price tags of 25 dollars and up.

Cut-out gingerbread shapes were a traditional part of the Christmas holidays. In the 1740s, Moravians from what is now southeastern Germany and southwestern Poland brought a love of gingerbread, especially in Christmas cookies, to the Delaware Valley. In Pennsylvania German homes of that period, cut-out gingerbread shapes were used to decorate the forerunner of the Christmas tree—literally translated as the Christmas May pole, a small tree set in a tub on a table, its greenery decorated with apples, decorated lebkuchen, marzipan, and ornamental *oblaten*, which were ancestors of springerle cookies, pressed into decorative molds and painted. *Kriss Kringle's Christmas Tree*, a children's book published in Philadelphia in 1845, shows a small tabletop mountain laurel Christmas tree decked out with marzipan cherries and what look like gingerbread cookies cut out into house and wagon shapes, as well as with toys. The Henry Francis DuPont Winterthur Museum in Delaware usually displays this type of tree during the Christmas holidays.

Besides a tree hung with gingerbread shapes, Philadelphia-area families also loved nativity sets and glass cake stands stacked into towers, displaying pyramids of cakes. Wealthy families could afford shimmery, translucent sugarwork houses (made by professional confectioners) as the centerpieces of Christmas tableaux on side or dining tables. In its vast collection of early Americana, the Winterthur Museum has fancy gingerbread house molds, circa 1800 to 1850, featuring tiled rooves and belfries. According to Weaver in *The Christmas Cook: Three Centuries of Yuletide Sweets*, the 1893 debut of Engelbert Humperdinck's children's opera *Hansel and Gretel* made the idea of a gingerbread house even more popular.

From late Victorian times on, the gingerbread house has been an American Christmas fixture. Museums and shopping centers showcase displays of decorated houses, each one unique and mouthwatering with its candy accouterments. You can buy kits for decorating your own gingerbread house, or purchase one already decorated from a bakery or confectioner's shop.

Cousin Jack Cookies

In the 1830s, groups of Cornish immigrants, known among themselves as "Cousin Jacks," began to settle in Dodgeville, Mineral Point, Linden, and Hazel Green in southwestern Wisconsin. They became miners, farmers, stonemasons, and business owners in their new land. When their wives and girlfriends emigrated, they brought this nutmeg-spiced heirloom cookie featuring dried currants, for which you could also substitute small raisins. **MAKES ABOUT TWENTY-EIGHT 3-INCH COOKIES**

1 cup dried Zante currants

$1/2$ cup hot water or milk

$2^1/2$ cups all-purpose flour, plus extra for rolling out dough

$1^1/2$ teaspoons baking powder

1 tablespoon freshly grated nutmeg

1 teaspoon salt

1 cup vegetable shortening, margarine, lard, or a combination

1 cup sugar

2 large eggs

1 teaspoon vanilla extract

1   Preheat the oven to 350 degrees F. Soak the dried currants in the hot water and set aside to soften.

2   Sift together the flour, baking powder, nutmeg, and salt into a medium-size mixing bowl. With an electric mixer, cream the shortening and sugar together in a large mixing bowl until light and fluffy. Beat in the eggs and vanilla and then add the dry ingredients, $1/2$ cup at a time, and continue beating until well blended. Stir in the currants and any remaining soaking water with a wooden spoon. Cover with plastic wrap and refrigerate for several hours or overnight.

3   Flour the dough, and on a heavily floured work surface, roll out the dough to a thickness of $1/4$ inch. Cut out the cookies with a 3-inch cookie cutter and place them on ungreased baking sheets. Bake until lightly browned, 10 to 12 minutes. Transfer to wire racks to cool.

Montana Snow Cookies

This is an old favorite from eastern Montana. Be sure to use only fresh snow with enough moisture so it will pack (avoid fresh powdery snow). The snow should be very clean, free of dirt and debris.

Yield: Makes as many cookies as you want.

Ingredient: Snow, slightly settled and wet.

Directions: Gather a handful of snow. Quickly mold into a small pancake no larger than the palm of your hand. Lightly rub the surface with your hands to ensure a crispy glaze. Eat.

Pine Tree Shillings

These thin, crisp molasses cookies have a very old pedigree—similar cookies were turned out by early nineteenth-century New England bake houses. In seaport towns, these establishments baked hard biscuits and crackers for ships' provisions on long voyages. Bake houses farther inland concentrated on bread, biscuits, small "cakes" (cookies), and larger cakes raised with yeast, eggs, pearlash (potassium carbonate), and saleratus (baking soda)— baking powder had not yet been invented. This very old recipe—still made today at the Bake House at Sturbridge Village in Sturbridge, Mass-achusetts—appeals to the modern cook because he or she can make the dough in a saucepan (less cleanup) and the cookies still taste great. In this adaptation of the recipe baked in Sturbridge Village, I have substituted pure cane syrup—a lighter form of molasses—and butter instead of shortening to be more true to the times.

MAKES ABOUT 4 DOZEN COOKIES

3 cups all-purpose flour

$1/2$ teaspoon baking soda

$1/2$ teaspoon salt

1 teaspoon ground cinnamon

$1/2$ teaspoon ground ginger

1 cup pure cane syrup or light molasses

$1/2$ cup (1 stick) unsalted butter

$1/2$ cup packed light brown sugar

1   Sift the flour, baking soda, salt, and spices together into a medium-size mixing bowl. In a large saucepan over medium-high heat, melt the cane syrup and butter together, stirring until blended. Remove from the heat and stir in the brown sugar. Beat in the flour mixture, $1/2$ cup at a time, until you have a stiff dough. Divide the dough in half, and with your hands, form each portion into a log 1 inch in diameter and wrap well in plastic. Refrigerate for 8 hours or overnight. (This dough will keep for weeks in the refrigerator.)

2   When ready to bake, preheat the oven to 375 degrees F. Coat several baking sheets with nonstick cooking spray or line with parchment paper and set aside.

3   Using a sharp knife, cut the logs into $1/4$-inch-thick slices. Place the slices on the prepared baking sheets, about 1 inch apart. Bake until browned, about 10 minutes. Transfer to wire racks to cool. Store in an airtight container.

Crisp, Lemony Sugar Cookies

At Annedore's Fine Chocolates in Kansas City, I finally found my favorite crisp, slightly lemony sugar cookie, which can transform itself into any shape. At Annedore's they become Valentine hearts, Easter chicks, Fourth of July flags, Halloween pumpkins, and Christmas ornaments—and I eat them all. After a few experiments, I duplicated the taste and texture. The secrets to crispness are the sugar content (corn syrup), the thickness of the dough after it is rolled out (very thin), and a high baking temperature. If you prefer a strong lemony flavor, add another teaspoon or 2 of zest. Use Decorating Icing to gild the lily, if you like. **MAKES 3 DOZEN COOKIES**

$\frac{1}{2}$ teaspoon baking powder

$\frac{1}{2}$ teaspoon baking soda

$\frac{1}{2}$ teaspoon salt

$2\frac{1}{2}$ cups all-purpose flour

$\frac{1}{2}$ cup (1 stick) unsalted butter at room temperature

$\frac{1}{2}$ cup sugar, plus more for dusting

Grated zest and juice of 1 lemon

$\frac{1}{3}$ cup light corn syrup

1 large egg

1 recipe Decorating Icing (optional, page 128)

1 Sift together the baking powder, baking soda, salt, and flour into a medium-size mixing bowl. With an electric mixer, cream together the butter, $\frac{1}{2}$ cup granulated sugar, and grated lemon zest in a large mixing bowl until light and fluffy. Beat in the lemon juice, corn syrup, and egg and continue beating until smooth. Beat in the dry ingredients, 1 cup at a time, and continue beating until you have a smooth and soft dough. Cut the dough in half, form each half into a disk, and cover with plastic wrap. Freeze for at least 30 minutes.

2 Preheat the oven to 400 degrees F. Sprinkle a flat work surface with sugar and roll out half the dough to a thickness of $\frac{1}{8}$ inch. (If the dough is too soft, cover and return it to the freezer for a while longer.) Use cookie cutters to cut out the dough and place the cookies on ungreased baking sheets. Repeat the process with the remaining half of the dough.

3 Bake the cookies until lightly browned at the edges, 6 to 8 minutes. Transfer to wire racks to cool. Decorate the cookies with the icing, if desired.

Decorating Icing

This icing is perfect for piping with a pastry bag. Or thin it and use it as a paint to decorate cookies, cakes, and cupcakes. **MAKES 1 CUP**

2 cups confectioners' sugar

1 tablespoon unsalted butter, melted

2 teaspoons light corn syrup

2$\frac{1}{2}$ tablespoons hot water, or more as necessary

Several drops of food coloring for tinting icing (optional)

1 Place all the ingredients in a medium-size mixing bowl and beat with an electric mixer on medium speed until thick and well blended.

2 If you wish to color the icing, add a little more hot water, and beat until the icing is smooth and has the consistency of oil paint. Add any food coloring you wish and beat again. Add more hot water, if necessary, to achieve the consistency of thin paint. If you wish to use the icing for piping, use a rubber spatula to transfer the icing to a pastry bag fitted with the appropriate tip. The icing keeps, covered, in the refrigerator for up to 2 weeks.

Chocolate Shortbread Cookies

These classic cookies came to America from the border country of northern England and the southern highlands of Scotland during the eighteenth and early nineteenth centuries. The "short" in shortbread means there is a high percentage of fat, and that makes for a crumbly dough. These substantial cookies require a lower baking temperature and a longer baking time than normal to attain their crispy texture. Intensely chocolaty and sturdy enough to line a trifle bowl or hold a brick of ice cream in a sandwich, these cookies are an essential building block in a dessert maker's repertoire. They're also the ancestors of the popular Hydrox and Oreo cookies.
MAKES 12 TO 15 COOKIES

$\frac{1}{4}$ cup plus 1 tablespoon unsweetened cocoa powder

1 cup all-purpose flour

$\frac{1}{4}$ teaspoon salt

$\frac{1}{2}$ cup (1 stick) unsalted butter at room temperature

5 tablespoons sugar, plus more for dusting

1 teaspoon vanilla extract

1   Preheat the oven to 275 degrees F. Line a baking sheet with parchment paper and set aside.

2   Sift together the cocoa powder, flour, and salt into a small mixing bowl. In a food processor or a large mixing bowl using an electric mixer, cream the butter until pale yellow. Add the sugar and vanilla and process or beat until fluffy. Add the dry ingredients, $\frac{1}{2}$ cup at a time, processing or beating until well blended but crumbly. Press the crumbles of dough onto a piece of plastic wrap, fold the wrap over the dough, and chill for 20 minutes.

3   On a lightly sugared work surface, roll out the dough to a thickness of $\frac{1}{2}$ inch. If the dough splits, just press it together with your fingers. Use sugar as you would flour to keep the dough from sticking to the work surface or the rolling pin. With a 2-inch cookie cutter, cut out the cookies and place on the prepared baking sheet, about 1 inch apart.

4   Bake the cookies until firm to the touch, 40 to 45 minutes. Let cool in the pan.

> **SANDWICH SHORTBREAD COOKIES** Sandwich 2 cookies together with a smear of Cocoa Mocha Frosting (page 147); Creamy, Fluffy Frosting (page 142); or Marshmallow Cream Filling (see page 114).

Icebox Shortbread Cookies

This easy, versatile cookie dough can be made in the food processor, then formed into a log and wrapped with wax or parchment paper and stored in the refrigerator. From this one basic shortbread cookie recipe, you can make a variety of cookie flavors and colors—pistachio, orange, chocolate spice, and vanilla. **MAKES ABOUT 40 COOKIES**

$\frac{3}{4}$ cup ($1\frac{1}{2}$ sticks) unsalted butter at room temperature
1 cup confectioners' sugar
2 teaspoons vanilla extract

$\frac{1}{4}$ teaspoon salt
1 cup all-purpose flour
Granulated sugar for rolling

1   In a food processor or a large mixing bowl using an electric mixer, cream the butter with $\frac{1}{2}$ cup of the confectioners' sugar, the vanilla, and the salt until light and fluffy. Sift the remaining $\frac{1}{2}$ cup of confectioners' sugar and the flour into the work bowl or mixing bowl, then process or beat again until blended. Cover and chill the dough until firm enough to shape, about 1 hour.

2 Transfer the dough to a sheet of plastic wrap. With your hands, roll the dough into smooth 10-inch log. Cover completely with the plastic and wrap a second time in aluminum foil. Place the log in the freezer until very firm, about 2 hours, before baking. (The dough will keep in the refrigerator for up to 1 week or in the freezer for 1 month.)

3 Preheat the oven to 375 degrees F. Coat a baking sheet with nonstick cooking spray or line with parchment paper and set aside.

4 Sprinkle a work surface with granulated sugar and roll the dough in it, then cut the log into ¼-inch-thick slices. Place the slices, 2 inches apart, on the prepared baking sheet. Bake until the edges are golden, about 10 minutes. Transfer to wire racks to cool.

> **ORANGE SHORTBREAD** In step 1, omit the vanilla extract and add 1 tablespoon plus 1 teaspoon grated orange zest and 1 teaspoon vanilla extract to the dough, then proceed with the recipe.

> **PISTACHIO SHORTBREAD** In a preheated 350 degree oven, lightly toast ¾ cup chopped pistachios. Let cool. In step 1, add the toasted pistachios to the dough with the flour mixture, plus ⅛ teaspoon salt, and 1 or 2 drops of green food coloring. Then proceed with the recipe.

> **CHOCOLATE SPICE SHORTBREAD** In the top of a double boiler, melt 3 ounces unsweetened chocolate over simmering water. In step 1, add the melted chocolate after you have creamed the butter and sugar. Omit the vanilla and add ½ teaspoon ground cinnamon, ¼ teaspoon ground allspice, ⅛ teaspoon salt, and ⅛ teaspoon freshly ground black pepper along with the flour and confectioners' sugar. Then proceed with the recipe.

Frosted Easter Egg Sugar Cookies

When her then-fiancé David was overseas during the Vietnam War, Bonnie Knauss sent him these cookies, which she wrapped in plastic, two at a time, then packed carefully in a box filled with popcorn to make the long haul. Her cookies sustained him, and he returned home safely to marry her. Bonnie still makes these cookies, sending them to relatives or giving them to neighborhood children. "I always have cookies in the freezer, because you never know when you're going to need a quick dessert," she says. "The only trick is to freeze them without frosting. Layer them in a plastic container or coffee can and place waxed paper or foil between the layers. After they thaw, then you can frost them if you want." These vanilla-flavored, egg-shaped sugar cookies can be frosted with a rainbow of colors. Simply divide the frosting among small ramekins and tint each one a different color. **MAKES 4 DOZEN COOKIES**

COOKIES

$2\frac{1}{2}$ cups all-purpose flour

1 teaspoon baking soda

1 teaspoon cream of tartar

1 cup (2 sticks) unsalted butter at room temperature

$1\frac{1}{2}$ cups confectioners' sugar

1 large egg, beaten

1 teaspoon vanilla extract

$\frac{1}{2}$ teaspoon almond extract

FROSTING

$\frac{1}{3}$ cup unsalted butter at room temperature

3 cups confectioners' sugar

1 teaspoon vanilla extract

2 tablespoons milk or cream

Colored sugars, sweetened flaked coconut, or colored sprinkles for decorating

1   In a medium-size mixing bowl, sift together the flour, baking soda, and cream of tartar. With an electric mixer, cream the butter and sugar together in a large mixing bowl until fluffy. Mix in the egg and flavorings. Beat in the dry ingredients, a little at a time. Cover the dough with plastic wrap and let rest in the refrigerator for 3 to 4 hours or overnight.

2   When ready to bake, preheat the oven to 350 degrees F. Coat several baking sheets with nonstick cooking spray or line with parchment paper and set aside.

3   Divide the dough in half and roll out on a lightly floured work surface to a thickness of $\frac{3}{8}$ inch, which is thicker than normal for sugar cookies. Cut the dough with a 3-inch Easter egg cookie cutter and place the cookies on the prepared baking sheets. Bake until barely browned at the edges, 7 to 10 minutes. Remove from the oven and let cool for 2 to 3 minutes in the pan before transferring to a wire rack to cool completely. When the cookies have cooled, either package and freeze or frost.

4   To make the frosting, with an electric mixer, beat the ingredients together in a large mixing bowl until light and fluffy. Spread a thin layer on each cookie and decorate with colored sugars, flaked coconut, or colored sprinkles.

Coriander Spice Cookies

A melia Simmons made a lot of "firsts" when her first cookbook, *American Cookery*, was published in 1796. It was the first truly American cookbook. Judging from her assertion that her recipes were "adapted to this country and all grades of life," she was voicing her frustration that English cookbooks, which called for unobtainable ingredients and were written for wealthy householders, were not of practical use to American women, even though they were reprinted in Boston and Philadelphia for the American market. Simmons was the first cookbook author to use the Dutch word *cooky* in a printed recipe instead of the English "biscuit," the first to list a recipe for cranberry tart, to use American molasses instead of English treacle, to give not one but three recipes for Indian Pudding, and to include pumpkin pudding made in a crust—in other words, pumpkin pie.

When I looked through the facsimile edition of *American Cookery* for a recipe I could use in this book, I came across these spice cookies and was immediately intrigued. Although our sugar is so refined now that we don't have to follow Simmons's instructions to "scum well," this recipe is still very doable—and very delicious—more than 300 years later. How many cookbook authors today could claim that? Simmons's method follows the accepted one for making gingerbread, though we replace her pearlash (potassium carbonate) with baking soda. This recipe produces a soft, rounded cookie known as a "jumble," with a crisp exterior and a cake-like center. The dough can be made in a saucepan and rolled out while still warm. It is easy to work with, and the cookies don't spread on the baking sheet as they bake. In other words, they're ideal for an American history lesson for kids in the kitchen. For a finishing touch, I like lemon icing, but it's not essential. These cookies are best eaten the day they're made.

MAKES 15 COOKIES

COOKIES

1 cup granulated sugar

1/2 cup water

1 teaspoon baking soda

1/2 cup milk

1/4 cup (1/2 stick) unsalted butter at room temperature

1 tablespoon ground coriander

1/4 teaspoon salt

3 cups all-purpose flour

LEMON ICING (OPTIONAL)

1 cup confectioners' sugar

1 teaspoon grated lemon zest

Juice of 1 lemon

1   Preheat the oven to 350 degrees F. Coat a baking sheet with nonstick cooking spray or line with parchment paper and set aside.

2   In a medium-size saucepan over medium-high heat, combine the granulated sugar and water, stirring to dissolve the sugar. Bring the mixture to a boil and continue boiling for 5 minutes. In a small bowl, whisk the baking soda and milk together and then whisk into the sugar mixture. Whisk in the butter, coriander, and salt and continue whisking until well blended. Remove from the heat and whisk or stir in the flour, 1 cup at a time, and continue mixing until you have a soft dough that holds together.

3   Transfer the dough to a floured work surface and roll out to a thickness of $\frac{1}{2}$ inch. Using a $2\frac{1}{2}$-inch cookie cutter, cut out 12 cookies and place them on the prepared baking sheet. Gather up the scraps of dough, roll out again, cut out 3 more cookies, and place on the baking sheet.

4   Bake the cookies until lightly browned, about 15 minutes. While they are slightly warm, make the icing, if desired.

5   To make the icing, whisk the confectioners' sugar and lemon zest and juice together until you have a thick frosting. Spread about 1 teaspoon on each cookie.

Grossmutter's Date-Filled Cookies

This old German recipe, which originally called for lard in the pastry and cooking instructions for a wood stove, traveled with the Miller family when they emigrated to Cleveland, Ohio. Bob Miller, an old house restorer, substituted shortening for the lard and baked the cookies in an electric oven. The cookies resemble miniature filled pies.

MAKES 2 DOZEN COOKIES

4 cups all-purpose flour

$\frac{1}{4}$ teaspoon salt

2 cups packed light brown sugar

1 cup vegetable shortening

3 large eggs, beaten

1 teaspoon baking soda

1 tablespoon hot water

2 teaspoons vanilla extract

DATE FILLING

1 cup packed light brown sugar

1 tablespoon all-purpose flour

$\frac{1}{2}$ cup walnuts or pecans

$\frac{3}{4}$ cup chopped dates

1 cup water

1   To make the cookies, whisk the flour and salt together in a medium-size mixing bowl. With an electric mixer, cream the brown sugar and shortening together in a large mixing bowl until light and fluffy. Beat in the eggs, one at a time, then beat in the flour mixture, 1 cup at a time, mixing well after each addition. Combine the baking soda and hot water in a small bowl and mix into the dough, then beat in the vanilla. Cover with plastic wrap and refrigerate while you make the filling.

2   To make the filling, put all the ingredients, except the water, in a food processor and chop the pecans and dates finely. Transfer the contents to a medium-size saucepan. Stir in the water, bring to a boil, and continue stirring until thick.

3   Preheat the oven to 350 degrees F. To assemble the cookies, roll out the dough on a floured board to a thickness of $\frac{1}{4}$ inch. With a biscuit cutter or the drinking end of a glass, cut the dough into 2-inch circles. Lay 12 dough circles on a tray. Put a teaspoonful of filling in the center of each circle, then lay a second circle on top of the filling. With a fork, press the edges of the circle together. Repeat the process with the remaining pastry and filling. Place on ungreased baking sheets, about 1 inch apart. Bake until browned, about 8 minutes. Transfer to wire racks to cool.

Cranberry, Almond, and Orange Rugelach

I love rugelach, the rolled crescents of sour cream or cream cheese pastry enclosing a spiced, nut, or fruit filling. Brought to this country by Eastern European immigrants of Jewish descent, these pastries have become as much a part of the Hanukkah celebration in some households as potato latkes, those crisp shredded potato pancakes often served with sour cream or applesauce. Now rugelach are so mainstream that you can buy them in containers at discount stores. But nothing, of course, beats homemade, especially this version of rugelach, adapted from a recipe distributed by Odense Almond Paste. You can use packaged almond paste or homemade marzipan. Besides tasting good and keeping well in an airtight container, these pastries also freeze well, unbaked. I like to freeze them in disposable pie pans (popped into a resealable plastic freezer bag), so they can go right from the freezer into the oven. What a surprise for holiday guests—rugelach warm from the oven! These taste great paired with Spiced Persimmon Ice Cream (page 433) or vanilla ice cream dusted with gingerbread or ginger cookie crumbs.

MAKES 5 DOZEN RUGELACH

1 cup Marzipan made with almond extract (page 481) or one 7-ounce package almond paste

2 cups all-purpose flour

1/4 teaspoon salt

One 8-ounce package cold cream cheese, cut into 1/2-inch pieces

1 cup (2 sticks) cold unsalted butter, cut into 1/2-inch pieces

ALMOND, CRANBERRY, AND ORANGE FILLING

1 cup flaked almonds

One 5-ounce package sweetened dried cranberries

1 teaspoon grated orange zest

1 recipe Fresh Orange Marmalade (page 6) or one 12-ounce jar orange marmalade

1 large egg, beaten

Sugar for dusting

1 To make the pastry dough, put the almond paste in a food processor and process until you have a uniform mixture with no large lumps. Add the flour and salt and pulse to combine. Add the cream cheese and butter and pulse until the mixture resembles coarse crumbs. Transfer the mixture to a lightly floured work surface. Press and knead into a ball. Divide the ball into four equal portions. Form each one into a ball and wrap with plastic wrap. Refrigerate the dough while you make the filling.

2 Preheat the oven to 375 degrees F. Coat several baking sheets with nonstick cooking spray or line with parchment paper and set aside.

3 To make the filling, combine the almonds, cranberries, and orange zest in the food processor and process until very finely chopped. Set aside.

4 On a lightly floured work surface, roll out a portion of pastry into a 9-inch circle, using an inverted 9-inch cake or pie pan as a guide. Trim the edges and reserve the trimmings to use for the fifth circle of dough. Spread 3 tablespoons of orange marmalade over the dough circle with an offset or rubber spatula. Sprinkle 1/2 cup of the filling over the marmalade and press firmly into the dough. With a pizza wheel or a sharp knife, cut the dough into 12 equal pie-shaped wedges. Starting with the wide end of each wedge, roll up the pastry, shape into a crescent, and place the crescents, 1 inch apart, on a prepared baking sheet. Brush each rugelach with the beaten egg and sprinkle with sugar. Repeat the process with the remaining dough portions. Gather all the trimmings together, press them into a ball, then roll out for a fifth dough circle and repeat the process of preparing the rugelach.

5 Bake the rugelach until puffed and golden, 21 to 23 minutes. Transfer to wire racks to cool.

Let's Eat Cake!

I've often wondered why cake and other dessert recipes greatly outnumber any other category in vintage American cookbooks. E. Mae Fritz, who wrote about her Nebraska farming and homesteading adventures in *Prairie Kitchen Sampler*, suggests a reason: "It wasn't long, even as a beginning cook, until I no longer relied on recipes. Once I had developed 'an eye' for judging proportions and for recognizing when pie crusts and fillings, biscuits and breads 'looked right,' I only needed recipes for cakes, cookies, candy and desserts."

Like Fritz, American women tended to write down their cake and dessert recipes because these dishes required more precision. From the earliest yeast-risen cake recipes brought to this country—Hartford Election Cake (page 234) and Moravian Sugar Cake (page 233)—to the richest, almost flourless French Chocolate Cake (page 242), cakes mean a special occasion and thus, extra care. The range of cakes in the American repertoire is astounding—layer, angel, sponge, pound, Bundt, sheet, fruit and keeping cakes, yeast-risen, and cheese cakes—a reflection of our melting-pot culture.

Tips for Great Cakes Every Time

* Use good quality ingredients: real unsalted butter; pure extracts, such as vanilla and almond; freshly grated nutmeg; and fresh citrus juices and zests.

* Measure accurately. Spoon the flour from the bag or canister into the measuring cup; don't scoop with the measuring cup, which compacts it. Then level off the flour with the blade of a knife or your finger.

* Set the timer, then check to see if your cake is done 5 minutes before the timer goes off (or set the timer to ring 5 minutes before the recipe's baking time). You can always put an underdone cake back in the oven; an overdone cake has no remedy. But don't keep checking the cake in the oven, or the change in oven temperature may prevent the cake from rising properly.

Classic Yellow Cake

The English are known for their sponge cakes, the French for their sponge-like *genoise*, the Germans and Scandinavians for their flourless tortes. But the high-rising and light-textured layer cake is uniquely American. Creaming the butter and sugar, folding the flour and milk into the batter, and then the beaten egg whites yields a higher, more tender cake. Use this cake as a template for your own unique dessert "designs." With the variety of fillings in this book—Warm Spiced Berries (see page 348), Cranberry-Chokecherry Conserve (page 7), Fresh Orange Marmalade (page 6), Wildflower Honey Curd (see page 322)—you can have a different cake each time you make it. Using Brown Butter Frosting (recipe follows) and Garden Candy (page 482), you can make a unique homespun plaid cake by threading candied strips of yellow and green zucchini and orange carrot in a basket-weave pattern on top. With Creamy, Fluffy Frosting (see page 142) and a dusting of sweetened flaked coconut, you've got a moist and delicious coconut cake. The possibilities are endless.

MAKES TWO 8-INCH CAKE LAYERS; 8 TO 10 SERVINGS

2 cups cake flour

¾ teaspoon salt

2 teaspoons baking powder

½ cup (1 stick) unsalted butter at room temperature

1 cup sugar

3 large eggs, separated

⅔ cup milk

1 teaspoon vanilla extract

½ teaspoon almond extract

1   Preheat the oven to 375 degrees F. Grease and lightly flour two 8-inch round or square cake pans, tapping out the excess, and set aside.

2   Sift together the flour, salt, and baking powder into a medium-size mixing bowl and set aside. With an electric mixer, cream the butter and sugar together in a large mixing bowl until light and fluffy. Beat in the egg yolks. With a rubber spatula, fold in the sifted dry ingredients, alternating with the milk, until you have a smooth batter. Then fold in the extracts.

3   Carefully wash and dry the beaters well, then beat the egg whites in a medium-size mixing until they hold stiff peaks. Fold the egg whites into the cake batter until you can no longer see them. Divide the batter evenly between the prepared pans.

4 Bake the layers until a cake tester inserted in the middle comes out clean and the cake has pulled away from the side of the pan, 22 to 25 minutes. Invert the cake layers onto wire racks, then carefully turn them right side up to finish cooling on the racks. Let cool completely before frosting.

> **BOSTON CREAM PIE** Spread the bottom layer with Classic Pastry Cream (page 163). Place the top layer over the pastry cream. Spread the top layer with Chocolate Ganache (page 213) so that the top of the cake is completely covered and the chocolate drips down the sides. Refrigerate until ready to serve.

Brown Butter Frosting

I love the vintage look and rich flavor of this frosting, which is the color of tea-dyed linen. **MAKES ABOUT 3 CUPS, ENOUGH TO FROST A 3-LAYER CAKE**

¾ cup (1½ sticks) unsalted butter, cut into pieces

3 cups sifted confectioners' sugar

¼ teaspoon salt

2 teaspoons vanilla extract

⅓ cup heavy cream

1 Melt the butter in a medium-size saucepan over medium-high heat until it begins to turn golden brown, about 5 minutes. Watch the pan carefully because the butter can easily burn.

2 Remove from the heat. Whisk in the confectioners' sugar, salt, and vanilla until smooth. Whisk in enough of the cream to achieve a spreadable consistency.

Glazes, Icings, and Frostings

★ A *clear glaze* can be a flavored sugar syrup, a very thin mixture of confectioners' sugar and a liquid, or warmed clear fruit jelly (such as apricot). A glaze is drizzled or brushed over the surface of cookies, cakes, or fruit tarts for heightened flavor and appearance.

★ An *icing* is a little thicker and more opaque than a glaze. Icings are made with butter and cream, milk, or another liquid, blended with confectioners' sugar. An icing may be drizzled or spread thinly for heightened flavor and appearance.

★ A *frosting* is a thick, opaque, and spreadable topping. Some part of it may be cooked in advance, such as the sugar syrup in fondant and buttercream frosting, the confectioners' sugar mixture in Creamy, Fluffy Frosting (see page 142), Italian meringue in classic Seven-Minute Frosting (see page 161), or the caramel mixtures in 3-6-9 Frosting (see page 171) or Caramel Cream Frosting (see page 173). A frosting is spread on a cake or cookies to hold layers together, give a cake a unified appearance, and create designs.

Classic Birthday Cake

The birthday cake as we know it—a two-layer creation with pastel or white frosting, decorations, and candles—is a relatively recent entrant in our collection of American desserts. It had to wait for the mass availability of good quality all-purpose flour, baking powder, vanilla extract, and confectioners' sugar. From the late nineteenth century onward, the classic homemade two-layer cake—or frosted cupcakes—reigned at children's birthday parties, peaking in the 1950s. When my children were in elementary school, I made my fair share of birthday cakes as well as cupcakes for classroom parties. Today, true homemade birthday cakes have a lot of noisy competition: cake mixes, frozen whipped topping, frosting in a tube, and grocery store bakery sheet cakes, which taste more than faintly of chemicals. But maybe nostalgia can bring it back. The Magnolia Bakery in New York City has had great success with its Traditional Vanilla Birthday Cake, a pink-frosted, two-layer confection with lots of colored sprinkles. "Feel as though you're at your seventh birthday party all over again!" is their savvy marketing ploy. Here is my version of the Magnolia Bakery's birthday cake, which I think will please anyone of any age. It's one of those culinary common denominators and well worth having in your dessert arsenal.

Self-rising flour is a combination of all-purpose flour, baking powder, salt, and baking soda. If you don't have it on hand, sift together 1 cup of all-purpose flour, 1 teaspoon of baking powder, ½ teaspoon of salt, and ¼ teaspoon of baking soda as a substitute for 1 cup of self-rising flour. **MAKES ONE 9-INCH 2-LAYER CAKE; 8 TO 10 SERVINGS**

1½ cups self-rising flour

1¼ cups all-purpose flour

1 cup (2 sticks) unsalted butter at room temperature

2 cups sugar

4 large eggs, at room temperature

1 cup milk

½ teaspoon vanilla extract

½ teaspoon almond extract

1 recipe Creamy, Fluffy Frosting (see page 142)

Colored sprinkles (optional) for decorating

1 Preheat the oven to 350 degrees F. Grease the bottoms of two 9-inch round cake pans, line with parchment paper, and grease and flour the pans and paper.

2 In a medium-size mixing bowl, combine the flours. With an electric mixer, cream the butter and

sugar together in a large mixing bowl until light and fluffy. Add the eggs, one at a time, beating well after each addition. Add the flour mixture a little at a time, alternating with the milk and beating well after each addition. Add the extracts and beat until you have a smooth batter. Pour or spoon half the batter into each prepared pan.

3   Bake the layers until the tops spring back when lightly touched, 20 to 25 minutes. Invert the cake layers onto wire racks, the immediately turn right side up, and let cool completely before frosting them. Use a fourth of the frosting between the layers, then the rest to frost the top and sides. Decorate with colored sprinkles, if desired.

> **CLASSIC YELLOW BIRTHDAY CUPCAKES** Line two 12-cup muffin tins with paper liners. Fill each muffin cup three quarters full. Bake until the tops of the cupcakes spring back when lightly touched, 20 to 22 minutes. Let cool in the pans, then frost. Makes 2 dozen cupcakes.

Creamy, Fluffy Frosting

The classic French buttercream and ganache, marzipan filling, and fondant icing beloved by the British all now have their place in our dessert collection. But this creamy, fluffy style of frosting is unique to America, topping traditional birthday cakes or becoming the surprise center for chocolate layer cakes or cupcakes. When I was sixteen, I worked at the Wyoming Bakery in Cincinnati, Ohio, after school and on weekends. For me, it was fascinating to go behind the scenes to see how the artfully decorated cakes that had been the centerpiece of first communions, family celebrations, and childhood birthdays were made. The white frosting had an elusive flavor, somewhat like coconut, piped in delicate ribbons and borders. Pale pastel sugar roses and pale green leaves made each cake look like a romantic Victorian valentine. I couldn't wait to meet the cake decorator, who usually arrived in the early mornings when I was at school. I imagined her to be tall, thin, and delicate. One day, however, when I carried a tray of cookies to the back of the shop, I saw the foot pedals pumping, whirling a cake around on a turntable, and I thought "at last!" To my shock, a small, wiry, heavily tattooed man with a pack of cigarettes rolled up in his T-shirt sleeve growled, "What do you want?" I was speechless. Although I can't recreate his artful designs, I've come close to the taste and texture of that pure white, creamy frosting. It keeps, covered, in the refrigerator for up to 1 week.

Let the frosting come to room temperature before using. (If you have health concerns about using raw egg white, substitute reconstituted dried or pasteurized egg white and proceed with the recipe.)

MAKES ABOUT 3 CUPS, ENOUGH TO FROST AND FILL A 2-LAYER CAKE

$\frac{1}{2}$ cup (1 stick) unsalted butter at room temperature

$\frac{1}{2}$ cup vegetable oil, such as canola or soybean

$\frac{1}{2}$ cup vegetable shortening

3 cups confectioners' sugar

1 teaspoon vanilla extract

$\frac{1}{2}$ teaspoon coconut extract (optional)

1 large egg white

$\frac{1}{4}$ teaspoon salt

With an electric mixer, cream together the butter, vegetable oil, and shortening in a large mixing bowl. Beat in the confectioners' sugar, vanilla, and coconut extract, if using, and beat on high speed for 3 minutes. Add the egg white and salt and beat until you have a fluffy, creamy frosting, about 2 minutes more.

Happy Birthday to You!

Americans love to celebrate birthdays—almost two billion birthday cards are sent in the United States every year. August, July, and September are the most common birthday months, with over 9 percent of Americans claiming birthdays in August alone.

No American birthday would be complete without the traditional "Happy Birthday" song, which has slowly evolved into a mega-hit. It all began in the 1890s, when Mildred Hill composed a short, catchy melody. Mildred's sister Patti, a teacher, penned the lyrics, "Good morning to you, good morning to you, good morning, dear teacher, good morning to you" to go with the tune. The song became popular and was sung in schools all over the United States. But it wasn't until 1935 that Patti came up with those other, far more popular lyrics to her sister's melody: "Happy birthday to you, happy birthday to you, happy birthday, dear (name), happy birthday to you." The song became part of the Broadway production *As Thousands Cheer* in the late 1930s. Now it is as much a part of the birthday celebration as the cake and candles.

During the Eisenhower administration in the 1950s, First Lady Mamie Eisenhower organized lots of birthday celebrations in the White House. She always ordered a birthday cake from the White House kitchen whenever anyone on her staff had a birthday and personally selected a card.

Devil's Food Cake with Old-Fashioned Chocolate Frosting

Angel food cake was invented in the latter part of the 1800s, legend has it, by black cooks in St. Louis. Devil's food cake—its polar opposite in flavor, color, and texture—wasn't created until baking chocolate was readily available and affordable. Relatively inexpensive unsweetened cocoa powder for baking hit the American market in the early 1900s.

In the 1873 edition of the *Presbyterian Cook Book* from Dayton, Ohio, there are two "chocolate cake" recipes that are really yellow layer cakes with frosting flavored with "one-half cake of sweet chocolate, grated." In the 1906 edition of the *Capital City Cook Book* from Madison, Wisconsin, there is only one chocolate cake recipe, a version of Pacific cake, which included three tablespoons of grated sweet chocolate in the batter. However, a "devil's cake" recipe using melted squares of chocolate appeared in the 1903 edition of *The Settlement Cook Book*. This luscious, tender, chocolaty devil's food cake made with baking chocolate has been a perennial favorite in American kitchens ever since. Devil's food became a popular Betty Crocker cake mix flavor in 1948. Both the cake and the frosting recipes are adapted from Margaret Rudkin's 1963 *Pepperidge Farm Cookbook.* **MAKES ONE 2-LAYER 9-INCH CAKE; 8 SERVINGS**

DEVIL'S FOOD CAKE

$\frac{1}{2}$ cup (1 stick) unsalted butter at room temperature

2 cups sifted cake flour

$\frac{3}{4}$ teaspoon salt

1 teaspoon baking soda

$1\frac{1}{4}$ cups sugar

$\frac{3}{4}$ cup milk

3 ounces unsweetened chocolate, melted

1 teaspoon vanilla extract

2 large eggs

OLD-FASHIONED CHOCOLATE FROSTING

1 cup sugar

$\frac{1}{4}$ cup cake flour

4 ounces unsweetened chocolate, cut into small pieces

$1\frac{1}{2}$ cups milk

2 tablespoons unsalted butter

1   Preheat the oven to 350 degrees F. Grease and flour two 9-inch round cake pans, tapping out the excess flour, and set aside.

2   To make the cake, put the butter in a medium-size mixing bowl. Sift the flour, salt, baking soda, and sugar right over the butter. Add the milk and beat with an electric mixer until the batter is smooth. Beat in the melted chocolate, vanilla, and eggs and continue beating until smooth. Divide the batter evenly between the prepared pans.

3   Bake the layers until they have shrunk from the sides of the pans and a cake tester inserted in the center comes out clean, about 25 minutes. Invert the cakes onto wire racks, then immediately turn right side up. Let cool completely before frosting.

4   To make the frosting, whisk together the sugar, flour, and chocolate in a medium-size saucepan over medium-high heat. Pour in the milk and continue to whisk until the mixture thickens and the chocolate melts. Remove from the heat, whisk in the butter, and continue whisking until it melts and the frosting is smooth and creamy. Let cool, then frost the cake.

The Frosting on the Cake

A homemade cake should look as good as it tastes, with luscious, creamy frosting swirled all over it in a decorative pattern. For the best results:

1   Let the cake cool completely before frosting.

2   Use a pastry brush to gently remove any crumbs that could get caught up in the frosting, creating an uneven finish.

3   Place the bottom cake layer on a cake stand or cake plate. Insert pieces of parchment or waxed paper under the cake to keep the stand or plate clean as you frost.

4   To keep fresh cream frostings such as Whipped Frosting (see page 184) or sweetened whipped cream from soaking into the cake and making it soggy, brush the top of each layer with a sugar syrup, perhaps Homemade Vanilla Bean Syrup (page 486) or Almond Syrup (page 486).

5   Divide the frosting in half. For a two-layer cake, use one quarter of it to frost the top of the bottom layer. Use half of the remaining frosting on the sides of the cake, using an offset spatula to make a thin coat. Swirl the top edge of the icing about $1/4$ inch above the top of the cake with the flat side of the offset spatula or a table knife. Use the remaining frosting for the top of the cake, blending the frosting at the raised edge and swirling the frosting on top in a decorative pattern.

6   Remove the parchment or waxed paper and let the cake stand for an hour before slicing to let the frosting become firm.

Classic Sour Cream Chocolate Cake

Beat this cake batter with an electric mixer for best results. I like to add either a dash of cinnamon or coffee to enhance the chocolate flavor. I adapted this recipe from a back-of-the-box cake recipe on a container of Hershey's cocoa.

MAKES ONE 8-INCH 2-LAYER CAKE OR 24 CUPCAKES; 8 TO 10 SERVINGS

2 cups all-purpose flour

1½ teaspoons baking soda

1 teaspoon ground cinnamon

2 cups sugar

½ cup vegetable oil, such as canola, soybean, or corn

½ cup unsweetened cocoa powder

½ cup sour cream

2 teaspoons vanilla extract

1 cup hot water

1 recipe Cocoa Mocha Frosting (recipe follows) or Seven-Minute Frosting (see page 161)

1 Preheat the oven to 325 degrees F. Grease and flour two 8-inch round cake pans, tapping out the excess, or line two 12-cup muffin tins with paper liners and set aside.

2 Sift together the the flour, baking soda, and cinnamon in a medium-size mixing bowl and set aside. With an electric mixer, beat together the sugar, vegetable oil, and cocoa in a large mixing bowl until smooth. Beat in the sour cream, then beat in the sifted dry ingredients, ½ cup at a time, beating well after each addition. Beat in the vanilla and then the hot water to make a runny batter. Divide the batter evenly between the prepared cake pans or fill the paper-lined muffin cups halfway.

3 Bake the layers until a cake tester inserted in the middle comes out clean, 25 to 30 minutes for the cake layers and 20 to 25 minutes for the cupcakes. Remove from the oven and let cool in the pans for 5 minutes. Invert the cake layers onto wire racks, then immediately turn right side up to finish cooling. When the cakes or cupcakes have completely cooled, ice them with the frosting of your choice.

Cocoa Mocha Frosting

This is richly flavored, yet easy to make and tastes wonderful on Classic Sour Cream Chocolate Cake (page 146) or Classic Yellow Cake (page 139). If whisking will not make the frosting smooth, transfer it to the bowl of a food processor and pulse.

MAKES 3 CUPS, ENOUGH TO FROST AND FILL A 2-LAYER CAKE OR 24 CUPCAKES

$\frac{1}{2}$ cup (1 stick) unsalted butter

$\frac{1}{4}$ cup unsweetened cocoa powder

$\frac{1}{2}$ cup freshly brewed dark roast coffee, such as French roast or espresso

1 teaspoon vanilla extract

6 cups confectioners' sugar

Melt the butter in a large saucepan over medium heat. Whisk in the cocoa and continue whisking until you have a smooth paste. Whisk in the coffee and bring to a boil. Remove from the heat and whisk in the vanilla. Whisk in the confectioners' sugar, 1 cup at a time, until you have a smooth frosting. Set aside to cool slightly, then frost the cake of your choice.

Flour Power

Choosing the right type of flour can make a big difference in your desserts.

★ *Cake flour* is made from soft wheat, mainly grown in the South. This flour has a low protein content, 8 to 11 percent, which makes for a tender crumb in cakes.

★ *All-purpose flour* is made from hard winter wheat, mainly grown in the Great Plains. This flour has a medium protein content, 10 to 15 percent, which makes for a sturdy batter that can hold up to nuts, dried fruits, sour cream, eggs, or other heavy additions. It can also serve as a thickener in dessert sauces and puddings. All-purpose flour is used in pastries and pies, cookies, pound cakes, brownies, and cakes.

★ *Self-rising flour* is a convenience product made from a blend of all-purpose flour, baking powder, baking soda, and salt. This flour is used for easy sponge cakes, shortcakes, biscuits, and pancakes. If you are using self-rising flour in a recipe that does not call for it, do not add an extra leavener.

Chocolate

Chocolate was brought back to Europe in the 1500s by Spanish explorers, but it was so expensive that only the wealthy could enjoy it—at first drunk as a beverage, then later in candies.

The first chocolate mill was established in Massachusetts when Dr. Baker, a physician, went into partnership with a young Irish chocolate maker, John Hannon, in 1765. In 1780, they made a blend called Baker's chocolate. In 1852, Sam German created a sweeter milk chocolate–like baking bar for Baker's Chocolate Company. The product was named in his honor—Baker's German's Sweet Chocolate. (In most recipes and products today, the apostrophe and the "s" have been dropped.)

After the Civil War, when American domestic life was again on an even keel, ladies' benevolent groups compiled cookbooks as fundraisers for various causes. Cookbooks like *The Presbyterian Cook Book* (1875), *Buckeye Cookery and Practical Housekeeping* (1877), and the *Capital City Cook Book* (1906) all list a few cake, cookie, and pudding recipes calling for grated chocolate. Some specify Baker's chocolate in the ingredients list. But a tidal wave of chocolate engulfed American kitchens at the turn of the century.

In 1900, Milton Hershey developed a recipe for milk chocolate, which he manufactured in bar form. This recipe required extra cocoa butter for creaminess, leaving him with a surplus of cocoa powder, which he began to experiment with and eventually marketed. Hershey's affordable chocolate products for eating and baking prompted an explosion of chocolate desserts to delight the American consumer: brownies, fudge and chocolate pies, devil's food cakes, chocolate drop cookies, chocolate ice cream, and eventually the famous chocolate chip cookie.

By the 1920s, Baker's was also marketing several different kinds of baking chocolate—unsweetened, German's chocolate, semisweet, and bittersweet. In 1927, General Foods bought Baker's and in 1989, Kraft and General Foods merged into what is now Kraft Foods, Inc.

Today, the best chocolate has escaped from the mass manufacturer and taken refuge in boutiques, where chocolate bars, buttons, and chips are available in many different percentages of cacao—the more cacao, the merrier, chocoholics believe. Chocolate companies from Ghirardelli to Scharffen Berger keep supplying Americans with the confection they just can't live without.

German Chocolate Cake

What an interesting story this cake has to tell! First of all, there is nothing German about it but the name, a salute to Sam German, who concocted the milk chocolate–like baking bar in 1852 that still bears his name—German's chocolate, now usually called German chocolate. In the fall of 1957, a Texas homemaker sent in this recipe—using Baker's German's Sweet Chocolate and as well as the company's flaked coconut—to a Dallas newspaper, where the recipe was published. Dessert lovers soon flocked to grocery stores, buying out all the stocks of German's Sweet Chocolate. The immediate sales increase prompted General Foods (which then owned Baker's Chocolate) to send copies of the recipe and photos of the cake to newspapers across the nation. Soon there was a German chocolate cake frenzy. Sales of German's Sweet Chocolate jumped 73 percent in one year. Today, German chocolate cakes, as well as brownies, cheesecakes, mousses, and even crème brûlée, feature a milk chocolate base and a sweet pecan and flaked coconut topping, now a classic American combination.

MAKES ONE 3-LAYER 8-INCH OR 9-INCH CAKE; 12 SERVINGS

GERMAN CHOCOLATE CAKE

2$\frac{1}{2}$ cups sifted cake flour

1 teaspoon baking soda

$\frac{1}{2}$ teaspoon salt

One 4-ounce package German's sweet chocolate

4 large eggs, separated

1 cup (2 sticks) unsalted butter at room temperature

2 cups sugar

1 cup buttermilk

1 teaspoon vanilla extract

PECAN AND COCONUT FROSTING

1 cup evaporated milk (not sweetened condensed)

1 cup sugar

3 large egg yolks, lightly beaten

$\frac{1}{2}$ cup (1 stick) unsalted butter

1 teaspoon vanilla extract

1$\frac{1}{3}$ cups sweetened flaked coconut

1 cup chopped pecans

1   Preheat the oven to 350 degrees F. Line the bottoms of three 8- or 9-inch round cake pans with parchment or waxed paper and set aside.

2   To make the cake, sift together the cake flour, baking soda, and salt in a small mixing bowl and set aside. Melt the chocolate in the top of a double boiler set over simmering water; let cool

slightly. With an electric mixer, beat the egg whites in a medium-size mixing bowl until they hold stiff peaks; set aside. Still using the mixer, cream the butter and sugar together in a large mixing bowl until light and fluffy. Beat in the egg yolks, one at a time. Add the dry ingredients, $\frac{1}{2}$ cup at a time, alternating with the buttermilk. Beat in the melted chocolate and the vanilla and continue beating until you have a smooth batter. With a rubber spatula, fold the egg whites into the batter until you can no longer see them. Divide the batter evenly among the prepared pans.

3   Bake the layers until a cake tester inserted in the center comes out clean, about 35 minutes for 8-inch pans, 40 minutes for 9-inch pans. Invert the cake layers onto wire racks, then immediately turn right side up. Let cool completely before frosting.

4   To make the frosting, in a medium-size saucepan over medium-high heat, whisk together the evaporated milk, sugar, egg yolks, and butter and cook, whisking constantly, until the mixture thickens enough to coat the back of a spoon, about 12 minutes. Remove from the heat and stir in the vanilla, coconut, and pecans. Let cool until thick enough to spread.

5   Place the bottom cake layer on a cake plate and spread the top with one third of the frosting. Place a second layer on top and frost the top with another third of the frosting. Place the last layer on top and frost with the remaining frosting, leaving the sides unfrosted. Serve, and store any leftover cake at room temperature.

Lady Baltimore Cake

Owen Wister immortalized this dessert in his 1906 romance *Lady Baltimore*. Legend has it that Wister first tasted this cake at Charleston's Lady Baltimore Tea Room, managed by the Misses Florence and Nina Ottolengui. Some claim that these ladies dreamed up the recipe, but others insist that Lady Baltimore cake is simply an ingenue version of the older Lane cake, created in Clayton, Alabama, in 1888. Some frost between the layers and frost on top, but leave the sides of the cake bare. Others frost the whole cake. Despite these turf battles, this cake is a winner. The white cake can be doubled, tripled, or quadrupled and will still taste wonderful, which makes it perfect for celebratory wedding cakes. Frosted with a fantasy of sweetened Italian meringue blended with sherry-soaked dried fruits and nuts, this cake is adapted from one in the 1973 edition of the *Joy of Cooking* by Irma S. Rombauer and her daughter, Marion Rombauer Becker. **MAKES ONE 3-LAYER 8-INCH CAKE; 12 SERVINGS**

WHITE CAKE

3½ cups cake flour

1 tablespoon plus 1 teaspoon baking powder

½ teaspoon salt

8 large egg whites

1 cup (2 sticks) unsalted butter at room temperature

2 cups sugar

1 cup milk

1 teaspoon vanilla extract

½ teaspoon almond extract

ITALIAN MERINGUE FROSTING

8 dried figs, snipped into small pieces with kitchen shears

½ cup mixed dark and golden raisins

¼ cup sherry or rum

3 cups sugar

1½ cups water

3 large egg whites

¼ teaspoon salt

¼ teaspoon cream of tartar

1½ teaspoons vanilla extract

1 cup chopped pecans or walnuts

1 Preheat the oven to 375 degrees F. Grease and flour three 8-inch round cake pans, tapping out the excess flour.

2 In a medium-size mixing bowl, sift together the cake flour, baking powder, and salt and set aside. With an electric mixer, whip the egg whites in a large mixing bowl until they hold stiff peaks; set aside. In another large mixing bowl, still using the mixer, cream the butter and sugar together until light and fluffy. Beat in the sifted flour mixture, one third at a time, alternating with the milk, and continue beating until you have a smooth batter. Beat in the extracts. With a rubber spatula, fold the egg whites into the batter lightly; it's okay if some of the egg white still shows. Divide the batter evenly among the prepared pans.

3 Bake the layers until a cake tester inserted in the center comes out clean, about 25 minutes. Invert the cake layers onto wire racks, then immediately turn right side up. Let cool completely before frosting.

4 To make the frosting, in a small bowl, combine the dried fruits and sherry and let soak for 10 minutes.

5 Stir the sugar and water together in a medium-size saucepan until the sugar has dissolved. Cook over medium-high heat until a candy thermometer inserted in the syrup registers 238 to 240 degrees F, the firm ball stage (when a bit of the hot syrup forms a firm ball when dropped into a glass of ice water), 7 to 8 minutes.

6 With an electric mixer and clean, dry beaters, whip the egg whites, salt, and cream of tartar in a medium-size mixing bowl until the egg whites hold soft peaks. Pour the hot syrup in a thin stream into the egg whites, beating constantly on low to medium speed, until you have a thick, glossy frosting. Beat in the vanilla.

7 Reserve a third of the frosting in a small bowl. Into the remaining two thirds, fold in the softened fruit mixture (and any sherry not absorbed by the fruits) and the pecans. Place the bottom cake layer on a cake plate and frost the top with a third of the nut-and-fruit frosting. Place a second layer on top and frost with another third of the nut-and-fruit frosting. Place the third layer on top and frost the top with the reserved plain white frosting. Frost the sides of the cake with the remaining nut-and-fruit frosting. Serve at room temperature and do not refrigerate because the frosting will droop.

Please Release Me

You've measured all the ingredients accurately. You've creamed the butter and sugar until light and fluffy. You've beaten in the eggs and the dry ingredients, a little at a time. You've carefully spooned the batter into the prepared pans and baked the cake until lightly browned and slightly domed in the center.

Now comes the crucial part—releasing the cake from the pan.

If you've taken a preventive approach and prepared your pan by greasing and flouring or lining with parchment paper or both, chances are your cake will release easily and cleanly. Each cake recipe in *All-American Desserts* details how best to prepare the pan, release the cake from the pan, and cool the cake. Below are a few more tips.

Loosen the cake

Use a dampened kitchen towel. My friend Mary Pfeifer, a great baker, passed along a simple tip that works for getting all kinds of cakes out of their pans easily. She dampens a kitchen towel and lays it flat on a work surface. When she takes her cake pans out of the oven, she sets them down on the dampened towel. The instantaneous cooling and steaming effect loosens all kinds of cakes—layer, sponge, angel food, Bundt, and cheese—from their pans in seconds.

Loosen with a thin metal spatula or knife. When a cake is done, the perimeter of the cake should have pulled away from the sides of the pan slightly. Some cakes, such as sponge and angel food cakes, do this as soon as you take them out of the oven. Others, such as pound cakes with a higher proportion of butter, do this after they have cooled for up to 20 minutes. After the cake has pulled away from the sides of the pan, take a knife or a small metal or offset spatula and run it around the perimeter of the pan to loosen the sides of the cake from the pan. Press the spatula against the sides of the pan, not the cake.

Release the cake from the pan

Cakes baked in cake pans. Place a wire rack upside down (feet in the air) over the top of the cake pan and invert quickly. Tap the center of the bottom of the cake pan; the cake should release. If not, turn the cake

LORD BALTIMORE CAKE Substitute Classic Yellow Cake (page 139) for the white cake. Reserve a third of the Italian Meringue Frosting in a small bowl. Into the remaining two thirds, fold in ½ cup dry macaroon crumbs, ¼ cup chopped pecans, ¼ cup chopped blanched almonds, 1 teaspoon grated orange zest, 12 candied cherries cut into quarters, and 2 teaspoons fresh lemon juice. Place the bottom cake layer on a cake plate and frost as described in step 7.

right side up again and carefully loosen the bottom of the cake with a small spatula or knife. If, after most of the cake has come out intact, part of it remains in the pan, loosen it, remove it from the pan, and place it where it fits on the cake. This will probably be your bottom layer. Use a second wire rack to help you turn the cake layer right side up to cool.

Angel food, chiffon, and sponge cakes baked in tube pans. Simply invert the tube pan onto a flat surface if your pan has built-in legs that are high enough so that the top of the cake will not touch the surface. For higher rising angel food and chiffon cakes, invert the tube pan over a metal funnel or a glass bottle with a slim neck to get maximum volume for the cake (see page 159 for details).

Pound cakes baked in loaf or Bundt pans. These should cool in the pan for at least 10 minutes. Then invert the pan onto a wire rack and use a second wire rack to help you turn the cake right side up to cool.

Cakes baked in springform pans. As the cake, usually a cheesecake, bakes and then cools, it should pull away from the sides of the pan. If some of the cake still touches the pan, simply run the blade of a dinner knife or an offset spatula around the perimeter of the pan to make sure nothing sticks to the sides. Release the catch on the side of the springform pan and carefully lift the ring up and over the cake. If the cheesecake or cake is very moist or somewhat fragile, simply transfer the cheesecake or cake, still sitting on the bottom part of the springform pan, to a serving plate or cake stand. This is how I serve Macadamia-Crusted Mango Cheesecake (page 258) and French Chocolate Cake (page 242), for example.

If the cake is not too moist or fragile, and you would like to separate the cake from the metal bottom, carefully run the blade of a kitchen knife or an offset spatula between the bottom of the cake and the bottom of the springform pan. Place a wire rack over the top of the cake and invert the cake onto the wire rack. Invert again onto a serving plate so the cake is right side up. This is how I serve Sonoma Orange, Almond, and Olive Oil Cake (page 223) or Grandmother's Flower Garden Cake (page 176).

Cane Syrup Gingerbread with Sugar and Spice Streusel

The Crusades in the eleventh and twelfth centuries brought spices to northern Europe and made confections like gingerbread possible. English, French, and German settlers all brought their different versions of gingerbread to American shores, so we've had a taste for spice cake from the earliest days. European gingerbread was usually sweetened with honey, but in America the colonists switched to molasses, cane syrup, or even sorghum. I prefer to use pure cane syrup to make this gingerbread, as the syrup adds a slightly spicy note of anise and is lighter in texture than molasses. The Sugar and Spice Streusel adds a pleasing crunchiness to the smooth, very gingery cake that you will be tempted to gobble up. **MAKES ONE 9-INCH SQUARE CAKE; 9 SERVINGS**

GINGERBREAD CAKE

1/2 cup (1 stick) unsalted butter at room temperature

1/2 cup packed light brown sugar

1/2 teaspoon baking soda

2 large eggs

1 1/2 cups all-purpose flour

1/2 cup pure cane syrup, molasses, or sorghum

1 tablespoon ground ginger

1/2 teaspoon ground cinnamon

1/2 teaspoon ground allspice

1 teaspoon grated lemon zest

1/2 cup buttermilk

SUGAR AND SPICE STREUSEL

1/2 cup packed brown sugar

1/4 cup (1/2 stick) unsalted butter at room temperature

1 teaspoon ground ginger

2 teaspoons ground cinnamon

1 recipe Baked Lemon Spice Pears or Bourbon-Laced Sautéed Apples (optional, page 67 or 53)

1 To make the cake, preheat the oven to 350 degrees F. Grease a 9-inch square baking pan and set aside.

2 With an electric mixer, cream the butter and brown sugar together in a large mixing bowl until light and fluffy. Add the baking soda and eggs and beat again. The mixture will look curdled, but that will disappear. Add the flour, 1/2 cup at a time, beating well after each addition. Beat in the cane syrup, blending well, then beat in the spices and lemon zest. Finally, add the buttermilk and beat until the batter is smooth. Pour or spoon the batter into the prepared pan.

3 To make the streusel, mix the ingredients together in a small mixing bowl with a wooden spoon or your fingers until the mixture resembles large crumbs.

4 Bake the cake for 25 minutes, then sprinkle the streusel evenly over the top of the gingerbread and return to the oven. Continue baking until a cake tester inserted in the center comes out clean and the sides of the cake have pulled away from the pan, about 5 more minutes.

5 To serve, cut squares of gingerbread and serve with the pears or apples, if desired.

"I remember that at one time I saw two of my young mistresses and some lady visitors eating ginger-cakes, in the yard. At that time those cakes seemed to me to be absolutely the most tempting and desirable things I had ever seen and then and there resolved that, if I ever got free, the height of my ambition would be reached if I could get to the point where I could secure and eat ginger-cakes in the way I saw those ladies doing."

BOOKER T. WASHINGTON
UP FROM SLAVERY, 1901

Classic Angel Food Cake with Minted Berries

Angel food cake is a true classic, reportedly whipped up by black cooks in early nineteenth-century St. Louis households and made famous by Miss Hullings' Tea Room in the twentieth century. Like other American desserts that have stood the test of time, angel food cake has found a new reason to be—it's deliciously low in fat. Experiment a little and make this cake with a Flavored Sugar (see page 103) for a more elusive flavor. **MAKES ONE 10-INCH TUBE CAKE; 8 TO 10 SERVINGS**

ANGEL FOOD CAKE

7 large egg whites

1/4 teaspoon cream of tartar

1/4 teaspoon salt

1 cup sugar

1 teaspoon vanilla extract

1/2 teaspoon almond extract

3/4 cup cake flour

MINTED BERRIES

1 quart fresh blueberries, or other berry of your choice, picked over for stems

Juice of 1 lemon

1/2 cup sugar

1/2 cup fresh mint leaves, snipped

1 Preheat the oven to 350 degrees F. With an electric mixer, beat the egg whites, cream of tartar, and salt together in a large mixing bowl until the egg whites hold stiff peaks. Add the sugar, 1/4 cup at a time, beating constantly. When the mixture holds stiff, glossy peaks, beat in the vanilla and almond extracts. Carefully fold in the cake flour with a rubber spatula, a little at a time. Spoon the batter into an ungreased 10-inch tube pan.

2 Bake the cake until a cake tester inserted in the center comes out clean, about 20 minutes. Invert the cake (see page 153) and let cool completely before transferring it to a plate.

In the early 1950s, Konrad Egli introduced Swiss fondue to patrons at his Chalet Suisse restaurant in New York City. As both the chef and owner, Egli made sure that his creativity in the kitchen produced sales in the dining room. In 1956, he introduced fondue Bourguignonne, or skewered pieces of beef tenderloin cooked in hot oil right at the table, then served with various condiments and sauces. With "fondue-ized" appetizers and main courses, could dessert be far behind? Egli experimented until 1964, when he introduced chocolate fondue, into which diners dipped fresh strawberries, pieces of cake, or bananas. Now fondue restaurants are hot again, and it's time to bring those old fondue pots out of basement storage.

Bite-size pieces of homemade cake, such as angel food, pound, or loaf cake, are ideal to spear on the end of a fondue fork and dip into a warm dessert fondue—and then eat. Moist cakes that hold together well are much better than crumbly layer or sponge cakes. You don't want crumbs in the creamy, rich fondue.

Chocolate-Coconut-Almond Fondue

If you don't want to frost a cake, have your guests do it. Since the 1960s, dessert fondues have been popular with "do-it-yourself" Americans, who love dipping bite-size pieces of cake into a warm, sweet sauce. Serve this updated recipe as a convivial and casual dessert. **MAKES ABOUT 3 1/2 CUPS**

1 cup cream of coconut (available in the beverage or Hispanic foods section of supermarkets)

1/2 cup heavy cream

12 ounces semisweet or bittersweet chocolate, broken into pieces

1/2 cup sweetened flaked coconut

1/2 cup sliced almonds, toasted (see page 181), and finely chopped

Bite-size pieces of pound cake, angel food cake, peeled bananas, and/or large, whole strawberries with stems attached

1 In a medium-size heavy saucepan, combine the cream of coconut and heavy cream and bring to a simmer over medium heat. Stir in the chocolate and remove from the heat. Set aside until the chocolate has melted, then stir to blend well.

3   To make the Minted Berries, put the berries in a large serving bowl. Drizzle with the lemon juice and sprinkle with the sugar. Set aside for 15 minutes. Gently toss the berries with the mint and serve over slices of the cake.

2   Transfer the chocolate mixture to a fondue pot or chafing dish and keep warm over a burner. Set out bowls of flaked coconut, the chopped almonds, and cake and/or fruit. To serve, skewer a piece of cake or fruit, dip in the fondue, then dredge in the almonds and coconut and enjoy.

Caramel Rum Fondue

My friend Dee Barwick is Queen of the Crock-Pot, the slow cooker that was launched in Kansas City by Rival Manufacturing in 1971. Her slowly simmered soups and stews are legendary, and she always has willing volunteers who come over for a glass of wine and a taste of a new dish she has created. I've adapted this dessert, which can be made in a slow cooker, from Dee's recipe. It's perfect for casual entertaining on a winter evening, even if your team is behind in the Super Bowl. It's also decadently good over ice cream, apple pie, or a dark fudge brownie. **MAKES ABOUT 3 1/2 CUPS**

1 recipe Caramel Sauce (page 454)
1/2 cup miniature marshmallows
1 to 2 tablespoons dark rum, to your taste

Apple wedges for dipping
Bite-sized pieces of angel food cake, pound cake, or cake doughnuts for dipping

1   In a slow cooker or a medium-size heavy saucepan, combine the caramel sauce and marshmallows. On the LOW setting of the slow cooker or over low heat on the stove top, heat the mixture until the marshmallows melt, stirring occasionally, about 1 hour in the slow cooker or 30 minutes on the stove top.

2   Stir in the rum to taste. To serve, skewer pieces of apple and cake or doughnut and dip into the warm fondue.

Lemon Chiffon Cake

In May 1948, *Better Homes and Garden* magazine proclaimed chiffon cake the "first really new cake in 100 years." With the help of a mystery ingredient—vegetable oil—chiffon cakes combine the airiness of angel food with the rich moistness of pound cake. The cake was really about 20 years old, however, by the time it created a nationwide sensation. Harry Baker, who made cakes at the Brown Derby restaurant in Los Angeles, had invented the chiffon cake in 1927. He created it for famous Hollywood stars, but kept the recipe secret, even though he was constantly asked for it. An avid listener to the Betty Crocker radio program, Baker finally decided that Betty was the one who could best understand his secret recipe, and he offered to share it with her in 1948. Of course, there was no real Betty Crocker, but instead a team of home economists to greet Baker when he came to the General Mills office in Minneapolis. A few years later, General Mills introduced chiffon cake mixes in several flavors. Here is the lusciously easy, homemade version with a moist, soft texture. If you don't want to make the Italian Buttercream, the cake is delicious simply dusted with confectioners' sugar or drizzled with Vanilla-Rum Glaze (see page 205). Chiffon cake can also be wrapped and frozen for up to 2 months. The buttercream can be flavored any way you'd like, and it will keep, covered, in the refrigerator for a week, or frozen, for several months, making this an ideal frosting for just about any cake. **MAKES ONE 10-INCH TUBE CAKE; 12 SERVINGS**

CHIFFON CAKE

8 large egg whites

$\frac{1}{2}$ teaspoon cream of tartar

$2\frac{1}{4}$ cups cake flour

$1\frac{1}{2}$ cups superfine sugar

1 tablespoon baking powder

1 teaspoon salt

$\frac{3}{4}$ cup cold water

$\frac{1}{2}$ cup vegetable oil

1 tablespoon grated lemon zest

Juice of $\frac{1}{2}$ a lemon

5 large egg yolks

ITALIAN BUTTERCREAM

1 pound (4 sticks) unsalted butter at room
  temperature

1 cup vegetable shortening

8 large egg whites

Juice of $\frac{1}{2}$ a lemon

$\frac{3}{4}$ teaspoon cream of tartar

1 cup sugar

$\frac{1}{4}$ cup water

1 tablespoon vanilla extract or grated lemon zest

1. Preheat the oven to 325 degrees F. To make the cake, with an electric mixer, beat the egg whites with the cream of tartar in a large mixing bowl until they hold fairly stiff peaks—the peaks should fall over slightly as you lift the beaters; set aside. In another large mixing bowl, sift the flour, superfine sugar, baking powder, and salt together; set aside. In a medium-size mixing bowl, whisk together the cold water, vegetable oil, lemon zest and juice, and egg yolks. Stir the lemon mixture into the dry ingredients to make a smooth batter. Pour the batter over the beaten egg whites, a third at a time, folding the batter into the egg whites with a rubber spatula until you cannot see the egg whites. Pour the batter into an ungreased 12-cup Bundt or 10-inch tube pan.

2. Bake the cake until the top springs back when lightly touched and is a golden color, 1 to $1\frac{1}{4}$ hours. Invert the cake (see page 153) and let cool completely before transferring it to a plate.

3. To make the buttercream, put the butter and shortening in a food processor and process until smooth; set aside in a cool area. Using a stand mixer, whip the egg whites, lemon juice, and cream of tartar together until the egg whites hold soft peaks; set aside.

4. Stir the sugar and water together in a medium-size saucepan until the sugar has dissolved. Cook over medium-high heat until a candy thermometer inserted in the syrup registers 250 degrees F, about 10 minutes. (This is a little different than other Italian meringue frostings; the sugar syrup is firmer because of the addition of the butter and shortening at the end.) Pour the hot syrup in a thin stream into the beaten egg whites, beating constantly at low speed, until you have a thick, glossy frosting. Beat in the vanilla or lemon zest. Beat the meringue on medium speed until the bottom of the bowl feels as warm as your face, about 98 degrees F. This will make a more stable buttercream. Set aside to cool for 5 minutes. Using the paddle attachment, add the butter-and-shortening mixture, 2 tablespoons at a time, beating well after each addition until smooth and creamy. If the frosting breaks, continue to beat at medium-low speed and the mixture will become uniform again. Let cool for about 1 hour before using the frosting.

5. With a rubber spatula, frost the cake. Serve, and store any leftover cake at room temperature.

Cooling and Cutting Angel Food and Chiffon Cakes

While the angel food or chiffon cake is baking, place a large metal funnel with the pointed side up or an empty, clean wine bottle on the kitchen counter. When the cake is done, invert the tube pan over the funnel or wine bottle so the cake does not touch the counter. Leave to cool for about $1\frac{1}{2}$ hours. When completely cool, run a knife around the sides to release them, then with your fingers, pull the cake away from the bottom and run the knife under the bottom of the cake. Reinvert the released cake onto a cake plate so that it is right side up. The cake should be completely cool before frosting.

Because angel food cake is so spongy, cutting it with a knife can be a lesson in futility; the cake will collapse and compress. Use a combed cake divider, serrated knife, or two forks inserted back to back to pry the cake apart.

Maryland Fresh Coconut Cake

Tourists visiting the venerable Lexington Market in Baltimore are dazzled by the number of choices and wide variety of all types of foods, including fresh seafood from the Chesapeake and outstanding Maryland lump crab cakes, available from 140 individual stalls. Since 1782, Lexington Market has purveyed the best regional products, from soft-shell crabs in late spring to oysters in the fall. When Ralph Waldo Emerson visited the market in the mid-nineteenth century, he proclaimed Baltimore the "gastronomic capital of the world." During the height of immigration before World War I, a peanut war between Greek and Italian merchants cut prices to 3 cents a quart and prompted a stall sign proclaiming, "Remember, We Do Not Sell Common Peanuts Here." Nor do they sell common sweetened flaked coconut. At several different stalls, you can watch with fascination as women process the shaggy whole brown coconuts into airy mountains of fresh white flaked coconut. And there's no better way to enjoy it than in this deliciously light cake. Sometimes flaked fresh coconut is available frozen at Asian markets. Or buy a whole coconut and make your own, with visions of Tom Hanks and *Cast Away* in your head. **MAKES ONE 3-LAYER 8-INCH CAKE; 8 TO 10 SERVINGS**

2 teaspoons vanilla extract

1¼ cups fresh coconut milk (see Note) or canned unsweetened coconut milk (not cream of coconut)

3 cups cake flour

1 tablespoon baking powder

¼ teaspoon salt

4 large egg whites

1 cup (2 sticks) unsalted butter at room temperature

2 cups sugar

1 cup finely grated fresh coconut or frozen (thawed) unsweetened shredded coconut, plus extra for garnish

1 recipe Seven-Minute Frosting (recipe follows)

1   Preheat the oven to 325 degrees F. Grease and flour three 8-inch round cake pans, tapping out the excess, and set aside.

2   In a small mixing bowl or a glass measuring cup, combine the vanilla and coconut milk; set aside. In a medium mixing bowl, whisk together the flour, baking powder, and salt; set aside. With an electric mixer, beat the egg whites until they hold stiff peaks; set aside. With clean beaters, cream the butter and sugar together in a large mixing bowl. Beat the dry ingredients into the creamed

mixture in thirds, alternating with the coconut milk, beginning and ending with the dry ingredients and beating well after each addition. Beat in the grated coconut. Using a rubber spatula, fold in the beaten egg whites until you can no longer see them. Divide the batter equally between the prepared pans.

3 Bake the layers until a cake tester inserted in the center comes out clean, 35 to 40 minutes. Invert the cake layers onto wire racks, then immediately turn right side up. Let cool completely before frosting.

4 Spread the frosting evenly between the layers and on the sides and top of the cake. Generously sprinkle the cake with more freshly grated coconut. This is best eaten within a day or two.

> **NOTE** To make 1 cup of fresh coconut milk, put 1 cup of grated coconut and 1 cup of hot water in a food processor or blender and puree. Strain the mixture and discard the pulp.

Seven-Minute Frosting

A perennial favorite from the early twentieth century for coconut cake.

MAKES 5 CUPS, ENOUGH TO FILL AND FROST A 3-LAYER CAKE

1½ cups sugar

2 large egg whites

¼ cup plus 1 tablespoon water

1 tablespoon light corn syrup

¼ teaspoon salt

1 teaspoon vanilla extract

Combine the sugar, egg whites, water, corn syrup, and salt in the top of a double boiler set over simmering water. With an electric mixer, beat the mixture on high speed until the frosting turns a bright white and triples in volume, 5 to 7 minutes. Beat in the vanilla and remove from the heat. This frosting can be made a day ahead and kept in a covered container in the refrigerator.

Cracking the Coconut

Freshly grated coconut makes a luscious addition to cakes, cookies, and macaroons. To crack a mature coconut, use an ice pick or sturdy knife and a mallet to pierce the three black dots at the coconut's peak. Drain off the coconut water. Then use a hammer to tap the nut briskly all over. The coconut should break up into large pieces. With a knife, remove the brown shell and discard. Reserve the white coconut meat. Grate the coconut by hand with a microplane grater for small amounts, or in a food processor for larger amounts. Freshly grated coconut can be stored in a resealable plastic bag in the freezer for up to 9 months. A medium coconut will yield between 3 and 3¾ cups of grated coconut.

Classic Meringue-Covered Cake with Coffee Cream Filling

After looking through *250 Classic Cake Recipes* from the 1950s, a booklet of recipes that both my mother and my grandmother used with great success, I was inspired to come up with my own creation. For me, recipes are blueprints to be modified and adapted based on the season, what I have available in the pantry, or my own whim. Starting with a basic two-layer yellow cake that I cut into four layers, I envisioned an all-season fairy-tale confection with a really delicious flavor. And this is it. What's more, the possibilities are endless for toothsome variations. How about two layers spread with Classic Pastry Cream (recipe follows) folded together with whipped cream, alternating with two layers spread with Fresh Orange Marmalade (page 6), Strawberry Spoon Fruit (page 5), or Golden Apple Compote (page 18)? Or spread all the layers with Tart and Tangy Lemon Curd (page 321), folded together with whipped cream. Yum!

MAKES ONE 4-LAYER 9-INCH CAKE; 12 SERVINGS

CAKE
1 recipe Classic Yellow Cake (page 139), cooled

FILLING
1 cup heavy cream
1 recipe Coffee-Flavored Pastry Cream variation
(see variations, recipe follows), at room
temperature

MERINGUE FROSTING
4 large egg whites
$\frac{1}{4}$ teaspoon cream of tartar
1 cup plus 1 tablespoon sugar
1 teaspoon vanilla extract

1 Slice each layer of cake in half horizontally with a serrated knife or a piece of dental floss held taut between your hands. Set the 4 layers aside.

2 To make the filling, with an electric mixer, whip the cream in a large mixing bowl until it holds stiff peaks. With a rubber spatula, fold the pastry cream into the whipped cream until well blended. Place the bottom cake layer on a baking sheet and spread with a fourth of the coffee filling, leaving a $\frac{1}{2}$-inch margin around the perimeter of the cake. Repeat with the next 3 layers, so that the top layer is spread with the last of the filling and the perimeter is bare. Set aside.

3 To make the frosting, wash and dry the beaters well, then beat the egg whites in a large mixing bowl with the cream of tartar until they hold soft peaks. Beat in 1 cup of the sugar, $\frac{1}{4}$ cup at a time, then the vanilla, and continue beating until you have a thick, glossy meringue that holds stiff peaks. Using a baker's spatula, spread the meringue on the top and sides of the filled cake. To make decorative swirls, press the spatula down on the meringue and then lift it straight up. Set aside to dry slightly.

4   Preheat the oven to 450 degrees F. Sprinkle the cake with the remaining 1 tablespoon of sugar, then place in the oven. Let the meringue brown for 4 to 5 minutes. Carefully remove the cake from the baking sheet and place on a serving plate. Chill until ready to serve.

Classic Pastry Cream

I tried many different recipes for pastry cream before I decided on this one. It's simply the best. With just a bare hint of lemon to take away any eggy taste, this lusciously rich pastry cream is a flavorful, yet somewhat neutral, ingredient to use as a filling for fruit tarts, cream pies, éclairs, Boston cream pie (see page 140) or layer cakes. It can be made ahead, covered, and chilled for up to 24 hours before using in a dessert. The technique of whisking the raw egg yolks with the sugar and flour helps break up the yolks and flour lumps for a smoother result—no need to strain or sieve the final product. The recipe can be doubled, but make it in a very large saucepan because the half-and-half could boil over in a smaller one. **MAKES ABOUT 2 CUPS**

1$\frac{1}{2}$ cups half-and-half	3 large egg yolks
One 2 x $\frac{1}{2}$-inch piece lemon zest	$\frac{1}{3}$ cup all-purpose flour
$\frac{1}{4}$ cup plus 3 tablespoons sugar	1 teaspoon vanilla extract

1   Combine the half-and-half, lemon zest, and $\frac{1}{4}$ cup of the sugar in a medium-size saucepan over medium-high heat and bring to a boil. Remove the lemon zest and set the mixture aside.

2   Whisk the egg yolks in a medium-size mixing bowl with the remaining 3 tablespoons sugar. Whisk in the flour and continue whisking until the mixture is smooth. Pour $\frac{1}{2}$ cup of the hot half-and-half mixture into the egg and flour mixture and whisk until smooth. Now pour the egg and flour mixture into the saucepan with the remaining hot half-and-half mixture and place over medium-low heat. Cook, whisking constantly, until the mixture begins to thicken and coats the back of a spoon. Continue to whisk and cook until very thick and an instant-read thermometer registers 170 degrees F, about 5 minutes more.

3 Remove the pastry cream from the heat and whisk in the vanilla. Transfer to a bowl, cover the top of the pastry cream with plastic wrap to keep a skin from forming, and let cool to room temperature. Chill until ready to use. It will keep for up to 1 week, tightly covered, in the refrigerator.

> **COFFEE-FLAVORED PASTRY CREAM** Use 1 cup half-and-half, add ½ cup freshly brewed dark-roast coffee, and proceed with the recipe.

> **RUM-FLAVORED PASTRY CREAM** Whisk in 2 tablespoons white, dark, or spiced rum instead of the vanilla extract.

> **CHOCOLATE PASTRY CREAM** Whisk in ¼ cup unsweetened cocoa powder with the half-and-half, lemon zest, and sugar and proceed with the recipe.

Cake Decorating Essentials

The right tools make any job easier, and cake decorating is no exception.

* *Offset spatulas.* The blade is lower than the handle, making this tool ideal for lifting a cake layer, spreading batter, or smoothing icing. Offset spatulas are available in several different sizes. A small, medium, and large offset spatula will allow you to get into tight corners, perfectly smooth the top and sides of a cake, and spread batter and smooth icing.

* *Pastry brush.* A good quality pastry brush, made of natural or nylon bristles, is used for brushing loose crumbs off a cake or brushing on a glaze. With a pastry brush, you can also brush beaten egg white on branches of rosemary, grapes, sage leaves, or cranberries, then sprinkle them with sugar to give a frosted effect, which makes a lovely garnish.

* *Candy thermometer.* When making glazes, syrups, and Italian Meringue (see page 351), use a candy thermometer to determine the exact temperature of the mixture, eliminating guesswork.

* *Concentrated food color pastes.* Experiment with different combinations of colors to get a wonderful range of hues for your frostings and icings. Start with just a little of the color paste, doled out with a toothpick, to be on the safe side.

* *Cake decorating, or piping, bag and tips.* For piping a decorative whipped cream border or rosettes on a torte, or for making leaves, blossoms, or a trail of vines on a quilt cake, this equipment is essential. A little practice makes perfect.

Baked Alaska

The period just after the Civil War continued political upheaval in American life. President Andrew Johnson, who acceded to the presidency in 1865 after Lincoln's assassination, was impeached. Johnson's secretary of state, William Seward, purchased Alaska from Russia in 1867 for $7 million, or about 2 cents an acre. Short-sighted pundits forgot the previous success of another huge plot of uncharted wilderness—Jefferson's Louisiana Purchase, which cost $3 million in 1803. Seward was vilified in the press. Newspapers dubbed Alaska "Seward's Folly," "Seward's Icebox," and "Icebergia." In 1880, gold was discovered near what is now Juneau, the gold rush years in Alaska began, and all of a sudden, Alaska was very, very interesting. Perhaps the popular fascination with the Klondike prompted the creation of baked Alaska, a layer of cake topped with a mound of ice cream, and the entire confection covered by meringue and baked in the oven. The first mention of this dessert came in the 1896 edition of Fannie Farmer's *The Boston Cooking-School Cook Book*.

Depending on how you make it, baked Alaska can look like an igloo or a snowy Mt. McKinley. Make the cake and Italian meringue a day ahead, then assemble the dessert and bake it at the last minute, for a dramatic and very American finale to a meal.

MAKES ONE 8-INCH CAKE; 8 SERVINGS

¾ cup self-rising flour

½ cup plus 1 tablespoon all-purpose flour

½ cup (1 stick) unsalted butter, softened

1 cup sugar

2 large eggs, at room temperature

½ cup milk

¼ teaspoon vanilla extract

¼ teaspoon almond extract

1 recipe Italian Meringue (page 351)

2 pints best-quality vanilla ice cream, or any flavor you prefer, slightly softened

1 Preheat the oven to 350 degrees F. Grease and flour the inside of a 9-inch cake pan and set aside.

2 In a small mixing bowl, sift together the flours.

3 In a large mixing bowl, cream together the butter and sugar with an electric mixer until light and fluffy. Add the eggs, one at a time, beating well after each addition. Add the flour mixture and the milk, beat well, and then beat in the vanilla and almond extracts until you have a smooth batter. Spread the cake batter evenly in the prepared pan.

4 Bake the cake until a cake tester inserted in the center comes out clean, 32 to 35 minutes. Remove from the pan and transfer to a wire rack to cool. (Once cooled, the cake may be covered with plastic wrap and kept at room temperature for 1 day before serving.)

5 Line an 8-inch-diameter metal mixing bowl with plastic wrap, leaving at least a 4-inch overhang of plastic wrap around the perimeter of the bowl. Pack the softened ice cream into the lined bowl, cover the top with the excess plastic wrap, and freeze until ready to assemble.

6 When ready to assemble and serve, preheat the oven to 450 degrees F. Place the cake on a parchment-lined baking sheet or on a cardboard circle. Unwrap the plastic from the top of the bowl of ice cream and invert the ice cream onto the cake, removing all the plastic wrap. To make an igloo, spoon the Italian meringue into a pastry bag fitted with a no. 8 tube. Starting at the base of the cake, pipe the frosting in concentric circles around the cake, ending where the ice cream begins. To make a mountain, use a spatula to spread the meringue over the cake and ice cream, swirling to created a pleasing design.

7 Bake until the meringue has browned, about 5 minutes. Carefully transfer the Baked Alaska to a serving plate and serve immediately.

Cream-Filled Devil's Food Cupcakes

Everyone from Girl Scouts to dinner guests will love these cupcakes, which bring out the kid in all of us. These are similar to the perennially popular Hostess cupcakes—devil's food cake with a creamy filling. **MAKES 30 CUPCAKES**

CREAM CHEESE CREAM FILLING
One 8-ounce package cream cheese at room temperature

1 large egg, beaten

$1/2$ teaspoon salt

$1/2$ cup confectioners' sugar

CHOCOLATE CUPCAKES
3 cups all-purpose flour

2 cups granulated sugar

1 teaspoon salt

$1/2$ cup unsweetened cocoa powder

$2/3$ cup vegetable oil

2 teaspoons baking soda

2 cups hot water

2 teaspoons cider vinegar

2 teaspoons vanilla extract

1 recipe Chocolate Ganache (see page 213) or Cocoa Mocha Frosting (see page 147) or your favorite chocolate frosting (optional)

1   Preheat the oven to 350 degrees F. Line 30 muffin cups with paper liners and set aside.

2   To make the filling, with an electric mixer, beat the cream cheese in a medium-size mixing bowl until smooth. Beat in the egg, salt, and confectioners' sugar. Set the filling aside.

3   To make the cupcakes, sift together the flour, granulated sugar, salt, and cocoa powder into a large mixing bowl. Beat in the vegetable oil and continue beating until smooth. Mix the baking soda with the hot water in a medium-size mixing bowl, then add the vinegar and vanilla. Pour this mixture into the dry ingredients and beat until smooth. Spoon enough batter in each cupcake cup so that it is one third full of batter. Spoon a heaping tablespoon of filling on top of the batter, and then top with more batter, dividing the remaining cake batter evenly among the cupcakes.

4   Bake the cupcakes until a cake tester inserted in the center comes out clean, 20 to 25 minutes. Cool completely, and if desired, frost the cupcakes.

Baby Cakes

Cupcakes appeal to the child in all of us. If you're looking for a charming and whimsical way to serve dessert, why not forego a more formal two-layer cake in favor of baby cakes mounded in a pyramid on a pedestal cake server?

Most layer or pound cake recipes can easily be converted into cupcakes. Add up the quantity of flour, sugar, butter or oil, and liquid in cups. Since you fill cupcake liners with only about $1/3$ cup of batter per cupcake, divide the volume of batter by one third, and you've got the number of cupcakes your cake recipe will provide. Usually the batter for a two-layer cake will also make 24 cupcakes. Pour the layer cake batter into paper-lined muffin cups until half full. Bake the cupcakes until a cake tester inserted in the center of a cupcake comes out clean, about 20 to 25 minutes.

For pound cake batter, I like to generously grease and flour my vintage metal gelatin molds, then pour in the batter to fill the molds three quarters full. I place the molds upside down in muffin cups to support them while they bake, usually 30 to 35 minutes. When they're cool, I release them from the molds, glaze them with a flavored icing or dust them with confectioners' sugar, and arrange them on a three-tiered server, garnished with fresh fruit, edible flowers, or whatever is in season.

Decorating cupcakes can also be an exercise in creativity. For chocolate or dark spice cupcakes like Mocha Spice Cupcakes (page 168), cut out a small stencil from parchment paper and place it over each cooled cupcake. Sift confectioners' sugar onto the stencil, then carefully lift it up and discard the sugar on it. A white design will appear on top of the dark cupcake. Place fresh or candied blossoms on top of a pale icing. Arrange ribbons of Garden Candy (page 482) in a bow to make the top of each cupcake look like a tiny wrapped gift.

Mocha Spice Cupcakes

Almost every child growing up in the 1950s went to school at least once with a cupcake in his or her lunch box. Even today, cupcakes are the top choice of room mothers in charge of seasonal celebrations in elementary school classrooms. But cupcakes aren't just for kids. Because these have the "grown-up" flavors of spice and mocha and are not very sweet, my excellent baker friend Mary Pfeifer of Kansas City calls these "adult cupcakes." Made with pure cane syrup from Louisiana (see Sources), the king of molasses, these are killer cupcakes. **MAKES 1 DOZEN CUPCAKES**

Which Came First—The Cupcake or the Muffin Tin?

If you asked seventeenth-century Margaret Winthrop, eighteenth-century Abigail Adams, and nineteenth-century Sophia Hawthorne each to bake a cupcake for you, the three cupcakes would be radically different from one another.

In 1632, when Margaret Winthrop, her husband, John, and other Puritans formed the Massachusetts Bay Colony, a "cake" could mean a yeast-risen cake, rich with lard, heavy with dried fruit, and sweetened with honey or precious sugar—similar to Hartford Election Cake (page 234) or Moravian Sugar Cake (page 233), which are still made today. Or "cake" could mean a classic sponge, which had been made in various forms in Elizabethan England. Leftover yeast dough or sponge batter might have been baked in a pottery cup—the predecessor of the cupcake—in a large beehive oven above the gigantic open fireplace, in the chimney stack.

By the time of Abigail Adams' term as First Lady (1797–1801), a new culinary product had become available—pearlash or potash (potassium carbonate), similar to what we now call baking soda. In the first truly American cookbook, published in 1796 by Amelia Simmons, the author offers several recipes for baked goods leavened by pearlash, which produces a carbon dioxide gas in the batter and causes the baked good to rise. Now American cooks could make muffins, with eggs and baking soda providing the leavening, or simple cookies. Abigail Adams' cupcake could either have been a muffin or leftover batter from a pound cake baked in a pottery cup.

In Sophia Hawthorne's time, Eliza Leslie's 1828 cookbook, simply titled *Seventy-Five Receipts*, makes the first reference to the "New York Cup Cake" in American culinary writing. By the mid-eighteenth century, Sophia's kitchen equipment would have included a metal muffin tin, which was also used to bake cupcakes. Baking powder was invented in 1857, which would have allowed Sophia to bake the fine-textured, layer cake–style cupcake we know today.

SPICE CUPCAKES

2½ cups sifted all-purpose flour

1½ teaspoons baking soda

1 teaspoon ground cinnamon

1 teaspoon ground ginger

½ teaspoon ground cloves

½ teaspoon salt

½ cup granulated sugar

½ cup (1 stick) unsalted butter at room
temperature

1 large egg, beaten

1 cup pure cane syrup or molasses

1 cup hot water

MOCHA FROSTING

3 ounces semisweet chocolate

1 tablespoon unsalted butter

¼ cup freshly brewed dark roast coffee

1 cup confectioners' sugar, or as needed

1 Preheat the oven to 350 degrees F. Line with paper liners or grease the inside of one 12-cup muffin tin and set aside.

2 To make the cupcakes, in a medium-size mixing bowl, sift together the flour, baking soda, spices, and salt. With an electric mixer, cream the granulated sugar and butter together in a large mixing bowl. Beat in the egg and cane syrup. Add the dry ingredients to the batter, 1 cup at a time, beating well after each addition. Pour the hot water in last and beat until you have a very soft batter.

3 Fill the muffin cups two thirds full and bake until a cake tester inserted in the center comes out clean, 15 to 20 minutes. Let cool completely before frosting.

4 To make the frosting, melt the chocolate in the top of a double boiler set over simmering water. With the electric mixer, cream the melted chocolate and butter together in a medium-size mixing bowl, then add the coffee and enough of the confectioners' sugar to achieve a spreadable consistency. Using a knife, spread the frosting over the top of each cupcake and serve.

Missouri Jam Cake

Food historian Katie Armitage looks at recipes the way other people look at antiques. She likes to know where they came from, where they've been, and what they say about the lives of the people who prepared them. When the Lawrence, Kansas, resident was involved in food consulting for director Ang Lee's Civil War–era movie *Ride with the Devil*, she brought a typical 1860s Missouri dinner for the director and his crew to taste: salt pork, cornbread, biscuits and gravy, hominy, pickles, butter, and both fresh and dried apple pies. "I told them that most Missourians had come west from Kentucky, and theirs was a typical 'hog and hominy' diet," Armitage says. She also came up with an 1860s wedding menu for one of the last scenes: several cakes, including this Missouri Jam Cake, which also originated in Kentucky. Still the province of home cooks, you won't find this cake in restaurants or bakeries; rather, you will find it at community bake sales, church suppers, bed and breakfast inns, and country cafes.

MAKES ONE 10-INCH TUBE CAKE; 12 SERVINGS

CAKE

3½ cups all-purpose flour, sifted

1 tablespoon unsweetened cocoa powder

1 teaspoon ground cinnamon

1 teaspoon ground cloves

2 cups buttermilk

2 teaspoons baking soda

1 cup (2 sticks) unsalted butter at room temperature

2 cups packed light brown sugar, sifted

3 large eggs, separated

1 cup blackberry or other tart jam with seeds

1 cup raisins

¾ cup chopped nuts, such as pecans, hickory nuts, or walnuts

CARAMEL FROSTING

¾ cup (1½ sticks) unsalted butter

1½ cups packed brown sugar

¼ cup plus 2 tablespoons milk

3 cups confectioners' sugar

1 teaspoon vanilla extract

1 Preheat the oven to 250 degrees F. Grease a 10-inch tube pan and line the bottom with parchment paper or waxed paper. Set aside.

2 To make the cake, in a large mixing bowl, sift together the flour, cocoa, and spices. In a glass measuring cup, stir the buttermilk and baking soda together.

3 With an electric mixer, cream the butter and brown sugar together in another large mixing bowl until light and fluffy. Beat in the egg yolks and continue beating until well incorporated, then beat in the blackberry jam until just blended. Add the flour mixture in thirds, alternating with the buttermilk and beating well after each addition. Fold in the raisins and nuts and set aside.

4 Wash and dry the beaters well. In a medium-size mixing bowl, beat the egg whites until they hold stiff peaks. With a rubber spatula, fold the egg whites into the jam cake batter until you can no longer see the whites. Pour the batter into the prepared pan.

5 Bake the cake until it pulls away from the sides of the pan, about 1 hour and 15 minutes. Remove from the oven and turn the cake out onto a serving plate to cool slightly.

6 To make the frosting, bring the butter, brown sugar, and milk to a boil in a large heavy saucepan over high heat. Remove from the heat and let cool. Whisk in the confectioners' sugar and vanilla and continue whisking until the frosting is smooth. Frost the top and sides of the cooled cake and serve.

Hickory Nut Cake

Many families hold a special place in their hearts for this cake. When hickory trees were common in the woods fringing farmland, families would gather these heart-shaped nuts in the fall and use the hickory wood for smoking hams and bacon. Now hickory nuts are available through American Spoon Foods and country sources like Jill Etzler, who lives near Dayton, Ohio. Her grandmother's hickory nut cake has a light and airy texture as well as a mellow flavor. Its crowning glory is a traditional 3-6-9 frosting of butter, cream, and brown sugar fortified with confectioners' sugar. I have substituted lemon zest for the lemon extract in the original recipe, but the rest is the Etzler family's original. Pecans can be substituted for the hickory nuts.

MAKES ONE 2-LAYER 8-INCH CAKE; 10 SERVINGS

CAKE
2$\frac{1}{2}$ cups cake flour

1 teaspoon baking powder

1 teaspoon salt

1$\frac{3}{4}$ cups granulated sugar

$\frac{2}{3}$ cup vegetable shortening

1 cup milk

1 teaspoon vanilla extract

1 teaspoon grated lemon zest

1 cup chopped hickory nuts or pecans, plus extra for garnish

5 large egg whites

3-6-9 FROSTING
3 tablespoons unsalted butter

$\frac{1}{4}$ cup plus 2 tablespoons heavy cream or evaporated milk

1 cup plus 3 tablespoons packed brown sugar

One 1-pound box confectioners' sugar, as needed

1 Preheat the oven to 350 degrees F. Grease and flour two 8-inch square cake pans and set aside.

2 To make the cake, sift together the flour, baking powder, salt, and 1$\frac{1}{4}$ cups of the sugar into a medium-size mixing bowl. With an electric mixer, cream the shortening in a large mixing bowl, then add the dry ingredients, $\frac{1}{2}$ cup at a time. Add the milk, vanilla, and lemon zest and beat for 2 minutes. Fold in the hickory nuts.

3 Wash and dry the beaters well. In another large mixing bowl, beat the egg whites until they hold soft peaks. Gradually add the remaining ½ cup of sugar and continue beating until the egg whites hold stiff peaks. Fold the egg whites into the cake batter until you can no longer see them. Divide the batter evenly between the prepared pans

4 Bake the cake layers until a cake tester inserted in the middle comes out clean, about 35 minutes. Invert the cake layers onto wire racks, then immediately turn right side up. Let cool completely.

5 While the cake is baking, make the frosting: In a medium-size heavy saucepan, stir together the butter, cream, and brown sugar and bring to a boil over medium-high heat. Immediately remove the saucepan from the heat and set it aside to cool. While the mixture is still warm, but not hot, whisk in enough of the confectioners' sugar to achieve a spreadable consistency.

6 When the cakes have cooled, place one layer on a cake plate. Using a metal offset or rubber spatula, spread the top with one quarter of the frosting. Place the second cake layer on top and spread the remaining frosting on the top and sides of the whole cake. Garnish with chopped hickory nuts and serve.

Tales of Hickory Nut Cake

The Yoder sisters in their *Yoder Sisters' Cookbook: A Family Heritage Cookbook* tell how their family's love of hickory nut cake went west from Ohio to Oregon. "Our father, who was born and raised in West Liberty, Ohio, told us how at 17, he left home to go West to the Dakota country. In North Dakota he worked in the wheat harvest in the fall, and worked in the coal mines the rest of the year. This is the cake his mother baked and sent with him on the train. She would carefully wrap it in a towel and put it in his lunch. He ate it sparingly. It would last the whole way back to his claim shanty near Kennmore, North Dakota. This was one of his favorite cakes. . . .The recipe was taken from my grandmother Delilah Troyer's *Inglenook Cookbook*, printed by the Brethren Publishing House, Elgin, Illinois, in 1901."

George Blacksmith of Delafield, Wisconsin, believes his affection for hickory nut cake is genetic. He recognized the beauty of these cakes early on. When he was a little boy, he would gather hickory nuts with his grandmother Sarah Baxter. After the first freeze in the fall, they would find the trees out in the woods. Sarah would sit beneath each tree, spreading out her long skirts and apron. George would shake the tree and the nuts would come raining down, to be caught up in Sarah's skirts and then gathered into a bag. Prying out the nut meats was a task carried out over many evenings. When there was enough for a cake, Sarah would first make what she called a "try cake," or a little test cake to make sure the oven temperature was right. Only then did she prepare the real thing, mellow with hickory nuts and caramel frosting. "It's still my favorite cake," George confesses.

Caramel Apple Cream Cake

Every fall, I can't wait for my first caramel apple of the season. When these confections are made well, the richness of the caramel and the tartness of the apple are a match made in heaven. This very extravagant cake sent to me by a Cleveland, Ohio, reader combines caramel and apple with a light and airy yellow layer cake—perfect for a special celebration. Both the caramel sauce and the cake can be made in advance. Frost the cake right before serving. Covered and refrigerated, it keeps for 2 days.

MAKES ONE 2-LAYER 9-INCH CAKE; 10 TO 12 SERVINGS

CAKE

2¾ cups cake flour

1½ teaspoons baking powder

½ teaspoon salt

4 large eggs

2½ cups sugar

1 cup vegetable oil

2 teaspoons vanilla extract

1 cup milk

1 cup Caramel Sauce (page 454)

CARAMEL CREAM FROSTING

2 cups cold heavy cream

1 teaspoon vanilla extract

1 cup Caramel Sauce (page 454) at room temperature

APPLE FILLING

2 large, tart apples, such as Jonathan or Granny Smith, peeled, cored, and finely chopped

1 tablespoon fresh lemon juice

1   Preheat the oven to 350 degrees F. Grease two 9-inch round cake pans and line the bottom of each pan with parchment or waxed paper. Grease the paper.

2   Sift together the flour, baking powder, and salt in a medium-size mixing bowl. Set aside. With an electric mixer, beat the eggs and sugar together in a large mixing bowl until light and fluffy, about 2 minutes. Slowly beat in the oil, vanilla, and milk. Beat in the flour mixture until just incorporated. Stir in the caramel sauce and continue beating until well blended. Divide the batter evenly between the prepared pans.

3   Bake the layers until a cake tester inserted in the center comes out clean, 55 to 60 minutes. They will be a rich mahogany brown. Let cool for 5 minutes in the pans, then invert onto wire racks and immediately turn upside down to cool completely. Discard the paper linings.

4   Wash and dry the beaters well. To make the frosting, beat the heavy cream and vanilla in a large

mixing bowl until the cream holds stiff peaks. Fold the caramel sauce into the whipped cream until the frosting has a marbleized look.

5   To make the filling, mix the chopped apple with the lemon juice and let sit for 5 minutes; drain off the juice. To assemble the cake, place one layer on a cake stand or cake plate. Spread 1 cup of the frosting over the top and spoon the chopped apples evenly over the frosting. Top with the second cake layer. Spread the remaining frosting on the top and sides of the cake, swirling the frosting on top. Cover and refrigerate for up to 2 days. Serve chilled.

Praise and Plenty Cake

Sometimes dessert inspiration comes from surprising sources. When I was looking through the pages of the *Home for the Holidays* pattern book by Missouri quilt designers Linda Brannock and Jan Patek, I found the germ of an idea. I wanted something more special than everybody's recipe for traditional carrot cake. Reading through their holiday dessert recipes, scattered among the quilt designs, made me hungry. And then I saw their "Praise and Plenty" quilt. Four squares of appliquéd pineapples and hearts in muted yellow, green, and orange on a creamy white background, surrounded by a border in homespun plaid. The wheels turned. I envisioned an autumn end-of-the-garden cake in those colors. A friendly, hospitable cake that everyone would like, but an original spin on an old recipe. So, here it is, a three-layer cake using garden "plenty" in a way that will garner "praise"—a gingered carrot layer complemented by layers of coriander-scented yellow squash and cinnamon-spiced green zucchini. Use small, trimmed zucchini and yellow squash and grate them whole. Traditional cream cheese frosting is the crowning glory, but you could also use Brown Butter Frosting (see page 140) for a homespun look.

MAKES ONE 3-LAYER 9-INCH CAKE; 8 SERVINGS

CAKE
3¾ cups all-purpose flour
1 tablespoon baking soda
1½ teaspoons salt
6 large eggs
3 cups granulated sugar

2 cups canola oil
1½ cups grated zucchini
1 teaspoon ground cinnamon
1½ cups grated yellow summer squash
1 teaspoon ground coriander
1½ cups cups grated carrots

1 teaspoon ground ginger

1½ cups raisins

1½ cups chopped pecans or walnuts

VANILLA CREAM CHEESE FROSTING

Two 3-ounce packages cream cheese at room
temperature

5 tablespoons unsalted butter at room
temperature

5 cups confectioners' sugar

1 tablespoon vanilla extract

1 Preheat the oven to 350 degrees F. Grease and flour three 9-inch round cake pans; set aside.

2 Sift together the flour, baking powder, and salt in a medium-size mixing bowl. With an electric mixer, beat the eggs and granulated sugar together in a large mixing bowl until light and frothy. Beat in the oil, then beat in the flour mixture, 1 cup at a time, beating well after each addition.

3 Transfer a third of the batter to each of two medium-size mixing bowls, so that you have 3 equal-sized portions of batter. In one bowl, stir in the zucchini and cinnamon until you have a stiff batter. In a second bowl, stir in the summer squash and coriander. In the third bowl, stir in the carrots and ginger. Fold ½ cup of the raisins and ½ cup of the chopped nuts into each bowl. Spoon each batter into a separate prepared cake pan.

4 Bake the layers until a cake tester inserted in the center comes out clean, about 35 minutes. Invert the cake layers onto wire racks, then immediately turn right side up. Let cool completely before frosting.

5 Make the frosting when the cake has cooled: Wash and dry the beaters well, and with the electric mixer, beat together the cream cheese and butter in a large mixing bowl. Add as much of the confectioners' sugar as needed to achieve a spreadable consistency, add the vanilla, and beat until smooth. Use the frosting right away, while it is soft.

6 To finish the cake, place one layer on a cake stand or serving plate and spread the top with a ½-inch-thick layer of frosting. Place another layer on the first layer and add an identical layer of frosting. Place the third layer on top. Frost the top and sides of the cake and serve.

Grandmother's Flower Garden Cake

The "Grandmother's Flower Garden," also called "French Bouquet" quilt pattern, features small hexagons, usually of pastel printed cottons, arranged in large geometric flower shapes. It offers endless possibilities for color combinations and the way the blocks can be set together, much like this cake. My lemon-scented sour cream cake is topped with colorful garden confetti in this summer dessert. But use your own creativity to change the flavoring to orange or vanilla or almond, and top it with whatever catches your fancy in the garden. I like to mix at least three different colors of edible flower blossoms and petals: lavender buds or bachelor's button petals, scented pink rose petals, and yellow pot marigold or coreopsis petals. These are tossed with granulated sugar or, even better, sanding sugar—clear sugar crystals available at specialty stores and through mail order.

MAKES ONE 9-INCH CAKE; 8 SERVINGS

2 cups sifted cake flour

1¼ teaspoons baking powder

¼ teaspoon salt

1 cup (2 sticks) unsalted butter at room temperature

2 cups granulated sugar

2 large eggs, beaten

One 8-ounce container sour cream

Grated zest and juice of 1 lemon

1 teaspoon vanilla extract

1 cup mixed fresh edible flower blossoms and petals

½ cup sanding or granulated sugar

1   Preheat the oven to 350 degrees F. Grease a 9-inch springform pan and set aside.

2   Sift together the flour, baking powder, and salt in a small mixing bowl. With an electric mixer on low speed, cream the butter and granulated sugar together in a large mixing bowl until light and fluffy. Beat in the eggs and sour cream, then beat in the dry ingredients, ½ cup at a time, beating well after each addition. Beat in the lemon zest and juice and the vanilla and blend well.

3   Pour the batter into the prepared pan and bake until a cake tester inserted in the center comes out clean, 50 to 60 minutes. Let cool in the pan on a wire rack.

4   Release and remove the sides of the pan. With a spatula or knife, separate the bottom of the cake

from the bottom of the pan, and invert the cake onto a wire rack. Then reinvert, so that it is right side up, onto a serving plate or cake stand lined with a paper doily. Toss the edible blossoms and petals with the sanding sugar in a small bowl and sprinkle over the cake.

Candied Flowers

Although I used to love the sugar roses and blossoms on my childhood birthday cakes, I now prefer more natural cake decorations. For a celebration cake that will be consumed the day it is made, I love to use fresh flowers. But for occasions when the cake has to last a few days, I sometimes use candied petals. In my baking cupboard, I have small bottles of commercially prepared candied rose petals, violets, and yellow acacia blossoms from France. What I like much better, though, are candied flowers from my own garden. The results are more natural and delicate looking than the vivid rose, purple, and bright yellow of the blossoms in the bottles.

I follow directions from a noted society florist, clipped from a Cincinnati newspaper in the 1960s. Frances Jones Poetker recommended picking flowers in dry weather "so that there is no dew nor condensed moisture on the surface of the petals." She then made royal icing by whipping an egg white until frothy, adding a drop of food coloring (red for pink petals, yellow for yellow or orange petals) and a drop of rosewater for fragrance, and whisking in enough confectioners' sugar to make a thin icing. She dipped each petal into the icing (I use tweezers to do this) and placed them on a wire rack to dry. Just before the icing set, she sprinkled the flowers with sugar and dried them in a preheated 100-degree-F oven with the oven door open. After they dried, she kept them in an airtight tin. I use my homemade candied petals on petit fours, cupcakes, Grandmother's Flower Garden Cake (page 176), Fresh Pineapple Sorbet with Honey Sabayon and Candied Rose Petals (page 462), or on cupcakes made from Classic Yellow Cake (page 139) and frosted with Creamy, Fluffy Frosting (page 142).

Lemon Rose Geranium Layer Cake

If you're going to go to the trouble of making a cake from scratch, why not make one that is truly singular? With a flavor, texture, and color that admiring friends will find hard to duplicate (unless you give them the recipe and the flavor secret), this moist, white layer cake harks back to Victorian times. The wonderful lemon-rose flavor comes from scented geraniums, or pelargoniums, indoor plants that came from South Africa to scent the parlors of our Victorian ancestors. Their scent is concentrated in the leaves. For this recipe, I like to use the leaves from Rober's Lemon Rose or Skeleton Rose (*Pelargonium graveolens* 'Rober's Lemon Rose' or *P. radens* 'Skeleton Rose') from plants I can get at my local nursery. You might also like to use the old-fashioned rose geranium (*P. graveolens*) or an apple- (*P. x fragrans* 'Old Spice'), nutmeg- (*P. x fragrans*) or lemon-scented variety (*P. x melissinum, crispum,* or *limoneum*). You can also use a combination of lemon and rosewater flavorings. If you want to use fresh flavorings, you will need to "steep" the geranium leaves in butter and confectioners' sugar the day before you begin the cake. Or you can substitute grated lemon zest and rosewater (see the Note below).

MAKES ONE 9-INCH 2-LAYER CAKE; 8 SERVINGS

16 scented geranium leaves (see Note), plus extra geranium leaves and blossoms for garnish

1 cup (2 sticks) cold unsalted butter, cut into cubes

4$\frac{1}{2}$ cups confectioners' sugar

3 cups sifted cake flour

1 tablespoon plus 1 teaspoon baking powder

1$\frac{1}{4}$ cups milk

$\frac{1}{2}$ cup water

1$\frac{3}{4}$ cups granulated sugar

6 large egg whites, at room temperature

6 tablespoons ($\frac{3}{4}$ stick) unsalted butter at room temperature

1 teaspoon vanilla extract

Food coloring (optional)

1   The day before you make the cake, rinse the scented geranium leaves and pat them dry. Place a layer of the cold butter cubes in a large mixing bowl and place 10 of the geranium leaves on top of them. Place the remaining butter cubes on top of the leaves, cover, and let sit overnight at room temperature. Put half the confectioners' sugar, which you will use for the frosting, in another large mixing bowl and place the remaining 6 geranium leaves on top of the sugar. Pour the remaining confectioners' sugar on top, cover, and let sit at room temperature overnight.

2   To make the cake the next day, preheat the oven to 350 degrees F. Grease and flour two 9-inch round cake pans, tapping out the excess flour, and set aside. Sift the flour and baking powder together into a medium-size mixing bowl; set aside. Stir 1 cup of the milk and the water together in a small mixing bowl; set aside.

3   Remove the geranium leaves from the butter cubes and discard. Add the granulated sugar to the butter, and with an electric mixer, cream them together until light and fluffy. Beat in the egg whites, one at a time, beating well after each addition.

4   Add the flour mixture, one third at a time, to the butter-and-sugar mixture, alternating with the milk mixture, and beating well after each addition. Begin and end with the flour mixture. Divide the batter evenly between the prepared pans and bake until a cake tester inserted in the center comes out clean, 30 to 35 minutes. Let cool in the pans on a wire rack for 10 minutes. Then invert the cake layers onto the racks, and immediately turn right side up. Let cool completely before frosting.

5   When the cake layers have cooled, make the frosting: Remove the geranium leaves from the confectioners' sugar and discard the leaves. With an electric mixer, beat the 6 tablespoons of butter in a large mixing bowl until light and fluffy. Sift half of the confectioners' sugar into the bowl and beat until smooth. Beat in the vanilla and the remaining $1/4$ cup of milk and continue beating until smooth. Sift and add as much of the remaining confectioners' sugar as it takes to make a thick, smooth frosting. Add drops of food coloring, if desired.

6   Arrange the bottom cake layer on a cake plate or cake stand. Frost the top with one quarter of the frosting. Place the second layer on top and frost the top and sides of the cake with the remaining frosting. Garnish with scented geranium leaves and blossoms.

> **NOTE** To substitute grated lemon zest and rosewater for the scented geranium leaves, add $1/2$ teaspoon grated lemon zest and $1/2$ teaspoon rosewater to the cake batter after you cream the granulated sugar and butter in step 3. Add another $1/2$ teaspoon grated lemon zest and $1/4$ teaspoon rosewater to the frosting along with the vanilla after you cream the butter and confectioners' sugar (see step 4).

Italian Cream Cake

Italian cream cake was on most American dessert tables during the late 1970s and is still popular today, with a texture that is cake-like, creamy, and crunchy in every bite.

MAKES ONE 3-LAYER 8-INCH CAKE; 12 SERVINGS

CAKE

2 cups sifted all-purpose flour

1 teaspoon baking soda

$\frac{1}{2}$ cup (1 stick) unsalted butter at room temperature

$\frac{1}{2}$ cup vegetable shortening

2 cups granulated sugar

5 large egg yolks

1 cup buttermilk

1 teaspoon vanilla extract

$\frac{1}{2}$ cup sweetened flaked coconut

1 cup chopped pecans

5 large egg whites

BUTTERY CREAM CHEESE FROSTING

One 8-ounce package cream cheese at room temperature

$\frac{1}{2}$ cup (1 stick) unsalted butter at room temperature

One 1-pound box confectioners' sugar, sifted

1 teaspoon vanilla extract

$\frac{1}{2}$ cup chopped toasted pecans (see page 181) for garnish

1   Preheat the oven to 350 degrees F. Generously grease and flour three 8-inch round cake pans, tapping out the excess flour, and set aside.

2   To make the cake, sift together the flour and baking soda into a small mixing bowl; set aside. With an electric mixer, cream the butter and shortening together in a large mixing bowl until light and fluffy. Add the granulated sugar and beat until smooth. Add the egg yolks, one at a time, beating well after each addition. Add the flour mixture, one third at a time, alternating with the buttermilk. Stir in the vanilla, coconut, and pecans.

3   Wash and dry the beaters well to remove any trace of the batter. Beat the egg whites in a medium-size mixing bowl until they hold stiff peaks. Fold the beaten egg whites into the batter until you can no longer see them. Divide the batter evenly among the prepared cake pans.

4   Bake the layers until a cake tester inserted in the center comes out clean, about 25 minutes. Invert the cake layers onto wire racks, then immediately turn right side up. Let cool completely before frosting.

5 While the cake is cooling, make the frosting: With the electric mixer, beat the cream cheese and butter together in a medium-size mixing bowl until soft and smooth. Add the confectioners' sugar, 1 cup at a time, add the vanilla extract, and continue beating until light and fluffy. Spread a third of the frosting between the cake layers, another third of the frosting on the sides, and the remaining frosting on the top of the cake. Sprinkle the top with the toasted pecans.

Toasting Nuts and Seeds

Toasting nuts and seeds brings out their wonderful, mellow flavor. Preheat the oven to 350 degrees F. Spread the nuts or seeds out in a single layer on a baking sheet. Toast in the oven until light golden brown, 5 to 10 minutes, or medium brown, about 15 minutes. Note that flaked or sliced almonds and whole pine nuts can go from golden to very dark brown in seconds, so watch them closely. Let the nuts cool completely before chopping them.

Wellesley Fudge Cake with Classic Fudge Frosting

This is an all-American chocolate cake, reputedly served to Wellesley College coeds at a tearoom in Wellesley, Massachusetts, outside of Boston. In Evan Jones's classic *American Food: The Gastronomic Story*, Wellesley Fudge Cake is made in a loaf pan and is not frosted. To my mind, if you're going to have chocolate cake, have your cake and frosting, too. **MAKES ONE 2-LAYER 9-INCH CAKE; 8 SERVINGS**

FUDGE CAKE

4 ounces unsweetened chocolate

1/2 cup freshly brewed coffee

1 3/4 cups granulated sugar

1 teaspoon vanilla extract

1 3/4 cups sifted all-purpose flour

1 teaspoon baking soda

1 teaspoon salt

1/2 cup (1 stick) unsalted butter at room temperature

3 large eggs

3/4 cup milk

CLASSIC FUDGE FROSTING

4 ounces unsweetened chocolate

2 tablespoons unsalted butter

4 cups confectioners' sugar

1/4 teaspoon salt

1/2 cup milk, plus extra as needed

1 teaspoon vanilla extract

1. Preheat the oven to 350 degrees F. Generously grease and flour two 9-inch round cake pans, tapping out the excess, and set aside.

2. Heat the chocolate and coffee together in a small heavy saucepan over very low heat, stirring until the mixture is smooth. Add ½ cup of the granulated sugar and cook the mixture, stirring, until the sugar is dissolved, about 2 minutes. Remove from the heat and let cool to lukewarm. Add the vanilla, stir to blend, and set aside.

3. Sift together the flour, baking soda, and salt into a small mixing bowl and set aside. With an electric mixer, cream the butter in a large mixing bowl. Gradually beat in the remaining 1¼ cups granulated sugar until the mixture is light and fluffy. Beat in the eggs, one at a time. Add the flour mixture and milk alternately, a little a time, beating after each addition. Blend in the chocolate mixture. Divide the batter evenly between the prepared cake pans.

4. Bake the layers until a knife inserted in the center comes out clean, 30 to 35 minutes. Let cool for 10 minutes, then invert the cake layers onto wire racks, and immediately turn right side up. Let cool completely before frosting.

5. To make the frosting, melt the chocolate and butter together in a small heavy saucepan over low heat, stirring to combine. Combine the confectioners' sugar, salt, milk, and vanilla in a large mixing bowl. Add the melted chocolate mixture and blend well. Let cool until the frosting is thick enough to spread. Work quickly to frost the cake, adding more milk if the frosting gets too thick. Put the bottom layer on a cake plate or cake stand. Frost the top with one quarter of the frosting. Place the second layer on top and cover the sides and top of the cake with the remaining frosting.

Maraschino Cherry Cake with Marshmallow Frosting

Make this pretty confection for President's Day or Valentine's Day—or any other special occasion when a glossy white cake trimmed with red cherries would be just the thing. **MAKES ONE 2-LAYER 8- OR 9-INCH CAKE; 8 TO 10 SERVINGS**

CAKE
2¼ cups sifted cake flour
1⅓ cups sugar
1 tablespoon baking powder
1 teaspoon salt
½ cup vegetable shortening
¼ cup maraschino cherry juice from the jar
16 maraschino cherries, drained, each cut into eighths, plus extra cherries for garnish
½ cup milk

4 large egg whites

½ cup chopped pecans, plus extra for garnish

MARSHMALLOW FROSTING

2 large egg whites

1½ cups sugar

¼ teaspoon cream of tartar or 1 tablespoon light corn syrup

⅓ cup water

1 teaspoon vanilla extract

¾ cup miniature marshmallows

1   Preheat the oven to 350 degrees F. Lightly grease and flour two 8- or 9-inch round cake pans, tapping out the excess flour, and set aside.

2   To make the cake, sift together the cake flour, sugar, baking powder, and salt into a large mixing bowl. Make a well in the center and add the shortening, cherry juice, cherries, and milk. With an electric mixer, beat for 2 minutes at medium speed, scraping down the side of the bowl. Add the egg whites and beat for 2 more minutes. Fold in the chopped pecans until well combined. Divide the batter evenly between the prepared pans.

3   Bake the layers until a cake tester inserted in the center comes out clean, 30 to 35 minutes. Invert the cake layers onto wire racks, then immediately turn right side up. Let cool completely before frosting.

4   Wash and dry the beaters well. To make the frosting, mix the egg whites, sugar, cream of tartar, and water together in the top of a double boiler set over boiling water. Beat with the electric mixer on high speed until the egg whites hold stiff peaks, 7 to 8 minutes, scraping the bottom and sides of the pan occasionally. Remove the top of the double boiler from the heat, beat in the vanilla and marshmallows, and continue beating until the marshmallows have melted and the frosting is smooth. When the frosting is cool, put the bottom cake layer on a cake plate or cake stand. Frost the top with one quarter of the frosting. Place the second layer on top and cover the sides and top of the cake with the remaining frosting. Garnish with maraschino cherries and pecans.

Red Rose Cake with Whipped Frosting

Also known as Waldorf Cake, Red Cake of the Waldorf, and Red Velvet Cake, this venerable American dessert has been around since the 1950s, and it still turns up in community cookbooks. The color of the cake itself is dark reddish brown—like chocolate-covered cherries—due to the red food coloring. The whipped frosting is a great substitute for a true whipped cream frosting because it keeps longer.

MAKES ONE 2-LAYER 9-INCH CAKE; 8 SERVINGS

CAKE
2 1/2 cups cake flour
1/2 teaspoon salt
1 teaspoon baking soda
1 cup half-and-half
2 tablespoons cider vinegar
1/2 cup vegetable shortening
1 1/2 cups sugar
2 large eggs
2 tablespoons unsweetened cocoa powder

Two 1-ounce bottles red food coloring
1 teaspoon vanilla extract

WHIPPED FROSTING
1 cup milk
1 tablespoon all-purpose flour
1 cup sugar
1 cup (2 sticks) unsalted butter at room temperature
1 teaspoon vanilla extract

1   Preheat the oven to 350 degrees F. Grease and flour two 9-inch round cake pans, tapping out the excess flour, and set aside.

2   To make the cake, sift together the flour, salt, and baking soda in a medium-size mixing bowl. Mix the half-and-half and vinegar together in a small bowl. With an electric mixer, cream the shortening and sugar together in a large mixing bowl until light and fluffy. Beat in the eggs, cocoa, food coloring, and vanilla. Beat in the dry ingredients, 1 cup at a time, alternating with the half-and-half mixture, until you have a smooth batter. Divide the batter evenly between the prepared pans.

3   Bake the layers until a cake tester inserted in the center comes out clean, about 25 minutes. Invert the cake layers onto wire racks, then immediately turn right side up. Let cool completely before frosting.

4   To make the frosting, whisk the milk and flour together in a medium-size heavy saucepan over medium-high heat. Bring to a boil and cook, whisking occasionally, until the mixture has thickened, about 5 minutes. Set aside to cool to room temperature.

5 With an electric mixer, cream the sugar and butter together in a medium-size mixing bowl until light and fluffy. Beat in the thickened milk mixture and the vanilla and continue beating until you have a smooth frosting. Put the bottom cake layer on a cake plate or cake stand. Frost the top with one quarter of the frosting. Place the second layer on top and cover the sides and top of the cake with the remaining frosting.

Wintertime Cranberry and Orange Cake

This is pudding in the sense of a slowly baked, English-inspired dessert, but made with cranberries from Wisconsin or New England and oranges from Florida, California, or Texas. Fragrant, luscious, and with a slightly crunchy, toothsome texture, it has become one of my favorite wintertime desserts, as long as I remember to buy my cranberries in November or December to keep in the freezer all winter.

MAKES ONE 8-INCH CAKE; 8 SERVINGS

CRANBERRY FILLING
2½ cups fresh cranberries, picked over for stems
½ cup sugar

SPONGE CAKE
1¼ cups self-rising flour
1½ cups sugar
½ teaspoon baking powder
¼ cup (½ stick) unsalted butter, melted and cooled a bit

2 large eggs, beaten
¼ cup heavy cream
Grated zest of 1 orange or 1 teaspoon pure orange oil
1 teaspoon vanilla extract
⅓ cup flaked almonds

1 cup heavy cream, whipped until it holds stiff peaks, for garnish

1 Preheat the oven to 325 degrees F. Coat the inside of an 8-inch springform pan with nonstick cooking spray and set aside.

2 In a medium-size heavy saucepan, heat the cranberries and sugar together over medium-high heat, stirring, until the sugar melts and the cranberries pop, about 10 minutes. Set aside to cool slightly.

3 In a large mixing bowl, stir together the flour, 1¼ cups of the sugar, and the baking powder. Whisk the melted butter, eggs, and cream together in the saucepan in which you melted the butter or in a small mixing bowl. Stir into the dry ingredients until well combined. Stir in the orange zest and vanilla.

4 With a rubber spatula, spread half the cake batter in the prepared pan. Spoon the cooked cranberries over the batter. Spread the remaining batter on top of the cranberries and sprinkle evenly with the flaked almonds and the remaining ¼ cup of sugar.

5 Bake the cake until browned on top and bubbling, about 1 hour. Let cool slightly in the pan. Release and remove the sides of the pan, and slice and serve the cake with a dollop of whipped cream.

Stars and Stripes Blueberry Sponge Cake

Every summer, we have blueberries, and blueberries, and more blueberries. After eating them plain, in pancakes and compotes, and on ice cream and pastry cream–topped tarts, I dug out an old recipe I had clipped from a magazine in the 1980s. The idea of a sponge cake striped like summer seersucker and filled with rich cream and a blueberry filling suddenly seemed very appealing. My version adds free-form patriotic stars of whipped cream topped with fresh blueberries in addition to the freeform stripes. **MAKES ONE 8-INCH 2-LAYER CAKE; 8 SERVINGS**

BLUEBERRY PUREE
½ cup fresh or frozen (thawed) blueberries
Juice of 1 lemon
2 teaspoons granulated sugar
2 tablespoons confectioners' sugar

SPONGE CAKE
¾ cup sifted cake flour
¾ teaspoon baking powder
¼ teaspoon salt

4 large eggs
¾ cup granulated sugar
Grated zest of 1 lemon

FILLING AND GARNISH
1½ cups heavy cream
¾ cup confectioners' sugar
1 recipe Warm Spiced Berries (see page 348) made with blueberries, cooled
Fresh blueberries for garnish

1 To make the puree, heat the blueberries, lemon juice, and granulated sugar in a small heavy saucepan over medium-high heat until the mixture begins to boil and the blueberries start to burst, about 5 minutes. Remove from the heat and pass through a sieve into a small bowl; add the confectioners' sugar, stir until smooth, and set aside.

2 Preheat the oven to 400 degrees F. Line two 8-inch round cake pans with parchment or waxed paper, and butter the paper. Set aside.

3 To make the cake, sift together the flour, baking powder, and salt into a small mixing bowl; set aside. Immerse the uncracked eggs in a bowl of hot (120 degrees F) water for 3 minutes. Rinse out a large metal mixing bowl with hot water. (This step helps cut down the beating time.) Crack the eggs into the warm metal bowl and, with an electric mixer, beat the eggs, granulated sugar, and lemon zest together until the mixture thickens, turns a very pale yellow, and ribbons from a whisk, 6 to 8 minutes. (This step ensures a light-textured cake.) With a rubber spatula or spoon, fold the flour mixture into the egg-and-sugar mixture until fully combined.

4 Transfer half of the batter to a small mixing bowl and fold in the blueberry puree. Use a spoon or a piping bag fitted with a no. 8 plain tube to make stripes of the plain batter in each prepared cake pan, leaving a 1-inch space between each stripe. If you are piping the stripes, end each stripe by pressing the tip down into the end of the stripe, then quickly release and resume piping. Fill the spaces with thin stripes of the remaining blueberry batter. (The stripes do not have to be perfect, and actually are more pleasing if they have a free-form appearance. If you wish, however, you can use the tip of a table knife to straighten out the rows.)

5 Bake the layers until the edges of the cake have browned and are starting to pull away from the pan, 10 to 13 minutes. Let cool in the pans for 5 minutes, then use a knife or a metal spatula to loosen the cake from the side of the pan and invert onto a wire rack. Carefully peel the paper off the bottoms and trim any dark or uneven edges with a sharp knife. Turn the cake layers right side up and let cool completely.

6 To make the filling and garnish, with the electric mixer, whip the cream with the confectioners' sugar in a medium-size mixing bowl until it holds stiff peaks. Place one of the cake layers on a serving plate and spread with the cooled spiced berries. Spread half the whipped cream on top of the berries. Place the other cake layer on top of the filling. Spoon the remaining whipped cream into a piping bag fitted with a star tip and pipe stars on top of the cake. Dot each star with a fresh blueberry and serve. The cake will keep, refrigerated, for 2 days.

Folding

The technique of folding is used to gently but thoroughly blend two different mixtures without losing volume. Cooked custards are folded into whipped egg whites to make soufflés. Cake flour is folded into airy egg-and-sugar mixtures to make sponge cake. And Italian meringue is folded into whipped cream or a gelatin mixture to form a mousse. Folding is done more easily when both mixtures are about the same consistency; for example, a cooked custard that is gently folded into firmly whipped egg whites.

To fold, use a large metal serving spoon or a large rubber spatula. Hold the spoon or spatula so that you slice down into the center of the bowl all the way to the bottom. Turn the spoon or spatula sideways, then scoop up the mixture from the bottom of the bowl and flip it upside down onto the surface. Repeat the motion until the two mixtures are well blended.

Raspberry Ribbon Cake Roll

In late June or early July, I rediscover why I put up with the unruly tangle of thorny raspberry canes in the garden on the side of my house. These tiny wild raspberries have an intense flavor and a brilliant color. This beautiful cake is great way to celebrate the all-too-brief fresh raspberry season.

MAKES ONE 11-INCH FILLED CAKE ROLL; 8 SERVINGS

RASPBERRY PUREE
½ cup fresh or frozen (thawed) raspberries

1 tablespoon fresh lemon juice

2 teaspoons granulated sugar

2 tablespoons confectioners' sugar

SPONGE CAKE
¾ cup cake flour, sifted

¾ teaspoon baking powder

¼ teaspoon salt

4 large eggs, at room temperature

¾ cup granulated sugar

1 teaspoon almond extract

Confectioners' sugar for sprinkling

FILLING AND GARNISH
2 cups heavy cream

1 cup confectioners' sugar

1¼ cups fresh raspberries, or as needed

Fresh lemon balm or mint leaves

1   To make the puree, combine the raspberries, lemon juice, and granulated sugar together in a small heavy saucepan over medium-high heat and cook until the mixture begins to boil and the raspberries start to burst, about 5 minutes. Remove from the heat and pass through a sieve into a small bowl; add the confectioners' sugar and stir until smooth. Set aside.

2   Preheat the oven to 400 degrees F. Line a 16½ x 11½ x 1-inch jelly-roll pan with parchment or aluminum foil; butter the paper or foil and set aside.

3   To make the cake, sift together the cake flour, baking powder, and salt in a small mixing bowl; set aside. Immerse the uncracked eggs in a bowl of hot (120 degrees F) water for 3 minutes. Rinse out a large metal mixing bowl with hot water. (This step helps cut down the beating time.) Crack the eggs into the warm bowl and, with an electric mixer, beat the eggs, granulated sugar, and almond extract until the mixture thickens, turns a very pale yellow, and ribbons from a whisk, 6 to 8 minutes. (This step ensures a light-textured cake.) With a rubber spatula or spoon, fold the flour mixture into the egg-and-sugar mixture.

4 Divide the batter evenly between two small mixing bowls. Fold the raspberry puree into one of the batters. Use a piping bag fitted with a no. 8 plain tube to make thin, vertical stripes of the plain batter in the prepared cake pan, leaving a 1-inch space between each stripe, or do this carefully with a spoon. If you are piping the stripes, end each stripe by pressing the tip down into the end of the stripe, then quickly release and resume piping. (The stripes do not have to be perfect, and actually are more pleasing if they have a free-form appearance. If you wish, however, you can use the square end of a plastic measuring teaspoon or the tip of a table knife to straighten out the rows.) Fill the spaces with thin stripes of the remaining raspberry batter.

5 Bake the cake until it has risen and browned and a cake tester inserted in the center comes out clean, 10 to 13 minutes. Invert the cake onto a tea towel sprinkled with confectioners' sugar, so that the paper or foil side faces up. Carefully peel off the paper and trim any dark or uneven edges on the cake with a sharp knife. Cover the cake with a dampened tea towel. Starting at a narrow end, roll up the cake and towel together. Let the cake cool, wrapped in the towel, so it will hold its shape.

6 Wash and dry the beaters well. To make the filling, whip the cream and confectioners' sugar in a large mixing bowl until the cream holds stiff peaks. Fold 1 cup of the raspberries into the filling with a fork, mashing them gently to release some of their juice. Unroll the cake, remove the dampened tea towel, and spread the filling over the surface of the cake, leaving a 1-inch margin all around. Beginning with a short end, roll up the cake firmly and place on a decorative serving plate. Garnish with the remaining fresh raspberries (as many as you like) and the lemon balm or mint leaves and serve. The cake will keep, refrigerated, for 2 days.

Wild Plum Jelly Roll with Lemon Curd Filling

The secret of a "next" generation jelly roll is to use a really good jelly, preferably homemade from wild or homegrown fruit, and a second luscious filling like home-made lemon curd. Dust the jelly roll lightly with confectioners' sugar, and you've got a true vintage American dessert in the making.

MAKES ONE 11-INCH FILLED CAKE ROLL; 8 SERVINGS

¾ cup sifted cake flour

¾ teaspoon baking powder

¼ teaspoon salt

4 large eggs

¾ cup granulated sugar

1 teaspoon vanilla extract

Confectioners' sugar for dusting

1 cup tart jelly, such as plum, red currant, or seedless raspberry

1 cup homemade (see page 321) or store-bought lemon curd or Classic Pastry Cream (see page 163), plus extra lemon curd (optional) for serving

Whipped cream for serving (optional)

1 Preheat the oven to 400 degrees F. Grease a 16½ x 11½ x 1-inch jelly-roll pan, line it with parchment paper or aluminum foil, then grease the parchment or foil. Set aside.

2 Sift together the flour, baking powder, and salt into a small mixing bowl; set aside. Immerse the uncracked eggs in a bowl of hot (120 degrees F) water for 3 minutes. Rinse out a large metal mixing bowl with hot water. (This step helps cut down the beating time.) Crack the eggs into the warm bowl, and with an electric mixer, beat the eggs and granulated sugar together until the mixture thickens, turns a very pale yellow, and ribbons from a whisk, about 4 minutes. (This step ensures a light-textured cake.) With a rubber spatula or spoon, fold the flour mixture into the egg-and-sugar mixture, then stir in the vanilla. Pour the batter into the prepared jelly-roll pan and smooth the batter with the spatula.

3 Bake until the cake has risen and is light brown and a cake tester inserted in the center comes out clean, about 13 minutes. When the cake is done, loosen the cake from the sides of the pan and invert it onto a tea towel sprinkled with confectioners' sugar so the parchment or foil side of the jelly roll faces up. Carefully peel off the paper or foil and trim any dark or uneven edges on the cake with a sharp knife. Starting at the narrow end, roll the towel and cake together. Let the cake cool, wrapped in the towel, so it will hold its shape.

4 When the cake has cooled, unroll it slowly and remove the towel. Carefully spread the jelly over the cake, then spread the lemon curd over the jelly. Reroll, but without using the dish towel. Dust with more confectioners' sugar and serve. If you like, pass a bowl of extra lemon curd and/or whipped cream at the table.

Quilter's Strawberry and Cream Roll

Barbara Brackman's career has combined her fascination with quilts and her passion for history. The author of several books on Kansas history and historic quilts, Brackman has a new project that involves designing a prairie wildflower appliqué quilt based on the letters and diaries of nineteenth-century prairie women. But she's also a great dessert maker. "Whenever I go to my quilt guild gatherings, I often bring this strawberry cake roll because it has a striking visual presentation—and it doesn't hurt that it tastes wonderful and that everybody likes it," she laughs.

MAKES ONE 11-INCH FILLED CAKE ROLL; 8 SERVINGS

CAKE
¾ cup cake flour

¾ teaspoon baking powder

½ teaspoon salt

4 large eggs, separated

¾ cup granulated sugar

1 teaspoon vanilla extract

¼ cup confectioners' sugar, plus extra for dusting

STRAWBERRY FILLING AND GARNISH
1 quart fresh strawberries, hulled

¼ cup granulated sugar

2 cups heavy cream

1   Preheat the oven to 375 degrees F. Grease a 16½ x 11½ x 1-inch baking sheet or jelly-roll pan, line it with parchment paper or waxed paper, and grease the paper. Set aside.

2   To make the cake, in a small mixing bowl, sift together the flour, baking powder, and salt. With an electric mixer, whip the egg whites in a large mixing bowl until they hold stiff peaks. Set aside.

3   Wash and dry the beaters well. In another large mixing bowl, beat the egg yolks and granulated sugar together until light and creamy. Beat in the vanilla. Add the flour mixture, ¼ cup at a time, beating until smooth. With a rubber spatula, fold the beaten egg whites into the egg batter until you can no longer see the egg whites. Pour the batter into the prepared baking sheet. With the spatula, smooth the batter to make a uniform layer.

4   Bake the cake until golden brown and a cake tester inserted in the center comes out clean, about 13 minutes. As soon as the cake comes out of the oven, carefully loosen the paper from the baking sheet and invert the cake onto a tea towel dusted with confectioners' sugar. Carefully peel off the paper from the cake and discard. If you wish, use a sharp knife to trim the cake to a neat rectangle.

Dust the top of the cake with the ¼ cup of confectioners' sugar and, starting at a short end, carefully roll up the cake in the towel. Let the cake cool rolled up in the towel so it will hold its shape.

5   While the cake is cooling, make the filling. Cut 10 strawberries in half and set aside to decorate the top of the cake. Slice the remaining strawberries and put in a medium-size mixing bowl. Sprinkle with 2 tablespoons of the granulated sugar and mash with a potato masher. Set aside for at least 30 minutes to let the juices run.

6   In a large mixing bowl, combine the cream and the remaining 2 tablespoons of sugar, and whip with the mixer until the cream holds stiff peaks. Carefully unroll the cake, remove the towel, and place the cake on a long serving plate or platter. (The cake will want to roll itself back up again.) With a rubber spatula, spread half of the juicy strawberries on top of the cake, leaving a 1-inch margin all around. Pour the rest of the juicy strawberries into a sauceboat or a small serving dish and set aside. Spread half of the whipped cream over the berry filling and reroll the cake. Carefully turn the cake so the seam is on the bottom. Frost the cake roll with the rest of the whipped cream and arrange the reserved strawberry halves artfully on the cake and the serving plate. To serve, slice the cake roll and serve it with a ribbon of juicy strawberries.

Pineapple Upside-Down Cake

Many of us remember Sunday dinners at Grandma's when the dessert was a pineapple upside-down cake, a recipe that pineapple producers developed and publicized in women's magazines during the 1920s. During the '50s and '60s, my grandmother made hers in a cast-iron skillet and placed maraschino cherries in the center of the pineapple slices for a little more color. She always served each slice with a generous dollop of whipped cream. **MAKES ONE 12-INCH CAKE; 8 SERVINGS**

½ cup (1 stick) unsalted butter

1 cup packed dark brown sugar

One 15-ounce can pineapple slices packed in juice, drained and ¼ cup plus 1 tablespoon of the juice reserved

½ cup maraschino cherries, drained

1 cup all-purpose flour

1 teaspoon baking powder

3 large eggs, separated

1 cup granulated sugar

1 teaspoon vanilla extract

Whipped cream for serving

1 Preheat the oven to 350 degrees F. In a 12-inch cast-iron skillet, melt the butter over medium-high heat, stir in the brown sugar, and continue stirring until the sugar melts and the mixture is well blended. Arrange whole pineapple circles in a single layer over the brown sugar–and-butter mixture. Place a maraschino cherry in the center of each pineapple ring. Cut the remaining pineapple circles in half and place around the sides of the skillet. Remove from the heat and set aside.

2 Sift the flour and baking powder together into a small mixing bowl. With an electric mixer, beat the egg yolks, granulated sugar, reserved pineapple juice, and vanilla together in a large mixing bowl until the mixture thickens, turns a very pale yellow, and ribbons from a whisk, 6 to 8 minutes. (This step ensures a light-textured cake.) Beat in the dry ingredients, $1/3$ cup at a time, beating well after each addition. Wash and dry the beaters well. In a medium-size mixing bowl, beat the egg whites until they hold stiff peaks. Fold the egg whites into the batter with a spatula. Spoon the batter over the fruit in the skillet.

3 Bake the cake until golden and a cake tester inserted in the center comes out clean, 45 to 55 minutes. Wear oven mitts to carefully invert the cake onto a serving plate and let cool on the plate. Touch up the pineapple and maraschino cherry arrangement as needed. Serve each piece with a dollop of whipped cream.

Peach and Almond Upside-Down Cake

This version of upside-down cake blends a caramelized peach "filling" and a hearty almond cake topping that present and future grandmothers will be proud to serve as a new tradition. It makes a moist, chewy, almondy cake with a caramelized peach topping—yum! **MAKES ONE 8-INCH CAKE; 8 SERVINGS**

1 cup (2 sticks) unsalted butter at room temperature

$1/2$ cup plus $2/3$ cup sugar

6 large ripe but firm peaches, peeled, pitted, and sliced

Juice of 1 lemon

$1/2$ cup unblanched whole almonds

1 cup self-rising flour

2 large eggs

$1/3$ cup heavy cream

1 teaspoon almond extract

Crème fraîche or whipped cream (optional) for serving

1   In a cast-iron or other ovenproof skillet over medium heat, melt ½ cup of the butter, then stir in ½ cup of the sugar. Cook, stirring, until the sugar has melted and the mixture is a caramel color, 20 to 30 minutes. Place the peach slices in a circular pattern in the butter-and-sugar mixture and drizzle them with the lemon juice. Remove from the heat.

2   Preheat the oven to 375 degrees F. Put the almonds and remaining ⅔ cup of sugar in a food processor and process to a fine consistency. Add the flour and pulse to blend. Add the remaining ½ cup butter, the eggs, cream, and almond extract and process again to make a stiff batter.

3   Pour the batter over the peaches and bake the cake until the top is browned and the cake has risen, about 45 minutes. Reduce the oven temperature to 350 degrees F and bake until a cake tester inserted in the middle comes out clean, 10 to 15 minutes more.

4   Remove from the oven and run a knife around the edges of the skillet. Let the cake cool for 10 minutes. Then wear oven mitts to place a serving plate over the top of the skillet and carefully invert the cake onto the serving plate. Serve with crème fraîche or whipped cream, if you like.

Coconut Upside-Down Cake with Star Fruit, Mango, Papaya, and Pineapple

Star fruit, also called carambola, is a bright yellow tropical fruit with a fluted exterior, which yields star shapes when it is sliced. My first experience with star fruit was on a trip to Hong Kong, where the fruit originated. Through centuries of East-West commerce, traders brought the fruit to Hawaii and then the Caribbean. Now star fruit is grown in Florida and is in season from August through March. When ripe, it has an aromatic flavor that reminds me of bubble gum. In this fusion recipe adapted from one by Chef Richard "Bingo" Starr of Cuvee, in New Orleans, a vintage American pineapple upside-down cake is married with other tropical fruits and a hint of coconut in the cake itself. Yummy! I like to arrange the fruits so the top of the cake looks like a profusion of fruits rather than a geometric pattern. **MAKES ONE 9-INCH CAKE; 8 SERVINGS**

1/2 cup (1 stick) unsalted butter, melted

1/2 cup packed light brown sugar

1 ripe star fruit, sliced into 1/8-inch-thick stars

1 cup sliced mango

1 cup sliced ripe papaya

1 cup sliced fresh pineapple (1/4-inch-thick slices)

CAKE

1 cup grated fresh coconut or frozen (thawed) unsweetened flaked coconut (available at Asian markets and health food stores)

2 1/2 cups cake flour

1 1/2 cups granulated sugar

1 tablespoon plus 1 teaspoon baking powder

1 teaspoon salt

1 teaspoon vanilla extract

1 teaspoon coconut extract

1/2 cup (1 stick) unsalted butter at room temperature

1 cup fresh or canned unsweetened coconut milk (not cream of coconut)

4 large egg whites

1   Preheat the oven to 350 degrees F. Grease and flour a 9-inch round cake pan, tapping out the excess flour, and set aside.

2   To make the topping, drizzle the melted butter over the bottom of the prepared pan and sprinkle evenly with the brown sugar. Arrange the fruits in the bottom of the pan. Set aside.

3   To make the cake, spread the flaked coconut on a baking sheet and toast in the oven until lightly browned, about 10 minutes. Set aside to cool.

4   In a large mixing bowl, sift the flour, granulated sugar, baking powder, and salt together. With an electric mixer on medium speed, beat the extracts, butter, and 1/2 cup of the coconut milk into the flour mixture and continue beating for 1 minute. Beat in the remaining 1/2 cup of coconut milk and the egg whites until smooth, about 2 minutes. Stir in the toasted coconut. Spoon the batter evenly on top of the fruit in the pan.

5   Bake the cake until a cake tester inserted in the center comes out clean, about 60 to 70 minutes. While still warm, run a knife around the perimeter to loosen the cake from the pan. Wear oven mitts to carefully invert the cake onto a serving plate. Let cool slightly before serving.

Blueberry Buckle with Pecan Streusel

A buckle is another one of those funny-sounding desserts—like slumps, grunts, betties, or cobblers—transplanted to New England from Great Britain. A buckle is a moist cake topped with fruit and sometimes nuts and sugar. Today, we would be more inclined to enjoy this as a coffee cake, but it makes a fine ending to any meal.

MAKES ONE 9 X 13-INCH CAKE; 8 SERVINGS

BLUEBERRY BUCKLE

2 1/4 cups all-purpose flour

2 teaspoons baking powder

1/2 teaspoon salt

1/2 teaspoon baking soda

3/4 cup (1 1/2 sticks) unsalted butter at room temperature

1 teaspoon grated lemon zest

3/4 cup sugar

1 teaspoon vanilla extract

2 large eggs

One 8-ounce container sour cream

2 cups fresh or frozen (thawed) blueberries

STREUSEL TOPPING

1/4 cup (1/2 stick) unsalted butter

1/4 cup all-purpose flour

1 teaspoon ground cinnamon

2/3 cup packed light brown sugar

2/3 cup chopped pecans or walnuts

1   Preheat the oven to 350 degrees F. Grease a 9 x 13-inch baking pan and set aside.

2   To make the buckle, in a small mixing bowl, sift together the flour, baking powder, salt, and baking soda, and set aside. With an electric mixer, cream together the butter, lemon zest, and sugar in a medium-size mixing bowl until light and fluffy. Beat in the vanilla and the eggs, one at a time. Beat in the dry ingredients a little at a time, alternating with the sour cream, and beating well after each addition, until you have a smooth batter. Pour half the batter into the prepared baking pan. Scatter the blueberries over the batter, then carefully spread the remaining batter on top of the fruit.

3   To make the streusel, combine all the ingredients in a small bowl. Work the butter into the dry ingredients with your fingertips until the mixture resembles large crumbs. Scatter evenly over the batter.

4   Bake until a cake tester inserted in the center comes out clean, about 45 minutes. Serve warm or at room temperature right from the pan.

Log Cabin Cake

The archetypal image of the log cabin has long been embedded in the American consciousness as a symbol of our pioneer roots. Candidates running for president long ago liked to claim they were born in log cabins. Nineteenth-century quilters liked to patch coordinating strips of fabric together to create a log cabin pattern to remind them of home. An old cookbook also made mention of a log cabin cake from Lincoln's hometown of Springfield, Illinois, but alas, no recipe! So I was on my own. I knew the cake had to be rectangular chocolate layers with a creamy filling and a dark mocha chocolate glaze to cover. This is what I came up with—and even Abe Lincoln would approve, I hope. The chocolate pound cake is best made a day ahead.

MAKES ONE 9 X 5-INCH 4-LAYER CAKE; 8 SERVINGS

CHOCOLATE POUND CAKE

$1\frac{1}{2}$ cups all-purpose flour

$\frac{1}{4}$ cup unsweetened cocoa powder

$\frac{3}{4}$ cup ($1\frac{1}{2}$ sticks) unsalted butter at room temperature

$1\frac{1}{2}$ cups granulated sugar

2 large eggs

$\frac{1}{2}$ cup freshly brewed dark roast coffee at room temperature

CREAM FILLING

1 cup heavy cream

$\frac{1}{2}$ cup confectioners' sugar

1 teaspoon vanilla extract

MOCHA CHOCOLATE GLAZE

1 cup heavy cream

1 teaspoon instant espresso powder

1 cup semisweet chocolate chips

Chocolate shavings (optional) for garnish

1   Preheat the oven to 350 degrees F. Grease a 9 x 5-inch loaf pan and set aside.

2   To make the cake, whisk the flour and cocoa powder together in a small mixing bowl. With an electric mixer, cream together the butter and granulated sugar in a large mixing bowl until light and fluffy. Beat in the eggs, then gradually beat in the flour mixture, alternating with the coffee, and beating well after each addition, until you have a smooth batter. Spoon the batter into the prepared pan.

3   Bake the cake until a cake tester inserted in the center comes out clean, about 1 hour and 10 minutes. Let cool in the pan. Invert the pound cake onto a cutting board and turn right side up. Using

a serrated knife or dental floss held taut between your hands, cut the pound cake horizontally into four layers.

4   Wash and dry the beaters well. To make the filling, with the electric mixer, whip the cream, confectioners' sugar, and vanilla together in a medium-size mixing bowl until the mixture holds stiff peaks. Place the bottom pound cake layer on a flat surface and spread with a third of the filling. Carefully place a second layer on top and spread with another third of the filling. Repeat the process with the third layer, then carefully lay the fourth layer on top of the filling. Wrap the cake with plastic wrap and refrigerate for at least 1 hour, or until ready to serve.

5   At least 1 hour before serving, make the glaze: Heat the cream in a heavy saucepan over medium heat until bubbles begin to form around the perimeter. Remove from the heat and whisk in the espresso powder and chocolate chips. Cover and let sit for 5 minutes to allow the chocolate to melt, then whisk again to form a smooth glaze.

6   Unwrap the cake and place on a wire cooling rack over a sheet of parchment or waxed paper. Spoon or pour the warm glaze over the cake so that the top and sides are completely covered. Let cool. Garnish the top with chocolate shavings, if desired, to form a "roof," and serve. Any leftover cake will keep, covered and refrigerated, for 2 days.

Making Chocolate Curls, Petals, and Leaves

Chocolate Curls

Melt about 8 ounces of dark or semisweet chocolate in the top of a double boiler. When the chocolate has melted, use a rubber or offset spatula to spread it out in a thin layer on a cool marble or laminated surface. Let the chocolate cool completely, about 30 minutes, just to be safe. Hold a chef's knife at a 45-degree angle and push the blade away from you across the surface of the chocolate. The chocolate will curl in different shapes and lengths. Carefully lift and place the curls on a wax- or parchment paper–lined baking sheet and keep in a cool place (but do not refrigerate) until ready to use.

Chocolate Petals and Leaves

Gather perfect rose petals and leaves in the morning. Refrigerate until ready to use. Line two baking sheets with aluminum foil and set aside. Melt about 8 ounces of dark or semisweet chocolate in the top of a double boiler. Dip one side of each rose petal in the hot, melted chocolate and place, chocolate side down, on one prepared baking sheet. Using a small pastry brush, brush one side of each leaf evenly with the melted chocolate, and place, chocolate side up, on the second baking sheet. Refrigerate until ready to use.

Arrange the chocolate petals by placing them, chocolate side down, on top of a cake. Peel the real petal away from the chocolate impression; arrange the chocolate leaves on top of the cake as well.

Citrus-Glazed Sweet Potato Pound Cake

Blacks from West African tribes, brought by force to work first on the seventeenth-century sugar plantations in the West Indies, then in the eighteenth-century tobacco and cotton fields in the South, sometimes had seeds or tubers with them when they were kidnapped and taken to the dreaded slave ships. After a terrible journey across the Atlantic, a few slaves managed not only to survive the unspeakable conditions, but also to bring benne (sesame) seeds, gombo (okra) seeds, and sweet potato tubers with them. Sweet potatoes were actually native to South America. They were first brought to Africa by sixteenth-century Spanish and Portuguese traders only a couple of centuries before the tubers recrossed the Atlantic Ocean to take root in North America. Today, sweet potato desserts like this one are still popular among black families, many of whom descended from those same West Africans. But the flavor and texture of this dessert appeals to a wide audience. Recently, I made this for a 40-student cooking class to taste test, and everyone gave a hearty thumbs-up.

MAKES ONE 12-CUP BUNDT OR 10-INCH TUBE CAKE; 12 SERVINGS

CAKE

3 cups cake flour

2 teaspoons baking powder

1/2 teaspoon baking soda

1 teaspoon ground cinnamon

1/4 to 1/2 teaspoon freshly grated nutmeg, to your taste

1/4 teaspoon salt

1 cup (2 sticks) unsalted butter at room temperature

2 cups granulated sugar

2 cups cooked sweet potatoes or one 16-ounce can sweet potatoes, drained and mashed

1 teaspoon vanilla extract

5 large eggs

CITRUS GLAZE

1 cup sifted confectioners' sugar

2 tablespoons fresh orange juice

1 tablespoon grated orange zest

1   Preheat the oven to 350 degrees F. Grease and flour the inside of a 12-cup Bundt or 10-inch tube pan, tapping out the excess flour, and set aside.

2   To make the cake, in a medium-size mixing bowl, sift together the flour, baking powder, baking soda, cinnamon, nutmeg, and salt. In a food processor, cream together the butter and granulated sugar until light and fluffy. Add the sweet potatoes and vanilla and puree. Add the eggs, one at a

time, pulsing to mix thoroughly after each addition. Slowly add the flour mixture to the sweet potato mixture, pulsing to combine. Pour the batter into the prepared pan.

3   Bake the cake until golden brown on top and a cake tester inserted near the center comes out clean, 60 to 75 minutes. Let the cake cool completely in the pan on a wire rack. Invert the cake onto the rack, and place the rack over a sheet of parchment or waxed paper.

4   To make the glaze, combine the ingredients in a small mixing bowl. Drizzle over the cooled cake so that it drips down the sides. Transfer the cake to a serving platter.

Creaming Butter and Sugar

One of the most essential techniques in the success of a cake is the simple process of creaming the butter and sugar together. Creaming creates air bubbles in the butter-and-sugar mixture, which are enlarged by the action of baking powder in the oven, according to food scientist Shirley Corriher in her book *Cookwise*. Creaming has a direct effect on how high your cake will rise.

Creaming butter and sugar together is simple. Just beat them together in a bowl, using an electric mixer. A hand-held mixer will take longer to cream the mixture than if you use a stand mixer. Generally, the butter and sugar have been adequately creamed when the mixture is very light and fluffy, 4 to 5 minutes with a stand mixer, 6 to 8 or 10 minutes with a hand-held mixer. If you use shortening, which is already aerated, you don't have to cream as long, but you won't have that buttery flavor.

Glazed Lemon-Berry Bundt Cake

There are Bundt cakes and there are Bundt cakes. The worst kind, from cheap mixes, taste like chemicals and have an oily texture. The best ones are like this—fresh tasting, satisfying, and a good keeper.

MAKES ONE 12-CUP BUNDT OR 10-INCH TUBE CAKE; 12 SERVINGS

CAKE

2 cups fresh or frozen whole raspberries, blackberries, blueberries, or cranberries

1 cup (2 sticks) unsalted butter at room temperature

1²⁄₃ cups sugar

5 large eggs

2 cups all-purpose flour

¹⁄₂ teaspoon salt

Grated zest and juice of 1 lemon

LEMON GLAZE

¹⁄₂ cup fresh lemon juice

¹⁄₂ cup water

1 cup sugar

1 Preheat the oven to 350 degrees F. Grease and flour the inside of a 12-cup Bundt or 10-inch tube pan, tapping out the excess flour, and set aside.

2 To make the cake, carefully separate the frozen berries, if necessary, and set aside in a bowl. With an electric mixer, cream the butter in a large mixing bowl, add the sugar, and continue to beat until light and fluffy. Beat in the eggs, one at a time. Gradually beat in the flour, salt, and lemon zest and juice until well blended. Fold in the berries and pour or spoon the batter into the prepared pan.

3 Bake the cake until a cake tester inserted near the center comes out clean, about 1 hour and 10 minutes. Let the cake cool in the pan on a wire rack for 20 minutes.

4 While the cake is cooling, make the glaze: Stir the lemon juice, water, and sugar together in a small heavy saucepan over medium-high heat. Bring the mixture to a simmer and let it reduce by half, but do not let it burn. Remove from the heat.

5 Invert the warm cake onto a cooling rack and place the rack over a sheet of parchment or waxed paper. Pour the warm glaze evenly over the cake. Allow the cake to cool completely before serving.

Almond Pound Cake

California vineyards are also home to groves of almond, fig, and pomegranate. Make your own marzipan from whole almonds or buy the best you can find because the almond paste provides most of the flavor and texture for this wonderful cake. Serve it on a large silver tray, the sugar-dusted cake in the middle, with a bowl of whipped cream on one side and a bowl of Strawberry and Lemon Compote on the other.

MAKES ONE 12-CUP BUNDT OR 10-INCH TUBE CAKE; 12 SERVINGS

3 cups sifted all-purpose flour

$\frac{1}{2}$ teaspoon salt

$\frac{1}{4}$ teaspoon baking soda

$2\frac{1}{2}$ cups granulated sugar

1 cup (2 sticks) unsalted butter at room temperature

4 ounces Marzipan made with almond extract (page 481) or store-bought almond paste

6 large eggs

$\frac{1}{2}$ to $\frac{3}{4}$ cup sour cream, as needed

$\frac{1}{2}$ teaspoon almond extract

$\frac{1}{2}$ teaspoon vanilla extract

1 cup golden raisins (optional)

Confectioners' sugar for sprinkling

1 recipe Strawberry and Lemon Compote (page 16) for garnish

1   Preheat the oven to 350 degrees F. Grease and flour a 12-cup Bundt or 10-inch tube pan very well, tapping out the excess flour, and set aside.

2   Sift together the flour, salt, and baking soda in a medium-size mixing bowl; set aside. In a large bowl with an electric mixer, or in a food processor, cream together the granulated sugar, butter, and marzipan until smooth. (If the marzipan is not soft, cream it first until smooth, then add the sugar and butter.) Add the eggs, one at a time, beating or processing until well blended after each addition. Add the flour mixture, $\frac{1}{2}$ cup at a time, alternating with the $\frac{1}{2}$ cup of sour cream and beating or processing well after each addition. Add the extra $\frac{1}{4}$ cup of sour cream if the batter seems too stiff. Mix in the extracts, then fold in the raisins by hand, if using. Pour the batter into the prepared pan.

3   Bake the cake until a cake tester inserted near the center comes out clean, about $1\frac{1}{2}$ hours. Let cool for 15 minutes in the pan on a rack. Then invert the cake onto the rack and cool completely. Transfer the cake to a serving plate and sprinkle with confectioners' sugar. To serve, slice the cake and garnish with a spoonful of the compote.

Luscious Cream Cheese Pound Cake

Pound cake comes to the American dessert repertoire from European roots. The French call it *quatre quarts*, or four fourths. The British just knew that a pound of four different ingredients—butter, flour, eggs, and sugar—was needed to make this cake and named it accordingly. With three different flavorings creating a trio of tastes, this moist and fragrant pound cake is wonderful served with sautéed apples, fresh berries, hot fudge, or a warm caramel sauce. You can also cut it into small pieces and dip them into a dessert fondue (see page 156).

MAKES ONE 12-CUP BUNDT OR 10-INCH TUBE CAKE; 12 SERVINGS

1½ cups (3 sticks) unsalted butter at room temperature

One 8-ounce package cream cheese at room temperature

3 cups granulated sugar

7 large eggs

3 cups sifted cake flour

2 teaspoons vanilla extract

2 teaspoons almond extract

2 teaspoons brandy

Confectioners' sugar for dusting

1 Preheat the oven to 325 degrees F. Grease and flour a 12-cup Bundt or 10-inch tube pan, tapping out the excess flour, and set aside.

2 With an electric mixer, cream the butter and cream cheese together in a large mixing bowl until smooth. Add the granulated sugar, and beat until fluffy. Add the eggs, one at a time, beating well after each addition. Add the flour, a little at a time, until well blended. Stir in the extracts and brandy by hand. Pour the batter into the prepared pan.

3 Bake the cake until a cake tester inserted near the center comes out clean, about 1 hour and 10 minutes. Let cool in the pan on a wire rack for 10 minutes, then invert the cake onto the rack and let cool completely. Transfer to a serving plate and dust with confectioners' sugar.

Buttermilk Pound Cake

Buttermilk adds a pleasing moistness and slight tartness to this classic pound cake. Serve drizzled with hot Chocolate Ganache (see page 213), White Chocolate Caramel Ganache (see page 214), fresh berries, or a fruit compote.

MAKES ONE 12-CUP BUNDT OR 10-INCH TUBE CAKE; 12 SERVINGS

$1/2$ teaspoon baking soda

1 cup buttermilk

3 cups all-purpose flour

$1/8$ teaspoon salt

$1/2$ cup (1 stick) unsalted butter at room temperature

$1/2$ cup vegetable shortening

2 cups sugar

4 large eggs

2 teaspoons lemon extract

1 teaspoon almond extract

1   Preheat the oven to 350 degrees F. Grease and flour a 12-cup Bundt or 10-inch tube cake, tapping out the excess flour, and set aside.

2   Dissolve the baking soda in the buttermilk and set aside. Whisk together the flour and salt in a medium-size mixing bowl and set aside. With an electric mixer, cream the butter and shortening together in large mixing bowl. Gradually add the sugar and beat until light and fluffy. Add the eggs, one at a time, beating well after each addition. Gradually add the flour mixture, alternating with the buttermilk mixture, beginning and ending with the flour, and beating well after each addition. Stir in the extracts by hand. Pour the batter into the prepared pan.

3   Bake the cake until a cake tester inserted near the center comes out clean, about 1 hour and 15 minutes. Let the cake cool in the pan on a wire rack for 15 minutes. Invert the cake onto the rack and cool completely. Transfer to a serving plate, add a topping or garnish, or serve with a fruit compote.

Kentucky Butter Cake

Lusciously rich, this Bundt cake with a buttery, sugary glaze tastes wonderful when paired with the best fresh fruits of the season. I like both vanilla and rum in the glaze. **MAKES ONE 12-CUP BUNDT OR 10-INCH TUBE CAKE; 12 SERVINGS**

CAKE

3 cups all-purpose flour

1 teaspoon baking powder

1 teaspoon salt

$\frac{1}{2}$ teaspoon baking soda

2 teaspoons vanilla extract

1 cup buttermilk

1 cup (2 sticks) unsalted butter at room temperature

2 cups sugar

4 large eggs

VANILLA-RUM GLAZE

1 cup sugar

$\frac{1}{4}$ cup water

$\frac{1}{2}$ cup (1 stick) unsalted butter, cubed

1 tablespoon vanilla extract

1 tablespoon rum

1 Preheat the oven to 325 degrees F. Grease and flour a 12-cup Bundt or 10-inch tube cake, tapping out the excess flour, and set aside.

2 To make the cake, sift together the flour, baking powder, salt, and baking soda in a medium-size mixing bowl and set aside. Stir the vanilla into the buttermilk and set aside. With an electric mixer, cream together the butter and sugar in a large mixing bowl until light and fluffy. Beat in the eggs, one at a time. Beat in the dry ingredients, one third at a time, alternating with the buttermilk mixture, and beating well after each addition, until you have a smooth, stiff batter. Spoon the batter into the prepared pan.

3 Bake the cake until a cake tester inserted near the center comes out clean, 60 to 70 minutes. Let cool in the pan for 10 minutes.

4 While the cake is still baking, make the glaze: In a medium-size, heavy saucepan over medium heat, combine the sugar, water, and butter. Remove from the heat immediately after the butter has melted, then stir to blend. Stir in the vanilla and rum. Invert the warm cake onto a cooling rack and place the rack over a sheet of parchment or waxed paper. Spoon or pour the hot glaze over the cake. Transfer the cake to a serving plate and serve warm or at room temperature.

Tunnel of Fudge Cake

In 1966, Ella Rita Helfrich of Houston, Texas, blew the socks off the judges and her competition when she won the 17th Pillsbury Bake-Off Contest and a prize of $5,000. The pan she used for her winning recipe caused an even greater stir than her unusual cake. She used a 12-cup Bundt cake pan, because her tunnel of fudge is created when the batter closest to the source of heat—the hot pan and the oven element—sets up first, forming an inner tube full of not-quite-so solid fudgy chocolate.

The Bundt pan was first manufactured by Nordic Products in 1950, after Minneapolis housewives requested an aluminum pan like the heavier cast-iron European kugelhopf pan to bake coffee cakes and kugelhopf. When the Tunnel of Fudge recipe was published, however, Pillsbury received over 200,000 requests for information on the Bundt cake pan.

Two things are essential to the success of this cake. You have to include the walnuts because they help set the "tunnel." And you have to spoon the flour into the measuring cup, then level it off. If you just scoop the flour out of the bag or canister, you might get too much flour and a dry cake. Because this cake has a tunnel of fudge in the middle, you judge its doneness by whether the cake is pulling away from the sides of the pan, not by whether a cake tester comes out clean.

MAKES ONE 12-CUP BUNDT CAKE; 12 SERVINGS

CAKE
¾ cup unsweetened cocoa powder
1¾ cups (3½ sticks) unsalted butter at room temperature
1¾ cups granulated sugar
6 large eggs
2 cups confectioners' sugar

2¼ cups all-purpose flour
2 cups chopped walnuts (essential)

CHOCOLATE GLAZE
¾ cup confectioners' sugar
¼ cup unsweetened cocoa powder
1 to 2 tablespoons milk

1   Preheat the oven to 350 degrees F. Grease and flour a 12-cup Bundt pan, tapping out the excess, and set aside.

2   To make the cake, sift the cocoa powder and set aside. With an electric mixer, cream the butter and granulated sugar together in a large mixing bowl until light and fluffy. Beat in the eggs, one at a time, beating well after each addition. Gradually beat in the confectioners' sugar, blending

well. With a wooden spoon, gradually stir in the flour, sifted cocoa, and then the walnuts, and continue stirring until well blended. Spoon the batter into the prepared pan and spread evenly.

3   Bake the cake until it has started to pull away from the sides of the pan, 58 to 60 minutes. Let cool in the pan on a wire rack for 1 hour.

4   To make the glaze, whisk together the ingredients in a small mixing bowl, adding enough of the milk to achieve a thin consistency. Invert the cake onto the cooling rack and place the rack over a sheet of parchment or waxed paper. Spoon the glaze over the top of the cake, allowing some to run down the sides. Transfer to a serving plate.

Williamsburg Orange Pecan Cake with Sherry Glaze

Colonial Williamsburg had been lost in the mists of time when historic preservationists got John D. Rockefeller interested in reviving this town, so important to early American history. A descendant of British fruitcakes, which were reserved for special occasions in the colonies, this cake can be made 2 or 3 days in advance and covered tightly in plastic wrap.

MAKES ONE 12-CUP BUNDT OR 10-INCH TUBE CAKE; 12 SERVINGS

CAKE

1 cup plus 2 tablespoons all-purpose flour

$1/2$ teaspoon baking powder

$1/2$ teaspoon baking soda

$1/8$ teaspoon salt

$1/2$ cup finely chopped pecans

$1/3$ cup finely chopped dates

6 tablespoons ($3/4$ stick) unsalted butter at room
temperature

$1/2$ cup sugar

1 large egg

$1/2$ cup buttermilk

Grated zest of 1 orange

SHERRY GLAZE

$1/3$ cup fresh orange juice

$1/4$ cup sugar

$1/3$ cup dry sherry

1   Preheat the oven to 350 degrees F. Grease and flour the inside of a 12-cup Bundt or 10-inch tube cake pan and set aside.

2   To make the cake, in a small mixing bowl, sift 1 cup of the flour with the baking powder, baking soda, and salt; set aside. In another small bowl, toss the pecans and dates with the remaining

2 tablespoons flour; set aside. With an electric mixer, cream the butter and sugar together in a large mixing bowl until light a fluffy. Beat in the egg, and then beat in the flour mixture, a little at a time, alternating with the buttermilk. Beat in the orange zest. Fold the pecan mixture into the cake batter and pour or spoon the batter into the prepared pan.

3   Bake the cake until a cake tester inserted near the center comes out clean, about 50 minutes.

4   While the cake is baking, make the glaze: In a small mixing bowl, whisk together the orange juice, sugar, and sherry until the sugar has dissolved. Remove the cake from the oven and, while it is still hot, poke the cake at intervals with a wooden skewer. Slowly pour the glaze over the cake. Let cool completely in the pan. Remove the cake from the pan, wrap it well in plastic wrap, and let rest at room temperature for 2 to 3 days to let the flavors develop.

Glazed Rum and Pecan Cake

W hen I worked at the Wyoming Bakery in Cincinnati, Ohio, as a teenager, the bakery made this wonderful rum cake—moist and delicious, heady with rum, and studded with toasted pecans. This recipe, made with cake mix, believe it or not, tastes just like it. Rum is one of those ingredients that can take the "cake mix taste" out of cake mix. **MAKES ONE 12-CUP BUNDT CAKE; 12 SERVINGS**

CAKE
1/2 cup chopped toasted pecans (see page 181)

One 18.5-ounce box yellow cake mix with pudding

4 large eggs

1/2 cup vegetable oil, such as canola, corn, or light olive oil

1/2 cup cold water

1/2 cup light, dark, or spiced rum

VERY RUM GLAZE
1/2 cup (1 stick) unsalted butter

1 cup sugar

1/4 cup light, dark, or spiced rum

1/4 cup water

1   Preheat the oven to 325 degrees F. Generously grease a 12-cup Bundt cake pan. Sprinkle the toasted chopped pecans over the bottom of the pan. Set aside.

2   With an electric mixer, mix together the cake mix, eggs, oil, water, and rum in a large mixing bowl and beat until you have a smooth batter. Pour the batter over the nuts in the pan.

3 Bake the cake until a cake tester inserted near the center comes out clean, 55 to 60 minutes.

4 About 10 minutes before the cake is done, make the glaze: Bring the butter, sugar, rum, and water to a boil in a medium-size heavy saucepan over medium-high heat, stirring constantly. Boil for 2 minutes. When the cake is done, poke holes in it with a skewer and pour all but $\frac{1}{4}$ cup of the hot glaze over the cake while still in the pan. Let cool for 30 minutes in the pan, then invert onto a serving plate. Reheat the glaze and drizzle over the top of the cake.

Glazed Lemon Sheet Cake

Sweet and tart, tender and moist, and a deep lemon yellow, this sheet cake actually starts with a cake mix. But you'd never know it. A square of this cake is fabulous all by itself, but if you want to truly go all out, serve it with a spoonful of Wild Berry Compote (see page 374), or Strawberry and Lemon Compote (page 16).

MAKES ONE 9 X 13-INCH CAKE; 8 SERVINGS

CAKE
One 18.5-ounce box lemon cake mix

One 3.4-ounce package instant lemon pudding

Grated zest and juice of 1 lemon

4 large eggs

1 cup water

$\frac{1}{3}$ cup vegetable oil, such as canola, corn, or light olive oil

LEMON GLAZE
$2\frac{1}{2}$ cups confectioners' sugar

$\frac{1}{4}$ cup fresh lemon juice

1 Preheat the oven to 350 degrees F. Grease and flour the inside of a 9 x 13-inch baking pan, tapping out the excess flour, and set aside.

2 To make the cake, combine the cake mix, pudding mix, lemon zest and juice, eggs, water, and oil in a large mixing bowl. With an electric mixer on low speed, beat until just blended. Then beat on medium speed for 4 minutes. Pour into the prepared pan.

3 Bake the cake until a cake tester inserted in the center comes out clean and the cake has shrunk from the sides of the pan, about 35 minutes.

4 While the cake is hot, prepare the glaze: Whisk the confectioners' sugar and lemon juice together in a small mixing bowl. Poke holes in the cake with a wooden skewer. Pour the glaze all over the hot cake and set aside to cool. Serve from the pan.

Thanks to Betty, Ann, and Duncan

Love 'em or hate 'em, cake mixes are another American success story.

In the early 1920s, when local flour mills continued their decline and mega-mills such as General Mills and Pillsbury put Minneapolis on the map, flour manufacturers and food scientists began experimenting with convenience mixes. The Duff Company in Pittsburgh developed a method for drying molasses and added that ingredient to create a gingerbread mix in 1929. Gingerbread was soon followed by mixes for spice, yellow, white, and chocolate cakes in the 1930s.

Then World War II broke out and, along with it, the rationing of ingredients essential to baking. Flour manufacturers developed baking mixes with ingredients such as dry milk and powdered eggs that would keep in combat conditions and sent them overseas for American troops. (These mixes produced very inferior results and didn't diminish the average GI's homesick yearning for Mom's cookies and cakes.)

Thankfully, the flour manufacturers also spent the war years in research and development, coming up with new and improved cake mixes. In 1947, General Mills introduced a single-layer Betty Crocker ginger cake mix, and devil's food and party cake mixes the next year. In 1948, Pillsbury joined the fray with white layer cake and chocolate fudge cake mixes, endorsed by the fictitious Ann Pillsbury. Duncan Hines, a real restaurant critic who published popular Duncan Hines travel guides, sold his name to Nebraska Consolidated Mills, which came up with its own cake mixes. (The Duncan Hines brand was later sold to Procter & Gamble in 1956, then to Aurora Foods of Columbus, Ohio, in 1998.) In 1951, a Duncan Hines cake mix known as the Three Star Special cornered the cake mix market, accounting for 48 percent of all cake mix purchases in just three weeks.

In the years that followed, General Mills, Pillsbury, and Duncan Hines reintroduced yellow cake and white cake mixes, and new angel food and chiffon cake mixes. In 1966, Bundt cake mixes hit the market, creating a demand for Bundt cake pans. And in 1977, pudding cake mixes became popular.

Since cake mixes are probably here to stay, perhaps now is a good time to learn to live with them, as Ann Byrn has so successfully done in *The Cake Mix Doctor*. The week her article on doctored-up cake mixes appeared in *The Tennessean* newspaper, she received over 500 doctored-up cake mix recipes. "Left untouched, cake mixes may be ho-hum," she admits. But a few ingredients such as citrus zest, bananas, apricot nectar, sherry, rum, and cream of coconut can take away the basic "cake-mix taste," which some people—Ann and myself included—find objectionable.

My favorite doctored-up cake mix recipes, culled from my own recipe box, include Glazed Rum and Pecan Cake (page 208) and Glazed Lemon Sheet Cake (page 209).

Double Chocolate Zucchini Cake

Anyone who has ever grown zucchini knows the true meaning of glut. Thrifty gardeners facing the inevitable have fought back with thousands of ingenious ways to use the vegetable, which seems to go from finger to submarine size overnight. This moist and delicious double chocolate cake is from Donna Vee Caraway, who bravely faces the yearly onslaught at her farm in Lamar, Missouri.

MAKES ONE 9 X 13-INCH CAKE; 8 SERVINGS

2$\frac{1}{2}$ cup sifted all-purpose flour

$\frac{1}{4}$ cup unsweetened cocoa powder

1 teaspoon baking soda

$\frac{1}{2}$ teaspoon baking powder

$\frac{1}{2}$ teaspoon ground cinnamon

$\frac{1}{2}$ cup (1 stick) unsalted butter at room temperature

$\frac{1}{2}$ cup vegetable oil

1 cup sugar

2 large eggs

$\frac{1}{2}$ cup buttermilk

1 teaspoon vanilla extract

2 cups finely grated zucchini (about 2 medium zucchini)

$\frac{1}{4}$ cup semisweet chocolate chips

1   Preheat the oven to 325 degrees F. Grease a 9 x 13-inch baking pan and set aside.

2   Sift the flour, cocoa, baking soda, baking powder, and cinnamon into a medium-size mixing bowl; set aside. With an electric mixer, cream together the butter, oil, and sugar in a large mixing bowl until light and fluffy. Beat in the eggs, buttermilk, and vanilla. Gradually beat in the dry ingredients, and continue beating until well blended. Stir in the zucchini and pour the batter into the prepared pan. Sprinkle the top evenly with the chocolate chips.

3   Bake the cake until a cake tester inserted in the center comes out clean, about 45 minutes. Let cool in the pan.

Iowa Foundation Sheet Cake

Light textured and almond scented, this Iowa cake can be transformed into diamond-shaped petit fours, or squares, triangles, or other geometric shapes of your choice. The combination of butter and shortening produces a light-textured white cake with good flavor. **MAKES ONE 9 X 13-INCH CAKE; 8 SERVINGS**

2 cups sifted cake flour

1 tablespoon baking powder

$\frac{1}{2}$ teaspoon salt

$\frac{1}{4}$ cup ($\frac{1}{2}$ stick) unsalted butter at room temperature

$\frac{1}{4}$ cup vegetable shortening

$1\frac{1}{4}$ cups sugar

1 teaspoon vanilla extract

$\frac{1}{2}$ teaspoon almond extract

$\frac{3}{4}$ cup milk

6 large egg whites

1 recipe Fondant Icing or Chocolate Ganache (recipes follow)

1 Preheat the oven to 375 degrees F. Grease a 9 x 13-inch pan, line it with parchment paper, grease the paper, and set aside.

2 Sift together the flour, baking powder, and salt in a medium-size mixing bowl. With an electric mixer, cream the butter and shortening together in a large mixing bowl. Beat in 1 cup of the sugar and the extracts and continue beating until the mixture is light and fluffy. Add the dry ingredients, a little at a time, alternating with the milk, and beating until smooth after each addition. Set aside.

3 Wash and dry the beaters well to remove any trace of cake batter. Beat together the egg whites and the remaining $\frac{1}{4}$ cup of sugar in a large mixing bowl until the egg whites hold soft peaks. With a rubber spatula, fold the egg whites into the cake batter until you can no longer see the egg whites. Pour the batter into the prepared pan.

4 Bake the cake until a cake tester inserted in the center comes out clean, 22 to 26 minutes. Let cool in the pan for 5 minutes, then invert the cake onto a wire rack and carefully remove the paper. Let cool completely before cutting or icing.

5 Cut the cake into the desired shapes and place on wire racks set over waxed or parchment paper. Pour or spoon the fondant icing or ganache over the entire surface of the cake. Add successive layers of icing, if you wish. When slightly warm, the icing is more transparent. It turns more opaque as it cools and hardens. Leave to set and slightly harden for 1 hour, then serve.

Fondant Icing

This is an easier version of traditional fondant, because it doesn't need to be worked and rolled on a marble slab. To create wonderful petit fours or small cakes, simply set the cut-up cake on wire racks over sheets of waxed or parchment paper and spread or pour the warm fondant over the cakes.

MAKES ABOUT 4 CUPS; ENOUGH TO FROST A 2-LAYER CAKE

4 cups granulated sugar

$1/4$ teaspoon cream of tartar

2 cups water

1 teaspoon vanilla extract

$1/2$ teaspoon almond extract

3 cups sifted confectioners' sugar, as needed

Food coloring (optional) for tinting

1 Combine the granulated sugar, cream of tartar, and water in a large heavy saucepan. Bring to a boil, stir to dissolve the sugar, and continue to cook until the mixture reaches the thin syrup stage, 226 degrees F on a candy thermometer.

2 Remove from the heat and let cool to lukewarm (about 110 degrees F). Whisk in the extracts and enough confectioners' sugar to reach a thickened but still pourable consistency. If necessary, process in a food processor to achieve a smooth icing. Add drops of food coloring, if desired.

Chocolate Ganache

As a warm sauce over ice cream or pound cake, or as a rich dark glaze poured over layer or loaf cakes, this ganache is simplicity itself. To glaze a cake, place waxed or parchment paper on a flat surface. Place a wire rack on top of the paper, and place the cake on the wire rack. Carefully pour the warm ganache over the cake, making sure the top and sides of the cake are covered. **MAKES ABOUT 1$1/2$ CUPS; ENOUGH TO COVER A SINGLE LAYER CAKE OR LOAF CAKE**

1 cup heavy cream

4 ounces best-quality semisweet or bittersweet chocolate, cut into pieces

1 teaspoon vanilla extract

In a small, heavy saucepan over medium heat, scald the cream until small bubbles form around the perimeter. *Do not let it boil*. Remove from the heat and whisk in the chocolate until it melts and the mixture is smooth and well blended. Whisk in the vanilla. This sauce keeps, covered, in the refrigerator indefinitely.

WHITE CHOCOLATE CARAMEL GANACHE Use white chocolate instead of dark and proceed with the recipe. Whisk in 1 cup Cajeta (page 485).

MINT CHOCOLATE GANACHE Whisk 1 teaspoon pure peppermint extract into the cream instead of the vanilla.

ORANGE CHOCOLATE GANACHE Substitute 1 teaspoon orange extract for the vanilla.

Seeing Stars

Stars and stripes debuted in 1776 on the first hand-sewn American flag, although historians now dispute the role of Betsy Ross. The first mention of "Stars and Stripes" came a year later in a resolution of the Continental Congress dated June 14, the day we now celebrate as Flag Day.

Ever since, American quilters have created many variations of the star pattern, stitched from thousands of fabric pieces. Of the 4,000 quilt patterns recorded in quilt historian Barbara Brackman's *Encyclopedia of Pieced Quilt Patterns*, almost 700 include stars. Sometimes star pattern names indicate places or regions where the quilt patterns were found: Kansas, Iowa, Chicago, Missouri, Michigan, Ohio, Texas, Arkansas, Oklahoma, Idaho, North Carolina, Mississippi, New Jersey, New Mexico, Prairie, Ozark, and Dakota.

Even today, the star pattern retains its special luster. Contemporary quilt designers like Linda Brannock, Gerry Kimmel-Carr, and Linda Patek favor rustic, asymmetrical stars in their folk art–influenced creations. "Starry, Starry Night," a Brannock-Patek design in muted colors, features a background of six-pointed stars and a foreground of appliquéd asymmetrical five-pointed stars along with snowmen, sledding children, a steepled church, and homespun houses. The Kimmel-Carr and Brannock design "Star Quilt" uses 25 blocks of asymmetrical stars, surrounded on three sides by a sawtooth border.

Find a star quilt pattern you like and use it as the inspiration for a unique presentation of brownies and bar cookies, sheet cakes, or petit fours. Simply cut the brownies, bars, or cakes into the shape called for on the pattern. You can find many star quilt pattern ideas from quilt pattern books in the library or in quilt shops.

Church Supper Pumpkin Sheet Cake

This is perhaps the quintessential American "take to a gathering" cake, mellow and spicy. My friend Pat Jordan, as a minister's wife, made this cake for meetings and socials at her husband's churches in Pennsylvania, Ohio, and Connecticut. This pumpkin cake is homey, comforting, flavorful, and has good keeping qualities. It's also easy to make and appeals to young and old alike. Cream cheese frosting is the only way to go with this one. **MAKES ONE 9 X 13-INCH CAKE; 8 SERVINGS**

CAKE

2 cups granulated sugar

2 cups all-purpose flour

$\frac{1}{2}$ teaspoon salt

2 teaspoons baking powder

2 teaspoons baking soda

2 teaspoons ground cinnamon

2 cups canned pumpkin

1 cup vegetable oil

4 large eggs, beaten

1 cup chopped walnuts (optional)

SWEET CREAM CHEESE FROSTING

One 1-pound box confectioners' sugar

One 8-ounce package cream cheese at room temperature

$\frac{1}{2}$ cup (1 stick) unsalted butter at room temperature

2 teaspoons vanilla extract

1   Preheat the oven to 325 degrees F. Grease the inside of a 9 x 13-inch baking pan and set aside.

2   To make the cake, in a medium-size mixing bowl, sift the granulated sugar, flour, salt, baking powder, baking soda, and cinnamon. With an electric mixer, beat the pumpkin and vegetable oil together in a large mixing bowl until smooth. Beat in the eggs, one at a time. Beat in the dry ingredients in thirds, beating well after each addition, and continue beating until you have a soft batter. Stir in the walnuts, if using. Spoon the batter into the prepared pan.

3   Bake the cake until a cake tester inserted in the center comes out clean, about 45 minutes. Let cool completely in the pan.

4   When the cake has cooled, make the frosting: With the electric mixer, beat together the confectioners' sugar, cream cheese, and butter in a large mixing bowl until smooth. Beat in the vanilla, and then spread the frosting evenly over the cooled cake.

No-Cholesterol Chocolate Cake

During the late 1980s Americans started to worry about their health. Newspapers began reporting almost daily on every new scientific study, no matter how narrow its scope or how limited its pool of subjects. First butter was bad, then sugar, then caffeine, and alcohol of any kind. No matter what the current study seems to say, it doesn't hurt to have a great-tasting cake like this one in your dessert file. Serve it dusted with confectioners' sugar and accompanied by fresh strawberries or raspberries in summer, or Cranberry-Chokecherry Conserve in winter.

MAKES ONE 9 X 13-INCH CAKE; 8 SERVINGS

3 cups all-purpose flour

2 cups minus 2 tablespoons granulated sugar

¼ cup plus 3 tablespoons unsweetened cocoa powder

2 teaspoons baking powder

1 teaspoon salt

½ teaspoon ground cinnamon

¾ cup canola or soybean oil

2 cups water

2 tablespoons distilled white or cider vinegar

1 tablespoon vanilla extract

Confectioners' sugar for dusting

Sliced strawberries, whole raspberries, or 1 recipe Cranberry-Chokecherry Conserve (page 7) for serving

1 Preheat the oven to 350 degrees F. Grease the inside of a 9 x 13-inch pan and set aside.

2 Sift together the flour, granulated sugar, cocoa powder, baking powder, salt, and cinnamon into a large mixing bowl. With an electric mixer, beat in the oil, water, vinegar, and vanilla and continue beating until well blended. Pour into the prepared pan.

3 Bake the cake until a cake tester inserted in the middle comes out clean, 35 to 40 minutes. Let cool completely in the pan. Sprinkle the top with confectioners' sugar and serve with sliced fresh berries or the conserve. (The cake may also be frosted, but this will add some cholesterol.)

Rootin' Tootin' Texas Chocolate Sheet Cake

Sometimes I just crave this homey, fudgy sheet cake. The "Texas" in the title means that it's a biggggg sheet cake. And the "rootin' tootin'" is for the exuberant flavor. I received a recipe for a Texas chocolate sheet cake from a minister's wife in the 1970s, and I dabbled with this recipe over the years until I got it just as I like it—with a hint of coffee to heighten the chocolate flavor; a moist, tender texture; and the perfect icing. This is the cake I would serve as a sweet ending to an all-American summer dinner of crispy fried chicken or burgers on the grill, homemade potato salad, and sliced garden tomatoes. Instead of a 17 x 12-inch jelly-roll pan, you could also use two 9 x 13-inch pans.

MAKES ONE 17 X 12-INCH SHEET CAKE; 12 SERVINGS

CAKE

2 cups granulated sugar

2 cups all-purpose flour

1/4 teaspoon salt

1 teaspoon baking soda

1/2 cup buttermilk

1 cup (2 sticks) unsalted butter

1/4 cup unsweetened cocoa powder

1 teaspoon ground cinnamon

1 cup freshly brewed dark roast coffee

2 large eggs

1 teaspoon vanilla extract

CHOCOLATE ICING

1/2 cup (1 stick) unsalted butter

1/4 cup plus 2 tablespoons milk

3 tablespoons unsweetened cocoa powder

One 1-pound box confectioners' sugar

1 teaspoon vanilla extract

1 Preheat the oven to 400 degrees F. Grease a 17 x 12-inch jelly-roll pan and set aside.

2 Sift together the granulated sugar, flour, and salt in a large mixing bowl. Stir the baking soda into the buttermilk. In a medium-size heavy saucepan over medium-high heat, combine the butter, cocoa, cinnamon, and coffee and bring to a boil. Pour the cocoa mixture over the flour mixture and stir to blend with a wooden spoon. In a small bowl, beat the eggs with a fork and add to the batter. Stir in the vanilla and buttermilk mixture and blend well. Spoon the batter into the prepared pan.

3 Bake the cake until it has pulled away from the sides of the pan and a cake tester inserted in the center comes out clean, 15 to 20 minutes.

4 About five minutes before the cake is done, make the icing: In a medium-size heavy saucepan over medium-high heat, combine the butter, milk, and cocoa and bring to a boil. Continue boiling for 2 minutes, then remove from the heat and whisk in the confectioners' sugar and vanilla. If necessary, transfer the icing to a food processor to get all the lumps out. Poke holes in the hot cake with a wooden skewer or fork and spread the icing over the cake. Let cool in the pan, then cut into squares to serve.

Kransekake (Norwegian Wedding Cake)

With a traditional crown as the cake topper, this towering cake adds a celebratory presence at birthdays, anniversaries, weddings, and other festive occasions. Decorated with fresh flowers for spring or holly and ivy for Christmas, *kransekake* looks more complicated to make than what it really is—basically an almond cookie dough piped onto circular patterns. After all the layers are baked, the cake is assembled by frosting each ring into place. Sharon Simington, who cooks on her family farm in Spencer, Iowa, makes this confection for special family occasions and holidays. She has made patterns for the 26 rings out of brown paper bags. The first circle is only 1¼ inches in diameter, and each circle gets ¼ inch larger in diameter, the 26th circle measuring 7¼ inches in diameter. Sharon stores her paper patterns in resealable plastic bags in the freezer until the next occasion. You can also buy *kransekake* molds at specialty gourmet stores. **MAKES ONE 25-LAYER CAKE; 24 SERVINGS**

CAKE

3 cups (6 sticks) unsalted butter at room temperature

10 ounces Marzipan (page 481) or store-bought almond paste

3 cups sifted confectioners' sugar

1 tablespoon almond extract

6 large egg yolks

7½ cups sifted all-purpose flour

ORANGE-ALMOND ICING

2 cups sifted confectioners' sugar

3 tablespoons unsalted butter at room temperature

¼ cup plus 3 tablespoons fresh orange juice

1 teaspoon grated orange zest

1 generous teaspoon almond extract

Fresh nontoxic greenery, flowers, or ribbons for decorating

1   Preheat the oven to 350 degrees F. Place the paper patterns or *kransekake* molds on lightly greased baking sheets and set aside.

2   To make the cake, with an electric mixer, cream together the butter, marzipan, confectioners' sugar, and almond extract in a large mixing bowl until smooth. Beat in the egg yolks all at once and blend well. Add the flour gradually, beating until the batter is very smooth.

3   Put the dough into a cookie press or a pastry bag. Press or pipe out the dough to make ½-inch-wide rings along the outer edge of each circular pattern or mold. Chill for 15 minutes, then bake until very lightly browned, about 15 minutes. Carefully remove the cake rings with the paper patterns from the baking sheets, and let the rings cool on the patterns. Repeat until all the rings have been baked.

4   To make the icing, with the electric mixer, cream the confectioners' sugar and butter together until light and fluffy. Beat in the orange juice and almond extract and continue beating until smooth.

5   To assemble the cake, spread a little of the icing on a platter to anchor it. Place the largest ring on top of the icing on the platter. Spread icing on the largest ring, then place the next largest ring on top of it. Continue the process of spreading the icing on a ring, then placing the next layer on the top of it, until all 25 layers have been placed. Decorate festively with fresh nontoxic greenery, flowers, or ribbons.

Greek Nut and Spice Cake

Also known as *karethopita*, this moist cake, cut into diamond shapes and served on frilly paper doilies, is an annual hit at Greek festivals around the country. Besides its heritage, though, this flavorful cake appeals to the modern cook because it's easy to make, stays moist, and is easily portable to the lake or a country home, where you and your guests can nibble it away during a three-day weekend. I love a diamond-shaped portion of this cake served with a few slices of fresh pear and rich, brewed coffee.

MAKES ONE 9 X 13-INCH CAKE; 8 SERVINGS

CAKE
1 tablespoon cider vinegar
1 cup milk
2 cups sifted all-purpose flour
1 tablespoon baking powder
$^1/_2$ teaspoon baking soda
1 teaspoon ground cinnamon
$^1/_2$ teaspoon ground cloves
1 cup vegetable oil

$1^1/_2$ cups sugar
3 large eggs
1 tablespoon vanilla extract
$1^1/_2$ cups chopped walnuts

SUGAR SYRUP
2 cups water
2 cups sugar
1 teaspoon fresh lemon juice

1   Preheat the oven to 350 degrees F. Grease a 13 x 9-inch baking pan and set aside.

2   To make the cake, in a small bowl, whisk the vinegar into the milk and set aside for several minutes to sour. In a medium-size mixing bowl, sift together the flour, baking powder, baking soda, cinnamon, and cloves. With an electric mixer, beat together the oil, sugar, and eggs in a large mixing bowl. Beat in the vanilla and sour milk. Add the dry ingredients gradually, beating well. Beat in the walnuts. Pour the batter into the prepared pan.

3   Bake the cake until a cake tester inserted in the center comes out clean, about 35 minutes. Allow the cake to cool completely in the pan while you make the syrup.

4   To make the syrup, bring the ingredients to a boil in a medium-size heavy saucepan over medium-high heat and boil for 5 minutes. With a wooden skewer, poke random holes halfway through the cake, then pour the hot syrup over the cake. Let the syrup soak into the cake, then cut it into squares or diamond shapes and serve.

Beekeeper's Honey Cake

According to Amy Bess Miller and Persis Fuller in *The Best of Shaker Cooking*, North Union Shaker Village was known for its "fine beehouse" and the honey that came from it. The honey that bees make has different characteristics every season, depending on what plants they visit. Fragrant with honey, moist with butter and sour cream, and flavorful with spices, this is a "keeping cake," or one that stays moist and fresh for weeks—if it lasts that long. Make it at least 2 days before you expect company; it needs that time in an airtight container to "ripen." I have adapted Miller's and Fuller's recipe to include more spices and some dried fruit and chopped nuts.

MAKES ONE 12-CUP BUNDT OR 10-INCH TUBE CAKE; 12 SERVINGS

2¾ cups all-purpose flour

1 teaspoon ground cloves

2 teaspoons ground cinnamon

¾ teaspoon freshly grated nutmeg

¾ teaspoon cream of tartar

¾ teaspoon baking soda

¼ teaspoon salt

6 tablespoons (¾ stick) unsalted butter, melted

1½ tablespoons canola or corn oil

3 tablespoons packed dark brown sugar

1 tablespoon granulated sugar

3 large eggs, beaten

1½ cups wildflower or other medium-colored honey

1 cup sour cream

1 cup dried cranberries or sour cherries

1 cup chopped walnuts or pecans

Sliced almonds for garnish

1   Preheat the oven to 350 degrees F. Grease and flour a 12-cup Bundt or 10-inch tube pan, tapping out the excess flour, and set aside.

2   Sift together the flour, spices, cream of tartar, baking soda, and salt in a medium-size mixing bowl. With an electric mixer, beat together the melted butter, oil, and both sugars in a large mixing bowl until well blended. Beat in the eggs, one at a time, then add the honey and sour cream all at once and beat until you have a smooth batter. Beat in the flour mixture, 1 cup at a time, beating well after each addition. Fold in the cranberries and walnuts. Pour the batter into the prepared cake pan.

3   Bake the cake until a cake tester inserted near the center comes out clean, 45 to 50 minutes. Invert the cake onto a wire rack and let cool. As soon as the cake is cool enough to handle, press the flaked almonds into the top. Place the cooled cake in an airtight container to ripen for 2 days before serving.

Altha's Cherry Pecan Fruitcake

I have never been much of a fruitcake lover. Most of them are too dark or too over-powered by the flavor of citron for my taste. But I love the lighter, pecan, candied cherry, and almond-flavored fruitcake that my former mother-in-law makes. I have been fortunate enough to be on Altha Fertig's holiday fruitcake gift list for many years, and I hope to stay in her good graces for many more. After Christmas, I use any excuse—the check wasn't in the mail, the weather is gloomy, my feet are cold—to leave my office in the afternoon for a pick-me-up. I head into the kitchen, where I cut a thin slice to have with a cup of tart and steaming rosehip and hibiscus tea. Suddenly, the world looks much better. By the time I've finished the whole fruitcake, months later, it's spring again. After years of my begging, Altha finally agreed to share her recipe.

MAKES ONE 12-CUP BUNDT OR 10-INCH TUBE CAKE; 24 SERVINGS

4 cups pecan halves (about 1 pound)

2 cups walnut halves (about 8 ounces)

2 cups candied red cherries (about 12 ounces)

2 cups candied pineapple (about 8 ounces)

1½ cups golden raisins

3 cups all-purpose flour

¾ teaspoon baking powder

1½ cups (3 sticks) unsalted butter at room temperature

1½ cups sugar

3 large eggs

One 1-ounce bottle or 2 tablespoons plus 1 teaspoon almond extract

1   Arrange an oven rack in the middle position and another rack in the lowest one. Preheat the oven to 300 degrees F. Grease and flour a 12-cup Bundt or 10-inch tube pan, tapping out the excess flour, and set aside.

2   In a large mixing bowl, combine the pecans, walnuts, cherries, pineapple, raisins, and 1 cup of the flour. Toss to blend and set aside.

3   Sift the remaining 2 cups of flour together with the baking powder into a medium-size mixing bowl. With an electric mixer, cream the butter and sugar together in a large mixing bowl until light and fluffy. Add the eggs, one at a time, beating well after each addition. Beat in the almond extract. Add the dry ingredients, about ⅔ cup at a time, beating well after each addition.

4   Fold the batter into the nut-and-fruit mixture with a rubber spatula or wooden spoon, mixing well to coat the nuts and fruit. Spoon the batter into the prepared pan and cover it tightly with aluminum foil. Place the pan on the middle rack of the oven. Fill a baking pan with hot water and place it underneath the Bundt pan on the bottom rack.

5   Bake the cake until it has pulled away from the pan, about 2½ hours. Remove the foil and continue baking until the top is slightly dry, about 5 minutes more. Remove the cake from the oven and let cool completely in the pan. Invert the cake onto a serving plate and serve. Store at room temperature, wrapped in aluminum foil, and enclosed in a resealable plastic storage bag. It will keep this way for months.

Sonoma Orange, Almond, and Olive Oil Cake

Before the Spanish missionaries came to California in the eighteenth century, it was a wilderness. Slowly, over time, parts of the California landscape have taken on a Mediterranean appearance. Orange and almond groves, vineyards, and orchards of pomegranate have adapted well to the West Coast climate. Now olive trees are taking root. In the late 1980s, Ridgely Evers and his wife, Colleen McGlynn, decided to try planting olive trees to make olive oil at their Olive Ridge Ranch in Sonoma. "There is a saying in Italy," Ridgely says philosophically. "You plant grapes for your children; you plant olives for your grandchildren." Their first true "vintage" of Da Vero olive oil, with a fruity character common to Lucchese olive oils in Tuscany, didn't happen until 1996. Ridgely expects their 4,500 olive trees to mature and produce up to 5,000 cases of "grand cru" olive oil. Da Vero olive oil is best used as a condiment, as its complex flavor breaks down during cooking, and it is expensive. But I couldn't resist including this recipe from Colleen, adapted for more mundane, yet fruity olive oils. A similar recipe, which includes whole boiled citrus fruit, almonds, and olive oil, appeared in *The New James Beard* years ago. **MAKES ONE 9-INCH CAKE; 8 TO 10 SERVINGS**

2 small oranges	4 large eggs
1 lemon	$1/2$ teaspoon salt
$1^1/_2$ cups sliced almonds	$1^1/_2$ cups granulated sugar
1 cup all-purpose flour	$2/_3$ cup good fruity olive oil
1 tablespoon baking powder	Confectioners' sugar for dusting

1 Preheat the oven to 350 degrees F. Place the oranges and lemon in a saucepan with water to cover and bring to a boil over medium-high heat. Reduce the heat to low and simmer the fruit until tender enough to be pierced by a fork, about 30 minutes. While the fruit is simmering, spread the almonds on a baking sheet and toast in the oven until golden brown, 10 to 15 minutes. Keep an eye on them and don't let them burn. Set the almonds aside, but keep the oven on. Drain and cool the citrus fruit until cool enough to handle.

2 Cut the lemon in half. Scoop out the pulp and seeds and discard, but reserve the lemon rind halves. Cut the oranges in half, but only discard the seeds. Place the lemon rind and orange halves in the food processor and chop fine.

3 Sift the flour and baking powder into a small mixing bowl. Combine the eggs and salt in a large mixing bowl and beat with an electric mixer until foamy. Beat in the granulated sugar, $1/_3$ cup at a time, beating well after each addition, then beat in the olive oil. Fold in the flour mixture. Stir in the almonds and chopped citrus fruit. Spoon or pour the batter into an ungreased 9-inch springform pan.

4 Bake the cake until the center has set and the cake is firm to the touch, about 40 to 50 minutes. Let cool completely in the pan on a wire rack. Release and remove the sides of the pan. Separate the cake from the bottom of the pan with a spatula or knife. Invert the cake onto the rack and re-invert, so that it is right side up, onto a serving plate. Dust the top with confectioners' sugar.

Blitz Torte

After I passed the bakery birthday cake phase of my childhood, this was the cake I wanted to celebrate with. In researching this book, I discovered that my mother had adapted the recipe from one in Ruth Berolzheimer's 1948 *The American Woman's Cook Book*. An Americanized version of a German torte, this cake tastes even better the second day. **MAKES ONE 9-INCH 2-LAYER CAKE; 8 SERVINGS**

CAKE

1 cup sifted cake flour

1 teaspoon baking powder

$\frac{1}{8}$ teaspoon salt

$\frac{1}{2}$ cup (1 stick) unsalted butter at room temperature

$\frac{1}{2}$ cup sugar

4 large egg yolks

1 teaspoon vanilla extract

3 tablespoons milk

TOPPING

$\frac{1}{2}$ cup chopped pecans

$\frac{3}{4}$ cup plus 1 tablespoon sugar

$\frac{1}{2}$ teaspoon ground cinnamon

4 large egg whites

FILLING

1 recipe Classic Pastry Cream (see page 163)

1 Preheat the oven to 350 degrees F. Grease and flour two 9-inch round cake pans, tapping out the excess flour, and set aside.

2 To make the cake, sift together the flour, baking powder, and salt into a small mixing bowl and set aside. With an electric mixer, cream the butter and sugar together in a large mixing bowl until light and fluffy. Add the egg yolks all at once and continue to beat for several minutes, until the mixture is pale. Beat in the vanilla, milk, and the sifted dry ingredients. Divide the mixture evenly between the prepared pans.

3 To make the topping, combine the pecans, 1 tablespoon of sugar, and the cinnamon in a small bowl. Wash and dry the beaters well to remove any trace of the batter. Whip the egg whites in a large mixing bowl until they form stiff peaks. Add the remaining $\frac{3}{4}$ cup of the sugar gradually and beat until the meringue is glossy. Spread half the meringue over the cake batter in each pan, and sprinkle the pecan mixture evenly over the meringue.

4 Bake the layers until a cake tester inserted in the center comes out clean, about 30 minutes. Let cool completely in the pans on wire racks.

5 To assemble the cake, invert the cake layers onto the wire racks and then immediately turn the layers right side up. Place one layer on a cake plate. Spread the pastry cream over it, then place the second layer on top. Cover with plastic wrap until ready to serve.

Chocolate Nut Torte

When George Kendall made his way across the prairie from St. Louis to Santa Fe, he kept a journal, which he eventually published in 1844. In what is now western Missouri, he noted, "The land lies in swells; the prairies are small . . . the crabapple, paw-paw, and persimmon are abundant, as also the hazel, pecan, and grape." Some of those wild groves of nut trees still stand, but now they're joined by orchards of pecan, walnut, butternut, and black walnut. The Pacific Northwest is also rich in wild nut groves and tamed orchards, where filbert, or hazelnut, trees are found. The hazelnuts add a wonderful flavor to this rich and elegant nut torte, adapted from a recipe by chef and restaurateur John Ash of California. Serve it with whipped cream, if you wish.

MAKES ONE 8-INCH TORTE; 8 SERVINGS

CRUST

$\frac{1}{2}$ cup hazelnuts

$\frac{1}{2}$ cup pecans

$3\frac{1}{2}$ tablespoons cake flour

3 tablespoons granulated sugar

6 tablespoons ($\frac{3}{4}$ stick) unsalted butter at room temperature

FILLING

1 cup plus $2\frac{1}{2}$ tablespoons packed light brown sugar

2 large eggs plus 1 large egg yolk

$\frac{1}{2}$ teaspoon baking powder

$\frac{1}{2}$ cup all-purpose flour

1 cup coarsely chopped walnuts

1 cup semisweet chocolate chips

Confectioners' sugar for dusting

1   Preheat the oven to 350 degrees F.

2   To make the crust, grind the hazelnuts and pecans together in a food processor to a medium crumb. In a large mixing bowl, mix together the ground nuts, cake flour, granulated sugar, and softened butter with a wooden spoon until the mixture is well blended but crumbly. Press this mixture into the bottom and halfway up the sides of an 8-inch springform or cake pan. Set aside.

3   To make the filling, with an electric mixer, beat together the brown sugar, whole eggs, egg yolk, baking powder, and all-purpose flour in a large mixing bowl. With a rubber spatula, fold in the walnuts and chocolate. Pour the filling into the prepared crust.

4   Bake the torte until a cake tester inserted in the center comes out clean, 50 to 55 minutes. Let cool

in the pan for 20 minutes. Release and remove the sides of the pan, and if you wish, transfer to a serving plate. Dust with confectioners' sugar and serve.

Black Kettle Double Fudge Torte

The Black Kettle Restaurant in Milwaukee, Wisconsin, is famous for this torte, which combines a German-style, thin-layered cake with a sinful amount of chocolate, an American trademark. The mayonnaise in the cake batter adds moistness.

MAKES ONE 4-LAYER 9-INCH CAKE; 12 SERVINGS

TORTE

2 cups all-purpose flour

$^2\!/_3$ cup unsweetened cocoa powder

$^1\!/_4$ teaspoon baking powder

1 teaspoon baking soda

$^1\!/_2$ teaspoon salt

3 large eggs

1$^2\!/_3$ cups granulated sugar

1$^1\!/_2$ teaspoons vanilla extract

1 cup good-quality mayonnaise

1$^1\!/_3$ cups water

CREAMY COCOA FROSTING

1$^1\!/_2$ cups heavy cream

One 8-ounce package cream cheese at room temperature

1 cup confectioners' sugar

$^1\!/_4$ cup unsweetened cocoa powder

1 teaspoon vanilla extract

1 recipe Classic Hot Fudge Sauce (see page 427) or 2 cups fudge ice-cream topping

1   Preheat the oven to 350 degrees F. Grease and flour two 9-inch round cake pans, tapping out the excess flour, and set aside.

2   To make the torte, in a medium-size mixing bowl, sift together the flour, cocoa, baking powder, baking soda, and salt. With electric mixer, beat the eggs lightly on low speed in a large mixing bowl, then slowly add the granulated sugar while mixing. Raise the speed to medium and beat until the mixture increases in volume and turns a pale yellow, about 5 minutes. Add the vanilla and mayonnaise and beat until well combined. On low speed, beat in the sifted flour mixture, alternating with the water and beating well after each addition. Mix 2 minutes longer on medium speed. Divide the batter evenly between the prepared pans.

3   Bake the layers until the center are firm, about 30 minutes. Let cool in the pans on wire racks for

10 minutes. Invert the cake layers onto the wire racks, then immediately turn right side up. Let cool completely before frosting.

4   Wash and dry the beaters well. To make the frosting, with the mixer, whip the cream in a medium-size mixing bowl until it holds stiff peaks. Beat the cream cheese, confectioners' sugar, cocoa, and vanilla in a large mixing bowl until smooth. Fold in the whipped cream a little at a time.

5   To assemble the torte, cut each cake layer in half horizontally with a serrated knife to create four layers. Put one layer on a cake stand or plate and spread with 1 cup of the hot fudge sauce. Place a second layer over that and spread with one quarter of the frosting. Top with the third layer and spread with the remaining 1 cup of hot fudge sauce. Add the fourth layer and spread the top and sides of the cake with the remaining frosting. Refrigerate until ready to serve.

Swedish Apple Torte with Vanilla Cloud Sauce

Whenever we celebrate Christmas at my sister Julie Fox's house, we know that this moist and delicious apple cake, adapted from a recipe by the late Adelma Grenier Simmons of Connecticut, will be on the menu. During the 1970s, Simmons was partially responsible for the resurgence of interest in herb gardening. Both my sister and I vividly remember the day we spent at Caprilands, Simmons' home and garden. Although she was known for her talents as a gardener and herbalist, rather than a cook, Simmons knew a good recipe when she saw one. This torte is simple to prepare and it's wonderful even without the sauce. If I have planned ahead, I make this cake with home-made toasted Wheat Country Zwieback (*Prairie Home Cooking*, page 345), which adds to the goodness. Layers of homemade applesauce and toasted buttered zwieback crumbs mark this dessert as another descendant of the European torte. The sauce is a northern European pouring custard, or crème anglaise, folded into whipped cream—ultra deca-dence with a cloud-like appearance. **MAKES ONE 10-INCH TORTE; 12 SERVINGS**

CAKE

4 cups sliced McIntosh or Red Delicious apples,
with some of the skin still on

1 cup sugar

$\frac{1}{2}$ cup (1 stick) unsalted butter

Two 6-ounce packages zwieback, crumbed in a
food processor, or homemade zwieback crumbs
(about 5 cups)

VANILLA CLOUD SAUCE

4 cups heavy cream

6 large egg yolks, beaten

$\frac{1}{4}$ cup plus 1 tablespoon sugar

$\frac{1}{2}$ vanilla bean, sliced lengthwise, or 1 tablespoon
plus 1 teaspoon vanilla extract

1 Preheat the oven to 350 degrees F. Grease the inside of a round 2-quart baking or soufflé dish and set aside.

2 To make the cake, in a large saucepan, combine the apples and sugar and cook over medium heat until the apples are softened, about 20 minutes. Meanwhile, melt the butter in a large skillet over medium heat and cook the zwieback crumbs until golden brown, stirring a few times.

3 Transfer the apple mixture to a blender or food processor and process until smooth; you should have about 3 cups of applesauce. Sprinkle the bottom and sides of the prepared dish with 1 cup of the toasted zwieback crumbs. Pour 1 cup of the applesauce into the dish and top with 1 generous cup of crumbs. Pour in another cup of applesauce and top with another generous cup of crumbs. Layer a third time in the same way, sprinkling all the remaining crumbs on top.

4 Bake the cake until it has pulled away from the sides of the dish, 35 to 40 minutes. Let cool in the dish on a wire rack. (The cake may be baked a day ahead and stored at room temperature.)

5 To make the sauce, warm 2 cups of the cream until hot and set aside. With an electric mixer, beat the remaining 2 cups of cream in a medium-size bowl and set aside. Whisk the egg yolks and sugar together in the top of a double boiler over simmering water. If using a vanilla bean, add this to the egg mixture. Stir in the hot cream and keep whisking until the mixture thickens, about 8 minutes. Remove from the heat; if using vanilla extract, whisk it into the sauce now. Let the sauce cool to room temperature, stirring occasionally. When ready to serve, remove the vanilla bean, fold the cooled sauce into the whipped cream and pour into a sauceboat.

6 When ready to serve, unmold the cake onto a serving plate. Serve each slice of cake topped with a small ladleful of sauce.

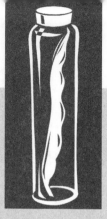

Vanilla

Vanilla planifolia, or vanilla, is the seed pod of a vining tropical orchid native to Mexico and was used by the Aztecs as a flavoring for their chocolate brews. Brought from Mexico to Spain by Hernando de Cortez in the late 1500s, vanilla slowly made its way into the kitchens of wealthy Europeans. Thomas Jefferson first encountered vanilla during his sojourn in France during the late eighteenth century. In 1791, he wrote to William Short, the American chargé d'affaires in Paris, asking him to send 50 pods of vanilla so Jefferson could introduce this flavoring to his friends at Monticello. In 1801, Jefferson became President, and his Monticello Vanilla-Flecked Ice Cream became legendary. Elizabeth Ellicott Lea's *A Quaker Woman's Cookbook*, first published in 1845, features desserts flavored mostly with rosewater, lemons, French and rose-flavored brandy, and nutmeg. Homemade "tincture of vanilla" (vanilla beans steeped in brandy) was used only in ice cream and blancmange.

By 1879, Marion Cabell Tyree, compiler of *Housekeeping in Old Virginia*, tried to steer her readers away from the readily available vanilla extract when making ice cream: "Instead of flavoring with extract of vanilla, it is much better to boil a vanilla bean in the milk, or to boil some peach leaves tied up in a piece of muslin (six to eight leaves to a quart of milk) or to flavor with burnt sugar." A century later, vanilla was so common that "basic vanilla" was a computer term, indicating generic equipment. In the late 1990s, vanilla was rediscovered as a flavoring in savory sauces and as an aromatic in perfumes and aromatherapy. Chefs continue to explore the uses of varietal vanilla—the distinct flavors of beans from Tahiti, Madagascar, and Bourbon.

Lingonberry Torte

Northern European tortes are flavorful cakes with a hint of texture from bread crumbs, ground nuts, or, in this case, dry farina cereal. Adapted from a recipe by Finnish-born caterer Soile Anderson of St. Paul, Minnesota, this buttery, vanilla-scented cake has a slightly chewy, cookie-like texture. Soile scatters lingonberries over the top of the batter before baking. I prefer to top the cake with a tart, ruby-colored glaze of lingonberry preserves and rosettes of stabilized whipped cream; it looks like a dessert out of a Parisian *patisserie* window. **MAKES ONE 8-INCH CAKE; 8 SERVINGS**

½ cup dry farina or Cream of Wheat cereal

1 cup all-purpose flour

1¼ teaspoons baking powder

¾ cup (1½ sticks) unsalted butter at room temperature

¾ cup sugar

1 large egg

1 tablespoon vanilla extract

1 cup lingonberry preserves or red currant jelly

1 recipe Stabilized Whipped Cream (recipe follows)

1   Preheat the oven to 350 degrees F. Grease and flour an 8-inch round cake pan, tapping out the excess flour, and set aside.

2   In a small mixing bowl, sift together the farina, flour, and baking powder. With an electric mixer, cream the butter and sugar together in a large mixing bowl until light and fluffy. Add the egg and vanilla and beat until smooth. Add the dry ingredients, ½ cup at a time, beating well after each addition, and continue beating until you have a smooth, stiff batter. Spoon the batter into the prepared pan.

3   Bake the cake until a cake tester inserted in the center comes out clean, about 20 minutes. Let cool in the pan on a wire rack for 5 minutes. Invert the cake onto the wire rack, then immediately turn right side up. Let cool completely.

4   Place the cake on a serving plate. Spoon the lingonberry preserves into a small glass bowl and microwave on HIGH until very warm, about 1 minute. Spread the preserves over the cake. Place a rosette tip on the end of a piping bag and fill the bag with the whipped cream. Pipe rosettes along the perimeter of the cake and pipe a large rosette in the center. Serve chilled or at room temperature.

Stabilized Whipped Cream

When you want to make a fancy dessert ahead of time, but worry that the whipped cream will fall, the answer is to stabilize it with gelatin. For every cup of heavy cream, use 1 teaspoon of powdered unflavored gelatin.

1 teaspoon unflavored gelatin

¼ cup warm water

1 cup heavy cream

1   Soften the gelatin in a small bowl with the warm water. Set the small bowl in a larger one containing enough hot water to come halfway up the sides of the smaller bowl. Set aside for several minutes until the gelatin is soaked through and has turned a translucent beige.

2 Pour the cream into a medium-size bowl. Pour the softened gelatin through a sieve into the heavy cream. With an electric mixer, whip the cream until it holds stiff peaks. Cover with plastic wrap and chill for 30 minutes. Now the whipped cream is ready to garnish your dessert.

Fresh Pear Torta

Waves of Italian immigration in the late nineteenth and early twentieth centuries brought families from Sicily and Calabria to this country, and with them, wonderful fresh fruit desserts like this one. Now it is my favorite pear dessert—easy, portable, and delicately delicious. The little bit of lemon zest helps bring out the fresh pear flavor.

MAKES ONE 9-INCH CAKE; 8 SERVINGS

$1/2$ cup (1 stick) plus 1 tablespoon (9 tablespoons) unsalted butter, melted

5 or 6 ripe but firm pears, such as Kieffer or Bartlett, peeled, cored, and thinly sliced

$2/3$ cup all-purpose flour

$1/2$ teaspoon baking powder

$1/2$ teaspoon salt

1 cup granulated sugar

2 large eggs plus 1 large egg yolk

1 teaspoon vanilla extract

$1/2$ teaspoon grated lemon zest

Confectioners' sugar for dusting (optional)

1 Preheat the oven to 375 degrees F. Grease and flour a 9-inch round cake pan with 2-inch sides, tapping out the excess flour, and set aside.

2 Pour 1 tablespoon of the melted butter into a large skillet over medium heat and cook the pears until softened, about 10 minutes. Set aside.

3 Sift together the flour, baking powder, salt, and granulated sugar into a large mixing bowl. In a small mixing bowl, whisk together the remaining $1/2$ cup of melted butter, the whole eggs, egg yolk, vanilla, and lemon zest. With a wooden spoon, stir the mixture into the dry ingredients and blend until smooth. With a rubber spatula, fold in the sautéed pears and their juices. Spoon the batter into the prepared pan and smooth the top with the spatula.

4 Bake the cake until the top is browned and a cake tester inserted in the center comes out clean, 30 to 35 minutes. Let cool completely in the pan. Transfer to a cake plate and dust with confectioners' sugar, if desired.

Moravian Sugar Cake

Both European and American cakes in the seventeenth and early eighteenth centuries were most likely raised with yeast. Privileged households with professional cooks began to use eggs to raise cakes by the mid 1700s, but these had to be beaten by hand and required a cook with muscles and stamina. The first baking powder, a mixture of an alkali and an acid to make carbon dioxide, was developed in England in 1835 and developed in America in 1842, but it was not available to home cooks until after 1850. This recipe is in the old yeast-raised cake tradition, brought to Salem, North Carolina, by the Moravians, a Protestant sect from Germany. This yeast cake is similar to a traditional *galette au sucre*, made with brioche dough, from the Champagne region of France, near the German border. Moravian Sugar Cake gets its moist texture from mashed potatoes, and you don't have to knead it. It is delicious served warm as a brunch pastry or as a dessert with fresh strawberries or peaches and cream. It is better to use freshly made, warm mashed potatoes for a more pliable dough. The recipe makes two cakes. You can serve one cake, and wrap and freeze the other after it has baked. It will keep, frozen, for up to 3 months. The cake requires two rising times of several hours each.

MAKES TWO 13 X 9-INCH CAKES; 24 SERVINGS

CAKE

18 ounces baking potatoes, peeled and cut into quarters

¾ cup (1½ sticks) unsalted butter, at room temperature

1 cup minus 1 tablespoon granulated sugar

2 large eggs, beaten

5 to 7 cups all-purpose flour, as needed

One ¼-ounce package or 2¼ teaspoons instant or bread machine yeast

TOPPING

2 tablespoons unsalted butter, cut into small pieces

1 cup packed dark brown sugar

1 teaspoon ground cinnamon

1 teaspoon freshly grated nutmeg

1 cup heavy cream

1   To make the cake, put the potatoes in a medium-size saucepan with enough water to cover and bring to a boil. Continue to boil until tender, about 15 minutes. Drain, reserving 1¼ cups of the potato water. Mash the potatoes in the pan. Measure 1 cup of mashed potatoes and place in the bowl of an electric stand mixer.

2 Using the balloon whisk attachment, cream the potatoes, butter, and granulated sugar together until smooth. Beat in the eggs and reserved potato water. Beat in 5 cups of the flour, 1 cup at a time, beating well after each addition. Add as much of the remaining flour as needed to achieve a soft, sticky dough. Beat in the yeast. Cover the bowl with plastic wrap and set aside to rise in a warm place, about 85 degrees F, until doubled in bulk, 2 to 3 hours.

3 Grease two 9 x 13-inch pans and set aside.

4 Punch down the dough, divide in half on a floured work surface, and pat each half in a prepared pan. Cover again with plastic wrap and let rise in a warm place until doubled in bulk again, 1 to 2 hours.

5 Preheat the oven to 400 degrees F. To make the topping, with a sharp knife, punch slits in the top of the dough and insert a piece of butter into each one. In a small mixing bowl, combine the brown sugar, cinnamon, and nutmeg and sprinkle half the mixture over each cake. Drizzle each cake with half of the cream.

6 Bake the cakes until puffed and browned and a cake tester inserted in the center comes out clean, 20 to 25 minutes. Let cool in the pans. Serve the cake warm or at room temperature. (This cake also reheats well.)

Hartford Election Cake

A yeast-risen sweet cake heavy with dried fruit and spices, Hartford Election Cake originated from a type of Lincolnshire plum bread found in northeastern England. In a journal entry dated April 17, 1631, founding Puritan father John Winthrop noted the "election cake" and "election beer" served at Election Day festivities that month, when Massachusetts Bay Company members met to elect their officers. By the early 1800s, election cakes were made and sold near Hartford, Connecticut. (Gingerbread, both the soft and hard kinds, was sold and consumed for the second day of civil obligation—Training Day, when citizens gathered to drill with weapons.) By 1949, Cora, Rose, and Bob Brown related in their *America Cooks* cookbook that election cake "ended the veal dinner that was as essential to this day as were turkey and pumpkin pie for Thanksgiving." The Browns also related that election cake was sometimes called "Raised Loaf Cake." Today, Hartford Election Cake seems like more of a coffee cake or cinnamon raisin bread to us, like the similarly old Moravian Sugar Cake (page 233). This recipe is adapted from one by Lydia Maria Child in the 1833 edition of *The American Frugal Housewife*. Her version makes a sort of dimpled flat coffee cake, but I've adapted it to produce an easier loaf form. It is still delicious, toasted and drizzled with a little cream and served with sautéed apples or pears—a sweet bite of history.

MAKES ONE 9 X 5-INCH LOAF CAKE; 8 SERVINGS

¼ cup lukewarm water

Two ¼-ounce packages or 1½ tablespoons dry yeast

¾ cup milk, heated until lukewarm

3 cups all-purpose flour, plus extra for kneading and forming cake

6 tablespoons (¾ stick) unsalted butter, melted and cooled

1 large egg

½ cup sugar

1 teaspoon freshly grated nutmeg

1 teaspoon ground cinnamon

1 teaspoon salt

1 cup dried currants

1 Grease a 9 x 5-inch loaf pan and set aside.

2 Pour the water into a large mixing bowl. Sprinkle the yeast over the top and set aside until it dissolves, about 3 minutes. Stir in the warm milk, then beat in 1½ cups of the flour, making a stiff batter. Cover the bowl with plastic wrap and set aside in a warm place for 30 minutes, but no longer.

3 Beat the butter, egg, sugar, spices, and salt into the yeast mixture. Then work in the remaining 1½ cups flour, making a soft, rough dough. Cover the bowl with plastic wrap and set aside for 15 to 30 minutes to rest.

4 Knead the dough until smooth on a lightly floured work surface, 5 to 10 minutes. It will be very soft and sticky. Gradually add more flour as necessary, a few tablespoons at a time, to form a smooth dough. Knead in the currants. Form the dough into a loaf, pinching any seams together with your fingers, and place the dough in the prepared loaf pan. Cover with plastic wrap and let rise in a warm place until slightly more than doubled, 1½ to 2 hours.

5 Preheat the oven to 375 degrees F. Bake the cake until puffed and richly browned, about 40 minutes. The cake is done when an instant-read thermometer inserted in the center registers at least 190 degrees F. Let the cake rest in the pan on a wire rack for 3 minutes. Invert the cake onto the wire rack, then immediately turn right side up. Serve warm, toasted, or at room temperature.

Rustic Brioche Galettes with Apricots and Almonds

One hot July afternoon, I did a book signing with Karen Adler, my co-author of *Fish & Shellfish, Grilled & Smoked* (Harvard Common Press, 2002), at Trotters to Go in Chicago. I wanted to move to Chicago when I saw and tasted some of the wonderful take-out food that this shop offers. Besides doing a great job with the grilled shellfish we passed out to customers as a sample from our book, Charlie Trotter's staff also did a fabulous job with individual galettes—small round dessert pizzas made with brioche dough and topped with fruits of all kinds. When I got home, I hurried into the kitchen to try my own version of their brioche galettes, and here is one, plus a variation. Turbinado sugar adds to the flavor and the rustic effect.

MAKES 1 DOZEN 6-INCH GALETTES; 12 SERVINGS

24 apricots, cut in half and pitted, or 48 canned apricot halves

1 cup white, dark, or spiced rum

1 recipe Buttery Brioche Dough (see page 32), made through step 3

2 large egg yolks

1 teaspoon water

$1/4$ cup heavy cream

$1/2$ cup turbinado sugar, "raw sugar," or organic sugar crystals

$1/2$ cup slivered almonds

1   Arrange the oven racks in the upper part of the oven. Preheat the oven to its lowest setting. Coat two baking sheets and two small pie pans with cooking spray or line with parchment paper and set aside. Combine the apricots and rum in a large mixing bowl and toss to blend. Let macerate for 30 minutes at room temperature, then drain. Reserve the rum for another use.

2   Divide the brioche dough into 12 equal portions on a lightly floured work surface. Press each portion into a disk, then roll out into a 6-inch circle. (The circles don't have to be perfect, just close enough.) Brush off any excess flour and place 10 circles on a prepared baking sheet and 2 in the pie pans. Place the dough circles in the oven. (You will have to wedge in the two pie pans, but this works. Shut the oven door, turn off the oven, and let the brioche rise for 30 minutes.

3   Whisk the egg yolks and water together in a small mixing bowl. Remove the galettes from the oven and brush each one with the egg wash. Place four apricot halves, cut side down, in the center of each galette, leaving a 1-inch perimeter around the circle. Brush each apricot with heavy cream, sprinkle with sugar, and then with almonds.

4   Bake the brioche until puffed and browned, 15 to 20 minutes. Serve warm or at room temperature with whipped cream or Wildflower Honey Cream (see page 348).

> **BROWN BUTTER NECTARINE GALETTES** Halve, pit, and cut 6 nectarines into $\frac{1}{2}$-inch slices, leaving on the peel. Melt $\frac{1}{2}$ cup (1 stick) unsalted butter in a medium-size skillet over medium-high heat until the butter turns light brown, about 5 minutes. Gently toss the nectarine slices in the butter to coat, then remove from the heat. Form the galettes as directed and let them rise for 30 minutes. Arrange the nectarine slices in a circular pattern on each galette, leaving a 1-inch perimeter. Brush the perimeter with the egg wash. Sprinkle each galette with about 1 tablespoon of turbinado sugar and chopped pistachios. Bake as directed above.

Individual Strawberry Charlottes

Making a great dessert can be as simple as putting a few well-made pieces together—in this case, slices of Buttery Brioche or a pound cake, fresh strawberries, sugar, and cream. **MAKES 12 INDIVIDUAL CHARLOTTES**

1 quart fresh strawberries

$\frac{1}{2}$ cup sugar

1 loaf Buttery Brioche (see page 32) or 1 recipe Luscious Cream Cheese Pound Cake (page 203)

2 cups heavy cream

1 recipe Vanilla Cloud Sauce (see page 229) or Classic Crème Anglaise (page 369)

Finely chopped strawberries for garnish

Finely chopped pistachios for garnish

1   Rinse the strawberries. Choose the 6 most perfect berries, cut them in half, and set aside. Hull the rest. Combine the hulled strawberries and sugar in a medium-size mixing bowl and mash the strawberries until they are in very small pieces. Set aside for 15 minutes to allow the strawberries to release their juices.

2   Line the cups of a 12-cup muffin or cupcake pan with $\frac{1}{4}$-inch-thick slices of brioche, cut to fit. Set aside.

3   With an electric mixer, whip the cream in a medium-size mixing bowl until it holds stiff peaks. Fold in the mashed strawberries with a rubber spatula until well blended. Spoon the strawberry mixture into each lined muffin or cupcake cup. Cover with plastic wrap and refrigerate for 1 hour.

4   Gently remove each charlotte from the pan, using a knife to loosen it. To serve, spoon a little Vanilla Cloud Sauce or Classic Crème Anglaise on each dessert plate. Center a charlotte on top and garnish with half of a reserved whole strawberry. Garnish the perimeter of the plate at intervals with little mounds of chopped strawberry and pistachio.

Chocolate Banana Loaf Cake with Caramel Sauce

In the 1990s, pastry chefs returned to their homey dessert roots, proudly serving individual crumbles and cobblers to restaurant patrons. They also used slices of loaf cakes or quick breads like this one, instead of pound cake, as platforms for flights of sweet fancy. I love the combination of flavors as well as the homemade comfort of this dessert, adapted from one served at Boudro's in San Antonio. For a trio of dessert delights, serve a slice of this loaf cake toasted and topped with a scoop of Toffee-Banana Ice Cream and a drizzle of warm caramel. Make one loaf for dessert and freeze the other. The sauce can be made a week ahead. For an even more chocolaty version, fold in 1 cup of chocolate chips right before baking.

MAKES TWO 9 X 5-INCH LOAF CAKES; 16 SERVINGS

LOAF CAKE

1 teaspoon baking soda

⅓ cup buttermilk

2 cups sifted all-purpose flour

1 teaspoon ground cinnamon

½ teaspoon freshly grated nutmeg

1 teaspoon salt

½ cup (1 stick) unsalted butter at room temperature

1 cup granulated sugar

½ cup packed brown sugar

2 large eggs

4 ripe bananas mashed

2 teaspoons vanilla extract

1 tablespoon unsweetened cocoa powder

1 cup chopped toasted pecans (see page 181), plus pecan halves to garnish

½ cup raisins or dried cherries, finely chopped

BUTTERY CARAMEL SAUCE

1½ cups granulated sugar

½ cup water

2 cups heavy cream

½ cup (1 stick) unsalted butter

1 recipe Toffee-Banana Ice Cream (page 439)

1   Preheat the oven to 375 degrees F. Grease and flour two 9 x 5-inch loaf pans, tapping out the excess, and set aside.

2 To make the cake, stir the baking soda into the buttermilk. Sift the flour, cinnamon, nutmeg, and salt into a medium-size mixing bowl. With an electric mixer, cream together the butter and both sugars in a large mixing bowl until light and fluffy. Add the eggs, beating until well blended. With a wooden spoon, stir in the mashed bananas, then the buttermilk mixture, the flour mixture, vanilla, cocoa, pecans, and raisins, and continue stirring until well blended.

3 Bake the loaves until a cake tester inserted in the center comes out clean, 40 to 45 minutes. Let cool in the pans on wire racks for 10 minutes. Invert the cakes onto the wire racks, then immediately turn right side up. Let cool completely.

4 Meanwhile, make the caramel sauce: Combine the granulated sugar and water in a medium-size heavy saucepan over medium-high heat. Bring to a boil and continue boiling until the mixture turns golden brown, 15 to 20 minutes. Wear an oven mitt to pour the cream into the sauce because the mixture may spatter. Reduce the heat to low and cook, whisking, until the mixture thickens, about 10 minutes. Whisk in the butter until melted, then remove the sauce from the heat. It can be made a week ahead of time and stored, covered, in the refrigerator.

5 To serve, cut slices of loaf cake and toast in the oven on a baking tray or in a toaster. Top each slice with a scoop of ice cream and a drizzle of warm caramel sauce. Garnish with pecan halves.

Cornish Saffron Loaf Cake

Mineral Point, a historic mining community surrounded by contour-ploughed cornfields, is the place where Wisconsin began. When Wisconsin was still part of Michigan Territory, British immigrants from the mining areas of West Cornwall—Camborne, Redruth, St. Just, and other small villages—left the depleted mines of the Old Country in 1827 to try their luck in the New World. When the miners did well enough to send for their families, Cornish saffron cake entered our culinary melting pot. Still available at local bake shops and restaurants, golden Cornish saffron cake has come a long way. Traders in Cornish tin, who traveled to and from the Mediterranean, were fond of saffron—the tiny orange stamens of the culinary crocus. Soon saffron slipped into the repertoire of Cornish cooking, largely in breads and cakes, and from there traveled to Wisconsin. Saffron imparts a deep, subtle flavor and golden color. You'll need to soak the saffron threads in water overnight before beginning the recipe.

MAKES ONE 9 X 5-INCH LOAF CAKE; 8 SERVINGS

⅛ teaspoon saffron threads

¾ cup boiling water

1½ cups all-purpose flour

2 teaspoons baking powder

¼ teaspoon salt

1½ cups raisins or dried Zante currants, soaked in boiling water to cover for 15 minutes and drained

½ cup (1 stick) unsalted butter at room temperature

1½ cups sugar

2 large eggs

1 teaspoon grated lemon zest or candied lemon peel

Whipped cream for garnish

1   Steep the saffron overnight in the ¾ cup of boiling water.

2   Preheat the oven to 325 degrees F. Grease and flour an 8½ x 4½- or 9 x 5-inch loaf pan, tapping out the excess, and set aside.

3   In a small mixing bowl, sift together the flour, baking powder, and salt. Dredge the raisins in the flour mixture. With an electric mixer, cream together the butter, sugar, eggs, and lemon zest in a large mixing bowl. Add the raisins-and-flour mixture gradually, alternating with the saffron and water, and beating well after each addition. Pour the batter into the prepared pan.

4   Bake the loaf until a cake tester inserted in the center comes out clean, about 1 hour. Let the cake cool completely in the pan, then transfer to a cake plate. Slice and serve with a dollop of whipped cream.

When Is My Cake Done?

Generally, cakes are done when the sides have pulled away from the pan, the center is somewhat firm, the color is golden, and a cake tester inserted in the middle comes out clean. A cake tester, while very handy, does not always work.

The Tunnel of Fudge Cake (page 206), for example, has that moist ribbon of fudge in the middle part of the cake, so using a cake tester won't be accurate—it will hit that fudgy layer and not come out of the cake clean. For this cake and other moist cakes and cheesecakes, the best indication of doneness is when the sides have pulled away from the pan and the center is somewhat firm.

Angel, sponge, or chiffon cakes, which are light and airy, and tortes made with ground nuts or crumbs, are done when the top springs back when lightly touched.

Each cake recipe has its own suggested test for doneness, so you'll know which method is best. The first time you make a cake recipe, start checking about 15 minutes before you expect the cake to be done. That way, if your oven is calibrated differently, your cake won't be overdone.

Fresh Pumpkin Cake

Although pumpkins are a New World vegetable, they had to travel to Europe, like the potato, before they were really accepted into American cuisine. This Puerto Rican version of a classic flan, made with the all-American pumpkin, shows a Spanish influence. Somewhere between a flan and a cheesecake in texture, this moist and delicious burnt orange–colored cake has a thin coating of caramel when it is turned out of the pan. Use small sugar or pie pumpkins, which come on the market in October, or, in a pinch, canned pumpkin. Fresh pumpkin adds the best flavor, though. This cake is gorgeous garnished with red, yellow, orange, or variegated nasturtium flowers and leaves.

MAKES ONE 8-INCH CAKE; 8 SERVINGS

$1\frac{1}{2}$ pounds fresh pumpkin, peeled, seeded, and cut into pieces

1 quart water

1 teaspoon salt

2 cups sugar

2 tablespoons unsalted butter

$\frac{1}{2}$ cup all-purpose flour

2 cups milk

$\frac{1}{2}$ teaspoon vanilla extract

4 large eggs

Fresh edible flowers for garnish

1   Put the pumpkin, water, and salt into a large saucepan and bring to a boil over high heat. Reduce the heat to medium-low, cover, and simmer until the pumpkin is tender, about 30 minutes.

2   Place a wire rack on a kitchen counter. Pour 1 cup of the sugar over the bottom of an 8-inch round metal cake pan. Place the pan directly on a burner over medium heat. When the sugar has melted and turned light gold, about 10 minutes, put an oven mitt on one hand and swirl the pan to coat the bottom and sides with the caramel. Transfer the pan to a wire rack. Preheat the oven to 350 degrees F.

3   Drain the pumpkin and put in a large mixing bowl. With an electric mixer, beat the pumpkin and butter together until smooth. Beat in the flour and milk a little at a time, alternating between the two. Beat in the vanilla and remaining 1 cup of sugar and continue beating until you have a smooth batter. Beat in the eggs, one at a time. Push the batter through a fine-mesh strainer into the pan with the caramelized sugar and place the pan in a large, shallow baking pan filled with 1 inch of hot water.

4 Bake the cake until it has pulled away from the sides of the pan and a cake tester inserted in the center comes out clean, about 2 hours. Remove the pan from the water bath and cool the cake completely in the pan. Carefully run a knife around the inside of the pan, if necessary, to loosen the cake. Invert onto a cake stand or serving plate. Garnish with fresh flowers and serve.

French Chocolate Cake

During the 1970s, after we had experienced the sophistication of the Kennedy White House years and had been introduced to the art of French cooking by Julia Child on public television, we were finally ready for this cake—dense, dark chocolate so rich you could only eat a small slice, and best served barely warm from the oven, dolloped with whipped cream. My sister and I still make this cake on occasion, adapted from a recipe served at the former Bakery Lane Soup Bowl in Middlebury, Vermont. Owners Marge Mitchell and Joan Sedgwick were ahead of their time with a local restaurant serving only their signature homemade soups, breads, salads, and desserts. Back then, Maillard Eagle Sweet Chocolate (really semisweet, not sweet), available at better grocery stores in bar form only, was the dark chocolate of choice. Now, you could use Valrhona, Scharffen Berger, or any rich, dark semisweet boutique chocolate you like. Boutique chocolates often state the percentage of cacao they contain. Use chocolate that contains at least 64 percent cacao in this cake—the richer and darker the chocolate, the better the cake. When making this recipe, remember to wash the hand mixer's beaters well to remove any butter before using them later on to whip the egg whites.

MAKES ONE 8-INCH CAKE; 8 SERVINGS

1 pound semisweet or bittersweet chocolate, broken into pieces

10 tablespoons (1¼ sticks) unsalted butter

1 tablespoon sugar

1 tablespoon all-purpose flour

1 tablespoon water

4 large eggs, separated

¼ teaspoon salt

Whipped cream for garnish

1 Preheat the oven to 450 degrees F. Line the bottom and sides of an 8-inch springform pan with waxed or parchment paper and set aside.

2   Place the chocolate pieces in a medium-size metal or glass mixing bowl over a larger bowl of very hot water so that the chocolate melts very slowly. Meanwhile, with an electric mixer, beat the butter in a small mixing bowl until fluffy. Wash and dry the beaters well. When the chocolate has melted, remove the bowl with the chocolate from the hot water and set aside to cool slightly.

3   Whisk the sugar and flour into the melted chocolate, and then the butter. In a small bowl, whisk the water into the egg yolks, then whisk the yolks into the chocolate. In a large mixing bowl, combine the egg whites and salt, then beat with the electric mixer, beat until the egg whites hold stiff peaks. Carefully fold them into the chocolate mixture with a rubber spatula until you can no longer see them. Spoon the batter into the prepared pan.

4   Bake the cake for 15 minutes, then turn off the heat, but leave the cake to cool slowly in the oven with the oven door ajar for about 45 minutes. Carefully release and remove the sides of the pan and transfer the cake to a serving plate. Serve slightly warm or at room temperature with a spoonful of whipped cream on each slice.

Brownie Pudding Cake

American cooks, pressed for time in a country where so many opportunities beckon, love to do at least two things at once. That's part of the appeal of pudding cakes, which form a sauce at the bottom of the pan as they bake. Either invert this moist, rich, and fudgy cake onto a serving platter so the sauce is on top, or cut the cake in the pan and spoon the sauce over each piece. **MAKES ONE 8-INCH SQUARE CAKE; 6 SERVINGS**

¾ cup packed brown sugar

½ cup plus 2 tablespoons unsweetened cocoa powder

1 cup all-purpose flour

½ teaspoon salt

¾ cup granulated sugar

2 teaspoons baking powder

¼ cup vegetable oil

½ cup milk

1 teaspoon vanilla extract

¾ cup chopped walnuts or pecans

1¾ cups hot water

1   Preheat the oven to 350 degrees F. Grease the inside of an 8-inch square baking pan and set aside.

2   In a small mixing bowl, mix the brown sugar with 2 tablespoons of the cocoa; set aside. In a large mixing bowl, sift together the flour, the remaining ½ cup of cocoa, the salt, granulated sugar, and baking powder. With a wooden spoon, stir in the vegetable oil, milk, and vanilla and continue stirring until well combined. Stir in the nuts. Pour the batter into the prepared baking pan. Sprinkle the reserved brown sugar mixture evenly over the batter in the pan. Pour the hot water over all. *Do not stir.*

3   Bake the cake until a cake tester inserted halfway through the center comes out clean, about 45 minutes. Serve warm.

Puckery Lemon Pudding Cake

This pudding cake rises higher than Brownie Pudding Cake (page 243), almost like a soufflé, because of the eggs. If you like your lemon desserts less puckery, use only 1 teaspoon of grated lemon zest. Garnish this low-fat dessert (only 10 percent of the calories are from fat) with blueberries, blackberries, or raspberries. **MAKES 6 SERVINGS**

2 large eggs, separated

2 teaspoons grated lemon zest

¼ cup fresh lemon juice

⅔ cup milk

1 cup sugar

½ cup all-purpose flour

¼ teaspoon salt

Fresh berries (optional) for garnish

Whipped cream (optional) for garnish

1   Preheat the oven to 350 degrees F. Grease the inside of a 1-quart soufflé or round baking dish with nonstick cooking spray and set aside.

2   With an electric mixer, beat the egg whites in a medium-size mixing bowl until they hold stiff peaks. In another medium-size mixing bowl, beat together the egg yolks, lemon zest, lemon juice, milk, sugar, flour, and salt until smooth. Fold the lemon mixture into the egg whites with a rubber spatula until well combined. Spoon the batter into the prepared dish. Place the soufflé dish in a deeper pan containing about 1 inch of very hot water.

3   Bake the cake until it has risen and pulled away from the sides of the dish, 45 to 50 minutes. To serve, spoon the warm pudding cake onto dessert plates and top with the sauce from the bottom of the pan. Garnish with berries and whipped cream, if desired.

Vanilla Bean Buttermilk Pudding Cakes

Adapted from a recipe by pastry chef Nancy Silver of MOD restaurant in Chicago's Wicker Park, these individual pudding cakes are part soufflé, part pudding, and all delicious in that unmistakable, homemade way. Serve each pudding on a dessert plate along with a small scoop of great ice cream. **MAKES 6 INDIVIDUAL PUDDING CAKES**

⅔ cup plus 2 tablespoons granulated sugar, plus extra for sprinkling the custard cups

1 vanilla bean or 1 teaspoon vanilla extract

2 tablespoons unsalted butter

3 large egg yolks

¼ cup plus 1 tablespoon all-purpose flour

½ cup buttermilk

½ cup heavy cream

¼ cup fresh lemon juice

¼ cup apple juice

4 large egg whites

Confectioners' sugar for dusting

6 scoops homemade or good-quality store-bought ice cream for serving

1 Preheat the oven to 375 degrees F. Grease the insides of six 8-ounce custard cups. Sprinkle the inside of each custard cup with granulated sugar and set aside.

2 If using a vanilla bean, slice it lengthwise with a sharp knife and scrape out the vanilla seeds into a mixing bowl; if using vanilla extract, pour it into the bowl. Add the butter and ⅔ cup of the granulated sugar. With an electric mixer, beat until light and fluffy. Add the egg yolks, one at a time, beating well after each addition and scraping down the sides of the bowl with a rubber spatula. Beat in the flour until just incorporated. Beat in the buttermilk and heavy cream, then the lemon and apple juices. Set aside the batter.

3 Wash and dry the beaters well to remove any trace of the batter. In a medium-size mixing bowl, beat the egg whites and remaining 2 tablespoons of granulated sugar until the egg whites hold stiff peaks. Using a spatula, gently fold half the egg whites into the batter at a time until well blended. Spoon the batter into the prepared cups. Place the cups in a deeper pan with enough hot water to reach halfway up the sides of the cups.

4 Bake the pudding cakes until they have risen and are golden brown on top, 30 to 40 minutes. Serve immediately for a soufflé-like texture. Let cool to room temperature before serving for a cake-like texture. Either way, carefully invert the cakes onto serving plates, dust each pudding cake with confectioners' sugar, and accompany with a scoop of ice cream.

Cinnamon Sugar–Pecan Pudding Cake

This Pennsylvania version of pudding cake has a mellow flavor that everyone loves and, of course, it makes its own sauce. This is another great potluck dessert, which is served chilled. **MAKES ONE 9 X 13-INCH CAKE; 8 SERVINGS**

BROWN SUGAR SAUCE
3 cups packed light brown sugar
2¼ cups water
½ cup (1 stick) unsalted butter
¼ teaspoon salt

CAKE
1⅔ cups all-purpose flour
2 teaspoons baking powder

2 teaspoons ground cinnamon
½ teaspoon salt
1 cup granulated sugar
2 tablespoons unsalted butter at room temperature
1 cup milk
½ cup chopped pecans
Whipped cream or ice cream for serving

1 Preheat the oven to 325 degrees F. Grease a 9 x 13-inch baking pan and set aside.

2 To make the sauce, combine the ingredients in a large heavy saucepan over medium-high heat. Bring to a boil, stirring occasionally. Set aside.

3 To make the cake, in a small mixing bowl, sift together the flour, baking powder, cinnamon, and salt; set aside. With an electric mixer, cream the granulated sugar and butter together in a medium-size mixing bowl until light and fluffy. Gradually beat in the dry ingredients, alternating with the milk, and continue beating until you have a smooth batter. Pour or spoon into the prepared pan. Pour the sauce over the batter and sprinkle the pecans on top.

4 Bake the cake until a cake tester inserted halfway through the cake comes out clean, about 45 minutes. Let cool completely in the pan, then cover with plastic wrap and chill at least 2 hours before serving. Serve with whipped cream or ice cream.

Cherry-Almond Poke Cake

In 1981, Jell-O introduced Moist and Fruity Rainbow Cake in an ad appearing in *Bon Appétit* magazine. The surface of the two-layer white cake was poked with a fork or cake tester, liquid Jell-O was poured into the holes, and the whole thing was chilled until the Jell-O set, and then frosted with Cool Whip—a dessert that became known as poke cake. More than 20 years later, we have more poke cake recipes than we know what to do with. There are Tropical (banana cake and orange Jell-O), Patriotic (white cake, strawberry and blue fruit Jell-O), Luscious Lemon (lemon cake and lemon Jell-O), and Holiday Poke Cakes (white cake and strawberry and lime Jell-O). You can make poke cake in two 8- or 9-inch layers or as a sheet cake in a 9 x 13-inch pan. I prefer a layer cake form because it looks more celebratory. I also prefer real whipped cream instead of whipped topping. MAKES ONE 2-LAYER 8- OR 9-INCH CAKE; SERVES 8

CAKE

One 18.5-ounce white cake mix with pudding

½ teaspoon almond extract

1 cup boiling water

One 3-ounce package cherry gelatin mix (Jell-O)

½ cup cold water

FROSTING

2 teaspoons cherry gelatin mix (Jell-O)

1 cup boiling water

2 cups heavy cream, whipped to stiff peaks, or one 12-ounce container whipped topping, thawed

Maraschino cherries for garnish

Flaked almonds for garnish

1   Grease two 8- or 9-inch round pans and set aside. To make the cake, preheat the oven and prepare the cake batter according to the package directions. Beat in the almond extract. Pour the batter into the prepared pans and bake according to package directions.

2   Remove the cake layers from the oven and let cool in the pans on a rack for 15 minutes. In a medium-size bowl, mix the boiling water with the gelatin mix and continue stirring until dissolved, about 2 minutes. Stir in the cold water. Place the cake layers, top sides up, in two clean cake pans. Pierce the cake layers with a fork at ½-inch intervals. Carefully pour half the gelatin mixture over each cake layer. Cover and refrigerate for 3 hours.

3   To make the frosting, in a small bowl, stir together the gelatin mix and the boiling water until dissolved, about 2 minutes. Chill until slightly thickened, about 1 hour. In a large bowl, blend the chilled cherry gelatin mixture with the whipped cream until well combined.

4   To assemble the cake, dip one cake pan in warm water for 10 seconds, then unmold the cake onto a serving plate and turn right side up. Spread the top of the cake with 1 cup of the whipped cream. Unmold the second cake layer and carefully place on top of the first layer. Frost the top and sides of the cake with the remaining whipped cream. Garnish with maraschino cherries and flaked almonds. Refrigerate until ready to serve.

Classic Sour Cream–Topped Cheesecake

Our collective passion for cheesecake was inflamed anew in the 1970s, when this Sara Lee–style recipe made the rounds of home cooks.

MAKES ONE 9-INCH CHEESECAKE; 8 SERVINGS

1 Crumb Crust (recipe follows), made with cinnamon graham crackers

FILLING

Two 8-ounce packages cream cheese at room temperature

⅔ cup sugar

3 large eggs

½ teaspoon almond extract

TOPPING

One 8-ounce container sour cream

3 tablespoons sugar

1 teaspoon vanilla extract

Toasted slivered almonds (see page 181) or sliced fresh strawberries (optional) for garnish

1   Preheat the oven to 350 degrees F. Press the crumb crust into a 9-inch pie pan and set aside.

2   To make the filling, with an electric mixer, beat the cream cheese and sugar together in a large mixing bowl until light and creamy. Add the eggs and almond extract and beat until smooth. Pour the filling into the prepared crust.

3   Bake the cheesecake until the middle has set, about 25 minutes. Leave the oven on, and cool the cheesecake slightly in the pan on a wire rack for 20 minutes.

4   In the meantime, make the topping: In a medium-size mixing bowl, whisk together the sour cream, sugar, and vanilla until smooth. Pour the topping over the surface of the cheesecake and smooth with a rubber spatula. Return to the oven to bake for 10 more minutes. Remove from the oven and let cool completely before serving. Garnish with toasted almonds or fresh strawberries, if desired.

Crumb Crust

As the foundation for cheesecakes, tarts, and pies destined to have a creamy filling, basic crumb crusts are a deliciously simple blend of three ingredients: graham crackers or thin cookies, melted butter, and sugar. Graham crackers are named after the mid-nineteenth-century health food guru Sylvester Graham, who touted the benefits of whole grains. During the 1860s, John Harvey Kellogg—a doctor who went on to create now-famous breakfast cereals like shredded wheat and corn flakes—had seven graham crackers and an apple for breakfast every day when he was in medical school. But it was Mrs. J. H. Kellogg who first concocted a crumb crust made with cereal crumbs, melted butter, and sugar. When I lived in England and was developing cheesecake recipes for an article for a London-based magazine, I had to use wheatmeal, digestive biscuits, or chocolate shortbread instead of these American staples. They were good, too; there is life beyond graham crackers! **MAKES ONE 8- OR 9-INCH CRUST**

1¼ cups chocolate wafer cookie, graham cracker, or Oreo or other cream-filled sandwich cookie crumbs

6 tablespoons (¾ stick) unsalted butter, melted

2 tablespoons sugar

In a medium-size mixing bowl, combine all the ingredients with your hands or a rubber spatula until the mixture holds together. Pat the crust mixture evenly into the bottom and up the sides of the pan.

Lemon Bisque Cheesecake with Raspberries

During hot and humid Ohio summers, my grandmother used to make a lemon bisque icebox dessert similar to a cheesecake. My updated version is cool, mildly tart, and creamy—with the added color and flavor surprise of an interior stripe of fresh raspberries. Keep this dessert chilled. **MAKES ONE 9-INCH CAKE; 8 SERVINGS**

¾ cup heavy cream

2 tablespoons buttermilk or sour cream

2 cups crushed graham cracker crumbs

½ cup plus 3 tablespoons sugar

1 teaspoon ground cinnamon

½ cup (1 stick) unsalted butter, melted

Grated zest and juice of 1 large lemon

One ¼-ounce package unflavored gelatin

Two 8-ounce packages cream cheese, at room temperature

8 ounces fresh or frozen (thawed) raspberries, plus extra for garnish

Fresh mint or lemon balm leaves for garnish

1   In a small mixing bowl, combine the heavy cream and buttermilk and leave out at room temperature for several hours, until the mixture has thickened to the consistency of a batter. Set aside.

2   In a medium-size mixing bowl, combine the graham cracker crumbs, 3 tablespoons of the sugar, the cinnamon, and the melted butter, blending with a rubber spatula. Press this mixture into the bottom and around the sides of a 9-inch springform pan and set aside.

3   Squeeze the lemon juice into a small ramekin and sprinkle the gelatin over the juice. Set aside for 5 minutes, until the gelatin is soaked through. Fill a small baking pan with enough hot water to come three quarters of the way up the sides of the ramekin. Set the ramekin in the pan of hot water for several minutes, until the gelatin mixture is clear. Set aside.

4   With an electric mixer, beat the cream cheese and remaining ½ cup of sugar in a large mixing bowl until smooth. Beat in the lemon zest and gelatin mixture. Wash and dry the beaters well. Beat the thickened heavy cream mixture until it holds soft peaks. Fold this into the cream cheese mixture with the spatula.

5   Pour half the filling into the prepared pan. Dot the raspberries over the surface of the filling. Carefully pour the rest of the filling over the raspberries. Cover with plastic wrap and chill until set, about 1 hour. If necessary, run a knife or spatula around the inside of the pan to loosen the cheesecake. Release and remove the sides of the pan and place the cake on a serving plate. Cut into wedges to serve, garnished with additional raspberries and a mint or lemon balm leaf.

How the Cookie Crumbles

For 1 cup of crumbs for a crumb crust, you will need about:

* ★ 14 individual graham crackers, *or*
* ★ 24 thin, crisp, round cookies, such as ginger, lemon, or chocolate, *or*
* ★ 14 vanilla wafers, *or*
* ★ 12 sandwich cookies

To make the cookie crumbs, use a food processor or place the cookies between two kitchen towels and roll with a rolling pin to crush.

Cream Cheese, Please

When I lived in London during the mid 1980s, I developed several American cheesecake recipes for *Taste* magazine, now no longer in print. The familiar silver-and-blue packages of Philadelphia cream cheese were not available, so I had to go to the local deli and buy cream cheese in bulk. After the fourth trip in as many days, the Pakistani owner looked at me strangely and asked, "What in the world are you doing with all of this?" How could I explain the American passion for cream cheese—transformed into a luscious, toothsome cheesecake?

Our love affair with cream cheese goes back a long way. The seventeenth-century family heirloom *A Book of Cookery* that Martha Washington cherished in Virginia contained a recipe for making cream or "slip coat" cheese made with a "quart of stroakings from ye cow" plus cream and rennet. Dutch, Welsh, and northern English settlers brought a love of cream cheese to this country when they began to settle around the Philadelphia area in the late 1600s. At that time, cream cheese was made by simply letting thick cream drain through layers of cheesecloth or linen for 1 to 2 weeks until partially dehydrated, thickened, and slightly soured. It must have had a flavor similar to today's sour cream or European *fromage frais*, a thick, slightly sour fresh cheese. Some cream cheese was also imported from Holland by Philadelphia merchants, establishing that city long ago as a cream cheese capital.

By the mid-nineteenth century, Elizabeth Ellicott Lea in *A Quaker Woman's Cookbook* offered a recipe for Pennsylvania cream cheese made with whole milk, separated into curds and whey with rennet, then pressed into a mold and left for a week to solidify. Today, Philadelphia-style cream cheese is made solid with gelatin for a smooth, creamy texture.

Although many Irish, German, Russian, Mennonite, English, and French immigrants brought their own unique recipes for cheesecake or curd cake made with curds or cottage cheese, cheesecake made with pasteurized cream cheese is an American invention. Philadelphia-style cream cheese first became available in 1880, produced by the Empire Cheese Company of New York. James L. Kraft invented pasteurized cheese in 1912, and that led to the development of pasteurized Philadelphia cream cheese.

When religious persecution forced the immigration of many European Jews to New York, they brought their love of sweet, creamy cheese with them. According to food historian Meryle Evans, towering, dense, crumbly textured cheesecakes made with cream cheese can be traced to Jewish delis—Leonard's on Manhattan's Upper East Side, Lindy's on Broadway, and Junior's in Brooklyn—which began to sell them during the 1920s. In 1949, Chicago baker Charles Lubin popularized a smoother, creamier, shorter cheesecake with a sour cream topping, and named his company Sara Lee, after his daughter. As their commercial states, "Nobody doesn't like Sara Lee." And it seems nobody doesn't like cheesecake, either. There is a flavor and texture to suit everyone's taste.

New York–Style Marbled Strawberry Cheesecake

Tall, dense, and filling, the New York–style cheesecake has been a staple of Big Apple delis since the turn of the century. This no-bake cheesecake gets a chocolate short-bread crust and a swirl of strawberry. **MAKES ONE 9-INCH CHEESECAKE; 8 SERVINGS**

CRUST

1½ cups crumbs made from Chocolate Short-bread Cookies (page 128) or store-bought chocolate wafer cookies

¼ cup (½ stick) unsalted butter, melted

STRAWBERRY MARBLING

¼ cup water

One ¼-ounce envelope unflavored gelatin

2 cups fresh or frozen strawberries (thawed), hulled

2 tablespoons sugar

CHEESECAKE

¼ cup water

One ¼-ounce envelope unflavored gelatin

Two 8-ounce packages cream cheese at room temperature

1 cup sugar

1 cup sour cream

1 To make the crust, lightly grease the inside of a 9-inch springform pan. With a rubber spatula, combine the crumbs with the melted butter in a small mixing bowl. Press the crumb mixture evenly over the bottom and up the sides of the prepared pan and set aside.

2 To make the strawberry marbling, pour the water into a small bowl and sprinkle the gelatin on top. Set the bowl in a larger pan of hot water and set aside until the gelatin is soaked through. Puree the strawberries and sugar together in a food processor. Transfer the puree to a medium-size mixing bowl and stir in the gelatin mixture. Set aside.

3 To make the cheesecake, pour the water into a small bowl and sprinkle the gelatin on top. Set the bowl in a larger pan of hot water and set aside until the gelatin is soaked through. With an electric mixer, beat together the cream cheese, sugar, and sour cream in a large mixing bowl until light and creamy. Beat in the gelatin mixture.

4 Pour the cheesecake mixture into the prepared crust. Place spoonfuls of the strawberry mixture around the perimeter of the cheesecake and swirl the mixture into a marble pattern with a knife. Cover with plastic wrap and chill for at least 1 hour before serving. If necessary, run a knife or spatula around the inside of the pan to loosen the cheesecake. Release and remove the sides of the pan and place the cake on a serving plate. Cut into wedges.

Key Lime Cheesecake

Through the years, cheesecakes have gotten more sophisticated and more regional. When I lived in England and wanted to invite friends over for an American meal, this is one dessert I made that was always well received.

MAKES ONE 9-INCH CHEESECAKE; 8 SERVINGS

PECAN–GRAHAM CRACKER CRUST

1 cup graham cracker crumbs

¾ cup finely chopped pecans

3 tablespoons sugar

1 teaspoon ground cinnamon

¼ cup (½ stick) unsalted butter, melted

FILLING

8 Key limes, or 5 domestic limes

Two 8-ounce packages cream cheese at room temperature

⅔ cup sugar

4 large eggs

1 teaspoon vanilla extract

One 8-ounce container sour cream

TOPPING

One 8-ounce container sour cream

1 teaspoon vanilla extract

3 tablespoons sugar

Thin slices lime for garnish

Whipped cream to garnish

Lime zest for garnish

1   Preheat the oven to 375 degrees F. To make the crust, blend the ingredients together with a rubber spatula in a small mixing bowl and press into the bottom of a 9-inch springform pan.

2   To make the filling, grate the zest of 7 of the Key limes or 4 of the domestic ones. Juice all 8 of the Key limes or 5 domestic ones. With an electric mixer, beat the cream cheese until light and creamy in a large mixing bowl, then beat in the sugar and the eggs, one at a time. Beat in the vanilla and lime juice and zest, then the sour cream. Pour or spoon the filling into the prepared crust. Whisk the topping ingredients together and set aside.

3   Bake the cheesecake for 40 minutes or until the center seems firm. Remove it from the oven and pour the topping over it, smoothing the topping carefully. Return the cheesecake to the oven for another 10 minutes. Turn off the oven, open the oven door, and let the cheesecake cool in the oven for 1 hour to prevent cracking.

4   If necessary, run a knife or spatula around the inside of the pan to loosen the cheesecake. Release and remove the sides of the pan and place the cake on a serving plate. Decorate with thin lime slices and swirls of whipped cream dusted with lime zest and serve.

Hood River Valley Hazelnut Cheesecake

Pair the dense texture of a New York cheesecake with the incomparable taste of toasted hazelnuts from Oregon and Washington, and this dessert is the happy result. If you wish, serve each slice drizzled with Classic Hot Fudge Sauce (see page 427).

MAKES ONE 9-INCH CHEESECAKE; 8 SERVINGS

1½ cups hazelnuts

⅓ cup graham cracker crumbs

Four 8-ounce packages cream cheese, at room temperature

1¾ cups sugar

¼ cup heavy cream

4 large eggs

1½ teaspoons vanilla extract

1 Preheat the oven to 350 degrees F. Spread the hazelnuts on a baking sheet and toast the nuts in the oven until golden brown and fragrant, about 15 minutes. Immediately wrap the hot nuts in kitchen towels and rub vigorously to remove the skins. Set aside to cool slightly. In a nut grinder or food processor, grind the nuts until fine. Set aside.

2 Grease a 9-inch springform pan, then sprinkle the graham cracker crumbs over the bottom and sides. Set aside. Reduce the oven temperature to 300 degrees F.

3 With an electric mixer, beat the cream cheese, sugar, heavy cream, eggs, and vanilla in a large mixing bowl until smooth. Fold in the ground hazelnuts until well blended. Pour the filling into the prepared pan. Set the pan in a larger pan with enough water to reach ½ inch up the sides of the springform pan.

4 Bake the cheesecake until the center seems firm, about 2 hours. Turn the oven off, open the oven door, and let the cheesecake cool for 1 more hour to prevent cracking. Remove the cheesecake from the oven and the water bath and let sit for another 2 hours before serving. If necessary, run a knife or spatula around the inside of the pan to loosen the cheesecake. Release and remove the sides of the pan and place the cake on a serving plate. Serve at room temperature or chilled.

Autumn Apple Cheesecake

When the apples have ripened and the nuts have fallen from the trees, it's time to make this homey dessert, which no one ever refuses. It combines mellow cream cheese with tart apples, spicy cinnamon, and crunchy pecans. It's just one of the many luscious permutations of the classic American cheesecake.

MAKES ONE 9-INCH CHEESECAKE; 8 SERVINGS

1 Pecan-Graham Cracker Crust (see page 253)

Two 8-ounce packages cream cheese at room temperature

$1/2$ cup sugar

1 teaspoon vanilla extract

2 large eggs

TOPPING

4 cups thinly sliced Jonathan or Granny Smith apples

$1/2$ teaspoon ground cinnamon

$1/3$ cup sugar

$1/2$ cup chopped pecans

The Festival of Shavuot and Cheesecake

I have often wondered why cheesecake is such a staple of Jewish delicatessens that also turn out wonderful corned beef sandwiches and chicken soup with kreplach. I know something about keeping a kosher kitchen—separate preparation areas and utensils for meat and dairy—from interviewing many Conservative, Orthodox, and Hasidic Jewish cooks. But I didn't know why cheesecake was so much a part of Jewish culture until I learned about Shavuot from cookbook author and syndicated columnist Faye Levy, who lives in California.

Shavuot, the Jewish festival held in mid-May, highlights dairy foods. "The official purpose of the two-day holiday is to commemorate Moses's receiving the Scriptures on Mount Sinai," says Levy. "Its unofficial *raison d'etre* is that on this day you're supposed to indulge in creamy delights—noodle kugels with sour cream, cheese filo pastries, cheese blintzes, and, most important of all, cheesecakes." She adds, "When I lived in Israel, my neighbors began discussing their favorite cheesecake recipes weeks before Shavuot."

According to Jewish tradition, the Scriptures that Moses received, called the Torah, included the *kashrut* or kosher dietary rules. When Moses came down from the mountain with these new laws, the Jews realized that all of their cooking pots and utensils had been used for both meat and dairy, and so were unclean. There were no towns, no markets nearby to purchase new ones during the years of wandering in the desert. Nothing, therefore, could be cooked. The only "safe" things to eat that didn't require cooking were the fresh dairy foods, such as sheep's milk and fresh cheese.

Another practical reason for including more dairy foods at Shavuot was that late spring brought rain, the lushest grazing, and the best milk from the herds during biblical times.

1 Preheat the oven to 325 degrees F. Press the crust into the bottom of a 9-inch springform pan. Bake for 10 minutes, then remove from the oven to cool. Leave the oven on.

2 To make the filling, with an electric mixer, beat together the cream cheese, sugar, and vanilla in a large mixing bowl until light and creamy. Blend in the eggs, one at a time. Pour this mixture over the crust.

3 To make the topping, put the sliced apples in a large mixing bowl and toss with the cinnamon and sugar. Spoon the apple mixture over the filling and sprinkle evenly with the pecans.

4 Bake the cheesecake until the center seems firm, about $1\frac{1}{4}$ hours. Let the cheesecake cool before removing it from the pan. For the best flavor, let the flavors develop by covering and chilling the cheesecake for at least 4 hours (and up to 1 day) before serving. If necessary, run a knife or spatula around the inside of the pan to loosen the cheesecake. Release and remove the sides of the pan and place the cake on a serving plate.

Espresso and Chocolate Cheesecake

The years have not dimmed this dessert's infinite variety, from the mid 1600s, when William Penn's wife, Gulielma, made a cheesecake studded with dried currants and flavored with rosewater, until today, when the taste of dark, rich coffee is better appreciated. I developed this recipe when I was living in London, and it was photographed for the cover of *Taste* magazine. **MAKES ONE 9-INCH CHEESECAKE; 8 SERVINGS**

ALMOND-CHOCOLATE CRUST

$1\frac{1}{2}$ cups crumbs made from Chocolate Short-bread Cookies (page 128) or store-bought chocolate wafer cookies

$\frac{1}{4}$ cup sliced almonds

$\frac{1}{2}$ cup (1 stick) unsalted butter, melted

CHEESECAKE

$\frac{1}{2}$ cup boiling water

$\frac{1}{4}$ cup plus 2 tablespoons finely ground espresso coffee

$\frac{1}{2}$ cup semisweet chocolate chips

Two 8-ounce packages cream cheese at room temperature

$1\frac{1}{4}$ cups sugar

1 cup sour cream

4 large eggs, beaten

1 recipe Stabilized Whipped Cream (see page 231) for garnish

Chocolate-covered coffee beans for garnish

1   Preheat the oven to 350 degrees F. To make the crust, combine the ingredients in a small mixing bowl, blending with a rubber spatula. Pat the crust mixture over the bottom and up the sides of a 9-inch springform pan and set aside.

2   To make the cheesecake, in a small mixing bowl, pour the boiling water over the espresso, cover, and set aside to infuse for 5 minutes. Melt the chocolate chips in the top of a double boiler over simmering water.

3   Meanwhile, with an electric mixer, beat the cream cheese in a large mixing bowl until light and creamy. Beat in the sugar, then strain the brewed espresso into the cream cheese mixture and beat well. Beat in the melted chocolate, sour cream, and eggs, one at a time, and continue beating until smooth. Pour the mixture into the prepared crust.

4   Bake the cheesecake until the center seems firm, 50 to 55 minutes. Turn the oven off, open the oven door, and let the cheesecake cool inside for 1 hour to keep it from cracking. If necessary, run a knife or spatula around the inside of the pan to loosen the cheesecake. Release and remove the sides of the pan and place the cake on a serving plate. To garnish, fill a piping bag fitted with a rosette tip with Stabilized Whipped Cream and pipe rosettes of cream around the perimeter of the cheesecake. Top each rosette with a chocolate-covered coffee bean.

Sour Mash Cheesecake

Like jazz and peanut butter, bourbon and sour mash whiskey are all-American, homegrown and original. Adapted from a recipe served at the Wild Boar in Nashville, Tennessee, this regional version of classic cheesecake will make you sit up and say "yee-haw!" MAKES ONE 9-INCH CHEESECAKE; 8 SERVINGS

OREO CRUMB CRUST
1½ cups finely crushed Oreo or other cream-filled chocolate cookie crumbs
2 tablespoons unsalted butter, melted

FILLING
Three 8-ounce packages cream cheese at room temperature
One 14-ounce can sweetened condensed milk
3 large eggs

2 teaspoons vanilla extract
1 teaspoon ground cinnamon
¾ cup sour mash whiskey or bourbon
1 cup sour cream

CHOCOLATE CREAM GLAZE
2 ounces semisweet chocolate
⅓ cup heavy cream

1   Preheat the oven to 350 degrees F. To make the crust, combine the cookie crumbs and butter in a small mixing bowl, blending with a rubber spatula. Press into the bottom of a 9-inch springform pan. Set aside.

2   To make the filling, with an electric mixer, beat the cream cheese in a large mixing bowl until light and creamy. Beat in the condensed milk, then the eggs, one at a time, the vanilla, cinnamon, and whiskey. Pour into the prepared pan.

3   Bake the cheesecake until the center seems firm, about 1 hour. Remove from the oven, run a knife or spatula around the inside of the pan to loosen the cheesecake, and let cool completely. Release and remove the sides of the pan and place the cake on a serving plate. Spread the top of the cheesecake with the sour cream.

4   To make the glaze, in a small heavy saucepan, stir the chocolate and cream together over low heat until the chocolate has melted and the mixture is well blended and smooth. Drizzle the chocolate glaze over the cheesecake. Chill at least 2 hours before serving.

Macadamia-Crusted Mango Cheesecake

Native to Australia and named after Scots-born chemist John Macadam, macadamia nuts were first introduced to Hawaii in the 1890s. By the 1930s, the nuts were commercially viable and mainland Americans slowly started discovering them. This easy and fabulous dessert from my friend Karen Adler is also delicious made with fresh pears or apples. Whenever Karen and I make this dessert for our cooking classes, it always gets rave reviews. For more of a wow factor, sprinkle each slice with bits of crystallized ginger. MAKES ONE 9-INCH CAKE; 8 TO 10 SERVINGS

1 Nut Crust (recipe follows) made with macadamia nuts, baked in a 9-inch springform pan

One 8-ounce package cream cheese at room temperature

1/2 cup sugar

1 large egg

1 teaspoon vanilla extract

2 small, ripe mangoes, peeled, pitted, and sliced

1 teaspoon pumpkin pie spice, or substitute a mixture of 1/2 teaspoon ground cinnamon, 1/4 teaspoon freshly grated nutmeg, and 1/4 teaspoon ground cloves

1 teaspoon fresh lemon juice

1   After the crust has baked, remove it from the oven and increase the oven temperature to 400 degrees F.

2 With an electric mixer, beat the cream cheese, ¼ cup of the sugar, the egg, and vanilla in a medium-size mixing bowl until smooth. Pour into the prepared crust.

3 Using the same bowl, toss the mango slices with the pumpkin pie spice, the remaining ¼ cup of sugar, and the lemon juice with your hands or a rubber spatula. Arrange the mango slices attractively in a circle on top of the filling. Pour any sugared juice left in the bowl on top of the mangoes.

4 Bake the cheesecake until the center seems firm, 20 to 25 minutes. Let cool in the pan for 20 minutes. If necessary, run a knife or spatula around the inside of the pan to loosen the cheesecake. Release and remove the sides of the pan and place the cake on a serving plate.

Nut Crust

For cheesecakes and tarts, a nut crust adds both texture and flavor. Vary this basic recipe to include the nuts of your choice. Almonds and cashews from California, peanuts from the South, hickory nuts from the Midwest, pecans from the Midwest and the South, hazelnuts from the Pacific Northwest, and macadamia nuts from Hawaii all make delicious nut crusts.

MAKES 1 CRUST FOR A 9-INCH SPRINGFORM PAN OR A DEEP-DISH PIE

1½ cups all-purpose flour
½ cup (1 stick) unsalted butter, melted

½ cup sugar
½ cup chopped nuts (see Note)

1 Preheat the oven to 350 degrees F. In a medium-size mixing bowl, combine all the ingredients with your hands or blend with a rubber spatula. Pat evenly over the bottom and up the sides of a 9-inch springform or deep-dish pie pan.

2 Bake until the crust is just beginning to brown, about 12 minutes. Remove from the oven and continue with the recipe of your choice.

NOTE Use flaked almonds, unsalted dry-roasted cashews and peanuts, whole macadamia nuts or pistachios, chopped hickory nuts or pecans, or whole hazelnuts. Chop the nuts in a hand-cranked nut grinder or in a food processor.

What was pie and what was pudding doesn't really seem clear from early seventeenth-century British receipt books. During that time period, fillings such as cooked custards, fresh sliced apples, vegetables sweetened with sugar and dried fruit, and rich beef marrow flavored with sack (a sherry-like fortified wine) could be called either "pie" or "pudding," with or without a crust. The British were adept at making pie pastry, or what old cookbooks referred to as "paste." According to Hilary Spurling, the editor of *Elinor Fettiplace's Receipt Book*, "Jacobean and Stuart cooks were expert at both [flaky and puff paste], giving any number of variations on what have remained essentially unchanged techniques for trapping air between the layers of their meltingly light and fragile sweet pastries."

From these culinary traditions sprang the American pie. Wrote Harriet Beecher Stowe in her 1869 novel, *Oldtown*

American Pie (and Tarts, and Tartlets, and Pastries)

Folks, "The pie is an English institution which, planted on American soil, forthwith ran rampant and burst forth into an untold variety of genera and species. Not merely the old mince pie, but a thousand strictly American seedlings from that main stock, evinced the power of American housewives to adapt old institutions to new uses. Pumpkin pies, cranberry pies, huckleberry pies, cherry pies, green-currant pies, peach, pear, and plum pies, custard pies, apple pies, Marlborough-pudding pies, pies with topcrust, and pies without—pies adorned with all sorts of fanciful flutings and architectural strips laid across and around, and otherwise varied, attested the boundless fertility of the feminine mind, when once let loose in a given direction."

Today in Britain, "pudding" is the generic term for dessert. "Pie" to the Brits most often brings to mind a savory pie, like shepherd's pie; chicken and bacon pie served at the Savoy in London, or the pub favorite, raised veal pie made with a hot water crust. The most common dessert pies are Bramley apple pie with an applesauce-like filling and mincemeat pie, not too far off from those made in Lady Fettiplace's day (although Bramley apples had not yet been developed).

In America today, pudding is one thing and pie is most emphatically another. Pie used to be a kind of common denominator. In the 1940s and '50s, a cake made from scratch usually meant a special occasion, while a good homemade pie was a friendly kind of everyday dessert. When neighbors came to call, when travelers stopped at a local cafe to refresh during a long trip, or when friends gathered to gossip, it was pie and coffee. Slices of pie are still sold at antique auctions, community events, and school functions.

Some people have pie phobia, though, mainly because of that darned crust. At one time, mothers and grandmothers taught kids early on how to make a pie crust from scratch, and eventually those kids learned it by sight and by feel. Not so today. People don't make pies as often as they used to when we were a more rural society. We now have a wider range of desserts we can choose to prepare, as well. Panna cotta? Tiramisu? Chocolate mousse?

Generally, we make pies for Thanksgiving and Christmas and then again in the summer, when fresh berries and other fruits are in season, plus maybe an apple pie or two in the fall. Months may go by before we make another pie. So every time we make one, it's like the first time all over again. See Tips for Making a Tender, Flaky Pie Crust on page 265 to help you through the process once more.

Think "rustic." You want your pie looking homemade instead of something that *Gourmet* would photograph. Pie is really about texture and flavor—the flaky tenderness of the pastry, the sweet toothsomeness of the filling—not about perfection. Give yourself permission to make an imperfect pie crust and go on from there. If you are still absolutely terrified, start with Pat-a-Pan Pie Crust (page 267), which you pat into the pie pan. When you're comfortable with that, move on to Jack's Vinegar Pie Crust (page 266), then to Basic Flaky Double-Crust Pastry (page 264).

Soon, you will begin to see how the crust interacts with the filling. The sweetness of southern pecan pie needs a crust with a light tartness, like Jack's Vinegar Pie Crust. Fruit-filled pies have so much flavor that you want a crust that will take a back seat like Basic Flaky Double-Crust Pastry. Pies with even more assertive flavor like Shaker Lemon Pie (page 284), do well with Farmhouse Lard Double-Crust Pastry (page 263).

Now that you have permission to experiment, let me lure you further into the irresistible world of American pies and tarts: There are fruit and custard-based pies, in which crust and filling are baked together; and icebox and cream pies, in which the crust is prebaked, the filling cooked, and the whole thing chilled before serving. A tart is generally made with a prebaked crust—usually crisper and sweeter than a pie crust—with a pastry cream and fresh fruit filling.

Now you're ready for the tart coolness of Florida Key Lime Pie (page 295); the sweet creaminess of Hoosier Sugar Cream Pie (page 288); the cheery fruitiness of Sparkly-Top Sour Cherry Pie (page 275), Bumbleberry Pie (page 274), or Black Raspberry Pie (page 270); and the mellow spiciness of Deep-Dish Sweet Potato Pie (page 313). And the tarts! Try ooey, gooey Transparent Tartlets (page 327) and everyone's late spring favorite, Fresh Strawberry Tart (page 314). Now, get out there and start rolling!

Farmhouse Lard Double-Crust Pastry

The English practice of using beef fat or suet for pastry crusts enclosing baked or steamed desserts eventually died out in America. In a country with lots of wilderness, pigs could forage better than cattle, and thus lard became the pastry fat of choice. Country cooks swear by a lard crust for flakiness, and this type of crust really stands up to a cream filling. This recipe uses a mixture of lard and a little butter for a great flavor. **MAKES ENOUGH FOR ONE 9-INCH DOUBLE-CRUST PIE**

2 cups all-purpose flour

$\frac{1}{2}$ teaspoon salt

$\frac{1}{2}$ cup lard, chilled

2 tablespoons cold unsalted butter

$\frac{1}{4}$ cup plus 2 tablespoons milk

Whisk the flour and salt together in a medium-size mixing bowl. With a pastry blender or two knives, cut in the lard and butter until the mixture resembles coarse meal. Stir in enough milk with a fork so that the dough forms a mass. Shape the dough into a ball, cover with plastic wrap, and chill for 15 to 30 minutes before proceeding with the pie recipe.

Basic Flaky Double-Crust Pastry

This classic pastry, made with vegetable shortening, produces a flaky crust that browns evenly and resists turning soggy. You can freeze unbaked fruit-filled pies made with this crust for up to a year and bake them right out of the freezer. Or use this pastry to make miniature tarts (which should not be frozen). Cincinnati-based Procter & Gamble introduced Crisco all-vegetable shortening to the American market in 1911. Today, Crisco is owned by Smucker's, based in Orrville, Ohio. **MAKES ENOUGH FOR ONE 8- OR 9-INCH DOUBLE-CRUST PIE OR 2 DOZEN MINIATURE TARTS**

3 cups all-purpose flour

$\frac{1}{2}$ teaspoon salt

1 cup vegetable shortening, preferably Crisco, chilled

$\frac{1}{3}$ to $\frac{1}{2}$ cup ice water, as needed

Sift the flour and salt together into a large mixing bowl. Using a pastry blender or two knives, cut in the shortening until the mixture resembles coarse crumbs. With a fork, stir in as much of the ice water as you need so that the dough forms clumps. With your hands, combine the clumps and knead together quickly into a smooth ball. Handle the pastry as little as possible to keep a tender crust. Cover with plastic wrap and refrigerate for at least 20 to 30 minutes. Then proceed with the recipe.

Frozen Assets

Basic Flaky Double-Crust Pastry (page 264) freezes very well. If you are making a fruit-filled pie made with this dough, for example Black Raspberry Pie (page 270) or Fresh Orange Marmalade Pie (page 292), how about an extra pie for the freezer? Assemble the unbaked pie in a disposable aluminum pie pan, wrap it well in aluminum foil, then place in a large resealable plastic freezer bag and freeze. To bake while still frozen, unwrap the pie and place it on a baking sheet. Bake the pie in a preheated 375-degree-F oven for $1\frac{1}{2}$ hours, or until the filling is bubbling and the crust is browned.

Tips for Making a Flaky, Tender Pie Crust

Making flaky, tender pie crust is a real achievement that takes patience and practice. Even an imperfect pie can taste great, however. Homemade crust, however funky looking, still tastes much better than already prepared pastry from a package. And if your homemade pie crust just doesn't want to behave, follow the suggestions below.

★ Don't skip steps in a recipe or try to hurry the procedure along. (I am sometimes as guilty of this as the next person.) If the recipe says that the dough needs to rest for 30 minutes, let it rest for that long. If you try to roll it out too soon, it will resist you. The resting time allows the dough to become more elastic.

★ Have all your ingredients at the correct temperature. Butter, lard, and shortening should be chilled. This ensures that the fat will remain in distinct tiny pockets in the dough, producing a flakier crust on baking.

★ Touch the pastry as little as possible to keep it tender and flaky. Only cut in the fat until the mixture resembles coarse crumbs or small peas. If you use a food processor, then pulse the butter, shortening, or lard into the flour mixture in short bursts. Then blend in only enough ice water to enable the dough to form a ball. Wrap it in plastic and let it rest in the refrigerator. If making a double crust, take the dough out of the refrigerator, divide it in half, and quickly press each half into a disk. When you roll out the dough, again, do so quickly and on a generously floured work surface using a generously floured rolling pin.

★ To transfer the crust to the pie pan, place the rolling pin in the center of the dough circle. Flip half of the dough back over the rolling pin, then carefully lift the rolling pin and place it over the pie pan, letting the dough fall back from the rolling pin and onto the pie pan. Some veteran pie makers now use a flexible plastic cutting board—lightly floured—to scoop up the whole crust and deposit it into the pie pan. With your fingers, gently fit the dough into the bottom and up the sides of the pan.

★ Add the filling at the last minute, so the bottom crust will not become soggy.

★ If disaster strikes and you have a recalcitrant pastry (perhaps on too warm a day), press the bottom crust into the pie pan as well as you can. Then, roll out the top crust and cut out star, heart, or leaf shapes (or the shape of your choice) with floured cookie cutters and place on top of the filling. No one will notice that your pie crust wasn't perfect; your family and friends will admire your creativity instead.

★ To keep your pie crust from getting too brown, especially if the pie bakes at 400 degrees F or more, cover the edges of the pie crust with aluminum foil.

★ To prebake a tart or pie crust, line the pastry with aluminum foil, then fill with pie weights (special metal balls), dried beans, or even raw rice. Bake for about 15 minutes, or until the edges of the pastry are golden brown. Then carefully remove the foil and pie weights and let the pastry cool.

Jack's Vinegar Pie Crust

When my dad retired, he got interested in all kinds of activities—golf, yoga, computers, and cooking. My mom has always been the pie maker in the family, but soon my dad also got into the act. He even formulated his own pie crust recipe, which is adapted from an old-fashioned German pastry dough called *murbe Teig*. He then printed out his recipe and passed it around to friends and family. We teased him that soon he'd be accosting strangers at the mall with "Are you totally satisfied with your current pie crust?" and then handing them the recipe. Before he accosts you, here it is. The dough is very workable. It makes one single crust, but you can double this recipe for a double-crust pie or even triple it.

MAKES ENOUGH FOR ONE 9-INCH SINGLE-CRUST PIE

1 cup all-purpose flour

¼ teaspoon salt

¼ cup vegetable shortening, preferably Crisco, chilled

3 tablespoons cold unsalted butter, cut into cubes

1½ tablespoons ice water

1 tablespoon beaten egg

1 teaspoon distilled white vinegar

(put in freezer then grate)

In a large mixing bowl, sift the flour and salt together. Cut in the shortening and butter with a pastry blender or two knives until the pieces are the size of small peas. In a small mixing bowl, combine the ice water, egg, and vinegar. Sprinkle the egg mixture into the flour mixture a little at a time, mixing with a fork until all the flour mixture is moistened and the dough will form a ball. Knead the dough briefly and divide into 3 balls. Cover each with plastic wrap, and chill for at least 30 minutes.

Pat-a-Pan Pie Crust

Sometimes the thought of making a pie or tart is too daunting—mixing, chilling, and rolling out the dough alone can take an hour. Use this alternative, easy method for making *pâte sucrée*, or a sweet pie or tart crust, suitable for fruit-, custard-, or cream-filled pies and tarts. Just mix the dough with a fork, pat it into the pan, and bake.

MAKES ENOUGH FOR ONE 8- OR 9-INCH SINGLE-CRUST PIE

½ cup (1 stick) unsalted butter, melted

2 tablespoons sugar

1 cup all-purpose flour

In a large mixing bowl, combine the melted butter, sugar, and flour with a fork and stir until smooth.

Cookie Crust Pastry

This adaptation of the classic French *pâte sucrée* is the basis for delicious fruit and custard tarts. The crust tastes something like a sugar cookie, and hence the name. The unbaked tart shell may be frozen in the pan for up to 3 months.

MAKES ENOUGH FOR ONE 9- OR 10-INCH TART

½ cup (1 stick) cold unsalted butter, cut into cubes

1 large egg yolk

1 cup all-purpose flour

¼ teaspoon salt

½ teaspoon vanilla or almond extract

¼ cup sugar

Put all the ingredients in a food processor and process until the dough forms a ball, about 10 seconds.

Fats of the Land

"Good pastry should smell good," insist Ari Weinzweig and Mo Frechette, butter fanatics and partners in Zingerman's Deli in Ann Arbor, Michigan. "The bottom line on baked goods' flavor is that butter tastes better." The wonderful flavor of butter in cookies, for example, is often what sets the superior homemade product apart from the cheaper, commercially baked variety.

There are occasions, however, when vegetable shortening wins out over butter. With a lower melting point (90 degrees F) than vegetable shortening, butter can make pie doughs more difficult to roll out and can cause some cookie doughs to flatten and spread out too much on the baking sheet. Lard and vegetable oil are also used in pastries when a particular texture is desired. Here are some of your choices:

★ *American butter:* Most butter produced in the United States comes from Wisconsin and is 80 percent butterfat, 18 percent water, and 2 percent milk solids. Unsalted butter has a fresher flavor and is preferred for making the desserts in this book.

★ *American Plugra:* First introduced to American food professionals in 1989, this butter is 82 percent butterfat. The increased butterfat content results in a satiny smooth texture, a fresher flavor, and a higher cost—about 6 dollars per pound. American Plugra is available at gourmet shops and better health food stores.

★ *Cultured butter:* This is butter to which active cultures have been added for a slight tang. The flavor of this butter, made by the Vermont Butter and Cheese Company, ripens over time, getting better and bigger, like a fine cheese. Perfect for spreading on good bread, but expensive to use in baking, this butter is available at gourmet shops and better health food stores.

★ *Lard:* This is rendered hog fat. Many pie bakers swear by a lard pie crust for a very flaky texture, good workability, and flavor. Ask your butcher for leaf lard, which is lighter and fresher tasting than the blocks of lard available at the supermarket.

★ *Margarine:* This butter substitute developed in France has been produced on a large scale in this country since 1880. Like butter, margarine is 80 percent fat, 18 percent water, and 2 percent solids. However, the fat comes mainly from soybean or corn oils and is colored with synthetic carotene, or annatto. Selling yellow margarine was illegal in Wisconsin until 1967. Margarine is not recommended for pie crust because many brands have extra water or air beaten into the mixture.

★ *Vegetable oil:* The oil extracted from soybean, corn, safflower, and other seed kernels, it is used for crumbly textured pie crusts and in chiffon cakes for a moist texture.

★ *Vegetable shortening:* This is a solid vegetable fat that has been hydrogenated—combined with hydrogen—to improve its keeping qualities. Vegetable shortening produces a flaky pie crust, and because of its superior ability to cream with sugar, it makes a light-texture cake. Its higher melting point allows cookies and other doughs to retain their shape longer while baking.

Citrus-Scented Pastry

Crisp, sweet, and subtly flavored with citrus, this pastry is delicious for fresh fruit and custard tarts or a luscious Wildflower Honey Curd Tart (page 322) strewn with fresh berries.

MAKES ENOUGH FOR ONE 9-INCH ROUND OR 13 X 4-INCH RECTANGULAR TART

2 tablespoons flaked almonds

1$\frac{1}{2}$ cups all-purpose flour

$\frac{1}{4}$ cup sugar

2 teaspoons grated lemon or orange zest

6 tablespoons ($\frac{3}{4}$ stick) cold unsalted butter, cut into cubes

$\frac{1}{2}$ teaspoon vanilla extract

1 large egg yolk

3 tablespoons cold water

In a food processor, grind the almonds into powder. Add the flour, sugar, and zest and pulse to blend. Add the butter cubes and pulse until the mixture resembles coarse crumbs. Add the vanilla, egg yolk, and water and pulse just until the dough just forms a ball. Cover with plastic wrap, shape into a disk, and chill for 30 minutes.

Pastry Flowers

If you're pressed for time or don't yet have a feel for homemade pastry, try making pastry flowers from packaged phyllo dough, available in the frozen food section of the grocery store. These are delicious filled with Plum and Port Mousse (page 351), Harvest Moonshine (page 421), Wildflower Honey Cream (see page 348), or Lemon Curd (see page 321). Scatter with fresh berries and garnish with fresh mint leaves and rose petal confetti. **MAKES 1 DOZEN PASTRY SHELLS**

Nine 16 x 11-inch sheets frozen phyllo pastry, thawed according to package directions

$\frac{1}{2}$ cup (1 stick) unsalted butter, melted

$\frac{1}{4}$ cup sugar

1   Preheat the oven to 350 degrees F. Brush the inside of 12 muffins cups with some of the melted butter and set aside.

2   Carefully unwrap the sheets of phyllo dough. Take one sheet at a time and lay on a flat work surface. Trim to a 10-inch square with kitchen shears. Cut each trimmed sheet into 5-inch squares.

3   Brush 3 squares with melted butter, sprinkle with sugar, and arrange them attractively in a single muffin cup so that you have a petal effect. Repeat the process with the remaining phyllo sheets, butter, and sugar. Place a ball of aluminum foil in each cup to hold the shape of the phyllo. Bake until the pastry flowers have browned, 8 to 10 minutes.

4   Carefully remove the pastry flowers from the cups and let cool completely. Fill the cups right before serving so the pastry stays crisp.

Black Raspberry Pie

Altha Fertig picks black raspberries every year at a farm near Wilmington, Ohio. Those buckets of berries are destined for pies, and lots of them. Before she leaves to pick early in the morning, she makes up at least 6 batches of the double-crust pastry, wraps each ball of dough well, and chills it all until she gets home. Then she makes up each pie, wraps it well, and freezes it unbaked; these pies will keep for up to a year. Having at least one pie like this one in the freezer is a wonderful dessert insurance policy. (See page 264 for suggestions on wrapping a pie for the freezer and baking it frozen.) Blackberries and raspberries work well in this recipe, too.

MAKES ONE 9-INCH DOUBLE-CRUST PIE; 8 SERVINGS

FILLING
1 quart fresh black raspberries, blackberries, or red raspberries, picked over for stems

1/2 to 1 cup sugar, or to taste

3 tablespoons instant tapioca

1/2 teaspoon ground cinnamon

1 recipe Basic Flaky Double-Crust Pastry (page 264)

2 tablespoons unsalted butter, cut into small pieces

1   In a large mixing bowl, combine the berries with 1/2 cup of the sugar, the tapioca, and cinnamon and set aside for 30 minutes.   *(continued on page 272)*

Mix and Match Desserts

Creative dessert makers like to experiment. A trip to the berry patch, your own herb garden, or the farmer's market can be the inspiration for wonderful desserts—especially if you have some of the basics on hand:

★ A batch of Italian Meringue (see page 351), Wildflower Honey Cream (page 348), Strawberry Spoon Fruit (page 5), Classic Hot Fudge Sauce (see page 427), Caramel Sauce (see page 454), Cajeta (page 485), Wildflower Honey Curd (see page 322), or Lemon Curd (see page 321) in the refrigerator.

★ Disks of pastry and bags of fruit in the freezer

★ Meringues, Amaretti (page 96), or Chocolate Shortbread Cookies (page 128) in airtight containers.

Try a few of these Mix and Match Desserts:

Fresh Berry and Wildflower Honey Cream or Lemon Curd Tart: Line a tart pan with Citrus-Scented Pastry, pre-bake, and cool. Fill with about 2 cups of Wildflower Honey Cream or Lemon Curd. Top with fresh blueberries and blackberries or black, red, or golden raspberries.

Pound Cake with Wildflower Honey Cream and Strawberry Spoon Fruit: Cut a frozen and thawed pound cake into three layers horizontally. Spread the layers with about 1½ cups Wildflower Honey Cream. Chill, then slice and serve with Strawberry Spoon Fruit drizzled over it.

Marbled Frozen Fruit Mousse: Puree 2 cups of berries of your choice, add sugar and fresh lemon juice to taste, and pass the mixture through a sieve into a bowl to remove the seeds. Whip 1 cup of heavy cream until it holds stiff peaks and fold it into 2 cups of Italian Meringue. Lightly fold in the pureed fruit until the mixture looks marbleized. Spoon the mousse into ramekins or a loaf pan lined with plastic wrap, cover, and freeze. To serve, remove the plastic-wrapped mousse from the ramekins or pan, peel off the plastic, and arrange the mousse on dessert plates.

Coffee Cream Meringues with Classic Hot Fudge Sauce: Whip 1 cup of heavy cream with ¼ cup of sugar and 1 teaspoon instant espresso powder. Sandwich meringues together with the coffee-flavored cream and serve in a pool of chocolate sauce.

Individual Apple or Pear Tartlets with Caramel Sauce or Cajeta: From thawed sheets of frozen puff pastry, cut 5-inch circles. Peel, core, and thinly slice dessert apples or pears and arrange some slices on each puff pastry circle in a pretty pattern. Sprinkle the top of each tart with a little sugar. Bake in a preheated 400-degree-F oven until the pastry has puffed and the fruit is tender, 10 to 15 minutes. Serve drizzled with Caramel Sauce or Cajeta.

Thickeners for Fruit Fillings

Fruit fillings intended for cakes, pies, and tarts need to be thick enough to hold the filling together and clear enough to see through so the beauty of the fruit isn't masked. Veteran pie bakers have their favorites, whether it be instant tapioca granules or tapioca flour, cornstarch, or a new product called Instant Cleargel. Most thickeners are made from starchy root vegetables, which are processed to a dry powder.

★ *Cornstarch.* Whisk a few teaspoonfuls with a liquid until smooth, then blend into the fruit to be cooked. Cornstarch provides the thickening for most commercially prepared pie filling, but it can taste gluey.

★ *Instant Cleargel.* This thickener produces a smooth, clear filling. Mix with superfine sugar first, then stir into the fruit; that way the gel will not clump. Use about ¼ cup of Cleargel with ½ to 1 cup of sugar, depending on the sweetness of the berries, in a filling for a 9-inch pie.

★ *Instant tapioca granules or tapioca flour.* Combine about 3 tablespoons of dry tapioca granules or flour with sugar and stir into the fruit before cooking it in a saucepan on top of the stove or in a double-crust pie. Tapioca granules thicken with no perceivable flavor and give you clearer result than cornstarch.; however, you will get those tiny tapioca lumps.

(continued from page 270)

2   If you are going to bake this pie right away, preheat the oven to 450 degrees F. Remove the dough from the refrigerator and cut it in half. Roll out half of the dough on a floured work surface to a circle about 11 inches in diameter. Carefully place the circle of dough in the bottom of a 9-inch pie pan. (If you are going to freeze the pie, use a disposable aluminum pie pan.)

3   Taste the berry filling and add more sugar if necessary. Pour the filling into the prepared pie shell and set aside. Dot the filling with the butter pieces. Roll out the remaining half of the dough on a floured surface to a circle about 10 inches in diameter. Carefully place the circle of dough on top of the filling. Trim and crimp the edges of the two crusts together. Cut steam vents into the top crust with a paring knife. Place the pie on a baking sheet and bake for 10 minutes. Reduce the oven temperature to 350 degrees F and bake until the filling is bubbling and the crust has browned, 40 to 45 minutes more. Let cool before slicing.

Zinfandel's Concord Grape Streusel Pie

A piece of Concord grape pie was one of the things Susan Goss looked forward to when she visited her grandmother Louise Smith Dawson at her farm in Kokomo, Indiana. "One of my favorite childhood memories is the aroma of Concord grapes cooking in my grandmother's kitchen. This pie was one of her specialties, and she made it every fall when the grapes were ripe," remembers the chef and co-owner of Zinfandel restaurant in Chicago. At home, Goss uses a pie crust made with shortening; at the restaurant, she uses *pâte brisée* because it holds up better. My children also look forward to this treat when their grandmother Altha visits, bringing her own homemade Concord grape pies. **MAKES ONE 9-INCH DOUBLE-CRUST PIE; 8 SERVINGS**

FILLING

5 cups Concord or dark purple wine grapes

1 cup sugar

1/4 cup all-purpose flour

CRUST

1 1/2 cups all-purpose flour

1/4 teaspoon salt

1/2 cup vegetable shortening, chilled

3 to 4 tablespoons ice water, as needed

STREUSEL TOPPING

1 cup all-purpose flour

1/2 cup old-fashioned rolled oats

1/2 cup granulated sugar

1/2 cup packed dark brown sugar

1 cup (2 sticks) cold unsalted butter, cut into pieces

1 To make the filling, wash and stem the grapes. Slip the skins from the grapes with your fingers, letting the grape pulp drop into a medium-size heavy saucepan. Reserve the skins. Bring the pulp to a boil over medium heat and simmer until soft, about 10 minutes. Pass the pulp through a food mill or a fine-mesh sieve set over a bowl to remove the seeds. Stir the reserved skins into the puree. Whisk the sugar and flour into the grape puree and set aside to cool.

2 Meanwhile, make the crust: Whisk the flour and salt together in a large mixing bowl. Using a pastry blender or two knives, cut in the shortening until the mixture resembles coarse crumbs. Stir in enough of the ice water with a fork so that the dough forms clumps. With your hand, combine the clumps and knead together quickly into a smooth ball. Handle the pastry as little as possible to keep a tender crust. Cover the dough with plastic wrap and refrigerate for 20 to 30 minutes.

3 To make the streusel topping, whisk together the flour, oats, and both sugars in a large mixing bowl. With your fingertips, work in the butter pieces until you have a uniformly crumbly mixture. Set aside.

4 Preheat the oven to 450 degrees F. Remove the dough from the refrigerator. Roll out the dough on a floured work surface to an 11-inch circle. Carefully place the circle of dough in the bottom of a 9-inch pie pan.

5 Pour the filling into the prepared pan and sprinkle evenly with the streusel. Place on a baking sheet and bake for 15 minutes. Reduce the oven temperature to 350 degrees F and bake until the filling is bubbling and the streusel has browned, about 20 minutes more. Let cool before serving.

Bumbleberry Pie

When summertime guests of innkeepers Terri and Chris Milligan watch the sun set over Green Bay, the perfect accompaniment is a warm slice of Bumbleberry Pie, with a filling that is a jumble of berries, hence the quirky name. At their Inn at Kristofer's in Sister Bay, Wisconsin, the Milligans "make about twenty of these pies every week," says Terri, "and we always use Door County sour cherries with whatever berries are best at the time." My family prefers the combination of sour cherries, blackberries, and raspberries, but choose the berries to suit your taste and take advantage of what's freshest in the market. **MAKES ONE 9-INCH DOUBLE-CRUST PIE; 8 SERVINGS**

CRUST
2¼ cups all-purpose flour
½ teaspoon salt
½ cup (1 stick) cold unsalted butter, cubed
¼ cup vegetable shortening
4 to 6 tablespoons ice water, as needed

FILLING
1½ pounds (about 3 cups) fresh, frozen (thawed), or drained canned pitted sour cherries
1½ pints assorted fresh berries, such as blackberries, raspberries, blueberries, and/or hulled strawberries, sliced

¼ cup cornstarch
2 tablespoons all-purpose flour
1 cup sugar

GLAZE AND TOPPING
3 tablespoons heavy cream
1 large egg, beaten
2 teaspoons sugar

1 recipe Monticello Vanilla-Flecked Ice Cream (optional, page 425) for serving

1   To make the crust, sift the flour and salt into a large mixing bowl. Using a pastry blender or two knives, cut the butter and shortening into the dry ingredients until the mixture resembles coarse crumbs. Sprinkle the cold water, 1 tablespoon at a time, over the mixture, mixing lightly with a fork until the dough clumps together. Form the dough into 2 balls, one slightly larger than the other, and cover both with plastic wrap. Chill for 30 minutes. Meanwhile, preheat the oven to 425 degrees F.

2   To make the filling, pick over the berries for stems and slice the strawberries, if using. In a large mixing bowl, stir together the cherries, berries, cornstarch, flour, and sugar until well blended.

3   On a lightly floured work surface, roll out the larger ball of dough to a 10½-inch circle. Carefully line the bottom of a 9-inch pie pan with the dough and spoon in the filling. Roll out the smaller ball of dough to a 10-inch circle and center the circle of dough over the filling. With a paring knife, trim the overlapping dough to leave a ½-inch perimeter beyond the pie pan. Trim and crimp the edges of the 2 crusts together. Cut vents in the top crust to let the steam escape.

4   To make the glaze, in a small bowl, whisk the cream and egg together and brush this glaze over the top of the pie. Dust with the sugar and place on a baking sheet.

5   Bake the pie for 20 minutes, then reduce the oven temperature to 375 degrees F and bake until the crust has browned and the filling is bubbling, 55 to 60 minutes more. Serve warm with Monticello Vanilla-Flecked Ice Cream, if desired.

Sparkly-Top Sour Cherry Pie

If you're lucky enough to have a cherry tree in your back garden, take a tip from a veteran pie maker: Remove the cherry pits with a hairpin or paper clip to help the cherries keep their shape. You can "officially" freeze a well-wrapped unbaked fruit pie for up to 4 months, but I've frozen them for a year and then baked them with no discernible difference in taste. It's all in how well they're wrapped. Brush milk over the top of the pie crust, then dust with sugar for a sparkly top.

MAKES ONE 9-INCH DOUBLE-CRUST PIE; 8 SERVINGS

1 recipe Basic Flaky Double-Crust Pastry (page 264) or Farmhouse Lard Double-Crust Pastry (page 263)

4 cups fresh, frozen (thawed) or drained canned sour cherries, pitted

1 cup sugar, plus extra for sprinkling

3 tablespoons quick-cooking tapioca

1 tablespoon fresh lemon juice

1 teaspoon almond extract

1 tablespoon cold unsalted butter, cut into tiny pieces

2 tablespoons milk or heavy cream

1 Preheat the oven to 425 degrees F. Remove the dough from the refrigerator and cut it in half. Roll a half on a floured work surface into an 11-inch circle. Place in a 9-inch pie pan.

2 In large mixing bowl, combine the cherries, sugar, tapioca, lemon juice, and almond extract. Fill the pastry shell with the mixture. Dot the filling with the butter. Roll out the remaining half of the dough on a floured work surface to a circle about 10 inches in diameter. Set the top crust over the filling. Trim and crimp the edges together. Cut steam vents into the top crust. Brush the top with the milk and sprinkle lightly with sugar.

3 Place the pie on a baking sheet and bake for 15 minutes, then reduce the oven temperature to 350 degrees F and bake until the crust is golden, 45 to 60 minutes longer. Let cool before slicing.

Star-Spangled Peach and Red Currant Pie

By the Fourth of July, I had already picked my red currants and frozen them in 2-cup bags. I also had ripe peaches in a "use them or lose them" state. Luckily, I remembered cookbook author Ken Haedrich's recipe for peach and red currant pie, and I decided to adapt it. For the occasion, I used a cookie cutter to make star shapes to arrange for the top crust, a technique that can also save an unruly top crust that just won't roll out right. Warm from the oven with a scoop of Monticello Vanilla-Flecked Ice Cream (page 425) on top, you'll have the red and white of the day, and no one will feel a bit blue. MAKES ONE 9-INCH DOUBLE-CRUST PIE; 8 SERVINGS

1 recipe Basic Flaky Double-Crust Pastry (page 264) or Farmhouse Lard Double-Crust Pastry (page 263)

4 cups peeled and sliced ripe peaches (about 8 large peaches)

1 pint fresh or frozen (thawed) red currants

1 cup sugar, plus more for sprinkling

1/4 cup quick-cooking tapioca

1 tablespoon fresh lemon juice

1/2 teaspoon ground cinnamon

1 tablespoon heavy cream

1. Preheat the oven to 425 degrees F. Take the dough out of the refrigerator and cut in half. On a floured work surface, roll out the bottom crust to make an 11-inch circle. Line the bottom of a 9-inch pie pan with the pastry circle and trim the crust around the perimeter of the pan with a paring knife.

2. In a large mixing bowl, combine the peaches, currants, sugar, tapioca, lemon juice, and cinnamon. Spoon the filling into the pie shell and set aside.

3. Roll out the top crust to make a rough 9-inch square. Use a star-shaped cookie cutter to cut out star shapes. Arrange them attractively on top of the filling. Brush the stars with the cream and sprinkle with a little sugar.

4. Place the pie on a baking sheet and bake for 20 minutes. Reduce the oven temperature to 375 degrees F and bake until the crust has browned and the filling is bubbling in the middle, 40 to 45 minutes more. Let cool on a wire rack before slicing.

Pie Toppers

* *Basic top crust with vents.* After the top crust has been placed over the filling, use a paring knife to cut 5 to 7 vents, about $1/2$ to 1 inch long, in a decorative pattern.

* *Decorative dough disks.* At kitchen and gourmet shops, you can buy special circular dough disks—each with a different cut-out design—that you press into the top crust or roll with a rolling pin over the crust. These disks cut out designs in the top crust for a decorative finish; it's like having 20 small cookie cutters to cut out apples, hearts, leaves, or whatever shape you want, all at once.

* *Lattice.* Roll out the top crust to a 12-inch square about $1/8$ inch thick. Then, using a paring knife or a pastry wheel, cut strips about $1/2$ inch wide. On a baking sheet lined with parchment paper, carefully weave the strips of pastry together. Top the lattice with another piece of parchment paper and chill the pastry for at least 30 minutes on the baking sheet. When ready to use, remove the baking sheet from the refrigerator. Keeping the lattice pastry between the parchment papers, fold it in half. Remove what was the bottom parchment paper and place the bottom half of the folded lattice on the filled pie. Carefully unfold the lattice so it covers the whole pie. Discard the top sheet of parchment paper. With a paring knife, trim the excess lattice. Use your fingers to crimp the edges.

    For an easy, wide-lattice pie, cut the lattice strips 3 to 4 inches wide and weave them together.

* *Decorative shapes.* Roll out the top crust. Use small, decorative cookie cutters to cut out leaf, star, heart, or other shapes of your choice. Place the pastry shapes in a decorative design over the filling. This is a great way to "save" a recalcitrant top crust. You can also cut out shapes and arrange them in a kind of tableau in the center of a pie like pumpkin or sweet potato that is really not meant to have a top crust. Use large autumn leaves, tiny hands, a jack'o'lantern, a partridge in a pear tree, mittens, a quilt block, or other cookie cutter shapes of your choice, and simply arrange the cut-out pastry in the center of the pie and bake.

Mom's Prize-Winning Apple Pie

Now, this is a recipe title that makes professional food writers just titter. Whose mom? What prize? Well, this recipe has a true provenance. The winner is my mother, Jean Merkle, who won a $100 prize in 1980 for this version of classic apple pie. I look at the photograph of her standing proudly with her first-place ribbon and realize that she was the same age that I am now.

MAKES ONE 9-INCH DOUBLE-CRUST PIE; 8 SERVINGS

CRUST

2 cups all-purpose flour

1 teaspoon salt

1 teaspoon sugar

1/2 cup vegetable shortening, chilled

1/4 cup (1/2 stick) cold unsalted butter, cubed

1/4 cup plus 1 tablespoon ice water

FILLING

2 tablespoons dried Zante currants

1 tablespoon fresh lemon juice

7 medium-size tart, full-flavored apples, such as Northern Spy (Mom's pick) or Jonathan

2/3 cup sugar

2 tablespoons all-purpose flour

3/4 teaspoon ground cinnamon

1/4 teaspoon freshly grated nutmeg

1/4 teaspoon salt

1 large egg, beaten

Sugar for sprinkling

1   To make the crust, combine the flour, salt, and sugar in a large mixing bowl. Using a pastry blender or two knives, cut in the shortening and butter until the mixture resembles coarse crumbs. Gradually stir in the ice water with a fork until the dough forms clumps. With your hands, combine the clumps and knead together quickly into a smooth ball. Handle the pastry as little as possible to keep a tender crust. Cover with plastic wrap and chill for at least 1 hour.

2   Preheat the oven to 450 degrees F. To make the filling, put the currants in a small dish and sprinkle the lemon juice over them. Microwave on MEDIUM until the lemon juice is hot, about 30 seconds; set aside. Peel and core the apples, and thinly slice into a large mixing bowl. Toss them with the sugar, flour, cinnamon, nutmeg, and salt. Stir in the currants and lemon juice. Set aside.

3   Butter the inside of a 9-inch pie pan and set aside. Remove the dough from the refrigerator and cut it in half. Roll out one piece on a floured work surface to an 11-inch circle. Carefully fit the circle in the bottom of the prepared pie pan. Spoon in the filling. Roll out the other piece of dough

to a 10-inch circle. Carefully place the circle of dough on top of the filling. Crimp the edges of the pastry together and cut steam vents into the top crust with a paring knife. Brush the crust with the beaten egg and sprinkle with sugar.

4 Place the pie on a baking sheet and bake for 15 minutes. Reduce the oven temperature to 350 degrees F and bake until the filling is bubbling and the crust has browned, 35 to 40 minutes more. Let cool on a wire rack before slicing.

Pie Mary

Holmes County, Ohio, is known for three reasons: its stunningly graphic vintage Amish patchwork quilts from the 1930s and '40s, snapped up by New York City antique dealers; as the location of Winesburg, Ohio, the setting and title of the novel by Sherwood Anderson; and Pie Mary.

Now in her 80s, Mary Yoder of Holmesville, Ohio, started her adult life as a farm wife over 60 years ago. When one of her sons took over the family farm in 1973, she began her first cottage industry—quilting. When her fingers became too stiff to quilt, however, she switched to her current career as a baker in the late 1970s.

Known as Pie Mary, she and her husband, Andy, who is also in his 80s, bake up to 100 pies a day, 6 days a week, and sell them out of their kitchen. They know the drill well. "We make all the dough first," she says, "in four big batches. I put all my filling in hot, all from scratch. We never measure anything. We've done it so many times already." They also don't set timers or watch the clock while the pies bake in the oven. "Just keep them in there until they're nice and brown. That's all," advises Mary.

The sheer variety is amazing—cherry, apple, peach, pecan, raisin, peach pineapple, blueberry, black raspberry, elderberry, grape, Dutch apple, shoestring apple (a custard-style apple), ground cherry (a bland fruit usually flavored with lemon), banana, peanut butter, coconut cream, chocolate, butterscotch, pumpkin, and lemon. Some of the varieties, like elderberry in July, ground cherry in August, and pumpkin in November, are strictly seasonal.

"I just hardly ever use a recipe," Mary says. "I just know them by heart."

Wisconsin Cheddar-Crusted Apple Pie

The combination of a wedge of apple pie and a chunk of cheddar cheese, an English tradition, gets a contemporary makeover in this recipe. **MAKES ONE 9-INCH PIE**

FILLING

4 Granny Smith apples, cored, peeled, and sliced

$1/2$ cup sugar

$1/2$ teaspoon ground cinnamon

TOPPING

$3/4$ cup all-purpose flour

$1/2$ cup sugar

$1/2$ cup finely grated medium-sharp cheddar cheese, preferably aged Wisconsin cheddar

$1/2$ cup (1 stick) unsalted butter at room temperature

Good-quality ice cream for serving

1 Preheat the oven to 400 degrees F. To make the filling, in a large mixing bowl, combine the apples, sugar, and cinnamon. Put the filling into a 9-inch pie pan.

2 To make the topping, mix the flour, sugar, grated cheese, and butter together with your fingers in a medium-size mixing bowl until crumbly. Sprinkle this mixture evenly over the apple filling. Bake until browned and bubbling, 45 to 55 minutes. Let cool, then slice and serve with ice cream.

Appalachian Dried Fruit Stack Cake with Gingerbread Pastry

In the late 1960s, Eliot Wigginton founded the Foxfire educational program in Rabun Gap, Georgia. Students involved in Foxfire went into the southern mountains to interview the people who lived there and study their way of life, as many of the mountain folkways were dying out. The result was *Foxfire* magazine, which eventually became a series of Foxfire books, detailing methods of making candles, butchering hogs, spinning and weaving, building a log cabin, and gathering wild plants for medicinal tea. All of this information was accompanied by the engaging life stories of the Appalachian people who still did those things. Along the way, the students picked up many recipes that were later published in *The Foxfire Book of Appalachian Cookery*. This recipe is adapted from one in that book and is related to plate-pies from England.

MAKES ONE 9-INCH 3-LAYER PIE; 8 SERVINGS

2 cups all-purpose flour

1 teaspoon ground ginger

1 teaspoon ground allspice

2 teaspoons baking soda

1 teaspoon salt

½ cup vegetable shortening, chilled

½ cup granulated sugar

1 large egg

½ cup dark molasses

FILLING

2 cups mixed dried fruit, such as dried cherries, apple slices, apricots, and/or raisins

1 cup packed brown sugar

1 teaspoon ground cinnamon

Confectioners' sugar for dusting

1 Preheat the oven to 350 degrees F. Make a template: Invert a 9-inch cake pan and place a piece of parchment or waxed paper on top. Trace the perimeter of the bottom of the pan with a pencil. Cut out the circle and set aside. Grease three 9-inch cake pans and set aside.

2 To make the pastry, sift together the flour, ginger, allspice, baking soda, and salt in a large mixing bowl. Make a well in the center and set aside.

3 In a food processor or in a medium-size bowl with an electric mixer, cream the shortening and granulated sugar together until fluffy. Add the egg and molasses and beat until smooth. Spoon the creamed mixture into the well in the center of the dried mixture. Blend well with a fork, gradually stirring the dry mixture into the creamed ingredients to make a dough. Divide the dough into 3 equal portions. Turn out a portion of dough out onto a floured work surface and roll out to a rough 10-inch circle. Using the template, cut out a 9-inch circle of dough and place in a prepared cake pan. Prick the dough all over with a fork. Repeat with the remaining 2 portions of dough. Bake the pastry until lightly browned, 10 to 12 minutes. Let cool in the pans.

4 To make the filling, put the dried fruit in a medium-size saucepan with enough water to barely cover. Bring to a boil, then reduce the heat and simmer the fruit until softened, about 15 minutes.

Stack Cake

"There were always two apple stack cakes at every Christmas celebration and family reunion, one made by my mother and one made by my grandmother Virginia. Mom would make her cake the day before, then she'd set it out on the porch in a cake box, so all the juices from the cooked, dried apples would soak into it. It never failed that when she brought the cake back in there was at least one slice missing. One of the boys—there were nine of us kids—had sneaked a piece out, because, well, with all those relatives around, sometimes seventy-five or a hundred, that might be the only way you'd get to taste it."

MARY HESTER, IN EASTERN KENTUCKY, 1999

Mash the fruit with potato masher and stir in the brown sugar and cinnamon. Stir and cook for 5 more minutes. Remove from the heat and set aside to cool.

5 To assemble the stack pie, place one pastry layer on a cake plate and top with half of the dried fruit filling. Place the second pastry layer on top and spread with the remaining half of the filling. Place the third pastry layer on top and dust with confectioners' sugar.

Drying Apples

The earliest colonists had to wait years before their first orchards yielded apples. In those times, feast and famine, glut and dearth, were part of the normal cycle of life, even for the likes of Washington, Jefferson, and Adams. They divided their time between city life and their official duties, and country life at Washington's Mount Vernon, Jefferson's Monticello, and John Adams's farm in Braintree (now Quincy), Massachusetts. When the colonists finally did have apples ripening on the trees, they had a lot of them. Orchard fruit not eaten fresh or kept in a cold cellar to be baked (a favorite New England way with apples) was dried.

Some colonists sliced apples horizontally, removed the core, and dried the apple rings with the skin still on. Others quartered and cored the apples, then dried them in slices. Ideally, this was done outside, the apple rings or slices spread out on fine, sheer dimity or other cheesecloth-like fabric during a spell of warm, dry weather. If the weather did not cooperate, the apples were dried on trays in a slack or low beehive oven after the bread or cakes had already been baked. The dried apples might then by sewn into long strings with needle and stout thread, and the rings stored in the attic or hanging from the kitchen ceiling. Dried apples were used in compotes, in stuffings for roast pork or chicken, and in dishes like the Pennsylvania Dutch *schnitz und kneppe*—dried apple pieces (*schnitz*) cooked with ham and brown sugar for hours until finally a kind of dumpling batter (*kneppe*) was steamed on the top.

Long after others had given up the practice of drying apples, when iceboxes and refrigeration made fresh apples available for most of the year, people in the more isolated Appalachian Mountains still dried them. Today, you can buy small bags of dried apple slices at the grocery store for snacking or cooking.

To dry apples in the oven: Arrange the apples in a single layer on a baking sheet in a preheated 175-degree-F oven. Let dry until slightly chewy or longer, until brittle, about 12 hours.

To dry in a dehydrator: Follow the manufacturer's instructions.

To store dried apples: Put them in a resealable plastic bag and put them in the refrigerator, where they will keep indefinitely.

To cook dried apples: Reconstitute them with water, wine, cider, or another liquid in a saucepan over medium-high heat until softened, then drain.

Rustic Stone Fruit Pie

The free-form appearance of the pastry belies the extravagant flavor in the filling. Who wants to spend time crimping pastry when there are all those fresh stone fruits—peaches, nectarines, and plums—to enjoy in just a few weeks? Three different stone fruit varieties—white, yellow, and fragrant peaches or red, yellow, and Italian plums—team up with dried cherries and almonds to create a sumptuous dessert. This recipe is just as delicious using all of one variety.

MAKES ONE 9-INCH, SINGLE-CRUST, DEEP-DISH PIE; 8 SERVINGS

FILLING

¼ cup dried cherries

¼ cup amaretto

3 pounds ripe peaches (white, yellow, and fragrant varieties) or plums (red, yellow, and Italian)

1 cup packed light brown sugar

2 tablespoons fresh lemon juice

3 tablespoons quick-cooking tapioca

¼ cup sliced almonds

½ recipe Basic Flaky Double-Crust Pastry (page 264)

3 tablespoons cold unsalted butter, cut into small pieces

2 tablespoons milk

2 tablespoons sugar

1 Preheat the oven to 400 degrees F. To make the filling, put the cherries in a small heat-proof bowl. In a saucepan, heat the amaretto until hot, but not boiling, and pour over the dried cherries. Set aside to steep for several minutes.

2 Peel, pit, and slice the fruit and put in a large mixing bowl. Toss with the brown sugar, lemon juice, and tapioca. When the dried cherries have softened, drain them and fold into the peach mixture along with the almonds.

3 Take the dough out of the refrigerator. On a well-floured work surface, roll out the pastry to form a 14-inch circle. Use a well-floured flexible plastic cutting board to slip under the pastry and gently slide the pastry into a 9-inch deep-dish pie pan. Or fold the crust loosely around a rolling pin and unfold onto the pie pan. Line the pie pan with the pastry, leaving the excess pastry to hang over the pan. Heap the peach filling into the pie pan. Dot the filling with the butter. Carefully fold the outer edges of the circle of dough inward over the filling, pleating the dough when necessary. Brush the milk over the top crust and sprinkle with the granulated sugar.

4 Bake for 10 minutes, then reduce the oven temperature to 350 degrees F and bake until the crust is golden brown and the filling is bubbling, 35 to 40 minutes more. Allow to cool completely in the pan. Using two pancake turners, remove the pie from the pan and transfer to a cake plate or stand to serve.

Shaker Lemon Pie

For lemon lovers, there's nothing better than a warm slice of Shaker Lemon Pie. Puckery and rich, the filling is made with paper-thin slices of whole lemons. The simple yet ingenious nineteenth-century recipe from North Union Shaker Village, in northern Ohio, needs no updating—it's a classic.

MAKES ONE 9-INCH DOUBLE-CRUST PIE; 8 SERVINGS

1 recipe Farmhouse Lard Double-Crust Pastry (page 263) or Basic Flaky Double-Crust Pastry (page 264)

2 large lemons

2 cups sugar

4 large eggs, well beaten

1 Preheat the oven to 450 degrees F. Take the dough out of the refrigerator and cut it in half. On a floured work surface, roll out the pastry for the bottom crust into an 11-inch circle. Line a 9-inch pie pan with the pastry and set aside. Roll out the top crust to a 10-inch circle and set aside. Slice the lemons paper-thin with a sharp knife or mandolin; remove and discard the seeds.

2 Put the lemon slices and their juice in a large mixing bowl and blend with the sugar. Blend in the eggs and mix well. Spoon the filling into the pastry shell. Cover with the top crust and crimp the edges of the two crusts together. Cut several slits near the center of the pie to let steam escape.

3 Put the pie on a baking sheet and bake for 15 minutes, then reduce the oven temperature to 375 degrees F and continue baking until a knife inserted near the edge of the pie comes out clean, about 20 minutes more. Let cool. This pie slices best when it's just faintly warm or room temperature.

What a Peach!

A few months after my culinary book club read David Matsumoto's *Epitaph for a Peach* (HarperCollins, 1998), I ordered some of his Suncrest peaches when we met at my house in August. Picked ripe, right off the tree, they had the perfect peach flavor—sugar crisp, aromatic, and so full of juice that it would run down your arm. For me, a fresh peach is a perfect dessert.

Originating in China, peaches came to Europe in the 1600s. Peach orchards appear in early sketches of seventeenth-century farms in the Carolinas, and Jefferson grew them at Monticello in the eighteenth century. These antique peaches were probably white, with a more floral and aromatic flavor. In 1850, horticulturist Charles Downing introduced Chinese Cling peaches to the United States. Most of our peaches descend from that variety.

Today, about 25 different peach varieties are grown in the more temperate parts of the United States. About 50 percent of them come from California, although "Georgia" and "peaches" remain a combination that's hard to beat. Early summer peaches tend to be clingstones, in which the peach flesh adheres to the pit. Later peaches are usually of the freestone variety; the stone is easily removed from the fruit, which has a fuller flavor. The differences between the varieties have more to do with growing conditions than with taste. The longer a peach has to ripen, the better the flavor. Here are some of my favorite varieties:

★ *Belle of Georgia:* Creamy, white fruit with crimson streaks and a very peachy flavor.

★ *Biscoe:* A hardy peach that can withstand the vagaries of Midwestern and New England weather, it has a flavor that is slightly tart and aromatic.

★ *Glohaven:* A later summer peach, a little less juicy and more meaty, but full of peach flavor.

★ *Raritan Rose:* White-fleshed with a bright red skin, this peach has a honeyed flavor and a texture that almost melts in your mouth.

★ *Suncrest:* A crisp, slightly tart, and aromatic fruit.

★ *White Lady:* White-fleshed with a floral, aromatic taste.

Bear Lake Raspberry, Lemon, and Buttermilk Pie

Jackson Hole, Wyoming, is situated in a protected valley just south of the Grand Teton Mountains and the Snake River Range. Winter descends heavily here—to the delight of skiers—with lots of snow, arctic temperatures, and grazing elk that come down from the mountains. Still, the first warm days of summer are very welcome, as are the first wild berries of the year from nearby Bear Lake. Pastry chef Deno Marcum of the Snake River Grill developed this recipe, a pairing of traditional buttermilk pie with the best freshly picked berries. **MAKES ONE 9-INCH SINGLE-CRUST PIE; 8 SERVINGS**

1 recipe Jack's Vinegar Pie Crust (page 266) or Pat-a-Pan Pie Crust (page 267)

1 pint fresh raspberries, boysenberries, huckleberries, blueberries, or blackberries

1 1/2 cups sugar

1/4 teaspoon salt

4 large eggs

1/4 cup grated lemon zest (5 or 6 lemons)

1/3 cup all-purpose flour

1/2 cup (1 stick) unsalted butter, melted

1 1/2 cups buttermilk

3 tablespoons heavy cream

2 tablespoons fresh lemon juice

1/4 teaspoon vanilla extract

1/4 teaspoon freshly grated nutmeg

1   Preheat the oven to 350 degrees F. If using Jack's Vinegar Pie Crust, remove from the refrigerator. On a floured work surface, roll it into an 11-inch circle and transfer it to a 9-inch pie pan. Trim and crimp the edges of the crust. Or press the Pat-a-Pan Pie Crust over the bottom and up the sides of the pie pan. Carefully line either pastry with aluminum foil and fill with pie weights. Bake until the crust is golden brown, about 15 minutes. Remove the pie weights and foil, and cool the pie shell in the pan.

2   Reduce the oven temperature to 325 degrees F. Scatter the berries over the bottom of the pie shell. In a large mixing bowl, whisk the sugar, salt, eggs, lemon zest, flour, and melted butter together. Whisk in the buttermilk, cream, lemon juice, vanilla, and nutmeg and continue whisking until smooth. Pour the buttermilk mixture over the berries.

3   Place the pie on a baking sheet and bake until a cake tester inserted in the center comes out clean, 35 to 40 minutes. Let cool before slicing.

Sour Cream Raisin Pie

Rich, moist, and delicious, this old-fashioned pie is great to make in the winter, when fresh fruits are out of season. Somehow, when paired with sour cream, raisins taste a bit like chocolate chips. The brown sugar and oatmeal crust just pats into the pan.

MAKES ONE 9-INCH SINGLE-CRUST PIE; 8 SERVINGS

BROWN SUGAR–AND-OATMEAL CRUST

1/2 cup packed brown sugar

3/4 cup old-fashioned rolled oats

3/4 cup all-purpose flour

1/2 cup (1 stick) unsalted butter, melted

1/2 teaspoon baking soda

FILLING

2 cups raisins

3 large egg yolks

1 cup granulated sugar

1 1/2 cups sour cream

2 1/2 tablespoons cornstarch

1 teaspoon vanilla extract

1 Preheat the oven to 350 degrees F.

2 To make the crust, mix together the ingredients in a medium-size mixing bowl with your hands or a rubber spatula until the mixture holds together. Pat three quarters of it over the bottom and up the sides of a 9-inch pie pan. Reserve the rest. Bake for 7 minutes, then remove from the oven, but leave the oven on.

3 While the crust is baking, make the filling: In a small saucepan, boil the raisins in just a little bit of water until plumped, about 5 minutes. Drain and set aside to cool.

4 Blend the egg yolks, granulated sugar, sour cream, and cornstarch together in a large saucepan and whisk over medium heat until the mixture thickens, about 10 minutes. Remove from the heat, whisk in the vanilla, and fold in the raisins. Pour the filling over the partially baked crust. Sprinkle the remaining brown sugar–and-oat crumbs evenly on top of the filling

5 Place the pie on a baking sheet and bake until the top has browned, about 30 minutes. Let cool completely before cutting.

Hoosier Sugar Cream Pie

If Indiana had a state pie, this would be it. Not quite a custard pie, sugar cream pie is a relative of the chess and transparent pies from England by way of Kentucky. The recipe probably came to Indiana through the nineteenth-century Shaker communities that spread from New England to Pleasant Hill, Kentucky, and then northward to Harrison and Lebanon, Ohio, near the Indiana border.

When I made the original recipe, full of heavy cream and butter, I understood why some recipes have to evolve over time. The old version is just too rich for modern tastes. Thankfully, Hoosier cooks have given it a lighter touch. Directions in the earliest receipts call for mixing the filling in the unbaked crust, then stirring it with the fingers as it baked. This contemporary version saves fingers from burning by combining the ingredients in a bowl and baking the filling without stirring.

MAKES ONE 9-INCH SINGLE-CRUST PIE; 8 SERVINGS

½ recipe Basic Flaky Double-Crust Pastry (page 264)
1 cup heavy cream
1 cup half-and-half
1 cup sugar

½ cup all-purpose flour
3 tablespoons unsalted butter, cut into small pieces
¼ teaspoon freshly grated nutmeg

1   Preheat oven to 425 degrees F. Take the dough out of the refrigerator and on a floured work surface, roll out the pastry into an 11-inch circle. Line a 9-inch pie pan with the pastry, trim and crimp the edges, and set aside.

2   In a medium-size mixing bowl, stir together the heavy cream, half-and-half, sugar, and flour and mix well. Pour into the unbaked pie shell. Dot with the butter, then sprinkle with the nutmeg.

3   Place the pie on a baking sheet and bake for 15 minutes. Reduce the oven temperature to

I'll Take My Pie with Creme and Sugar

In 1944, Mr. and Mrs. "Wick" Wickersham began baking and selling sugar-creme pies based on his great-grandmother's recipe from their home base of Winchester, Indiana. The sugar-creme pies, and 18 other varieties, were made by hand and delivered to customers in the family's 1934 Buick sedan. Milk, sugar, flour, shortening, vanilla, and nutmeg combine to form a single-crust pie with a sweet, custard-like filling subtly scented with spice. (The "creme" indicates that although creamy in texture, the pie filling does not contain real cream.) Sugar-creme pie is still their best-seller, although Wick's Pies, Inc., makes 10,000 pies daily of several different varieties: pumpkin cheese, southern pecan, German chocolate, and peanut butter creme.

350 degrees F and continue baking until a cake tester inserted in the center comes out clean, about 45 minutes more. Let cool completely before slicing.

Deep-Dish Cider Cream Pie

Before electricity came to rural areas in the 1930s and '40s, farm families had to boil and then can cider to keep it from fermenting. The dark, sweet-tart boiled cider syrup was used on pancakes and in desserts like this one. If the top browns too quickly, remove the pie from the oven and cover the filling loosely with aluminum foil, then continue to bake. **MAKES ONE 8-INCH, SINGLE-CRUST, DEEP-DISH PIE; 8 SERVINGS**

2 cups apple cider

$\frac{1}{2}$ recipe Basic Flaky Double-Crust Pastry (page 264)

3 large eggs, separated

1 cup sugar

$1\frac{1}{2}$ tablespoons all-purpose flour

1 cup milk

1 teaspoon ground cinnamon

2 tablespoons unsalted butter, melted

1 In a medium-size heavy saucepan, bring the cider to a boil and continue to boil until it has reduced to 1 cup, about 10 minutes. Set aside to cool.

2 Preheat the oven to 450 degrees F. Take the dough out of the refrigerator and on a floured work surface, roll out the pastry into an 11-inch circle. Line an 8-inch deep-dish pie pan with the pastry, trim and crimp the edges, and set aside.

3 With an electric mixer, beat the cooled cider, egg yolks, sugar, flour, milk, cinnamon, and melted butter in a large mixing bowl. Wash and dry the beaters well. Still using the electric mixer, whip the egg whites in a medium-size mixing bowl until the egg whites hold stiff peaks. Fold the beaten egg whites into the cider mixture with a rubber spatula until you can no longer see them. Pour the filling into the prepared pie shell and place the pie on a baking sheet.

4 Bake the pie for 10 minutes. Reduce the oven temperature to 350 degrees F and continue to bake until a cake tester inserted in the center of the pie comes out clean, about 30 minutes more. Remove from the oven and let cool before serving.

Caramelized Banana Cream Icebox Pie

This is adapted from a recipe by popular television chef Caprial Pence, who co-owns Caprial's Bistro in Portland, Oregon. Caprial gives a classic banana cream pie a new twist with a chocolate crumb crust, caramelized bananas, and pastry cream instead of a plain cooked custard. Basic banana cream pie is good, but this has a definite "wow" factor. At her bistro, Caprial serves each slice topped with decoratively piped whipped cream, several slices of roasted banana, and a mint sprig. "We always run out of this pie," she says. And no wonder! **MAKES ONE 10-INCH SINGLE-CRUST PIE; 8 SERVINGS**

CHOCOLATE CRUMB CRUST

2½ cups crumbs from Chocolate Shortbread Cookies (page 128) or store-bought chocolate wafers

¼ cup granulated sugar

1 teaspoon ground cinnamon

5 tablespoons unsalted butter, melted

FILLING

¼ cup (½ stick) unsalted butter

¾ cup packed dark brown sugar

1 teaspoon ground cinnamon

¼ teaspoon freshly grated nutmeg

½ teaspoon ground allspice

4 ripe but firm bananas, peeled and cut into 1-inch-thick slices

2 recipes Rum-Flavored Pastry Cream (see variation, page 164)

TOPPING

1 cup heavy cream

Fresh mint sprigs for garnish

1   Grease the inside of a 10-inch springform pan. To make the crust, in a medium-size mixing bowl, combine the ingredients with a fork. Press the mixture over the bottom and up the sides of the pan. Chill for 30 minutes.

2   To make the filling, melt the butter with the brown sugar in a large skillet over medium-high heat. Stir in the spices and bananas and cook, stirring, until the bananas are tender, about 3 minutes. Remove from the heat and let cool to room temperature. Then spoon the filling into the chilled crumb crust. Spoon the pastry cream over the banana mixture. Cover with plastic wrap and chill the pie until firm, 2 to 3 hours.

3   Right before serving, release and remove the sides of the pan and transfer the pie to serving plate. With an electric mixer, whip the cream in a medium-size bowl until it holds stiff peaks. Spoon or pipe the whipped cream over the top of the pie. To serve, garnish each slice with a mint sprig.

Nutmeg-Scented Coconut Custard Pie

This is one of my favorite pies, a sweet indulgence. I have adapted this recipe from *The Margaret Rudkin Pepperidge Farm Cookbook*, published in 1963. There actually was a real Pepperidge Farm, a 125-acre plot in rural Connecticut that Margaret and her husband, Henry, bought in 1926. When Margaret developed concerns about her family's health in 1937 and wanted more natural foods in their diet, she started experimenting with recipes for homemade stone-ground whole-wheat bread. Thus, the Pepperidge Farm empire was born. I am a big fan of their frozen layer cakes, especially the coconut, and it's good to know that Margaret herself was a great cook.

MAKES ONE 9-INCH SINGLE-CRUST PIE; 8 SERVINGS

1 recipe Jack's Vinegar Pie Crust (page 266) or Pat-a-Pan Pie Crust (page 267)

1 large egg white

4 large eggs

1/4 cup plus 1 tablespoon sugar

1/4 teaspoon salt

3 cups half-and-half

1 teaspoon vanilla extract

1/4 teaspoon freshly grated nutmeg

1/2 cup sweetened flaked coconut, plus extra for garnish

1 cup heavy cream

1   Preheat the oven to 450 degrees F. If using Jack's Vinegar Crust, remove it from the refrigerator. On a floured work surface, roll it into an 11-inch circle and transfer it to a 9-inch pie pan. Trim and crimp the edges of the crust. Or press the Pat-a-Pan Pie Crust over the bottom and up the sides of the pie pan. Whisk the egg white in a small bowl until frothy, then brush the inside of the pie pastry with the egg white. Chill for 15 minutes.

2   To make the filling, whisk the eggs, 1/4 cup of the sugar, and the salt together in a large mixing bowl until the egg mixture is smooth. Whisk in the half-and-half until well blended. Whisk in the vanilla, nutmeg, and coconut. Pour the filling into the pie shell.

3   Place the pie on a baking sheet and bake for 10 minutes, then reduce the oven heat to 300 degrees F and bake until a cake tester inserted in the center comes out clean, about 50 minutes more. Let the pie cool completely. To make the topping, with an electric mixer, whip the cream and remaining 1 tablespoon of sugar together in a medium-size mixing bowl until the cream holds stiff peaks. Spoon or pipe the whipped cream over the top of the cooled pie and sprinkle with sweetened flaked coconut.

Fresh Orange Marmalade Pie

This is a great pie to make during the winter months, when citrus fruit is in season. Because the marmalade makes about 2 cups, why not bake and enjoy one pie and wrap and freeze the other? A pie in the freezer is a cook's best insurance for feeding surprise guests. **MAKES TWO 9-INCH SINGLE-CRUST PIES; SERVES 16**

1 recipe Basic Flaky Double-Crust Pastry (page 264)

2 cups sugar

$^1\!/_4$ cup plus 1 tablespoon cornstarch

$^1\!/_2$ cup (1 stick) unsalted butter at room temperature

6 large eggs

1 recipe Fresh Orange Marmalade (page 6)

1   Preheat the oven to 425 degrees F. Take the dough out of the refrigerator and cut in half. Roll out each half on a floured work surface into an 11-inch circle. Carefully place each one in a 9-inch pie pan. Set aside.

2   With an electric mixer, beat together the sugar, cornstarch, and softened butter in a large mixing bowl until light and fluffy. Beat in the eggs, one at a time, beating well after each addition. With a rubber spatula, fold in the marmalade. Spoon half of the filling into each pie shell.

3   Place the pies on a baking sheet and bake for 10 minutes, then reduce the oven temperature to 350 degrees F and bake until the pies are lightly browned and a cake tester inserted in the middle comes out clean, 35 to 40 minutes longer. Let cool before slicing.

Luscious Lemon Meringue Pie

I have worked with this recipe to get every aspect of this beloved pie close to perfection: crisp and fragrant *pasta frolla* pastry that can be patted into the pie pan and doesn't get soggy; a tart yet sweet and buttery lemon custard filling that is a close cousin to lemon curd; and a gossamer meringue with just the right touch of chewiness. Both the pastry and the filling can be made ahead. The trick with this pie is to keep the meringue from "weeping," or oozing a clear liquid after it has baked. The late cookbook author Michael Field opted to beat half a teaspoon of calcium phosphate (available in drugstores) into his five—egg white meringue. Food guru and cookbook author Shirley

Corriher recommends adding a cooked cornstarch mixture to the meringue before adding the sugar, a method I use here. I love the way the in-house bakeries in Draeger's California grocery stores make whimsical meringue loop-de-loops on their pies—like Esther Williams diving backward into a Hollywood pool.

MAKES ONE 9-INCH SINGLE-CRUST PIE; 8 SERVINGS

PASTA FROLLA
2 large egg yolks

$\frac{1}{2}$ cup granulated sugar

1 cup all-purpose flour

$\frac{1}{4}$ cup ($\frac{1}{2}$ stick) unsalted butter at room temperature

$\frac{1}{2}$ teaspoon grated lemon zest

1 teaspoon Marsala or dry sherry

FILLING
Grated zest of 2 lemons

$\frac{1}{3}$ cup fresh lemon juice (about 2 large lemons)

3 large egg yolks

1 large egg

$\frac{1}{3}$ cup granulated sugar

$\frac{1}{2}$ cup heavy cream

2 teaspoons cornstarch

5 tablespoons unsalted butter, cut into small pieces

MERINGUE
2 teaspoons cornstarch

2 tablespoons water

5 large egg whites

$\frac{1}{2}$ teaspoon cream of tartar

1 teaspoon vanilla extract

$\frac{2}{3}$ cup superfine sugar

1   To make the pastry, in a food processor, blend the egg yolks and granulated sugar together until thick and pale yellow. Add $\frac{1}{2}$ cup of the flour, the butter, lemon zest, and Marsala and pulse to blend. Add just enough of the remaining $\frac{1}{2}$ cup of flour to make a soft dough, pulsing to blend. Do not overwork the dough. Cover the pastry with plastic wrap and chill for 30 minutes.

2   Preheat the oven to 375 degrees F. Pat the pastry evenly over the bottom and up the sides of a 9-inch pie pan. With a paring knife, trim the pastry flush with the rim of the pie pan. Cover with plastic wrap and chill for 15 minutes.

3   Prick the dough all over with a fork, then with the tines, crimp the edges of the pastry. Bake until light golden brown, 10 to 12 minutes. Let cool on a wire rack.

4   To make the filling, combine the lemon zest and juice in a small ceramic or plastic bowl and set aside. In a medium-size nonreactive saucepan, whisk together the egg yolks, whole egg, and granulated sugar until thick and lemon colored. In a small jar, combine the cornstarch and cream, secure the lid, and shake to blend. Whisk the cornstarch mixture into the saucepan. Whisk in the lemon juice mixture and place the saucepan over medium heat. Cook, whisking constantly, and

add the butter, one small piece at a time. The custard is done when it is slightly thickened and coats the whisk, about 8 minutes. Remove from the heat and transfer to a bowl. Cover and let cool to room temperature, or cover and chill for up to 2 weeks before serving.

5   Preheat the oven to 325 degrees F. To make the meringue, combine the cornstarch and water in a small saucepan over medium heat. Whisk until the cornstarch has dissolved into the water and then thickened, about 3 minutes. Remove from the heat and let cool for 5 minutes. With an electric mixer on high speed, beat the egg whites and cream of tartar in a large mixing bowl until the egg whites are foamy. Beat in the cornstarch mixture, then the vanilla. When the egg whites hold soft peaks, start adding the superfine sugar, ⅓ cup at a time, beating until the egg whites turn glossy and have tripled in volume.

6   Spoon the cooled filling into the pie shell. Using a rubber spatula, spread the meringue on top of the filling without touching the pie crust. To make decorative swirls, press the spatula down on the meringue and then lift it straight up. Make sure you cover all the filling, so it doesn't seep out.

7   Place the pie on a baking sheet and bake until the meringue has browned, 25 to 30 minutes. Let cool completely before cutting.

Tales of Lemon Meringue Pie

Jane Grigson speculated in *The Observer Guide to British Cookery* that the precursor to American lemon meringue pie might be Chester pudding, popular in northwestern England in the 1860s. The lemon filling in Chester pudding, however, features blanched and grated almonds, which do not appear in American versions of lemon meringue pie. But there could be a link.

By 1879, in Marion Cabel Tyree's *Housekeeping in Old Virginia*, there were four different versions of a lemon dessert with meringue topping; some were baked in a pie shell. A dessert called "lemon meringue" seems to be a missing link between Chester pudding, Bakewell Tart (page 319), and modern lemon meringue pie. It featured a custard-like pudding made with bread crumbs soaked in milk, sugar, egg yolks, and lemon zest; the pudding was then topped with fruit jelly and meringue and baked again. Most of our American pies began as puddings baked in a pastry shell, and they were indeed called "puddings" in the earliest cookbooks. You have to look closely at the end of the directions to see where the pastry comes in. Over time, the almonds or bread crumbs used as a thickener were discarded in favor of the lighter cornstarch or tapioca because they became readily available to home cooks.

By the early 1900s, lemon meringue pie had become a public eating house staple, served coast to coast in establishments such as Boston's Parker House and Salt Lake City's Lion House Social Center. In a 1997 poll of *Bon Appétit* readers, lemon meringue pie rated third among favorite old-fashioned desserts, just behind apple pie à la mode and strawberry shortcake.

Florida Key Lime Pie

Key limes are smaller and sharper in flavor than the Persian limes that you usually see at the grocery store, and they have seeds. When the sharp juice meets a creamy filling, you get a dessert so good it can stand the test of time. Since at least 1939, when a Key lime pie recipe first appeared in a Key West community cookbook, this pie has been a Floridian favorite. When Key limes are not available, use a mixture of common Persian limes and lemons to get that characteristic tangy flavor. Although Key lime juice is available bottled, I prefer to use fresh fruit for a better taste. You'll need about 1¼ pounds of fruit or about 24 Key limes. **MAKES ONE 9-INCH SINGLE-CRUST PIE; 8 SERVINGS**

1 recipe Crumb Crust made with cinnamon graham cracker crumbs (see page 249), patted over the bottom and up the sides of a 9-inch pie pan

3 large egg yolks

One 14-ounce can sweetened condensed milk

½ cup plus 2 tablespoons fresh Key lime juice, or half fresh lime juice and half fresh lemon juice

Grated zest of 1 lime, plus extra for garnish

1 cup heavy cream

¼ cup confectioners' sugar

1 teaspoon vanilla extract

1 Preheat the oven to 350 degrees F. Bake the crust for 5 minutes and let cool. Do not turn off the oven.

2 To make the filling, with an electric mixer on high speed, beat the egg yolks and condensed milk in a large mixing bowl until light and fluffy, about 5 minutes. Gradually beat in the lime juice and zest. Pour the filling into the prepared crust and bake until a cake tester inserted in the center comes out clean, 7 to 8 minutes. Set aside to cool completely. Wash and dry the beaters well.

3 To make the whipped topping, with an electric mixer, beat together the heavy cream, confectioners' sugar, and vanilla in a medium-size mixing bowl until the cream holds stiff peaks. Mound the topping over the cooled pie and sprinkle with grated lime zest. Refrigerate for at least 2 hours, or until ready to serve.

Secret Lemon Pie

In the late nineteenth and early twentieth centuries, canned milk was a staple in most households. Fresh milk was not always available, and canned milk sold well. By 1928, however, the Borden Company needed to push their canned milk products, so they produced the "Borden Condensed Milk Magic Recipes" booklet, with a version of this pie recipe made with sweetened condensed milk. By the late 1960s, my mother was making this chilled and creamy pie for summer gatherings. Her secret? A filling made with frozen lemonade, fresh lemon juice and zest, and whipped cream, but no eggs (unlike the Key lime version). I blend the condensed milk mixture and the whipped cream just until it looks marbleized, then I fill the pie shell.

MAKES ONE 9-INCH SINGLE-CRUST PIE; 8 SERVINGS

1 recipe Crumb Crust made with cinnamon graham crackers (see page 249), patted over the bottom and up the sides of a 9-inch pie pan

One 14-ounce can sweetened condensed milk

One 6-ounce can frozen lemonade, thawed

Grated zest and juice of 2 lemons

1 or 2 drops yellow food coloring

1 cup heavy cream

Paper-thin lemon slices for garnish

1   Preheat the oven to 350 degrees F. Bake the crust for 5 minutes and let cool.

2   To make the filling, with an electric mixer on high speed, beat the condensed milk and lemonade in a large mixing bowl and beat until light and fluffy, about 5 minutes. Beat in the lemon zest and juice and the food coloring.

3   Wash and dry the beaters well. Still using the electric mixer, whip the heavy cream in a medium-size mixing bowl until it holds stiff peaks. Using a rubber spatula, fold the whipped cream into the condensed milk mixture, then spoon the filling into the prepared crust. Garnish with lemon slices. Cover and chill for at least 2 hours, or until ready to serve.

Frozen Margarita Pie

Folks who like an occasional sojourn in Margaritaville will love this pie, a boozy riff on the now-classic combination of citrus and sweetened condensed milk. This no-bake pie from Texas assembles in minutes, but needs at least 2 hours to freeze. It also tastes great simply refrigerated for a couple of hours, or until well chilled, instead of frozen. This one is not for the kids. **MAKES ONE 9-INCH SINGLE-CRUST PIE; 8 SERVINGS**

1 recipe Crumb Crust made with graham cracker crumbs (see page 249), patted over the bottom and up the sides of a 9-inch pie pan

2 tablespoons tequila

1 tablespoon orange curaçao liqueur

1 tablespoon blue curaçao liqueur

One 14-ounce can sweetened condensed milk

1/4 cup fresh lime juice

1 cup heavy cream

Grated lime zest for garnish

1   Preheat the oven to 350 degrees F. Bake the crust for 5 minutes and let cool.

2   To make the filling, combine the tequila, liqueurs, and condensed milk in a large mixing bowl and beat with an electric mixer on high speed until light and fluffy, about 5 minutes. Gradually beat in the lime juice.

3   Wash and dry the beaters well and beat the heavy cream until it holds stiff peaks. Fold the whipped cream into the condensed milk mixture. Spoon the filling into the prepared pie crust and freeze until solid, about 2 hours.

4   To serve, remove the pie and let soften for about 15 minutes. Sprinkle with grated lime zest, then cut into individual servings.

Mile-High Strawberry Pie

In the early 1970s, Americans were in love with Julia Child. The Vietnam War had ended. College students who weren't busy burning their bras or flags took advantage of a great exchange rate and traveled to Europe. And mile-high pies—pastry or crumb crusts piled at least 6 inches high with clouds of meringue and whipped cream—were offered at every trendy casual restaurant. This pie is still fabulous, but if you have concerns about un-cooked egg whites, use the powdered form and follow the package instructions. Allow 8 hours for the pie to freeze. **MAKES ONE 9-INCH SINGLE-CRUST PIE; 8 SERVINGS**

One 16-ounce package frozen sweetened strawberries, partially thawed

1/2 cup granulated sugar

1 tablespoon fresh lemon juice

1/8 teaspoon salt

4 large egg whites

1 cup heavy cream

1/4 cup confectioners' sugar

1 teaspoon vanilla extract

1 recipe Nut Crust (see page 259) made with almonds, patted over the bottom and up the sides of a 9-inch springform pan and baked

1 With an electric mixer on low speed, beat the strawberries, granulated sugar, lemon juice, salt, and egg whites in a large mixing bowl until just blended. Gradually increase the speed of the mixer to high and beat until the strawberry mixture is light and fluffy, about 18 more minutes.

2 Wash and dry the beaters well and in a medium-size mixing bowl, beat the heavy cream, confectioners' sugar, and vanilla until the cream mixture holds soft peaks. Using a rubber spatula, fold the whipped cream into the strawberry mixture and spoon the filling into the prepared crust. Cover with plastic wrap and freeze for 8 hours or overnight.

3 Remove from the freezer about 30 minutes before serving, and release and remove the sides of the pan.

French Chocolate Silk Pie

Creamy, smooth, and chocolaty French chocolate silk pie probably entered the American pie pantheon in the 1960s, when, thanks to Julia Child and Jacqueline Kennedy, we were discovering the French delights of chocolate mousse and *pots de crème*. Early recipes for this pie filling resemble a whipped *pot de crème*, made with uncooked egg yolks. This version starts with a chocolate ganache enriched with egg yolks, butter, and sugar, which is then cooked to a thin custard. Finally, the custard is whipped to get the light texture characteristic of French silk. My daughter Sarah, the French major, counts this pie as her favorite. Remember, the better the chocolate, the better the pie. **MAKES ONE 9-INCH SINGLE-CRUST PIE; 8 SERVINGS**

½ recipe Basic Flaky Double-Crust Pastry (page 264)

1 cup heavy cream

1 cup good quality semisweet chocolate pieces or chips

3 tablespoons unsalted butter

⅓ cup sugar

2 large egg yolks

3 tablespoons crème de cacao (optional)

Whipped cream for garnish

1 Preheat the oven to 350 degrees F. Take the dough out of the refrigerator and on a floured work surface, roll out the pastry into an 11-inch circle. Line a 9-inch pie pan with the pastry, and trim and crimp the edges.

2 Carefully line the pastry with aluminum foil and fill with pie weights. Bake until the crust is golden brown, about 15 minutes. Remove the pie weights and foil, and cool the pie shell in the pan.

3 In a medium-size heavy saucepan, combine the heavy cream, chocolate, butter, and sugar over low heat. Cook, stirring, until the chocolate and butter melt and the mixture is smooth, about 10 minutes.

4 Beat the egg yolks lightly in a medium-size bowl. Whisk half of the hot chocolate mixture into the egg yolks, then whisk this egg yolk–and-chocolate mixture back into the saucepan. Continue to cook over medium heat, whisking occasionally, until the custard thickens, about 5 minutes. Remove from the heat and stir in the crème de cacao, if using.

5 Place the saucepan in a large bowl of ice water. Stir the custard until it becomes stiff and hard to stir, about 20 minutes.

6 Transfer the mixture to a medium-size mixing bowl. Beat with an electric mixer on medium to high speed until the filling is light and fluffy, about 3 minutes. Spoon into the prepared pie shell and chill for at least 5 hours.

7 To serve, either spread whipped cream over the filling, or serve each wedge of pie with a dollop.

Iron Skillet Chocolate Pie

Some American pie fillings, like butterscotch and chocolate, are best made in a heavy, seasoned cast-iron skillet, as our grandmothers used to do. Somehow, the flavor is richer and the color darker. If you don't have an iron skillet, make this in a heavy saucepan instead. The flavor is wonderfully fudgy. This pie would also be delicious with a chocolate wafer Crumb Crust (see page 249). Instead of the meringue topping, you could also pipe rosettes of sweetened whipped cream on top of the cooled pie.

MAKES ONE 9-INCH PIE; 8 SERVINGS

1 recipe Jack's Vinegar Pie Crust (page 266) or Pat-a-Pan Pie Crust (page 267)

3 tablespoons unsalted butter

3 tablespoons unsweetened cocoa powder

1 cup plus 2 tablespoons sugar

3 tablespoons all-purpose flour

2 large eggs, separated

1 cup milk

1 teaspoon vanilla extract

1   Preheat the oven to 350 degrees F. If using Jack's Vinegar Pie Crust, remove from the refrigerator. On a floured work surface, roll it into an 11-inch circle and transfer it to a 9-inch pie pan. Trim and crimp the edges of the crust. Or press the Pat-a-Pan Pie Crust over the bottom and up the sides of the pie pan. Carefully line either pastry with aluminum foil and fill with pie weights. Bake until the crust is golden brown, about 15 minutes. Remove the pie weights and foil, and cool the pie shell in the pan. Position a rack at the top of the oven and raise the oven temperature to 450 degrees F.

2   Melt the butter in a seasoned cast-iron skillet over medium heat. Whisk in the cocoa powder until well blended. In a small mixing bowl, whisk together 1 cup of the sugar and the flour, then whisk this mixture into the cocoa butter. In the same bowl, whisk the egg yolks and milk together, then whisk this into the skillet. Continue to cook the mixture over medium heat, whisking, until it thickens, about 10 minutes. Whisk in the vanilla, then pour the filling into the prepared pie shell and set aside to cool for 1 hour.

3   With an electric mixer, beat the egg whites and remaining 2 tablespoons of sugar in a medium-size mixing bowl until the egg whites hold stiff peaks. Using a rubber spatula, mound the meringue over the chocolate filling. Bake the pie at the top of the oven until the meringue browns, about 5 minutes.

Chocolate-Crusted Brownie Pie with Mocha Glaze

This is the ultimate brownie from the more-more-more-'80s, adapted from a recipe by cookbook author Lee Bailey.

MAKES ONE 9-INCH SINGLE-CRUST PIE; 8 SERVINGS

CHOCOLATE CRUST

¾ cup all-purpose flour

3 tablespoons packed light brown sugar

6 tablespoons (¾ stick) unsalted butter, frozen and cut into small pieces

6 tablespoons vegetable shortening, frozen and cut into small pieces

1 tablespoon unsweetened cocoa powder

1 teaspoon vanilla extract

1 to 2 tablespoons cold milk

FILLING

3 ounces unsweetened chocolate

2 ounces semisweet chocolate

¾ cup (1½ sticks) unsalted butter at room temperature

1 cup plus 2 tablespoons granulated sugar

¼ teaspoon salt

2 large eggs

2 teaspoons vanilla extract

½ cup coarsely chopped pecans or walnuts (optional)

½ cup plus 1 tablespoon all-purpose flour

TOPPING

1 cup packed light brown sugar

½ cup heavy cream

2 tablespoons unsalted butter

1 teaspoon instant espresso powder

½ cup confectioners' sugar

1 Preheat the oven to 350 degrees F. To make the crust, in a food processor, combine the flour, brown sugar, butter, shortening, and cocoa powder and pulse until the mixture resembles coarse meal. Add the vanilla and 1 tablespoon of the milk and process until just combined. Add a little more milk if the mixture still seems dry. Flour your hands and press the sticky mixture evenly into the bottom and up the sides of a 9-inch pie pan. Set aside.

2 To make the filling, melt both chocolates in the top of a double boiler over simmering water. Whisk in the butter, 1 tablespoon at a time, until well blended. Remove from the heat and whisk in the granulated sugar, salt, and eggs. Stir in the vanilla and nuts, if using, then stir in the flour, ¼ cup at a time. Pour the filling into the pastry shell. Bake until a toothpick inserted in the center comes out clean, about 30 minutes. Let cool.

3 To make the topping, combine the brown sugar, heavy cream, and butter in a medium-size heavy

saucepan over medium-high heat and bring to a boil. Sift the espresso powder and confectioners' sugar into the work bowl of a food processor. When the cream mixture begins to boil, take it off the heat and pour it into the food processor. Process until smooth. Pour the topping over the pie. The topping sets up quickly and the pie will be ready to serve in 30 minutes.

Montana Three-Layer Chokecherry Pie

Chokecherries (*Prunus virginiana*) are small, bitter-tasting wild fruits that are more pit than pulp. They are too bitter to eat raw, but they make excellent syrups and jellies. Chokecherry trees grow wild over much of the United States, but if you don't know what they look like, they just blend into the unnoticed fringes of yards, parking lots, creek sides, and riverbanks. The community of Lewistown, Montana, celebrates their chokecherry harvest every fall with a festival on the first Saturday after Labor Day. This three-layer pie is adapted from one served at the Lewistown Chokecherry Festival. It can be made with similar bitter fruits, such as lingonberries and cranberries.

MAKES ONE 9-INCH SINGLE-CRUST PIE; 8 SERVINGS

½ recipe Basic Flaky Double-Crust Pastry (page 264)

CHOKECHERRY FILLING
1 pint chokecherries, lingonberries, or cranberries, picked over for stems

2½ cups water

3 tablespoons cornstarch

1 cup granulated sugar

Juice of ½ lemon

½ teaspoon almond extract

CREAM CHEESE FILLING
Two 3-ounce packages cream cheese at room temperature

¾ cup confectioners' sugar

½ cup heavy cream

TOPPING
½ cup heavy cream

1 Preheat the oven to 350 degrees F. Take the dough out of the refrigerator and on a floured work surface, roll out the pastry into an 11-inch circle. Line a 9-inch pie pan with the pastry, and trim and crimp the edges.

2 Carefully line the pastry with aluminum foil and fill with pie weights. Bake until the crust is golden brown, about 15 minutes. Remove the pie weights and foil, and cool the pie shell in the pan.

3 To make the chokecherry filling, line a strainer with a layer of cheesecloth and place it over a

medium-size mixing bowl. Combine the chokecherries and water in a large saucepan and bring to a boil over medium-high heat. Mash with a potato masher, then reduce the heat to low and simmer for 30 minutes, mashing occasionally. Pour the chokecherry mixture through the lined strainer. Press the fruit with a rubber spatula to extract as much juice as possible. Measure 2 cups of chokecherry juice into a measuring cup. Discard the solids left in the sieve and any remaining juice.

4   Pour $\frac{1}{2}$ cup of the reserved juice into a jar. Add the cornstarch, secure the lid, and shake to blend. Set aside. Pour the remaining $1\frac{1}{2}$ cups of juice into a clean medium-size saucepan, stir in the granulated sugar, and bring to a boil. Whisk in the cornstarch mixture and cook, whisking constantly, until the mixture thickens, about 5 minutes. Remove from the heat and stir in the lemon juice and almond extract. Set aside to cool to room temperature.

5   To make the cream cheese filling, with an electric mixer, beat the cream cheese and confectioners' sugar together in a medium-size mixing bowl. Beat in the heavy cream and continue beating until the cream cheese mixture is light and fluffy, about 3 minutes. Spread this over the bottom of the prebaked pie shell and smooth the top with a rubber spatula. Spoon or pour all but $\frac{1}{2}$ cup of the thickened chokecherry mixture over the cream cheese layer.

6   Wash and dry the beaters well. To make the topping, beat the heavy cream in a medium-size mixing bowl until it holds stiff peaks. Fold the reserved $\frac{1}{2}$ cup of chokecherry mixture into the cream and spoon this on top of the pie. Serve immediately or chill until ready to serve.

Pennsylvania Dutch Shoofly Pie

This pie inspired the American song "Shoofly Pie and Apple Pan Dowdy," which Dinah Shore sang in 1946. Traditionally made during late winter, when the supply of fresh fruits stored in the root cellar had been depleted, shoofly pie is still rich and good. Our collective taste for a heavy molasses flavor has diminished over the years, so I have reduced the amount of it in this pie. Pure cane syrup is my first choice because it is lighter in texture, but just as flavorful as molasses.

MAKES ONE 9-INCH SINGLE-CRUST PIE; 8 SERVINGS

½ recipe Basic Flaky Double-Crust Pastry (page 264) or Farmhouse Lard Double-Crust Pastry (page 263)

TOPPING

⅔ cup packed light brown sugar

½ cup all-purpose flour

1½ teaspoons ground cinnamon

½ teaspoon freshly grated nutmeg

¼ cup (½ stick) unsalted butter at room temperature

FILLING

2 large eggs

½ cup light corn syrup

½ cup pure cane syrup, molasses, or sorghum

½ teaspoon baking soda dissolved in 1 cup warm water

1 cup raisins

1 Preheat the oven to 400 degrees F. Take the dough out of the refrigerator and on a floured work surface, roll out the dough into an 11-inch circle. Line a 9-inch pie pan with the pastry, trim and crimp the edges, and set aside.

2 To make the topping, combine the brown sugar, flour, spices, and butter in a small mixing bowl, working the butter into the mixture with your fingers. Set aside.

3 To make the filling, whisk together the eggs, corn syrup, and cane syrup until well blended. Whisk in the baking soda mixture and blend well. Sprinkle the raisins evenly over the bottom of the pie shell. Pour the filling over the raisins and sprinkle the filling with one third of the topping.

4 Place the pie on a baking sheet and bake for 25 minutes. Sprinkle the pie with the rest of the topping and bake until browned and bubbling, about 5 more minutes. Serve warm or at room temperature.

Dear Abby Pecan Pie

Ann Landers and Abigail Van Buren were what the British call "agony aunts" or as we say, "advice columnists." These twin sisters from Iowa practically invented the genre in their daily columns appearing in competing newspaper syndicates. I always read both of them in the *Kansas City Star*. The year 2002, however, saw a sad but expected change. Ann Landers passed away, and her column ended. Abigail Van Buren passed the torch to daughter Jeanne Phillips, who continues to write as "Dear Abby."

Almost every year, a reader would write to Dear Abby, requesting her recipe for pecan pie. I have adapted this recipe from the one I clipped in the newspaper.

MAKES ONE 8-INCH SINGLE-CRUST PIE; 8 TO 10 SERVINGS

1 recipe Jack's Vinegar Pie Crust (page 266)

1 cup light corn syrup

1 cup packed dark brown sugar

3 large eggs, lightly beaten

5 1/2 tablespoons unsalted butter, melted

1/2 teaspoon salt

1 teaspoon vanilla extract

1 1/4 cups pecan halves

1   Preheat the oven to 350 degrees F. Take the dough out of the refrigerator and on a floured work surface, roll out the dough into an 11-inch circle. Line an 8-inch pie pan with the pastry, trim and crimp the edges, and set aside.

2   In a large mixing bowl, stir together the corn syrup, brown sugar, eggs, melted butter, salt, and vanilla until smooth and well blended. Scatter the pecans over the bottom of the pie shell and pour the filling on top.

3   Place the pie on a baking sheet and bake until a cake tester inserted in the center comes out clean, 45 to 55 minutes. Serve warm or at room temperature.

A Season of Pies in the Ozarks

In the *Ozarks Collection: The Best Recipes from the Heritage and Traditions of a Storied Region* (The Ozarks Mountaineer, 1987), co-authors Billy Joe Tatum and Ann Taylor Packer follow the seasons in the "hills and hollers" of the Ozark Mountains. This area encompasses the four corners of Missouri, Arkansas, Kansas, and Oklahoma. Beginning about 1830, settlers traveling westward mainly from the Southern states of Virginia, North Carolina, Kentucky, and Tennessee arrived in the region to scratch a bare living in the mountains. Their main diet was "hog and hominy," plus whatever wild game could be shot and whatever wild greens or fruits could be foraged.

Until electricity and modern highways invaded, the Ozarks was an area of isolation and wild beauty. The authors recount, "There was a time when the season could be told by the pies being served . . . In the country, we are more attuned to nature, as we are closer to it . . . So when strawberries are ripe in our region, we make strawberry pie. Later come peaches. Still later, or overlapping in time, the wild blackberries ripen. Singly or in combination, in pan pie or cobbler, pies are the dessert of choice. Comes later summer and it's apples, pumpkins and persimmons."

During the winter months when there was no fresh fruit, enterprising Ozarks cooks made desserts like vinegar cobbler, which had a filling made of vinegar, molasses, butter, sugar, and cinnamon. Other choices were pinto bean pie, made with cooked and mashed pinto beans mixed with egg yolks, sugar, and cinnamon, baked in a pie shell, and covered with meringue; and oatmeal pie, made with a filling of toasted oats, sugar, corn syrup, eggs, salt, and vanilla.

Maple Walnut Pie

In the mid 1970s, when I lived in South Burlington, Vermont, I discovered the culinary delights of fiddlehead ferns, corn cob–smoked cheese, and Grade B maple syrup, which is darker and heartier than the usual Grade A. My then-husband was working in a small animal veterinary practice owned by Dr. Harold Brown. Harold and his wife, Janice, had worked hard for their own little piece of heaven—acreage and a camp in a sugarbush a few miles away. In the spring, the whole family and lots of friends like us gathered to tap their maple trees and make enough syrup to last the rest of the year. In addition to treasured jugs of the syrup, Janice gave me this recipe, which, to my mind, tastes best made with the darker Grade B. If you like pecan pie, you'll love this.

MAKES ONE 9-INCH SINGLE-CRUST PIE; 8 SERVINGS

$\frac{1}{2}$ recipe Basic Flaky Double-Crust Pastry (page 264)

3 large eggs

$\frac{1}{2}$ cup plus 1 tablespoons sugar

$\frac{1}{2}$ teaspoon salt

$1\frac{1}{2}$ cups pure maple syrup

$1\frac{1}{8}$ teaspoons vanilla extract

1 cup chopped walnuts or pecans

1   Preheat the oven to 350 degrees F. Take the dough out of the refrigerator and on a floured work surface, roll out the pastry into an 11-inch circle. Line a 9-inch pie pan with the pastry, and trim and crimp the edges.

2   Carefully line the pastry with aluminum foil and fill with pie weights. Bake until the crust is golden brown, about 15 minutes. Remove the pie weights and foil, and cool the pie shell in the pan. Raise the oven temperature to 375 degrees F.

3   To make the filling, with an electric mixer, beat the eggs in a medium-size mixing bowl. Beat in the sugar, salt, maple syrup, and vanilla. Sprinkle the walnuts in the bottom of the pie shell and pour the filling over the nuts.

4   Place the pie on a baking sheet and bake until a cake tester inserted in the center comes out clean, 35 to 40 minutes. Serve warm or at room temperature.

Derby Pie with Bourbon Whipped Cream

Rich and sweet with chocolate, nuts, and sugar and topped with bourbon-laced whipped cream, this pie is traditionally served during the Kentucky Derby festivities the first weekend in May. But it's also delicious any other time of year.

MAKES ONE 9-INCH SINGLE-CRUST PIE; 8 SERVINGS

$\frac{1}{2}$ recipe Basic Flaky Double-Crust Pastry (page 264)

3$\frac{1}{4}$ cups granulated sugar

$\frac{3}{4}$ cup packed brown sugar

$\frac{1}{2}$ cup (1 stick) unsalted butter at room temperature

$\frac{1}{2}$ cup all-purpose flour

2 large eggs, beaten

One 6-ounce bag semisweet chocolate chips

1 cup walnuts, chopped

1 teaspoon vanilla extract

1 cup cold heavy cream

$\frac{1}{4}$ cup bourbon, such as Early Times, Knob Creek, Maker's Mark, Wild Turkey Kentucky Spirit, or Elijah Craig 12-Year-Old

1   Preheat the oven to 350 degrees F. Take the dough out of the refrigerator and on a floured work surface, roll out the pastry into an 11-inch circle. Line a 9-inch pie pan with the pastry, and trim and crimp the edges.

2   Carefully line the pastry with aluminum foil and fill with pie weights. Bake until the crust is golden brown, about 15 minutes. Remove the pie weights and foil, and cool the pie shell in the pan.

3   With an electric mixer, beat together both sugars, the butter, and flour in a large mixing bowl until well blended. Beat in the eggs, then stir in the chocolate chips, walnuts, and vanilla and blend well. Spoon the mixture into the prepared pie shell and bake until a cake tester inserted in the center comes out clean, 35 to 45 minutes. Let cool. Wash and dry the beaters well.

4   Right before serving, with an electric mixer, whip the cream in a medium-size mixing bowl until it holds soft peaks. Gradually add the bourbon and whip until the mixture holds stiff peaks. To serve, spoon a generous dollop of cream onto each piece of pie.

Butternut Squash Pie

Golden colored and mellow with spices, this classic autumn pie tastes lighter to me than sweet potato pie. If you don't want to bother cooking squash, use frozen cooked squash. **MAKES ONE 9-INCH SINGLE-CRUST PIE; 8 SERVINGS**

$^1/_2$ recipe Basic Flaky Double-Crust Pastry (page 264)

$1^1/_2$ cups cooked and pureed butternut squash (see Note)

$^3/_4$ cup sugar

1 tablespoon all-purpose flour

$^1/_4$ teaspoon salt

$^1/_2$ teaspoon ground ginger

$^1/_4$ teaspoon freshly grated nutmeg

1 teaspoon ground cinnamon

1 large egg, beaten

$1^1/_2$ cups milk

2 tablespoons unsalted butter, melted

1   Preheat the oven to 450 degrees F. Take the dough out of the refrigerator and on a floured work surface, roll out the pastry into an 11-inch circle. Line a 9-inch pie pan with the pastry, trim and crimp the edges, and set aside.

2   With an electric mixer, beat the squash, sugar, flour, salt, and spices in a large mixing bowl until well combined. Beat in the egg, milk, and melted butter, and continue beating until smooth. Spoon the filling into the pie shell.

3   Place the pie on a baking sheet and bake for 15 minutes, then reduce the oven temperature to 325 degrees F and bake until the filling is firm and a cake tester inserted in the center comes out clean, about 40 more minutes.

> **NOTE** To cook the fresh butternut squash, cut the squash in half lengthwise and remove the seeds with a fork. Preheat the oven to 350 degrees F. Place the squash, cut side down, on a baking sheet lined with aluminum foil. Bake for 45 minutes, or until the squash seems tender when pierced with a fork. Using oven mitts, scrape the squash from the rind into a food processor. Puree the squash, let cool, and measure out $1^1/_2$ cups.

Pumpkin Pecan Streusel Pie

I am not a fan of your basic pumpkin pie made with filling from a can and loads of spices. It's too heavy for me. I either like pumpkin pie made with fresh pumpkin (see *Prairie Home Cooking*, page 389) or this recipe from Bev Fertig, my former sister-in-law. With its pecan crust and streusel topping, this pie is truly worthy of the holiday dinner spotlight. What's even better, this recipe makes 2 pies or 2 dozen tartlets, so you'll be sure to have enough. **MAKES TWO 8-INCH SINGLE-CRUST PIES OR 2 DOZEN TARTS**

PECAN CRUST

2 cups all-purpose flour

¼ cup finely chopped pecans

1 teaspoon salt

⅔ cup plus 2 tablespoons vegetable shortening

4 to 5 tablespoons ice water, as needed

FILLING

One 15-ounce can pumpkin puree

1 large egg

One 14-ounce can sweetened condensed milk

STREUSEL TOPPING

½ cup packed brown sugar

¼ cup all-purpose flour

¼ cup chopped pecans

¼ cup (½ stick) unsalted butter at room temperature

½ teaspoon ground cinnamon

1   To make the crust, combine the flour, pecans, and salt in a medium-size mixing bowl. Using a pastry blender or two knives, cut in the shortening until the mixture resembles coarse crumbs. Sprinkle the ice water, 1 tablespoon at a time, over the crumb mixture, stirring it into the mix with a fork. Add enough ice water so that the dough almost cleans the bowl. Divide the dough in half, cover with plastic wrap, and refrigerate for 30 minutes.

2   Preheat the oven to 375 degrees F. Roll out each portion of dough on a lightly floured work surface into an 11-inch circle. Fit each dough circle into the bottom of an 8-inch pie pan, trim, and crimp the edges of the crust. Set aside. Or, to make tartlets, use a 3-inch biscuit cutter to cut rounds of pastry from each dough circle. Line each of 24 tartlet pans with a small round and crimp the edge of the crust.

3   To make the filling, in a large mixing bowl, blend the ingredients until smooth. Pour half of the mixture into each prepared pie shell.

4 Combine the topping ingredients in a medium-size mixing bowl, working in the butter with your fingers or with a fork until crumbly. Sprinkle half this mixture over the top of each pie.

5 Place the pies or tartlets on a baking sheet and bake until a cake tester inserted in the center comes out clean, 50 to 55 minutes for pies, 30 to 35 minutes for tartlets.

James Beard's Pumpkin Pie with Candied Ginger

With cream and cognac in the filling, this is not your ordinary pumpkin pie, so it would be a shame to use ordinary canned pumpkin. Buy small sugar or pie pumpkins, which come on the market around Halloween, and save them in your refrigerator for Thanksgiving. One medium-size sugar pumpkin will yield 3 cups of puree. Fresh pumpkin really makes a difference in the flavor and texture of this pie. The late, great James Beard—the culinary guiding light for whom the James Beard House and James Beard restaurant and cookbook awards are named—would definitely approve. This recipe is adapted from a classic James Beard pumpkin pie.

MAKES TWO 9-INCH SINGLE-CRUST PIES; 16 SERVINGS

1 recipe Farmhouse Lard Double-Crust Pastry (page 263) or Basic Flaky Double-Crust Pastry (page 264), or a double recipe Jack's Vinegar Pie Crust (page 266)

2 cups cooked and pureed pumpkin (see Note)

6 large eggs

2 cups heavy cream

$\frac{2}{3}$ cup sugar

$\frac{1}{2}$ cup cognac

1 teaspoon ground cinnamon

$\frac{1}{4}$ teaspoon freshly grated nutmeg

$\frac{1}{4}$ teaspoon ground cloves

$\frac{1}{4}$ teaspoon salt

$\frac{1}{2}$ cup finely chopped crystallized ginger

Whipped cream for garnish

1 Preheat the oven to 425 degrees F. Remove the dough from the refrigerator and cut it in half. Roll half of the dough on a floured work surface into a circle about 11 inches in diameter. Place on the bottom of a 9-inch pie pan. Repeat with the other portion of dough.

2 Carefully line the pie shells with aluminum foil and fill with pie weights. Bake the pie shells for 12 minutes. Remove the foil and pie weights and set the pie shells aside. Reduce the oven temperature to 375 degrees F.

3 To make the filling, in the work bowl of a food processor, combine the pumpkin, eggs, heavy cream, sugar, cognac, spices, and salt and pulse to blend. Taste for seasoning and add more spices if desired. Spoon or pour half the filling into each pie shell. Dot the surface of the filling of each pie with pieces of crystallized ginger.

4 Bake the pies until a cake tester inserted in the center comes out clean, 35 to 40 minutes. Serve each slice with a dollop of whipped cream.

> **NOTE** To cook fresh pumpkin, simply stem, and then cut sugar pumpkins in 3 or 4 pieces and remove the seeds. Place them, flesh side down, on a parchment paper–lined baking sheet and roast in a preheated 350-degree-F oven until tender, 45 to 60 minutes. Scoop out the flesh and puree in a food processor.

The Quest for Pie

When the late writer Michael Dorris was a child, he loved to go on long summer trips with his mother and aunt, driving cross-country to visit relatives. Although he was too young to drive, he was old enough to navigate. The Dorris family took their trips in 400-mile-a-day segments, respecting the 50 miles an hour the car would go and the 8 hours a day the driver and passengers could tolerate. He described their trips in an article that appeared in *Gastronomica*, a food magazine.

"Looking back," he wrote, "I realize now that our journeys could quite accurately be described as a quest for pie. For instance, like experienced surfers who chart odd itineraries (Laguna to Capetown by way of The Big Island) in order to snag a reliable wave en route, I always had to include Paoli, Indiana, in any cross-country trip. There was a café off the square in that otherwise undistinguished hamlet where was found, according to my mother the connoisseur, a lattice crust like no other. Woven in intricate patterns across a sea of blueberry or peach, each segment was crisp and melting, studded with just the right amount of sugar, laced with a subtle jolt of almond extract, and browned to perfection. If I brought us through Paoli too soon after a major meal, we might order our twenty-five-cents-apiece slices for the crust alone, reluctantly leaving the fruit on the green plastic plates."

If you envision 50 black-garbed Pilgrims sitting down with 90 Wampanoags to a slice of pumpkin pie during the first Thanksgiving feast at Plymouth in 1621, you're in for a shock.

Pumpkin pie as we now know it had not yet been concocted in the early seventeenth century. And besides, there were no forks. Each Pilgrim sat down to the communal table with a personal knife, a spoon, and a large napkin, as was the custom of the time. Each diner had his or her own wooden plates, or trencher, which was sometimes shared with another diner (or "trenchermate"). They served themselves from each platter.

You would think that such a momentous occasion would be very well documented, but such is not the case. (As in modern days, hindsight is 20/20.) Very few written references to this historic dinner remain. Historians do know, however, that wild fowl and venison were served at this 3-day feast, a fact related in Edward Winslow's 1621 letter, the only surviving description of the event itself. The other elements of the meal must be surmised from knowledge of English precedents, such as harvest festivals held in the fall, usually around the English holiday of Michaelmas on September 29. (Historians theorize that the first Thanksgiving might have been held on that date, or somewhere between September 21 and November 11.) During these festivals, held after the harvest had been safely gathered in, the manor or village held a community feast featuring rather simple foods—meat, bread, and beer, for example. In addition to the large mid-day meals (leftovers were served later in the day), the feast included time for leisure and recreation. The Puritans didn't go in for card games and dancing, but they were all for physical games and tests of strength.

The food for the first Thanksgiving would have been prepared by the four surviving Pilgrim housewives, all steeped in the English cookery techniques of Elizabethan and Jacobean England. Imagine making it through a difficult year in the wilderness only to have to cater a three-day event for 140 people! And all of this without grocery stores, appliances, or convenience products of any kind.

The foods the housewives did have to work with included stores of grain and spices left over from the voyage; wild fruits and vegetables; the squash, beans, and corn the Wampanoags grew; wild game and fowl; some not-very-good barley from the first harvest; and fish and shellfish from the sea. I wonder how many were homesick for the traditional Michaelmas goose, a hunk of bread, and good mug of beer.

The housewives would have used spits to roast the meats; cauldrons of boiling water to cook puddings wrapped in cloth, along with meat and vegetables in earthenware vessels; and iron saucepans and three-legged skillets to cook still more vegetables and sauces.

Researchers at Plimoth Plantation, the living history museum on the site of the Pilgrim's first settlement at Plymouth, propose that desserts similar to furmenty and prune tart were served for the first Thanksgiving. Furmenty (also spelled "frumenty"), is a spiced pudding made with cracked grains, cream, and eggs. This is a dish that goes back to medieval times and is the antecedent of the more sophisticated steamed English Christmas pudding and our Indian Pudding. Prune tarts may have been filled with dried wild beach plums or even fox grapes, and flavored with rosewater. The tart, which would have used up precious wheat flour, would have been a special treat that first year, until wheat could be planted and harvested the next year. Pumpkin pie had to wait another century.

Deep-Dish Sweet Potato Pie

"I was probably about 25 years old before I ever tasted pumpkin pie," confesses Southern food expert John T. Edge of Mississippi, the author of *A Gracious Plenty* (Penguin, 1999). "We always had sweet potato pie for Thanksgiving and Christmas," he says. I adore this version, with a lighter texture from the eggs and half-and-half, but with that sweet spiciness that we love in pumpkin pie. Indeed, you can substitute canned pumpkin for the sweet potato here for yet another variety of pumpkin pie.

MAKES ONE 9-INCH DEEP-DISH PIE; 8 SERVINGS

1 recipe Pat-a-Pan Pie Crust (page 267) or Jack's Vinegar Pie Crust (page 266), or ½ recipe Basic Flaky Double-Crust Pastry (page 264)

3 medium-size sweet potatoes, baked or boiled until tender

⅔ cup packed dark brown sugar

1 teaspoon ground cinnamon

½ teaspoon ground ginger

¼ teaspoon freshly grated nutmeg

2 large eggs

2 cups half-and-half

Whipped cream for garnish

1   Press the Pat-a-Pan Pie Crust into the bottom and up the sides of a 9-inch pan. Or, if using Jack's Vinegar Pie Crust or Basic Flaky Double-Crust Pastry, remove the dough from the refrigerator and on a floured work surface, roll out the pastry into an 11-inch circle. Line the pie pan with the pastry, and trim and crimp the edges. Place the pie shell on a baking sheet and set aside.

2   Preheat the oven to 450 degrees F. With a paring knife, peel the skin from the baked sweet potatoes and place the potatoes in a food processor. Process until smooth, then measure 1½ cups of the puree and place in a large mixing bowl. With an electric mixer, beat in the brown sugar and spices until smooth. Then add the eggs, beating until well blended, and then the half-and-half. Carefully pour the filling into the prepared pie shell.

3   Bake the pie for 10 minutes, then reduce the oven temperature to 350 degrees F. Bake until a cake tester inserted in the center comes out clean and the custard is set, about 45 minutes more. Let cool. Serve warm or at room temperature, garnished with rosettes of whipped cream.

Fresh Berry Cookie Crust Tart

Here is another mix-and-match dessert that is simply delicious. Because the cookie crust pastry is easy to work with, you could try patting it into a heart- or petal-shaped tart pan for a different look. This is wonderful served with Monticello Vanilla-Flecked Ice Cream (page 425). **MAKES ONE 9- OR 9¹/₂-INCH TART; 8 SERVINGS**

1 recipe Cookie Crust Pastry (page 267) or
   Citrus-Scented Pastry (page 269)

1 quart fresh raspberries, blueberries, blackberries,
   or loganberries

Confectioners' sugar

1   Preheat the oven to 350 degrees F. Pat the Cookie Crust Pastry over the bottom and up the sides of a 9- or 9¹/₂-inch tart pan. Or take the Citrus-Scented Pastry out of the refrigerator and roll it between two sheets of parchment paper into a circle about 12 inches in diameter. Carefully remove one sheet of paper and drape the pastry, paper side up, over the tart pan. Remove the second sheet of paper. Press the pastry carefully into the pan. Roll the rolling pin over the perimeter of the pan to trim the edges of the pastry neatly. Cover the pie shell with plastic wrap and refrigerate for 15 minutes.

2   Pick over the berries for stems and spoon them into the pastry-lined tart pan.

3   Place the pie on a baking sheet and bake until the pastry has browned, about 45 minutes. Sprinkle with confectioners' sugar while still warm. Serve warm, at room temperature, or cold.

Fresh Strawberry Tart

This is one of my favorite desserts in late May or early June, when our first locally grown strawberries come into season. I use a recipe I got years ago from Maddelena Riggi, known to devoted friends, family, and restaurant patrons as Mamma Francesca. Born near Rome, Riggi brought her home-style Italian cooking to Cincinnati in the late 1960s and developed a loyal following long before Italian cooking gained the prominence it has today. The *pasta frolla* is very easy to work with for either a tart or tartlets. You just press it into the pan. Although Mamma Francesca made her pastry dough by hand, I use the food processor for a gloriously beautiful dessert requiring very little work. **MAKES ONE 9-INCH TART OR 8 TARTLETS; 8 SERVINGS**

1 recipe *Pasta Frolla* (see page 293, step 1)

1 quart fresh strawberries, hulled

One 10-ounce jar strawberry or red currant jelly

1 tablespoon Marsala or dry sherry

TOPPING

1 cup heavy cream

2 tablespoons confectioners' sugar

1   Preheat the oven to 375 degrees F. Remove the pastry from the refrigerator.

2   With your hands, press the dough into the bottom and up the sides of a 9-inch tart pan or 8 small tartlet pans. Flute the edges, if desired. Prick the dough all over with a fork. Bake the large tart shell for 12 to 15 minutes, the smaller tartlet shells for 8 to 10 minutes, until golden brown. Let cool completely on a wire rack and release the tart or each tartlet crust from the pan (see page 323).

3   To make the filling, place the strawberries, hulled side down, on the cooled pastry in a pleasing pattern. In a saucepan, heat the jelly and Marsala together over low heat until melted and transparent. Carefully pour or brush the glaze over the berries. Chill the pie for 1 to 2 hours to set the glaze.

4   Right before serving, make the topping. With an electric mixer, whip the heavy cream in a medium-size mixing bowl until it holds soft peaks, then whip in the confectioners' sugar and continue beating until the cream holds stiff peaks. Using a spoon or a pastry bag fitted with a star tip, pipe a whipped cream border around the pie.

Sour Cream Peach Tart

The rolling dairy country of southern Wisconsin produces not only fresh butters and lush and creamy cheeses, but also wonderful orchard fruits like apples and peaches. The summer flavors of fresh peach, almond, and cream come together in this easy dessert. Fresh plums also work well in this recipe.

MAKES ONE 10-INCH ROUND TART OR 1 DOZEN TARTLETS; 10 TO 12 SERVINGS

1 recipe *Pasta Frolla* (see page 293, step 1) or Pat-a-Pan Pie Crust (page 267)

1 cup sour cream

2 large egg yolks

¼ cup sugar

2 tablespoons fresh lemon juice

4 large ripe peaches, peeled, pitted, and sliced

¼ cup sliced almonds

1 tablespoon cold unsalted butter, cut into small pieces

1   Preheat the oven to 350 degrees F. Press the pastry into the bottom and up the sides of a 10-inch tart or 12 tartlet pans. Roll the rolling pin over the top of the tart rim(s) to trim the crust evenly. Chill for 30 minutes.

2   Prick the pastry all over with a fork. Carefully line the pastry with aluminum foil and fill with pie weights. Bake until the pastry turns golden brown, 12 to 15 minutes. Carefully remove the foil and pie weights. Cool completely and release the tart or tartlet crusts from the pans (see page 323).

3   Make the filling by whisking together the sour cream, egg yolks, 3 tablespoons of the sugar, and 1 tablespoon of the lemon juice in a medium-size mixing bowl. In another medium-size mixing bowl, toss the sliced peaches with the remaining 1 tablespoon each of sugar and lemon juice. Spoon the sour cream mixture into the pie shell. Arrange the peach slices on top. Sprinkle the almonds on top of the peaches and dot with the butter. Place the tart or tartlet pans on a baking sheet and bake until the center barely wobbles when you shake the pan, about 20 minutes for the tart and 10 minutes for the tartlets. Do not let the filling bubble and overcook because the sour cream will separate and turn grainy. The filling will firm as it cools.

Apple, Apple, Apple Tart with Cinnamon Cream

Three different varieties of apple go into the making of this luscious tart, and the recipe idea comes from Jill Vorbeck of Applesource in Chapin, Illinois. When I went to visit her and her husband, Tom, at their extensive orchards, she told me about their custom of giving away crab apples to customers who visit them at the nearby Jacksonville Farmer's Market on Saturday mornings in late summer and early fall. The only hitch is that the takers have to bring back a jar of homemade crab apple jelly for the Vorbecks in return. Jill uses the jelly to glaze an apple tart like this one. For this recipe, besides the crab apple jelly, you will need an early season apple like Transparent or Lodi for the applesauce at the base, and a fall apple like Jonathan, Red Delicious, or McIntosh for decoration. If you don't want to make your own applesauce, use 3 cups of good quality sweetened applesauce instead. **MAKES ONE 9- OR 9¹/₂-INCH TART; 8 SERVINGS**

1 recipe Cookie Crust Pastry (page 267) or Citrus-Scented Pastry (page 269)

FILLING

4 cups sliced tart cooking apples, such as Transparent, Lodi, or Rhode Island Greening

1 cup sugar

3 large red apples, such as McIntosh, Jonathan, or Red Delicious

2 tablespoons fresh lemon juice

¹/₂ cup crab apple jelly

CINNAMON WHIPPED CREAM

1 cup heavy cream

1 tablespoon sugar

1 teaspoon ground cinnamon

1 Preheat the oven to 350 degrees F. Pat the Cookie Crust Pastry over the bottom and up the sides of a 9- or 9¹/₂-inch tart pan with a removable bottom. Or take the Citrus-Scented Pastry out of the refrigerator and roll between two sheets of parchment paper into a circle about 12 inches in diameter. Carefully remove one sheet of paper and drape the pastry, paper side up, over the tart pan. Remove the second sheet of paper. Press the pastry carefully into the pan. Roll the rolling pin over the perimeter of the pan to trim the edges of the pastry neatly. Cover the tart shell with plastic wrap and refrigerate for 15 minutes.

2 Carefully line the tart shell with aluminum foil and fill with pie weights. Bake the tart shell for 7 minutes, then carefully remove the weights and foil. Bake the shell for another 7 to 10 minutes, until the edges have turned golden. Cool completely and release the tart crust from the pan (see page 323). Place on a serving plate.

3 In a large saucepan, combine the tart apples and sugar and cook over medium heat until they are softened, about 20 minutes. Transfer to a blender or food processor and puree; you should have about 3 cups of applesauce. Set aside.

4 When ready to serve, spoon the applesauce into the pastry shell and smooth with a rubber spatula. Set aside. Peel and quarter the red apples, then core and thinly slice. Put the slices in a large mixing bowl. Drizzle the lemon juice over the apples and toss to coat. Arrange the apple slices in an attractive, overlapping, circular pattern on top of the applesauce. Warm the crab apple jelly in a small heavy saucepan over low heat or in the microwave and brush it over the apples.

5 To make the Cinnamon Whipped Cream, combine the heavy cream, sugar, and cinnamon in a medium-size mixing bowl. With an electric mixer, beat the cream until it holds stiff peaks. Serve slices of the tart garnished with a dollop of the whipped cream.

Perfect Fruit Slices

When you're making an apple or pear tart or another type of dessert that requires uniform slices of fruit, two tools will make your life a lot easier. An apple peeler/corer/slicer is an all-in-one hand-cranked gadget that will peel, core, and thinly slice an apple in seconds. It is available in many different kitchen and gourmet catalogs and also at better hardware stores. Practice with a few apples first, both to get the hang of it and to adjust the settings.

A melon baller works with either apples or pears to get uniform slices when you are peeling and cutting with a paring knife. After peeling the fruit and cutting it into wedges, use the melon baller to core each wedge of fruit. Then cut the wedge into thinner slices, if necessary.

Fresh Apple Tart with Honeyed French Cream

Use your favorite amber-colored varietal honey—wildflower, sourwood, tupelo, or perhaps white clover—to get the elusive flavor that makes this tart such a winner.

MAKES ONE 10-INCH TART; 8 TO 10 SERVINGS

PASTRY

2 cups all-purpose flour

¼ cup sugar

¾ cup (1½ sticks) unsalted butter at room temperature

2 large egg yolks

FILLING

3 large tart apples, such as Jonathan, Braeburn, or Granny Smith

4 large egg yolks

¼ cup wildflower or other amber honey

1 teaspoon vanilla extract

2 teaspoons ground cinnamon

½ cup heavy cream

½ cup sour cream

1   Preheat the oven to 425 degrees F. Butter a 10-inch tart pan and set aside.

2   To make the pastry, sift the flour and sugar together into a large mixing bowl. Cut in the butter with a pastry blender or two knives until the mixture resembles coarse crumbs. Add the egg yolks and blend well with the pastry blender or a fork. The dough will be a little crumbly. Take a handful of dough (about 1/2 cup) and shape it into a ball with your hands; this helps melt the butter and makes the pastry easier to work with. Press the ball of dough into part of the tart pan. Repeat the process until all the dough has been worked into the bottom and up the side of the tart pan. Set aside.

3   To make the filling, peel and quarter the apples, then core and cut into thin slices. Arrange the apple slices over the pastry in the tart pan, working from the outside in to form a semblance of a rose. Bake for 15 minutes, then remove from the oven, but leave the oven on.

4   With an electric mixer, beat together the egg yolks, honey, vanilla, and cinnamon in a medium-size mixing bowl until smooth. Beat in the heavy cream and sour cream. Carefully pour this mixture over the apples, return the tart to the oven, and bake until the apples are tender, about 35 minutes more. Let cool completely before slicing.

Bakewell Tart

Family recipes for Bakewell tart came over with the first generations of Puritans in seventeenth-century Massachusetts, and eventually traveled down the coast to the South. The 1950 edition of *Charleston Receipts* contains this recipe, which I have adapted. Bakewell tart is still made to rave reviews at the Green Gateau, a restaurant and tearoom in Lincoln, Nebraska. Over time, ground almonds have sometimes been replaced with cake or bread crumbs in versions of this recipe, but I prefer the almonds. Good quality seedless raspberry jam is essential.

MAKES ONE 9-INCH TART; 8 SERVINGS

1 recipe Pat-a-Pan Pie Crust (page 267)

1/2 cup sugar

1/2 cup (1 stick) unsalted butter

4 large egg yolks

2 large egg whites

1/2 cup ground almonds

1 teaspoon almond extract

1/2 cup seedless raspberry jam

Transparent tarts, also known as transparent puddings baked in a single crust, traveled from the British Midlands—primarily from the area around Bakewell (see Bakewell Tart, page 319) and Cambridge, England—to the American South, where they are still popular in the Carolinas, Georgia, and Kentucky. "The typical transparent filling consists of sugar solidified with eggs and butter," wrote the late Jane Grigson in *The Observer Guide to British Cookery*. "It survives, just, in some versions of syrup tart [in England] and also in modern American cookery books where you will also find, embedded like fossils, quite a few of our forgotten dishes."

Fossils like plate-pie, for instance.

"A plate-pie is frugal, much pastry, little filling, the art is all in the pastry," explained Grigson. Made in Yorkshire and Northumbria for centuries, plate-pies start with a circle of pie dough made with a combination of butter and lard on an 8-inch metal plate. The pie dough is pricked all over with fork, then spread with uncooked fruit or rhubarb, mincemeat, or cottage cheese and sprinkled with sugar and spices, leaving the perimeter of the dough plain. A second circle of pie dough is placed over the filling, the edges crimped, and a hole cut out of the top circle of dough. The plate-pie is baked for 10 to 15 minutes at 425 degrees F, then for 20 minutes or so at 350 degrees F, until the pastry has browned.

Dressed-up versions of plate-pie appear in various recipes. Cynthiana (Kentucky) Strawberry Short Cake, for example, in Elizabeth Kremer's *Welcome Back to Pleasant Hill*, is made with two 8-inch circles of pie dough pricked and baked at 475 degrees F on a baking sheet until browned. When done, one circle is placed on a serving plate, topped with fresh strawberries and a little Seven-Minute Frosting (see page 161). Then the second circle of crust is placed on top and more frosting is spooned over it and down the sides.

Other versions still reflect the frugality of the original English plate-pies, made with dried fruit or preserves when fresh fruit was unavailable. Sidney Saylor Farr recalls in *More Than Moonshine*, "We filled a twenty-five pound flour sack with dried apples every summer. Dried apples are tasty to eat as a snack, but we liked them especially used in Mother's Dried Apple Stackcake." Farr's southeastern Kentucky family's seven-layer stackcake also starts with a basic pie crust, which is flavored with molasses, buttermilk, and spices, and then layered with a cooked dried apple filling that is also sweetened and spiced. The top is sprinkled with confectioners' sugar. "Prepare cake at least a day before you serve it. Slice thin," Farr recommends. It's very similar to a simpler version from the Georgia mountains, collected by Eliot Wigginton's Foxfire students—Appalachian Dried Fruit Stack Pie with Gingerbread Pastry (page 280).

1   Preheat the oven to 350 degrees F. Pat the pastry into a 9-inch tart pan. Or push the Pat-a-Pan Pie Crust over the bottom and up the sides of the pan. Set aside.

2   In a food processor, cream the sugar and butter together. Add the egg yolks and egg white and process until smooth. Add the ground almonds and almond extract and process until you have a granular batter.

3   Spread the raspberry jam over the bottom of the pastry. Spoon the almond batter on top of the jam and smooth it over. Bake until browned on top and a knife inserted in the center comes out clean, about 30 minutes. Let cool before slicing.

Tart and Tangy Lemon Curd Tart

English in origin, lemon curd, or lemon "cheese," was brought to America during colonial days, when British trade in the West Indies brought tropical fruits of all kinds to ports like Boston and Charleston. Today, our lemons and limes come from Florida and California, but the lure of this dessert staple has not diminished—a great homemade lemon curd is the best kind of convenience food. For instance, fold 1 cup of this curd together with 1 cup whipped cream for a quick lemon mousse to serve with fresh or cooked and sweetened berries. Lemon curd will keep, covered, in the refrigerator for about 2 weeks. This recipe includes just a hint of lime for extra tartness.

MAKES ONE 9- OR 10-INCH TART; 8 SERVINGS; 2 CUPS OF LEMON CURD

1 recipe Cookie Crust Pastry (page 267)

LEMON CURD
$\frac{1}{2}$ cup (1 stick) unsalted butter
$1\frac{1}{2}$ cups sugar
$\frac{1}{2}$ cup fresh lemon juice
2 teaspoons grated lemon zest

1 teaspoon fresh lime juice
1 teaspoon grated lime zest
5 large eggs, beaten

Fresh berries or Candied Citrus Peel (page 483) for garnish

1   Preheat the oven to 350 degrees F. Pat the dough over the bottom and up the sides of a 9- or 10-inch tart pan with a removable bottom. Carefully line the tart with aluminum foil and fill with pie weights. Bake for 15 minutes, or until golden brown. Carefully remove the weights and

the foil. Cool completely and release the tart from the pan (see page 323). Transfer the tart to a serving plate.

2   To make the lemon curd, melt the butter in a medium-size heavy saucepan over medium-low heat. Whisk in the sugar, lemon juice and zest, and lime juice and zest. Cook, stirring, until the sugar has dissolved, about 5 minutes. Whisk in the eggs and continue to cook, whisking, until the mixture has thickened and an instant-read thermometer registers 160 degrees F, 5 to 7 minutes. Remove from the heat and let cool for several minutes. (If not using immediately, transfer to a container and cover the surface of the curd with plastic wrap while still hot to prevent a "skin" from forming on the top. Then cover the container and store in the refrigerator.)

3   Spoon the curd into the tart shell. Let cool, then refrigerate for at least 2 hours, until completely chilled. Before serving, garnish with berries or lemon peel.

Wildflower Honey Curd Tart

Wildflower honey gets its mellow, not-too-sweet flavor from summer wildflowers, and has more color and depth than blossom honey made in the spring. As a filling for tartlets, as a spread between delicate Homemade Ladyfingers (see page 406), or as a sweet surprise filling in the middle of a layer cake or petit four, the thick, honey-colored curd in this tart has the golden taste of summer. I could just sit and eat it with a spoon. Tupelo, sourwood, or any other varietal honey of your choice would also be delicious in this. **MAKES ONE 9- OR 10-INCH TART; 8 SERVINGS; 2 CUPS OF WILDFLOWER HONEY CURD**

1 recipe Citrus-Scented Pastry (page 269)

WILDFLOWER HONEY CURD
6 tablespoons (¾ stick) unsalted butter, cubed
1 cup wildflower or other amber honey
Finely grated zest and juice of 1 lemon

Finely grated zest and juice of 1 orange

3 large eggs, beaten

3 nectarines or peaches, peeled, pitted, and sliced for garnish

1   Preheat the oven to 350 degrees F. Take the pastry out of the refrigerator and roll it between two sheets of parchment paper into a circle about 12 inches in diameter. Carefully remove one sheet

of paper and drape the pastry, paper side up, over a 9- or 10-inch tart pan with a removable bottom. Remove the second sheet of paper. Press the pastry carefully into the pan. Roll the rolling pin over the perimeter of the pan to trim the edges of the pastry neatly. Cover with plastic wrap and refrigerate for 15 minutes.

2　Carefully line the pie shell with aluminum foil and fill with pie weights. Bake the tart shell for 7 minutes, then carefully remove the weights and foil. Bake the shell for another 7 to 10 minutes, until the edges have turned golden. Cool completely and release the tart crust from the pan (see below). Place on a serving plate.

3　To make the curd, melt the butter in a large heavy saucepan over medium heat. Stir in the honey, juices, and zests. Pour the eggs through a fine-mesh strainer into the mixture and whisk to blend. Cook, whisking constantly, until the mixture thickens and begins to boil, 8 to 10 minutes.

4　Remove the curd from the heat and let cool for several minutes. (If not using immediately, pour into a jar or plastic container. Cover and refrigerate for up to 3 weeks.)

5　Spoon the honey curd into the tart and let cool, then refrigerate for at least 2 hours, until completely chilled. When ready to serve, garnish the top of the tart with the fruit slices.

Please Release Me, Part II

To release a prebaked tart crust from a pan with a removable bottom, first let it cool completely. The crust should have pulled away from the sides of the pan, but some crust may still stick to the fluted sides. Use a knife or a thin spatula to carefully separate the crust from the pan. Press the knife or spatula against the sides of the pan, not the tart crust.

When all the crust has been loosened from the sides of the pan, use one hand to press upwards in the middle of the bottom of the tart pan. This should elevate the bottom up and away from the sides of the pan. Transfer the tart crust to the other hand and remove the sides of the tart pan. Transfer the tart crust, still sitting on the metal bottom of the pan, to a serving plate and fill.

Festive Cranberry Tart

I love the vibrant color and fresh cranberry flavor of this tart. The slight hint of lemon in the crust and the addition of almond in the filling help round out the total flavor package. Serve wedges of this tart during the holidays, each festooned with a generous dollop of whipped cream. This tart can be prepared a day ahead and kept, covered, in the refrigerator. For a festive garnish, brush beaten egg white over small branches of fresh rosemary, then dredge the branches in sugar. Put 2 sugared rosemary branches and a fresh cranberry on each serving for edible "holly." **MAKES ONE 10-INCH TART; 8 SERVINGS**

1 recipe Citrus-Scented Pastry (page 269)

Two $1/4$-ounce packages unflavored gelatin

$1/2$ cup cold water

Three 12-ounce bags fresh cranberries, picked over for stems and rinsed

$1^3/4$ cups sugar

1 cup red currant jelly

1 teaspoon almond extract

1 Preheat the oven to 350 degrees F. Take the pastry out of the refrigerator and roll it between two sheets of parchment paper into a 12-inch circle. Carefully remove one sheet of paper and drape the pastry, paper side up, over a 10-inch tart pan with a removable bottom. Remove the second sheet of paper. Press the pastry carefully into the pan. Roll the rolling pin over the perimeter of the pan to trim the edges of the pastry neatly. Cover with plastic wrap and refrigerate for 15 minutes.

2 Carefully line the pie shell with aluminum foil and fill with pie weights. Bake the tart shell for 7 minutes, then carefully remove the weights and foil. Bake the shell for another 7 to 10 minutes, until the edges have turned golden. Cool completely and release the tart crust from the pan (see page 323). Place on a serving plate.

3 Sprinkle the gelatin over the cold water in a small bowl and set aside to soak through.

4 Combine the cranberries, sugar, and jelly in a large heavy saucepan and cook over low heat until the sugar and jelly have melted, about 10 minutes. You don't want the cranberries to pop or burst, but soften instead. Remove from the heat and stir in the almond extract and gelatin mixture until well blended. Set aside to cool completely.

5 Spoon the filling into the prebaked tart shell and chill for at least 1 hour, covered, before serving. Serve slightly chilled or at room temperature.

Lemon-Blueberry-Strawberry Tart

When U-pick farms begin their busy season in the middle of June, you can pick all you want, then enjoy a fresh summer fruit dessert like this one, which assembles in minutes. With homemade lemon curd already on hand, it goes even faster. Serve each slice on a pool of rosy strawberry sauce for a great visual effect.

MAKES ONE 8-INCH ROUND OR 13 X 4-INCH RECTANGULAR TART; 8 SERVINGS

1 recipe *Pasta Frolla* (see page 293, step 1) or
  Cookie Crust Pastry (page 267)

1½ cups Lemon Curd (see page 321)

2 cups whipped cream or whipped topping

1 pint fresh blueberries, picked over for stems

1 pint fresh strawberries, hulled

3 tablespoons sugar

1   Pat the dough over the bottom and up the sides of an 8-inch round or 13 x 4-inch rectangular tart pan with a removable bottom. Prick the pastry all over with a fork and chill in the refrigerator for 30 minutes. Preheat the oven to 350 degrees F.

2   Bake the pastry until pale brown, 15 to 20 minutes. Cool completely and release the tart crust from the pan (see page 323). Place on a serving plate.

3   In a large mixing bowl, fold the lemon curd into the whipped cream and pile this mixture into the tart pan. Toss the blueberries and strawberries with the sugar in a medium-size bowl, then arrange attractively on top of the tart.

Razzle-Dazzle Raspberry Tart

Most tarts look better than they taste. The French don't seem to mind bland desserts as long as they look good, but Americans have come to want flavor as well as appearance. This tart has both. The pastry cream flavored with cooked sugared raspberries has a wonderful fruit taste. With a fragrant, crisp tart shell and the juicy goodness of fresh berries, you've got definite razzle-dazzle.

MAKES ONE 9-INCH ROUND OR 13 X 4-INCH RECTANGULAR TART; 8 SERVINGS

1 recipe Cookie Crust Pastry (page 267) or Citrus-
   Scented Pastry (page 269)

4 cups fresh raspberries

¼ cup sugar

Juice of 1 lemon

1 recipe Classic Pastry Cream (see page 163)

1 Preheat the oven to 350 degrees F. Pat the Cookie Crust Pastry over the bottom and up the sides of a 9-inch round or 13 x 4-inch rectangular tart pan with a removable bottom. Or take the Citrus-Scented Pastry out of the refrigerator and roll it between two sheets of parchment paper into a 12-inch circle or a 15 x 6-inch rectangle. Carefully remove one sheet of paper and drape the pastry, paper side up, over the tart pan. Remove the second sheet of paper. Press the pastry carefully into the pan. Roll the rolling pin over the perimeter of the pan to trim the edges of the pastry neatly. Cover with plastic wrap and refrigerate for 15 minutes.

2 Carefully line the pie shell with aluminum foil and fill with pie weights. Bake the tart shell for 7 minutes, then carefully remove the weights and foil. Bake the shell for another 7 to 10 minutes, until the edges have turned golden. Cool completely and release the tart crust from the pan (see page 323). Transfer to a serving plate.

3 Place 2 cups of the raspberries in a medium-size heavy saucepan with the sugar and lemon juice. Bring to a simmer over medium-high heat until the berries begin to release their juices. Remove from the heat. Place the berry mixture in a food processor and puree. Strain the puree through a fine-mesh sieve into a bowl to remove the seeds. Discard the seeds and let the strained puree cool to room temperature.

4 In a large mixing bowl, fold the raspberry puree into the pastry cream. Spoon the flavored pastry cream into the prebaked tart shell and smooth the top with a rubber spatula. Arrange the remaining 2 cups of raspberries on top of the pastry cream and serve.

Razzle-Dazzle Raspberries

Of all the berries prized by gardener and gourmet alike, the raspberry is queen. The tiny ruby berries must be carefully plucked from thick, thorny tangles that always try to escape the most carefully constructed arbor, frame, or fence. Raspberries ripen in late June and early July, with perhaps a second harvest in September, especially for golden raspberries. Because the berries are very perishable, they must be used the day they are picked or frozen. Sally Calvin, an organic market gardener on her Wigeonwood Farm near Jefferson City, Missouri, manages to "collect enough golden raspberries every season, a very few at a time," and freezes them individually on a baking sheet, then puts them in plastic bags for later use.

All this effort goes into ambrosial black raspberry pies, red raspberry tarts, golden raspberry preserves, or perhaps an easy jam that tastes delicious slathered over homemade bread. A honey-sweetened cream cheese torta might hide a secret, delicious layer of raspberry preserves, ready to be scooped, then spread on a breakfast bagel.

Among the hardy raspberry varieties that do well in the United States are Boyne and Killarney, which provide red summer raspberries; Royalty, Jewel Black, and Estate, which produce summer black raspberries; Honey Queen yields yellow summer raspberries; Autumn Bliss, Heritage, and Red Wing give up their red raspberries in autumn; and Golden Harvest produces yellow raspberries that ripen in the fall. Wild red raspberries do well in spring, but wilt in the heat of summer and must be watered well if you bring them into the garden.

Transparent Tartlets

When my parents owned a weekend home in the sleepy river town of Augusta, Kentucky, I loved to visit them there. Crossing the Ohio River on the ferry, I always felt like I was leaving one world behind and entering another, stepping from North to South, city to country. In this hilly place, where valleys and flatlands are given over to growing tobacco, small towns with late eighteenth-century brick buildings still flourish. Visiting Washington, Kentucky, one Saturday, we tasted these transparent tartlets made from a recipe by local culinary legend Mary Greene. The granddaughter of former slaves, Greene cooked countless dinners for guests at the Harbeson, a hotel and local landmark. She was known for her yeast rolls, beaten biscuits, and these tartlets, or "puddings," as she called them. Transparent tartlets are still made for church bake sales in this area; they're less rich than a big slice of transparent pie, but only just! Once baked, the filling turns a semi-transparent dark gold. MAKES 30 TARTLETS

3 recipes Jack's Vinegar Pie Crust (page 266)

4 large eggs

2 cups sugar

1 cup (2 sticks) unsalted butter, cubed

$\frac{1}{4}$ cup light corn syrup

$1\frac{1}{2}$ teaspoons vanilla extract

1   Preheat the oven to 375 degrees F. Take the pastry out of the refrigerator and divide it in half. Roll out one half on a well-floured surface to a thickness of $\frac{1}{4}$ inch. Use a 3-inch biscuit cutter to cut the individual tart pastries, then press them into individual tartlet pans or minimuffin cups. Repeat the process with the remaining dough. Place the tartlet pans on baking sheets and set aside.

2   In the top of a double boiler over simmering water, whisk the eggs and sugar together. Add the butter and corn syrup and whisk until the butter has melted and the filling has thickened, become shiny and semi-translucent, and you can see the bottom of the pan when you whisk, about 12 to 15 minutes. Stir in the vanilla. Spoon the filling into the pastry-lined tart pans until two thirds full.

3   Bake for 5 to 6 minutes, watching carefully. If the filling starts to puff up, remove the pans from the oven for a few seconds, then return. When the filling is set around the edges (the middle will jiggle), and the crust has browned, they're done. Leave in the pans to cool completely. The filling will continue to solidify. If you used minimuffin cups, remove from the pans before serving.

Miniature Toasted Pecan Tartlets in Cream Cheese Pastry

Pecan pie is so ooey, gooey good, but also so rich that I prefer to eat it in small bites, as in these tartlets. My mother, Jean Merkle, has been making them since the 1970s. For novice pie bakers, this is a great recipe to start with because the pastry is easy to manage and delicious. For best results, the dough needs to rest in the refrigerator for several hours before you're ready to bake. These tiny tartlets are great to have on hand for the holidays, bridal showers, or family reunions. They can be made ahead and kept for a week or so in an airtight container. **MAKES 5 DOZEN TARTLETS**

CREAM CHEESE PASTRY

1 cup (2 sticks) unsalted butter at room temperature

Two 3-ounce packages cream cheese at room temperature

2 cups all-purpose flour

FILLING

4 large eggs

3 cups packed brown sugar

2 teaspoons vanilla extract

$\frac{1}{4}$ cup ($\frac{1}{2}$ stick) unsalted butter, melted

$\frac{1}{8}$ teaspoon salt

2 cups chopped pecans

1   To make the pastry, blend the butter and cream cheese together in a food processor or with an electric mixer in a large mixing bowl. Add the flour and blend together until you can form the dough into a smooth ball. Cover the dough with plastic wrap, and let rest in the refrigerator for 3 to 4 hours or overnight. Let it come to room temperature before using.

2   Preheat the oven to 350 degrees F. To make the filling, in a food processor or a large mixing bowl with an electric mixer, process or beat the eggs until pale yellow. Add the brown sugar, vanilla, butter, and salt and process or beat until you have a smooth filling. Set aside.

3   With the dough at room temperature, cut into 4 equal portions. Form each one into 15 tablespoon-size balls. Press each ball into a minimuffin cup to form the bottom and sides of each tartlet. Fill each tartlet with about 1 tablespoon of the filling and sprinkle the tops with the chopped pecans.

4   Bake until the pastry has browned lightly and the filling has firmed, 25 to 30 minutes. Let cool in the pans, then carefully remove the tartlets from the pans and serve.

> **VARIATION** To make pecan pie, cut the dough in half and press each portion into an 8-inch pie pan to form the crust. Divide the filling and pecans between the two pies. Bake until the filling has firmed, about 35 to 40 minutes.

Miniature Crab Apple Tarte Tatins

In September, tiny orchard fruits appear at farmers' markets and better grocers throughout the Midwest. The many varieties of crab apples, Seckel and Forelle pears, and lady apples have the same flavor as the larger fruit varieties. They're ideal to use in this recipe—8 individual tarte tatins made of shortcake batter dropped on top of caramelized fruit in muffin pans. If crab apples are not available in your area, use the smallest fruits you can find. **MAKES 8 TARTLETS**

½ cup (1 stick) unsalted butter

½ cup sugar

8 crab apples, Seckel or Forelle pears, lady apples, or other small orchard fruit

SHORTCAKE
¾ cup all-purpose flour

¼ cup cake flour

1½ teaspoons baking powder

¼ teaspoon salt

¼ cup sugar

¼ cup (½ stick) unsalted butter at room temperature

1 large egg

3 tablespoons milk

1 recipe Wildflower Honey Cream (page 348) or whipped cream for serving

1   Preheat the oven to 400 degrees F. Grease 8 muffin cups and set aside. Place 1 tablespoon of butter and 1 tablespoon of sugar in the bottom of the muffin cups. Slice and core, but do not peel, each fruit and arrange the slices on top of the butter and sugar in each muffin cup. Bake for 10 minutes, then remove from the oven and set aside.

2   To make the shortcake, sift the all-purpose flour, cake flour, baking powder, salt, and sugar into a medium-size mixing bowl. Cut in the butter with a pastry blender or two knives until the mixture resembles coarse crumbs. With a fork, beat the egg with the milk in a small bowl. Make a well in the center of the dry ingredients and pour in the egg mixture. Using a circular motion, blend the dry ingredients into the egg mixture with a fork until you have a moist dough; do not overmix.

3   Drop about 2 tablespoons of the dough onto the fruit in each muffin cup. Bake for 12 to 15 minutes, or until the tarts have risen and browned. Remove from the oven, run a knife around each tart, and invert the muffin tin onto a plate. Serve the tarte tatins fruit side up on individual dessert plates, accompanied by Wildflower Honey Cream or whipped cream.

Greek Deep-Dish Custard Pastry

At summertime Greek festivals, large pans of this mellow custard-filled pastry known as *galatobouriko* are cut up into many diamond-shaped servings. Farina is used as a thickener, which is also typical of some dessert recipes of Eastern European origin, such as *rote grütze* ("red groats"), a berry pudding thickened with farina. For a variation, try Fresh Orange Syrup (page 488) drizzled over this instead of the lemon.

MAKES ONE 9 x 13-INCH TART; 8 TO 10 SERVINGS

CUSTARD

6 cups milk

2 cups sugar

¾ cup minus 1 tablespoon dry Cream of Wheat or other farina cereal

9 large egg yolks, beaten

1 tablespoon unsalted butter, melted

1 teaspoon vanilla extract

PASTRY

Sixteen 16 x 11-inch sheets frozen phyllo pastry, thawed

½ cup (1 stick) unsalted butter, melted

LEMON SYRUP

1¼ cups sugar

¼ cup fresh lemon juice

½ cup water

1 Preheat the oven to 350 degrees F. Grease a 9 x 13-inch baking pan and set aside.

2 To make the custard, in a large heavy saucepan, scald the milk over medium heat until bubbles form around the edge of the pan, then stir in the sugar. Add the Cream of Wheat gradually, stirring constantly, until thickened. Stir ¼ cup of the hot farina mixture into the beaten egg yolks, then transfer the egg yolk mixture to the farina mixture and stir to blend. Remove from the heat. Beat in the melted butter and vanilla and set aside to cool.

3 To assemble, lay a sheet of phyllo in the prepared pan and brush it with melted butter. Repeat this process with 7 more sheets of phyllo. Pour or spoon the custard mixture over the pastry. Lay 7 more sheets of phyllo, each brushed with melted butter, over the custard filling.

4 Bake until the pastry is lightly browned, about 45 minutes.

5 While the pastry is baking, make the syrup. Bring the sugar, lemon juice, and water to a boil in a medium-size heavy saucepan. Boil for 5 minutes, then remove from the heat. When the custard pastry is done, take it out of the oven and let cool for 5 minutes. Cut into diamond-shaped portions with a pizza wheel or sharp knife. Pour over the hot syrup. Serve warm or at room temperature.

Fruit-Filled Custard Tartlets

When you want a homemade fruit tart, but you don't have time to make pastry and pastry cream, this simplified recipe is a good pick. Paper-thin phyllo dough, available in the frozen food section of the grocery store, makes a thin and crackly free-form crust. A thin pouring custard is spooned over the fresh fruit and then baked. Go to a farm stand, a good greengrocer, or a farmers' market and select the best seasonal fruit, then come home and improvise. Instead of the plums, you could use one cup of pitted tart red cherries, gooseberries, blackberries, or blueberries; four small crab apples, lady apples, or small pears, peeled, cored, and thinly sliced; or four small peaches, peeled, pitted, and thinly sliced. Dried fruits like tart red cherries, apricots, or raisins plumped in hot water also make a delicious filling. **MAKES 4 FREE-FORM TARTLETS**

Four 16 x 11-inch sheets frozen phyllo pastry, thawed

3 tablespoons unsalted butter, melted

4 small plums, pitted, left unpeeled, and thinly sliced

2 large eggs, beaten

¾ cup whipping cream

¼ cup granulated sugar

4 teaspoons light brown sugar

1   Preheat the oven to 325 degrees F. Grease four 4-inch tart pans or the insides of 4 muffin cups and set aside.

2   Place a sheet of phyllo dough on a lightly floured work surface and brush the surface with melted butter. Fold the phyllo in half lengthwise to form a 16 x 5½-inch rectangle. Brush the surface again with butter. Fold in half again to form an 8 x 5½-inch rectangle. Gently press the folded phyllo into a tart pan or muffin cup. Repeat with the remaining phyllo and melted butter. Arrange one quarter of the fruit in each phyllo crust and set aside.

3   In a small mixing bowl, whisk together the eggs, whipping cream, and granulated sugar until smooth. Spoon this mixture evenly over the fruit. Sprinkle 1 teaspoon of the brown sugar over each tart.

4   Place the tarts on a baking sheet and bake until the custard has set, 30 to 35 minutes. Let cool in the pans for 5 minutes. Remove from the pans and serve warm or cover and refrigerate for up to 1 day and serve cold.

Tiny Berry Tartlets

Berries are the jewels of the summer garden, from the first tiny strawberries in June through a profusion of blueberries, golden raspberries, blackberries, and black and red raspberries. Any of these will taste delicious in this dessert, which takes minutes to assemble before serving. Both the berry syrup and the phyllo can be prepared in advance. These tartlets look wonderful on a three-tiered dessert stand, a footed cake stand, or a Depression glass plate. This recipe is adapted from one by Janet Trefethen of Trefethen Winery in California. **MAKES 12 TARTLETS**

CRUST

2½ tablespoons slivered almonds

Three 16 x 11-inch sheets frozen phyllo pastry, thawed

2 tablespoons unsalted butter, melted

1 tablespoon granulated sugar

1 tablespoon confectioners' sugar

FILLING

1 cup Wildflower Honey Cream (page 348)

4 cups fresh berries

1 recipe Fresh Berry Syrup (page 487)

1   Preheat the oven to 350 degrees F. Grease a 12-cup muffin pan and set aside.

2   To make the crust, put the almonds is a food processor and grind until fine; set aside. Place a sheet of phyllo on a flat work surface and brush with a third of the melted butter. In a small bowl, mix the almonds and granulated sugar together and sprinkle half of this mixture over the buttered sheet. Place a second sheet of phyllo on top of the first, brush with another third of the butter, and sprinkle with the remaining almond and sugar mixture. Place the third phyllo sheet on top, brush with the remaining melted butter and sprinkle with the confectioners' sugar.

3   With a sharp paring knife or kitchen shears, cut the layered dough into 12 squares. Gently press each square into a prepared muffin cup to create a free-form tartlet. Bake until just golden, about 5 minutes. Let cool in the pans completely. The crusts can be made up to 2 days in advance and kept in an airtight container.

4   To fill the tarts, gently remove them from the muffin cups and place on a serving tray or plate. Place a generous tablespoon of honey cream in each tartlet. Dip the berries into the berry syrup with a slotted spoon and mound them on the honey cream. Serve immediately.

Prairie Apple Strudel

Among German, Russian, Austrian, and Czechoslovakian families that settled mainly in the Midwest, apple strudel was saved for special occasions such as the Christmas holidays or weddings. I like to use a mixture of tart and sweet apples such as Granny Smith or Jonathan and Golden Delicious for a well-rounded flavor. Strudel dough is surprisingly easy to make and roll out. **MAKES 3 STRUDELS; 30 SERVINGS**

STRUDEL DOUGH

1 cup warm water

2 tablespoons corn or canola oil

3 cups all-purpose flour

$\frac{1}{2}$ teaspoon salt

FILLING

6 to 8 apples, such as Jonathan, Empire, Golden Delicious, Fuji, or Braeburn, cored, peeled, and thinly sliced

1 cup sugar

1 tablespoon ground cinnamon

$\frac{1}{4}$ teaspoon salt

$\frac{1}{2}$ cup (1 stick) unsalted butter, melted

Whipped cream or ice cream (optional) for serving

1   To make the dough, mix the water and oil together in a large mixing bowl. Add the flour and salt and stir to make a soft dough. Cover and let stand for 10 minutes.

2   Preheat the oven to 375 degrees F. Coat a large baking sheet with nonstick cooking spray or line it with parchment paper and set aside.

3   To make the filling, mix the apples, sugar, cinnamon, and salt together in a large mixing bowl.

4   Transfer the dough to a floured work surface and cut it into 3 equal portions with a serrated knife. Roll out each portion into a circle about 10 inches in diameter and $\frac{1}{8}$ inch thick. Brush the dough with one quarter of the melted butter, leaving a 1-inch border around the perimeter without butter. Place a third of the filling on a circle of dough and roll up like a jelly roll. Carefully pinch the long seam closed, pinch the ends shut, and tuck them under. Repeat the process with the remaining 2 portions of dough and filling. Place on the prepared baking sheet with the seam to the side of each strudel. Brush the tops with the remaining melted butter.

5   Bake the strudels until the crust just begins to turn brown, about 45 minutes. Leave on the pan to cool. Serve warm with whipped cream or ice cream, or just by itself.

Apple Patches

Small "hand pies" are a traditional Southern dessert and are also popular in German-American communities. These miniature pies, also known as *Hemetschwenger*, are easy to make and delicious to eat. They're great picnic or take-in-the-car fare. Use any kind of filling you like. For Apple Patches, I sometimes use a small, apple-shaped cookie cutter to cut out an apple shape from the top "patch" of each square pie or turnover. When my pears ripen, I make a pear filling and use a pear cookie cutter to make the top design. Use your imagination. These patches can be frozen, unbaked; when you're ready, bake them from frozen in a preheated 350-degree-F oven until the crust has browned, 45 minutes to 1 hour. **MAKES ABOUT 20 MINIATURE DOUBLE-CRUST PIES**

4 tart apples, such as Granny Smith, peeled, cored, and cut into small dice

1 cup sugar

2 teaspoons ground cinnamon

1 recipe Farmhouse Lard Double-Crust Pastry (page 263) or Basic Flaky Double-Crust Pastry (page 264)

1 Preheat the oven to 350 degrees F. Coat a baking sheet with nonstick cooking spray or line with parchment paper and set aside.

2 Put the apples in a large mixing bowl. In a small bowl, mix the sugar and cinnamon together. Reserve ¼ cup of the cinnamon sugar for sprinkling the baked patches, and mix the rest with the apples. Set aside.

3 Remove the dough from the refrigerator and cut it in half. Wrap one half in plastic and return to the refrigerator. Roll out the other half into a 12-inch square on a lightly floured work surface. Using a 3-inch biscuit cutter, cut the dough into circles. Spoon about 1 tablespoon of apple filling in the center of each circle. Save the scraps of dough, cover with plastic wrap, and chill in the freezer until firm.

4 Roll out the remaining portion of dough into a 12-inch square and cut it into circles. Place a circle over each filled circle on the prepared baking sheet. With the tines of a fork, press the 2 circles together around the perimeter. Reroll and cut the remaining scraps of dough and use the remaining filling to make more patches.

5 Bake the patches until the crusts have browned, 25 to 30 minutes. Sprinkle with the reserved cinnamon sugar while still warm.

Sweet Empanaditas

This dessert evolved in old Santa Fe from the different ethnic groups who settled there. The native Pueblo Indians had long been drying wild game, wild fruits, and the trinity of corn, beans, and squash for winter use. The conquering Spanish brought wheat flour, orchard fruit, and the little meat pies known as empanadas. The Anglo-American newcomers, especially those from the South, brought a love of little fried pies filled with dried fruit. Today, these small fried pies filled with peach butter and pine nuts bridge all these cultures. The biscuit-style dough traditionally was made with home-rendered lard, but you could also use shortening. The oil needs to be hot so that the pastries turn out flaky and crisp. This is adapted from a recipe by cookbook author Huntley Dent of Santa Fe. **MAKES 16 MINIATURE PIES**

DOUGH

2 cups all-purpose flour

$1/2$ teaspoon ground cinnamon

$1/4$ teaspoon freshly grated nutmeg

2 teaspoons granulated sugar

$1/2$ teaspoon salt

$1/2$ teaspoon baking powder

6 tablespoons cold lard or vegetable shortening, cut into pieces

6 tablespoons ice water

FILLING

$1/2$ cup chopped toasted pine nuts (see page 181)

$1/2$ cup peach butter or thick peach preserves

1 teaspoon fresh lemon juice

Vegetable oil for frying

Confectioners' sugar for dusting

1   To make the dough, combine the flour, spices, granulated sugar, salt, and baking powder in a food processor and pulse to blend. Add the lard and pulse to blend until the mixture resembles coarse crumbs. Sprinkle the water, 1 tablespoon at a time, on the flour mixture and pulse until the dough holds together but does not yet form a ball. Remove the dough from the processor and transfer to a floured work surface. Work the dough with your fingers until it just forms a ball. Cover with plastic wrap and refrigerate for 30 minutes.

2   To make the filling, combine the chopped pine nuts, peach butter, and lemon juice in a small mixing bowl and stir until well blended. Set aside.

3   Remove the chilled dough from the refrigerator and cut it in half, and then in half again to make 4 portions. Cut each portion of dough into 4 pieces. Roll out each piece on a floured work surface

to make a circle about 3¾ inches in diameter. Use a 3-inch biscuit cutter to make a neat circle of dough. Place 1 teaspoon of filling in the middle of each circle. Moisten the perimeter of the circle with water and fold the dough over to make a semicircle. Press the edges together, then crimp with the tines of a fork.

4 When all the empanaditas have been formed, heat ½ inch of vegetable oil in a large skillet over medium-high heat to a temperature of 375 degrees F. The oil should be hot enough so that a scrap of dough placed in the oil will bubble immediately. If the oil starts to smoke, reduce the heat. Fry the empanaditas in small batches, turning them once, until browned on both sides, 2 to 4 minutes total. Drain on paper towels and dust with confectioners' sugar. These are best served warm.

Domestic Science

In the 1957 movie *Desk Set* starring Spencer Tracy and Katherine Hepburn, we see our culture's reaction to the blessing and curse of new technology. Hepburn plays the head of the research department at a large company; she has a remarkable photographic memory but no luck with men. Tracy plays an efficiency expert who thinks his enormous computer (before the days of the microchip) can "help" all the researchers—right out of a job, they believe. This clash of human versus machine was a major theme in an American postwar society that was becoming increasingly technical.

In 1950 both the first commercial color television and the first commercial computer—a huge machine known as UNIVAC—had come on the market. Every year afterward, there was some kind of new advance, from a pocket transistor radio to the FORTRAN computer system.

Science fiction movies of the time reflect our interest in—and fear of—science and technology. In *The Day the Earth Stood Still* (1950), an alien from outer space proves to earthlings that they're still not ready for peace, despite the recent devastation of World War II. In the *Invasion of the Body Snatchers* (1956), human beings are quietly replaced by giant zucchini-like pods that suddenly appear in one's basement—don't go to sleep! One of the best science fiction films is the *Forbidden Planet* (1956) inspired by Shakespeare's play *The Tempest*, showing that human behavior is just as deadly as an alien attack. Robby the Robot became the forerunner of C3PO, and *Forbidden Planet* was the first film to have an all-electronic score.

You even see an emphasis on machine-like precision and technology in cookbooks of that era, especially in *The American Family Cook Book* by Lily Wallace, published in 1954. Her theme through the whole book is "domestic *science*." Her curious introduction provides a little human feeling but mostly fear, mentioning casually that "those with a tendency to stray will spend more time in homes where every meal is an event to look forward to," a statement guaranteed to rattle any new bride. The "laboratory-developed and tested" recipes are numbered, with no explanatory headnotes to tempt us to make them or to offer help along the way. Lily was our taskmistress, not our friend in the kitchen. We, the readers, might as well have been robots.

Coffee-Filled Éclairs with Caramel Icing

Éclairs have been a hometown bakery staple since the 1940s, but to get really good ones these days, you have to make them yourself. I have adapted this recipe from recipe numbers 3023, 3160, and 3183 in *The American Family Cook Book* by Lily Wallace, published in 1954. They're actually quite good, despite the off-putting format of the book. The éclair is simply *choux* pastry made in a saucepan. The traditional éclair filling is Classic Pastry Cream (see page 163), and the traditional icing is Chocolate Ganache (see page 213)—also delicious. **MAKES 2 DOZEN ÉCLAIRS**

CHOUX PASTRY

½ cup (1 stick) unsalted butter, cubed

1 cup water

1 cup all-purpose flour

1 teaspoon salt

4 large eggs

FILLING

6 tablespoons all-purpose flour

⅔ cup sugar

1 teaspoon instant espresso powder

¼ teaspoon salt

2 cups milk

2 large eggs, beaten

1 teaspoon vanilla extract

1 tablespoon unsalted butter

1 recipe Coffee-Flavored Pastry Cream (see variation, page 164)

CARAMEL ICING

6 tablespoons (¾ stick) unsalted butter

¼ cup plus 2 tablespoons packed dark brown sugar

¼ cup heavy cream

½ teaspoon vanilla extract

1 cup confectioners' sugar

1 Preheat the oven to 450 degrees F. Line a baking sheet with parchment paper. With a pencil, mark twenty-four 4-inch-long lines spaced 2 inches apart. Turn the parchment paper over on the baking sheet so the penciled side is on the bottom, but you can still see the guidelines. Set aside.

2 To make the pastry, bring the butter and water to a boil in a medium-size saucepan over medium-high heat. Vigorously whisk in the flour and salt all at once and continue whisking until the dough forms a ball in the middle of the pan. Remove from the heat and transfer to a food processor. Add the eggs, one at a time, pulsing to blend after each addition, until you have a smooth, shiny, golden dough.

3 Fit the end of a pastry bag with a no. 8 tube (½ inch in diameter). Fill the bag with the *choux* pastry, twist closed, and squeeze the bag, pushing the pastry down until it reaches the tube. Hold your finger over the tube to keep the pastry from flowing out. To pipe the dough onto the marked lines on the parchment paper, press the tip of the tube against the top of a line and gently squeeze the pastry bag while you trace down its length. You should have a line of *choux* pastry dough about 1 inch wide and 4 inches long. Start and stop the dough by pressing the tip of the tube firmly onto the parchment paper. Lift up the pastry bag to begin a new line. Or, instead of using a pastry bag, simply spoon the mixture with a spoon-shaped spatula.

4 Bake the éclairs for 15 minutes, then reduce the oven temperature to 350 degrees F and bake until the éclairs have puffed and turned a shiny golden brown, 25 to 30 minutes more. Let cool completely on the baking sheet.

5 To make the filling, mix the flour, sugar, espresso powder, and salt together in the top of a double boiler. Whisk in the milk and eggs and cook over medium heat, stirring, until the mixture thickens. Stir in the vanilla extract and butter, and remove from heat.

6 To make the icing, melt the butter with the brown sugar in a medium-size heavy saucepan over medium-high heat and cook until the mixture bubbles, about 2 minutes. Remove from the heat and stir in the cream and vanilla. Whisk in the confectioners' sugar.

7 To fill the éclairs, cut each one in half horizontally with a serrated knife and spoon or pipe the filling into the bottom half of the éclair. Place the top half over the filling. Drizzle each filled éclair with a spoonful of the icing. Set aside for the icing to cool and harden. Eclairs are best eaten the day they're made.

Homemade Cannoli Shells with Sweet Cheese Filling

During the volatile 1960s, home cooks seemed to realize that truly homemade foods were going the way of pin curls and stockings with seams. Perhaps that's one reason why the '60s saw such a proliferation of community cookbooks in which women formally recorded their mothers' and grandmothers' recipes. In the 1969 *The American Daughters of Columbus Cook Book*, for example, you'll find recipes for homemade ricotta used as cannoli filling. You'll also find a version of this recipe for cannoli shells, with instructions to "roll dough as thin as a dime." This versatile dough, however, doesn't need to be limited to the tube-shaped cannoli. Circles of dough can also be placed between larger and smaller Chinese mesh ladles, then plunged into hot oil to fry up as crispy pastry baskets. Fried pastries can be kept in an airtight container or frozen, then wrapped in foil and reheated in a preheated 350 degree oven until warm and crispy.

MAKES ABOUT 30 CANNOLI OR PASTRY BASKETS

SWEET CHEESE FILLING

2 pounds ricotta cheese

$\frac{1}{2}$ cup heavy cream

1 cup sugar

1 teaspoon vanilla extract

2 tablespoons candied cherries, snipped into small pieces

$\frac{1}{4}$ cup semisweet chocolate chips

CANNOLI SHELLS

2 cups all-purpose flour

$1\frac{1}{2}$ tablespoons sugar

$\frac{1}{4}$ teaspoon salt

$\frac{1}{3}$ cup plus 2 tablespoons cold vegetable shortening

$\frac{1}{3}$ cup plus 2 tablespoons milk

Vegetable oil for frying

1 large egg white beaten with 1 tablespoon water

1   Drain the ricotta in a colander placed over a large mixing bowl for about 2 hours at room temperature. Press the cheese with a spatula to release more of the whey. Transfer the drained cheese from the colander to a large mixing bowl; discard the whey in the bowl.

2   With an electric mixer, whip the cream in a small mixing bowl until it holds stiff peaks; set aside.

3   Beat the sugar and vanilla into the ricotta until smooth. Fold in the whipped cream with a rubber spatula, then the cherries and chocolate chips. Cover and chill until ready to use.

4   To make the cannoli shells, sift the flour, sugar, and salt together into a large mixing bowl. With a pastry blender or two knives, cut in the shortening until the mixture resembles coarse crumbs. With a fork or your hands, mix in the milk, and continue mixing until you have a soft dough. Cut the dough in half. Roll out each half on a floured work surface to a thickness of $\frac{1}{8}$ inch. Using a $3\frac{1}{2}$-inch biscuit or cookie cutter, cut out circles of dough.

5   Heat the oil to a depth of 4 inches in a deep saucepan or deep fryer until it registers 325 degrees F on a meat or candy thermometer. Wrap each circle of dough around a metal cannoli tube, sealing any overlapping dough with the beaten egg white. Or place each circle in a large mesh ladle and top with a second, smaller mesh ladle to form a basket shape. Fry in the hot oil until golden brown, about 4 minutes. Remove carefully and place on paper towels to drain and cool.

6 When the cannoli shells have cooled, fit a pastry bag with the largest tube or snip ½ inch off the corner of a resealable plastic bag. Pressing one finger over the tube opening or pinching the corner of the bag shut, spoon the filling into the bag. Fill each cannoli tube with the cheese filling. Cover and refrigerate until ready to serve, up to 1 hour.

Cinnamon-Sugar Sopaipillas

Glenn Parker knows his way around a defense. He played football at the University of Arizona, where he developed a love of southwestern cuisine. Over the years, he has played professionally for the Buffalo Bills, the Kansas City Chiefs, and most recently for the New York Giants. Parker also loves to "get in the kitchen and have fun," he says. "I like to experiment with things even when they don't turn out. You learn more from your mistakes than the things that come out right." Thanks to off-season stints working in restaurant kitchens, Parker's hits greatly outnumber the misses. This fried pastry, from the dessert tradition of the Tex-Mex cuisine of Texas and New Mexico, is one he makes for his two daughters, Madeleine and Emily. Parker serves these with vanilla ice cream and hot fudge sauce, but they're also tasty with Mexican Chocolate Ice Cream or after-dinner coffee. **MAKES 8 SOPAIPILLAS**

2 large flour tortillas

Vegetable oil for frying

2 tablespoons sugar

2 teaspoons ground cinnamon

1 recipe Mexican Chocolate Ice Cream (page 443) or good quality vanilla ice cream (optional)

1 recipe Classic Hot Fudge Sauce (see page 427) or store-bought hot fudge sauce (optional)

1 With a pizza wheel or a sharp knife, cut each tortilla into quarters.

2 Heat 2 inches of vegetable oil in a large deep skillet over medium-high heat until it registers 350 degrees F on a candy or meat thermometer. When the oil is hot (a bread cube placed in the hot oil should immediately sizzle), fry the tortilla wedges, a few at a time, until golden and puffy. Remove the tortilla wedges from the oil with a slotted spoon and place on paper towels to drain.

3 Combine the sugar and cinnamon in a small bowl. While the tortilla wedges are still hot, sprinkle with the cinnamon sugar. Serve with ice cream and hot fudge sauce, if desired.

County Fair Funnel Cakes

Most of us have memories of Ferris wheels, merry-go-rounds, and success at the fish-pond embedded in our collective conscious. If you're not a child or accompanied by a child, you don't even think about these types of entertainment. Maybe that's why we overindulge ourselves when we do go to carnivals—on wispy cotton candy, chocolate-covered frozen bananas, thick-cut French fries in a cup, and funnel cakes. I love good funnel cakes, the light and crispy kind with a dusting of confectioners' sugar that also dusts your nose. These spiral-shaped fritters are meant to be shared, which is part of the fun. Make these on a rainy day when your kids or grandchildren are restless and hungry. I like to use an electric skillet for this to maintain the right temperature. Known as *drechter kucha* in Pennsylvania Dutch communities, funnel cakes were originally made using a large tin funnel when adding the batter to the hot oil. **MAKES 6 TO 8 SMALL FUNNEL CAKES**

1⅓ cups all-purpose flour

¼ teaspoon salt

¾ teaspoon baking soda

½ teaspoon cream of tartar

2 tablespoons granulated sugar

1 large egg

1 cup milk

1 teaspoon vanilla extract

Vegetable oil for frying

Confectioners' sugar for dusting

1   Sift together the flour, salt, baking soda, cream of tartar, and granulated sugar into a large mixing bowl. Whisk the egg and milk together in a small dish, then stir this mixture into the dry ingredients until smooth. Stir in the vanilla.

2   In a large, deep skillet, heat 1 inch of vegetable oil over medium-high heat until it registers 375 degrees F on a candy or meat thermometer. Hold your finger over the bottom of a large kitchen funnel and pour in enough batter to reach the top of the funnel. Hold the funnel over the center of the skillet, remove your finger, and with a circular motion, let the batter create a spiral in the hot oil. Fry until the funnel cake is light brown on one side, then carefully flip and fry on the other side. Remove with a slotted spoon and drain on paper towels. Dust with confectioners' sugar while the funnel cake is still hot. Repeat the process with the remaining batter, letting the oil reheat to the proper temperature between cakes.

Crisp Swedish Rosettes

I loved these when I was a child and they're still delicious warm from the pan, a wonderful weekend treat to make with your own children or grandchildren. You'll need a Swedish rosette iron, a long metal handle on which a decorated metal form is attached (available in some hardware stores and culinary shops). The secrets to great rosettes are to dip the iron rosette form in 400-degree-F oil to heat it, then into the smooth crepe-like batter, then quickly into hot oil again to fry. I use a deep electric frying pan or a deep saucepan and a meat or candy thermometer to check the temperature of the oil before frying the rosettes. Once golden brown, the rosettes easily slip off the iron and onto paper towels to drain. While still warm, dust them with confectioners' sugar. A Scandinavian tradition, these crisp pastries are best enjoyed warm.

MAKES ABOUT 1 DOZEN ROSETTES

2 large eggs, beaten	¼ teaspoon salt
1 tablespoon granulated sugar	1 teaspoon vanilla extract
1 cup milk	About 5 cups vegetable oil for frying
1 cup all-purpose flour	Confectioners' sugar for dusting

1   Make the batter by whisking the eggs and sugar together in a large mixing bowl until smooth. Whisk in the milk, flour, salt, and vanilla and continue whisking until smooth.

2   Heat the vegetable oil in an electric skillet or large deep saucepan. Place paper towels near the skillet.

3   When the oil registers 400 degrees F on a candy or meat thermometer, dip the rosette form into the hot oil to heat it. Drain off the excess oil on paper towels, then immediately place the rosette form in the batter, but only three quarters of the way, so that the rosette form is not immersed in the batter. Immediately plunge the rosette form back in the hot oil and fry until golden brown, about 1 minute. Use a fork to gently remove the rosette from the form and onto paper towels to drain. Dust with confectioners' sugar while still warm. Repeat the process with the remaining batter.

If you're confused about the difference between custard and pudding, you're not alone. Like other types of foods, both custard and pudding have so evolved over the years that they're very different than their origins. "Custard" comes from the Old French *croustade*, meaning a crust or pastry shell in which a filling was usually baked. "Pudding" comes from the Middle English *poding*, a length of intestine or a piece of cloth in which a mixture of grains, meats, and fruits was sewn up and boiled—sort of like the Scottish haggis.

In Britain, "custard" can mean two things—the set custard dessert that you eat with a fork or spoon and the pouring custard (crème anglaise) people love over apple pie. The word "pudding" is a generic term for dessert in England, as in "What are we having for pudding?"

Until the nineteenth century, Americans didn't really distinguish between pie and pudding—a pie was simply a

Gelat

Custard's Last Stand Puddings, Custards, Mousses, Flans, and Soufflés

flavored custard baked in a pastry crust, or "paste," and called a "pudding." In the United States today, we have custard, and from custard we get pudding, usually a soft, smooth, creamy dessert thickened with eggs, cornstarch, flour, tapioca, cornmeal, rice, bread, or sometimes gelatin. And pie is pie.

Within the custard category, there are many subtle variations:

* Bavarian cream A cold, creamy custard, set with gelatin.

* Blancmange In eighteenth-century France, a cream dessert thickened with ground almonds. In the United States, beginning in the late nineteenth century, it was a cream dessert thickened with cornstarch.

* Crème Anglaise This is what the Amish call "English custard" (a translation of the French name) or "pouring custard." It's a cream slightly thickened with eggs, meant to be used as a dessert sauce.

* Crème brûlée French for "burnt cream," which is what it is called in England. This very old dessert is made in three steps: The custard is baked in the oven, then chilled, and finally a layer of sugar is sprinkled on the top and broiled or caramelized with a torch.

* Crème caramel or flan A custard dessert enjoyed in France and Spain. The custard is baked on top of a thin, simple sugar-and-water caramel, then inverted and served with the caramel on top.

* Crème patissière or pastry cream A thicker custard than crème anglaise, with more eggs and perhaps flour or cornstarch added. This type of pastry cream is used as a filling.

* Curd This filling is made with fruit juice, usually lemon or lime, and zest cooked with sugar, eggs, and sometimes butter until it becomes a thick mass.

* Custard An egg and milk dish, sometimes baked and sometimes stirred on the stove top until it thickens to a smooth, creamy mass.

* Mousse A light and airy dessert made with whipped cream, a thin custard or fruit puree, and sometimes Italian meringue. It may also be thickened with gelatin or frozen.

* Panna cotta Old Italian versions were cooked, hence the name "cooked cream." Today, most pastry chefs use gelatin to set this creamy dessert.

* Pots de crème French in origin, these individual portions of flavored custard are served in tiny pots with lids.

* Pudding A custard-like dessert that may be thickened with flour or cornstarch. The term also includes bread, rice, tapioca, and Indian cornmeal puddings, which feature a custard as a binding agent.

* Pudding cakes These pair a custard-like pudding with sponge cake to make a dessert with its own built-in sauce or creamy filling.

* Soufflé A custard base folded into whipped egg whites, then baked.

Americans love pudding in all its shapes, sizes, and flavors, from the earliest New England Maple Indian Pudding (page 394) to Appalachian Sweet Potato Pone with Kentucky Bourbon Pouring Custard (page 388) to vintage Iron Skillet Butterscotch Pudding (page 377) and Everyone's Favorite Banana Pudding (page 379). We love the whole range of bread and rice puddings brought to this country by German, Scandinavian, and Bohemian immigrants. We crave baked custards such as French Valley Scented Custard (page 384) or Persimmon Flan with Honeyed Whipped Cream (page 382), which show a Spanish influence on American ingredients.

We just have to have kugels, charlottes, and homey batter puddings (sweeter relatives of the savory Yorkshire pudding) and any dessert topped with flavorful Classic Crème Anglaise (page 369) poured over it. We've also discovered a yen for Tiramisu (page 380), Crème Brûlée (page 364), and Almond Panna Cotta (page 363), all relatively recent additions to the American dessert repertoire.

Wildflower Honey Cream with Warm Spiced Berries

One day, when a friend was recovering from an automobile accident and I wanted to bring her something, I came up with this. Sweetened with wildflower honey and thickened with gelatin, this dessert with a crème fraîche base marries elements of both Swedish and French cream confections. As an alternative dessert, I like to layer Wildflower Honey Cream parfaits with Strawberry Spoon Fruit (page 5) and garnish them with tiny fresh strawberries and leaves of lemon balm from my garden. The cream is also delicious served with Martha's Vineyard Summer Pudding (page 34), as a filling for Charlotte Russe (page 405), on top of fresh peaches, or you name it.

MAKES 8 SERVINGS

WILDFLOWER HONEY CREAM
One $1/4$-ounce package unflavored gelatin

$1/4$ cup water

2 cups heavy cream

2 cups sour cream

$1/2$ cup wildflower or other medium-colored honey

WARM SPICED BERRIES
3 cups fresh or frozen (thawed) blackberries, blueberries, or black raspberries

$1/2$ cup wildflower or other medium-colored honey

1 teaspoon ground cinnamon

1   To make the Wildflower Honey Cream, sprinkle the gelatin over the water in a small bowl. Set aside for several minutes until the gelatin is soaked through. Set the bowl in a small pan of hot water for several minutes, until the gelatin mixture is clear. Pour the heavy cream into a large mixing bowl, remove the bowl of gelatin from the water, and whisk the gelatin into the cream. With an electric mixer, whip the cream until it holds soft peaks. Beat in the sour cream and honey and continue beating for 2 minutes. Cover the bowl with plastic wrap and chill until ready to serve.

2   To make the Spiced Berries, right before serving, combine the berries, honey, and cinnamon in a medium-size saucepan over medium-high heat. Cook, stirring occasionally, until the berries just begin to release their juice, about 5 minutes, then remove from the heat.

3   To serve, spoon the honey cream into parfait glasses or dessert bowls and top with the warm berries.

Rum and Banana Cream

This is an adult gourmet's version of a quick dessert, easy to whip up for guests.
MAKES 6 SERVINGS

1 cup heavy cream

2 tablespoons white, dark, or spiced rum

2 tablespoons packed light brown sugar

2 very ripe bananas, peeled and mashed

Freshly grated nutmeg for garnish

Grated chocolate for garnish

1   With an electric mixer, whip the cream with the rum and brown sugar in a medium-size mixing bowl until the cream holds stiff peaks. Fold in the mashed bananas.

2   Spoon into 6 chilled martini glasses or bowls. Dust with grated nutmeg and chocolate and serve.

Brandied Apricot Fool

Margaret Tilghman Carroll presided over Mount Clare, a pink brick Georgian-style home completed in 1763. It used to sit on 848 acres overlooking the Patapsco River. Now the house is in downtown Baltimore. Margaret's husband, Charles Carroll (the "barrister," not the Charles Carroll who signed the Declaration of Independence), indulged his wife's interest in horticulture. Margaret had a greenhouse and an orangery, where she experimented with growing tropical pineapples, lemons, oranges, and temperamental apricots. In a letter written in 1767, Charles Carroll notes: "My wife takes much Pleasure in gardening and sends you a List of Peaches each of which she would be glad if you would send some of the stones of those of them that can be met with, Tied up in Different Parcels and the names of each wrote on the Parcel and Likewise Some of the Stones of your best Apricots and Nectarines." Although none of Margaret's horticultural notes survive, her receipt book does, and it's filled with recipes for all kinds of desserts and cordials. Interestingly, her desserts do not feature vanilla and chocolate, but are flavored heavily with lemon, spices, brandy, and peach cordial, like this updated one—a sophisticated American take on old-fashioned English fool.

MAKES 6 TO 8 SERVINGS

Two 29-ounce cans apricots, drained

Grated zest of 1 lemon

¼ cup Plantation House Peach Cordial (page 501) or brandy

1 cup heavy cream

½ cup sugar

Crystallized ginger for garnish

Crisp spice cookies for serving

1   Put the apricots in a food processor and process until smooth. You should have about 3 cups. In a large mixing bowl, stir together the pureed apricots, lemon zest, and cordial.

2   With an electric mixer, whip the cream and sugar together in a medium-size mixing bowl until the cream holds stiff peaks. With a rubber spatula, fold the cream into the apricot mixture. Spoon into parfait or dessert glasses and chill for at least 2 hours before serving. Garnish each glass with a piece of crystallized ginger and accompany with a crisp spice cookie.

A Trifling Fool

The English love for the spoken word and their dry sense of humor infuse some of our earliest desserts with names that bespeak silliness, puffery, and insignificant things that can be utterly delightful. Many of these have to do with whipped cream, and perhaps the inflated nature of that dessert staple helped the names along. Although Lady Fettiplace does not use the term "trifle" in her 1604 receipt book, she does include a recipe for what we would recognize as a trifle, titled "Creame Called a Foole." A fool, to her, could also be a baked batter pudding.

Today, a fool is a simple concoction of whipped cream blended with stewed fruit. In England, you can buy little pots of fruit fool like you do fruit yogurt here. My young son loved fruit fool packed in his lunch when we lived there.

A trifle, a term added later on, is a layered dessert of pieces of sponge cake or ladyfingers, stewed fruit, custard, and whipped cream. Trifle recipes called "tipsy squire" or "tipsy parson" in eighteenth-century New England were also flavored liberally with sherry, sack, or rum.

After the English Civil War was over in the mid 1600s, travel between the American colonies and England resumed. Abigail Adams was one of many American women to bring back an English cookbook or recipes from her sojourn there. Up until the American Civil War, we continued to draw heavily on English precedents in matters of taste in architecture, furniture, clothing, and cookery. And to some degree, we still do.

Despite that ongoing influence, the fool faded away, but the trifle held on in this country.

Plum and Port Mousse

In creek banks and low-lying areas in the rural western prairie of Kansas and Nebraska, small wild plums ripen in late July. At that same time, wild beach plums beckon pickers on the New England coast. Generations of home cooks have gathered both kinds of plums to make jelly, preserves, and summer desserts. Either wild or domestic plums work well in this recipe, which blends regional ingredients with French techniques. Plum puree and port are swirled with Italian Meringue to create a light, refreshing dessert. Serve this with a drizzle of dark fruit syrup or accompany it with a crisp cookie. This mousse is also delicious served in a Pastry Flower (page 269), garnished with fresh mint or lemon verbena sprigs. **MAKES 8 SERVINGS**

1 pound plums	1 teaspoon vanilla extract
¼ cup sugar	1 cup heavy cream
¼ cup port	1 recipe Italian Meringue (recipe follows)

1   Place the plums and sugar in a large, heavy-bottomed saucepan and cook over low heat, covered, until the plums are soft, stirring a few times, about 15 minutes. Remove from the heat and let cool.

2   When the plums have cooled, discard the pits. Place the plums in a food processor, add the port, and puree. Press the puree through a strainer into a bowl to remove the skins. Stir in the vanilla.

3   With an electric mixer, whip the cream in a large mixing bowl until it holds stiff peaks. Fold the plum puree and meringue into the whipped cream, but not completely, so the mixture looks swirled. Divide the mousse between 8 dessert glasses or into one decorative serving bowl. Cover with plastic wrap and chill for at least 2 hours, and up to 6 hours, before serving.

Italian Meringue

This type of meringue, which is a component of many American desserts, provides a light and airy texture and good keeping qualities. You incorporate a heavy sugar syrup into stiffly beaten egg whites for a glossy, ethereal mixture that will keep, covered, in the refrigerator for days before you need it. Soak the saucepan in hot water to melt off any hardened syrup. **MAKES ABOUT 4 CUPS**

$\frac{1}{2}$ cup water	$\frac{1}{4}$ teaspoon cream of tartar
1 cup sugar	4 large egg whites

1   In a heavy-bottomed saucepan, heat the water and sugar together over low heat until the sugar dissolves. Increase the heat to medium-high and bring the mixture to a boil. Cook, without stirring, until the mixture registers 248 degrees F on a candy thermometer, or the hardball stage (when a bit of the hot mixture forms a hard ball when dropped into a glass of cold water), 12 to 15 minutes. Remove from the heat.

2   While the sugar syrup is cooking, with an electric mixer, beat the egg whites with the cream of tartar in a large mixing bowl until they hold stiff peaks. Set aside.

3   Wearing an oven mitt on the hand holding the saucepan, gradually pour the hot sugar syrup into the egg whites and continue to beat with an electric mixer on low until all the syrup is incorporated and the meringue is thick and glossy.

Get with the Beat

Beating whole eggs, egg whites, or egg yolks to the proper consistency can be crucial to the success of a dessert recipe. Having the eggs at room temperature before beating helps create more volume and speeds up the process. Delicious sponge cakes, angel food cakes, and meringues are the payoff for eggs that have been beaten properly. Use a clean bowl and utensils. When beating egg whites, any speck of butter, egg yolk, or fat of any kind can deflate the meringue.

Eggs can do great things for your desserts if you become familiar with the techniques described below.

Slightly beaten eggs. Beat the eggs in a small bowl with a fork until the whites and yolks are blended and no streaks remain.

Beating egg whites until they hold soft peaks. Using an electric mixer with clean, dry beaters, beat the egg whites on high speed until they turn opaque white and have a soft, cloud-like appearance. When you lift the beaters out of the egg whites, the egg white mixture should form a peak, with the tip of the peak falling over slightly.

Beating egg whites until they hold stiff peaks. Using an electric mixer with clean, dry beaters, beat the egg whites on high speed until they turn opaque white and have a soft, cloud-like appearance. At this point, you usually add cream of tartar or sugar, depending on the recipe. Continue to beat the egg whites until they are firm, glossy, and form stiff peaks when you lift the beaters out of the egg whites.

Beating egg yolks until they're thick, lemon-colored, and ribbon off the beaters. With an electric mixer on high speed, beat the egg yolks until they are thick and lemon colored, about 5 minutes. When you lift the beaters out of the egg yolks, the mixture should fall from the beaters in thick, ribbon-like streams, like pancake batter.

Raspberry Amaretti Frozen Mousse

Also called a *semifreddo* (Italian for "half frozen"), this delicious frozen pink concoction is made in a loaf pan. It is wonderful sliced and served with fresh raspberries and amaretti or fresh raspberry sauce. Ice cream novelties abound in grocery store freezers, but homemade is still best. **MAKES 16 SERVINGS**

4 cups fresh or frozen (thawed) raspberries, plus extra for garnish

1 cup sugar

1 tablespoon fresh lemon juice

1 cup heavy cream, plus extra for garnish

1 teaspoon vanilla extract

1 recipe Italian Meringue (page 351)

1 cup crushed homemade (page 96) or store-bought amaretti, plus extra for garnish

Fresh mint or berry leaves for garnish

1   Line two 9 x 5-inch loaf pans with long sheets of plastic wrap so that the mousse can be covered completely. Set aside.

2   In a food processor, combine the raspberries and sugar and process until smooth, then rub the puree through a strainer into a bowl to remove most of the seeds. Discard the seeds. Stir the lemon juice into the berry puree.

3   With an electric mixer, whip the cream and vanilla together in a large mixing bowl until the cream holds stiff peaks. Add the raspberry puree, meringue, and amaretti, and mix gently to blend. Spoon the mixture into the prepared loaf pans. Carefully drop the filled loaf pans onto the counter several times to remove any large air pockets. Cover with plastic wrap and freeze for at least 6 hours or overnight.

4   Unwrap the mousse, invert onto a serving platter or plate, and peel off the plastic wrap. Slice and garnish with fresh berries, amaretti, whipped cream, and mint leaves.

Crazy Quilt Chocolate Mousse with Fresh Orange Syrup

The poet Gerard Manley Hopkins extolled "pied beauty"—anything that is brindled, spotted, or patterned, a haphazard charm also appreciated by American crazy quilt makers in the late nineteenth century. That's just one of the virtues of this dessert. What you end up with is a variegated crazy quilt pattern of white, medium, and dark chocolate and a workout for your taste buds with flavors of chocolate, mocha, and orange. Although this recipe may look complicated, you actually repeat the same procedure three times, and the mousse assembles in an hour. Just be sure to clean out the top of the double boiler after each use. The mousse is best made ahead early in the day or the night before so it chills thoroughly. **MAKES 8 SERVINGS**

MOCHA CHOCOLATE MOUSSE

¾ cup semisweet chocolate chips

2 teaspoons instant espresso powder

½ cup (1 stick) unsalted butter at room temperature

2 tablespoons sugar

¾ cup heavy cream

WHITE CHOCOLATE MOUSSE

¾ cup white chocolate chips

½ cup (1 stick) unsalted butter at room temperature

Grated zest of 1 large orange

¾ cup heavy cream

DARK CHOCOLATE MOUSSE

¾ cup semisweet chocolate chips

½ cup unsweetened cocoa powder

½ cup (1 stick) unsalted butter at room temperature

2 tablespoons sugar

¾ cup heavy cream

1½ teaspoons vanilla extract

1 recipe Fresh Orange Syrup (page 488)

Whipped cream for garnish

1 recipe Candied Citrus Peel (page 483) or fresh orange segments for garnish

Fresh mint leaves for garnish

1   Line a 9 x 5-inch loaf pan with a long sheet of plastic wrap so that the mousse can be covered completely. Set aside.

2   Make the Mocha Chocolate Mousse: Combine the chocolate and espresso powder in the top of a double boiler over just simmering water, stirring until the chocolate melts. Remove from the heat and whisk in the softened butter until smooth. Set aside. With an electric mixer, beat the sugar and cream together in a large mixing bowl until the cream holds soft peaks. Using a rubber

spatula, fold 1 cup of the whipped cream into the chocolate mixture, then carefully fold in the remaining whipped cream until well blended. Set aside.

3   Make the White Chocolate Mousse: Put the white chocolate in the top of a double boiler over just simmering water until it melts. Remove from the heat and whisk in the softened butter and orange zest until smooth. Set aside. With an electric mixer, beat the cream in a large mixing bowl until it holds soft peaks. Using a rubber spatula, fold 1 cup of the whipped cream into the chocolate mixture, then carefully fold in the remaining whipped cream until well blended. Set aside.

4   Make the Dark Chocolate Mousse: Combine the chocolate and cocoa powder in the top of a double boiler over just simmering water until the chocolate melts. Remove from the heat and whisk in the softened butter until smooth. Set aside. With an electric mixer, beat together the sugar, cream, and vanilla in a large mixing bowl until the cream holds soft peaks. Using a rubber spatula, fold 1 cup of the whipped cream into the chocolate mixture, then carefully fold in the remaining whipped cream until well blended. Set aside.

5   Spoon about 1/2 cup of each mousse into the bottom of the prepared loaf pan, making a variegated pattern. Using a rubber or offset spatula, gently press down and smooth the bottom layer. Spoon about 1/2 cup of each mousse to create a second layer, press and smooth down, then make a third layer. Cover with the plastic wrap and chill until firm, 2 to 3 hours.

6   Remove the mouse from the refrigerator about 15 minutes before serving. To serve, unwrap the mousse, invert onto a serving platter, and peel off the plastic wrap. Slice into 8 equal portions. Drizzle the orange syrup on the bottom of each plate and top with a slice of mousse. Garnish each plate with a dollop of whipped cream, candied orange peel or fresh orange segments, and mint leaves.

Holiday Eggnog Mousse

As a teenager growing up in Cincinnati, I went on holiday shopping jaunts with my mother that always included a stop at an exclusive women's clothing store downtown—the kind that had liveried elevator operators and deep couches for weary husbands. The conservative and designer clothes were not for us, but the holiday eggnog sure was! Served from an ornate silver punch bowl, this eggnog was rich with cream and wicked with rum. A small cup was all we could manage without swaying as we walked to the next store. Serve this elegant mousse with a fruit compote or surround it with sugared fruits.

MAKES 8 TO 10 SERVINGS

Two $\frac{1}{4}$-ounce envelopes unflavored gelatin

$\frac{1}{3}$ cup water

1 quart dairy eggnog

$\frac{1}{4}$ teaspoon freshly grated nutmeg

$\frac{1}{3}$ cup white or dark rum

1 recipe Chocolate Curls (see page 198) for garnish

1 Sprinkle the gelatin over the water in a small saucepan until it is soaked through. Then whisk in 1 cup of the eggnog and warm over medium-low heat until the gelatin has completely dissolved, about 5 minutes.

2 Remove from the heat and whisk in the remaining 3 cups of eggnog, the nutmeg, and the rum. Pour into a metal bowl, cover with plastic wrap, and chill until partially set, about 1 hour.

3 Using an electric mixer, whip the mousse until light and fluffy. Using a rubber spatula, transfer the mousse to a glass serving bowl. Cover and chill for 2 more hours or until ready to serve. Garnish with chocolate curls.

Green Mountain Frozen Maple Mousse

Use real maple syrup for this dessert, which tastes best served with a nut cookie. I like the richer, darker flavor of Grade B syrup when I can find it. This is also wonderful made with Vermont apple syrup. **MAKES 8 SERVINGS**

3 large eggs, separated

1 cup pure maple syrup

1 teaspoon vanilla extract

2 cups heavy cream

1 In a medium-size heavy saucepan, whisk the egg yolks and maple syrup together. Cook the mixture over low heat, whisking constantly, until it has slightly thickened, about 15 minutes. Whisk in the vanilla and set aside to cool.

2 With an electric mixer, whip the egg whites in a medium-size mixing bowl until they hold stiff peaks. Set aside. In a large mixing bowl with the mixer, whip the cream until it holds stiff peaks. Fold the egg whites and egg yolk mixture into the whipped cream. Spoon into 8 individual parfait or dessert glasses, decorative bowls, or a large soufflé dish and freeze for at least 1 hour before serving.

Molasses, Pure Cane Syrup, and Maple Syrup

The sweeteners that most distinguish American desserts from those of other countries are molasses and pure cane syrup made from sugar cane, and maple syrup from the sap of the sugar maple tree. Each provides a distinctive flavor and a different quality of sweetness. All three were commonly used in American cooking and baking before refined sugar was readily available, and they still hold an important place in our collective repertoire of American desserts.

Molasses, a by-product of sugar refining, has a dark history in America. Sugar cane, a giant perennial grass native to Asia and brought to the West Indies, requires a tropical climate and lots of hard, intensive hand labor. From the seventeenth century onwards, that labor was provided by African slaves, kidnapped by slave traders from the western coast of Africa and brought to the West Indies and to American shores to work on plantations. American slaves were sold in exchange for molasses and sugar in the West Indies. These were made into rum in New England, and the rum was shipped to West Africa and traded for still more slaves, in what became known as the triangular trade route. Today, sugar cane is cultivated in the United States in the tropical climates of Florida, Louisiana, Texas, and Hawaii.

Deep, dark brown molasses has a dark, almost sulfurous taste. It's what's left over after sugar is pressed and the resulting syrup is boiled to crystallize the sugar. The molasses syrup is blended with uncrystallized sugar syrup, and the mixture is then crystallized and centrifuged or "cooked." Different grades of molasses are produced from subsequent "cookings." Lighter molasses is made from the first and second cookings, and very dark blackstrap molasses (from the Dutch word *stroop*, for syrup) from the third cooking, when the sugars have been highly caramelized. Final molasses, made from a fourth cooking, is used as animal feed.

Pure cane syrup, made in Louisiana, is just that—syrup pressed from sugar cane with nothing else added. Dark brown pure cane syrup has a licorice-like flavor and a less viscous consistency than that of molasses. Both molasses and pure cane syrup are essential to Shoofly Pie, spice and molasses cookies, gingerbread, and some old-fashioned crisps and cobblers.

Maple syrup was first made by Native Americans, who extracted the sweet sap of the sugar maple, which was boiled until greatly reduced. English settlers observed this springtime rite and soon were doing it themselves, learning the right time to tap the trees. It takes between 30 and 35 gallons of maple sap to make 1 gallon of maple syrup. The longer and harder the syrup is boiled, the more heavily concentrated it is. Grade A Fancy and Grade A are lighter in color and flavor, while Grade B is darker and more robustly flavored. In the late eighteenth century, some Americans found a moral reason for preferring maple to cane sugar. Benjamin Rush wrote to Thomas Jefferson in 1791: "I cannot help contemplating a sugar maple tree with a species of affection and even veneration, for I have persuaded myself to behold in it the happy means of rendering the commerce and slavery of our African brethren in the sugar islands as unnecessary as it has always been inhuman and unjust."

New Jersey Applejack Mousse

Use the best local apples you can find at your farmers' market and pair them with a spirited applejack to make this lusciously soft mousse for a celebratory harvest dinner. MAKES 8 SERVINGS

1½ cups half-and-half or light cream

4 large egg yolks

½ cup sugar

3 cups homemade applesauce (see Swedish Apple Torte with Vanilla Cloud Sauce, page 229, step 5)

1 tablespoon fresh lemon juice

2 teaspoons ground cinnamon

½ cup applejack, hard cider, or Calvados

One ¼-ounce envelope unflavored gelatin

1 cup heavy cream

Candied apple peel (see Note), fresh apple slices, or cinnamon sticks for garnish

1   In a large heavy saucepan over medium heat, whisk the half-and-half, egg yolks, and sugar together. Cook, whisking constantly, until the mixture thickens enough to coat the back of a wooden spoon, about 10 minutes. Stir the applesauce, lemon juice, and cinnamon into the custard. Set aside to cool slightly.

2   Pour the applejack into a small bowl and sprinkle the gelatin on top. Set the bowl in a pan of hot water until the gelatin has dissolved. Whisk the gelatin mixture into the custard. Cover with plastic wrap and refrigerate for 1 hour.

3   With an electric mixer, whip the cream in a medium-size mixing bowl until it holds stiff peaks, then fold the cream into the custard mixture. Mound the mousse into a serving bowl, cover with plastic wrap, and refrigerate for 2 hours or until set.

4   To serve, spoon the mousse onto individual dessert plates. Garnish with a curl of candied apple peel.

NOTE To make candied apple peel, stir together 1 cup of water and 1 cup of sugar in a heavy saucepan over medium-high heat. Bring to a boil, then remove from the heat and stir in the juice of 1 lemon. Set aside. With a mechanical apple peeler or with a sharp paring knife, peel several apples so that you get thin, curling strips of apple peel. Place the strips of peel into the simple syrup in the saucepan, then bring to a boil again over medium-high heat. Cook for 5 minutes, then remove with a slotted spoon and let cool on waxed paper or parchment paper. Use as an edible garnish.

Jacqueline Kennedy's Cold Chocolate Soufflé

In 1961, this recipe appeared in *House Beautiful* magazine as *Soufflé Froid au Chocolat*. Mrs. Kennedy had served this at small dinner parties at the Kennedy home in Georgetown when her husband was a senator. Although the dish, which I have adapted here, looks like a risen soufflé within its collar, it is really a mousse made airy with whipped cream and semisolid with gelatin. Like everything else about Jacqueline Kennedy, the dessert remains an understated classic. **MAKES 8 SERVINGS**

SOUFFLÉ

One ¼-ounce envelope unflavored gelatin

3 tablespoons water

2 ounces unsweetened chocolate, cut into pieces

½ cup confectioners' sugar

1 cup milk

¾ cup granulated sugar

1 teaspoon vanilla extract

¼ teaspoon salt

2 cups heavy cream

CHOCOLATE CURLS

One 4-ounce block bittersweet chocolate, chilled

1 To make the soufflé, sprinkle the gelatin over the water in a small bowl. Set aside for several minutes until the gelatin has soaked through.

2 Put the chocolate pieces in the top of a double boiler over barely simmering water and let the chocolate melt very slowly. Remove the top of the double boiler from the water and whisk in the confectioners' sugar. Set aside.

3 Scald the milk in a medium-size saucepan over medium-high heat until small bubbles form around the perimeter. Slowly stir the milk into the chocolate mixture. Mix thoroughly and transfer the chocolate mixture to the saucepan. Cook over low heat, stirring constantly, until the mixture begins to simmer, but not boil, about 10 minutes.

4 Remove the pan from the heat and mix in the softened gelatin, granulated sugar, vanilla, and salt. Pour the mixture into a large mixing bowl and refrigerate until slightly thickened, about 45 minutes.

5 Remove the chocolate mixture from the refrigerator and beat the mixture with a whisk until light and airy. With an electric mixer, whip the cream in a medium-size mixing bowl until it holds soft peaks. With a rubber spatula, fold the cream into the chocolate mixture.

6   Fold a long sheet of aluminum foil over lengthwise to make a 4-inch-wide collar. Coat the inside of the collar with nonstick cooking spray and paper clip or tie the collar around the perimeter of a 1-quart soufflé dish so that the collar stands at least 2 inches above the rim of the dish. Spoon the chocolate mixture into the prepared dish. Refrigerate for at least 3 hours before serving. The soufflé can be made a day ahead, covered, and stored in the refrigerator.

7   To make the chocolate curls, scrape the bittersweet chocolate block with a vegetable peeler. To serve, remove the collar from the soufflé and garnish the top with chocolate curls.

Orange Blossom Honey Mousse with Fresh Fruit

This is a delightfully light dessert from Fripp Island, off the coast of South Carolina. Orange blossom honey is made in March and early April, when orange trees begin to blossom in Florida, Arizona, and California. Combined with citrus juice and sour cream, the honey lends a gentle flavor and the mousse is luscious. Nondairy or low-fat sour cream also works well. Use a decorative ring mold and garnish with fresh seasonal fruit.

MAKES 10 TO 12 SERVINGS

$\frac{1}{2}$ cup cold water

Two $\frac{1}{4}$-ounce packages unflavored gelatin

$\frac{1}{4}$ cup fresh lemon juice

$\frac{1}{2}$ cup orange juice

$1\frac{1}{2}$ cups sour cream

$\frac{1}{2}$ cup orange blossom, clover, or other light-colored honey

Seasonal fresh fruits, such as strawberries, pineapple, blackberries, grapes, or melon balls, for garnish

Fresh mint or lemon balm leaves for garnish

1   Pour the water into a small bowl and sprinkle the gelatin over it. Set the bowl in a pan of hot water and set aside until the gelatin has soaked through, about 5 minutes.

2   Transfer the dissolved gelatin to a large mixing bowl. With an electric mixer, beat in the juices, sour cream, and honey until light, fluffy, and smooth, about 2 minutes. Lightly brush the inside of a 4-cup mold with vegetable oil or water. Spoon the mousse mixture into the prepared mold and smooth the top with a rubber spatula. Cover with plastic wrap and chill in the refrigerator until firm, 3 to 4 hours.

3   Unmold the mousse onto a serving platter and garnish with fresh fruit and mint leaves.

Honey, Honey

When I was at La Varenne Ecole de Cuisine in Paris during the 1980s, I walked miles and miles around the city, discovering all the wonderful markets and food purveyors. One day I walked into La Maison du Miel, or "the House of Honey," in the ninth *arrondissement*. What a revelation! The small shop featured rows and rows of turquoise containers filled with all different types of honey, from lavender to linden blossom to heather—like sweetened flavors of the French countryside. I brought a jar of the assertive lavender honey home with me.

Of course, it makes sense that what bees graze upon makes a difference in the flavor of the resulting honey. While food manufacturers try to keep the taste and texture of their products consistent from day to day, bees don't. When I returned home to Kansas, I decided to educate my taste buds a little more and find out about American varietal honeys.

I already knew and loved sourwood honey—made from the nectar of sourwood tree blossoms—from childhood vacations in the Smoky Mountains. After a bit of searching, I discovered locally produced wildflower honey from the W. F. Matthes Bee Farms in Pleasant Hill, Missouri, and this has become my hands-down favorite.

Honey lovers in other parts of the country become attached to the sweet and lightly fragrant orange blossom varietal from Florida and Arizona, the delicate and clear white tupelo from Mississippi and Alabama, basswood or clover honey from New England, mellow alfalfa or fireweed from Idaho, dark amber sunflower from the Dakotas, assertive sagebrush from Nevada, and cat's claw or prickly pear honey from Arizona.

The process of making honey is fascinating. The bees designated as foragers have special cavities in their bodies to mix the sweet flower nectar they "drink" with enzymes that convert the sucrose into more highly concentrated glucose and fructose. On the way back to the hive, the forager bees perform a stylized dance—like moving runes—to communicate the location and type of flower to their fellow foragers. Back at the hive, they become part of a tag team. They pass the converted nectar on to house bees and head back out to the flowers again.

The house bees take the nectar to a central location in the hive, where hundreds of bees fan their wings to evaporate the moisture from the nectar. When the moisture content has been reduced to below 20 percent, the nectar has become honey. It is then stored in honeycombs, ready to feed the bees or be taken by the beekeeper. Each pound of honey reflects the amazing collective work of the hive—over two million flowers visited, thousands of miles flown.

Tasting regular bottled honey at the grocery store might leave you with the thought "so what?" That's because most of those honeys are blended from many different kinds, heated, and filtered into bland sweetness. Look for varietal honeys made with cold-processing techniques and that are never blended.

When baking, substitute about ¾ cup of honey for 1 cup of sugar in a recipe. Honey improves the keeping properties of cookies and cakes.

White Chocolate and Pasilla Chile Mousse

Here is a Southwestern twist on classic chocolate mousse adapted from a recipe by chef Jeffrey Axell of Phoenix. Fresh dark brown pasilla chiles add a medium-hot burst of flavor to the cool and creamy mousse flavored with rum. When the cooking of the American Southwest began to eclipse California cuisine in the late 1980s, chefs began to experiment with all the "new" chiles—even adding them to chocolate desserts, like this one. Serve with Warm Spiced Berries (see page 348) or fresh fruit.

MAKES 8 SERVINGS

8 ounces white chocolate, broken into pieces

2 tablespoons sugar

2 cups heavy cream

½ vanilla bean

2 tablespoons dark rum

2 tablespoons water

One ¼-ounce package unflavored gelatin

2 tablespoons seeded and chopped fresh pasilla chile

1   Put the chocolate and sugar in a medium-size heatproof mixing bowl. In a small heavy saucepan, heat 1 cup of the cream with the vanilla bean half and the rum.

2   As soon as the cream starts to boil, remove from the heat. Strain through a sieve over the chocolate and sugar in the bowl and discard the vanilla bean. Whisk the mixture to melt the chocolate and dissolve the sugar. Set aside to cool to room temperature.

3   Pour the water into a small bowl and sprinkle the gelatin on top. Set the bowl in a pan of hot water and set aside until the gelatin has dissolved. Whisk the gelatin mixture into the chocolate mixture, then fold in the pasilla chile. With an electric mixer, whip the remaining 1 cup of cream in a small mixing bowl until it forms stiff peaks. Fold the cream into the chocolate-chile mixture. Spoon the mousse into a glass bowl and chill for at least 2 hours before serving.

Almond Panna Cotta

San Francisco pastry chef and cookbook author Emily Lucchetti is very passionate about how she wants her restaurant desserts to look and taste. "The primary thing is flavor," she says. "Desserts shouldn't be a lot of work. You shouldn't get a plate in front of you and say: 'What is it? How do I eat it? What's it supposed to be? How do things all relate together?' Dessert should be easier. You should say, 'Gosh, that looks great!' And then you should be able to dig right in and eat it." The home cook can certainly do that with this panna cotta, adapted from Lucchetti's recipe. *Panna cotta* is Italian for "cooked cream," which is thickened with gelatin and served chilled. **MAKES 8 SERVINGS**

1 cup sliced almonds, toasted (see page 181)

3 cups heavy cream

½ cup milk

1 tablespoon unflavored gelatin

3 tablespoons water

⅔ cup sugar

¼ teaspoon salt

1 recipe Northwest Sweet Cherry Compote (optional, page 15)

1   Combine the almonds, cream, and milk in a large heavy saucepan over medium heat. Scald the mixture until small bubbles form around the perimeter, then remove from the heat. Cover the pan and let steep for 15 minutes.

2   Meanwhile, sprinkle the gelatin over the water in a small bowl and set aside until it is soaked through. Then place the bowl in a small pan of hot water and set aside until the gelatin completely dissolves.

3   Strain the almond mixture into a bowl, discard the almonds, then return it to the saucepan. Stir in the sugar and scald again over medium heat. Whisk in the dissolved gelatin and salt. Pour the warm almond mixture into a bowl and allow to cool slightly, stirring occasionally. Pour into eight 4- to 6-ounce ramekins or custard cups. Refrigerate until set, at least 3 hours or overnight.

4   To serve, run a knife around the inside of each ramekin and invert each panna cotta onto a dessert plate. Serve with the compote, if desired.

Crème Brûlée

The origins of crème brûlée lie in Europe, but whether in Spain, France, or England, we may never know. The Spanish have taken credit for this dessert in the form of *crema catalana*, or crème brûlée without the sugar topping, since the eighteenth century. The English claim it originated in seventeenth-century Britain, where it was known as "burnt cream" and famously served on formal occasions at Trinity College at Cambridge University. A salamander, or shovel-like metal cooking implement, was heated in the fire, then held over the sugar topping on the custard to produce its characteristic crunch. Recipes for burnt cream began appearing in eighteenth-century British cookery books, featuring flavorings such as a strip of lemon or orange peel and a cinnamon stick. It wasn't until the end of the nineteenth century that common usage of the French term came into vogue. But when crème brûlée came to this country is still somewhat of a mystery because it was more in the realm of restaurant food than a dish that home cooks would make. New Orleans residents will tell you that their city has been quietly enjoying a version of this classic dessert for more than 60 years. Before Le Cirque owner Sirio Maccioni added crème brûlée to the menu of his Manhattan restaurant in 1982, few Americans had ever heard of it. Today, the dessert appears in an astonishing variety of flavors, from cranberry and maple in New England to coconut in Hawaii. Although a fixture on restaurant dessert menus, it's not difficult for the home cook to make—especially this easy version, which just bakes in the oven. This recipe makes a classic vanilla-flavored crème brûlée with a caramelized granulated sugar topping. Make sure you use pure cane sugar (not sugar made from sugar beets) so that the top caramelizes evenly. You can also use a small kitchen torch to caramelize the sugar, rather than putting the custards under the broiler. **MAKES 6 SERVINGS**

8 large egg yolks
⅓ cup granulated sugar
2 cups heavy cream

1 teaspoon vanilla extract
¼ cup packed light brown sugar

1   Preheat the oven to 300 degrees F. In a large bowl, whisk the egg yolks and granulated sugar together until the sugar has dissolved and the mixture is thick and pale yellow, about 5 minutes. Whisk in the cream and vanilla. Strain the mixture into a large mixing bowl, skimming off any egg

solids, bubbles, or foam. Place six 4-ounce ovenproof ramekins or custard cups in a baking pan with enough water to come halfway up the sides of the ramekins. Divide the custard among the ramekins.

2   Bake for 50 to 60 minutes, or until the custard is set around the edges, but still jiggles in the center. Remove from the oven and leave in the water bath until cooled. Remove the ramekins from the water bath and refrigerate for at least 2 hours and up to 2 days before serving.

3   When ready to serve, preheat the broiler. Sprinkle about 2 teaspoons of brown sugar on top of each custard. Place the ramekins on a heavy baking sheet, and broil for 2 minutes, or until the tops have browned. Keep the oven door open and watch carefully, as the sugar can caramelize quickly. Serve immediately.

CHOCOLATE CRÈME BRÛLÉE Melt 4 ounces of good quality bittersweet or dark chocolate in the top of a double boiler over simmering water. Whisk the melted chocolate into the egg and cream mixture in step 1, then proceed with the recipe.

Saffron Crème Brûlée with Rosy Strawberry Compote

I have a late eighteenth- or early nineteenth-century glazed chintz quilt from Pennsylvania in gorgeous earthy colors of pale gold, warm brown, and rose red, the colors of this dessert. A spoonful of brûlée together with a rosy-flavored strawberry is simply wonderful. This dish, which I have adapted, is based on a recipe by chef Chris Elbow of Kansas City. Both the crème brûlée and the compote can be made a day ahead. When strawberries are not in season, serve this with a scattering of pomegranate seeds and a drizzle of grenadine mixed with a drop or two of rosewater, available at gourmet shops and Asian markets. MAKES 8 SERVINGS

SAFFRON CRÈME BRÛLÉE
4 cups heavy cream
1 cup granulated sugar
¼ teaspoon saffron threads
10 large egg yolks
8 to 10 tablespoons packed light brown sugar

ROSY STRAWBERRY COMPOTE
2 pints fresh strawberries, hulled
1 recipe Homemade Vanilla Bean Syrup (page 486)
Grated zest of 1 orange
Grated zest of 1 lemon
2 tablespoons rosewater

1   To make the crème brûlée, preheat the oven to 375 degrees F. Whisk the cream, ½ cup of the granulated sugar, and the saffron together in a large heavy-bottomed saucepan over medium heat. Scald the cream until small bubbles form around the perimeter of the pan. Do not let the cream boil. Remove from the heat, cover, and let steep for 5 minutes.

2   Meanwhile, with an electric mixer, beat the egg yolks with the remaining ½ cup of granulated sugar in a large mixing bowl until the mixture turns pale yellow, about 3 minutes. Slowly beat in the hot cream, then pour this mixture through a fine-mesh strainer into a bowl. Ladle the mixture into eight 6-ounce ramekins or small ovenproof bowls. Set the ramekins in a baking pan and fill with enough hot water to reach halfway up the sides of the ramekins. Cover the baking pan with aluminum foil and place in the oven. Immediately reduce the oven temperature to 325 degrees F.

3   Bake until the crèmes brûlées are just set but the center still jiggles a bit when gently shaken, about 30 minutes. Remove the ramekins from the water bath and let cool to room temperature. Cover with plastic wrap and refrigerate for at least 4 hours or overnight.

4   To make the compote, combine the strawberries, syrup, zests, and rosewater in a large mixing bowl. Cover with plastic wrap and refrigerate for at least 4 hours or overnight.

5   To serve, preheat the broiler. Place the ramekins in a baking pan with enough cool water to reach halfway up their sides. Sprinkle 1 tablespoon of brown sugar evenly over the top of each ramekin and broil until the sugar bubbles and melts. Remove immediately and serve with the compote.

Pumpkin Crème Brûlée with Warm Spiced Berries

For me, this dessert is November on a spoon—the pale flame of falling leaves with the dark purple of a late autumn nighttime sky and a mellow, spicy flavor. A more sophisticated alternative to holiday pumpkin pie, this dessert also has the advantage of being prepared a day ahead of the feast. **MAKES 8 SERVINGS**

3 cups heavy cream

1 cup granulated sugar

¼ cup dark rum

10 large egg yolks

2 cups cooked and pureed pumpkin (see Note, page 311) or one 15-ounce can pumpkin puree

½ teaspoon salt

½ teaspoon ground cinnamon

8 to 10 tablespoons packed light brown sugar

1 recipe Warm Spiced Berries (see page 348)

Rosewater

Rosewater was distilled from fragrant rose petals and used to flavor milk-based puddings, fruit desserts, and cakes from the time of the first American kitchens in the 1620s. Ladies of well-run households of the period made their own rosewater for both culinary and medicinal purposes. William Bradford mentions "the fragrant rose" in Plymouth gardens, and in a letter to John Winthrop, Jr., in 1634, Joseph Downing in London offers, "If you write word that you have no roses there, I will send you over some damask, red, white, and province rose plants." Gulielma Penn, the wife of William Penn, made a curd cheesecake with rosewater and currants. By the mid 1800s, rosewater is infrequently listed as a flavoring ingredient in receipt books and cookbooks. Today, however, it is enjoying a renaissance because of the popularity of Middle Eastern food. Rosewater is most often used in rice puddings or compotes of red fruits.

1   To make the crème brûlée, preheat the oven to 375 degrees F. Whisk the cream, ½ cup of the granulated sugar, and rum together in a large heavy-bottomed saucepan over medium heat. Scald the cream until small bubbles form around the perimeter of the pan. Do not let the cream boil. Remove from the heat, cover, and let steep for 5 minutes.

2   Meanwhile, with an electric mixer, beat the egg yolks with the remaining ½ cup of granulated sugar, the salt, and cinnamon in a large mixing bowl until the mixture is smooth. Slowly beat in the hot cream, then pour the mixture through a fine-mesh sieve into a bowl. Ladle the mixture into eight 6-ounce ramekins or small oven-proof bowls. Set the ramekins in a baking pan and fill with enough hot water to reach halfway up the sides of the ramekins. Cover the baking pan with aluminum foil and place in the oven; immediately reduce the oven temperature to 325 degrees F.

3   Bake until the crème brûlées are just set, but the center still jiggles a bit when gently shaken, about 30 minutes. Remove the ramekins from the water bath and let cool to room temperature. Cover with plastic wrap and refrigerate for at least 4 hours or overnight.

4   To serve, preheat the broiler. Place the ramekins in a baking pan with enough cool water to reach halfway up the sides of each ramekin. Sprinkle 1 tablespoon of brown sugar evenly over the top of each ramekin and broil until the sugar bubbles and melts. Remove immediately and serve with the warm berries.

Blackberry Floating Islands

As landlocked Midwesterners, my family has always gone in the opposite direction on vacation. We love to be surrounded by water. In the Great Lakes, we've vacationed on Mackinac, Manitoulin, and Beaver Islands. In the South, we've headed to beachfront houses on Fripp and Bald Head Islands in the Carolinas. Perhaps that's the appeal of this *trompe l'oeil* dessert, which looks like a meringue island surrounded by a blackberry-dotted sea of homemade pouring custard. I also love the fresh flavor and the fact you can make the custard ahead of time and keep it chilled until serving.

MAKES 6 SERVINGS

CUSTARD

3 large egg yolks

¼ cup sugar

2 cups half-and-half

1 teaspoon vanilla extract

MERINGUE

3 large egg whites

⅓ cup plus 2 tablespoons sugar

1 teaspoon vanilla extract

3 cups fresh blackberries, blueberries, black raspberries, or other berry in season

1   In a medium-size heavy saucepan, whisk the egg yolks and sugar together. Whisk in the half-and-half. Over low heat, bring to a boil, whisking occasionally. Cook, whisking constantly, until the custard thickens enough to coat the back of a spoon, about 5 minutes. Remove from the heat and stir in the vanilla. Set aside.

2   Arrange one rack in the middle of the oven and another at the bottom. Preheat the oven to 275 degrees F. With an electric mixer, beat the egg whites in a large mixing bowl until they hold soft peaks. Then sprinkle in ⅓ cup of the sugar and beat until they hold stiff peaks. Beat in the vanilla.

3   Butter a 9-inch square baking pan and sprinkle evenly with the remaining 2 tablespoons of sugar. Carefully spoon the meringue, in 6 portions, onto the prepared baking pan. Fill a large pan with hot water to a depth of 1 inch. Sit the prepared baking pan on the middle rack of the oven and the pan of water on the bottom rack.

4   Bake the meringues, or islands, until firm and lightly browned, 25 to 30 minutes.

5   To serve, pour or spoon the custard into 6 dessert or soup bowls and sprinkle each serving with ½ cup of the blackberries. Top each with a meringue island.

Classic Crème Anglaise

This is the classic pouring custard, which can be used warm or chilled, and spooned or poured over fruit tarts and desserts of all kinds. **MAKES ABOUT 1¹/4 CUPS**

1 cup heavy cream

3 large egg yolks

¹/4 cup sugar

¹/8 teaspoon salt

1 teaspoon vanilla extract

1 In a medium-size heavy saucepan, scald the cream over medium-high heat until small bubbles begin to form along the perimeter. Whisk the egg yolks, sugar, and salt together in a medium-size heat-proof mixing bowl.

2 Pour the warm cream through a fine-mesh strainer into the egg yolk mixture, whisking constantly. Return the mixture to the saucepan and cook over low heat until it has thickened and coats the back of a spoon, 10 to 15 minutes. Whisk in the vanilla.

3 Pass the cream again through a fine-mesh strainer to remove any lumps. Cover with plastic wrap and chill until ready to serve. Let it come to room temperature before using in a recipe.

COFFEE CRÈME ANGLAISE Add 1 tablespoon of instant espresso powder to the cream, scald, and proceed with the recipe.

CHOCOLATE CRÈME ANGLAISE Put ³/4 cup of semisweet chocolate chips in a heat-proof bowl, pour the scalded cream over the chips, and set aside to melt for 5 minutes, stirring occasionally. Proceed with the rest of the recipe.

Spiced Pear Crème Anglaise

Every year I face the question, "What will I do with all these pears?" The two Kieffer pear trees on the side of my house give bushels of pears, which are great for baking and poaching, but not for eating raw. One creative solution is this dessert sauce. Unlike the pale and sophisticated crème anglaise served at upscale restaurants or the more plain English pouring custard still popular at Amish tables, this prairie version is the color of pale caramel, fragrant with pear and rich with cinnamon and nutmeg. It makes a wonderful sauce to pour over warm bread pudding. With an extra egg yolk whisked in with the others, it can also be a delicious cake filling. **MAKES ABOUT 3 CUPS**

4 large ripe pears, such as Kieffer, Bartlett, or Anjou

⅓ cup wildflower or clover honey

1 teaspoon ground cinnamon

½ teaspoon freshly grated nutmeg

1 cup light cream or half-and-half

⅓ cup sugar

⅛ teaspoon salt

6 large egg yolks, beaten

1   Preheat the oven to 350 degrees F. Butter a baking dish and set aside.

2   Peel, core, and quarter the pears, and put them in the prepared baking dish. Pour the honey over the pears and sprinkle with ½ teaspoon of the cinnamon and ¼ teaspoon of the nutmeg. Cover and bake until the pears have softened, about 30 minutes. Set aside to cool.

3   Put the pears, their baking liquid, and the remaining ½ teaspoon of cinnamon and ¼ teaspoon of nutmeg into a food processor and process until smooth; set aside.

4   Bring the cream, sugar, and salt to a boil in a medium-size saucepan. Whisk in the pear puree. Whisk in the egg yolks and cook over medium-high heat, stirring constantly, until the sauce coats the back of a spoon, about 10 minutes. Pass the sauce through a fine-mesh strainer and serve warm or chilled. Refrigerate any leftover sauce.

Blueberry Batter Pudding

Maude Peterson, the grandmother of my neighbor Elaine Munyan, is known for two things—bingo and Blueberry Batter Pudding. Maude owned a sheep ranch near Britton, South Dakota. "The entertainment highlight of Grandma's week was going into town on Friday night and playing chicken-sh*t bingo," recalls Elaine. This involved a well-fed chicken strutting over a wire grid on the floor in a barn. When the chicken responded to the call of nature, the bingo caller would identify the appropriate square as "B12" or "O48," and people played their bingo cards accordingly. **MAKES 8 SERVINGS**

2 cups fresh or frozen (thawed) blueberries

Grated zest and juice of 1 lemon

1⅓ cups sugar

3 tablespoons unsalted butter

½ cup milk

1 cup all-purpose flour

½ teaspoon baking powder

½ teaspoon salt

1 cup water

1 tablespoon cornstarch

1   Preheat the oven to 350 degrees F. Butter an 8-inch square baking pan. Arrange the berries in the bottom of the pan and drizzle with the lemon juice.

2   With an electric mixer, cream together ⅓ cup of the sugar and the butter in a medium-size mixing bowl. Mix in the milk, flour, baking powder, and salt to make a smooth batter. Spoon the batter over the berries.

3   Bring the water to a boil in a medium-size saucepan. Remove from the heat and whisk in the remaining 1 cup of sugar, the cornstarch, and the lemon zest and continue whisking until the sugar and cornstarch are dissolved. Pour this mixture over the batter. Bake until browned and bubbling, about 30 minutes. Serve warm.

Rustic Cherry Batter Pudding

The simple yet sophisticated Checkerberry Inn—a beacon of Heartland hospitality in the Amish country around Goshen, Indiana—makes a wonderful black raspberry clafouti, or batter pudding, a happy marriage of local ingredients and European savoir faire. In this recipe, based on a technique that cookbook author Anne Willan uses, the tart red cherry batter pudding bakes in a cabbage leaf–lined dish. Although the cabbage leaves give the batter a light and sweetly perfumed flavor, the presentation is what counts here. If you don't feel adventurous, simply bake the batter pudding without the cabbage leaves. It still tastes delicious. **MAKES 8 SERVINGS**

¾ cup all-purpose flour

½ teaspoon salt

1 cup sugar

4 large eggs, beaten

1 cup half-and-half

8 to 10 large, perfect green cabbage leaves

4 cups pitted fresh, frozen (thawed), or canned (drained) sour cherries or black raspberries

2 tablespoons kirsch, 1 teaspoon almond extract, or 1 teaspoon Princess Cake and Cookie flavor (see Sources, page 505)

1   Sift the flour into a large mixing bowl. Stir in the salt and sugar and make a well in the center. Pour the eggs and ½ cup of the half-and-half into the center of the well, and using a circular motion, whisk the dry ingredients into the liquids until you have a smooth, thick batter. Whisk in the remaining ½ cup half-and-half and continue whisking until the batter is smooth and pourable. Cover and set aside at room temperature for 30 minutes.

2   Preheat the oven to 400 degrees F. Butter a large 10 x 16-inch oval baking pan and set aside. Bring a large pot of water to the boil. Blanch the cabbage leaves for 2 minutes. Drain immediately in one layer on paper towels. With a paring knife, trim away any tough stems. Line the baking pan with the cabbage leaves, curling the leaves over the rim, like a frill. Trim the leaves, if necessary, to create a pleasing appearance.

3   Stir the cherries and kirsch into the batter. Pour the batter into the prepared pan, place on a baking sheet, and bake until the cabbage leaves have browned and a cake tester inserted in the middle of the pudding comes out clean, 35 to 45 minutes. The filling will rise, but then fall when the dish comes out of the oven. Serve warm or at room temperature. This is best eaten the day it is made.

Swedish Sour Cream Dessert Crepes with Golden Raspberries

Roll 3 of these thin, lacy Swedish pancakes, from Lindsborg, Kansas, into cylinders and arrange them on a dessert plate. During the summer, spoon warmed golden raspberries on top. During cold weather months, use tart red lingonberry preserves or Cranberry-Chokecherry Conserve (page 7). The crepes can be made ahead, cooled between layers of waxed paper, and frozen for up to 3 months in resealable plastic storage bags. Thaw them and warm on a griddle to serve. **MAKES 4 SERVINGS**

CREPES
¼ cup all-purpose flour
½ teaspoon baking powder
⅛ teaspoon salt
2 cups sour cream
2 large eggs, lightly beaten
2 tablespoons unsalted butter

GOLDEN RASPBERRIES
2 tablespoons unsalted butter
2 tablespoons sugar
2 cups golden raspberries

1 recipe Wildflower Honey Cream (page 348),
    whipped cream, or crème fraîche for serving

1   To make the crepes, sift the flour, baking powder, and salt into a small bowl. In a large mixing bowl, whisk together the sour cream and eggs until smooth. Add the dry ingredients to the bowl and whisk to blend.

2   Melt the butter in a large skillet over medium heat. Pour 2 tablespoons of the batter into the hot skillet. When air bubbles rise to the surface, gently turn the crepe with a metal spatula. Cook until both sides are golden brown, about 2 minutes total. Continue in this fashion, transferring the cooked crepes to a warm plate and covering them with a tea towel while you make the rest.

3   To prepare the raspberries, in a small saucepan, melt the butter and add the sugar. Stir until the sugar has dissolved. Remove from the heat, add the raspberries, and toss the raspberries in the pan to coat them with the butter mixture. Set aside.

4   Roll the crepes into cylinders and place 3 on each plate. Top with the warm raspberry mixture and serve with a dollop of the Wildflower Honey Cream, whipped cream, or crème fraîche.

Ginger Pecan Applesauce Crepes

In the 1970s, Americans were in love with all things French, and that included creperies, which served appetizer, main course, and dessert crepes like this one. Creperies such as Magic Pan popped up in every major suburban shopping center until the craze died out in the mid to late 1980s. Crepes make an elegant dessert and are "make-aheadable."

MAKES 4 TO 6 SERVINGS

3 cups homemade applesauce (see page 318, step 3)

¾ cup sour cream

½ cup chopped toasted pecans (see page 181)

2 tablespoons chopped crystallized ginger

⅓ cup sugar

2 teaspoons grated lemon zest

½ teaspoon ground ginger

1 recipe Swedish Sour Cream Dessert Crepes (see above, steps 1 and 2)

Confectioners' sugar for dusting

1   Preheat the oven to 350 degrees F. Butter a 9 x 13-inch baking dish and set aside.

2   Place the applesauce in a large saucepan over medium-high heat and bring to a boil, stirring frequently. Let the applesauce cook down, stirring, until it is reduced to 2½ cups, about 5 minutes.

Remove from the heat and stir in the sour cream, pecans, crystallized ginger, sugar, lemon zest, and ground ginger.

3   Place 2 tablespoons of the applesauce filling in the middle of each crepe and fold the crepe over the filling to make a cylinder. Place the crepes, seam side down, in the prepared baking dish. Reserve the remaining filling.

4   Heat the crepes in the oven until warmed through, about 10 minutes. Serve each crepe with more filling spooned over it and a dusting of confectioners' sugar.

Indian Corn Cakes with Wild Berry Compote

Native American tribes grew several different types of corn, along with beans and squash—the "three sisters" of native agriculture. Flint corn was ground between two stones for cornmeal, while other types of corn were eaten boiled, pounded into flour, or dried and then boiled in a wood ash and water mixture to make hominy. Many tribes also made a kind of "fruitcake," parched cornmeal mixed with dried wild berries, animal fat, and sometimes honey, then formed into bricks or cakes to keep through the winter. In this contemporary dessert, sweetened cornmeal is cooked, then cooled flat on a tray, cut into chevrons, and sautéed in butter. **MAKES 8 SERVINGS**

CORN CAKES
4 cups half-and-half

¼ cup honey

¼ cup sugar

1 teaspoon ground cinnamon

1 teaspoon ground ginger

½ teaspoon freshly grated nutmeg

1 teaspoon salt

1 cup yellow cornmeal or a mixture of yellow and white cornmeal

6 tablespoons (¾ stick) unsalted butter

WILD BERRY COMPOTE
3 cups fresh wild berries, such as blackberries, mulberries, wild raspberries, elderberries, or juneberries, or fresh or frozen (thawed) cultivated berries

½ cup wildflower or other medium-colored honey

1 teaspoon ground cinnamon

1   Line a rimmed baking sheet with a sheet of plastic wrap at least twice its length; set aside.

2   Bring the half-and-half, honey, sugar, spices, and salt to a boil in a medium-size saucepan over high

heat. Gradually pour in the cornmeal, whisking constantly, then remove from the heat and continue whisking until smooth. Reduce the heat to low, return the saucepan to the heat, and continue whisking until the mixture has thickened, about 3 minutes. Add 2 tablespoons of the butter and whisk until completely incorporated into the cornmeal mixture.

3   Spoon or pour the hot cornmeal mixture into the prepared baking sheet and smooth with a rubber spatula to a thickness of $\frac{1}{2}$ inch. Let cool to room temperature, then cover with the overhanging plastic wrap and refrigerate for at least 2 hours to firm up.

4   About 30 minutes before serving, make the compote: Put the berries, honey, and cinnamon in a medium-size saucepan over medium-high heat. Cook, stirring occasionally, until the berries just begin to release their juices, then remove from the heat.

5   Remove the baking sheet from the refrigerator and slice the cornmeal mush into 3-inch triangles. Melt the remaining 4 tablespoons of butter in a large skillet over medium-high heat and sauté the triangles on both sides until golden brown, about 5 minutes per side. Transfer the triangles to a paper towel–lined plate or platter to keep warm while you sauté the remaining triangles.

6   To serve, arrange 3 triangles on each place and top with about $\frac{1}{4}$ cup of compote. Serve warm.

Rich Dark Chocolate Pudding with Coffee Crème Anglaise

This relative of the soufflé is a great dessert for entertaining because you can make both the pudding and the sauce ahead of time. The pudding may still look a bit underdone after baking, but it firms up as it cools. **MAKES 8 SERVINGS**

1 pound good quality dark or plain chocolate, such as Maillard, Scharffen Berger, or Godiva, cut into pieces

$\frac{1}{4}$ cup sugar

$\frac{1}{2}$ cup (1 stick) unsalted butter, cut into pieces

1 tablespoon all-purpose flour

4 large eggs, separated

1 recipe Coffee Crème Anglaise (see page 369)

1   Preheat the oven to 400 degrees F. Butter the inside of a 1-quart soufflé dish and set aside.

2   Place a metal mixing bowl over the top of a saucepan of simmering water, taking care that the bottom of the bowl does not touch the water. Put the chocolate in the bowl to soften. When it is soft, remove the bowl from the saucepan and whisk in the sugar and butter. Sift the flour into the

chocolate mixture and whisk to blend. Add the egg yolks, one at a time, whisking after each addition until well blended.

3   With an electric mixer, beat the egg whites in a large mixing bowl until they hold stiff peaks. Using a rubber spatula, fold the egg whites into the chocolate mixture. Pour the batter into the prepared dish and bake until the pudding has risen, about 15 minutes. Set aside to cool.

4   Serve warm or at room temperature with crème anglaise spooned over it.

Mississippi Mud Chocolate Puddings

Cousin of the volcano cake, with its hot, lava-like chocolate center, this little pudding combines the flavor of dense chocolate with the pleasure of a molten center. It is delicious served on a pool of Classic Crème Anglaise (page 369). **MAKES 4 SERVINGS**

½ cup (1 stick) unsalted butter

6 ounces bittersweet chocolate, broken into pieces

2 large eggs

2 large egg yolks

¼ cup sugar

¼ teaspoon salt

2 tablespoons all-purpose flour

1   Preheat the oven to 450 degrees F. Butter and lightly flour four 6-ounce ramekins, tapping out the excess flour. Set the ramekins on a baking sheet.

2   In a medium-size saucepan, melt the butter and chocolate together, stirring until smooth. Remove from the heat.

3   With an electric mixer on high speed, beat the whole eggs, egg yolks, sugar, and salt in a medium-size mixing bowl until thickened and pale. Add the chocolate mixture, whisking until smooth, then whisk in the flour. The batter can be refrigerated for several hours; bring to room temperature before baking.

4   Spoon the batter into the prepared ramekins and bake until the sides of the puddings are firm but the centers are soft, about 12 minutes. Let the puddings cool in the ramekins for 1 minute, then cover each with an inverted dessert plate. Carefully turn each one over, let stand for 10 seconds, unmold, and serve.

Heirloom Gooseberry Pudding

Pale green and tart, this pudding from the 1868 Kansas cookbook *The Ladies' Floral Calendar and Household Receipt Book* is updated with a splash of vanilla. When the bottled extract was not available, knowledgeable prairie pioneer ladies would have cooked the gooseberries with large Queen Anne's lace–like heads of elderflower blossoms to get a vanilla-like flavor. If you can only find canned gooseberries, pass them through a sieve, add vanilla and sugar to taste, and proceed with the recipe.

MAKES ABOUT 8 SERVINGS

4 cups fresh or frozen (thawed) gooseberries

1/4 cup water

1 cup sugar

2 teaspoons vanilla extract

3 large eggs, beaten

2 drops green food coloring

Whipped cream for garnish

1   Cook the gooseberries and water together in a medium-size saucepan over medium-high heat until the skins soften and burst, about 10 minutes. Press the cooked gooseberries through a fine-mesh sieve into a bowl until you have about 1¾ cups gooseberry pulp. Stir in the sugar and vanilla.

2   Return the gooseberry mixture to the saucepan and bring to a simmer over medium-high heat. Whisk the eggs in a small bowl, add a little of the hot gooseberry mixture, and whisk the mixture back into the saucepan. Lower the heat and simmer for several minutes, until the custard coats the back of a spoon. Whisk in the green food coloring. Remove from the heat and serve warm, or cover and chill to serve later. Serve in bowls with a dollop of whipped cream.

Iron Skillet Butterscotch Pudding

My late grandmother's recipe for this butterscotch pudding is written in an old school exercise book with a crinkled and torn brown cover. Her directions say, "Take butter the size of an egg." Her handwriting, in blue fountain pen ink, has faded over the 60 years since she started her "receipt book." But this dessert remains a family favorite, enjoyed as a pudding served in a bowl or as the filling in a butterscotch pie topped with meringue (my mother's favorite pie). For the best color and flavor, make this in a seasoned cast iron skillet (one that has developed a black coating over time; manufacturer's directions tell you how to season the skillet). I like to serve this warm on a chilly winter evening, accompanied by buttery shortbread or crisp spice cookies and a mug of rich, dark coffee.

MAKES 6 SERVINGS OR ENOUGH FILLING FOR ONE 8-INCH PIE

2 large egg yolks

2 cups plus 2 tablespoons milk

2 1/2 tablespoons all-purpose flour

1/4 cup (1/2 stick) unsalted butter

2 cups packed brown sugar

1   In a medium-size mixing bowl, whisk together the egg yolks, 2 cups of the milk, and the flour until smooth. Set aside.

2   In a cast-iron skillet or a large heavy-bottomed saucepan, melt the butter over medium-high heat. Stir in the brown sugar and continue stirring until it melts. Then stir in the remaining 2 tablespoons of milk. When this mixture comes to a boil, whisk in the egg yolk mixture. Cook, whisking occasionally, until the mixture boils and then thickens, about 2 minutes. Remove from the heat and serve warm in bowls or use as a pie filling.

Back in Thyme to Heirloom Desserts

Sitting back from the road, the white-painted Italianate farmhouse looks like so many of the other "white ladies" that still dot the rural Midwestern landscape. But this family homestead northeast of Eudora, Kansas, is special to Nancy and Richard Smith. It's the place they call home.

The farmhouse was built in 1875 by Richard's great-great-grandmother, Caroline Mackie, a fortyish widow who moved here from upstate New York with her teenage son. Today, Nancy and Richard have "recycled" a farmhouse and traditional farm life into a home and a country lifestyle with a new purpose. Instead of growing wheat and raising livestock as Caroline did a century ago, Nancy grows heirloom and prairie plants as part of her business Back in Thyme. The farmhouse parlor is now the office where Nancy designs gardens, produces a newsletter, manages a Web site, and published a facsimile edition of an 1868 Kansas cookbook, *The Ladies' Floral Calendar and Household Receipt Book*. The old threshing barn functions as a shop where visitors can buy seeds and plants on open house days. The old livestock barn shelters garden equipment. "A farm has to find a reason for being that will work today," Nancy says.

Likewise, heirloom dessert recipes like Nancy's Lavender Lemonade (page 497) need a "reason for being" and a fresh interpretation if they are to remain part of our culinary repertoire. Happily, that's the case with most of them. Our love of things sweet—the first taste we recognize as infants—endures, generation after generation.

Everyone's Favorite Banana Pudding

This is another back-of-the-box dessert loved by generations of American children. Vanilla wafers hit grocery store shelves in the early 1900s, and added another convenience food to the home cook's dessert repertoire. Although you could use a package of vanilla pudding mix to make the pudding, I prefer to make mine from scratch in the microwave. Today, this is a staple dessert at Texas barbecue joints. **MAKES 8 SERVINGS**

¼ cup cornstarch

⅓ cup sugar

2 cups milk

1 large egg, beaten

1 teaspoon vanilla extract

2 tablespoons unsalted butter

½ cup heavy cream

One 16-ounce box vanilla wafer cookies

5 or 6 ripe bananas, peeled and sliced ½ inch thick

One 14-ounce can sweetened condensed milk

1   In a microwave-safe bowl, whisk the cornstarch and sugar together. Whisk in 1 cup of the milk and continue whisking until the mixture resembles a smooth paste. Whisk in the remaining 1 cup of milk and microwave on HIGH for about 6 minutes total, stopping the microwave to stir the pudding every 1½ minutes, until the pudding has slightly thickened. Transfer ¼ cup of the hot pudding to a small bowl and whisk in the egg. Whisk this mixture back into the pudding. Micro-cook for 2½ more minutes on HIGH, whisking at 30-second intervals, until the pudding is thick enough to coat the back of a spoon. Or, cook in a heavy medium-size saucepan over medium-high heat, stirring constantly. Whisk in the egg as described above and continue cooking, stirring, until thick. When the pudding has thickened, whisk in the vanilla and butter. Set aside to cool to room temperature.

2   With an electric mixer, whip the cream in a small bowl until it holds soft peaks. In the bottom of a 9 x 13-inch pan, arrange the vanilla wafers in a single layer and add a row of cookies, standing on their edge, around the sides. Top with the banana slices and set aside. In a large mixing bowl, mix together the cooled pudding, whipped cream, and condensed milk until smooth. Pour or spoon this mixture over the bananas. Cover with plastic wrap and chill for 1 hour before serving.

Pineapple Icebox Pudding

Combining two commercially popular foods—canned pineapple and vanilla wafers—this vintage recipe from the 1920s still makes a darn good dessert. I have substituted macadamia nuts to be more true to the Hawaiian flavor, but pecans or walnuts are also delicious. This dessert needs to be chilled for 8 hours or overnight before serving. **MAKES 8 SERVINGS**

One 14-ounce can crushed pineapple, left undrained

½ cup (1 stick) unsalted butter, cut into pieces

1 cup sugar

One 16-ounce box vanilla wafer cookies

1 cup chopped macadamia nuts, pecans, or walnuts

1 cup heavy cream

1   In a large heavy saucepan, stir together the crushed pineapple, butter, and sugar. Bring to simmer over medium heat and cook, stirring, until the mixture has thickened, about 15 minutes. Set aside to cool.

2   Grind the vanilla wafers into fine crumbs in batches in a food processor. Sprinkle three quarters of the crumbs over the bottom of a 9 x 13-inch baking pan. Stir the nuts into the pineapple filling and spoon into the pan. Sprinkle the remaining cookie crumbs on top of the filling. Cover with plastic wrap and chill overnight.

3   Before serving, with an electric mixer, whip the cream in a medium-size mixing bowl until it holds stiff peaks. Swirl over the top of the pudding.

Tiramisu

During the last few decades, this Italian dessert has become part of the American repertoire. Europeans prefer rich desserts as an afternoon treat, but Americans like to end an evening meal with a sweet extravagance. Restaurant chefs and good home cooks now make this "pick-me-up" (that's how *tiramisu* translates from the Italian), which pairs especially well with after-dinner espresso. **MAKES 6 TO 8 SERVINGS**

1 large egg yolk, beaten

1/4 cup coffee-flavored liqueur

1/4 cup hot brewed coffee

3 large egg whites

1/4 cup sugar

1 pound mascarpone cheese at room temperature

1 recipe Homemade Ladyfingers (see page 406) or 8 ounces savoiardi biscuits or store-bought ladyfingers

4 to 6 cups freshly brewed espresso, as needed

Unsweetened cocoa powder for garnish

1   In a small microwave-safe bowl, whisk together the egg yolk, coffee liqueur, and hot coffee until well blended. Microwave for 60 seconds on HIGH to heat the mixture. Or, cook, stirring, in a medium-size heavy saucepan over medium-high heat until hot, 4 to 6 minutes. Let cool to room temperature.

2   With an electric mixer, beat the egg whites and sugar in a medium-size mixing bowl until they hold stiff peaks. Beat the coffee mixture with the mascarpone cheese in a large mixing bowl. Fold the egg whites into the mascarpone mixture. Taste and add more sugar if necessary. Set aside.

3   Layer half the ladyfingers on the bottom of a 9-inch square baking pan and drizzle with half of the espresso. Spread the moistened ladyfingers with half of the mascarpone mixture. Repeat the process, adding another layer of ladyfingers and using the remaining espresso and mascarpone mixture. Dust the top with the cocoa, cover, and chill until firm, 2 to 3 hours, or until ready to serve.

Puerto Rican Pumpkin Pudding

Known in Puerto Rico as *cazuela*, this mellow and spicy dessert with a hint of coconut could make an interesting alternative to traditional pumpkin pie at the Thanksgiving table. **MAKES 6 TO 8 SERVINGS**

One 15-ounce can pumpkin pie filling

3 cups mashed boiled sweet potatoes (about 1 pound sweet potatoes)

1/2 cup sugar

1/8 teaspoon salt

1/4 teaspoon ground ginger

1/4 teaspoon ground cinnamon

1/8 teaspoon ground cloves

2 large eggs

3/4 cup canned unsweetened coconut milk (not cream of coconut)

1/4 cup cream sherry

1 Preheat the oven to 350 degrees F. Coat the inside of a 2-quart mold or soufflé dish with nonstick cooking spray and set aside.

2 With an electric mixer, beat together the pumpkin, sweet potatoes, sugar, salt, and spices in a large mixing bowl until well blended. Beat in the eggs, coconut milk, and sherry. Pour into the prepared dish.

3 Bake the pudding until a knife inserted in the center comes out clean, 50 to 60 minutes. Serve warm.

Persimmon Flan with Honeyed Whipped Cream

This dessert marries regional ingredients like native persimmon and wildflower honey with traditional Mexican flan and French *crème caramel*. As an alternative to the heavier pumpkin pie, add persimmon flan to your cold weather or holiday menu repertoire. Even better than pie for holiday entertaining, the flans can be made the night before and actually improve in flavor. Cinnamon, coriander, and nutmeg add an aromatic interest to the sweet and mellow persimmon; wildflower honey completes the trio of flavors. **MAKES 12 SERVINGS**

2 1/2 cups sugar

1 teaspoon ground cinnamon

1 teaspoon ground coriander

1/4 teaspoon freshly grated nutmeg

6 large eggs

1 cup pureed native persimmon pulp or pulp of 3 or 4 ripe Asian persimmons

One 12-ounce can evaporated milk (not condensed)

1 teaspoon vanilla extract

Juice of 1 large lemon

1/2 cup water

1 cup heavy cream

1/2 cup wildflower, tupelo, clover, or other amber honey

1 Preheat the oven to 350 degrees F. Assemble twelve 6- to 8-ounce custard cups or ramekins on a kitchen counter.

2 In a large mixing bowl, whisk together 1 cup of the sugar with the cinnamon, coriander, and nutmeg. With an electric mixer on medium speed, add the eggs, one at a time, beating constantly. Add the persimmon pulp and beat just until blended. Beat in the evaporated milk, vanilla, and lemon juice and mix until the batter is smooth. Set aside.

3   In a medium-size heavy-bottomed saucepan, combine the remaining 1½ cups of sugar and the water and cook, without stirring, over medium heat until the mixture caramelizes, 15 to 20 minutes. When the sugar has caramelized to a medium brown, immediately remove it from the heat.

4   Wearing an oven mitt on the hand that holds the saucepan, carefully pour a little caramel into the bottom of each custard cup. Spoon about ⅓ cup of the persimmon batter on top of the caramel. Set the custard cups in a deep-sided baking dish and pour enough water around them to reach halfway up the sides of the cups. Cover the baking dish with aluminum foil and bake until the flans are set and a cake tester inserted in the center of a flan comes out clean, 35 to 40 minutes. Remove the flans from the oven and from the water bath and set aside to cool. Cover each flan with plastic wrap and chill for up to 2 days, until ready to serve.

5   Just before serving, with the mixer, whip the cream in a medium-size mixing bowl until it holds soft peaks. Blend in the honey and whip again until the mixture holds stiff peaks. Remove the flans from the refrigerator and run a small paring knife around the rim of each. Hold a dessert plate over the flan and invert so that the flan is in the center of the plate and the caramel runs down the flan to pool on the plate. Repeat the process with the remaining flans. Place a dollop of Honeyed Whipped Cream on each portion and serve.

Rum and Pineapple Flan

From the Spanish culinary influence in the Caribbean and the American Southwest, we get dessert recipes like flan. Most flans have a very smooth, velvety texture. This one does, too, but it also has caramelized bits of baked pineapple as a wonderful foil. Serve this drizzled with a little heavy cream if you want to gild the lily. **MAKES 8 SERVINGS**

2 cups 1-inch chunks fresh pineapple

1½ cups milk (regular or 2 percent, but not skim)

1 vanilla bean, split lengthwise

½ cup rum

3 large eggs

3 large egg yolks

⅔ cup sugar

2 tablespoons all-purpose flour

2 tablespoons heavy cream

1   Preheat the oven to 400 degrees F. Butter a 10-inch shallow baking dish or soufflé dish and scatter the pineapple chunks over the bottom. Bake until the pineapple has slightly caramelized, about

20 minutes. Remove from the oven and let cool slightly. Reduce the oven temperature to 350 degrees F.

2　Pour the milk into a medium-size heavy saucepan. Scrape the vanilla seeds into the milk, then add the vanilla bean. Bring to a simmer over medium heat until small bubbles form around the perimeter of the pan. Remove from the heat, cover, and let steep for 15 minutes. Remove the vanilla bean and whisk in the rum.

3　In a medium-size mixing bowl, whisk together the whole eggs, egg yolks, sugar, flour, and cream until smooth. Gradually whisk in the hot milk mixture. Pour the custard over the pineapple.

4　Bake the custard until a knife inserted in the center comes out clean, about 30 minutes. Serve warm or at room temperature by spooning the flan into individual bowls.

French Valley Scented Custard

In 1778, as the American Revolution continued, George Rogers Clark was sent westward to secure the French outposts of Cahokia and Kaskaskia in what is now southwestern Illinois. When Clark and his troops arrived at the forts, they were not prepared for the culture shock. The language, dress, architecture, and foodways of the French settlers were all very different from what the Anglo-American Clark had experienced before. If you've only tasted plain English-style custard, you'll feel like Clark when you encounter the vivid flavor of this one, flavored with the fennel seed that settlers in the French Valley loved so well. I've also added vanilla for smoothness and lemon for zing. The whole eggs and egg yolks give this custard a voluptuous texture. **MAKES 6 SERVINGS**

2 teaspoons fennel seeds

Grated zest of 1 lemon

2 cups milk

$\frac{1}{2}$ cup heavy cream

$\frac{1}{3}$ cup sugar

3 large eggs plus 5 large egg yolks, beaten together

$\frac{1}{8}$ teaspoon salt

1 teaspoon vanilla extract

1　Preheat the oven to 350 degrees F. With a mortar and pestle or a spice grinder, coarsely grind the fennel seeds. In a saucepan, bring the crushed fennel seeds, lemon zest, and milk to a boil. Remove from the heat, cover, and let steep for 10 minutes.

2 Whisk in the cream, sugar, beaten eggs, salt, and vanilla. Pour the custard mixture through a fine-mesh strainer into another bowl, then ladle the custard into 6 custard cups or small baking dishes. Set the cups in a deep baking dish. Fill the baking dish with enough water to reach halfway up the sides of the custard cups. Bake until a knife inserted near the edge of a custard cup comes out clean, 20 to 30 minutes. Remove the custards from the oven and from the water bath to cool. Cover with plastic wrap and chill in the refrigerator until ready to serve.

3 To serve, run a knife around the inside of each custard cup and invert each custard onto a dessert plate or serve from the cup.

Marzipan Custards

A light-tasting yet luscious dessert garnished with a fruit compote or fresh summer fruit, this recipe makes a perfect foil for richer holiday desserts. Waves of German immigrants landed in eastern American cities from the 1840s to the 1880s. Besides good beer, yeast-risen coffee cakes, and sauerkraut, German cooks also brought us marzipan—a sweet confection of ground almonds, egg white, sugar, and flavorings.

MAKES 8 SERVINGS

3 cups heavy cream

1/4 teaspoon salt

2/3 cup sugar

1/2 cup Marzipan (page 481) made with almond flavoring or store-bought almond paste, cut into pieces

1 teaspoon vanilla extract

6 large egg yolks, beaten

1/2 cup sliced almonds

1 recipe Dried Fruit Compote with Brown Sugar Syrup (page 9), Quince Compote (page 10), Cranberry-Chokecherry Conserve (page 7), or fresh strawberries, peaches or pears for garnish

1 Preheat the oven to 350 degrees F. Butter the insides of eight 4-ounce ramekins and set aside.

2 In a large heavy-bottomed saucepan, whisk together the cream, salt, sugar, marzipan, and vanilla over medium heat. Continue whisking until the almond paste has dissolved and the mixture has small bubbles starting to form around the perimeter of the pan. Remove from the heat and whisk in the egg yolks. Return to the heat and cook, whisking constantly, until the mixture thickens enough to coat the back of a spoon.

3   Pour the custard into the prepared ramekins and sprinkle the tops with the sliced almonds. Bake until a knife inserted in the center comes out clean and the custards have set, 12 to 15 minutes. Let cool completely.

4   To serve, invert the ramekins on dessert plates and garnish with a dollop of compote or conserve or with fresh fruit.

Too Many Egg Whites

Home cooks who make custards or pastry creams have one complaint: too many egg whites left over. What do you do with them? Sometimes you don't have the opportunity to make a meringue dessert or angel food cake right away. But you can store egg whites in a closed container in the refrigerator for 2 to 3 weeks, and they can also be frozen.

But another problem emerges when you want to use them. How do you know how much of the bulk egg white represents one egg? I never remember to mark on the container how many egg whites I have stored in it, so I came up with another way. I measured a large egg white and discovered it comes to about 2 tablespoons. If you store or freeze your egg whites in bulk, simply let them come to room temperature and measure out what you need. Four egg whites would measure ½ cup. For the Classic Angel Food Cake on page 155, which calls for 7 large egg whites, that means a scant cup. Or freeze your egg whites in ice cube trays, 2 tablespoons to each partition. When frozen, remove the cubes to a plastic freezer bag. Then defrost whatever quantity you need.

Warm Grits Pudding with Roasted Apples

In the South, people love their grits, the coarsely ground grain made from yellow or white hominy. When I read about this dessert served at the Mimosa Grill in Charlotte, North Carolina, I knew grits had finally gone uptown. Although I've never eaten there, I imagine that their dessert is similar to this creation. To me, a tapioca lover, it tastes like Southern tapioca. Instead of roasting the apples, you can serve Bourbon-Laced Sautéed Apples (page 53) as an accompaniment. **MAKES 6 TO 8 SERVINGS**

ROASTED APPLES

8 Jonathan, Winesap, or Braeburn apples

$\frac{1}{4}$ cup ($\frac{1}{2}$ stick) unsalted butter, melted

$\frac{1}{2}$ cup sugar

1 tablespoon ground cinnamon

$\frac{1}{4}$ teaspoon freshly grated nutmeg

GRITS PUDDING

4 cups water

1 teaspoon salt

1 cup traditional or instant grits

One 8-ounce container mascarpone cheese

$\frac{1}{2}$ cup sugar

3 large eggs, beaten

1 teaspoon vanilla extract

1   To roast the apples, preheat the oven to 425 degrees F and butter a 9 x 13-inch baking pan; set aside. Core and cut each apple into quarters. Pour the melted butter into a small bowl and mix the sugar, cinnamon, and nutmeg together in another one. Toss the apple wedges in the butter, then the sugar and spice mixture and place in the prepared baking pan. Roast, turning once, until the apples have softened and browned, 25 to 30 minutes.

2   While the apples are roasting, make the pudding: Bring the water and salt to a boil in a medium-size saucepan over high heat. Gradually pour in the grits, whisking constantly, then remove from the heat and whisk until smooth. Reduce the heat to low, return the saucepan to the heat, and continue cooking, whisking constantly, until the grits have thickened, about 3 minutes. Whisk in the mascarpone cheese, sugar, eggs, and vanilla and continue whisking until completely incorporated. Cook for another 3 minutes.

3   To serve, spoon the grits pudding onto serving plates or into bowls and garnish with roasted apple wedges. Drizzle with a little of the cooking liquid from the apples.

Grapenut Pudding

This homey New England dessert is good for you. It's the kind of virtuous dessert you might imagine Norman Rockwell or one of his wholesome characters enjoying. And indeed, this dessert is on the menu at the Red Lion Inn in Rockwell's hometown of Stockbridge, Massachusetts. Grapenut pudding has been popular in that part of the country since the 1930s. In fact Brooke Dojny, an expert on New England's regional cuisine, claims, "If Grapenut Pudding is on the menu, you can probably trust the place to serve honest home-style food." Although made with Grape-Nuts cereal, the pudding is spelled "grapenut" for unknown reasons. This cold weather dessert is good served with sweetened, stewed fruit, such as apples—especially the local Macoun—or cranberries.

MAKES 8 SERVINGS

2 cups warm milk

$1/2$ cup Grape-Nuts cereal

2 large eggs, beaten

$1/2$ cup sugar

1 teaspoon vanilla extract

$1/4$ teaspoon salt

$1/8$ teaspoon freshly grated nutmeg

$1/8$ teaspoon ground cinnamon

1   Preheat the oven to 350 degrees. Butter a 9 x 5-inch loaf pan and set aside. Pour the warm milk over the cereal in a medium bowl and leave until softened, about 2 to 3 minutes.

2   Stir in the beaten eggs, sugar, vanilla, salt, and spices. Spoon into the prepared loaf pan. Set the loaf pan in a baking pan filled with enough water to come halfway up the sides of the loaf pan.

3   Bake for 50 to 60 minutes, or until a knife inserted in the center comes out clean. Slice and serve hot.

Sweet Potato Pone with Kentucky Bourbon Pouring Custard

The earliest colonists learned to make hoe cake, cornmeal mush baked on the blade of a hoe in a hot fire, and corn pone, cornmeal mush formed into cakes and fried in a skillet. Since then, Appalachian cooks have always found ways to put dinner on the table, even when supplies were scanty. This recipe grew out of necessity, when sweet potatoes planted around the homestead, a jug of molasses or sorghum, and maybe a secret stash of moonshine were about all a cook had to work with. Over time, white sugar, spices, and good butter took the basic idea and made it divine. Somehow, "crème anglaise" is too fancy a term for the pouring custard accompanying this dessert, but that's what it is. It's also good over sautéed apples, spiced pound cake, a warm chocolate brownie, or baked pears. **MAKES 6 TO 8 SERVINGS**

KENTUCKY BOURBON POURING CUSTARD

1 cup heavy cream

3 large egg yolks

¼ cup sugar

⅛ teaspoon salt

¼ cup Kentucky bourbon, such as Early Times, Knob Creek, Maker's Mark, Wild Turkey Kentucky Spirit, or Elijah Craig 12-Year-Old

SWEET POTATO PONE

3 cups peeled and grated raw sweet potatoes (about 2 large sweet potatoes)

½ cup sugar

¼ cup all-purpose flour

2 large eggs

½ cup pure cane syrup, dark molasses, or sorghum

1 teaspoon freshly grated nutmeg

1 teaspoon ground cinnamon

1 teaspoon vanilla extract

¼ cup (½ stick) unsalted butter, melted

1 To make the custard, scald the cream in a medium-size heavy saucepan until small bubbles start to form around the perimeter. Whisk together the egg yolks, sugar, and salt in a medium-size mixing bowl. Pour the warm cream into the egg yolk mixture, whisking constantly. Transfer the egg yolk and cream mixture to the saucepan and cook over low heat until it has thickened and coats the back of a spoon, 10 to 15 minutes. Stir in the bourbon (use less or more if you prefer). Pass the pouring custard through a fine-mesh strainer to remove any lumps. Cover with plastic wrap and chill the pouring custard until ready to serve. Let it come to room temperature before serving.

2 To make the sweet potato pone, preheat the oven to 350 degrees F. Generously butter the inside of a 10-inch cast iron skillet or round casserole dish. Set aside.

3 In a large mixing bowl, combine the sweet potatoes, sugar, flour, eggs, cane syrup, spices, and vanilla. Pour in the melted butter and mix well. Spoon the sweet potato mixture into the prepared skillet. Bake until a knife inserted in the center comes out clean, about 50 minutes. Serve warm with the pouring custard.

Sweet Squash Kugel with Cinnamon Sugar

Jewish immigration to America, like that of other religious and ethnic groups, has been largely prompted by religious persecution elsewhere. During the Russian pogroms of the late nineteenth and early twentieth centuries, many Jews from Eastern Europe settled in Eastern and Midwestern cities. Those who wanted to keep a kosher kitchen, in which cooking utensils and areas for meat meal and dairy meal preparation are kept separate, had an easier time in the city than in more rural areas. Today, Orthodox Jewish cooks throughout the United States have a repertoire of delicious nondairy desserts that can be served as part of the meat-based Sabbath meal on Friday evenings. Many of these desserts fall into the kugel category—baked sweet or savory puddings made with noodles, apples, squash, or sweet potatoes and flavored with cinnamon. Serve this with a crisp spice cookie or a scoop of ice cream, if you're not concerned with dairy restrictions. **MAKES 6 SERVINGS**

¾ cup sugar

2 tablespoons ground cinnamon

6 large eggs, beaten

½ cup (1 stick) margarine, melted

2 cups liquid nondairy creamer

Two 10-ounce packages frozen winter squash, thawed

1 cup all-purpose flour

1   Preheat the oven to 350 degrees F. Coat a 9 x 13-inch baking pan with nonstick cooking spray and set aside. Mix the sugar and cinnamon together in a small bowl. Remove 2 tablespoons for the topping and set aside.

2   In a food processor or in a large mixing bowl with an electric mixer, blend the eggs with the melted margarine. Add the nondairy creamer, squash, and cinnamon sugar, pulsing or beating to blend. Gradually add the flour, blending to make a thick batter. Pour the batter into the prepared baking pan and sprinkle the top with the reserved 2 tablespoons of cinnamon sugar.

3   Bake the kugel until a cake tester inserted in the center comes out clean, about 1 hour. Serve warm.

Making Sorghum

It's 4 a.m. on a cool, starlit September morning. In Rich Hill, Missouri, an Old Order Mennonite community, the men are up feeding the horses, getting ready for the first day of the sorghum harvest.

With their traditional clothing, horse and buggy travel, and old-fashioned ways, these very conservative Mennonites seem the epitome of nineteenth-century Missouri pioneers, but they've only been in Rich Hill since the early 1990s. They moved here from Kentucky when their community there became overpopulated. Today, they're harvesting and processing their main crop—by hand—to make about 9,000 gallons of "Bates County Pure Sorghum."

The sorghum cycle begins in May, when sorghum cane seeds are planted. The Rich Hill Mennonites hoe the 30-acre sorghum fields by hand all summer, until the sorghum canes are 10 to 12 feet high.

The harvest begins in late September and lasts through October. Workers use special cane knives to cut the leaves from the sorghum stalks. A horse-drawn implement cuts the stalks, which are then bundled and laid out to dry for several days. The bundles are then loaded onto carts and taken to the press shed above the mill.

Farmers feed the dried cane into the sorghum roller press powered by 10 huge Belgian and Percheron draft horses. Green sorghum juice trickles down a pipeline to the mill, where it undergoes its first cooking. The green juice boils in a purification pan, where the foam and impurities are scooped away. When the juice looks right to the cooker, he lets it run into the next pan, where the juice is cooked further to allow some of the moisture to evaporate.

Determining when the juice is ready is a tricky business because no one has a recipe for sorghum. Every year, the sorghum canes are different in composition—even varying from field to field—so the cooker's job is to consider all the variables and come up with a consistently delicious product, much like blending grapes for wine or wheats for flour.

One such cooker is Matthew Brubaker, who didn't learn this skill from his father. "My father didn't know spit about making sorghum," he says. "I just got interested as a boy and started hanging around the pans."

When Brubaker sees the perfect amber color, he takes a sample and nods his head in satisfaction. "You can see why I put on a few pounds this time of year," he says of his frequent sampling. He then releases the sorghum to the third or finishing pan, where it will begin the cooling process. When the sorghum is cooled, it is poured into Mason jars and plastic jugs.

"The work is hard, but we like it," Brubaker says.

Apricot Noodle Kugel

This Jewish dessert, with its cream and butter and milk, would be considered a dairy dish to eat with a nonmeat meal in observant Jewish households. Kugels were originally brought to America from Eastern Europe at least 100 years ago. You can tell this one has been Americanized, perhaps three or four times over, because it includes cream cheese and canned apricot nectar. It's delicious and is great to bring to a potluck dinner.

MAKES 10 TO 12 SERVINGS

6 tablespoons (³/₄ stick) unsalted butter, melted

One 12-ounce packages medium egg noodles, cooked according to the package directions and drained

One 8-ounce package cream cheese at room temperature

¹/₄ cup plus 2 tablespoons granulated sugar

2 tablespoons packed brown sugar

3 large eggs, beaten

One 12-ounce can apricot nectar

¹/₂ cup dried apricots, snipped with scissors into small pieces

³/₄ cup milk

Salt to taste

TOPPING

1 cup sliced almonds

¹/₄ cup (¹/₂ stick) unsalted butter, melted

1 teaspoon ground cinnamon

1 teaspoon freshly grated nutmeg

¹/₄ cup granulated sugar

1 Pour the melted butter into a 9 x 13-inch baking pan. Mix the noodles with the butter in the pan and spread evenly over the bottom. Set aside.

2 With an electric mixer, cream together the cream cheese and granulated and brown sugars in a medium-size mixing bowl. Beat in the eggs and apricot nectar. Stir in the snipped apricots by hand. Pour this mixture over the noodles, then the milk, and stir to blend. Add salt to taste. Cover the kugel with plastic wrap and refrigerate for 3 to 4 hours or overnight.

3 When ready to bake, preheat the oven to 350 degrees F. To make the topping, mix the ingredients together in a small mixing bowl. Remove the noodles from the refrigerator and sprinkle evenly with the topping. Bake until bubbling, 1¹/₂ to 2 hours. Serve warm.

Bess Truman's Ozark Pudding

If violins, Vermeer paintings, and homemade dolls can inspire novels that follow the object from owner to owner down through history, then this dessert could also. When the French revoked religious freedom with the Edict of Nantes in 1685, thousands of Protestant Huguenots (among them were James Beard's ancestors) fled religious persecution in France for Charleston, South Carolina. Recipes for a *gâteau aux noisettes* came with them. Hazelnuts were not available in the Carolinas, but pecans were, so the recipe was adapted. Gradually, this airy, cake-like dessert became known as Huguenot torte and traveled up and down the coastal South. When Southerners traveled westward to settle the hilly Ozarks of southern Missouri and northeastern Arkansas, they substituted black walnuts for the hazelnuts and changed the name to Ozark pudding.

When Winston Churchill joined President Harry Truman in Fulton, Missouri, in 1946 and gave his famous "Iron Curtain" speech, trying to alert Americans to the danger of a Communist takeover in East Germany, this dessert was on Bess Truman's dinner menu. When the Berlin Wall finally came down in 1989, a portion of it came back to Fulton as a tangible piece of history. While walls are built and then taken down, this recipe has lasted for hundreds of years, and still held a prominent place in the Junior League of Charleston's famous *Charleston Receipts* of 1950. I love the combination of apples and black walnuts in the Ozark version, but you could also use pecans or hazelnuts and stay truer to the Huguenot roots. **MAKES 9 SERVINGS**

1 large egg

¾ cup sugar

⅓ cup all-purpose flour

1¼ teaspoons baking powder

⅛ teaspoon salt

1 teaspoon vanilla extract

1 large apple, peeled, cored, and chopped

½ cup chopped black walnuts or pecans

1 cup heavy cream

3 tablespoons rum

1 Preheat the oven to 325 degrees F. Butter a 9-inch square baking pan and set aside.

2 With an electric mixer, cream the egg and sugar together in a medium-size mixing bowl. Sift the flour, baking powder, and salt into the creamed mixture and beat until well blended. Beat in the vanilla. Fold in the apple and black walnuts and spoon the batter into the prepared pan. Bake until the top is browned, about 30 minutes. Let cool until warm or at room temperature.

3   Just before serving, with the electric mixer, whip the cream in a small bowl and gently stir in the rum. Cut the pudding into squares, and serve each piece with a dollop of rum-flavored whipped cream.

Maple Indian Pudding

Indian Pudding is a great example of a very early American dessert that has evolved to suit the tastes of the times. Traditionally, it was made with molasses, but maple syrup gives this dessert a lighter and more delicate flavor that is better appreciated today. The long baking time remains—it is necessary to soften the cornmeal and caramelize the milk and sugar—so this is a dessert best made in cool weather. Stone-ground yellow cornmeal is preferable for its wonderful texture, but regular cornmeal is fine, too.

MAKES 8 SERVINGS

4 cups milk

1 cup stone-ground yellow cornmeal

$\frac{1}{2}$ cup packed light brown sugar

1 cup heavy cream

$\frac{1}{2}$ cup pure maple syrup

2 large eggs

$\frac{1}{2}$ teaspoon baking powder

$\frac{1}{4}$ teaspoon salt

$\frac{1}{4}$ teaspoon freshly grated nutmeg

Whipped cream or vanilla ice cream for serving

1   Arrange a rack in the middle of the oven. Preheat the oven to 275 degrees F. Butter the inside of a 1$\frac{1}{2}$-quart baking dish and set aside. Fill a larger pan with 2 inches of water and set aside.

2   In a medium-size saucepan over medium-high heat, scald the milk until small bubbles form around the perimeter of the pan. Whisk in the cornmeal and cook, whisking occasionally, until the mixture has thickened, about 10 minutes. Remove from the heat.

3   In a medium-size mixing bowl, whisk together the brown sugar, $\frac{1}{2}$ cup of the cream, the maple syrup, eggs, baking powder, salt, and nutmeg. With a wooden spoon, stir the maple mixture into the cornmeal and continue stirring until well blended. Spoon the mixture into the prepared baking dish. Pour the remaining $\frac{1}{2}$ cup cream over the top. Cover the baking dish with aluminum foil, place in the larger pan of water, and place the pan in the center of the oven.

4   Bake the pudding until it is bubbling and the top has browned, about 3$\frac{1}{2}$ hours. Serve warm with whipped cream or vanilla ice cream.

Tales of Indian Pudding

Before John Winthrop left his comfortable Groton Manor in Suffolk, England, for the raw New England wilderness in 1630, his younger son Henry came back home after trying to make a success of a tobacco plantation in Barbados. The business of running these Caribbean plantations accounted for the largest English settlements in the New World during the seventeenth century. Sugar, molasses, oranges, limes, almonds, slaves, and even watermelon from the West Indies arrived by ship in Boston during the mid- to late-seventeenth century.

During this time, especially in the years of colonial "neglect," when the English were preoccupied by their own civil war (1642–1649), trade with England was disrupted. British dishes were transformed—by necessity—with the use of New World ingredients. One such dish was Indian pudding, made with West Indian molasses and locally grown corn or maize ground into meal. The British word "corn" was applied to any grain, but most often wheat. So maize was called "Indian corn," and lent its name to this dish. Early versions were probably a sweetened gruel like frumenty, perhaps flavored with carefully hoarded spices.

Benjamin Franklin made the first mention of Indian pudding in *The New England Courant* in 1722. Indian pudding increased in popularity during the eighteenth and nineteenth centuries, and methods for its preparation proliferated. Maple syrup, cane sugar, and dried fruits took the basic sweetened gruel to a new level. In Amelia Simmons' 1796 *American Cookery*, one version of Indian pudding included raisins, another was spiced, and still a third was boiled for 12 hours.

Late nineteenth–century cookbooks also feature a wealth of Indian pudding recipes, which were recommended for the autumn dinner table. Durgin-Park, a Boston restaurant that has been serving up Yankee cooking for over 170 years, still serves Indian pudding to 200 diners every day. Yet in recent years, when Massachusetts residents were asked to vote on a state dessert, Indian pudding lost to Boston cream pie (see page 140).

Chilled Cinnamon and Raisin Rice Pudding

This deliciously fragrant rice pudding, cooked on the stove top, harks back to the flavoring and technique of the earliest rice pudding recipes in this country. Today, we would ditch the rosewater and keep the cinnamon, but in ground, not stick, form. Instead of pounding raw rice into flour, we would use already cooked rice. And unlike the hearty Pilgrim women who cooked the first Thanksgiving dinner, we have the luxury of chilling this dessert in the refrigerator before serving. This recipe is adapted from one in Ruth Berolzheimer's *The American Woman's Cook Book* from 1948. Because this dessert is served cold, I have increased the quantities of cinnamon and nutmeg called for in the original recipe. MAKES 6 SERVINGS

2 cups milk

$1/2$ cup golden or dark raisins

2 large eggs, separated

$1/4$ teaspoon salt

$1/2$ cup sugar

$1 1/4$ cups cooked white rice

$1/2$ teaspoon ground cinnamon

$1/4$ teaspoon freshly grated nutmeg

1   Scald the milk in the top of a double boiler placed directly over medium-high heat until bubbles form around the perimeter of the pan. (Don't use the bottom part of the double boiler yet. If the top can't be placed directly over the heat, fashion a double boiler out of two saucepans and put the smaller one over the heat.) Remove from the heat, add the raisins, and let them steep for 15 minutes.

2   Meanwhile, with an electric mixer, beat the egg whites in a medium-size mixing bowl until they hold stiff peaks. Set aside.

3   With the mixer, beat the egg yolks, salt, and sugar together in another medium-size mixing bowl until thick and lemon colored. Whisk the egg yolk mixture into the milk-and-raisin mixture, then stir in the rice and spices and continue stirring until well blended. Place the top of the double boiler over simmering water and cook the pudding, stirring occasionally, until thickened, about 15 minutes.

4   Remove from the heat and fold in the egg whites with a rubber spatula. Spoon the pudding into individual custard cups or a serving bowl, cover, and chill for at least 1 hour before serving. Serve chilled.

Hungarian Rice Pudding

The triangle formed by Cleveland and Toledo in northern Ohio and Detroit in southern Michigan has become a Hungarian-flavored slice of the Midwestern pie. In addition to their sweet paprika-laced goulash and stuffed cabbage rolls, Hungarians have also added wonderful strudels and Dobos tortes to the culinary scene here. Even diners who enjoy the traditional German fish fries on Friday nights, featuring locally caught lake perch, know that a Hungarian dessert like this home-style rice pudding beats a ho-hum cake mix any day. **MAKES 8 SERVINGS**

2$\frac{1}{2}$ cups cooked long-grain rice

$\frac{1}{2}$ teaspoon salt

$\frac{1}{2}$ cup sugar

2 large eggs, separated

1$\frac{1}{2}$ cups milk

1 teaspoon vanilla extract

2 tablespoons unsalted butter, melted

1 teaspoon grated lemon zest

1 cup dried tart cherries, cranberries, or raisins

Whipped cream for garnish

1   Preheat the oven to 375 degrees F. Butter a 1$\frac{1}{2}$- or 2-quart round baking dish and set aside.

2   Place the rice in large mixing bowl and blot it with a paper towel to remove extra moisture, if necessary. In a medium-size mixing bowl, whisk together the salt, sugar, egg yolks, milk, vanilla, melted butter, and lemon zest. Fold in the dried cherries. Pour this mixture over the rice and combine well with a rubber spatula or wooden spoon. With an electric mixer, whip the egg whites in a small mixing bowl until they hold stiff peaks, then fold them into the rice mixture.

3   Spoon the rice into the prepared baking dish and bake until the top is golden brown and a cake tester inserted in the center comes out clean, about 1 hour. Serve warm, cold, or at room temperature with a dollop of whipped cream.

North Woods Wild Rice Pudding with Dried Cranberries

In the hours before a blizzard threatens, hearty Minnesotans hurry out to stock up on groceries before the storm hits. After all, they could be housebound for days if the conditions are bad enough. When the winds are howling outside—no matter where you are—make this rustic pudding with a slightly crunchy texture from the best of the Upper Midwest larder. Wild rice is not a true rice, but rather an aquatic grass that has been harvested by Native American tribes for centuries. Some Minnesota tribes now cultivate wild rice, which has smaller grains than true wild rice, and package it under the Grey Owl brand. A cup of cooked wild rice stashed away in the freezer will save time with the first step. The day after you make this, use up the leftover egg whites in a meringue dessert. **MAKES 6 SERVINGS**

The World of Rice Pudding

Europeans were already cooking whole grains with water or milk in a pot over a fire when rice became available to upper class households in the Middle Ages. In 1604, Lady Fettiplace recorded four rice puddings in her book *Elinor Fettiplace's Receipt Book*. Lord Ruthven, an English gentleman, published a book of recipes and household hints titled *The Ladies Cabinet, Containing Many Rare Secrets* in 1658 with this recipe for "A Rice Pudding":

"Take thin Creame, or good milk of what quantity you please, boil it on the fire with a little Cinnamon in it, and when it hath boiled a while, take out the cinnamon and put in Rosewater and sugar enough to make it good and sweet; then having your rice ready beaten as fine as flour (and searced as some do it) throw it in, till it be of a thickness, of a hasty pudding; then pour it into a dish and serve it at the Table."

The earliest rice puddings in this country were also made this way—in a pot over a fire. Later versions were started on the stove top, then poured into a baking dish and baked until done. Almost every European immigrant group added its own touches to this basic English rice pudding over the centuries. Families of Scandinavian heritage flavor theirs with lemon or serve it with a red fruit sauce. For Christmas they hide a whole almond in the pudding for Christmas; whoever gets it has a year of good luck. Those of French descent might go for a *riz à l'impératrice*, or "the Empress's rice," a molded Bavarian cream with cooked rice, fruits, and kirsch. Those with Belgian relatives might have a recipe for *vlaamse rÿsttaart*, a creamy, vanilla-scented rice pudding tart. Italian families might turn theirs into a *risotto gelato*, made with cooked rice blended with a lemon-and-vanilla-scented custard and frozen.

1 cup cooked wild rice

1 cup cooked long-grain rice

1 cup dried cranberries, blueberries, or tart cherries

2 cups half-and-half

5 large egg yolks

$\frac{1}{2}$ cup wildflower, sunflower, or other amber honey

1 teaspoon ground cinnamon

$\frac{1}{4}$ teaspoon salt

1 Preheat the oven to 350 degrees F. Butter a 9-inch round or square baking dish, spoon the cooked rices and dried cranberries over the bottom, and set aside.

2 In a medium-size saucepan, scald the half-and-half over medium-high heat until small bubbles form around the perimeter. In a medium-size mixing bowl, whisk the egg yolks and honey until smooth. Whisk in the warm half-and-half until well blended. Whisk in the cinnamon and salt. Strain the custard mixture through a fine-mesh strainer over the wild rice and fruit.

3 Bake the pudding until slightly browned on top and bubbling around the edges, about 45 minutes.

Blueberry Frumenty

Frumenty is a very old dish of a whole grain cooked with milk and sweetened to a slightly thickened pudding. The name derives from the Latin *frumentum*, meaning "wheat," and the Middle English *frumenty*, meaning "a kind of pudding." Today, we would consider frumenty either a very hearty cold weather dessert, perhaps after a soup supper, or a deliciously substantial breakfast dish. Whole wheat berries are available at health food stores. **MAKES 8 SERVINGS**

1 cup wheat berries

2 cups half-and-half

$\frac{1}{4}$ cup sugar

1 teaspoon vanilla extract

1 teaspoon grated lemon zest

2 cups fresh or frozen (thawed) blueberries or huckleberries

Fresh berries for garnish

1 In a large saucepan, bring the wheat berries, half-and-half, and sugar to a boil over medium-high heat. Reduce the heat to medium-low and simmer until the wheat berries are soft, but still a little chewy, about 45 minutes.

2 Stir in the vanilla, lemon zest, and 2 cups of blueberries and cook for 10 minutes more. Serve warm in bowls garnished with fresh berries.

Lemony Baked Apple Tapioca

Whole pearl tapioca came into common household usage in the 1870s. Dry and transportable, it traveled across the country as President James Madison's idea of the country's Manifest Destiny—to settle America from coast to coast—was slowly realized. At first, pearl tapioca had to be soaked overnight, then cooked with liquid. Later, quick-cooking tapioca made the process a lot faster. I happen to love tapioca; for me it's a real comfort food, but not everyone feels that way. When badly made, tapioca can have a thick, glutinous, lumpy texture reminiscent of school paste. But forget that! This version is light, airy, and flavorful. **MAKES 8 SERVINGS**

2 tart, crisp apples, such as Granny Smith or Jonathan, peeled, cored, and sliced

$\frac{1}{3}$ cup quick-cooking tapioca

Grated zest and juice of 1 lemon

4 cups milk

1 cup sugar

2 large eggs, separated

1   Preheat the oven to 350 degrees F. Butter the bottom of a 2-quart baking dish. Arrange the apple slices over the bottom of the dish.

Hasty Pudding

"Hasty pudding" is a very old culinary term designating a mixture of grain, milk, and sweetener cooked together in a pot over a fire. The English Lord Ruthven's 1658 *The Ladies Cabinet, Containing Many Rare Secrets* included a recipe for rice pudding, with instructions to cook it until it has the thickness "of a hasty pudding."

In 1795, Harvard students formed a secret society known as the Hasty Pudding Club, which was supposed to encourage patriotism and friendship. The club's constitution stipulated that members, going in alphabetical order, had to bring a hasty pudding—basically an Indian pudding made with cornmeal, milk, and molasses—to serve in its pudding pot (a small cauldron) at each meeting. Indian pudding was hasty because it set up as soon as the cornmeal cooked into a kind of mush. Over the years, the fun of consuming the hasty pudding paled, so the group added amateur theatricals, which continue today. The Hasty Pudding Club also gives out annual Man and Woman of the Year awards to deserving actors and actresses.

2 In a large mixing bowl, stir together the tapioca, lemon zest and juice, milk, sugar, and egg yolks. With an electric mixer, whip the egg whites in a small mixing bowl until they hold stiff peaks. Fold the egg whites into the tapioca mixture, and pour the mixture over the apples.

3 Bake until the tapioca has firmed and the apples are soft, about 30 minutes. Serve warm.

The Next Best Thing to Robert Redford

During the late 1960s and early '70s, women went on the Pill, wore miniskirts, burned their bras, went for a career and not just a job, and declared war on the antiquated notion that women were not interested in sex. This recipe reflects the spirit of the times, and it's still good today. To make another version of this dessert—Can't Leave It Alone—substitute lemon instant pudding for the pistachio called for here.

MAKES 10 TO 12 SERVINGS

CRUST

1½ cups all-purpose flour

¾ cup (1½ sticks) unsalted butter at room temperature

½ cup finely chopped pecans or walnuts

¼ cup plus 2 tablespoons confectioners' sugar

FILLING

Two 3.4-ounce boxes pistachio instant pudding

2½ cups milk

One 8-ounce package cream cheese at room temperature

1 cup confectioners' sugar

One 8-ounce container Cool Whip, thawed, or 2 cups whipped cream

TOPPING

One 8-ounce container Cool Whip, thawed, or 2 cups whipped cream

Toasted sweetened flaked coconut or chopped pistachios for garnish

1 Preheat the oven to 350 degrees F. To make the crust, combine the ingredients with your hands in a medium-size mixing bowl until well blended. Pat the mixture evenly into the bottom of a 9 x 13-inch baking pan. Bake until lightly browned, about 15 minutes. Let cool.

2 To make the filling, whisk the instant pudding and milk together in a medium-size mixing bowl until the pudding thickens. Set aside. With an electric mixer, beat the cream cheese and confectioners' sugar together in large mixing bowl until smooth and creamy. Fold in the Cool Whip.

The Next Best Thing to Robert Redford

The year was 1966.

The Beatles were working on their groundbreaking Sergeant Pepper album.

The Hollywood Squares and *Batman* debuted on network television.

Robert Redford was about to become a Hollywood heartthrob by starring in *Barefoot in the Park* with Jane Fonda.

General Foods Corporation launched Cool Whip nondairy whipped topping.

Almost immediately, American cooks, freed from the not-so-arduous task of whipping real cream, became almost giddy with this sense of dessert freedom—and with the smooth, creamy taste of this nondairy whipped topping.

Desserts with improbable names like "The Next Best Thing to Robert Redford" or "Can't Leave It Alone"—the two I have in my recipe collection—were hastily written down on recipe cards. All are layered desserts made in 9 x 13-inch pans. Most follow a similar format—a baked cookie or graham cracker crumb crust and a filling made with instant pudding, milk, and Cool Whip. Here are two other examples:

For a mock éclair, 2 small boxes of instant vanilla or chocolate pudding are mixed with milk, then Cool Whip is folded in. Three layers of this pudding mixture, alternating with layers of graham crackers, broken into their natural rectangles, are arranged in a baking pan. The "éclair" is then drizzled with chocolate sauce or syrup. This recipe even showed up in a community cookbook from a Dakota Sioux reservation in South Dakota.

Kansas Dirt or Mississippi Mud Cake starts off with an Oreo or Hydrox cookie crumb crust. Half of the crushed cookies line the bottom of the pan. The filling is made with cream cheese at room temperature, butter, milk, 2 packages of instant pudding (vanilla or chocolate), Cool Whip, and confectioners' sugar, all beaten together. The topping is the rest of the crushed cookies.

Spread the cream cheese mixture over the cooled crust. Spread the pudding over the cream cheese layer.

3   For the topping, spread the Cool Whip over the pudding layer and garnish with coconut or pistachios. Chill for 1 hour, then cut into squares and serve.

Warm Sour Cherry Charlotte with Sour Cherry Sauce

Sour cherries are the glory of Great Lakes orchards, celebrated in recipes like this one adapted from a dessert created by Chicago chef Gale Gand. Rich brioche lines the charlotte mold, a sour cherry custard provides the filling, and a warm sour cherry sauce flavored with almond finishes this cherry-lover's feast. Like Martha's Vineyard Summer Pudding (page 34), this charlotte is best assembled early in the day or the night before to let the filling soak into the bread. When I want to make this, I bake a loaf of Buttery Brioche ahead of time. A loaf of brioche is better than individual ones for cutting into uniform slices to line the charlotte mold. You can also make this using a loaf of challah or pound cake. If you use smaller store-bought brioche, make the dessert in eight 4-ounce ramekins, first lined with plastic wrap. The plastic wrap will not burn at 300 degrees F, and the charlotte will unmold beautifully. Instead of the Sour Cherry Sauce, you could also serve this with Sour Cherry and Almond Compote (page 15).

MAKES 8 SERVINGS

CHARLOTTE

1 loaf Buttery Brioche (see page 32) or 8 medium-size brioches from a bakery

2 cups half-and-half

2 cups heavy cream

1/8 teaspoon salt

6 large eggs, beaten

1 cup sugar

2 teaspoons almond extract

3 cups pitted sour cherries, fresh, frozen (thawed), or canned, juice reserved

SOUR CHERRY SAUCE

1 cup pitted sour cherries, fresh, frozen (thawed), or canned, juice reserved

1 cup cranberry juice cocktail, plus more as needed

2 tablespoons fresh lemon juice

2 tablespoons cornstarch

1/2 teaspoon almond extract

1   To make the charlotte, slice the loaf or individual brioches into 1/2-inch-thick slices and remove the crusts. Line the bottom and sides of a 2-quart charlotte mold or 8 individual ramekins with plastic wrap, and then line the plastic wrap with the larger slices of brioche. Chop enough of the remaining brioches to measure 3 cups. Set aside.

2   Combine the half-and-half, cream, and salt in a medium-size saucepan over medium heat and

scald until bubbles form around the perimeter of the pan; remove from the heat. In a large mixing bowl, whisk the eggs and sugar together until smooth. Add ½ cup of the hot cream mixture to the eggs and whisk to blend. Pour the tempered eggs through a fine-mesh strainer back into the hot cream mixture, whisking to blend. Whisk in the almond extract and set aside.

3   In a large mixing bowl, using a rubber spatula, fold together the cubed brioche, cherries, and custard (if using canned cherries, drain the cherries, reserving their juice for the sauce). Spoon this mixture into the prepared charlotte mold or ramekins. (All the filling might not fit at this time. Reserve the rest of the filling, covered, in the refrigerator.) Cover the charlotte mold or ramekins with plastic wrap and refrigerate for at least 4 hours or overnight to let the brioche absorb the custard.

4   When ready to bake, arrange a rack in the middle of the oven and preheat to 300 degrees F. If there is leftover filling, spoon it into the charlotte mold or ramekins to reach the top. Place the charlotte mold or ramekins in a deep baking pan and fill with hot water to reach a depth of 2 inches.

5   Place in the center of the oven and bake until a cake tester inserted in the center comes out clean and the custard has set, about 1 hour and 45 minutes for the charlotte mold and 1 hour for the ramekins. Remove from the oven and the water bath and let cool for 15 minutes.

6   Meanwhile, make the sauce: Pour the cranberry juice into a saucepan and bring to a boil (if using canned cherries, combine the cherry juice with cranberry juice to make 1 cup). Mix the lemon juice and cornstarch together until it makes a smooth paste, then whisk the paste into the liquid. Keep whisking until the sauce has thickened enough to coat the back of a spoon, then whisk in the almond extract and fold in the cherries. Keep warm over low heat.

7   To serve, unmold the charlotte while still hot onto a serving plate and pass the sauce at the table.

Charlotte Russe

One of food historian Katie Armitage's favorite "antique" recipes is charlotte russe, which tells a little story all by itself. "Kansas, opened to settlement in 1854, consumed by the free state versus slave state struggle, and parched by an 18-month drought in 1860–61, probably did not join the passion for fancy dining as early as the eastern United States," says Armitage. "By 1870, however, a menu at a fancy dinner party at Fort Leavenworth included charlotte russe. After the Civil War, the rigors of the Indian campaigns, and the beginning of a new decade, the officers and their ladies were ready to have a good time. Rebecca Richmond, then visiting her cousin Libbie Custer (wife of ill-fated General George Custer), recorded the menu in her diary. She wrote down all the foods, but also mentioned that she only ate a little of each of the six courses: soup for the first course; fish for the second; turkey, oysters, and a great variety of vegetables; birds and veal, with jellies and pickles; ham and salad; charlotte russe, ice cream, blancmange, and cake, concluding with nuts, oranges, and coffee." Presidential wives of Midwestern small colleges still serve charlotte russe for faculty teas and dessert parties. It remains an easy, elegant, do-ahead dish. The influence of Libbie Custer lives on.

MAKES 8 TO 10 SERVINGS

1 recipe Homemade Ladyfingers (see page 406) or three 3-ounce packages store-bought ladyfingers

Four ¼-ounce packages unflavored gelatin

½ cup water

4 cups heavy cream

¾ cup confectioners' sugar

Grated zest of 1 lemon

Fresh fruit, such as strawberries, raspberries, or blueberries, for garnish

1 Line the bottom and sides of a 9-inch springform pan with the ladyfingers, rounded sides facing out. Sprinkle the gelatin over the water in a small bowl. Set aside for several minutes until the gelatin is soaked through.

2 Fill a small baking pan with enough hot water to come three quarters of the way up the sides of the bowl of gelatin mixture. Set the bowl in the pan of hot water for several minutes, until the gelatin mixture is clear.

3 With an electric mixer, whip the cream in a large mixing bowl until it holds soft peaks. Add the gelatin and continue whipping. Add the confectioners' sugar, a little at a time, then the lemon zest, and continue beating until the cream holds stiff peaks. Pour the whipped cream mixture over the ladyfingers, cover, and refrigerate for up to 3 hours before serving.

4 Release and remove the sides of the pan. Garnish the top of the dessert with fresh fruit. Cut into wedges to serve.

Homemade Ladyfingers

Gentle and delicate, these elegant lengths of sponge cake are latter-day descendents of old English sippets. Their taste is fresh and light, not dusty the way packaged ladyfingers can taste. Moistened with liqueur and used to line the bottom and sides of a springform pan, they can provide the framework for any number of desserts. Once you are comfortable with the technique of folding, ladyfingers are easy to make. They can be flavored with almond extract, citrus zest, or unsweetened cocoa powder. Sift the flour first, then measure it, before using in this recipe. **MAKES 4 DOZEN 4-INCH LADYFINGERS**

4 large eggs, separated

$\frac{1}{2}$ cup granulated sugar

$1\frac{1}{2}$ teaspoons vanilla extract

$\frac{3}{4}$ cup plus 2 tablespoons sifted all-purpose flour

Superfine sugar for dusting

1 Preheat the oven to 325 degrees F. Line two baking sheets with parchment paper. With a pencil, make twenty-four 4-inch-long lines, about $1\frac{1}{2}$ inches apart, on each piece of parchment paper. Turn the parchment paper over on the baking sheet so the penciled side is on the bottom but you can still see the guidelines. Set aside.

2 With an electric mixer, beat together the egg yolks and 3 tablespoons of the granulated sugar in a medium-size mixing bowl until the mixture thickens and turns light yellow, about 5 minutes. (This step ensures a light texture.) Stir in the vanilla and set aside.

3 Wash and dry the beaters well. Beat the egg whites with 1 tablespoon of the granulated sugar in a large mixing bowl until the egg whites hold soft peaks. Do not overbeat. With a hand whisk, blend in the remaining $\frac{1}{4}$ cup of granulated sugar and the egg yolk mixture.

4 Using a rubber spatula, fold in the sifted flour, $\frac{1}{2}$ cup at a time, until the mixture is light and well blended.

5 Fit a pastry bag with a no. 8 tube (½ inch in diameter) or cut a ½-inch opening from the tip of a large squeeze bottle used for condiments. Fill halfway with the batter. Using a downward motion, pipe 4-inch-long fingers about ½ inch apart onto the guidelines on the parchment paper–lined baking sheet. To end each ladyfinger, press the tip down into the end of the ladyfinger, then quickly release and resume piping the next ladyfinger. Sift superfine sugar over the ladyfingers.

6 Bake the ladyfingers until the edges just begin to brown, 10 to 12 minutes. Let cool for 1 minute in the pan, then carefully slide the parchment paper off the baking sheet and onto a wire rack. When the ladyfingers have cooled completely, use a metal spatula to remove them from the paper. Ladyfingers can be stored in an airtight container in layers, separated by waxed paper, for 1 week; they may be frozen for up to 3 months.

Rich Chocolate Charlotte in a Ladyfinger Mold

Made in two stages, this relatively easy dessert makes a stunning presentation. Prepare the ladyfingers the day before and keep them in an airtight container. Make the chocolate mousse the day you want to serve the charlotte. When the dessert has chilled and you release it from the springform pan, carefully but firmly tie an organdy or French wire ribbon around the middle, and voila! (Remove the ribbon before cutting the charlotte into wedges to serve.) Instead of using chocolate to flavor the mousse, experiment with raspberry, boysenberry, or apricot purees for different flavors and colors. The mousse filling makes about 5 cups. **MAKES 8 TO 10 SERVINGS**

1 recipe Homemade Ladyfingers (see page 406) or five 3-ounce packages store-bought ladyfingers

8 ounces semisweet chocolate

1 cup (2 sticks) unsalted butter at room temperature, cut into pieces

¼ cup sugar

1½ cups heavy cream

1 tablespoon vanilla extract

1 Using your best ladyfingers, line the sides of a 9-inch springform pan, turning the ladyfingers so that the rounded side is against the pan. Completely cover the bottom with the remaining ladyfingers, cutting to fit. Set aside.

2 Put the chocolate in the top of a double boiler over barely simmering water until it melts. Remove from the heat, whisk in the butter, and continue whisking until smooth. Set aside.

3   Put the sugar, cream, and vanilla in a large mixing bowl. With an electric mixer, whip until the cream holds soft peaks. Using a rubber spatula, fold 1 cup of the whipped cream into the chocolate mixture. Carefully fold the remaining whipped cream into the chocolate mixture until well blended. Spoon the mousse into the ladyfinger-lined springform pan, cover with plastic wrap, and chill for 2 to 3 hours or overnight.

4   To serve, remove the sides of the springform pan. Cut a length of ribbon and tie it carefully but firmly around the circumference of the charlotte.

Montmorency Bread Pudding

In June, when tart, red Montmorency cherries ripen, home cooks in the North and Midwest get busy picking, pitting, and then freezing these fruits or turning them into wonderful summertime desserts. At my local farmers' market, I can buy quarts of locally grown, already pitted (what a luxury!) frozen Montmorency cherries. If you pit the cherries yourself, a clean hairpin or even a large paper clip works well. The idea is to remove the pit while preserving the round shape of the cherry.

MAKES 10 TO 12 SERVINGS

3 large eggs, lightly beaten

1/4 cup sugar

1 teaspoon vanilla extract

1/2 cup mascarpone cheese or cream cheese at room temperature

2 cups warm milk

1/4 cup (1/2 stick) unsalted butter, melted

1/8 teaspoon freshly grated nutmeg

1/2 teaspoon ground cinnamon

1 cup pitted tart red cherries, fresh, frozen (thawed), or canned (drained)

1/2 cup sour cherry preserves

1 loaf Buttery Brioche (see page 32), challah, or other good quality bread, cut into 12 slices, and crusts trimmed

1   Preheat the oven to 350 degrees F. Butter a 9 x 13-inch baking dish and set aside.

2   In a large mixing bowl, stir together the eggs, sugar, vanilla, mascarpone, milk, melted butter, nutmeg, cinnamon, and cherries. Set aside.

3   Generously spread cherry preserves on each slice of bread. Place a layer of prepared bread slices in the baking dish, cherry side up. Pour in enough of the cherry mixture to just cover the surface, making sure the cherries are equally distributed. Add another layer of the prepared bread, and pour over the remaining cherry mixture. Set aside for 20 minutes.

4   Place the baking pan in a larger, deeper pan. Add enough water to come halfway up the sides of the baking dish. Bake until a cake tester inserted in the center comes out clean, 50 to 60 minutes. Serve immediately.

Coffee Bread and Butter Pudding

How could anyone resist this pudding of brandy-soaked raisins, buttery brioche, and coffee-flavored custard? I know I can't. It is great for entertaining because you can make it ahead of time, and your guests will go home happy. Enjoy leftovers for an indulgent breakfast the morning after. **MAKES 10 TO 12 SERVINGS**

⅔ cup raisins

½ cup brandy or cognac

6 cups half-and-half or light cream

¾ cup finely ground French roast or espresso coffee beans

1 loaf Buttery Brioche (see page 32), challah, or other egg-rich bread, cut into 12 slices, and crusts trimmed

½ cup (1 stick) unsalted butter at room temperature

½ cup granulated sugar

4 large eggs

6 large egg yolks

Confectioners' sugar for dusting

1   Several hours or the night before baking, macerate the raisins in the brandy until plump.

2   In a large saucepan, heat the half-and-half and ground coffee together. Slowly bring to a boil, then remove from the heat, cover, and let steep for 30 minutes.

3   Butter the inside of a 9 x 13-inch baking dish and set aside. Butter both sides of 6 slices of brioche and cover the bottom of the prepared pan. Sprinkle evenly with the raisins and their soaking liqueur and ¼ cup of the granulated sugar. Top with 6 more slices of buttered brioche and sprinkle with the remaining ¼ cup of granulated sugar. Set aside.

4   In a large mixing bowl, whisk the whole eggs and egg yolks together. Strain the coffee cream through a fine-mesh strainer into the egg mixture and whisk until well blended. Pour the egg-and-cream mixture through a strainer over the buttered brioche in the pan. Leave to soak for at least

30 minutes before baking. (The bread pudding can be made up to this point a few hours or the night before serving, and stored, covered, in the refrigerator. It will need to bake a little longer.)

5   Preheat the oven to 350 degrees F. Bake until browned and bubbling and the filling has set, 30 to 40 minutes. Serve warm or cold, dusted with confectioners' sugar.

Bohemian Bread Pudding

Minnesota immigrants whose roots were in the German-speaking area of Bohemia make this winter bread pudding with bread crumbs instead of larger bread pieces. Some Bohemian bread puddings are flavored with candied lemon peel, others with raisins or more simply, vanilla. This version from the area around New Ulm, Minnesota, includes a variety of dried fruits for a richer flavor. The better the quality of the bread you use, the better this dessert tastes. **MAKES 6 SERVINGS**

1 cup fine dry bread crumbs from Buttery Brioche (see page 32) or a good quality bread

2 cups milk

¼ teaspoon salt

1 large egg

½ cup sugar

1 teaspoon vanilla extract

1 tablespoon unsalted butter at room temperature

1 cup assorted dried fruits, such as raisins, currants, tart cherries, apricots, and/or prunes, snipped with kitchen scissors into small pieces, if necessary

1   Preheat the oven to 325 degrees F. Butter a 1-quart soufflé dish or baking pan and set aside.

2   Put the bread crumbs in a large mixing bowl. Heat the milk to almost boiling in a small saucepan. Pour the milk over the bread crumbs, whisking to blend. Set aside to cool.

3   In a small bowl, whisk the salt, egg, and sugar together. When the bread crumb mixture is warm, but not hot, whisk in the egg mixture. Whisk in the vanilla and butter. Pour the bread crumb batter into the prepared dish. Sprinkle the dried fruit evenly on the top.

4   Bake the pudding until a cake tester inserted in the center comes out clean, 30 to 35 minutes. Serve warm.

New Orleans Bread Pudding with Rum Sauce

A really good south Louisiana bread pudding should be light and airy, not dense like a brick. Sinfully rich, this one is well worth serving (after guests have had time for their dinners to digest), along with a cup of dark, rich coffee—chicory coffee, to be authentic. Use fresh French bread for this recipe, rather than stale. It's much easier to slice, trim away the crusts, and cut into cubes. Simply let the fresh bread cubes air-dry or arrange them on a baking sheet and dry in a 200-degree-F oven for 15 minutes before using in this recipe. **MAKES 8 SERVINGS**

PUDDING

16 cups lightly packed very dry French bread cubes with crusts trimmed (about 3 loaves)

$1/2$ cup (1 stick) unsalted butter, melted

3 large eggs

$1^1/2$ cups granulated sugar

2 tablespoons vanilla extract

1 teaspoon freshly grated nutmeg

$1^1/2$ teaspoons ground cinnamon

3 cups milk

1 cup golden raisins

1 cup chopped toasted pecans (see page 181)

RUM SAUCE

1 cup (2 sticks) unsalted butter, cut into pieces

$1/3$ cup confectioners' sugar

$1^1/2$ cups granulated sugar

2 large eggs, beaten

$1/2$ cup dark rum

1 Preheat the oven to 350 degrees F. In a large mixing bowl, toss the bread cubes with the melted butter until well blended. Arrange them in a 9 x 13-inch baking pan.

2 With an electric mixer, beat together the eggs and granulated sugar in another large mixing bowl until the mixture is thick, lemon colored, and ribbons from the beaters, about 4 minutes. (This will ensure a light texture.) Beat in the vanilla, spices, and milk. Stir in the raisins and pecans and pour this mixture over the bread cubes. With a rubber spatula or a spoon, press the bread cubes down into the custard to moisten all of them.

3 Bake the bread pudding until the top is golden and crusty and a cake tester inserted in the center comes out clean, 45 to 55 minutes.

4 While the pudding is baking, make the rum sauce. Cream the butter and sugars together in a large mixing bowl with an electric mixer until light and fluffy. Transfer the mixture to the top of a double

boiler, set over simmering water, and cook, whisking often, until silken, smooth, and light colored, about 20 minutes. Whisk 2 tablespoons of the hot butter mixture into the eggs, then slowly whisk the eggs into the butter mixture. Cook, stirring, until thickened, about 5 minutes. Remove from the heat and stir in the rum. Keep the sauce warm over hot water until ready to serve.

5 Serve each square or spoonful of warm bread pudding topped with warm rum sauce.

Tropical Fruit Bread Pudding

Whether fresh or canned, many tropical fruits have a sweet, slightly perfumed taste. Some are now grown in Florida and are available fresh or canned at groceries and Asian markets. Yellow jackfruit, available canned in Asian markets, has a slightly crunchy texture and tastes like a blend of apricot, honey, and melon. Make this exotic bread pudding in summer, suggests recipe creator Dr. Lillian Pardo, who grew up in the Philippines, came to America for medical school, and stayed. "Everyone in my family loves tropical fruits, even my granddaughter Olivia," says Pardo. "When the weather is hot, there's nothing more soothing or cooling than a dessert made with tropical fruit." **MAKES 8 SERVINGS**

6 to 7 cups lightly packed very dry French bread cubes with crusts trimmed (about 1½ loaves)

One 8-ounce can jackfruit in syrup, drained and coarsely chopped, syrup reserved

One 8-ounce can mandarin oranges in syrup, drained and syrup reserved

½ cup (1 stick) unsalted butter at room temperature

¾ cup sugar

4 large eggs

1 teaspoon vanilla extract

½ cup milk

Ice cream (optional) for serving

1 Put the bread cubes in a large mixing bowl. Pour the reserved jackfruit and mandarin orange syrups over the bread and toss to blend well. Let sit at least 30 minutes to allow the bread to absorb the syrups.

2 Preheat the oven to 350 degrees F. Butter a 1½-quart soufflé or baking dish and set aside.

3 With an electric mixer, cream the butter and sugar together in a large mixing bowl until light and fluffy. Beat in the eggs, vanilla, and milk. Fold in the jackfruit and mandarin oranges. Fold in the juice-soaked bread cubes. Pour the mixture into the prepared dish and bake until the top is golden brown and a knife inserted in the center comes out clean, 35 to 45 minutes. Serve warm with ice cream, if desired.

A World of Bread Puddings

In Lady Fettiplace's 1604 book of receipts from her English manor house, sweet puddings are made with ground almonds or rice, thin cream, and sugar; a batter of eggs, flour, cream, spices, and suet; and bread. The bread she would have used was called "manchet," a fine white loaf that would have been several days old in order to make good crumbs. In her recipe for what we would now call bread and butter pudding, she used "the top of the morning milke" or cream beaten together with eggs, a little flour, ground cloves and mace, a little salt, and melted butter. This was poured over bread crumbs and raisins. Although some of her puddings were steamed, this one was baked.

Ladies raised in homes with similar kitchens would have brought their bread pudding recipes to the first settlements in New England and the South from 1620 until the civil war began in England in 1642. The problem was, until other areas of the country were settled and wheat could be reliably grown, wheat flour for bread was scarce. Instead of going to the trouble of making cornbread first for a bread pudding, these early cooks made hasty, or Indian, pudding instead, thus saving a step. Why bake cornbread when it would just go soggy and lose its shape in a bread pudding? Wheat bread held up better to the custard in a bread and butter pudding.

By the Revolutionary War, when trade between the colonies made regional products like wheat flour available in larger cities, bread pudding recipes were a way for thrifty cooks to make use of stale homemade or bake-house (bakery) bread and serve a delicious dessert at the same time.

Peanut Butter Bread Pudding with Hot Fudge Sauce

I love not-too-sweet chocolate-covered peanut butter candy. That same flavor comes through in this dessert. Made from peanuts grown in the South, peanut butter first debuted as a health food at the 1904 World's Fair in St. Louis. Soon, however, adults and children both discovered that a peanut butter sandwich was hard to beat, healthy or not. Today, peanut butter is one of those foods that separate Americans from Brits and Australians, who prefer their Marmite and Vegemite spreads, made from malt and brewer's yeast. When I lived in London, while others purchased wheels of Stilton and braces of pheasant upstairs in Harrod's Food Hall, I bought our peanut butter in the basement, where other American products like Oreos, Marshmallow Fluff, and Cheerios beckoned Yanks wanting a taste of home. Some things you just can't live without.

MAKES 10 TO 12 SERVINGS

1 cup crunchy peanut butter

1 loaf Buttery Brioche (see page 32) or challah bread, cut into 12 slices and crusts trimmed

4 cups half-and-half

3 large eggs

2 large egg yolks

¾ cup sugar

1 tablespoon vanilla extract

¼ teaspoon salt

1 recipe Classic Hot Fudge Sauce (see page 427) or good quality store-bought hot fudge sauce, warmed

1   Butter a 9 x 13-inch baking pan and set aside. Spread the peanut butter on one side of each bread slice. Arrange the slices in the bottom of the baking pan, peanut butter side up.

2   In a large mixing bowl, whisk together the half-and-half, whole eggs, and egg yolks. Whisk in the sugar, vanilla, and salt. Pour this mixture over the bread in the pan. Cover with plastic wrap and refrigerate for at least 1 hour or overnight.

3   Preheat the oven to 350 degrees F. Place the baking pan in a larger pan filled with enough hot water to come halfway up the sides of the baking pan. Bake until a knife inserted in the center comes out clean, 45 to 55 minutes. Let the pudding cool in the water bath for 30 minutes before serving. To serve, place a portion of the bread pudding on a serving plate and drizzle it with hot fudge sauce.

Get Yer Peanuts Here...

Americans love their peanuts, whether consumed in the shell at baseball games, roasted and shelled for party snacks, or ground into peanut butter. We eat peanuts in candy bars of all kinds, on top of ice cream sundaes, and in little packages of airline snacks. In convenience stores along the coasts of the Carolinas, you can buy bags of boiled peanuts, definitely an acquired taste for this Yankee girl. But we can all agree that Americans have a love affair with the common peanut, which Europeans—who prefer almonds, walnuts, or hazelnuts—find puzzling.

Peanuts are native to Brazil and Peru, were brought to Africa by Portuguese traders, and came to America through the slave trade. Legumes that grow underground, rather than true nuts that grow on trees, peanuts were also called "groundnuts" and "goobers" throughout the South. Slaves originally from the Congo used a Gedda word, *nguba*, which soon became Americanized as "goober." For a long time, peanuts were regarded as food fit only for slaves or livestock.

Some slaves and free blacks grew these underground nuts for their own personal use because they were a familiar African food, a good source of extra nutrition, and would keep through the year. During the cotton harvest and cotton ginning, slaves boiled peanuts to eat. In winter, they were roasted. Free blacks in Charleston, South Carolina, blended roasted and shelled peanuts with molasses, brown sugar, and butter to make groundnut cakes, a kind of candy. "Formerly these groundnut cakes were sold by our Maumas (free black women who dressed in colorful turbans) on street corners or on the Battery on the Fourth of July and other special occasions. The Maumas were picturesque, with their turbaned heads, waving a short fly brush made of dried grasses," writes Miss Ellen Parker in the 1950 *Charleston Receipts*.

It took a descendant of slaves, George Washington Carver, to rid the peanut of its lower class reputation and bring it to the forefront of American agriculture. At Tuskegee Institute in Alabama, Carver began experimenting with peanuts in 1903, coming up with over 300 peanut products. Peanuts were then grown for personal consumption and for peanut butter, a product introduced as a health food at the St. Louis World's Fair in 1904. During the 1920s and '30s, the boll weevil wreaked havoc on the cotton fields of the South, and more farmers turned to growing peanuts. Today, Georgia produces over 40 percent of the all the peanuts in the United States.

The Queen of Bread Puddings

Queen of Puddings is an old English dessert with three layers: a deep custard thickened with bread crumbs and generally flavored with grated lemon zest; a thin layer of raspberry or blackcurrant jelly; and, finally, clouds of meringue. I was intrigued to find this version in *Good Things to Eat*, compiled and published in 1929 by the Pastors Aid Society of the Roanoke Presbyterian Church in Kansas City. Mrs. Ham, the contributor, felt that either a generous layer of "fruit jelly, jam, or cocoanut" would taste delicious with her orange-scented custard. Today, this makes a great dessert to take to a potluck gathering. If I make a lemon-scented pudding, I use raspberry, red currant, or blackberry jelly. If I make an orange-scented version, I use apricot or peach preserves, cranberry conserve or relish, or sweetened flaked coconut.

MAKES 10 TO 12 SERVINGS

2 cups fine dry bread crumbs, preferably homemade

1 quart milk

1½ cups sugar

1 tablespoon unsalted butter at room temperature

5 large eggs, separated

1 teaspoon vanilla extract

1 teaspoon grated orange or lemon zest

1 cup good quality fruit jelly

1   In a large mixing bowl, soak the bread crumbs in the milk for 1 hour.

2   Preheat the oven to 350 degrees F. Butter a 9 x 13-inch baking pan and set aside.

3   In a food processor, combine 1 cup of the sugar and the butter, pulsing to blend. Add the egg yolks, one at a time, and process until the mixture is smooth and creamy. Whisk this mixture into the bread crumb mixture, and continue whisking until smooth. Whisk in the vanilla and zest and pour into the prepared baking pan.

4   Bake until set (the center may still be a bit wobbly), about 1 hour. Remove the pudding from the oven and carefully spread the jelly over the top of the hot pudding.

5   With an electric mixer, beat together the egg whites and remaining ½ cup of sugar in a large mixing bowl until the egg whites hold stiff peaks. Spread the meringue over the pudding and return to the oven to brown, about 10 minutes. Serve warm, at room temperature, or cold.

Old-Fashioned Steamed Chocolate Pudding

Deacon Porter's Hat is a classic nineteenth-century steamed molasses, spice, and raisin pudding with accompanying hard sauce, served at Mount Holyoke College in Massachusetts. It got its name because its shape reminded students of the tall hat worn by an early college trustee, Deacon Porter, around the late 1830s. Today, Deacon Porter's Hat is more likely to be a steamed chocolate pudding, more amenable to current college student tastes. The pudding must be brought to the table whole, with sauce, and sliced after it has been placed on the table, or it is not considered a Hat. Instead of hard sauce, I would serve this with Classic Hot Fudge Sauce or Raspberry Sauce (see page 61). Because it needs to be steamed for an hour, this is an ideal dessert for winter, when the furnace is blasting away and the house feels dry. I adapted this from a recipe in the 1943 edition of Irma Rombauer's *The Joy of Cooking*. This steamed pudding really does look like a hat and, better yet, it has a satiny texture, somewhere between a cake and a pudding. **MAKES 4 SERVINGS**

1 cup all-purpose flour

$^{1}/_{2}$ teaspoon baking powder

1 teaspoon vanilla extract

$^{1}/_{2}$ cup milk

2 ounces unsweetened chocolate

$^{1}/_{2}$ cup sugar

1 large egg

1 tablespoon unsalted butter, melted

1 recipe Classic Hot Fudge Sauce (see page 427, optional)

1   Fill a large saucepan with 3 inches of water. Butter the inside of a heat-proof ceramic, glass, or metal round-bottomed small mixing bowl or pudding mold that fits inside the saucepan. Cut out a circle of waxed paper to cover the top of the bowl with some overhang and set aside.

2   Sift the flour and baking powder into a small mixing bowl. Mix the vanilla into the milk. In the top of a double boiler over simmering water, melt the chocolate. In a medium-size mixing bowl, whisk the sugar and egg together until creamy. Add the melted chocolate and butter and whisk to blend. Stir the flour mixture into the chocolate mixture, alternating with the milk mixture, and continue stirring until you have a smooth batter.

3   Pour the batter into the prepared bowl. Place the waxed paper over the top and secure with a rubber band or kitchen string. Place the bowl in the saucepan of water and bring to a boil. Reduce the heat to simmer, cover, and let steam for 1 hour. Let cool slightly, remove the waxed paper, and tip the pudding out of the bowl onto a serving plate. Serve with the fudge sauce, if desired.

Fresh Mint Soufflés with Warm Chocolate

Chocolate and mint is a favorite American dessert and candy combination. For an ultimate version of this pairing, try this recipe. These miniature pale green soufflés come to the table right from the oven. You press your spoon down into the middle, pour a little warm dark chocolate into the center, and take a bite. The taste? Smooth, rich chocolate. Then cloud-like meringue, slightly crunchy. And finally, the flavor and aroma of mint. Made in four stages, the dessert sounds more difficult than it actually is. The soufflés are delicious in springtime, when you have fresh mint in your garden, or during the holidays, when it is again available at the grocery store. Make a double batch of the Fresh Mint Syrup to keep in the refrigerator indefinitely. **MAKES 6 SERVINGS**

4 large eggs, separated

1 cup Fresh Mint Syrup (page 487)

⅛ teaspoon salt

¾ cup heavy cream

1 recipe Chocolate Ganache (see page 213)

1   Whisk together the egg yolks, ½ cup of the mint syrup, and the salt in a medium-size bowl.

2   In a medium-size heavy saucepan, bring the cream to a boil. Whisk ¼ cup of the hot cream into the egg yolk mixture, whisking constantly. Transfer that mixture back to the saucepan, whisking constantly. Cook over low heat until the pastry cream has thickened enough to coat the back of a spoon, 10 to 15 minutes. Pass through a fine-mesh strainer into a bowl to remove any lumps. If not using right away, cover and chill until ready to serve. Let it come to room temperature before using in the recipe.

3   To assemble the soufflés, preheat the oven to 400 degrees F. Butter the insides of 6 ramekins or small soufflé dishes, sprinkle with sugar, and set them in a deep baking pan. With an electric mixer, beat the egg whites in a large mixing bowl until they hold soft peaks. Beat in the remaining ½ cup of mint syrup, a little at a time, until the egg whites are glossy. With a rubber spatula or large metal spoon, fold the pastry cream into the meringue mixture until well blended but not deflated. Spoon this mixture into each prepared ramekin. Pour enough hot water into the deep baking pan to come halfway up the sides of the ramekins.

4   Bake the soufflés in the pan of water until they have risen, browned, and pulled away from the sides of the ramekins, 18 to 20 minutes.

5   Meanwhile, warm the Chocolate Ganache in the top of a double boiler over barely simmering water, stirring until smooth. Pour into a warmed sauceboat. To serve, press a spoon deep into the center of each soufflé and pour in a little of the warmed ganache.

Marzipan Soufflé with Vanilla Sauce

Soufflé as a homey dessert? If you think of a soufflé as a homemade pudding blended with a meringue, then yes. Vintage American cookbooks from the 1920s abound with marzipan desserts flavored with almond or almond and maraschino cherry. When I developed this recipe in the late 1980s, based on a hazelnut I enjoyed at the bistro La Coquille in Paris, I was delighted with its flavor, airiness, and the slightly crunchy texture from the with California almonds, which I substituted for the hazelnuts. Enjoy it right out of the oven, puffed and golden, with a luscious ribbon of Vanilla Sauce. The soufflé may be partially made ahead, then folded with whipped egg whites and baked, making it easier to serve while entertaining. The sauce can be made hours ahead of time as well.

MAKES 6 SERVINGS

SOUFFLÉ

1¼ cups milk

1 vanilla bean or 1 teaspoon vanilla extract

6 large eggs, separated

2 tablespoons all-purpose flour

8 ounces Marzipan made with almond flavoring (page 481) or store-bought almond paste at room temperature

¼ teaspoon salt

Two 2.25-ounce packages sliced almonds (about ½ cup)

VANILLA SAUCE

2 cups heavy cream

3 large egg yolks, beaten

2 tablespoons sugar

1 teaspoon vanilla extract

1 tablespoon cognac or brandy (optional)

1   To make the soufflé, combine the milk and vanilla bean in a medium-size saucepan over medium heat and bring to a boil. Remove the pan from the heat and let steep for 5 minutes. Remove the vanilla bean. (If using vanilla extract, simply whisk the vanilla into the hot milk at this point.)

2   In a small mixing bowl, whisk the egg yolks and flour together. Pour in ½ cup of the hot milk, whisking all the while, then transfer the egg mixture to the hot milk in the saucepan, whisking constantly. Return the saucepan to the heat. Break off pieces of the marzipan and whisk into the hot milk. Keep whisking until the pieces dissolve into the milk and the mixture thickens enough to coat the back of a spoon, about 10 minutes.

3   Remove from the heat, cover, and let cool. The recipe may be made ahead to this point. If you like, refrigerate the marzipan custard for several hours. Remove from the refrigerator and bring to room temperature before baking.

4   Preheat the oven to 325 degrees F. Butter the inside of a 1-quart soufflé dish and set aside.

5   With an electric mixer, beat the egg whites with the salt in a large mixing bowl until they hold stiff peaks. Gently fold the egg whites into the marzipan custard and pour into the prepared soufflé dish. Sprinkle the top with the sliced almonds and bake until risen and golden brown, 35 to 40 minutes.

6   While the soufflé is baking, make the sauce. In a medium-size saucepan, scald the cream by heating it until small bubbles form around the perimeter. Pour the cream into the top of a double boiler placed over simmering water. Whisk in the egg yolks and sugar and keep whisking until the sauce has thickened, about 10 minutes. Remove from the heat and whisk in the vanilla and cognac or brandy, if using. Serve warm or cold. (If you are making the sauce ahead of time, store in the refrigerator.)

7   Serve the soufflé straight from the oven, and pass the sauce in a sauceboat.

Harvest Moonshine

Long ago, a quick dessert meant something a lot different than our 60-second puddings tasting not-so-faintly of chemicals. In the 1877 edition of *Buckeye Cookery and Practical Housekeeping*, a compilation of recipes from Midwestern home cooks, I found this recipe from Cambridge City, Indiana. Made from ingredients most home cooks would have on hand, it can be literally whipped up in about 30 minutes. Moonshine is modestly described as having a "pretty appearance with palatable flavor." If you've ever seen a large, glowing harvest moon in the autumn night sky, that's the sort of dreamy, golden color this mousse achieves on the plate. It looks even better accented by deep purple, fruit-like grapes, plums, and blackberries and dark orange bittersweet vines. If you like, freeze this dessert in one 2-quart mold or 8 individual molds for at least four hours. **MAKES 8 SERVINGS**

8 ounces dried apricots

¼ cup sugar

1 tablespoon dry sherry

1 teaspoon vanilla extract

1 cup heavy cream, chilled

1 recipe Italian Meringue (see page 351)

1   Place the apricots and sugar in a medium-size heavy-bottomed saucepan and cook over low heat, covered, until the apricots are soft, about 15 minutes. Remove from the heat and let cool. Put the apricots in a food processor, add the sherry and vanilla, and process until smooth. Set aside.

2   With an electric mixer, whip the cream in a large mixing bowl until stiff. Add the apricot puree and Italian meringue and fold in just enough to give the mixture a swirled appearance. Divide the mousse between 8 dessert glasses or spoon into one decorative serving bowl. Cover with plastic wrap and chill for at least 2 hours and up to 6 hours before serving.

Italians love their *gelato*, the French their *glace*. The English have fabulous double cream and lovely soft fruits that would make incredible ice creams, but they seem to be fairly lukewarm—like Germans and Scandinavians—about the frosty treat.

Americans, on the other hand, are simply wild about ice cream and have been for 200 years. They are the biggest consumers of ice cream in the world, eating 15 to 20 quarts per person of the 800 million gallons made in this country every year.

Why? Aside from the fact that ice cream tastes wonderful, I think it's a combination of factors. For one thing, ice cream is democratic and convivial—unlike crème brûlée, for instance, another kind of cold custard. There is at least one ice cream flavor that will appeal to almost everyone, and though it's a treat that can be relished solo, it is so much better enjoyed in a group at an ice-cream parlor or standing around a hand-cranked ice-cream machine just waiting, waiting, waiting with every turn of the handle.

Ice cream is also portable, fitting in with Americans' on-the-go lifestyles. And it's something you can enjoy with kids, who go almost everywhere with their parents in this country. (Just try taking a 5-year-old child to dinner at a restaurant in London or Paris, and you'll see what I mean.)

After the first real ice cream was prepared and served in Paris in 1775—with Thomas Jefferson sampling it—ice cream made the big leap over the Great Pond. Jefferson had it prepared at Monticello, and later on at the White House.

The first ice-cream parlor is said to have opened in New York City in 1776. Nearby Philadelphia was also known for its ice-cream parlors as well as vendors—many of them African American. Soon, there were two different styles of ice cream in the United States, both with their own devotees: one type made with cream and eggs, as Jefferson's cooks made it at Monticello; the other, Philadelphia style, made with only cream, fruit or flavorings, and sugar.

In 1843, American homemaker Nancy Johnson invented the hand-cranked ice-cream maker, which allowed more middle class households to make and enjoy this treat. You didn't have to have a special cold room filled with ice and snow, as Jefferson did at Monticello, in order to make ice cream. In 1851, Jacob Fussell converted his Baltimore milk plant into the world's first ice cream factory, which allowed anyone with a few pennies to sample this frozen confection.

Ice cream sodas happened by accident in the late nineteenth century, when a scoop of ice cream fell into a fizzy soda. Someone sampled it, and the rest is history.

In 1904, ice cream was first served in a cone—by a happy accident—at the World's Fair held in St. Louis, where the hot dog and peanut butter were also introduced to American palates. Vendor Charles Menches was doing a brisk business selling scoops of ice cream in dishes—until he ran out of dishes. Determined not to let this gold mine cave in, Menches found his friend Ernest Hamwi, who was selling a Syrian wafer-like cookie called *zalabia*. The thin, waffled cookie could be shaped into a cone or a bowl when it came hot off the waffle iron. And so the ice cream cone was born.

Today, Americans enjoy many different ice creams, sherbets, sorbets, and water ices, made from all kinds of regional products.

Monticello Vanilla-Flecked Ice Cream

In May 1784, the household ledger of George Washington recorded the first ice-cream freezer in America. After the Revolutionary War was over and trade relations began again with England, Washington had his factor, or agent, in London purchase "a cream machine for ice" for 2 pounds British sterling. It was Thomas Jefferson, however, who introduced the exotic vanilla bean and vanilla ice cream to the American palate. This recipe is an adaptation of one served at Jefferson's Monticello at the end of the eighteenth century. Jefferson served his vanilla ice cream in decorative molds, leaving instructions to "put it in moulds, jostling it well down in the knee, then put the mould into the same bucket of ice, leave it there to the moment of serving it. To withdraw it, immerse the mould in warm water, tossing it well until it will come out & turn it into a plate." Quite a production! It tastes just as good scooped into a bowl.

MAKES 2 QUARTS

4 cups heavy cream

1 vanilla bean, split lengthwise

6 large egg yolks

1 cup sugar

1   In a large heavy saucepan, combine the cream and vanilla bean over medium heat. Scald the cream until small bubbles form around the edge. Remove from the heat, carefully remove the vanilla bean, and scrape the seeds into the cream with a paring knife. Set aside. Discard the bean.

2   In a large mixing bowl, whisk the egg yolks and sugar together until smooth. Slowly whisk in the hot cream, about ½ cup at a time. Transfer the cream-and-egg mixture to the top of a double boiler set over simmering water. Cook, whisking constantly, until the custard is thick enough to coat the back of a spoon, about 10 minutes.

3   Let the custard cool to lukewarm, then transfer to an ice-cream maker and freeze according to the manufacturer's directions.

Farmhouse Vanilla Pudding Ice Cream

The thickening and coagulating agent for dairy cheeses and desserts has changed over time. Farm wives of long ago used rennet from a cow's stomach to make cottage cheese and ice cream. When packaged rennet (Junket) became available, they switched to that. And now that rennet can be hard to find, this third-generation farmhouse ice-cream recipe from central Kansas relies on vanilla pudding mix to thicken the milk-based custard. **MAKES 1 GALLON**

4 cups milk

$1/4$ teaspoon salt

3 large eggs, well beaten

2 tablespoons packaged vanilla pudding mix (not instant)

1 to $1\frac{1}{2}$ cups sugar, to your taste

1 tablespoon vanilla extract

One 13-ounce can evaporated (not condensed) milk

2 cups heavy cream

1   In a medium-size heavy saucepan, heat the milk until warm. Whisk in the salt, eggs, and pudding mix. Whisk in the sugar and continue whisking until it dissolves and the pudding is slightly thickened.

2   Remove from the heat and let cool slightly. Whisk in the vanilla, evaporated milk, and cream. Pour the custard into an ice-cream maker and freeze according to the manufacturer's directions.

Burnt Sugar Ice Cream

Burnt sugar ice cream and crème brûlée, which are both based on caramelized sugar, were popular in the United States in the late eighteenth and early nineteenth centuries. They've made a comeback because Americans love caramel flavors. This caramel ice cream is a wonderful accompaniment to fruit tarts of all kinds and is delicious with Classic Hot Fudge Sauce (see page 427). The egg yolks give this a voluptuous and soft texture, so you don't have to take it out of the freezer ahead of time. The recipe looks complicated, but it's not. First you make the custard, then you make a caramel, then you freeze it all. **MAKES ABOUT 1$1/2$ QUARTS**

1 cup milk

2½ cups heavy cream

10 large egg yolks

⅛ teaspoon salt

1½ cups sugar

½ cup cold water

½ cup boiling water

1   In a large heavy saucepan, scald the milk and cream together until small bubbles form around the edge of the pan. Remove from the heat and set aside to cool to room temperature.

2   With an electric mixer, beat the egg yolks and salt in a large bowl until thick and creamy. Set aside.

3   Bring the sugar and water to a boil in a medium-size heavy saucepan over high heat. Stir with a wooden spoon until the sugar dissolves, then cook for 5 more minutes without stirring. Occasionally rotate the pan to swirl the syrup around. Watch the pan carefully, as the sugar syrup will caramelize quickly and can get too dark in seconds. When the syrup begins to turn a golden brown, after 8 to 10 more minutes, remove it from the heat.

4   Carefully pour the boiling water into the caramel. The boiling water will be colder than the caramel, so some of it may harden in the pan. Return the caramel to the heat and whisk to blend and melt any hardened caramel.

5   With the mixer running, gradually pour the hot caramel into the egg yolks, blending well. Whisk this egg yolk mixture into the cream-and-milk mixture in the saucepan. Heat the custard over medium heat, whisking constantly, until it thickens enough to coat the back of a spoon, about 7 minutes. Remove from the heat, cover with plastic wrap, and chill.

6   Transfer to an ice-cream maker and freeze according to the manufacturer's directions.

Classic Hot Fudge Sauce

A great hot fudge sauce is one of America's stellar contributions to the dessert world— a luscious dark brown lava that slides off a big scoop of ice cream. A true hot fudge sundae lover, I wish I could have eaten this treat from the very place the hot fudge sundae was invented in 1906—C. C. Brown's in Hollywood, now closed, or maybe Bailey's, in Boston, which also claims this culinary invention. Use either regular or Dutch process cocoa powder, whichever you prefer. **MAKES ABOUT 1 PINT**

2/3 cup sugar

1/2 cup unsweetened cocoa powder

3/4 cup heavy cream

1/2 cup light corn syrup

2 tablespoons instant espresso powder

2 tablespoons unsalted butter at room temperature

1 teaspoon vanilla extract

Combine the sugar, cocoa, cream, corn syrup, and espresso powder in a medium-size heavy saucepan. Bring to a boil and continue boiling, stirring constantly, for 4 minutes. Remove from the heat, whisk in the butter and vanilla, and continue whisking until smooth. Serve warm over ice cream, pound cake, or other desserts. Or transfer to a jar, let cool, cover tightly, and refrigerate. Keeps indefinitely.

Iced Berries 'n' Cream

I like to vary my ice cream–making methods to suit the ingredients. For ripe but bland fruits, squash, or nuts, I prefer a crème fraîche base. For peaches, bananas, blackberries, and rhubarb, I like to bake the fruit first with a little sugar and lemon juice to concentrate the flavors and add a touch of caramelization. When working with strawberries, raspberries, and melon, I like to keep the taste as fresh as possible, so I use a fresh fruit puree, simple syrup, and very little cream, as in this recipe. With a consistency somewhere between a sorbet and an ice cream, this frozen confection is heavenly served in the middle of a warm berry compote or in a cannoli "basket" (see page 340, steps 4 and 5) with a dollop of whipped cream and a sprinkling of fresh berries. This dish is adapted from a nineteenth-century Ohio Shaker recipe. It is a Philadelphia-style ice cream, which means it is made without a custard base. **MAKES 1 GENEROUS QUART**

2 cups sugar

2 cups water

3 pints hulled ripe strawberries, raspberries, blackberries, or black raspberries

Juice of 2 lemons

1/2 cup heavy cream

1   Bring the sugar and water to a boil in a large heavy saucepan. Remove from the heat and let the simple syrup cool.

2   In a food processor, puree the berries and pass through a fine-mesh strainer to remove any seeds. In a large mixing bowl, mix the berry puree with the simple syrup and lemon juice and set aside. In a small bowl, mix ½ cup of the puree with the cream. Cover with plastic wrap and refrigerate.

3   Pour the reserved berry puree into an ice-cream maker and freeze according to the manufacturer's directions. When the ice cream is almost frozen, pour in the cream-and-berry mixture and continue freezing the ice cream. This two-step procedure will keep the color of the fruit from darkening.

Peaches and Cream Ice Cream

Georgia peaches deserve every bit of their fame. That sugar-crisp flavor, voluptuous texture, and aromatic scent are unforgettable. Sometimes we can get Georgia peaches in Kansas City, a summertime treat. When our family vacations in the South, we always buy a bushel and just eat, eat, eat. Those who grow peaches in their gardens know that not every year is a good peach year in northern reaches of the country. Bad storms, late frosts, severe winters, and baseball-sized hail can take their toll on the Belle of Georgia, Red Haven, Briscoe, Pink Pearl, and Summer Haven varieties. So when it is a good peach year and I've eaten enough to make my arms and chin sticky with juice, I like to make this simple and delicious ice cream. MAKES 1 GENEROUS QUART

4 cups peeled, pitted, and chopped ripe peaches (about 1 pound)

1 cup sugar, or to taste

2 tablespoons fresh lemon juice

2 cups heavy cream

1   Arrange a rack in the lower third of the oven and preheat the oven to 350 degrees F. Put the peaches in a large, shallow baking dish and sprinkle with the sugar and lemon juice. Place the dish on the oven rack and bake until the juice released from the peaches has cooked down to about 2 tablespoons and the peaches are slightly shriveled, 25 to 30 minutes. Remove from the oven and let cool. Transfer the peach mixture to a food processor and process until smooth. Stir the cream into the peach puree.

2   Pour the peach mixture into an ice-cream maker and freeze according to the manufacturer's directions.

Democracy and Philadelphia-Style Ice Cream

The City of Brotherly Love was not only the home of the first American government, but it was also the place where democratic ideals were deliciously translated through ice cream.

Ice cream fame came to Philadelphia in a rather unusual and roundabout way. In 1795, a successful slave rebellion on San Domingo (now Haiti) had prompted the many French and Creole inhabitants (those of mixed European and African birth) to emigrate to New Orleans and to Philadelphia, at a greater distance. The émigrés sought to regain their former wealth by taking jobs and opening small shops. Monsieur Collot, most likely a Creole and the son of a high San Domingan government official, was one of these newly arrived émigrés. Collot advertised in Philadelphia newspapers in 1795, announcing that he had moved his business into larger quarters near the German Catholic Church and would continue to make ice cream "in all the perfection of the true Italian mode" from the finest local cream. He almost certainly bought his ice from the Philadelphia House of Correction, which sold its excess ice. Like most Americans, Philadelphians stored their ice in specially insulated icehouses.

Augustus Jackson, an African American confectioner, continued the city's ice cream–making tradition. Jackson had been a chef at the White House, but moved to Philadelphia in the late 1820s and started his own successful business. He created several popular ice-cream flavors, which he distributed in tin cans to the many ice-cream parlors in the Philadelphia area, especially two black-owned parlors on South Street. Jackson ran a successful business well into the 1850s and became one of Philadelphia's wealthiest African American citizens.

Philadelphia-style ice cream, as it became known, was made with cream and flavorings—such as fruit or vanilla—and nothing else. There was no cooked custard, as was typical of the French style exemplified by Monticello Vanilla-Flecked Ice Cream (page 425). The two most popular Philadelphia flavors were vanilla and lemon.

A now-anonymous observer recorded some of the secrets to the success of Philadelphia's ice-cream entrepreneurs. "It is really country ice cream, fresh from the farm, and although cried and sold in the streets, the market, and the public squares, it will please the most fastidious palate. The loudest criers . . . are the coloured gentlemen, who carry tin cans containing it, about the streets on their shoulders. They sing a . . . song in praise of their lemon ice cream and their vanilla too. . . it is a pretty good fip's worth."

Pleasure gardens, open to the public all throughout nineteenth-century Philadelphia, became places where rich and poor would stroll, enjoy a balmy evening, and have a dish of ice cream from one of many black vendors.

If you visit Philadelphia now, you'd be hard pressed to find an ice-cream parlor owned by blacks. The sad change came slowly. An 1838 survey listed 5 confectioners—Augustus Jackson among them—in the city and surrounding districts. By 1849, there were 46. By 1857, only 7 confectioners were listed, along with this explanation: "Less than two-thirds of those who have trades follow them. A few of the remainder pursue avocations from choice, but the greater number are compelled to abandon their trades on account of the unending prejudice against their color."

By the time that black ice-cream entrepreneurs were fading from the scene, other Philadelphia businessmen took their places. In 1861, a Quaker farmer and schoolteacher from Salem, New Jersey, moved to Philadelphia to pursue his ice-cream dream. Louis Dubois Bassett opened his shop in the Reading Terminal in 1893. Later, grandson Louis Lafayette offered flavors such as yellow tomato, kiwi, and papaya—well beyond vanilla and lemon. Great-granddaughter Ann Lafayette, known for her business acumen, expanded the business beyond Philadelphia. Even Nikita Khrushchev, of Sputnik-launching and shoe-bashing fame, enjoyed a borscht sherbet during a visit in 1961.

Back in 1866, William Breyer hand-cranked ice cream in his kitchen, then traveled the Frankford and Kensington areas of Philadelphia, selling ice cream from his horse-drawn wagon. Breyer eventually opened 6 ice-cream shops before he died in 1882, leaving the business to his sons Henry and Fred, who expanded it over the years. The Breyer family still insisted on making Philadelphia-style ice cream—no custard—only milk, cream, sugar, and flavorings.

How can home cooks make such ice cream? In the nineteenth century, Sarah Tyson Rorer, a mother of three who taught cooking classes in her home town, discovered the secret and taught it to others in her cooking school. In her *Philadelphia Cook Book*, published in 1886, she tells readers: "To make good Philadelphia ice cream, use only the best materials. Avoid gelatine, arrowroot, or any other thickening substance. Good, pure cream, ripe fruit, or the best canned in winter, and granulated sugar make a perfect ice cream."

The Philadelphia-style ice creams in *All-American Desserts* include Iced Berries 'n' Cream (page 428), Peaches and Cream Ice Cream (page 429), Fresh Mango Ice Cream (page 432), Summer Melon Ice Cream (page 433), Toffee-Banana Ice Cream (page 439), Caramelized Sour Cherry and Apricot Ice Cream (page 442), Chicago Fire Ice Cream (page 442), White Chocolate Ice Cream (page 445), Almond Macaroon Ice Cream (page 446), Amaretti Apricot Ice Cream (page 447), and Lemony Blackberry Crumble Ice Cream (page 450).

Indiana melon ... Indiana melon ...

According to novelist Henry James, the most perfect words in the English language were "summer afternoon, summer afternoon." When you say them, it's like a murmur that conjures up thoughts of sunny afternoons in a quiet garden, listening to the hum and buzz of bees, with nothing to do but be lazy.

The taste that conjures up that same thought for me is the luscious, sweet, summery flavor of a salmon-fleshed cantaloupe or pale green honeydew. Cool, juicy, and perfect by itself, melon stands alone, like the ideal summer day. To me, the best melons—casaba, Crenshaw, Ogen, Charentais—are grown in Indiana, where the humid summer climate and rich soil are optimal conditions. And I'm not alone. As I looked through the *Seed Savers Yearbook*, a publication from a group of dedicated gardeners who save rare and heirloom seeds, I saw a notation for a variety of oblong muskmelon called Indiana. The gardener wrote beside it, "best I ever had."

Old Midwestern cookbooks recommend the Nutmeg melon, an heirloom variety dating back to the 1830s, which has green flesh and a distinctive spicy flavor and perfume, and is still available from specialty seed houses. It's sometimes called Early Hanover or Green Nutmeg; a Seed Savers gardener noted that its flavor was "ambrosial." Another antique melon called Jenny Lind, which dates back to the 1830s, has green flesh and a turbaned end. Seek it out at farmers' markets and farm stands.

Fresh Mango Ice Cream

This recipe from the Menger Hotel in San Antonio's Riverwalk area couldn't be simpler or fresher tasting. It's just what you want after a spicy meal or a long after-noon of shopping or sight-seeing on a hot day. **MAKES ABOUT 1 QUART**

2 large, ripe mangoes	1 cup heavy cream
½ cup sugar	1 tablespoon fresh lemon juice

1   Cut the mangoes in half and cut the flesh away from the pits. With a spoon, scoop the mango flesh away from the skin and drop into a food processor. Add the sugar, cream, and lemon juice and process until smooth.

2   Pour the mixture into an ice-cream maker and freeze according to the manufacturer's directions.

Summer Melon Ice Cream

For the best flavor in this ice cream, a variation on the Iced Berries 'n' Cream on page 428, use a ripe melon with a sweet perfume. **MAKES 1 GENEROUS QUART**

2 cups sugar

2 cups water

Juice of 2 lemons

1 large, ripe cantaloupe, seeded, peeled, and cut into small pieces (about 6 cups)

1 cup heavy cream

1 Bring the sugar, water, and lemon juice to a boil in a medium-size heavy saucepan. Remove from the heat and let the simple syrup cool.

2 Puree the melon in a food processor or blender. Pass the mixture through a fine-mesh strainer to remove any seeds and fibers. In a medium-size mixing bowl, mix the melon puree with the simple syrup and set aside. In a small bowl, combine 1 cup of the puree mixture with the cream; cover with plastic wrap and refrigerate.

3 Pour the reserved melon puree into an ice-cream maker and freeze according to the manufacturer's directions. When the ice cream is almost frozen, pour in the melon-and-cream mixture and continue freezing the ice cream. This two-step procedure will keep the color of the fruit from darkening.

Spiced Persimmon Ice Cream

The pale apricot color and spicy flavor of this ice cream earn it a place at your holiday table. Native persimmon pulp is readily available at grocery stores in Indiana or through mail order. The name "persimmon" (*Diospyros virginiana*) derives from an Algonquin word. The fruit was mentioned by Captain John Smith of Pocahontas fame in 1607. "When it is ripe," he noted, "it is as delicious as an apricot." You can also use Asian persimmon puree or canned pumpkin for this recipe. **MAKES 1 GENEROUS QUART**

¾ cup heavy cream

2 tablespoons buttermilk or sour cream

6 large eggs, beaten

⅔ cup sugar

2 cups milk

1 teaspoon ground coriander

1 teaspoon ground cinnamon

⅛ teaspoon freshly grated nutmeg

1 cup pureed persimmon pulp from 3 to 4 ripe Asian or native persimmons

1 teaspoon vanilla extract

1   In a small bowl or measuring cup, mix the cream and buttermilk together and set aside in a warm place to thicken for several hours or overnight.

2   With an electric mixer, beat the eggs and sugar together in a medium-size mixing bowl until the mixture turns pale yellow, about 5 minutes. Transfer to a medium-size heavy saucepan and stir in the milk and spices. Bring to a simmer and whisk the mixture constantly until it thickens enough to coat the back of a spoon, about 8 minutes. Whisk in the persimmon pulp and vanilla and set aside to cool.

3   When the custard has cooled, fold in the buttermilk mixture until well blended. Freeze in an ice-cream maker according to the manufacturer's directions.

Black Walnut and Honey Ice Cream

This is perfect for an apple pie à la mode with a country twist, using two of America's best-loved ingredients—black walnuts and regional or varietal honey. Even people like me, who don't swoon over black walnuts, love this ice cream—especially when served with Bourbon-Laced Sautéed Apples (page 53). Black walnuts are available in grocery stores in the Midwest and the South or through mail order. You can also make this recipe with common walnuts, which are called English walnuts.

MAKES ABOUT 1 QUART

¾ cup heavy cream

2 tablespoons buttermilk or sour cream

6 large eggs, beaten

⅔ cup wildflower, tupelo, or other amber honey

2 cups milk

1 cup black or English walnuts, finely chopped

1 teaspoon vanilla extract

1　In a small bowl or measuring cup, mix the heavy cream and buttermilk together and set aside in a warm place to thicken for several hours or overnight.

2　With an electric mixer, beat the eggs and honey together in a medium-size mixing bowl until the mixture turns golden, about 5 minutes. Transfer to a medium-size heavy saucepan and stir in the milk and walnuts. Bring to a simmer and whisk the mixture constantly until it thickens enough to coat the back of a spoon, about 8 minutes. Whisk in the vanilla and set aside to cool.

3　When the custard has cooled, fold in the buttermilk mixture until well blended. Freeze in an ice-cream maker according to the manufacturer's directions.

Sundaes Will Never Be the Same

Go to many ice-cream parlors today, and the sundae you get will be a dish of ice cream topped with a caramel or hot fudge sauce "fresh" out of a big can. You might get a squirt or two of imitation, pressurized whipped cream, a sprinkling of stale mixed nuts, which are mostly peanuts, and a lone maraschino cherry on top.

It wasn't always like that.

When the first ice-cream sundae arrived on the American scene in 1881, the 5-cent treat was served—on Sundays only, hence the name—at Ed Berners's ice-cream parlor in Two Rivers, Wisconsin. This ice-cream treat became so popular that it eventually spread across the country. By 1906, hot fudge sauce was invented and the hot fudge sundae, my personal favorite, was launched. During those years, the ice cream itself was a treat, made with real cream, sugar, vanilla, and other quality ingredients. Fillers, additives, extenders, and imitation flavorings became more common as ice cream left the environs of the parlor for the grocery store freezer.

To enjoy the best sundaes today, you can do one of two things. Frequent a family-owned ice-cream parlor known for their locally made ice cream and sauces. When I was growing up in Cincinnati, that meant Aglamesis's or Graeter's, still known for their outstanding ice-cream sundaes today. Or make your own. Although ice cream of any flavor can be used in a sundae, a good quality vanilla ice cream drizzled with homemade hot fudge or warm caramel is a match made in heaven.

To assemble ice-cream sundaes, place about a tablespoon of sauce in the bottom of each sundae glass. Top with a medium scoop of ice cream, then drizzle over more warm sauce and sprinkle with chopped toasted nuts (almonds, pecans, or peanuts, see page 181). Add a dollop of real whipped cream and a stemmed maraschino cherry. And dig right in!

Spiced Fig Ice Cream

Fig trees, transplanted to Atlantic barrier islands like Ocracoke off the shore of North Carolina and to the California wine country, love the heat. When fresh, figs have a juicy sweetness. Drying intensifies their flavor and gives them a little more body. Spiced fig recipes, from cakes to pies to ice creams, abound in the coastal South. This ice cream, made with homemade crème fraîche, is luscious. It was inspired by one in *Charleston Receipts*. **MAKES 1 GENEROUS QUART**

¾ cup heavy cream

2 tablespoons buttermilk or sour cream

6 large eggs, beaten

⅔ cup sugar

2 cups milk

½ teaspoon ground cinnamon

½ teaspoon ground ginger

⅛ teaspoon freshly grated nutmeg

Juice of 1 lemon

1 teaspoon vanilla extract

1 cup finely chopped dried figs

1   In a small bowl or measuring cup, mix the heavy cream and buttermilk together and set aside in a warm place to thicken for several hours or overnight.

2   In a medium-size mixing bowl with an electric mixer, beat the eggs and sugar together until the mixture turns pale yellow and falls in ribbons, about 5 minutes. Transfer to a medium-size heavy saucepan and stir in the milk and spices. Bring to a simmer and whisk the mixture constantly until it thickens enough to coat the back of a spoon, about 8 minutes.

3   Stir the lemon juice, vanilla, and dried figs into the custard and set aside to cool.

4   When the custard has cooled, fold in the buttermilk mixture until well blended. Freeze in an ice-cream maker according to the manufacturer's directions.

Medjool Date Ice Cream

Medjool dates, originally from Morocco, have been grown since the early 1900s around the town of Indio in southeastern California, an area 20 feet below sea level. Formerly a desert, this area was transformed into lush farmland after irrigation canals running from the Hoover Dam on the Colorado River provided the needed water. Date palms grow in harems, with one male able to pollinate up to 50 surrounding female palms. It takes 10 years for a date palm to first bear fruit, usually in April or May. By August, the dates are ripe. The best ones are picked soft (they are not allowed to cure on the tree) and are then frozen and sold throughout the year. As the market demands, the dates are thawed and shipped to grocery stores. In this recipe, the dates already provide a rich taste, so you can lower the fat content by using half-and-half instead of heavy cream. A drizzle of pomegranate molasses makes a lovely finishing touch; it is available at Middle Eastern and Asian markets. **MAKES 1 1/2 QUARTS**

6 large egg yolks

1/2 teaspoon salt

1 cup sugar

1 vanilla bean

5 cups half-and-half

1/4 teaspoon ground cardamom

4 ounces Medjool dates, pitted and snipped into 1/4-inch pieces

1   In the top of a double boiler over simmering water, whisk the egg yolks, salt, and sugar together until smooth. In a large heavy saucepan over medium-high heat, split and scrape the seeds of the vanilla bean into the half-and-half, add the vanilla bean pod, and bring the mixture to a boil. Whisking constantly, pour the half-and-half into the egg mixture and cook, stirring, until the mixture thickens enough to coat the back of a spoon, about 8 minutes. Remove from the heat and stir in the cardamom and dates. Set aside to cool to room temperature.

2   Freeze in an ice-cream maker according to the manufacturer's directions.

Cannoli Ice Cream

On special occasions, Sicilian families love cannoli—crispy pastry tubes filled with sweetened ricotta mixed with preserved fruits. In this recipe, the filling is transformed into an ice cream, which is delicious served in bowls or in homemade cannoli shells formed into tubes, cups, or funnel-shaped "cones." I am not fond of citron, so I use only candied red and green cherries and pineapple. Contemporary Italian families have added chocolate to the traditional recipe. Here it is complemented with cinnamon oil, which can be found at drug stores and in gourmet shops. This is a recipe that Kansas City chef and restaurateur J. J. Mirabile loves to make for special occasions.

MAKES 2 GENEROUS QUARTS

1 pound ricotta cheese

2 quarts good quality vanilla ice cream, softened

1 cup heavy cream

1/2 cup sugar

1/2 teaspoon vanilla extract

1 cup semisweet chocolate chips

2 drops cinnamon oil

1/2 cup mixed candied fruit, such as cherries and pineapple

1   Drain the ricotta in a cheesecloth-lined strainer for 30 minutes, pressing the cheese to release the liquid.

2   Put the softened ice cream in a large mixing bowl and fold in the drained cheese. Cover with plastic wrap and refrigerate while you complete the next step.

3   With an electric mixer, whip the cream in a medium-size mixing bowl until it holds soft peaks. Add the sugar and vanilla and beat until the cream holds stiff peaks.

4   Fold the whipped cream into the ice-cream mixture and stir in the chocolate chips, cinnamon oil, and candied fruit. Pack the ice cream into a container, cover, and freeze until firm, about 2 hours. Or, using a spoon, fill cannoli shells (see page 340, steps 4 and 5) with the ice cream and put the filled shells in the freezer for 30 minutes before serving.

Toffee-Banana Ice Cream

Bananas and plantains from the Caribbean islands often made their way to ports such as Charleston and Boston in the early nineteenth century. When New England clipper ships packed with missionaries and merchants went to the Hawaiian Islands in 1820, bananas and pineapples became even better known. The trouble was, if a clipper ship was becalmed for several days before reaching port, bananas could rot in the hold. When the clipper ships were replaced by steam ships, the banana enterprise became much more viable. After the transcontinental railway linked the West with the East Coast, bananas become increasingly available to American home cooks, who loved them. In this recipe, adapted from one in the 1933 edition of the *Home Comfort Cook Book* (from the Wrought Iron Range Company in St Louis), the brown sugar and lemon juice add complementary flavors of caramel and citrus, which really bring out the best in the banana. I like to add a few drops of yellow food coloring to make the ice cream a pale yellow, and accompany a scoop with a crisp spice cookie. **MAKES 1 GENEROUS QUART**

5 large ripe bananas, peeled and sliced (about 4 1/2 cups)

Juice of 1 lemon

1/2 cup packed dark brown sugar

2 cups heavy cream

Yellow food coloring (optional)

1   Arrange an oven rack in the bottom third of the oven. Preheat the oven to 350 degrees F. Put the bananas in a large shallow baking dish and toss with the lemon juice and brown sugar. Bake in the lower part of the oven until the banana slices are shriveled and the juices are brown, 25 to 30 minutes. Transfer the bananas and their cooking juices to a food processor and process until smooth. Cover with plastic wrap and chill for 1 hour.

2   Stir the cream into the banana puree, and add several drops of yellow food coloring, if desired. Pour the mixture into an ice-cream maker and freeze according to the manufacturer's directions.

Toasted Piñon and Caramel Ice Cream

Adapted from a recipe from Café Pasquale in Santa Fe, New Mexico, this rich ice cream needs to freeze hard before serving. Piñon, or pine nuts, native to the Southwest, are harvested from certain pine cones. Early native Americans who settled along the canyons and carved out homes in the stone bluffs harvested this wild bounty. Today pine nuts, like native hickory nuts and black walnuts, can be pricey because the nuts are difficult to remove from their outer covering. They are available in bulk at health food or deep discount stores. This is not a quick ice cream to make, but the voluptuous texture and spiced caramel flavor make it worthwhile for a special occasion. If you wish, you can gild the lily with hot fudge, caramel, or butterscotch sauce.

MAKES ABOUT 2 QUARTS

½ cup pine nuts

3 cups heavy cream

1 cup sugar

1¼ cups water

12 large egg yolks

2 teaspoons ground cinnamon

2 teaspoons vanilla extract

1   Preheat the oven to 250 degrees F. Spread the pine nuts on a baking sheet and toast, stirring occasionally, until they begin to turn golden, 8 to 10 minutes. Do not let them burn; remember, they will continue to cook as they cool. Remove from the oven and set aside.

2   With an electric mixer, beat the heavy cream in a large mixing bowl until it holds stiff peaks. Cover with plastic wrap and refrigerate.

3   In a small heavy saucepan, combine the sugar and water and heat over medium-high heat, stirring, until the sugar has dissolved. Continue to cook without stirring until the mixture turns deep amber and has caramelized, 20 to 25 minutes more.

4   While the sugar is caramelizing, with the mixer, beat the egg yolks, cinnamon, and vanilla together in another large mixing bowl until the mixture turns light yellow and has thickened, about 5 minutes. With the mixer on high speed, begin to beat the egg yolk mixture again. Wearing an oven mitt on the hand that holds the saucepan, slowly drizzle the hot caramel into the egg yolk mixture as you continue to beat it. Using an instant-read thermometer, make sure the temperature of the mixture reaches 160 degrees F to "cook" the eggs. (If you don't succeed, set the mixing bowl

over a pan of hot water and continue to whisk until the temperature reaches 160 degrees F.) Continue to beat until the mixture cools to room temperature and is as light and fluffy as whipped cream, about 10 minutes.

5   Remove the whipped cream from the refrigerator and gently fold the egg yolk mixture into the whipped cream, using a rubber spatula or large metal spoon. Fold in the toasted pine nuts.

6   Place the mixture in an ice-cream maker and freeze according to the manufacturer's directions. Cover and freeze for at least 8 hours before serving.

Ice Cream Sandwiches, Eskimo Pies, Klondike Bars, and the Good Humor Man

Go to the freezer section of the grocery store today and you will see boxes and boxes of ice cream novelties—ready-made ice cream cones, sandwiches, pops, bars, and individual cups. Novelties are big business; they first came on the American scene during the 1890s when New York City street vendors solved a tricky sanitation problem and started serving ice cream sandwiched between two thin cookies.

The Eskimo Pie, invented by Chris Nelson in Onawa, Iowa, in 1920, was first called the "I-Scream-Bar." Nelson had seen a young customer having trouble deciding between an ice cream sandwich and a chocolate bar. Nelson simply covered a small block or bar of vanilla ice cream in chocolate. Soon to follow was another famous chocolate-dipped ice cream bar.

The Klondike Bar must be from the frozen tundra of—Youngstown, Ohio? Yep, that's where it originated. In 1918, William Isaly opened Isaly's Dairy Store in Youngstown, and included his children, Chester, Charlie, Sam, Henry, Selma, and Josephine in the family business. In 1922, the Isaly family created the Klondike Bar— thick squares of vanilla ice cream hand-dipped in rich Swiss chocolate. Today, Klondike Bars can be found in most grocery store freezer sections, but Isaly's stores keep to their northern Ohio roots.

Which came first, the Good Humor Man or the Good Humor Bar? The bar, created in 1920 by Harry Burt, another Ohio entrepreneur who owned an ice-cream parlor and had already invented a lollipop known as the Jolly Boy Sucker. The smooth chocolate coating on the vanilla ice cream was delicious, but the Good Humor Bar was messy to eat. Young Harry Burt, Jr., came up with the solution—using extra wooden sticks from the Jolly Boy Suckers to turn the Good Humor Bar into a treat on a stick. When Burt senior sent out a fleet of 12 chauffeur-driven trucks with bells to sell the treats door to door, the Good Humor Man was born. Many kids growing up in suburbs recall the tinkling of those bells and the ensuing arguments with their mothers as to whether eating a Good Humor Bar would ruin their appetites for dinner. By 1976, direct selling was phased out in favor of increased grocery store presence and the Good Humor Man quietly faded away.

Caramelized Sour Cherry and Apricot Ice Cream

California apricots and Montmorency cherries from Michigan orchards baked with a little sugar and spice produce an ice cream the color of a lakeside sunset, with a flavor just as fabulous. This is based on a recipe by Larry Forgione of An American Place in New York City. **MAKES 1 GENEROUS QUART**

2 cups pitted fresh or frozen (thawed) sour cherries

6 small fresh apricots, pitted and sliced

1/2 cup sugar

1 1/2 teaspoons ground cinnamon

1/4 teaspoon ground ginger

1 tablespoon fresh lemon juice

2 cups heavy cream

1 teaspoon vanilla extract

1   Arrange an oven rack in the lower third of the oven. Preheat the oven to 350 degrees F. Scatter the fruits in a large shallow baking dish. Sprinkle with the sugar and spices and drizzle with the lemon juice. Bake in the lower part of the oven until the fruits have started to give off their juices and the sugar has caramelized, 10 to 15 minutes. Remove from the oven and let cool. Transfer the fruits and the caramelized sugar to a food processor and process until smooth. Stir in the heavy cream and vanilla.

2   Pour the mixture into an ice-cream maker and freeze according to the manufacturer's directions.

Chicago Fire Ice Cream

I first had this heady combination of creamy, spicy, tart, cool, yet fiery ice cream at an IACP gathering held at the Chicago Art Institute several years ago. The title of the recipe alludes to the legacy of the infamous Mrs. O'Leary's cow, which supposedly kicked over a lantern and started the calamitous Chicago Fire, which destroyed most of the city in 1871. While some ice creams are meant to complement another dessert, this one can stand alone (although a chocolate cookie is a worthy match). It is adapted from a Tabasco recipe. **MAKES ABOUT 1 QUART**

½ cup milk

1 medium-size cinnamon stick, plus extra for garnish

Zest of 1 medium-size orange, peeled in one strip (see Note), plus extra for garnish

4 cloves

2 cups heavy cream

2 teaspoons vanilla extract

One 14-ounce can sweetened condensed milk

1½ teaspoons Tabasco sauce

1 In a small heavy saucepan over medium heat, bring the milk, cinnamon stick, orange zest, and cloves to a boil. Reduce the heat to low, cover, and simmer for 5 minutes. Remove from the heat and set aside, covered, to cool.

2 With an electric mixer, whip the cream in a medium-size mixing bowl until it holds stiff peaks; set aside. Strain the cooled milk mixture into a large mixing bowl and whisk in the vanilla, condensed milk, and Tabasco. Fold in the whipped cream. Pour the mixture into an ice-cream maker and freeze according to the manufacturer's directions.

3 To serve, scoop the ice cream into glasses or dessert dishes and garnish each one with a cinnamon stick and orange zest twist.

NOTE To peel the orange in one strip, using a paring knife, start at the stem end of the orange and cut a ¼-inch-wide strip in a continuous circular motion.

Mexican Chocolate Ice Cream

The Latino population is one of the fastest growing in the United States today. In towns across the country, this ice cream is becoming a staple flavor. At Mexican grocers, you can buy packages of Mexican chocolate—a flavorful blend of chocolate, ground almonds, and cinnamon. My favorite is the Ibarra brand, which makes an incredible ice cream. If you can't find Mexican chocolate in your area, use a mixture of semisweet chocolate, ground cinnamon, and ground toasted almonds (see below). **MAKES 1½ QUARTS**

2 cups milk

1 vanilla bean, split lengthwise

8 large egg yolks

1 cup sugar

1 pound Mexican chocolate, grated, or a mixture of 12 ounces semisweet chocolate, grated, ¼ teaspoon ground cinnamon, and ⅓ cup ground toasted almonds (see page 181)

Grated chocolate and toasted sliced almonds for garnish

1   In the top of a double boiler over simmering water, scald the milk and vanilla bean until small bubbles form around the edge of the pan.

2   With an electric mixer, beat the egg yolks and sugar together in a medium-size mixing bowl until light yellow, about 5 to 7 minutes. Pour 1 cup of the hot milk into the egg mixture and whisk to blend, then pour the egg mixture into the top of the double boiler and whisk again to blend. Cook, whisking occasionally, until the mixture coats the back of a spoon, about 10 minutes.

3   Remove from the heat and pour the custard into a large stainless-steel mixing bowl. Mix in the Mexican chocolate or chocolate-cinnamon-almond mixture and stir until well blended. Sit the bowl in a larger bowl full of ice to chill the chocolate custard.

4   When the custard has chilled, remove the vanilla bean, pour the custard into an ice-cream maker, and freeze according to the manufacturer's directions.

5   To serve, scoop the ice cream into glasses or dessert dishes and garnish each one with grated chocolate and a sprinkling of toasted almonds.

Ice Cream Social

In many rural communities of the late 1800s and early 1900s, homemade hand-cranked ice cream heralded the beginning of summer. A block of ice from the farm's icehouse, or one delivered by the iceman in the city, was chopped into pieces and poured, along with rock salt, around the perimeter of the ice-cream freezer. Kids each took turns with the cranking until the cream mixture became so stiff that an adult had to take over. On a blazingly hot day, ice cream was eaten right then and there, with plenty of homemade pie.

In communities across America, ice-cream socials sponsored by churches, schools, and community organizations bring back this homemade tradition. Vanilla ice cream is still the hands-down favorite, but fresh strawberry or peach runs a close second. At festivals honoring a locally grown specialty, you'll find some great ice-cream flavors: pumpkin in Circleville, Ohio; native persimmon in Brown County, Indiana; tart red cherry in Traverse City, Michigan; cranberry in Warrens, Wisconsin; honey in Hamilton, Ohio; highbush blueberry in Montrose, Michigan; raspberry in Hopkins, Minnesota; huckleberry in Jay, Oklahoma; and chokecherry in Montana.

Because homemade ice cream lacks the preservatives and emulsifiers that keep the texture soft even after it has been frozen hard, it's best eaten quickly. But that's the whole point, isn't it?

White Chocolate Ice Cream

In the aftermath of the glitzy, big-hair, big-shoulders, Trump-dominated, more-is-better 1980s, chefs around the country became enamored of decadent white chocolate in cakes and cheesecakes, cookies, and ice creams like this one. Served at Stephan Pyles's former Routh Street Cafe in Dallas, this easy-to-make ice cream goes with almost anything—fresh strawberries or raspberries; hot fudge sauce; roasted pineapple; and fruit crisps, crumbles, pandowdies, slumps, grunts, buckles, and cobblers. **MAKES ABOUT 1 QUART**

¾ cup milk

10 ounces white chocolate, broken into small pieces

1 teaspoon vanilla extract

2 cups heavy cream at room temperature

1   In a small heavy saucepan over low heat, combine the milk and white chocolate and stir occasionally until the chocolate melts, about 7 minutes. Remove from the heat and set aside to cool to room temperature.

2   Stir in the vanilla, and then the cream. Pour the mixture through a fine-mesh strainer into an ice-cream maker and freeze according to the manufacturer's directions.

Chocolate Chip Cookie Dough Ice Cream

Ben Cohen and Jerry Greenfield met in seventh grade gym class and became fast friends. After college and several dead-end jobs, they decided to try their luck making ice cream in Burlington, Vermont. They bought a college textbook and paid $2.50 each for an ice cream–making correspondence course. Then they started making ice cream. They opened their first shop in a renovated gas station on May 5, 1978, and revolutionized American ice cream with "big chunks and lots and lots of them," according to Cohen. Cherry Garcia, Chunky Monkey, and Chocolate Chip Cookie Dough ice creams soon became household favorites. Chocolate Chip Cookie Dough ice cream can be hard to find now, so when you're in the mood, make your own. Be sure to use an egg substitute instead of raw eggs when you make the cookie dough, since it will not be baked. **MAKES 2 QUARTS OR A HALF-GALLON**

1 recipe Monticello Vanilla-Flecked Ice Cream (page 425) or 2 quarts good quality store-bought vanilla ice cream, softened

3 cups Classic Chocolate Chip Cookie dough (page 112), made with egg substitute

Spoon the softened ice cream into a large mixing bowl. Drop the cookie dough by teaspoonfuls into the ice cream. Fold with a rubber spatula until the cookie dough nuggets are dispersed through the ice cream. Cover and freeze until firm, about 3 hours.

OREO COOKIE CRUMBLE CREAM United Dairy Farmers in Cincinnati, Ohio, won a national taste contest with this ice cream flavor. Simply crumble enough Oreos or another cream-filled chocolate cookie to measure 3 cups. Substitute the cookie crumbs for the cookie dough and proceed with the recipe.

Almond Macaroon Ice Cream

Recipes are artifacts. Reading through old cookbooks is like taking a tour of an archaeological dig, only better. No bugs. No searing heat or pouring rain, but you still get glimpses of real life in the past. At a local antiques mall, I found a hardcover copy of *Good Things to Eat*, compiled and published in 1929 by the Pastors Aid Society of the Roanoke Presbyterian Church in Kansas City. Here you have a look at fare in Middle America right before the Depression hit. Lots of lemon pies; shortening instead of lard in pie crusts; cookies and homemade doughnuts; baked, boiled, and icebox puddings; and liberal use of the new convenience food—Knox gelatin. Prunes feature in whips, puddings, dessert loaves, and pies. There are no cheesecakes, but there is a recipe for "Plain Cake for Any Emergency." What kind of emergency that could be, I'm not sure, but I would guess it's of the dreaded "unexpected guests" variety.

When you are actually expecting guests, make this palest pink ice cream, adapted from *Good Things to Eat*, and serve it in Depression-glass sherbet cups. Amaretti (almond macaroon) crumbs thicken this ice cream instead of eggs.

MAKES 1 GENEROUS QUART

12 homemade (page 96) or store-bought amaretti

4 cups heavy cream

¾ cup sugar

1 teaspoon almond extract

¼ cup finely chopped maraschino cherries

2 tablespoons maraschino cherry syrup (from the jar)

1   Preheat the oven to 350 degrees F. Coat a baking sheet with nonstick cooking spray or line it with parchment paper and crumble the amaretti over the bottom. Dry in the oven for 10 to 15 minutes, but do not brown. Place the crumbled amaretti in a food processor and pulse until reduced to fine crumbs. Set aside.

2   In a large mixing bowl, whisk together the cream, sugar, almond extract, chopped cherries, and cherry syrup until well blended. Pour into an ice-cream maker and freeze according to the manufacturer's directions until the ice cream is partly frozen. Mix in the amaretti crumbs and continue to freeze until the ice cream is frozen.

Amaretti Apricot Ice Cream

Ice creams made with macaroons were popular in the United States from around 1920 to 1950. Lusciously easy, this classic Southern dessert harks back to a time when every household had a recipe for almond macaroons, which we now call amaretti.

MAKES 1 GENEROUS QUART

2 cups heavy cream

2 cups crumbs made from homemade (page 96) or store-bought amaretti (16 small or 12 large)

2 cups canned apricots with their syrup

¼ cup sugar

Juice of 1 lemon

1   With an electric mixer, whip the heavy cream in a large mixing bowl until it holds stiff peaks. Fold in the amaretti crumbs and let sit to soften slightly.

2   In a food processor, process the apricots with their syrup until smooth. Pass the puree through a fine-mesh strainer, then stir in the sugar and lemon juice. Fold the apricot puree into the whipped cream mixture.

3   Spoon the apricot cream into an ice-cream maker and freeze according to the manufacturer's directions.

Many families have stories of how they coped with economic hardship during the Great Depression, beginning with the stock market crash in the fall of 1929 and ending soon after the United States entered World War II in 1942. My out-of-work grandfather, Raymond Vanderhorst, used to wait until dark, then climb on top of slow-moving railroad coal cars near his home in Arlington Heights, Ohio. He rolled lumps of coal off the car and onto the gravel track bed below, then jumped off and hurried home with the fuel he couldn't afford to buy.

Like my grandfather, millions of other people were also out of work. Thousands of banks closed and the gross national product was almost cut in half. Despite the economic and social turmoil, the glass industry, amazingly, manufactured more glass than during any other period of American history.

The first company to make Depression glass was the Fostoria Glass Company of Fostoria, Ohio. Other Midwestern glass companies—The Fenton Art Glass Company in Martins Ferry, Ohio; A.H. Heisey Glass Company in Newark, Ohio; Hocking Glass Company in Lancaster, Ohio; and Indiana Glass Company in Dunkirk, Indiana—soon took advantage of Fostoria Glass's popularity, and made their own, less expensive versions. Other companies in the Glass Belt—the border area of Ohio, West Virginia, and Pennsylvania—followed suit. Unlike the handblown or cut glass prevalent until then, this new type of glass was produced by "tank molding." Soda ash, silica sand, and limestone were first heated together and then passed into pressing molds, where the mixture cooled to form the various glassware pieces.

More than 200 patterns such as "American Pioneer," "Princess," "Sunflower," "Tea Room," "Pretzel," "Cloverleaf," and "Petal Swirl" were often acid-etched or carved directly into these pressing molds. The clear, pastel-tinged colors so characteristic of this type of glass—pink, green, blue, amber, and yellow—were created by the addition of metallic elements such as manganese, copper, cobalt, and chromium, as well as nonmetallic agents like sulfur, tellurium, and phosphorus.

During this time, when a dark cloud seemed to hover over the country, the silver lining, actually pastel, seemed to be inexpensive Depression glass, which almost anyone could afford. If you could pay for a box of oatmeal or a tank of gas, you would receive a piece of Depression glass as a free premium. That's how my grandmother acquired a small collection, which I now treasure. As a child, I remember sipping lemonade from the footed, V-shaped green glasses and the ice clinking in the tall green pitcher etched with a winged design.

Today, Depression-glass pieces are mixed with white or floral patterned china, lacy napkins, and silver. Their softer, summery look is perfect for serving desserts. I like to pour iced Summertime Almond Tea (page 493) or Lavender Lemonade (page 497) from the pastel green pitcher and pass a selection of homemade cookies on the handled sandwich plate. A piece of the fancy cake I've spent the morning making shows off well on a Depression-glass dessert plate or cake stand. And scoops of homemade ice cream seem to taste best in a lime-green sherbet glass.

Toasted Hazelnut Ice Cream

I first had this drizzled with a deep and rich hot fudge sauce at a luncheon celebrating the guest of honor—Julia Child. I was so excited to be there that I could hardly eat, but this ice cream was too good to pass up. Although hazelnuts grow wild over much of the Heartland, it is in the rainy, temperate climate of the Pacific Northwest that this wonderfully aromatic nut grows best. Buy the freshest hazelnuts you can find. You will also need hazelnut butter, available in health food stores, or Nutella, a chocolate and hazelnut spread sold in most supermarkets. Serve this with Classic Hot Fudge Sauce (see page 427) for true decadence. If you like an ice cream with a smoother texture, sieve the custard and reserve the chopped hazelnuts for a cheesecake.

MAKES ABOUT 1¹/₂ QUARTS

1 scant cup shelled hazelnuts (about 4 ounces)

1 cup milk

2 large eggs

³/₄ cup sugar

2¹/₂ cups heavy cream

1 cup hazelnut butter or Nutella

1 teaspoon vanilla extract

1   Preheat the oven to 350 degrees F. Spread the hazelnuts on a baking sheet and toast until golden brown and fragrant, about 15 minutes. Immediately wrap the hot nuts in kitchen towels and rub vigorously to remove the skins. Set aside to cool slightly. Using a nut grinder or pulsing a food processor, finely grind the nuts.

2   In a medium-size heavy saucepan, heat the milk and hazelnuts together until the mixture begins to steam, but before it simmers, about 5 minutes. In a medium-size mixing bowl, whisk the eggs and sugar together until a light lemon color, about 2 minutes. Whisk in the hot milk mixture, then return the mixture to the saucepan. Cook over medium heat, whisking constantly, until the custard is thick enough to coat the back of a wooden spoon, about 8 minutes. Transfer the custard to a large stainless-steel bowl and let cool slightly, then refrigerate until the custard has chilled, about 1 hour.

3   When the custard has chilled, whisk in the cream, hazelnut butter, and vanilla. Pour into an ice-cream maker and freeze according to the manufacturer's directions.

Lemony Blackberry Crumble Ice Cream

Every time I serve my Lemony Rhubarb Crumble Ice Cream from *Prairie Home Cooking*, people ooh and aah. So I thought I would substitute blackberries for the rhubarb and see if the ice cream is equally delicious. It is! This version includes a lemon-zested streusel, which adds little crunchy bits to the smooth creaminess of the ice cream itself. Blackberries are very all-American, whether garden raised or picked from the wild. Baked with a little sugar, they take on a slight caramelized flavor. It all comes together in this fabulous, reddish purple ice cream. **MAKES 1 GENEROUS QUART**

CRUMBLE

¼ cup all-purpose flour

1 teaspoon grated lemon zest

¼ cup sugar

2 tablespoons unsalted butter at room temperature

ICE CREAM

4 cups fresh or frozen (thawed) blackberries

1 cup sugar

1 tablespoon fresh lemon juice

2 cups heavy cream

1   Arrange a rack in the middle of the oven and another in the bottom third. Preheat the oven to 350 degrees F. To make the crumble, in a small bowl, whisk together the flour, lemon zest, and sugar. Using your fingers, rub the butter into the flour mixture to form large crumbs. Sprinkle them in a baking dish and bake in the middle of the oven until they begin to brown, 7 to 10 minutes. Set aside to cool, but keep the oven on.

2   To make the ice cream, scatter the berries in a large, shallow baking dish. Sprinkle with the sugar and drizzle with the lemon juice. Bake in the lower part of the oven until the berries start to give off their juice, 15 to 20 minutes. Remove from the oven and let cool. Transfer the berries to a food processor and process until smooth.

3   Before finishing the ice cream, use your hands to break up the cooled crumble into small, pea-sized pieces (if they're too big, the pieces are difficult to eat in the ice cream; if they're too small, they disappear). Next, stir the heavy cream into the berry puree, pour into an ice-cream maker and freeze until it has the consistency of softly whipped cream. Then quickly stir in the crumble pieces and finish freezing the ice cream.

Soft Vanilla Ice Cream

Soft-serve ice cream—ice cream that is extruded or spooned out rather than scooped—debuted in 1938, when J. F. McCullough developed a soft vanilla ice cream in Green River, Illinois. Because it does not include heavy cream or full-fat milk, soft-serve is less expensive than regular ice cream, making it even more democratic. Today, the smallest American hamlet probably has a soft-serve ice cream stand, which may also serve burgers and fries or chicken strips in a basket. Whether it's Dairy Queen, Creamy Whip, or Tastee-Freeze, it becomes a community gathering spot on summer nights, when the line snakes out the door or away from the take-out windows outside. This is a version you can make at home, in air-conditioned but community-less comfort. **MAKES ABOUT 1 QUART**

2 cups 2-percent milk	One 14-ounce can condensed milk
2 large egg yolks, lightly beaten	1 tablespoon plus 1 teaspoon vanilla extract

1 Bring the 2 percent milk to a simmer in a medium-size heavy saucepan. In a medium-size heat-proof mixing bowl, slowly beat the hot milk into the egg yolks. Return the entire mixture to the pan and place over low heat. Whisk constantly until the custard thickens enough to coat the back of a spoon, about 10 minutes.

2 Remove the custard from the heat and pour it through a fine-mesh strainer into a large, clean stainless steel bowl (so that it cools faster). Allow the custard to cool slightly, then whisk in the condensed milk and vanilla. Cover and refrigerate until cold, for several hours or overnight.

3 Stir the chilled mixture, then pour into an ice-cream maker and freeze according to the manufacturer's directions.

Fudgy Ice-Cream Torte

Glamorous ice-cream tortes made with cookie crumb or nut crusts, designer ice-cream sauces, crumbled candy bars, and ice cream in every imaginable flavor made a big splash on casual restaurant menus in the late 1980s and early 1990s. These no-bake desserts are just as easy for the home cook to make, and the variations are endless. **MAKES 12 TO 14 SERVINGS**

2 cups crumbs made from Oreos or other cream-filled chocolate cookies (about 24)

1/4 cup (1/2 stick) unsalted butter, melted

1 cup heavy cream

2 quarts vanilla, coffee, chocolate chip, or fudge ripple ice cream, softened

1 recipe Classic Hot Fudge Sauce (see page 427) at room temperature or one 12-ounce jar hot fudge sauce

2 cups crushed salted dry-roasted peanuts

1 Combine the cookie crumbs and melted butter well in a small mixing bowl. Press three quarters of the mixture into the bottom of a 9 x 13-inch baking pan. Reserve the remaining for the topping. With an electric mixer, whip the cream until it holds stiff peaks; set aside.

2 Spread the softened ice cream evenly over the crust with a rubber spatula, dipping it periodically into hot water. Spread the hot fudge sauce over the ice cream, then sprinkle with the peanuts. Spread the whipped cream over the peanuts and sprinkle with the reserved cookie crumb mixture.

3 Cover the torte with plastic wrap and freeze for at least 4 hours, or overnight. When ready to serve, let the torte thaw out for 15 minutes before cutting.

Pig Stands, Big Boys, and Dairy Queens

In 1920, there were 8 million automobiles on American roadways, and the number was increasing every year by over a million. The automobile radically changed the pattern of American life. Entrepreneurs who could foresee the opportunities that a freer, more mobile society would bring made a fortune.

J. G. Kirby, a candy and tobacco wholesaler in Dallas, was struck by the wisdom of his own sarcastic comment: "People with cars are so lazy they don't want to get out of them to go eat." Bingo. With financing from a local physician, Kirby designed and opened the first circular Pig Stand in 1921, serving barbecued pork sandwiches and banana pudding to people sitting in their cars. By the early 1930s, there were 60 Pig Stands in Texas and 6 other states.

In 1922, Roy Allen and Frank Wright opened 3 walk-up A & W root beer stands in Houston; there the root beer float was born. In 1934, A. H. "Gus" Belt started the Steak 'n' Shake chain in Normal, Illinois. In 1936, Robert C. Wian opened his 10-stool restaurant in Glendale, California, which would eventually become the first of Bob's Big Boy drive-ins.

In 1938, J. F. McCullough developed a soft ice cream in Green River, Illinois. This new confection was test marketed that summer during an all-you-can-eat-for-10-cents promotion at a store in Kankakee, Illinois. Over 1,600 servings were sold in 2 hours. McCullough called his dairy product "Dairy Queen," and the first franchise was launched in June 1940.

During World War II, drive-ins held on despite rationing, which impacted both food and auto supplies. When the war was over, however, business exploded. Five years after the war ended, there were 40 million cars. Many were owned by the millions of young families buying houses in new suburbs and getting around by car.

Candy Bar Ice-Cream Pie

During the late 1970s and early 1980s, boutique ice-cream parlors began to spring up in suburban shopping malls, offering ice cream custom mixed with your choice of crumbled candy bars, cookies, dried fruit, individual fruit gum candies, or chocolate chips. Soon, soft-serve ice cream emporiums developed ice-cream shakes with candy bar pieces mixed in, and casual restaurants began serving candy bar–ice cream pies.

These are easy to make at home—you just assemble all the parts—and they are great for entertaining because you can make an ice-cream pie a day or 2 ahead of time.

MAKES ONE 9-INCH PIE

1 recipe Crumb Crust (see page 249) made from Chocolate Shortbread Cookies (page 128) or Oreos, patted over the bottom and up the sides of a 9-inch pie pan, or a store-bought crumb crust

2 pints ice cream, any flavor, at room temperature

Two 1½-ounce candy bars of your choice, chopped into small pieces

1 recipe Caramel Sauce (recipe follows) or store-bought caramel sauce

1 recipe Classic Hot Fudge Sauce (see page 427) or store-bought hot fudge sauce

1   If you are making the crumb crust, preheat the oven to 350 degrees F. Bake the crust for 5 minutes and let cool completely. (Skip this step if using a store-bought crust.)

2   Spoon 1 pint of the softened ice cream into the prepared crust and smooth with a rubber spatula, dipping it once or twice into hot water. Sprinkle the ice cream with the candy bar pieces and press them into the ice cream with the spatula. Spoon the remaining pint of ice cream over the candy bar filling and smooth with the spatula so that the ice cream layer mounds in the middle. Cover with plastic wrap and freeze until ready to serve.

3   To serve, remove the ice-cream pie from the freezer and let soften for about 30 minutes before cutting. Serve each slice in a pool of caramel sauce and drizzle the top with the hot fudge sauce.

How to Soften Ice Cream

Ice cream is easiest to scoop out when it has just started to soften. If you take it out of the freezer to thaw at room temperature and then forget about it, you could have a goopy mess. If you take it out right before serving, it's likely to be rock hard and difficult to scoop.

Use your microwave on the lowest or THAW setting to soften ice cream quickly. Soften each pint just until the ice cream begins to separate from the perimeter of the container. In my microwave, this takes about 1 minute.

Caramel Sauce

This is a rich, luscious sauce to drizzle over ice cream, individual apple tarts, pound cake, fresh fruit, or to use in Caramel Cream Frosting for Caramel Apple Cream Cake (page 173) or in White Chocolate Caramel Ganache (see variation, page 214). **MAKES 2 CUPS**

1 cup sugar

¾ cup water

1 teaspoon vanilla extract

1 cup heavy cream or evaporated milk (evaporated low-fat or skim works well)

1 Combine the sugar, water, and vanilla in a medium-size heavy saucepan. Stir over low heat to dissolve the sugar, then increase the heat to medium-high and bring to a boil. Without stirring, keep a careful watch on the mixture until it begins to turn golden, 15 to 18 minutes. Remove from the heat.

2 While the sugar mixture is cooking, heat the cream in a small saucepan over low heat and keep warm. When the caramel reaches a golden brown, remove from the heat immediately so it does not darken and become bitter. With heavy-duty oven mitts on each hand, pour in the warm cream and whisk to blend. (The hot caramel may splatter a bit as you do this.) If the caramel seizes up in the cream, simply return the sauce to the heat and whisk until blended. Serve warm, cold, or at room temperature. Keeps, covered, up to 2 weeks in the refrigerator.

Tart Red Cherry Sorbet

The lake effect helps fruit trees along the Great Lakes bear delicious crops each year. Festivals in Michigan and Wisconsin celebrate the tart red cherry season during late June. Even as far west as Newton, Kansas, you'll find tart red cherry trees in Mennonite farm gardens, their fruit destined for sour cherry mooss, a cold fruit dessert soup (see *Prairie Home Cooking*, page 380). At farmers' markets in Kansas City, I can buy bags of frozen tart red cherries for recipes like this, adapted from one by Harlan "Pete" Peterson of Tapawingo, a restaurant in Ellsworth, Michigan. **MAKES 1 GENEROUS QUART**

4 cups pitted fresh or frozen (thawed) tart red cherries (do not use sweet cherries)

½ cup sugar

1 cup dry white wine

Juice of ½ lemon

1   Put the cherries in a food processor and process until smooth. Set aside.

2   Combine the sugar and wine in a medium-size saucepan and bring to a boil, then set aside to cool. Stir in the cherry puree and lemon juice.

3   Transfer the mixture to an ice-cream maker and freeze according to the manufacturer's directions.

Gunflint Lodge Blueberry and Orange Sorbet

Rustic Gunflint Lodge, located at the edge of Minnesota's famed Boundary Waters Canoe Wilderness Area, is also known for its sophisticated regional cuisine. When Bruce and Sue Kerfoot's guests aren't canoeing, hunting, fishing, hiking, cross-country skiing, snowshoeing, or dog sledding, they are probably enjoying themselves in the dining room. The challenge for Chef Ron Berg is to create 4-star meals when the nearest "town"—Grand Marais—is 43 miles away. He excels at using local ingredients such as wild rice, walleye pike, duck, venison, and salmon in his entrees, and local produce and wild berries in the desserts. Each night, his meals are accompanied by a different sorbet, and this is one of the best. **MAKES 2 QUARTS**

4 cups water

2 cups sugar

4 cups fresh or frozen (thawed) blueberries, picked over for stems

Juice of 3 lemons

4 cups orange juice

¼ cup Triple Sec or other orange-flavored liqueur

1   In a large heavy saucepan, bring the water, sugar, and blueberries to a boil and continue boiling for 5 minutes. Pass the mixture through a fine-mesh strainer into a large mixing bowl, pressing down hard on the blueberries to get as much juice as possible. Set aside to cool and discard the solids in the strainer.

2   Stir the lemon juice, orange juice, and Triple Sec into the blueberry puree. Transfer to an ice-cream maker and freeze according to the manufacturer's instructions.

Shaker Coffee Ice

We might think that boutique ice cream and coffee are relatively new, but they're not. I was surprised to find this nineteenth-century coffee ice cream recipe from North Union Shaker Village in what was to become Cleveland, Ohio. It takes very little adaptation to fit well into the millennium kitchen. Halfway between a smooth ice cream and a sorbet or granita, but with more pronounced ice crystals, this coffee ice is, as the original recipe states, "very refreshing," and delicious accompanied by a chocolate or spice cookie. **MAKES ABOUT 2 QUARTS**

4 cups freshly brewed dark roast coffee, such as
   French roast or espresso, cooled
1 cup heavy cream

2 cups milk
¼ cup sugar

Whisk all the ingredients together in a large mixing bowl. Transfer to an ice-cream maker and freeze according to the manufacturer's directions.

Meyer Lemon Ice

Wherever Italian immigrants settled in America, especially those from Sicily, you could be sure there were granitas and gelatos of all kinds. From the North End of Boston to the Hill in St. Louis and North Beach in San Francisco, a different kind of ice-cream parlor enlarged the scope of traditional American ice cream and fruit ice. This refreshing Meyer lemon ice, or granita, is made with a lemon syrup, resulting in a wonderfully slushy texture and a gentle lemon taste. **MAKES ABOUT 1 QUART**

1 cup sugar

4 cups water

1 tablespoon grated Meyer lemon zest or 2
  teaspoons regular lemon zest

⅔ cup fresh Meyer lemon juice or ½ cup regular
  lemon juice

¼ teaspoon salt

1 In a large heavy saucepan over medium-high heat, stir together the sugar and water until the sugar dissolves. Bring to a boil, then remove from the heat. Stir in the lemon zest and juice and salt. Let cool to room temperature.

2 Transfer the mixture to an ice-cream maker and freeze according to the manufacturer's directions.

Lemon Water Ice

Water ice" is a nineteenth-century term for a sorbet or fruit ice. Tarter and more lemony than the Meyer Lemon Ice (page 456), most of the lemon flavor in this ice comes from the oils in the rind. In most other dessert recipes, you would grate the zest to release the oils. The technique here is to rub sugar cubes over the rind to trap the flavorful oils in the sugar, giving this water ice an intense lemon flavor without the added texture of zest. **MAKES 1½ QUARTS**

1½ cups superfine sugar

4 cups water

1 cup sugar cubes

12 lemons, washed and patted dry

1 In a medium-size saucepan, combine the superfine sugar and water over medium heat, stirring until the sugar dissolves. Bring to a boil and continue boiling until the syrup has reduced by a third, about 20 minutes. Remove from the heat and set aside.

2 Rub each sugar cube over a lemon so that they are all scented with lemon oil. Put the cubes in the syrup. Halve the lemons and juice them through a strainer held over the syrup. Mix well, stirring until the sugar cubes have all dissolved.

3 Transfer the mixture to an ice-cream maker and freeze according to the manufacturer's directions.

Citrus

As a result of the growing West Indies trade during the late 1600s and early 1700s, port cities in the American colonies received shipments of citrus fruits in time for the Christmas holidays and the winter months. Some wealthy plantation owners, such as Charles and Margaret Tilghman Carroll of Maryland, built greenhouses or orangeries to grow their own supply of citrus fruits. Lemon juice began to replace vinegar and verjus (the sour juice of unripe grapes) to sharpen flavors in both sweet and savory dishes. A recipe for lemon tea cakes in Eliza Smith's *The Compleat Housewife*, published in 1742, and recipes for "lemon cheese" (lemon curd) from Pennsylvania cooks are indicative of how lemons were used in dessert cookery early on.

In 1804, Franciscan monks planted the first sizable orange grove at the San Gabriel Mission, east of what today is Los Angeles. During the 1800s, more California groves were established. When the transcontinental railway system was completed in 1869, citrus fruit from California could be shipped all over the country. In 1873, the first navel oranges were grown in a Riverside, California, backyard from seedlings sent by an American Presbyterian missionary living in Brazil. Today, we prize Valencia oranges for their juice and navel oranges for peeling and eating. Cooks also look for unique varieties of citrus fruits, such as Meyer lemons, blood oranges, and kumquats.

Blood Orange Water Ice

Amerian dessert chefs love to serve a trio of lozenge-shaped portions of their homemade ice creams and sorbets, especially those made from American fruits. So when blood oranges are in season during the winter months and available at my local market, I love to make this tart and dramatic dark orange and red ice as a foil for a richer, buttery cake or cookie. For high-style presentation, use 2 large soup or serving spoons to shape the water ice into *quenelles*, or lozenge-shaped servings, and place them alongside an individual charlotte or custard or a slice of pound cake.

MAKES 1¹/₂ QUARTS

1¹/₂ cups superfine sugar

4 cups water

1 cup sugar cubes

10 blood oranges, washed and patted dry

Juice of 1 or 2 lemons, to your taste

1   In a medium-size saucepan, combine the superfine sugar and water over medium heat, stirring until the sugar dissolves. Bring to a boil and continue boiling until the syrup has reduced by a third, about 20 minutes.

2   Meanwhile, rub each sugar cube over a blood orange so that they are all scented with orange oil. Place the cubes in the hot syrup and stir to dissolve. Halve the oranges and juice them through a strainer held over the syrup, mixing well. Taste, then stir in enough lemon juice to give a tart flavor. This granita tastes sweeter when it's frozen.

3   Transfer the mixture to an ice-cream maker and freeze according to the manufacturer's directions.

Watermelon Ice

Native to the Kalahari Desert in Africa, where they were a prized source of water, watermelons have an ancient past. The first recorded watermelon harvest happened 5,000 years ago, and the fruit appears in hieroglyphics on the walls of the pyramids. Pharoahs and other royalty started their journeys to the Other World with watermelon as one of the ceremonial foods. Much later, African slaves brought watermelon seeds to the United States. The first mention of watermelon in American gardens was in 1629 in Charleston, South Carolina. We have been in love with it ever since. "When one has tasted watermelons, one knows what angels eat," Mark Twain once wrote. "It was not a Southern watermelon that Eve took; we know it because she repented." As simply delicious as a wide slice of crisp, cold, juicy watermelon on a hot summer night, this slushy ice comes close to capturing the taste, without the seeds. Serve with a crisp spice cookie. **MAKES ABOUT 1 QUART**

2 cups sugar

2 cups water

Juice of 2 lemons

1 small, ripe watermelon, flesh cut from the rind, seeded, and cut into small pieces (about 6 cups)

1   Bring the sugar, water, and lemon juice to a boil in a medium-size heavy saucepan. Remove from the heat and let the simple syrup cool.

2   Puree the watermelon in a food processor or blender. Pass the mixture through a fine-mesh strainer into a large mixing bowl to remove any stray seeds or fibers. Add it to the simple syrup and stir until well blended.

3   Transfer the mixture to an ice-cream maker and freeze according to the manufacturer's directions.

Summery Apricot Ice

I'm always tempted to buy fresh apricots, and I'm always sorry. Grocery store apricots look good, but they just don't have any flavor. Why? For one thing, grocery store buyers favor varieties like Tilton, Castelbrite, and Patterson, which are more prolific and sturdier to ship. These apricots are also picked before they're ripe. To my mind, they don't improve much afterwards. If you can find tree-ripened Blenheim apricots (see Sources), then you're in for a treat, and you can make this ice with fresh fruit. If you can't find Blenheims, then use dried. First grown in America along the southeastern seaboard, apricots today are grown commercially in California. What I love about this sorbet-like ice is that you can make it at any time, it's low in fat, and it has a lovely color when made with fresh apricots. **MAKES ABOUT 2 QUARTS**

1 pound fresh or unsulfured dried apricots
2 cups water
1 cup sugar

¾ cup fresh lemon juice
Three 5.5-ounce cans apricot nectar (about 2¼ cups)

1   Bring the apricots, water, and sugar to a boil in a large heavy saucepan over medium-high heat. Stir to dissolve the sugar, then reduce the heat to medium-low and simmer until the apricots have softened and most of the liquid has evaporated, about 15 minutes. Stir in the lemon juice and set aside to cool. If you are using fresh apricots, press them through a strainer or food mill to remove the skins and pits.

2   Place the apricot mixture in a food processor and process until smooth. Transfer the puree to a bowl and stir in the apricot nectar.

3   Transfer the mixture to an ice-cream maker and freeze according to the manufacturer's directions.

Fresh Peach Sherbet

There's nothing like a Georgia peach, so fresh and ripe that the juice runs down your arm when you take a bite. Peach season in Georgia runs from the middle of May through August, as different varieties ripen and are picked by hand. But this sherbet tastes wonderful whether your peaches come from Georgia or Ohio or California. Low in fat and luscious in color, this is a great summer dessert. **MAKES 1 GENEROUS QUART**

2 cups peeled, pitted, and sliced ripe peaches (about 5 or 6 peaches)

1 cup sugar

¼ cup fresh lemon juice

¼ teaspoon salt

1½ cups orange juice

1   In a blender or food processor, process the peaches, sugar, lemon juice, salt, and orange juice until smooth.

2   Transfer the mixture to an ice-cream maker and freeze according to the manufacturer's directions.

A World of Ice Cream in America

Americans have eagerly welcomed a variety of ice creams and fruit ices over the years, as European immigrants brought their own unique styles and savvy inventors created new ones.

★ *Frozen yogurt:* A frozen confection made with yogurt as its base, with flavorings that vary from coffee and vanilla to chocolate, fruits, and spices.

★ *Gelato:* Italian-style ice cream, usually deeply colored and vibrantly flavored.

★ *Glace:* French-style ice cream with an icy texture.

★ *Granita:* A coarsely textured, more granular Italian ice made in a flat pan rather than in an ice-cream freezer. The mixture is stirred only occasionally as it freezes to get the desired texture.

★ *Ice cream:* Cream and flavorings or a cream-based custard, frozen in an ice-cream maker for a smooth texture. Ice cream can take on any number of flavorings, from fruit to coffee to spices and even vegetables!

★ *Ice, fruit ice, and water ice:* Frozen confections made with fresh fruit, a simple syrup, and perhaps a squeeze of lemon juice, processed in an ice-cream maker or sorbetier for a smooth texture.

★ *Sherbet:* A fruit-based confection that might also contain egg white or fruit juice to give it a softer texture and more opaque appearance.

★ *Soft-serve ice cream:* Ice cream with a lower butterfat content and a softer texture than regular ice cream. Too soft to scoop, this ice cream is usually extruded from special machines into a cone or bowl.

★ *Sorbet, sorbetto:* The French and Italian words for a smooth fruit ice.

Frozen Lemonade Pops

There's only one thing better than a cold lemonade on a hot day—and that's a frozen lemonade pop! Plastic pop molds are available, in season, at grocery and discount stores. **MAKES 12 POPS**

2 cups boiling water

Juice of 4 lemons

1 cup sugar, or to taste

2 cups cold water

1   Pour the boiling water into a large heat-proof bowl or pitcher. Stir in the lemon juice and sugar. Taste, then add more sugar if necessary. Stir in the cold water.

2   Ladle the mixture into frozen pop molds and freeze for at least 4 hours.

Fresh Pineapple Sorbet with Honey Sabayon and Candied Rose Petals

Alice Waters's Chez Panisse in Berkley, California, has been a groundbreaking restaurant since it first opened in 1971. A former Montessori teacher, Waters lived and traveled in France, a formative experience. "At the age of nineteen I went eating in France—the best description of my year of study abroad," she writes in the introduction to the *Chez Panisse Menu Cookbook*. When she returned to California, her mission was clear: "Doing the very best we could do with French recipes and California ingredients." She adds, "My one unbreakable rule has always been to use only the freshest and finest ingredients available." Chez Panisse's early desserts were simple and delicious—homemade ice creams, fresh fruits and regional cheeses, fresh cherries and almond cookies, raspberries and crème fraîche. This recipe, adapted from one served at Chez Panisse, is in that tradition. Use only the very freshest, ripest pineapple. **MAKES 1 GENEROUS QUART**

PINEAPPLE SORBET

1 large, very ripe pineapple, peeled, cored, and cut into pieces

⅔ cup sugar

Juice of ½ lemon

HONEY SABAYON

3 large egg yolks

1/2 cup orange blossom, clover honey, or any light-colored varietal honey

Juice of 1/2 lemon

Homemade (see page 177) or bottled candied rose petals

1   To make the sorbet, puree the pineapple in a food processor. Measure out 4 cups of puree and discard the rest. Place 1 cup of puree in a medium-size heavy saucepan and mix with the sugar over low heat until the sugar dissolves. Remove from the heat and stir in the remaining 3 cups of puree and the lemon juice. Transfer to an ice-cream maker and freeze according to the manufacturer's directions. The sorbet can be made 1 day ahead and kept in a container in the freezer.

2   Make the sabayon right before serving: In the top of a double boiler set over simmering water, whisk together the egg yolks, honey, and lemon juice, using an up-and-down motion to beat air into the mixture. Keep whisking until the egg mixture has increased in volume to become a fluffy cream, about 5 minutes.

3   To serve, arrange the candied rose petals on dessert plates. Place 1 or 2 scoops of the sorbet in the center of the petals and spoon the sabayon over the sorbet.

How the Epperson Kids Named the Popsicle

In the winter of 1923, on a very cold night in New Jersey, Frank Epperson was showing friends how he could make instant lemonade from a powdered mix, instead of laboriously squeezing real lemons and mixing the juice with sugar and water. He stirred the mix and water together with a spoon, then gave his friends a sip. They were impressed.

But Epperson was a little absent-minded. He left the glass of lemonade, with the spoon still in it, on a windowsill. After his friends left, he went to bed. This was in the days before efficient central heating and storm windows, and the next morning, the lemonade was frozen solid, with the spoon standing up straight in the glass. After the room had warmed a little, Frank took the handle of the spoon and pulled the frozen cylinder of lemonade out of the glass. He licked it. He liked it. And the frozen pop was born.

A year later, in 1924, Epperson had a patent on the "Epsicle," as he first called his frozen treat. But his kids called it "Pop's sicle." The name stuck.

During the next 14 years, Epperson also invented the Fudgsicle, a chocolate ice bar on a stick; the twin Popsicle, popular during the Depression because two kids could share it; and the Creamsicle, a bar of vanilla ice cream coated with orange sherbet.

By 1938, kids all over America were listening to 15-minute weekly adventures of "Popeye" on radio, 25 of which were sponsored by Popsicle/Fudgsicle/Creamsicle. Kids who saved sticky Popsicle wrappers could exchange them for a Popeye pipe toss game, a bubble pipe set, a harmonica, Popeye figurines, or other "hot" toys at designated retailers.

sugar

When Captain John Smith's adventurers, the Pilgrims, and then the Puritans, established colonies in the New World by 1630, their idea of candy included sugarplums, which were whole fruits preserved in sugar syrup; sweetmeats, such as

quince juice cooked with sugar to a paste; and candied peel from oranges and lemons. Chocolate was for drinking only. There were "wet suckets," or candied fruit pieces that were kept in their syrup, and "dry suckets," such as *marrons glaces*, or candied chestnuts. All of these were the exclusive preserve of the wealthy. Both the sugar and the fruits were too expensive for lower class households. Candy was a luxury and was usually served as part of a decorative tableau for a multicourse meal.

Early American colonists learned to like maple sugar, which only required some know-how and patience to produce. After maple trees were tapped in the spring,

The American Sweet Tooth Candy and Flavored Syrups

maple syrup could be boiled down and dried and crystallized into maple sugar.

The term "candy," from the French word *candir*, which means to preserve by cooking with sugar, didn't come into American usage until the eighteenth century. Tall cones of sugar wrapped in paper, available at that time, were again the province of wealthy households. Southern plantations often had a piece of wooden furniture known as a sugar chest for locking the precious sugar away for safekeeping. Sturdy metal sugar nippers were used to cut off pieces of the sugar cone, to be used in cooking or candying. Early recipes often included instructions for skimming the sugar as it cooked, as it was sometimes full of impurities.

Candy makers often used barley sugar, which was cheaper than cane sugar, until the early nineteenth century. Barley sugar candy, made by professional confectioners in metal molds, has been an American favorite for over 300 years. Candy makers of Dutch or German descent produced marzipan from almonds and sugar, which William Woys Weaver calls "a cornerstone of early American Christmas cookery" because it had both culinary and decorative uses.

Between 1855 and 1875, candy making became industrialized. Gumdrops and other hard candies were made in large quantities. New methods of sugar processing brought the price down further, so that even pioneer children like Laura Ingalls Wilder in her *Little House* books could reasonably hope for a piece or two of candy in a Christmas stocking. Candy was also made at home as part of the preparation for the holidays and as a pastime for children.

In the late nineteenth century, the first candy bars came on the market. Soon candy was inexpensive enough for almost anyone to enjoy. Candy making at home continued, with taffy, peanut brittle, divinity, fudge, and candied peel among the favorites. Sugar rationing during World War II temporarily put a halt to this activity, but after the war, the American sweet tooth reasserted itself. During the 1950s and '60s, my sister and I learned to make fudge from a back-of-the-cocoa-box Hershey's recipe (Classic Fudge, page 469), and we love it still.

Today, candy making at home generally occurs as a prelude to Thanksgiving, Christmas, Hanukkah, or Valentine's Day; it's a special-occasion activity. Sometimes families and friends make candies together or separately, then have the same kind of candy exchange that people organize for cookies. Everyone gets a certain weight of different kinds of homemade candies without going through the trouble of making them all!

Cherry-Almond Divinity

I love divinity—soft white candy pillows that melt in your mouth. Before the days of television, VCRs, and computers, people made candy as something to do on a weekend evening. Today, candy making is becoming a lost art. It deserves a comeback, because what you can make at home tastes far better than what you can buy. **MAKES ABOUT 2 DOZEN CANDIES**

2½ cups sugar

½ cup light corn syrup

½ cup water

2 large egg whites

2 teaspoons almond extract

¾ cup candied cherries, snipped into small pieces

¾ cup chopped sliced almonds

1   Line a rimmed baking sheet with parchment paper and set aside.

2   In a medium-size heavy saucepan over medium-high heat, stir together the sugar, corn syrup, and water and continue stirring until the sugar has dissolved. Bring to a boil, without stirring, and continue boiling until the mixture reaches 260 degrees F on a candy thermometer, or the hard-ball stage (when a drop of the hot syrup makes a hard ball when dropped into a glass of ice water).

3   While the mixture is boiling, with an electric mixer, beat the egg whites in a large mixing bowl until they hold stiff peaks. When the syrup is ready, pour it slowly into the egg whites, beating constantly on low to medium speed, until you have a thick, glossy, and creamy mixture, about 3 minutes. Beat in the almond extract, then the cherries and nuts. Beat on high speed until the candy starts to lose its sheen, about 6 more minutes.

4   Dip a large soup spoon in water, then into the candy, and drop spoonfuls of the divinity onto the prepared baking sheet. Let cool for 1 hour. Store, covered, in an airtight container, layered between sheets of waxed paper, for up to 1 month.

Ideal Conditions for Making Candy

Veteran candy makers know a few tricks that you won't often find in a candy recipe. For one thing, there's the weather to consider. Any candy with a high sugar and water content, like brittle, divinity, or marshmallows, is best made on a dry day or a day with low humidity. A dry atmosphere keeps the candy from getting sticky.

Old cookbooks assume their readers have a piece of marble handy for kneading fudge and taffy or pulling cream candies. Granite or other solid-surface countertops work fine today. If you're serious about making candy, you can also shop for a marble remnant at a building supply store. Marble and granite stay cool and are ideal for the task of getting the warm candy mixture to the right texture. Placing a tray for cooling brittle or toffee on marble or granite helps the candy cool faster.

New Orleans–Style Pecan Pralines

Pralines, candies made by coating hazelnuts with a caramelized-sugar-and-water mixture, were brought to New Orleans by French settlers. In New Orleans, the brittle French candy slowly became voluptuous. Creole confectioners nixed the unavailable hazelnuts and substituted local pecans, creating a creamier, smoother, more seductive praline. Its pronunciation slowly changed to the drawl-y "PRAH-leen." In a 1978 issue of *Bon Appétit* magazine, food writer M. F. K. Fisher, who knew all about seduction, wrote about eating her fair share of these candies. "Once I drove slowly across the southern part of this country from California to Florida," she wrote, "and for a lot of the trip, my partner and I treated ourselves to a mid-afternoon praline, a fresh brown patty of melted sugar spread over some pecans, that we had bought yesterday or today at a roadside stand." Make one batch to eat, and another to crumble and use in cheesecakes, ice cream, or frostings. **MAKES 2 DOZEN PRALINES**

Saltwater Taffy

Boxes of pastel-colored sticks or bite-sized squares of saltwater taffy wrapped in twists of waxed paper have become the quintessential souvenir of a beach vacation—at least on the Atlantic side. Vanilla, chocolate, strawberry, lemon, peanut butter—my sister and I certainly gobbled up our share when we vacationed as kids with our family at Nag's Head and Ocracoke Island, Jekyll Island, and the beach communities in Florida.

But why is this candy called "saltwater"? If you look at the ingredients on the package, saltwater is not listed. And if you've ever made and pulled taffy—a combination of sugar, corn syrup, water, cornstarch, butter, salt, and flavoring—you know that saltwater doesn't go into the recipe.

The answer comes from Atlantic City, New Jersey. In 1870, railroad executive Alexander Boardman had the Atlantic City Boardwalk built to prevent sand from drifting into hotel lobbies and the passenger cars of the Camden and Atlantic Railroad. Atlantic City became the first American seaside resort, and by the 1880s it was the most famous. Shops built along the boardwalk did a brisk business in the summer.

After a summer storm in 1883, however, one shopkeeper was not too happy. David Bradley's shop was damaged by a tidal surge that submerged his goods in seawater. The story goes that during the cleanup, a girl walked into his store and asked for taffy. Grumpily, Bradley offered her his "saltwater taffy." Bradley's mother saw the silver lining to the dark cloud and encouraged her son to market his candy with that name. The first mention of saltwater taffy in Atlantic City business directories did not come until 1889, but it's a good story, anyway. No matter how saltwater taffy got started, it is definitely associated with Atlantic City.

2 cups granulated sugar

1 cup packed light brown sugar

½ cup (1 stick) unsalted butter

1 cup milk

2 tablespoons light corn syrup

3 cups pecan halves

2 teaspoons vanilla extract

1   Line two baking sheets with parchment paper and set aside.

2   In a heavy 2-quart saucepan over medium-high heat, stir together both sugars, and the butter, milk, corn syrup, and pecans with a wooden spoon. Bring to a boil, stirring often, until the mixture reaches 234 degrees F on a candy thermometer, or the soft-ball stage (when a drop of the hot syrup makes a soft ball when dropped into a glass of ice water), about 18 to 20 minutes.

3   Remove the mixture from the heat and stir in the vanilla. Stir rapidly until the mixture loses its glossiness. Working very quickly, drop the praline mixture, 1 tablespoon at a time, onto the prepared baking sheets. Let cool completely. Store, covered, in an airtight container, layered between sheets of waxed paper, for up to 2 weeks.

Classic Fudge

When Americans think of fudge, they think chocolate, as in hot fudge sundae. Of course, we know there are other kinds of fudge—peanut butter, vanilla, penuche, and marshmallow, for example. But chocolate is the first kind we think of. This is the fudge I grew up making, adapted from a 1950s Hershey's cocoa back-of-the-box recipe. We didn't have a candy thermometer, so I had to judge when the mixture hit the soft-ball stage (when a drop of the hot mixture forms a soft ball when dropped into a glass of ice water). Even if you goof and stop cooking the fudge before it reaches the soft-ball stage, you still have a great hot fudge sauce. The first mention of fudge in American cookery came when Emelyn Hartridge, a student at Smith College in Massachusetts, made 30 pounds of it for a senior auction in 1888. **MAKES 12 SERVINGS**

⅔ cup unsweetened cocoa powder

3 cups sugar

⅛ teaspoon salt

1½ cups milk

¼ cup (½ stick) unsalted butter

1 teaspoon vanilla extract

1 Butter a 9-inch square baking pan and set aside.

2 In a large heavy saucepan, whisk together the cocoa powder, sugar, and salt. Over medium-high heat, whisk in the milk and bring to a boil. Continue to cook until the mixture reaches 234 degrees F on a candy thermometer, or the soft-ball stage (when a drop of the hot fudge makes a soft ball when dropped into a glass of ice water), about 10 minutes.

3 Remove from the heat and drop in the butter and vanilla, but do not stir because this will cause the fudge to be runny. Let the fudge cool to about 110 degrees F or warm room temperature, then whisk or stir in the butter and vanilla and continue stirring until the fudge has thickened and loses its gloss. Pour or spread into the prepared pan.

4 When the fudge has cooled, cut into squares. Store in an airtight container for up to 6 months.

Mamie Eisenhower's Million Dollar Fudge

Okay, maybe Dwight Eisenhower wasn't the most exciting president we've ever had, but at least First Lady Mamie popularized the birthday cake (page 141) and gave us an easy recipe for fudge. This is adapted from her recipe in *Who Says We Can't Cook!*, a spiral-bound collection of recipes by the Women's National Press Club in Washington, D. C., published in 1955. **MAKES 12 SERVINGS**

One 12-ounce bag semisweet chocolate chips

12 ounces Baker's German's sweet chocolate, cut into pieces

One 16-ounce jar marshmallow creme

2 cups chopped nuts (optional), such as peanuts, pecans, walnuts, or cashews

4$\frac{1}{2}$ cups sugar

$\frac{1}{4}$ teaspoon salt

2 tablespoons unsalted butter

One 14-ounce can sweetened condensed milk

1 Butter the inside of a 9 x 13-inch baking pan and set aside. Put the chocolate chips and pieces, marshmallow creme, and chopped nuts (if using) in a large heat-proof mixing bowl and set aside.

2 In a large heavy saucepan over medium-high heat, combine the sugar, salt, butter, and condensed milk. Bring to a boil, stir to blend, and boil for 6 minutes.

3 Pour the hot sugar mixture over the ingredients in the bowl, stirring to melt the chocolate until the fudge is well blended. Pour into the prepared pan.

4 Let cool for at least 1 hour, then cut into squares and serve. Store in an airtight container for up to 1 month.

Old-Fashioned Peanut Butter Fudge

In the days before television changed American life in the 1950s, kids and teenagers liked to get in the kitchen after dinner and the subsequent dishwashing duties were over and make cookies or fudge. Before the 1960s, cookbooks were replete with home-made candy recipes for just this reason. Now we'd have to pull kids away from their computers or Nintendo or soccer practice, but maybe they wouldn't mind after they tasted this fudge. It is adapted from a recipe in *Favorite Recipes*, compiled in the early 1940s by the Smithfield Woman's Club in Smithfield, North Carolina.

MAKES 12 SERVINGS

2 cups sugar

1 cup water

1/4 teaspoon cream of tartar

1 teaspoon vanilla extract

1 cup creamy peanut butter

1 Butter the inside of an 8- or 9-inch square baking pan and set aside.

2 Combine the sugar and water in a medium-size heavy saucepan. Bring to a boil over medium-high heat and continue to boil until the mixture reaches 235 to 240 degrees F on a candy thermometer, or the soft-ball stage (when a drop of the hot syrup makes a soft ball when dropped into a glass of ice water). Remove from the heat and let cool for 15 minutes.

3 With an electric mixer on low speed, beat the cream of tartar and vanilla into the cooled syrup. Gradually increase the speed and keep beating until the mixture turns white. Beat in the peanut butter and continue beating until well blended. Transfer the mixture to a smooth work surface and knead by patting the candy into an oval, folding it in half, pressing the candy all over with the heel of your hand or your knuckles, turning the candy a quarter turn, and repeat the kneading process until the candy is no longer sticky, about 2 minutes. Pat into the prepared pan and cut into squares. Store in an airtight container for up to 1 month.

Microwave Peanut Brittle

By the beginning of the twentieth century, American cooks were making peanut brittle, a version of the original French praline, which contained hazelnuts. Brittle is named for the texture of the finished candy, which breaks into delicious, lumpy shards. This easier version of an old classic comes from my friend Mary Ann Duckers.

MAKES 12 SERVINGS

1 cup sugar

½ cup light corn syrup

⅛ teaspoon salt

1 cup skinned raw peanuts

1 teaspoon unsalted butter

1 teaspoon vanilla extract

1 teaspoon baking soda

1   Butter the inside of a rimmed baking sheet or tray, or line with parchment paper, and set aside.

2   Combine the sugar, corn syrup, salt, and peanuts in a large glass bowl. Microwave on HIGH. Stir the mixture, then cook on HIGH for 8 minutes more, until the mixture has turned a light golden color. Stir in the butter and vanilla. Stir in the baking soda, which will make the mixture foam.

Old-Fashioned Penny Candy

From the mid nineteenth century onward, American kids have had a taste for penny candy, old-fashioned confections like peppermint twists, horehound drops, licorice shoestrings, waxed paper–wrapped taffy, sourballs, fireballs, jelly worms, candy necklaces, Boston baked beans (candy-coated peanuts), jaw breakers, rock candy on a stick, jelly beans, and candy cigarettes. General stores of a bygone era (although some still exist, such as the Vermont General Store in Weston) used to have barrels or large glass jars full of each kind of penny candy. Some offered these sweets behind a large glass display case.

"Clear toys," or hard candy made in toy-like shapes, are still made in the Moravian town of Lititz, Pennsylvania. A flavored and colored sugar syrup is boiled to the hard-crack stage, then poured into oiled metal molds in the shapes of chickens, birds, reindeer, sailing ships, scissors, baskets, and zoo animals. Before the candy hardens, a cardboard stick is inserted in the bottom of each mold. When the candy cools, the finished lollipops are released, to be wrapped in cellophane and handed to a lucky child.

Today, candy certainly costs more than a penny, but kids still go for the same things that their parents and grandparents did.

3 Pour the mixture onto the prepared baking sheet. Working quickly, spread to the desired thickness. Let cool, then break into pieces. Store in an airtight container for up to 6 months.

> **STOVETOP VARIATION** Combine the sugar, corn syrup, salt, and peanuts in a medium-size heavy saucepan. Bring to a boil over medium-high heat and continue to boil until it reaches 329 to 338 degrees F on a candy thermometer, when the mixture turns a golden brown, about 15 minutes. Remove from the heat. Wearing mitts, stir in the butter, vanilla, and baking soda. The mixture will foam up. Pour onto the prepared baking sheet and proceed as directed above.

Chocolate-Covered Cashew Butter Toffee

There is pulled taffy, like the saltwater kind, and then there is hard toffee, like this recipe, adapted from one in *A Pinch of Salt Lake* published by the Junior League of Salt Lake City in 1986. This is addictive when made with lightly salted, roasted cashews and good quality or couverture ("covering") chocolate. **MAKES 24 SERVINGS**

3½ cups lightly salted dry-roasted cashews, whole or pieces

1 pound (4 sticks) unsalted butter, cut into pieces

2½ cups sugar

¼ cup light corn syrup

½ cup water

8 ounces good quality dark, semisweet, or couverture chocolate

1 Lightly butter the inside of a 16 x 11-inch jelly-roll pan. Sprinkle evenly with 3 cups of the cashews and set aside. In a food processor, coarsely grind the remaining ½ cup of cashews and set aside.

2 Combine the butter, sugar, corn syrup, and water in a large heavy saucepan. Bring to a boil over medium-high heat, then reduce the heat to low and continue to cook until the mixture reaches 310 degrees F on a candy thermometer, the hard-crack stage (when a drop of the hot syrup makes a hard crack or separates into hard, brittle shreds when dropped into a glass of ice water), about 20 to 25 minutes. The mixture should be a light brown color.

3 Meanwhile, melt the chocolate in the top of a double boiler set over simmering water.

4 Pour the hot butter mixture over the cashews on the prepared baking sheet. Pour the melted chocolate evenly over the hot butter mixture and sprinkle with the reserved ground cashews. Let cool. Break the toffee into pieces and store, layered between sheets of waxed paper, in an airtight container for up to 6 months.

Cooking Sugar

Cooked sugar plays a special role in creating desserts. A syrup starts out as a mixture of sugar and liquid, which is brought to a boil. As the liquid evaporates during cooking, the proportion of sugar to liquid increases, and this raises the boiling point higher and higher. The longer a sugar syrup is cooked, the higher its temperature rises and the greater its density. Here are the different stages of cooking sugar and water.

Simple syrup: This is a thin syrup with equal parts water and sugar, just brought to a boil at about 214 degrees F on a candy thermometer to completely dissolve the sugar. Then the syrup is removed from the heat. Use simple syrup to poach fruit and make granitas, sorbets, and sherbets. Brush the bottoms of prebaked pie and tart crusts and the tops of cake layers with a simple syrup to prevent creamy fillings from making the crust or cake soggy. Bundt cakes and bar cookies can also be glazed with a flavored simple syrup for an enhanced flavor and appearance.

Syrup: This refers to a thicker syrup, perhaps flavored with fruit, that has cooked to a temperature of 230 to 235 degrees F on a candy thermometer, or what's known as the thread stage, when a drop of hot syrup makes a thread when dropped into a glass of ice water. Fruit can be dipped into a warm syrup to glisten on top of a tart. Dessert crepes can be drizzled with a fruit syrup.

Soft-ball stage: This is a sugar-and-water syrup that has cooked to a temperature of 235 to 240 degrees F on a candy thermometer, or when a drop of hot syrup makes a soft ball when dropped into a glass of ice water. It is used to make fondant icings, buttercream frostings, and fudge.

Hard-ball stage: This is a sugar-and-water syrup that has cooked to a temperature of 248 degrees F on a candy thermometer, or when a drop of hot syrup makes a hard ball when dropped into a glass of ice water. It is used to make Italian Meringue (see page 351) and candies.

Hard-crack stage: This is a sugar-and-water syrup cooked to a temperature of 295 degrees F on a candy thermometer, or when a drop of hot syrup makes a hard cracked ball when dropped into a glass of ice water. It is used to make spun sugar garnishes.

Caramel: This is a sugar-and-water syrup cooked to a temperature of 329 to 338 degrees F on a candy thermometer. It is used to make caramel sauces and crème caramel or flan.

Red Candied Apples

This is an old-fashioned fall treat—whole apples dipped into a cinnamon-flavored red candy syrup, which dries to a crispy coating. **MAKES 9 APPLES**

9 medium-size red-skinned apples, such as McIntosh, Jonathan, or Red Delicious

9 wooden craft or Popsicle-style sticks

1 cup sugar

$\frac{1}{3}$ cup water

$\frac{1}{3}$ cup light corn syrup

$\frac{1}{4}$ cup tiny, hard, red cinnamon candies, such as Red Hots

1　Rinse and dry the apples. Insert a stick through the bottom up to the center of each apple and push about 2 inches into the core. Set aside. Line two baking sheets with waxed paper and set aside.

2　Combine the sugar, water, corn syrup, and cinnamon candies in a medium-size heavy saucepan. Bring to a boil over medium-high heat and continue to boil until the mixture reaches 300 degrees F on a candy thermometer, the hard-crack stage (when a drop of the hot syrup makes a hard crack when dropped into a glass of ice water), about 15 minutes.

3　Remove the syrup from the heat. Holding each apple by the stick, carefully and quickly dip and swirl each apple in the hot syrup until all of the apple is covered. Place the apple, stick side up, on a prepared baking sheet. Let the apples cool on the baking sheets. They will keep, uncovered, at room temperature for up to 3 days.

Homemade Caramel Apples

Every September, I can't wait until caramel apples arrive in the stores. My favorites are caramel-coated Jonathans sprinkled with chopped peanuts, a taste of my childhood. Of course, homemade caramel apples are even better. To make these, you start with a sugar-and-water syrup and blend it with a cream-and-sugar syrup for a heavenly caramel that will harden enough to coat the apples and stay that way. **MAKES 6 APPLES**

1 cup granulated sugar

½ cup boiling water

1 cup packed light brown sugar

½ cup heavy cream

2 tablespoons unsalted butter

6 craft or Popsicle-style sticks

6 tart red apples, such as Jonathan, Winesap, or Braeburn

½ cup chopped unsalted dry-roasted peanuts

1 Have a bowl of ice water ready. Line a baking sheet with parchment or waxed paper and set aside.

2 To make the simple syrup, place ½ cup of the granulated sugar in a small heavy saucepan and melt it over medium-high heat. Pour in the boiling water and boil until you have a smooth syrup, about 2 minutes. Keep warm.

3 Make the second syrup. In a medium-size heavy saucepan, blend the remaining ½ cup of granulated sugar, the brown sugar, heavy cream, and butter over medium-high heat. Bring to a boil and keep boiling until the syrup reaches 236 degrees F on a candy thermometer, about 7 more minutes. Pour the warm caramel into the sugar-and-water mixture and cook to 250 degrees F on a candy thermometer, or the soft-ball stage (when a drop of hot syrup makes a soft ball when dropped into a glass of water). Remove from the heat and let cool to lukewarm.

4 Insert a stick from the bottom up to the center of each apple and push about 2 inches into the apple core. Twirl the apples, stem facing down, in the lukewarm caramel until well coated. Dip each coated apple in ice water to harden. Press some chopped peanuts into each apple and place the apples, stick side up, on the prepared baking sheet to finish hardening and drying, about 1 hour. The apples will keep at room temperature for about 1 week.

Caramel Popcorn

On the west side of Chicago's Michigan Avenue, you'll see a long line of people snaking out of Garrett's tiny shop. They're waiting in line for popcorn, but just not any old popcorn—warm caramel corn, still sticky and crispy from all the butter and sugar. The workers at Garrett's stir up the popcorn and caramel in deep copper kettles. At home, you would use a different method: spread the popcorn in a large roasting pan, pour the caramel over, then toss and bake for a few minutes. **MAKES 8 CUPS**

7 to 8 cups popped popcorn

¾ cup packed dark brown sugar

¼ teaspoon salt

6 tablespoons (¾ stick) unsalted butter

3 tablespoons light corn syrup

¼ teaspoon baking soda

½ teaspoon vanilla extract

1   Preheat the oven to 300 degrees F. Line a baking sheet with aluminum foil and butter the foil; set aside. Remove all unpopped kernels from the popcorn and pour the popcorn into a large roasting pan; set aside.

2   In a small heavy saucepan over medium-high heat, stir together the brown sugar, salt, butter, and corn syrup, and continue stirring until the mixture begins to boil. Continue to boil, without stirring, for 5 minutes.

3   Remove the pan from the heat, and stir in the baking soda and vanilla. Pour the hot caramel over the popcorn and stir gently to coat.

4   Bake for 15 minutes, stirring once. Transfer the caramel popcorn to the prepared baking sheet and let cool. Store the caramel popcorn in an airtight container. It will keep indefinitely.

Coffee Cup Truffles

Flavored with coffee-flavored liqueur, these chocolate truffles are just the thing to enjoy with after-dinner coffee for just a little morsel of dessert. True French truffles are made with raw egg yolks for a voluptuous texture, but these—made without raw egg—are a close second. Without the yolks to hold the ingredients together, these truffles get very soft at room temperature. They should be served right from the freezer. The better quality the chocolate, the better the truffle. You can substitute rum, cognac, or other flavored liqueurs for the coffee-flavored liqueur, if you wish.

MAKES 5 TO 6 DOZEN TRUFFLES

¼ cup granulated sugar

¾ cup heavy cream

1 teaspoon instant espresso powder

8 ounces semisweet or dark chocolate, chopped

1 tablespoon coffee liqueur, such as Tia Maria or crème de cacao

½ cup chopped toasted sliced almonds (see page 181)

½ cup confectioners' sugar

1   Combine the granulated sugar, cream, and espresso powder in a medium-size heavy saucepan. Bring to a simmer over medium-high heat, then remove from the heat. Stir in the chocolate until it has melted. Stir in the liqueur. Let cool, then cover and freeze in the saucepan for 3 to 4 hours or overnight.

2   With a melon baller, scoop the frozen mixture into balls and roll in your hands. Then roll half of each truffle in the almonds and half in the confectioners' sugar. Place in a covered container, layered between sheets of waxed paper, and freeze until ready to serve. Truffles will keep for up to 1 month frozen.

Bourbon Balls

John T. Edge, the director of the Southern Foodways Alliance and a noted cookbook author, said I had to have bourbon balls in this book to represent the South. That was fine with me because my own great uncles had a particular fondness for this confection. Uncle Cliff and his brother-in-law, my Uncle Joe, used to arrive at family gatherings, each with a fifth of bourbon or scotch tucked under one arm. So these easy, bourbon-flavored confections were right up their alley. At the end of Thanksgiving or Christmas dinner, the fifths were empty and the bourbon balls were all gone. And the two of them walked in a straight line out the door, to the everlasting amazement of my father. You can substitute rum for the bourbon, if you wish.

MAKES ABOUT 3 DOZEN BOURBON BALLS

3 cups vanilla wafers

1 cup pecans

3 tablespoons light corn syrup

$1/2$ cup bourbon, or more as needed

Confectioners' sugar for dusting

1   Process the vanilla wafers and pecans together in a food processor until finely ground. Add the corn syrup and bourbon and pulse until the mixture forms a ball or sticks together. Add more bourbon if necessary.

2   Pinch off about 1 teaspoon of the mixture at a time and roll into a ball. Then roll each ball in confectioners' sugar. Store in the refrigerator in an airtight container, layered between sheets of waxed paper, for up to 1 month.

Mom's Homemade Marshmallows

Marshmallows were first made with the juice of the marsh mallow plant, then with gum arabic, and finally with unflavored gelatin powder. My mother remembers going to the candy store as a kid in the 1930s to buy individual homemade marshmallows wrapped in waxed paper. The first commercial marshmallows hit grocery store shelves in the late nineteenth century. They quickly became an integral part of the American family's outdoor cooking, from the simple marshmallow impaled on a stick and roasted over a fire to the sandwich of graham crackers, marshmallow, and a square of milk chocolate heated into a meltingly irresistible S'more. In the 1990s, chefs induced a wave of marshmallow nostalgia, bringing back this confection to restaurant dessert carts. For a revisionist dessert on a cold evening, make real hot chocolate—Rich, Dark Hot Chocolate (page 496)—and top it with one of these marshmallows. You can also dredge each homemade marshmallow in melted butter and cinnamon sugar, enclose it in small triangles of pie or puff pastry, and bake it in a muffin cup for an easy, gooey dessert. Or dip homemade marshmallows into melted chocolate or caramel sauce.

MAKES ABOUT 4 DOZEN MARSHMALLOWS

Four ¼-ounce packages unflavored gelatin

1½ cups cool water

1¼ cups light corn syrup

¼ teaspoon salt

3 cups granulated sugar

2 tablespoons vanilla extract

Confectioners' sugar for dusting

1   Line a 9 x 13-inch pan with parchment paper and coat the paper with nonstick cooking spray; set aside. Sprinkle the gelatin over ¾ cup of the water in a large mixing bowl. Set aside for several minutes, until the gelatin is soaked through.

2   In a large heavy saucepan over high heat, combine the remaining ¾ cup of water, the corn syrup, salt, and the granulated sugar and cook to a temperature of 240 degrees F on a candy thermometer, or the end of the soft-ball stage (when a drop of hot syrup makes a soft ball when dropped into a glass of ice water), about 10 minutes.

3   Pour the hot sugar mixture over the gelatin. With an electric mixer, beat until fluffy and pure white, about 15 minutes. Beat in the vanilla.

4   Spread the marshmallow into the prepared pan, smoothing the top well. Cover with plastic wrap and set aside to solidify at room temperature for 12 hours.

5   When the marshmallow has solidified, use a moistened knife to cut it into 1½-inch squares. Dust each square with a little confectioners' sugar. Store the marshmallows in the refrigerator in an airtight container, layered between sheets of waxed paper, where they will keep indefinitely.

Chewing and Doing

Industrious and optimistic Americans, believing they could pull themselves up by their bootstraps and achieve their life goals, have known from early on that they have to be able to do at least two things at once to succeed. Maybe that's why Americans invented and then popularized chewing and bubble gums. You can chew and do. Gum has become so much a part of our culture that it is even part of an old joke, as in "He can't even chew gum and [fill in the activity] at the same time."

Chewing gum was first marketed in this country in 1848 by John Curtis of Maine, who made his chewing gum from the sap of the spruce tree. By 1871, Thomas Adams was making chewing gum from chicle, the white sap of the tropical sapodilla tree, which was imported from South America (and also used to make rubber tires). His Black Jack chewing gum, licorice flavored and guaranteed to make your tongue black, has been on the market ever since.

In 1891, William Wrigley introduced Americans to spearmint and Juicy Fruit gum. By the early 1900s, we had colored gumballs and Chiclets, small squares of gum with a candy coating. In 1928, pink bubble gum hit the market, at the same time that the stock market's bubble had almost burst.

During the Depression in the 1930s, kids could escape the dreariness of everyday life for a few cents by buying a small rectangle of chewing gum enclosed in a pack of cardboard baseball cards depicting their favorite players.

Today, chewing gum is made from synthetic ingredients, but it still helps us do two things at once—whatever we're already doing plus getting fresher breath, losing weight, or kicking a nicotine habit.

Marzipan

When I lived in Europe, I fell in love with almond paste. Rolled into a thin layer and draped over cakes or used to flavor Danish pastries and *gâteau pithiviers*, it added a layer of sweet surprise. In the ninth century, when the Arabs brought almonds and cane sugar to southern Italy, France, and Spain, they brought their love of almond paste as well—a love that conquered Europe. When European bakers and confectioners later emigrated to the United States, they brought their talents for working with marzipan and eventually made it from California almonds. Like any other product you can think of, homemade marzipan tastes better than the commercially prepared counterpart—almond paste in a can. With this homemade marzipan and a little imagination, your dessert repertoire can include soft amaretti, a marzipan soufflé, marzipan custards, dark chocolate–dipped marzipan candies, and fillings for tarts and pastries of all kinds. Flavor the marzipan to suit your taste: vanilla for a Scandinavian version, rosewater for a more medieval take, orange flower water for a Moroccan style, or almond extract for an even more pronounced almond flavor. And keep it on hand for last-minute desserts. Wrapped well in plastic film, homemade marzipan will keep in the refrigerator for up to 6 months. For best results, let the flavors of the marzipan develop in the refrigerator for 2 days before using. **MAKES ABOUT 1 POUND**

8 ounces blanched whole almonds

1 cup plus 1 tablespoon superfine sugar

1 large egg white

1 teaspoon vanilla or almond extract, or 1 to 2 teaspoons rosewater or orange flower water, or more as needed

1   Heat the oven to 350 degrees F. Arrange the almonds on a baking sheet in a single layer and toast until they start to turn golden brown, 10 to 15 minutes.

2   Transfer the almonds to a food processor and add the sugar. Process until the mixture resembles fine crumbs. Add the egg white and flavoring of your choice and process until the mixture turns into a fine paste. Taste and add more flavoring, if you wish. Wrap the marzipan in plastic wrap and refrigerate for 2 days to allow the flavors to develop before using. It will keep for at least 6 months in the refrigerator.

Garden Candy

What if?" is the question that prompts all creativity, especially in my kitchen. After making the Praise and Plenty Cake (page 174), I still had fresh yellow squash, zucchini, and carrot left. I wondered what would happen if I cooked long ribbons of squash, carrot, and zucchini in a sugar syrup. Would I end up with an attractive garnish for cakes and tarts—or a mess? The result of my experiment: the vegetables become glisteningly transparent and the ribbons look like they're made of French wire—a wonderful and unique garnish. Garden Candy keeps in the refrigerator, covered with syrup, indefinitely, so you can let it warm to room temperature, then garnish your favorite custard tart, pudding, or pound cake. Strips or curling ribbons of citrus peel may be candied in the same way. **MAKES ABOUT 1 CUP OF CANDIES**

Long, thin yellow summer squash and zucchini

Carrots

2 cups water

2 cups sugar

Juice of 1 lemon

Sugar-on-Snow

Early spring is sugaring season in northern New England, when sugar maple trees are tapped, and the sap is boiled down to make maple syrup. It still snow at that time of year, and when it does, some New Englanders think "dessert," and they've been thinking that way for over 200 years. First, they head for the kitchen to heat up some new maple syrup. Then they go out and scoop up a pan of freshly fallen, clean snow, free of debris, and pack it down with mittened hands. When the hot maple syrup hits the packed snow, it forms a taffy-like coating that is tooth-rattlingly sweet. Everyone grabs a fork and twirls up both coating and snow. This confection is also known as "leather aprons" or "leather britches" because of its chewy brownness. No wonder the traditional accompaniments are sour pickles and saltines—to cut the sweetness.

Maple syrup

Pan of packed freshly fallen, wet snow

Heat the maple syrup in a saucepan over medium-high heat for about 5 minutes. In the meantime, go and get the snow. When the maple syrup registers 234 degrees F on a candy thermometer, remove from the heat and pour over the snow without stirring. Dig in.

1 To make vegetable ribbons, trim off the ends of the vegetables with a paring knife. Holding the squash and zucchini vertically with one hand, peel long ribbons from the vegetables with a vegetable peeler or mandolin to a thickness of $1/16$ inch. Discard the first slice, which is mostly skin.

2 Bring the water, sugar, and lemon juice to a boil in a large heavy saucepan. Add about 1 cup of prepared vegetables and lower the heat to a simmer. Cook, uncovered, until the vegetables have turned translucent, about 1 hour. Using a slotted spoon, remove the candied vegetables from the syrup. Lay in a plastic container, then top with the syrup in the saucepan. Let cool, then cover and store in the refrigerator, where it will keep for up to 6 months.

Candied Citrus Peel

For holiday giving, to accompany after-dinner espresso, or to garnish a homemade cake, candied citrus peel makes a great Saturday morning project. Make this, of course, during the winter months, when oranges, regular and Meyer lemons, and grapefruits are in season. Choose bright-skinned and unblemished fruit. But if you have some slices that are not as attractive as you'd wish, chop them up and use them in pound cake batter for a citrus twist. **MAKES ABOUT 4 DOZEN CANDIES**

3 medium-size to large navel oranges, or 6 regular or Meyer lemons, or 2 small grapefruits
$1\frac{1}{2}$ cups water

$1\frac{1}{2}$ cups sugar

3 tablespoons light corn syrup

1 With a sharp paring knife, trim a slice off the bottom and top of each fruit. Then score the peel into four sections and remove them with a paring knife by hand. Reserve the fruit for another use. Scrape away the white pith from each section of peel.

2 Place the peels in a saucepan with enough water to cover. Bring to a boil over medium-high heat and boil for 10 minutes. Drain off the water, but leave the peel in the pan. Add fresh water to cover and bring to a boil again. Boil for another 10 minutes. Drain off the water, add fresh, bring to a boil, and this time boil until the peel is tender, 15 to 25 minutes. This process gets rid of any bitterness from the peel and rind. Remove the peel with a slotted spoon and let cool on paper towels.

3 Cut each section of peel into thin slivers with a sharp knife.

An American Candy Timeline

Many candies that we see on grocery store shelves—or put in trick-or-treat bags—have been around for nearly a century. Find out when your favorite candy first caused a sensation in the timeline that follows.

1847 *NECCO Wafers.* These slender, pastel-colored candies debut in Cambridge, Massachusetts. In 1932, the company produces the Sky Bar, chocolate-covered segments of caramel, vanilla, peanut, and fudge.

1860s *Gumdrops and hard clear candies.* These show up in confectioner's shops.

1894 *Hershey Almond Bar and Hershey Milk Chocolate Bars.* The first American candy bars, made by Milton Hershey in Hershey, Pennsylvania.

1896 *Tootsie Roll.* Leo Hirschfield of New York City names his candy after his daughter, Clara, who is nick-named "Tootsie."

1907 *Hershey's Kisses.* According to company legend, Milton Hershey's teardrop-shaped chocolates wrapped in foil are named for a sound produced during the manufacturing process.

1912 *Life Savers.* These hard fruit candy shaped like a ship's lifesaver are made by Clarence A. Crane in Cleveland, Ohio.

1912 *Goo Goo Cluster.* Howard H. Cambell of Nashville, Tennessee, creates and markets this combination of caramel, marshmallow, peanuts, and milk chocolate.

1920 *Baby Ruth.* The Curtiss Candy Company of Chicago honors the young daughter of President Grover Cleveland (not the baseball great Babe Ruth).

1921 *Chuckles.* These jellied fruit candies covered in granulated sugar are first made by Fred W. Amend in Chicago.

1923 *Reese's Peanut Butter Cups.* H. B. Reese in Hershey, Pennsylvania, makes these peanut butter–filled chocolates.

1925 *Mr. Goodbar.* A chocolate-and–chopped peanut bar joins the Hershey family of candies.

1926 *Milk Duds.* These chocolate-covered caramel morsels are made by the Holloway Company in Chicago.

1930 *Snickers.* Frank C. Mars's candy bar—nougat and peanuts in caramel, covered with chocolate—comes out. He begins to compete with Milton Hershey for the unofficial "emperor of chocolate" title. Milky Way is introduced soon after and Three Musketeers in 1932.

1932 *Heath Bar.* Chocolate-covered hard toffee made by L. S. Heath comes on the market.

1940s *M & M's.* These are named for the candy's developers, Forrest Mars, son of Frank, and Bruce Merries. The candies are modeled after the Smarties candies in Britain. The candy coating kept them from melting in the hand, which made them a popular GI rations during World War II.

4 In the same saucepan, combine the 1½ cups of water, 1 cup of the sugar, and the corn syrup and bring to a boil over medium-high heat. Boil for 3 minutes, then add the slivers of peel. Boil gently, covered, until the peel looks translucent, about 5 minutes. Uncover and continue boiling until the syrup has cooked down to about 2 tablespoons, 2 to 3 minutes more. With a fork, remove the peels to wire racks to cool.

5 Sprinkle the remaining ½ cup of sugar on a baking sheet. Dredge each peel in the sugar, then return to the wire racks to dry. Store the candied peels, layered between sheets of waxed paper, in an airtight container. They will keep for at least 6 months.

Cajeta

A Mexican dessert sauce popular in the American Southwest, *cajeta* is delicious poured over peeled and sliced fresh oranges, fresh apple cake, or any pumpkin dessert. This tangy and not-too-sweet caramel is adapted from a recipe by Grady Spears, the chef-owner of Reata in Fort Worth. Traditionally, *cajeta* is cooked slowly for hours until it becomes a mellow caramel, but Spears prefers the hurry-up method, and it's equally good. Fresh goat's milk is often available at health food stores, but you can also substitute heavy or whipping cream. **MAKES ABOUT 4 CUPS**

4 cups sugar

1 cup water

¼ cup (½ stick) unsalted butter

2 cups fresh whole goat's milk or heavy cream

Juice of ½ lemon, or more to taste (optional)

1 In a large heavy saucepan, whisk the sugar and water together. Over medium-high heat, bring to a boil. Stir as the mixture comes to a simmer, but then do not stir again. Let the mixture cook until it is foamy and has turned golden brown, or until it reaches 325 degrees F on a candy thermometer, about 20 minutes.

2 Immediately remove from the heat and whisk in the butter, then the goat's milk, and continue whisking until the mixture has turned a mellow tan color and thickened. Whisk in the lemon juice, if desired. Serve warm or let cool. *Cajeta* will keep, covered, in the refrigerator indefinitely.

Homemade Vanilla Bean Syrup

This is a versatile syrup to use as a glaze over pound cakes, fruit cakes, or just drizzled over fresh fruit. **MAKES 1 CUP**

1 vanilla bean   1 cup sugar
1 cup water

1   Combine the vanilla bean, water, and sugar in a small heavy saucepan and bring to a boil. Continue boiling until the syrup registers 220 degrees F on a candy thermometer, or a drop placed on a chilled saucer and refrigerated for 1 minute is thick and syrupy.

2   Remove from the heat, cover, and let steep for 1 hour. Use immediately, or cool and store, covered, in the refrigerator. This syrup keeps indefinitely. Remove the vanilla bean when ready to use.

> **RUM AND VANILLA BEAN SYRUP** Stir ¼ cup of dark rum into the syrup at the end of step 1 and let steep.

Almond Syrup

A deliciously easy syrup for pouring over fresh fruit, for poaching fruit, or for drizzling over cakes. **MAKES 2 CUPS**

2 cups water   1½ teaspoons almond extract
2 cups sugar   Juice of 1 lemon

In a medium-size heavy saucepan, bring the water and sugar to a boil, stirring to dissolve the sugar. Stir in the almond extract and lemon juice. Return to a boil, then reduce the heat and simmer until the syrup registers 220 degrees F on a candy thermometer, or a drop placed on a chilled saucer and refrigerated for 1 minute is thick and syrupy. Remove from the heat. Use immediately, or let cool and store in the refrigerator. This syrup keeps indefinitely.

Fresh Berry Syrup

This is a great all-purpose syrup to have on hand for drizzling over pancakes, waffles, pound cake, savarin, ice cream, or berry tarts. I like a combination of berries, usually all red or a mix of blue and purple, but even a syrup made from one kind of berry tastes great. **MAKES ABOUT 2 CUPS**

3 cups fresh berries, such as blackberries, blueberries, red raspberries, black raspberries, hulled strawberries, or red currants

Juice of 1 lemon

⅔ cup sugar

1   Place the berries, lemon juice, and sugar in a large heavy saucepan. Bring to a boil, stirring. Reduce the heat to medium-low, and simmer until the sugar has dissolved and the berries have given off their juices, about 15 minutes. When the syrup is ready, the temperature will register 220 degrees F on a candy thermometer, or a drop placed on a chilled saucer and refrigerated for 1 minute should be thick and syrupy.

2   Remove from heat and pour the mixture through a fine-mesh strainer into a bowl. Discard the cooked berries. Let cool, then pour the syrup into a glass jar. Cover and chill until ready to use. It will keep for up to 1 week, covered, in the refrigerator.

Fresh Mint Syrup

If fresh mint is unavailable or you are pressed for time, substitute the peppermint extract for the fresh leaves and use the syrup right away without letting it steep. **MAKES 1 CUP**

1 cup sugar

1 cup water

½ cup packed fresh spearmint or peppermint leaves or ½ teaspoon peppermint extract

Juice of 1 lemon

1   Combine the sugar and water in a medium-size heavy saucepan and bring to a boil, stirring, until the sugar is dissolved. Reduce the heat to medium-low and simmer until the syrup registers 220 degrees F on a candy thermometer, or a drop placed on a chilled saucer and refrigerated for 1 minute is thick and syrupy. Remove from the heat.

2   Stir in the mint leaves or extract and lemon juice. If using mint leaves, cover, and let steep overnight. If using extract, use right away.

3   Strain and store in a covered jar in the refrigerator until ready to serve. It will keep indefinitely.

Peach Leaf Syrup

This is an almond-flavored syrup infused with fresh peach leaves. Make sure you use organic or unsprayed leaves from a friend's peach tree or an organic farm. You can freeze and use them later, straight from the freezer. Don't try to dry them like an herb; they will be unusable. Pears and peaches poached in this syrup are heavenly, and the syrup also makes a refreshing sorbet or glaze for a cake. You can substitute this syrup for the Vanilla Bean Syrup in Fresh Peach and Blueberry Gelatin (page 23). **MAKES 2 CUPS**

24 fresh peach leaves

2 cups boiling water

Juice of 1 lemon

2 cups sugar

1   Rinse the peach leaves gently and drain in a colander. Put the leaves in a small saucepan and pour the boiling water over them to cover. Cover the saucepan and let the mixture steep for 24 hours.

2   The next day, strain the cooled mixture into a bowl. Add the lemon juice and sugar. Bring the mixture to a boil, reduce the heat to medium-low, and simmer for 10 to 15 minutes, until the syrup registers 220 degrees F on a candy thermometer, or a drop placed on a chilled saucer and refrigerated for 1 minute is thick and syrupy. Remove from the heat, let cool, and pour into glass jars. The syrup will keep indefinitely.

Fresh Orange Syrup

This fresh-tasting syrup is delicious served with Crazy Quilt Chocolate Mousse (page 354). **MAKES ABOUT 1 CUP**

1 teaspoon cornstarch

1 cup fresh orange juice

1/2 cup sugar

1 tablespoon orange-flavored liqueur such as Triple Sec or Cointreau (optional)

Put the cornstarch and ¼ cup of the orange juice in a small jar with a lid. Close and shake until smooth. Pour the cornstarch-and–orange juice mixture into a small saucepan and stir in the remaining ¾ cup of orange juice and the sugar. Bring to a boil over medium heat, and continue boiling for 2 minutes, then remove from the heat and stir in the liqueur. Pour the syrup through a fine-mesh strainer into a sauceboat or a glass jar and let cool. Serve lukewarm or cold. The syrup will keep, tightly covered, in the refrigerator for up to 3 days.

Rosy Rhubarb Syrup

Rhubarb, also known by the old-fashioned name "pie plant," did not come over with the Pilgrims and Puritans, but by the early nineteenth century, it was well established in New England gardens and has thrived ever since. The only problem is that sometimes you have too much of a good thing. That's when you make this recipe. Rhubarb syrup is a pretty pink in the jar and has many uses, such as poaching fruits or making Lemony Rhubarb Cooler (page 499). To make rhubarb syrup, you first extract the juice by chopping up the rhubarb stalks and steaming them with just a little water. Then you strain the juice and mix it with equal parts sugar and lemon juice. And then cook away. **MAKES 2 CUPS**

4 cups chopped rhubarb stalks (not the leaves, which are poisonous)

1 cup water

Juice of 2 lemons

2 cups sugar

1 Place the rhubarb stalks and water in a large heavy saucepan over medium-high heat and bring to a boil. Reduce the heat to medium-low, cover, and cook the rhubarb until tender, about 10 minutes. Strain the juice, discarding the pulp. Measure the juice and add the lemon juice to it; you should have about 2 cups of liquid. If not, add enough water to equal 2 cups.

2 Return the liquid to the saucepan over medium-high heat and stir in the sugar. Bring to a boil and continue boiling until the syrup registers 220 degrees F on a candy thermometer, or a drop placed on a chilled saucer and refrigerated for 1 minute is thick and syrupy. Let cool, then cover and refrigerate. Serve at room temperature or chilled.

Beverages brewed from herbs, flowers, and fruit are what the French call *tisanes*. The subtle flavors infused in these warm or chilled drinks pair well with desserts. When you want to relax or revive, try pairing a complementary *tisane* with a homemade cake, cookie, or tart. Take a well-deserved winter afternoon break with rosehip and hibiscus tea and a slice of a keeping cake, and pore over the new garden catalogs while the weather is raw and bleak. Attune your senses to the rebirth of spring with a refreshing rhubarb or ginger brew and a sugar cookie flecked with lemon balm, one of the first herbs to come up in the garden. Relax in front of a log fire after a long day of vigorous yard work, enjoying a warm apple dessert and a *tisane* to help you drift off to sleep later on. Cool off on a hot day with an icy beverage and

Tisane
for Two
Teas, Coolers,
and Punches
to Enjoy
with Your
American
Dessert

something sweet to revive you. Or pair a favorite dessert with a well-matched *tisane*; here are some of my favorite combinations:

Apricot tarts or pastries with jasmine tea

Fruitcake or other keeping cake with rosehip and hibiscus tea

Chocolate cookies, brownies with Lavender Lemonade (page 497)

Quince or apple compotes or baked fruit with Lemon Verbena and Apple Peel Tea (page 492)

Pear or apple crumbles or crisps with Summertime Almond Tea (page 493)

Sugar or butter cookies with Lemony Rhubarb Cooler (page 499)

Spice cake or cookies with Spiced Cranberry Tea (page 493)

Vanilla layer cake with Shaker Fresh Gingerade (page 498)

Chocolate cake, orange desserts with Double Mint Tea (page 494)

Lemon Verbena and Apple Peel Tea

The French have long sworn by the restorative effects of herbal infusions, which are as much a part of their nightly bedtime ritual as a cup of Horlick's (a malted chocolate beverage) and a hot water bottle used to be for the British. Waves of European immigrants brought to the United States a similar love for herbal teas or *tisanes*, as they are more correctly called. Today, interest in alternative therapies and natural foods has revived an interest in *tisanes* like this one from Carol Vorbeck, who owns and operates the Applesource mail-order heirloom apple business with her husband, Tom, in Chapin, Illinois. When I want to relax and unwind, I brew this tea. Aromatic, citrus-flavored, and slightly sweet, it goes well with apple, almond, and custard desserts. **MAKES 4 CUPS**

Peel of 1 aromatic red apple, such as Jonathan or Winesap

6 to 8 fresh or 10 to 12 dried lemon verbena leaves

4 cups water

Fresh lemon juice for serving

Honey for serving

Combine the apple peel, lemon verbena, and water in a medium-size saucepan and bring to a boil. Remove from the heat, cover, and let steep for 5 minutes. Strain the tisane. Drink hot or cold with a squeeze of fresh lemon and a little honey to taste.

Summertime Almond Tea

A summertime staple in Tennessee, this sweetly fragrant tea will keep in the refrigerator for several weeks—a delicious beverage to have on hand for unexpected guests. A cup or glass of this tea, served hot or cold, is just the thing to sip in the rocker on the front porch. **MAKES A GENEROUS 1 1/2 QUARTS**

3 orange pekoe tea bags

2 cups boiling water

1 cup sugar

4 cups cold water

1/4 cup plus 2 tablespoons fresh lemon juice

1 tablespoon almond extract

1 teaspoon vanilla extract

Fresh mint or lemon balm sprigs for garnish

1 Steep the tea bags in the boiling water for 10 minutes.

2 Meanwhile, in a medium-size saucepan, bring the sugar and cold water to a boil and continue to boil for 5 minutes. Combine the steeped tea and sugar water. Stir in the lemon juice and extracts. Serve hot or chill and serve cold with a mint leave for garnish.

Spiced Cranberry Tea

Tart, dark rosy red, and spicy, this tea is just the thing to take the chill off an autumn afternoon or to serve family and friends at a holiday tea. **MAKES 8 SERVINGS**

4 cups water

4 cups cranberry juice cocktail

4 teaspoons loose leaf or 4 tea bags English breakfast tea

Peel of a Jonathan, Winesap, or other red apple

16 allspice berries

3/4 teaspoon ground cinnamon

1 tablespoon sugar

Fresh cranberries, picked over for stems, for garnish

1 In a large saucepan, combine the water and juice and bring to a boil. Add the tea, apple peel, and allspice, cover, and remove from the heat. Let the tea infuse for 10 minutes.

2 Stir in the cinnamon and sugar. Strain the tea into warmed teacups or mugs, garnish each with a couple of cranberries, and serve.

Lemon Garden Tea

I love sour, fragrant teas: hibiscus and rosehip, Spiced Cranberry Tea (page 493), and this one, redolent of a summer herb garden. In mine, the perennial lemon balm grows with tender lemon verbena until September. Since the lemon verbena can't withstand a prairie winter, and I have had mixed luck with growing the plant indoors, I usually harvest all the leaves at the end of the summer and dry them on a baking sheet in a very low oven. I also dry leaves of lemon balm this way. Then I can make this dried tea blend, package some of it in small cellophane bags to tie on holiday gifts, and save the rest for me. Working at home on a gloomy, dismal January day, I look forward to an afternoon break with a cup of Lemon Garden Tea and its reviving reminder of summer. A cup of this tea goes well with vanilla-scented pound cake and custards, fruit crisps, and spice cookies. **MAKES 2¹/₂ CUPS LOOSE TEA**

1 cup crumbled dried lemon verbena leaves   ¹/₂ cup dried lemon peel
1 cup crumbled dried lemon balm leaves

1   Mix all the ingredients together and store in tightly closed jar in a cool, dark place. This will taste best if used within 1 year.

2   To make tea, bring water to the boil. Swirl about 1 cup of hot tap water into a teapot to rinse it and warm it, then pour out the water. Measure 1 rounded teaspoon of tea for every cup and place it in the bottom of the teapot or in a metal mesh tea ball. Pour the boiling water over the tea, cover, and let steep for 10 to 15 minutes before straining and serving.

Double Mint Tea

Pale yellow and slightly sweet, mint tea brewed from dried herbs gets a flavor boost when you put a fresh leaf of orange mint, spearmint, or pineapple mint at the bottom of each teacup, then pour in the tea. This soothing *tisane* is delicious served with a chocolate dessert or Citrus Glazed Sweet Potato Pound Cake (page 199). **MAKES 4 CUPS**

4 teaspoons dried peppermint leaves

4 fresh orange mint, spearmint, or pineapple mint leaves

4 cups boiling water

Milk, sugar, or lemon for serving

1 Put the dried peppermint in tea ball or loose in the bottom of a teapot. Put a fresh mint leaf in the bottom of each of 4 teacups. Pour the boiling water into the teapot and let steep until at the desired strength, 5 to 7 minutes.

2 Strain the tea into the prepared teacups and serve with milk, sugar, or lemon.

An Herbal Tea Garden

Fragrant and comforting, herbal teas provide a delicious afternoon pick-me-up or a nighttime soother. Not surprisingly, the freshest herbal teas or *tisanes* have the best flavor. Who knows how long packages of herbal tea have been sitting on grocery store shelves or in a warehouse before that? A small cluster of plants, in a sunny windowsill or planted in the garden, can provide fresh herbs, flowers, and scented leaves to make the best-tasting *tisanes*. Grow several plants together in a large terra-cotta container, so you can easily slip outside to snip the makings for your favorite brew. Here are a few suggestions:

* *Golden lemon thyme (Thymus x citriodorus 'Aurea'):* Use the small, gold-tinged leaves to make a spicy tea.

* *Lavender (Lavandula angustifolia):* Pick the very fragrant deep purple blossom ends before they bloom into pale purple flowers. Lavender buds are delicious in lemonade as well as in hot lemon herb tea.

* *Lemon balm (Melissa officinalis):* Keep clipping this hardy perennial and using the leaves in teas or as a garnish for ice tea; once it has blossomed, the flavor is not as pronounced.

* *Lemon verbena (Citriodorus):* A tender plant, it must be brought indoors before the first frost. Its highly scented leaves make delicious lemony *tisanes*.

* *Mint. Peppermint (Mentha x piperita), spearmint (M. spicata), pineapple mint (M. graveolens 'Variegata'), and orange mint (M. citrata):* These are very hardy plants that can take over in the garden. Plant them where you can contain them. The leaves, either fresh or dried, are delicious in herbal teas or as garnishes for other beverages and desserts.

* *Pineapple sage (Salvia elegans):* This is another tender plant, with bright green foliage and spikes of scarlet flowers in the fall. The leaves make a quince- or pineapple-scented tea.

Iced Coffee Slushy

This is a cool and refreshing way to enjoy coffee even on the hottest day. To my mind, dark roast coffee tastes best in this drink because flavor dulls when something is chilled. The late novelist and cookbook author Laurie Colwin had a great tip—freeze leftover brewed coffee in ice cube trays to use for iced coffee. That way, when the ice melts, the coffee flavor is not diluted. Use a favorite syrup, such as Homemade Vanilla Bean Syrup or Rum and Vanilla Syrup (see main recipe and variation, page 486) or Almond Syrup (page 486) to further flavor your drink. **MAKES 2 SERVINGS**

1 cup ice cubes

1 cup freshly brewed French roast or espresso coffee, cooled

2 tablespoons flavored syrup, or to taste (optional)

Place the ice cubes in a blender or food processor and process until the ice is crushed. Add the cooled coffee and process until you have a slushy drink. Pour into 2 glasses. If you like, stir a tablespoon of flavored syrup into each drink and enjoy.

Rich, Dark Hot Chocolate with Peppermint Cream

When Nathaniel and Sophia Hawthorne were newlyweds living in their beloved Old Manse in Concord, Massachusetts, they often made real hot chocolate for their evening meal, prepared right at the hearth. It's simplicity itself—just shaved dark chocolate, a little sugar, and light cream. If you like, serve just a warm sip in demitasse cups, along with a thin, crisp cookie. Or indulge yourself and enjoy a full mug topped with peppermint-flavored whipped cream. The peppermint cream is also luscious on warm brownies or as the topping on a hot fudge sundae. **MAKES 4 SERVINGS**

HOT CHOCOLATE

2 cups half-and-half

4 ounces good quality milk, semisweet, or bittersweet chocolate, such as Maillard, Godiva, or Valrhona

¼ cup sugar

PEPPERMINT WHIPPED CREAM

One 6-inch stick peppermint candy or candy cane

1 cup heavy cream

1   To make the chocolate, in a medium-size saucepan over medium heat, scald the half-and-half until bubbles form around the edge of the pan. Using a microplane grater or the smallest holes on a box grater, finely shave the chocolate into the saucepan. Stir in the sugar and continue to cook, stirring often, until the chocolate melts. Stir again, then remove from the heat.

2   To make the peppermint cream, crack the candy into pieces, put in a food processor, and process until the candy is finely ground. With an electric mixer, whip the heavy cream and ground candy in a medium-size mixing bowl until the cream holds stiff peaks.

3   Serve the hot chocolate with a generous dollop of whipped cream.

Lavender Lemonade

A cool glass of lavender lemonade goes exceptionally well with a chocolate cookie, brownie, or piece of chocolate cake. Use only organic lavender buds bought from a health food store or harvested from your own garden. This is adapted from a recipe by Nancy Smith. **MAKES 6 TO 8 SERVINGS**

2 cups cold water

½ cup fresh or dried lavender blossoms

2 cups boiling water

Juice of 4 lemons

1 cup sugar, or to taste

1   Pour the cold water into a heat-proof pitcher. Put the lavender blossoms in a strainer and place over the mouth of the pitcher. Pour the boiling water over the lavender blossoms into the pitcher. Remove the strainer and discard the lavender blossoms.

2   Add the lemon juice and sugar to the pitcher and stir until well blended and the sugar is dissolved. Serve over ice.

Shaker Fresh Gingerade

In the late 1700s, Shaker religious communities in New England were founded on beliefs in celibacy, communal living, and the value of work, physical health, simplicity, and spirituality. By the early 1800s, Shaker communities had spread to Ohio and Indiana. The simple, symmetrical, Georgian-style architecture and clean-lined furniture that the Shakers produced were the physical evidence of their beliefs, and so were their thriving gardens, successful apothecary herb businesses, and well-made food. This fresh gingerade recipe from North Union Village in what is now Cleveland, Ohio, was originally concocted to revive flagging spirits on a hot day. It still works deliciously.

MAKES 1 GENEROUS QUART

5 cups water

One 2-inch piece of fresh ginger, coarsely chopped

Grated zest and juice of 2 lemons

1 cup sugar

Juice of 2 lemons

1   Bring 4 cups of the water to a boil in a medium-size saucepan, and add the ginger and lemon zest. Remove from the heat, cover, and let steep for 5 minutes. Strain through a fine-mesh sieve and let cool.

2   In a small heavy saucepan, bring the sugar and remaining 1 cup of water to a boil, then set aside to cool.

3   When both mixtures have cooled, stir the lemon juice into the ginger-infused mixture. Stir in sugar syrup to taste. Serve over ice.

Lemony Rhubarb Cooler

Here's a rosy and refreshing beverage that pairs well with a creamy dessert, such as cheesecake. **MAKES 1½ QUARTS**

Juice of 4 lemons

1 cup sugar, or to taste

2 cups boiling water

1 cup Rosy Rhubarb Syrup (page 489)

2 cups cold water

Stir the lemon juice and sugar together in a heat-proof pitcher until well blended. Pour in the boiling water and stir to dissolve the sugar. Then pour in the rhubarb syrup and cold water and stir again. Serve over ice with a twist of lemon.

Watermelon Agua Fresca

In Latino communities, *agua fresca*, or "fresh water," is served as a refreshing, fruit-based summer drink. Because watermelon is so sweet, I prefer lots of lime juice with this and just a touch of salt. Serve this pleasingly pink drink in a large pitcher with lots of ice. **MAKES ABOUT 1 QUART**

2 cups seeded and cubed fresh watermelon

1 cup sparkling spring water

¼ cup fresh lime juice

2 tablespoons sugar, or to taste

1   Combine the watermelon and sparkling water in a blender or food processor and process until smooth.

2   Strain the mixture through a fine-mesh strainer into a pitcher. Stir in the lime juice, then add the sugar to taste. Serve over ice in tall glasses.

Strawberry Agua Fresca

Fresh strawberries make a deliciously tart *agua fresca*, good with cold and creamy desserts. **MAKES ABOUT 1 QUART**

2 1/2 cups fresh strawberries, hulled

1 1/2 cups sparkling spring water

3 tablespoons fresh lime juice

2 tablespoons sugar, or to taste

1   Combine the strawberries and sparkling water in a blender or food processor and process until smooth.

2   Strain the mixture through a fine-mesh strainer into a pitcher. Stir in the lime juice, then add the sugar. Serve over ice in tall glasses.

Fresh Cantaloupe Agua Fresca

Immigrants to America from tropical climates in Mexico and the Philippines brought their repertoire of cool fresh-fruit drinks, perfect for a blisteringly hot summer day. **MAKES 1 GALLON**

1 ripe cantaloupe, seeded, peeled, and cut into chunks (about 6 cups)

1 gallon water

Juice of 2 lemons

1 cup sugar, or to taste

1   Puree the melon flesh in a food processor in batches. Transfer to a large pitcher, stir in the water, lemon juice, and sugar, and chill thoroughly.

2   To serve, stir again and strain through a fine-mesh strainer over crushed ice or ice cubes into tall glasses.

Plantation House Peach Cordial

Homemade cordials, eggnog, rum punch, sangaree (a sangria-like wine drink made with fruit), Madeira, and brandy were the usual drinks on offer at eighteenth-century society gatherings. Rum was distilled in New England from sugar cane grown in the West Indies, while Madeira and brandy were imported from Europe. Cordials were made at home. Although Southerners made scuppernong wine, it would be another 100 years before vineyards were planted in Ohio and Missouri and another 150 years before vineyards dotted the Napa and Sonoma Valleys of California. Homemade cordials, or ratafias, were usually flavored with stone fruits like peaches, apricots, and nectarines, as well as the kernels from the pits, which have an almond-like flavor. This recipe is adapted from an eighteenth-century one by Baltimore's Margaret Tilghman Carroll. **MAKES 3 QUARTS**

1 dozen ripe peaches

2 cups sugar

1 teaspoon allspice berries

2 quarts boiling water

1 quart brandy

1   Bring a large pot of water to a boil and drop in the peaches to scald for 1 minute. Remove the them with a slotted spoon and drain on paper towels. With a paring knife, peel the peaches, then cut in half and remove the pits. Reserve 6 peach pits. With a nutcracker, crack each reserved peach pit and remove the central kernel; discard the hard outer shell.

2   Place the peaches, reserved peach kernels, sugar, and allspice in the bottom of a large wide-mouth jar or plastic tub. Pour the boiling water over them. Pour in the brandy and cover tightly. Shake the jar to combine the ingredients. Cover and set aside in a cool, dark place for 4 to 5 months, shaking occasionally.

3   After 4 months, taste the cordial. If it is to your liking, line a colander with cheesecloth and set it over a large bowl. Pour out the contents of the jar, about a quart at a time, and strain through the colander into the bowl. Using a funnel, fill clean bottles with the strained cordial and cap tightly. The cordial will keep indefinitely at room temperature.

Making Rose Brandy in 1845

Elizabeth Ellicott Lea noted in *A Quaker Woman's Cookbook* that she flavored her cakes, cheesecakes, cookies, and puddings with the rose brandy she made in her own kitchen. She would have used dark red damask rose petals, which are very fragrant. Here is her recipe, a deliciously old-fashioned alternative to vanilla or almond extract:

"Fill a large bottle with damask rose leaves [petals] picked while they are still fresh; fill the bottle with brandy, or good spirits of any kind; cork it tightly and set it away for use. It will bear filling up several times."

Making Lemon Brandy in 1988

The late writer Laurie Colwin was a fan, like me, of sour flavors. She made her own lemon brandy, "a heavenly elixir," which she put in gingerbread and lemon icing. To make your own lemon brandy, pare the peel from 2 lemons without getting too much of the white pith. Bruise the peel with a rolling pin to help release the oils, then place in a ½-pint jar or bottle. Pour ½ cup of good brandy over the peel. Close the jar tightly, and let steep at room temperature. "I have had my bottle for thirteen years and have replenished the brandy many times," she wrote.

Mint Julep Slush

The running of the Kentucky Derby, a 1¼-mile race for 3-year-old horses that goes by in seconds, is still a big social occasion in the bluegrass country of Kentucky. Parties start at breakfast and continue all day long, and the weather during this first weekend in May usually cooperates. On a hot day, this refreshing semifrozen drink can sneak up on you, so serve it with caution. Adapted from the official drink of the Kentucky Derby celebration, this slush can also be served in a traditional silver julep cup, garnished with a sprig of mint. Make it about 8 hours before serving to allow plenty of time for it to freeze to its semisolid form. **MAKES 12 TO 16 SERVINGS**

1 cup sugar

1 cup water

12 sprigs fresh spearmint, plus extra for garnish

1 quart good quality Kentucky bourbon, such as Early Times, Knob Creek, Maker's Mark, Wild Turkey Kentucky Spirit, or Elijah Craig 12-Year-Old

1 In a medium-size heavy saucepan, heat the sugar and water together over medium heat, stirring, until the sugar has dissolved and the mixture has thickened. Remove from the heat and add the mint. Cover and let the mixture steep for 30 minutes.

2 Pour the bourbon into a large rectangular disposable aluminum foil pan and set aside. Remove the mint from the simple syrup, add the syrup to the bourbon, and blend well. Cover with plastic wrap and freeze for 2 hours.

3 With a large fork, rake through the slush to stir the ice crystals. Cover and freeze again for another 2 hours. Then repeat the process once more.

4 To serve, scoop the slush into a silver julep cup or a small wineglass. Garnish with a sprig of fresh mint.

New Jersey Stone Fence Punch

In colonial days, the area around Montclair, New Jersey, boasted acres of apple orchards, which yielded sweet cider for everyday drinking and a spirited applejack or hard cider for special occasions. These apple beverages combine for a potent party drink in this eighteenth-century punch. Supposedly, a man who drank 2 cups of this punch—usually from a large, imported Lowestoft bowl—could afterward easily leap one of the local stone fences. If you don't want your guests leaping about or hurdling over your furniture, serve it over ice, garnished with a lemon twist and a cinnamon stick. Served chilled or warmed. **MAKES 8 SERVINGS**

2 cups applejack, hard cider, scrumpy, or Calvados

1 quart fresh apple cider

Cinnamon sticks for garnish

Lemon twists for garnish

In a large pitcher or punch bowl, stir together the applejack and cider. Fill each cocktail glass or punch cup with ice and pour in the punch. Garnish with a cinnamon stick and a twist of fresh lemon.

Christmas Ratafia

When well-heeled colonists along the Eastern seaboard entertained during the early part of the eighteenth century, ratafia was one of the drinks served to guests. The lady of each plantation or manor home had her own receipt for this home-made spicy, aromatic liqueur, which she would put up when citrus fruit came in by clipper ship. Today, we can enjoy a nip of ratafia in coffee, drizzled on a fruit compote, sipped after dinner, or as a unique hostess gift. To stud the oranges and tangerines with whole cloves, first poke the skin of the fruit with the point of a cake tester, then push the stem of the clove into the hole. To get a complete twist of peel from a lemon, start at the top, using a paring knife, and carefully peel in a spiral motion. You will need a big glass jar with a wide mouth or a plastic tub for this recipe. I recycle large food jars from the wholesale club. **MAKES ABOUT 1¹/₂ QUARTS**

1 thin-skinned orange, preferably organic

2 tangerines, preferably organic

9 cloves

1 quart vodka

2 cups dry white wine

A complete twist of peel from 1 lemon, preferably organic

3 cinnamon sticks

8 coriander seeds

2 bay leaves

6 cardamom pods

1 vanilla bean

3 tablespoons sugar

1 Stud the orange and each tangerine with 3 cloves. Put all the ingredients into a large, wide-mouth jar or plastic tub, secure the lid, and shake to combine the ingredients. Keep in a cool, dark place for at least 3 weeks, shaking the jar occasionally.

2 To decant, pour the ratafia through a strainer lined with a double thickness of cheesecloth into a bowl. Pour through a coffee filter into a second large bowl. Funnel the ratafia into clean bottles, then cork and label. Keeps indefinitely at room temperature.

Sources

For over 20 years, Justin Rashid and Larry Forgione have purveyed the best of the Upper Midwest, including jellies, jams, dessert sauces, persimmon pulp, and hard-to-find hickory nuts and black walnuts.

American Spoon Foods
1668 Clarion Avenue
Petoskey, MI 49770-0566
(800) 222-5886
www.spoon.com

Besides producing yummy cookies and cakes, this bakery in Massachusetts also sells little pots of Earth-Grown Food Colors in natural shades of sage green, malt brown, yellow light, rose madder red, and orange nasturtium—colors that add a vintage look to cakes and cookies.

Dancing Deer Baking Co.
77 Shirley Street
Boston, MA 02119
(888) 699-DEER
www.dancingdeer.com

In addition to her flavored vinegars and unique spice blends and dried seasonings, owner Laura McCann has created wonderful organically infused sugars that taste terrific sprinkled on fresh fruit, sugar cookies, and shortbread or stirred into teas or hot chocolate. Flavored sugars include cardamom, cinnamon-orange, hibiscus, lavender-ginger, lemon-rosebud, rosemary, and vanilla.

Golden Fig Epicurean Delights
2010 East Hennepin Avenue
Minneapolis, MN 55413
(612) 378-2222
www.goldenfig.com

The company's Baker's Catalogue offers Queen Guinevere Cake Flour, a variety of pastry flours, European-style round cake pans, Nordic Ware Bundt pans, syrups, sugars, flours, pie filling, thickeners, Princess Cake and Cookie Flavor, and every piece of equipment you might need for baking. It is a wonderful retail and information resource for home bakers.

King Arthur Flour
P.O. Box 876
Norwich, Vermont 05055-0876
(800) 827-6838
Baker's hotline: (802) 649-3717
www.kingarthurflour.com

La Cuisine, The Cook's Resource
323 Cameron Street
Alexandria, VA 22314
Phone: (800) 521-1176
Fax: (703) 836-8925
www.lacuisineus.com

Nancy Purves Pollard has assembled the finest in cooking and baking products and utensils in her Washington, D.C.–area store. This is where I bought my Hammersong cookie cutters, the finest that are made, in my opinion. Pollard also publishes an informative quarterly newsletter/catalog distributed to more than 20,000 clients worldwide.

Maid of Scandinavia Co.
Division of Sweet Celebrations
3244 Raleigh Avenue
Minneapolis, MN 55416
(800) 328-6722 (out of state)
(800) 851-1121 (in Minnesota)
www.sweetc.com.

This is a treasure trove of pans, cutters, gel pastes and food colorings, piping bags and tips, tools, decorations, edible sprinkles, candy wraps, cupcake liners, baking chocolates, rolled fondant, cookbooks, doilies, you name it! The company offers hexagonal, Father Christmas, Père Noël, leaf, star, heart, and blossom cookie cutters; paper decorations; tart pans of all shapes and sizes; and springerle and shortbread molds.

Mariani Orchards
1615 Half Road
Morgan Hill, CA 95037
(408) 779-5467

Here you'll find many different and delicious varieties of apricot, including the Blenheim and a white apricot, which are grown in northern California.

Pumpkin Hill Farm
Pumpkin Hill
Sumerduck, VA 22742
(540) 439-4533

Try their flavored sugars that are wonderful for sprinkling on fresh fruits, or including in icings, frosting, or pastry creams. Rose-geranium sugar and lavender sugar are my favorites.

Steen's Pure Cane Syrup
The C. S. Steen Syrup Mill Inc.
P.O. Box 339
119 N. Main Street
Abbeville, LA 70510
(800) 725-1654
www.steensyrup.com

Lighter in color, texture, and flavor than molasses, and more pure, this Louisiana syrup is delicious in gingerbread, cookies, and any recipe calling for molasses. You can find this syrup at Dean & DeLuca and other fine food emporiums.

Reference Works

Arenstam, Clare, et al. *New England Begins: The Seventeenth Century*. Volume 2, *Mentality and Environment*. Boston: Museum of Fine Arts, 1982.

Corriher, Shirley. *Cookwise: The Hows and Whys of Successful Cooking*. New York: William Morrow and Company, 1997.

Danforth, Randi, et al., editors. *Culinaria: The United States: A Culinary Discovery*. Cologne, Germany: Konemann, 1998.

Fischer, David Hackett. *Albion's Seed: Four British Folkways in America*. New York: Oxford University Press, 1989.

Fisher, M. F. K. *The Art of Eating: Her Five Most Famous Books in One Volume*. London: Picador, 1983.

Jones, Evan. *American Food: The Gastronomic Story*. Second edition. New York: Vintage Books, 1981.

Langdon, Philip. *Orange Roofs, Golden Arches: The Architecture of American Chain Restaurants*. New York: Alfred A. Knopf, Inc., 1986.

Leighton, Ann. *Early American Gardens: "For Meate or for Medicine."* Boston: Houghton Mifflin Company, 1970.

Mariani, John. *The Dictionary of American Food and Drink*. New York: Hearst Books, 1994.

McGee, Harold. *On Food and Cooking: The Science and Lore of the Kitchen*. London: Unwin Hyman Limited, 1988.

——*The Curious Cook: More Kitchen Science and Lore*. New York: MacMillan, 1990.

Miller, Amy Bess. *Shaker Herbs: A History and a Compendium*. New York: Clarkson N. Potter, Inc., 1976.

Sokolov, Raymond. *Why We Eat What We Eat: How the Encounter Between the New World and the Old Changed the Way Everyone on the Planet Eats*. New York: Summit Books, 1991.

Stevens, Patricia. *Rare Bits: Unusual Origins of Popular Recipes*. Athens, Ohio: Ohio University Press, 1995.

Welsch, Roger L. and Linda K. *Cather's Kitchens: Foodways in Literature and Life*. Lincoln, Nebr.: University of Nebraska Press, 1987.

Cookbooks

American Daughters of Columbus Cook Book. Fourth edition. Kansas City, Mo.: Cookbook Publishers, Inc., 1997.

Anderson, Jean. *The American Century Cookbook: The Most Popular Recipes of the 20th Century*. New York: Clarkson Potter Publishers, 1997.

Bailey, Lee. *Lee Bailey's Good Parties*. New York: Clarkson N. Potter, Inc., 1984.

——*Lee Bailey's California Wine Country Cooking*. New York: Clarkson N. Potter, Inc., 1991.

Beard, James. *The New James Beard*. New York: Knopf, 1981.

Benson, Evelyn Abraham, editor. *Penn Family Recipes: The Cooking Recipes of William Penn's Wife Gulielma*. York, Pa.: George Shumway, 1966.

Berolzheimer, Ruth, editor. *250 Classic Cake Recipes*. Chicago: Consolidated Book Publishers, 1950.

——, editor. *The American Woman's Cook Book*. Chicago: Culinary Arts Institute, 1948.

Brown, Cora, Rose, and Bob, compilers. *America Cooks: Favorite Recipes from 48 States*. Garden City, N.Y.: Halcyon House, 1949.

Buckeye Cookery and Practical Housekeeping. Facsimile reproduction of the 1877 edition. Minneapolis, Minn.: Steck-Warleck Company, 1970.

Byrn, Ann. *The Cake Mix Doctor*. New York: Workman Publishing, 1999.

Capital City Cook Book. Madison, Wis.: 1906.

Child, Lydia Maria. *The American Frugal Housewife*. Boston: Carter, Hendel, 1833.

Colwin, Laurie. *Home Cooking: A Writer in the Kitchen*. New York: Harper Collins Publishers, Inc., 1988.

——*More Home Cooking: A Writer Returns to the Kitchen*. New York: Harper Collins Publishers, Inc. 1993.

Cusick, Heidi Haughey. *Soul and Spice: African Cooking in the Americas*. San Francisco: Chronicle Books, 1995.

Dent, Huntley. *The Feast of Santa Fe: Cooking of the American Southwest*. New York: Simon and Schuster, 1985.

Dojny, Brooke. *New England Cookbook: 350 Recipes from Town and Country, Land and Sea, Hearth and Home*. Boston: The Harvard Common Press, 1999.

Donovan, Mary, Amy Hatrak, Frances Mills, and Elizabeth Shull. *The Thirteen Colonies Cookbook*. Montclair, N.J.: Montclair Historical Society, 1975.

Edge, John T. *A Gracious Plenty: Recipes and Recollections from the American South*. New York: G. P. Putnam's Sons, 1999.

Elsah Landing Restaurant. *The Elsah Landing Restaurant Cookbook*. Elsah, Ill.: Elsah Landing Restaurant, 1981.

Episcopal Church Women of the Saint James Episcopal Church, compilers. *Our Daily Bread*. Waubay, S. Dak.: Enemy Swim Lake, 1991.

Farr, Sidney Saylor. *More Than Moonshine: Appalachian Recipes and Recollections*. Pittsburgh, Pa.: University of Pittsburgh Press, 1983.

Gillette, F. L., and Hugo Ziemann. *The White House Cook Book: A Comprehensive Cyclopedia of Information for the Home, Containing Etiquette, Care of the Sick, Health Suggestions, Facts Worth Knowing, Etc*. New York: The Saalfield Publishing Company, 1915.

German Village Society. *German Village Cook Book*. Columbus, Ohio: German Village Society, 1968.

Glenn, Camille. *The Heritage of Southern Cooking*. New York: Workman Publishing, 1986.

Griffith, Linda and Fred. *The Best of the Midwest*. New York: Viking Penguin, 1990.

Grigson, Jane. *The Observer Guide to British Cookery*. London: Michael Joseph, 1984.

Hess, Karen. *Martha Washington's Booke of Cookery; and Booke of Sweetmeats transcribed by Karen Hess with Historical Notes and Copious Annotations*. New York: Columbia University Press, 1995.

Kremer, Elizabeth. *We Make You Kindly Welcome: Recipes from the Trustees' House Daily Fare*. Harrodsburg, Ky.: Pleasant Hill Press, 1970.

——*Welcome Back to Pleasant Hill: More Recipes from the Trustees' House*. Harrodsburg, Ky.: Pleasant Hill Press, 1977.

Junior League of Charleston. *Charleston Receipts*. Charleston, S.C.: Walker Evans & Cogeswell, 1950.

Lea, Elizabeth Ellicott. *Domestic Cookery*. Baltimore, Md.: 1853.

——*A Quaker Woman's Cookbook*. 1845. Reprint, Philadelphia: University of Pennsylvania Press, 1982.

Lermon, Sue, and Simon Mallet, editors. *Cuisine de Terroir: The Lost Domain of French Cooking. Original Recipes Collected by the Master Chefs of France*. London: Corgi Books, 1987.

Leslie, Eliza. *Miss Leslie's House Book*. Philadelphia: Cary Hart, 1840.

Miller, Amy Bess, and Persis Wellington Fuller, editors. *The Best of Shaker Cooking*. New York: The MacMillan Company, 1970.

Mitchell, Marge, and Joan Sedgwick. *Bakery Lane Soup Bowl: One Hundred Recipes*. Middlebury, Vt: Bakery Lane Soup Bowl, 1976.

Moore, John Hammond, compiler and editor. *The Confederate Housewife: Receipts & Remedies, Together with Sundry Suggestions for Garden, Farm, and Plantation*. Columbia, S.C.: Summerhouse Press, 1997.

National Women's Press Club. *Who Says We Can't Cook!* Washington, D.C.: National Women's Press Club, 1955.

Pastors Aid Society of the Roanoke Presbyterian Church, compiler. *Good Things to Eat*. Kansas City, Mo.: Pastors Aid Society of the Roanoke Presbyterian Church, 1929.

Presbyterian Cook Book. Dayton, Ohio: 1873.

Prudhomme, Paul. *Chef Paul Prudhomme's Louisiana Kitchen*. New York: William Morrow and Company, 1984.

Putcamp, Luis, and Virginia Z. Goulet, compilers. *Key West Recipes*. Miami, Fla.: The Central Press, Inc., 1948.

Rudkin, Margaret. *The Margaret Rudkin Pepperidge Farm Cookbook*. New York: Grosset and Dunlap, 1963.

Schreiber, Cory. *Wildwood: Cooking from the Source in the Pacific Northwest*. Berkeley, Calif.: Ten Speed Press, 2000.

The Settlement Cookbook: The Way to a Man's Heart. Milwaukee, Wis., 1903. Reprint, Bedford, Mass.: Applewood Books, 1996.

Simmons, Amelia. *American Cookery*. Hartford, Conn., 1796.

Spurling, Hilary. *Elinor Fettiplace's Receipt Book: Elizabethan Country House Cooking*. London: Viking Salamander, 1986.

St. Ambrose Parish. *St. Ambrose Parish "On the Hill" Cookbook*. St. Louis, Mo.: St. Ambrose Parish, 1990.

Swedish Folk Dancers' Cookbook: A Collection of Sweets and Breads. Pipestone, Minn.: Nicollet Cookbooks, 1987.

Sykora, Lester, and John A. Kuba. *Our Favorite 106 Czech Pastry Recipes Cookbook*. Cedar Rapids, Iowa: Sykora Bakery.

Szathmary, Louis, compiler. *Midwestern Home Cookery: Introduction and Suggested Recipes by Louis Szathmary*. [A cookbook comprising the *Presbyterian Cookbook* compiled by the Ladies of the First Presbyterian Church, Dayton, Ohio, in 1875 and the *Capital City Cookbook* compiled by the Woman's Guild of Grace Church, Third Edition, in 1906.] New York: Promonotory Press, 1974.

Tatum, Billy Joe, and Ann Taylor Packer. *Ozarks Collection: The Best Recipes from the Heritage and Traditions of a Storied Region*. Branson, Mo.: The Ozarks Mountaineer, 1987.

Tyree, Marion Cabell, compiler. *Housekeeping in Old Virginia: Containing Contributions from Two Hundred and Fifty of Virginia's Noted Housewives, Distinguished for Their Skill in the Culinary Art and Other Branches of Domestic Economy*. Louisville, Ky.: John P. Morton and Company, 1879.

Valdejuli, Carmen Aboy. *Puerto Rican Cookery*. Gretna, La.: Pelican Publishing Company, 1989.

Wallace, Lily. *The American Family Cook Book*. New York: Books, Inc., 1954.

Waters, Alice. *Chez Panisse Menu Cookbook*. New York: Random House, 1982.

Weaver, William Woys, editor. *A Quaker Woman's Cookbook: The Domestic Cookery of Elizabeth Ellicott Lea*. Philadelphia: University of Pennsylvania Press, 1982.

——*The Christmas Cook: Three Centuries of Yuletide Sweets*. New York: HarperPerennial, 1990.

Wesleyan Service Guild of the Methodist Church. *Brown County Cookery*. Third Edition. Nashville, Ind.: Wesleyan Service Guild of the Methodist Church, 1961.

What's Cooking in St. George, Minnesota? Audubon, Iowa: Jumbo Jack's Cookbooks, 1996.

White, James Edson, editor. *The "Home Queen" Cook Book: Two Thousand Valuable Receipts on Cookery and Household Economy, Table Etiquette, Toilet, Etc*. Chicago: The Fort Dearborn Publishing Company, 1898.

Wolfer, Charity Yoder, Marjorie Yoder Larson, and Kathryn Yoder Miller. *Yoder Sisters' Cookbook: A Family Heritage Cookbook*. Salem, Ore: 1986.

Woodward, B. W., compiler. *The Ladies' Floral Calendar and Household Receipt Book*. Facsimile reproduction of the 1868 edition. Tonganoxie, Kans.: Back in Thyme, 1999.

Wrought Iron Range Company. *Home Comfort Cook Book*. 1933. Reprint, Kidron, Ohio: Lehman Hardware, 1988.

Unruh, Ruth, and Jan Schmidt, compilers. *From Pluma Moos to Pie*. Revised edition. Goessel, Kans.: Mennonite Heritage Museum, 1991.

Voth, Norma Jost. *Mennonite Foods & Folkways from South Russia, Vols. 1 & 2*. Intercourse, Pa.: Good Books, 1994.

Index